CASUALTY CLAIM PRACTICE

CASUALTY CLAIM PRACTICE

Sixth Edition

Donald J. Hirsch, J.D.
of the Wisconsin Bar

IRWIN
Chicago • Bogotá • Boston • Buenos Aires • Caracas
London • Madrid • Mexico City • Sydney • Toronto

Irwin Book Team

Sponsoring editor:	Gina M. Huck
Editorial coordinator:	Wendi L. Sweetland
Senior marketing manager:	Ron Bloecher
Project editor:	Karen M. Smith
Production supervisor:	Lara Feinberg
Designer:	Larry J. Cope
Art studio:	Alexander Graphics, Ltd.
Compositor:	Alexander Graphics, Ltd.
Typeface:	10/12 Times Roman
Printer:	R. R. Donnelley & Sons Company

Times Mirror
Higher Education Group

Library of Congress Cataloging-in-Publication Data

Hirsch, Donald J.
Casualty claim practice / Donald J. Hirsch. — 6th ed.
p. cm.
Includes bibliographical references and index.
ISBN 0-256-15199-7 ISBN 0-256-22424-2 (IIA Special edition)
1. Insurance, Casualty—Adjustment of claims—United States.
I. Title.
KF1215.H57 1996
346.73′0865—dc20
[347.306865] 95–16496

Printed in the United States of America
1 2 3 4 5 6 7 8 9 0 DO 2 1 0 9 8 7 6 5

To My Wife and Children,
who made this work possible
and necessary, this volume is
affectionately dedicated.

Preface

In recent years, we have seen increased public awareness, in certain areas, of the social impact caused by the application of current rules of law to the disposition of claims. This is especially true in cases arising out of the manufacture and use of automobiles and other products, the disposal of waste, the use of materials in construction, the manufacture and sale of pharmaceutical drugs, and the rendering of health care.

The legislative and judicial responses have been the enactment of new legislation and common-law rules. This places a burden on the claim department to amend its procedures of investigation and settlement to conform to the new rules. Because of the continuing nature of judicial and legislative pronouncements, an additional burden is placed on the claim representative, who must remain alert to new developments.

The purpose of this volume remains the same as that of previous editions: to present the basic legal knowledge that every claim representative should have, to suggest procedures for investigation and settlement, to provide a ready reference for the experienced claim representative, and to provide a starting point for those whose duty it is to research various phases of applicable law.

The author gratefully acknowledges the helpful suggestions received from claim representatives. The suggestions have received careful attention, contributing in large measure to the final result. The errors and omissions are, as usual, the author's own.

Donald J. Hirsch

Contents

1 Casualty Claims and the Claim Representative *1*

100 Casualty Claims Defined *1*
101 The Claim Representative *2*
102 Responsibilities of the Claim Representative *3*
103 Functions of the Claim Representative *4*
104 Duties of the Claim Representative *5*
105 Required Knowledge *7*

2 Common Law and Equity; Federal Jurisdiction and Authority; Trial *8*

LAW AND THE COURTS *9*

200 Common Law Defined *9*
201 Early Concepts *9*
202 Common-Law Rights and Duties *10*
203 Stare Decisis *11*
204 Statutory Modifications of the Common Law *11*
205 Statutory Construction *12*
206 The Common Law in the United States *12*
207 Judicial Authority *13*
208 Choice of Law *13*
209 Significant Contacts Rule *14*
210 Jurisdiction, Venue, and Forum Shopping *17*
211 Restatement of the Law *18*
212 Origin of Equity *18*
213 Equitable Remedies *19*
214 Appellate Courts *20*
215 Federal Jurisidiction and Authority—the Federal Judiciary *21*
216 Preemptive Statutes *22*
217 Code of Federal Regulations *22*

PROCEDURE IN A CIVIL SUIT *24*

218 Trial Preparation Generally *24*
219 The Summons *24*
220 The Complaint *25*
221 Duties of the Insured Receiving Process *27*
222 Duties of the Claim Representative Receiving Process *28*
223 Stipulation to Extend Time for Answer or Otherwise Plead *28*
224 Tender of an Overdue Process *29*
225 The Answer *29*
226 Discovery Proceedings *30*
227 Motions *32*
228 Subpoenas *33*
229 Functions of the Judge and Jury *33*
230 Waiver of a Jury *34*
231 Selection of the Jury *34*
232 Opening Statements *35*
233 The Trial *35*
234 The Court's Charge and the Verdict *36*
235 Motions after Verdict *37*
236 Responsibilities of the Claim Representative with Respect to Litigation *37*
237 Responsibilities of the Claim Representative with Respect to Trial Preparation *37*
238 Alternative Dispute Resolution *38*

3 Law of Torts *40*

TORTS AND NEGLIGENCE 40

TORT LAW—AN OVERVIEW *40*

300 Tort Defined *40*
301 Classification of Torts *42*

NEGLIGENCE *44*

302 Negligence Defined and Described *44*
303 Negligence Per Se *47*
304 Degrees of Care *48*
305 Gross Negligence *49*
306 Proximate Cause *49*
307 Intervening Cause *52*
308 Foreseeability *54*

APPLICATIONS OF NEGLIGENCE 55

FORESEEABILITY *55*

309 Foreseeability as Applied to Motor Vehicles *55*
310 Foreseeability as Applied to Premises *56*
311 Foreseeability as Applied to Products *57*
312 Rescue Doctrine *57*

OWNERS AND POSSESSORS OF PROPERTY *58*

313 Duties of the Possessor of Land *58*
314 Trespassers *59*
315 Licensees *60*
316 Social Guests *60*
317 Invitees *61*
318 Area of Invitation or License *62*
319 Revocation of Invitation or License *63*
320 Police Officers and Fire Fighters in the Line of Duty *63*
321 Modifications of Occupiers' Liability *64*
322 Landlord and Tenant *66*
323 "Attractive Nuisance" Doctrine *68*

EMOTIONAL DISTRESS *71*

324 Negligent Infliction of Emotional Distress *71*

4 Law of Torts, Continued *74*

INTENTIONAL TORTS *74*

400 Assault and Battery *74*
401 Defamation: Libel and Slander *75*
402 Right of Privacy *76*
403 Conversion *78*
404 Trespass *79*
405 False Imprisonment *80*
406 Malicious Prosecution *80*
407 Wrongful Civil Proceedings *82*
408 Nuisance as a Basis of Tort Liability *82*
409 Dram Shop Acts *83*
410 Intentional Infliction of Emotional Distress *84*

STRICT OR ABSOLUTE LIABILITY *86*

411 Dangerous Instrumentality Doctrine *86*
412 Animals as Dangerous Instrumentalities *87*
413 Ultrahazardous Operations Doctrine *89*

WRONGFUL DEATH AND SURVIVAL *90*

414 Survival Actions *90*
415 Death by Wrongful Act *91*

DEFENSES *94*

416 Contributory Negligence *94*
417 Comparative Negligence *97*
418 Assumption of Risk *98*
419 Unavoidable Accident *99*
420 Act of God *100*
421 Statute of Limitations *101*

5 Tort Parties and Immunities *104*

PARTIES *104*

500 Consortium *104*
501 Prenatal Injuries *106*
502 Minors and Insane Persons *107*

JOINT TORT–FEASORS *108*

503 Joint and Several Liability *108*
504 Release-of-One Rule *110*
505 Contribution and Indemnity *111*
506 Joint Tort–Feasors Contribution Law *112*

VICARIOUS LIABILITY *113*

507 Vicarious Liability or Imputed Negligence *113*
508 Employer–Employee *114*
509 Owner and Independent Contractor *114*
510 Parent–Child *114*
511 Husband–Wife *117*

IMMUNITIES *117*

512 Family Immunity *117*
513 Federal Tort Claims Act *122*
514 Governmental Immunity: Federal *123*
515 Governmental Immunity: State *124*
516 Governmental Immunity: Municipal *124*
517 Governmental Immunity: Effect of Insurance *128*
518 Charitable Immunity *129*

6 Law of Contracts, Agency, and Bailments *131*

CONTRACTS 132

CONTRACTS—ELEMENTS OF CONTRACTS *132*

600 The Elements *132*
601 Offer *133*
602 Duration of Offer *133*
603 Offer to an Attorney or Agent *134*
604 Offer Through an Authorized Agent *136*
605 Termination of Offer *137*
606 Acceptance *138*
607 Consideration *138*
608 Capacity to Contract *139*

DEFENSES TO CONTRACTS *140*

609 Void and Voidable Contracts *141*
610 Mistake of Fact *141*
611 Fraud *142*
612 Parol Evidence Rule *143*

INTERPRETATION OF CONTRACTS *143*

613 Representations *143*
614 Warranties *144*
615 Conditions *145*
616 Waiver and Estoppel *146*
617 Nonwaiver and Reservation of Rights *147*
618 Ambiguities *148*
619 Assignments *148*
620 Law Governing Contracts *148*

SOME TYPES OF CONTRACTS *149*

621 Contracts to Compound a Crime *149*
622 Contracts to Procure Evidence *150*
623 Attorney's Contingent Fee Contracts *150*
624 Exculpatory Contracts *151*
625 Hold Harmless Agreements *153*
626 Arbitration Agreements *155*
627 Beneficiary Contracts *155*
628 Leases *156*
629 Accord and Satisfaction *157*
630 Releases *158*
631 Covenant Not to Sue *160*

AGENCY 161

TYPES OF AGENCY RELATIONSHIPS *161*

632 Agency Defined *161*
633 Types of Agents *162*
634 Specific Agency Relationships *164*
635 Appointment of Subagents *166*
636 Agency by Emergency *166*
637 Special and General Employees *167*
638 Attorneys as Limited Agents *168*
639 Fiduciary Agents *168*
640 Trustees *169*
641 Independent Contractors *170*

LIABILITIES IN AGENCY RELATIONSHIPS *172*

642 *Respondeat Superior* *172*
643 Scope of Agency *172*
644 Deviation from the Scope of Agency *173*
645 Direct Liability of the Principal *174*
646 Liability of Agent to Principal *175*
647 Liability of Agent to Third Persons *175*

648 Liability of Principal to Agent *176*
649 Ratification or Adoption of Unauthorized Acts *176*

BAILMENTS 176

NATURE OF BAILMENTS *176*

650 Bailments Defined *176*

LIABILITIES IN BAILMENT SITUATIONS *179*

651 Kinds of Bailments *179*
652 Degrees of Care Required *179*
653 Liability, Bailor to Bailee *180*
654 Liability, Bailee to Third Persons *180*
655 Liability, Bailor to Third Persons *181*
656 Liability, Third Person to Bailee *181*
657 Liability, Third Person to Bailor *182*
658 Limitation of Liability *182*
659 Conversion or Unauthorized Use by the Bailee *183*
660 Exculpatory Contracts as Applied to Bailments *183*
661 Innkeepers' Liability *184*
662 Liability of Common Carriers *185*
663 Exculpatory Contracts, Common Carriers *186*
664 Private Carriers *186*

7 Law of Products *187*

700 Products Liability Generally *187*
701 Early Concepts *190*
702 Elimination of the Privity Requirement *191*
703 Effect of the Elimination of Privity *191*
704 Liability of the Retailer for Negligence *191*
705 Liability of the Retailer for Breach of Warranty *194*
706 Liability of the Manufacturer or Distributor for Breach of Warranty *195*
707 Duties of the Manufacturer *196*
708 Duty of Safe Design *197*
709 Duty to Warn *199*
710 Identification of Manufacturer *202*
711 Strict Liability for Retailers and Manufacturers *203*
712 A Seller Engaged in the Business *204*
713 Defective Condition *206*
714 An Unreasonable Danger *207*
715 User or Consumer *207*
716 Physical Harm *208*
717 Defenses: Use of Product for Unintended Purpose *208*
718 Defenses: Contributory Negligence *210*
719 Defenses: Allergy and Susceptibility *210*
720 Defenses: Third Party's Conduct *211*
721 Defenses: State of the Art *213*
722 Defenses: Government Specifications *213*
723 Defenses: Disclaimers *214*
724 Defenses: Statute of Limitations *214*
725 Indemnity and Contribution *215*
726 Long-Arm Statutes *216*
727 Products Liability Investigation *217*
728 Plan of Investigation *219*

8 Law of Automobiles *226*

RULES OF THE ROAD *227*

800 Rights and Duties of the Motorist *227*
801 Rules of the Road *228*
802 Assured Clear Distance Rule *228*
803 Compliance with Traffic Signs *229*
804 Failure to See Traffic Warning Signs *230*
805 Vehicles Traveling in the Same Direction *230*
806 Vehicles Traveling in Opposite Directions *232*
807 Vehicles Traveling at Right Angles *233*
808 Violating Rules of the Road in an Emergency *233*
809 Stop Signs *234*
810 Vehicles Entering the Highway from Private Way *234*

SPECIAL SITUATIONS *234*

811 Railroad Crossings *234*
812 School Buses *235*
813 Emergency Vehicles *235*
814 Motorcycles and Bicycles *236*
815 Parked Vehicles *236*
816 Disabled Vehicles *237*
817 Commercial Vehicles *238*
818 No-Contact Cases *238*
819 Seat Belt Defense *239*

OWNER AND VICARIOUS LIABILITY *240*

820 Vicarious Liability of the Owner *240*
821 Family Purpose Doctrine *242*
822 Statutory Liability of the Owner *243*
823 Vicarious Liability of Person Other than Owner *243*

PASSENGERS AND PEDESTRIANS *244*

824 Rights and Duties of Passengers *244*
825 Automobile Guest Statutes *245*
826 Guest Defined *246*
827 Driver's Negligence Not Imputed to Passengers *246*
828 Rights and Duties of Pedestrians *247*
829 Traffic Officers and Workers on the Roadway *248*

STATUTORY REQUIREMENTS *249*

830 State Licensing Regulations *249*
831 Unregistered Vehicles *250*
832 Financial Responsibility Acts *250*
833 Compulsory Automobile Insurance *250*
834 Statutory Policies of Automobile Liability Insurance *251*
835 Service of Process on Nonresident Motorists *251*

PERSONAL INJURY PROTECTION (PIP) NO-FAULT SYSTEMS *251*

836 Purpose and Scope *251*
837 Legislation *253*
838 Insurance *253*
839 Benefits Provided *254*
840 Tort Exemption *255*
841 Third-Party Claims *256*
842 Subrogation under No-Fault Statutes *256*
843 Arbitration under No-Fault Statutes *256*
844 Claims Administration under No-Fault *257*

9 Law of Evidence *262*

REQUIREMENTS FOR EVIDENCE *263*

900 Nature of Evidence *263*
901 Admissibility of Evidence *263*
902 Weight of Evidence *264*
903 Qualifications of Witnesses *265*
904 Expert Testimony *266*

SUBSTITUTES FOR EVIDENCE *270*

905 Presumptions and Inferences *270*
906 Irrebuttable Presumptions *271*
907 *Res Ipsa Loquitur* *272*
908 Judicial Notice *274*

THE HEARSAY RULE AND ITS EXCEPTIONS *276*

909 The Hearsay Rule *276*
910 *Res Gestae* Statements *277*
911 Declarations of Pain and Suffering *278*
912 Admissions against Interest *278*
913 Testimony in Prior Proceedings *279*
914 Prior Contradictory Statements *279*
915 Book Entries in the Regular Course of Business *280*

RULES OF EVIDENCE IN CERTAIN SITUATIONS *280*

916 Plea of Guilty at a Motor Vehicle Hearing *280*
917 Conviction in Traffic Court *281*
918 Conviction of Prior Crimes *281*
919 Admissions by Conduct *283*
920 Admissions by an Agent *284*
921 Deception Tests *284*
922 Subsequent Precautions to Prevent Harm *284*
923 Offers to Compromise and Similar Conduct *285*
924 Liability Insurance *285*

PRIVILEGES *286*

925 Privileged Communications *286*
926 Husband and Wife *286*
927 Attorney and Client *287*
928 Physician and Patient *287*
929 Priest and Penitent *288*

DEMONSTRATIVE EVIDENCE *289*

930 Photographs *289*
931 Videos *289*
932 X Rays *290*

PUBLIC RECORDS 291

933 Admissibility of Public Records *291*
934 Motor Vehicle Accident Reports *291*
935 Intoxication Tests *291*
936 Police Records *292*
937 Traffic Court Hearings *292*
938 Weather Reports *292*
939 Autopsy Reports *293*
940 Public Service Commission Accident Reports *293*
941 Civil Aeronautics Reports *293*
942 Federal Income Tax Returns *294*
943 Veterans Administration Records *294*
944 Selective Service Records *295*
945 Social Security Records *295*
946 Unemployment Compensation Records *295*
947 Workers' Compensation Records *296*
948 Vital Statistics: Birth, Marriage, Death *296*
949 Court Records: Divorce or Prior Proceedings *296*
950 Interstate Commerce Commission Records *297*

10 Principles of Investigation *298*

ESSENTIALS OF INVESTIGATION *298*

1000 Nature of Investigation *298*
1001 Purpose of Investigation *301*
1002 Scope of Investigation *301*
1003 Theory of Defense *302*
1004 Outline of Investigation *303*
1005 Critical Evidence *305*

WITNESSES *306*

1006 Witnesses—Defined *306*
1007 Classification of Witnesses *307*
1008 Finding the Witness *308*
1009 Interviewing the Witness *309*
1010 Evaluation of Witnesses *311*

STATEMENTS *312*

1011 Structure of Statements *312*
1012 The Signed Statement *314*
1013 Recorded Statements *317*
1014 Statements: Form and Substance *318*
1015 Automobile Statements *318*
1016 General Liability Statements *322*
1017 Workers' Compensation Statements *324*

STATEMENTS IN SPECIAL SITUATIONS *328*

1018 Statements Taken in Hospitals *328*
1019 Statements: Serious Injury and Death Claims *329*
1020 Statements of Illiterates *331*
1021 Statements through Interpreters *331*
1022 Statements of Persons with a Physical or Mental Disability *331*
1023 Statements of Children *332*
1024 Negative Statements *332*
1025 Multiple Statements *333*

PHYSICAL AND DEMONSTRATIVE EVIDENCE *333*

1026 Physical Facts *333*
1027 Photographs *334*
1028 Diagrams *335*

VERIFICATION *340*

1029 Verification Generally *340*
1030 Verification by Experts *340*
1031 Verification by Medical Examination *342*
1032 Verification of Disability *347*
1033 Verification through the Index Bureau *348*

11 Medical Aspects *349*

1100 Medical Knowledge in Relation to Personal Injury Claims *349*
1101 Causation *351*
1102 Trauma *352*
1103 Etiology *352*
1104 X Rays *353*
1105 Other Diagnostic Tests *353*
1106 Diagnostic Signs *354*
1107 Anatomy *354*
1108 Fractures *358*
1109 Head Injuries *360*
1110 Spinal or Back Injuries *362*
1111 Traumatic Neurosis *363*

1112 Disc Injuries *363*
1113 Whiplash *364*
1114 Hernia *364*
1115 Arthritis *364*
1116 Inflammatory Diseases *365*
1117 Common Injuries *366*
1118 Lengths of Disability *366*
1119 The Eye *367*
1120 The Heart *368*
1121 The Blood *370*
1122 Blood Grouping and Transfusions *373*
1123 Compressed-Air Disease *374*
1124 Lung Diseases *374*
1125 Hematoma *375*
1126 Infection *375*
1127 Blood Tests for Intoxication *376*
1128 Other Intoxication Tests *377*
1129 Intoxication Tests as Evidence *377*

12 Damages and Claims Evaluation *379*

LAW OF DAMAGES *379*

1200 Purpose and Scope of Claims Evaluation *379*
1201 Nature of Damages *380*
1202 Single Recovery Principle *382*
1203 Time of Valuation *382*
1204 Duty of the Claimant to Establish Damages *383*
1205 Duty of the Claimant to Mitigate Damages *384*
1206 Effect of a Religious Belief on Mitigation *386*
1207 Collateral Source Rule *387*
1208 Effect of a Preexisting Physical Disability *388*
1209 Loss of Consortium *389*

MEASURE OF DAMAGES *391*

1210 Measure of Damages: Property Damage *391*
1211 Measure of Damages: Personal Injury *395*
1212 Measure of Damages: Permanent Disability *399*
1213 Life Expectancy *401*
1214 Work-Life Expectancy *402*
1215 Present Value of Future Damages *404*

CLAIMS EVALUATION *408*

1216 Personal Injury: Tangible Items *408*
1217 Personal Injury: Intangible Items *415*
1218 Formula Methods of Evaluation *416*
1219 The "Three Times the Medical" Formula *416*
1220 The Unit of Time Formula *419*
1221 Factors Increasing Settlement Valuation *420*
1222 Factors Decreasing Settlement Valuation *422*
1223 Survival Claims *424*
1224 Wrongful Death *426*
1225 Settlement Valuation of Wrongful Death *430*

PUNITIVE DAMAGES *434*

1226 Nature of Punitive Damages *434*
1227 A Current Perspective on Punitive Damages *436*

13 Settlement Negotiations and Termination *438*

SETTLEMENT CONSIDERATIONS *439*

1300 Nature and Purpose of Settlement *439*
1301 Burden of Proof *439*
1302 Qualification for Settlement *440*
1303 Nuisance Settlements *441*
1304 Classification of Claims as to Liability *442*
1305 Relationship of Injury to Settlement *444*
1306 Liens *445*
1307 Satisfaction of Liens *446*
1308 Subrogation *448*
1309 Subrogation by the United States *448*

SETTLEMENT NEGOTIATIONS *449*

1310 Order of Settlement *449*
1311 Settlements by Joint Tort-Feasors *450*
1312 The Settlement Interview *451*
1313 First-Call Settlements *453*
1314 Control of the Claimant *453*
1315 Preparing for Settlement Negotiations *454*
1316 The Offer *455*
1317 When to Make An Offer *456*

1318 When Not to Make an Offer *457*
1319 Negotiations with Attorneys *457*
1320 Increasing Offers *459*
1321 Creating a Problem for the Claimant or Attorney *460*

RELEASES *460*

1322 What Is a Release? *460*
1323 Effect of a Release *462*
1324 Execution of the Release *463*
1325 Releases by Individuals *464*
1326 The Releasee *467*

SETTLEMENT IN SPECIAL SITUATIONS *467*

1327 Releases by or in Behalf of Minors *467*
1328 Indemnifying Releases by the Parents *469*
1329 Guardianship Proceedings and Friendly Suits *469*
1330 Nominal or No Consideration Releases *470*
1331 Releases by Partnerships or Corporations *470*
1332 Settlements: Survival and Wrongful Death *471*
1333 Covenants Not to Sue *477*
1334 Mary Carter Agreements *477*
1335 Loan Receipt Agreements *478*
1336 Form of Guarantee or Loan Agreement *479*
1337 Open-End Releases *479*
1338 Advance Payments *481*
1339 Settlement without Release *486*

14 A Note on Bibliography and Miscellaneous Areas of the Law *487*

1400 Bibliographical Note: Legal Reading and Research *487*
1401 Researching Various Areas of the Law *488*
1402 Computer-Assisted Legal Research *490*

Appendix Glossary of Legal and Insurance Terms *491*

Index *503*

Chapter 1

Casualty Claims and the Claim Representative

100 Casualty Claims Defined
101 The Claim Representative
102 Responsibilities of the Claim Representative
103 Functions of the Claim Representative
104 Duties of the Claim Representative
105 Required Knowledge

100 Casualty Claims Defined

A claim is the assertion of an alleged legal right, which carries with it a demand for appropriate relief. The legal right asserted may involve any right in the legal spectrum, and the relief demanded may be any one or more of the forms of relief afforded by the courts.

A casualty claim, for the purposes of this work, is one which arises out of, or is the subject matter of, an insurance contract of indemnification. In such a contract, the insurance carrier promises to hold the insured harmless against financial loss from an unknown or contingent event. The relief which may be demanded in a casualty claim is the payment of money or its equivalent.

The promise of indemnification may involve either or both of the following types of losses:

1. Losses sustained directly by the policyholder.
2. Losses sustained by others to whom the policyholder is legally liable.

1. Losses Sustained by the Policyholder. This type of promise is one whereby the policyholder obtains protection from financial loss which he would otherwise have to bear because of damage to, or destruction of, property that he owns or in which he has an interest, or because of injury to his person. There are only two parties to this contract—the policyholder (the first party) and the insurance carrier (the second party). Therefore, the insurance afforded is referred to as *first-party coverage,* and the losses as *first-party claims,* since the loss is suffered by the first party to the contract.

2. Losses Sustained by Others. The second type of promise is one whereby the policyholder obtains protection against the loss which he would be legally obligated to pay as damages to others because of bodily injury, sickness or disease, or death, or because of the injury to or destruction of their property, including damages for loss of use.

There are three parties involved in this situation: (1) the policyholder, or first party, (2) the insurance carrier, or second party, and (3) the party who has been injured or whose property has been damaged, the third party. Thus a promise of indemnification referring to this type of situation is called *third-party coverage,* and the claims are referred to as *third-party claims,* since the person asserting the alleged legal right against the insured is the third party.

101 The Claim Representative

A claim representative is one who represents an insurance carrier in the investigation, adjustment, negotiation, and trial preparation of claims arising under the policies of insurance written by the company that is represented. Various other titles are used to describe this position, such as an adjuster, investigator, claim auditor, or claim agent. The claim representative may be employed (1) directly by the insurance company; (2) by an independent adjuster; or (3) by a company-owned adjustment bureau.

1. Direct Employment by the Insurance Company. A salaried claim representative, employed directly by the insurance company, devotes his or her entire working time to the exclusive handling of claims made against the company and its insureds. Some companies use the term staff adjuster or staff claim representative to describe this type of employment.

2. Independent Adjuster. This term refers to a person, firm, or corporation which is held out to the insurance industry for employment in the handling of claims for more than one insurance company; does not work exclusively for one insurance company; and is paid in each case for the time devoted to the handling of the claim plus the expenses incurred. The claim representative may be the principal owner of the business or may be an employee of a person, firm, or corporation of this type.

3. Company-Owned Adjustment Bureau. This is a corporation whose stock is owned entirely and exclusively by one or more insurance companies. The claim representative employed by such a corporation handles the claims of the stockholder companies and of any other insurance companies to whom the directors of the corporation make its services available. Such services are paid on an individual fee basis per case or by means of an overall assessment.

102 Responsibilities of the Claim Representative

The responsibilities of the claim representative to the company he or she represents are the same whether the claim representative is employed by the company or undertakes to represent the company while employed by an adjusting organization. The relationship is one in which the company, as the principal, places special trust and confidence in the claim representative. The relationship requires that the representative maintain a high degree of fidelity and loyalty to the interests of the principal. Thus, the claim representative must treat the affairs, the money, or other property of the principal with a high degree of care at all times.

It is fundamental that an agent cannot serve two masters in the same transaction. He or she cannot on the one hand act as an agent for the principal and, at the same time, deal with himself or herself as an individual. Should this type of transaction be undertaken without the knowledge or consent of the principal, the transaction is in law conclusively presumed to be fraudulent, regardless of whether the claim representative personally profited from the transaction or not.

For example, if a stolen car is recovered after payment for it has been made by the insurance company, the claim representative may be instructed to sell the car to the highest bidder. If the claim representative made a bid on the car, which bid is the highest amount offered, permission must be secured from the principal before the sale is made at the figure offered in the bid. The claim representative must honestly and fairly disclose the amounts of the other bids and the sources from which they were received. It must appear that bids were invited from a representative group of salvage buyers. Should there be a failure on the part of the claim representative to disclose the full facts of the bid that he or she made on the car (no matter how honestly the bid was made), the transaction is conclusively presumed to be fraudulent and may be set aside or voided at the option of the insurance company.

The agent may not in any way deal with the principal's property with motives of self-interest. If, in the previous example, the claim representative simply solicited a friend to make the bid on his or her behalf—failing to disclose to the company these circumstances—the result would be the same. The transaction is fraudulent. The claim representative may not represent interests that are adverse to those of the principal. Using the above example, if the claim representative should disclose to a salvage buyer the amounts of the bids already received so that he or she could bid accordingly, the claim representative would be serving an interest that is adverse to that of the principal; this transaction is a breach of trust.

Likewise, if an independent adjuster or an employee of a company-owned adjustment bureau should accept an assignment from one company involving an accident, no other claim arising under the same transaction can be accepted unless both companies involved are made aware of the facts and give their permission to the dual representation. The acceptance of the later assignment and the failure to make full disclosure to the companies involved, with the representation of the adverse interests, amounts to a breach of trust against both companies. The claim representative may be liable in damages to the company whose interests are adversely affected.

Finally, a claim representative may never profit from an outside source as a consequence of actions and dealings taken for and in behalf of the principal. The claim representative may accept the salary or the fees agreed upon with the principal, but may not accept any gift, service, or other emolument from persons who provide services in connection with the claims handled. Acceptance of such gifts constitutes a breach of trust, even though the principal's interests are not adversely affected by the gift.

103 Functions of the Claim Representative

The general functions of the claim representative are to investigate, negotiate, evaluate, or prepare claims for trial. The representative also must keep the company's file on the claim up to date, so that it will reflect all of the actions taken by the claim representative and will also indicate the present status of the claim, whether it be in a preliminary, investigating, or negotiating stage. This latter duty of the claim representative is of vital importance to the company, because its business records and its decisions with respect to the claim are fashioned from the information in the file. Among the decisions to be made are questions of coverage, the amount of the reserve to be carried on the file, and—more important to the claim representative—the amount of the settlement authorization which will be given.

A decision is no better than the information on which it is based. Therefore, if there is evidence that has not been transmitted to the file or if the claim representative has information that has not been reported to the file, the decision based on only what is in the file may be faulty. If this should happen, the claim representative is to blame and not the person who was required to make the decision with insufficient information.

The reports to the file should be clear, concise, and as brief as they can be, but should contain all of the available information and evidence. In making the reports, the claim representative should confine the information transmitted to the file to the facts as supported by the available evidence. The claim representative should refrain from transmitting to the file unnecessary characterizations or opinions concerning the claimant and any other persons involved in the claim. He or she should be especially wary of making derogatory statements not supported by the evidence. In many instances, company files are seen by others, as when they are subpoenaed in court proceedings or reviewed by insurance examiners from various states. The reports should reflect the fairness and impartiality with which both the company and the claim representative view the evidence. There should be nothing in the file which could possibly form a basis for an action against either the company or the claim representative for defamation or bad faith.

104 Duties of the Claim Representative

The overall duty of the claim representative is to dispose of claims. This may be accomplished by payment of the full amount demanded, settlement on a negotiated basis, or an outright denial of liability. The ultimate objective is accomplished in three steps, as follows:

1. Investigation.
2. Evaluation
3. Termination.

1. Investigation. This consists of a reasonable inquiry into the facts of the accident or occurrence. Because the claim representative seldom, if ever, is an eyewitness to the accident, reliance must be placed upon secondary evidence in the form of statements from others who were present at the scene, as well as the physical facts. These physical facts may include skid marks, debris and other evidences of the accident, and the extent of the damage to the vehicles and the injuries sustained by the persons involved. In cases other than automobile, the investigation might include statements from eyewitnesses, a survey of the premises or an examination of the offending instrument, if any.

Every investigation starts out with some known evidence. This usually is in the form of a report of accident from the insured, giving his or her version of what occurred. The inquiry will start by verifying the known evidence and by establishing or uncovering whatever other evidence there may be. The extent of the inquiry will be dictated by the amount of believable evidence available, and the severity of the injuries claimed or the value of the property damage allegedly caused. In some cases much of this evidence can be secured by telephone without the necessity of making an inquiry in the field.

Among the first items of inquiry is the question of whether the accident or occurrence comes within the scope of the insurance contract. In some cases this will be established with a minimum of effort, and in others it will not. If the inquiry discloses any question as to whether the claim comes within the coverage afforded, the company must make a decision at that moment as to what position it will take in regard to coverage. If the accident is not covered because of its location or because it did not occur within the policy period—or if there has been a breach of a condition of the policy contract by the insured—the company cannot consistently continue with the investigation and at the same time deny coverage. Therefore, when the claim representative is aware that there is a coverage question, the claim representative must STOP the investigation and seek advice from the company as to what further activity should be undertaken. By continuing the investigation with the knowledge of the fact that the claim is not within the terms of the contract, the company may waive its right to deny coverage.

The form that the investigative inquiry will take will be conditioned by the evidence which is needed to reach a conclusion as to the possible liability of the insured and the probabilities of the claim. The claim representative must be informed of the applicable law and the statutes in the state which have a bearing on the possible liability of the insured.

2. Evaluation. The claim representative is expected to gather a sufficient amount of evidence concerning liability, the amount of damages claimed, and the specific details—consisting of out-of-pocket expenses, the claimed loss of earning capacity, and the injuries sustained or the property damage involved. He or she then will make some approximation of the value, or the lack of it, of the claim. Some companies give the claim representative blanket authority for settlement, subject to a maximum amount. Within that limit, the claim representative may exercise judgment as to settlement valuations, seeking advice from the supervisor where necessary. As to values above the settlement authorization, the claim representative will make recommendations to the company, supporting the conclusion reached with evidence of the injuries, details of the expenses claimed, and an evaluation of the applicable law. The claim representative will then proceed as instructed, whether the instructions are directed toward further investigation, denial of the claim, or further negotiation of a settlement within the limits authorized.

3. Termination. This is the ultimate objective of all claims handling. The two preliminary steps were taken solely to bring the claim to this stage. To dispose of the case, the claim representative may take one of the following three actions:

1. Acceptance.
2. Rejection.
3. Compromise.

1. Acceptance. This may mean that the claimant's demand is considered to be reasonable and it will be paid in full; or it may mean that it is in the company's best interest to dispose of the claim on that basis.

2. Rejection. This means that the claim representative will turn down the claim. By the rejection of the claim, the initiative has been transferred to the claimant. If he or she presses the claim, the claim representative should be prepared to offer sufficient evidence to defeat it, or to have sufficient evidence available to effectuate an attractive compromise. If the claimant takes no action and abandons the claim, the rejection has effectively terminated it.

3. Compromise. This action refers to negotiating a settlement of the claim for an amount which is consistent with its merits, and in accordance with and subject to the settlement authorization. Not all cases in which a compromise is attempted will result in a settlement. Where the claimant is unwilling to accept the top offer and the company is unwilling to meet the claimant's lowest demand, there will be a rejection of both offer and demand. Then, the same principles would apply as where the company has rejected the claim from the outset. When this impasse is reached—where the company refuses to increase its offer and the claimant has refused to decrease his or her demand—the initiative passes to the claimant, and the next move is up to him or her. The claimant (1) may engage counsel and bring the case to trial; (2) may continue to try negotiation; or (3) may finally accept the company's highest offer. On the other hand, with the passage of time, the company may be induced to increase its offer, especially if further investigation reveals facts that are not conducive to a successful defense.

105 Required Knowledge

The duties of the claim representative do not require admission to the bar or a complete legal education. They do require some knowledge of the basic rules of law which are applicable to the insurance claims industry. They also require some knowledge of medicine to the extent of being able to understand the nature of an injury, evaluate the periods of disability which will follow the infliction of an injury, and the costs and the type of treatment needed. In addition, some knowledge is necessary of the terms of the insurance policies written to provide first- and third-party coverages. The claim representative also will have to develop personal skills in investigation and claims negotiation.

Knowledge can be acquired; and it is the purpose of this volume to provide an insight into the basic principles and to point the way toward the development of the necessary skills.

Chapter 2

Common Law and Equity; Federal Jurisdiction and Authority; Trial

LAW AND THE COURTS

200 Common Law Defined
201 Early Concepts
202 Common-Law Rights and Duties
203 Stare Decisis
204 Statutory Modifications of the Common Law
205 Statutory Construction
206 The Common Law in the United States
207 Judicial Authority
208 Choice of Law
209 Significant Contacts Rule
210 Jurisdiction, Venue, and Forum Shopping
211 Restatement of the Law
212 Origin of Equity
213 Equitable Remedies
214 Appellate Courts
215 Federal Jurisidiction and Authority—the Federal Judiciary
216 Preemptive Statutes
217 Code of Federal Regulations

PROCEDURE IN A CIVIL SUIT

218 Trial Preparation Generally
219 The Summons
220 The Complaint
221 Duties of the Insured Receiving Process
222 Duties of the Claim Representative Receiving Process
223 Stipulation to Extend Time for Answer or Otherwise Plead
224 Tender of an Overdue Process
225 The Answer
226 Discovery Proceedings
227 Motions
228 Subpoenas
229 Functions of the Judge and Jury
230 Waiver of a Jury
231 Selection of the Jury
232 Opening Statements
233 The Trial
234 The Court's Charge and the Verdict
235 Motions after Verdict
236 Responsibilities of the Claim Representative with Respect to Litigation
237 Responsibilities of the Claim Representative with Respect to Trial Preparation
238 Alternative Dispute Resolution

LAW AND THE COURTS

200 Common Law Defined

Common law is court-made law. The common law of England, upon which the jurisprudence of most of our states is based, consists of a body of principles and rules of action which relate to the powers of government and to the security of persons or property. These principles and rules derive from usages and customs, and from judgments and decrees of the courts which enforced such usages and customs. The colonists brought the common law of England to this country, and during colonial days it was the rule of decision in all the courts. After the Revolution, the existing common law was adopted by the several states and has developed since that time through the decisions of the courts of the states. The common law continues to develop today, further refining and modifying existing common law and interpreting statutory law.

Statutory law, as distinguished from common law, is enacted by legislatures. Thus, statutory law represents the will of the people as expressed by their elected representatives.

201 Early Concepts

The jurisdiction originally assumed by the courts and the judges was that of a criminal nature. They heard and determined cases involving unreasonable or unlawful conduct in violation of the law, and assessed punishment. They made no distinction between a violation that involved the public as a whole and one that involved only one individual or group of individuals. Thus, if a man committed larceny, assault, or murder, he was punished as a criminal. If a man negligently injured his neighbor, he also was punished as a criminal. Gradually, the courts made a distinction between the two classes of cases. Acts offensive to the community and the public as a whole, such as larceny, assault, and murder, were classified as crimes and were punished accordingly. Acts not offensive to the public in general but which caused injury to another because of socially unreasonable conduct were classified as *torts* (that is, *wrongs*) and were considered to involve only the particular parties. These acts were punished only by an award of money damages in favor of the injured party and against the wrongdoer.

In addition to the determination of rights arising out of the social relationships, the courts also assumed jurisdiction over contractual relationships into which the parties entered. Where there was a breach of contract, the common-law courts would award damages.

The common-law courts adopted as a fundamental concept that each individual was endowed with certain rights which the law was bound to protect. These include the rights to: liberty; security of person, property, and reputation; and the services of a wife, unemancipated child, or servant. Any wrongful deprivation or diminution of the enjoyment of these rights could give rise to an action at law for damages against the wrongdoer.

202 Common-Law Rights and Duties

In its use in law, the word *duty* is also correlative of a right. For example, whenever a person has a right, there is a corresponding duty upon some other person or upon all persons generally. The common law imposes duties of performance, care, or observance in matters arising out of the social relationships of an individual in favor of (1) the *community* at large and (2) other *individuals*.

As to the community at large, the common law recognized that individual members of the community were obligated to regulate their conduct in such a way so as to be in conformity with the law, both human and divine. Any act done in violation of those duties which the individual owed to the community was a crime for which the individual was answerable to the community. The common law took the view that any acts which offended the community and which, if repeated, would undermine the peace and harmony of the community were violations of the duty owed to the community. Therefore, such acts as larceny, robbery, burglary, atrocious assault, mayhem, and homicide were regarded as offensive to the peace and dignity of the community and punishable by the community as crimes.

As for the individual, the common law imposed a duty on others to regulate their conduct with due care so as to avoid an infringement of the basic rights recognized by the law. Failure to exercise just, proper, and sufficient care which results in the invasion of the legal rights of another is a tort. The consequences of a tort, as we have said, are "private" in nature in the sense that they affect only the individual particular parties.

An act, or omission, may be both a crime and a tort. It may be an offense against the peace and dignity of the community at large, and it also may invade the rights of an individual. In such a case, the offender is subject to both criminal and civil liability. He is answerable to the public for his violation of his public duty and may be punished according to the penal law; he is also answerable to the individual for damages sustained as a result of his wrongful invasion of the individual's private right. These are separate and distinct liabilities as far as the offender is concerned, and the disposition of one will have no effect upon the disposition of the other.

A fairly common example of this situation is the automobile accident case where the death of an individual was caused by the culpably negligent operation of the vehicle. Under those circumstances, the driver would be answerable in damages to the estate of the victim. He could also be prosecuted for automobile homicide or manslaughter, and subjected to criminal liability if convicted. The fact that he settled the private claim of the deceased's estate will not relieve him of criminal liability, nor will his conviction or acquittal on the criminal charges relieve him of his liability in tort.

A tort is based on the rights and duties arising from social relationships. These rights and duties are recognized by law and ordinarily are not voluntarily acquired or assumed. A contract, on the other hand, is a voluntary agreement between parties which creates rights and duties on the part of each. These rights and duties are enforceable by the courts. The individual can avoid the obligations imposed by a contract by not making one.

203 Stare Decisis

This doctrine refers to a policy adopted by the courts holding that, where the court has once laid down a principle of law as applicable to a certain state of facts, it will adhere to that principle and apply it to all future cases where the facts are substantially the same. The doctrine is grounded on the theory that security and certainty require that an accepted and established legal principle, under which rights may accrue, be recognized and followed.

The doctrine is subject to the exception that the court may, in its discretion, modify or overrule a legal principle where public policy requires it or where the reason for the rule no longer exists. For example, the original common-law view with respect to the ownership of land contemplated that the owner of the property owned the land to the center of the earth and to the heavens above. Anyone who invaded any portion of this area was a trespasser. An aircraft, flying over the owner's property, committed a trespass. In the light of modern conditions and public necessity, the rule has been modified to the extent that the ownership of the land either upward or downward is limited to that portion of the land which has been reduced to possession by occupancy, plus the area needed for the enjoyment of that occupancy. Thus, if a man built a building 100 stories high, he then would have reduced to possession by occupancy the space from the ground to the top of the building. An intrusion by an aircraft into that area would be a trespass.

Where an aircraft is flown at a high altitude and does not interfere with the owner's right of possession or enjoyment, there is no trespass.

204 Statutory Modifications of the Common Law

Statutory law, as enacted by the legislature, can alter, amend, or abrogate any principle of the common law and can also create new causes of action which were not recognized by the common law. The rule is, however, that any legislation which is contrary to or "in derogation of" the common law is strictly construed, and the legislation changes the common law only in those areas where the statute specifically says it does. As an example of such a change, the common-law view was that a man ceased his legal existence at death. Therefore, he could not make a will which would call for the performance of an act after death, namely, the distribution of his property–nor could he sue or be sued. The theory was that, because the man had ceased to exist, he could neither perform nor be held accountable for any earthly actions. But, as a result of legislative enactment, a man may now make a will that effectively disposes of his property after his death in accordance with his wishes, and he may sue for damages through his personal representative to recover for injuries suffered prior to his death. He may also be sued, by means of an action brought against his personal representative, after his death.

At common law, an employee could recover damages for bodily injury from his employer only if the employer had failed in one of his common-law duties to the employee. Workers' compensation laws represent legislation that completely abrogates the common-law principles applicable to the relationship of master and servant, substituting a new remedy which was completely unknown to the common law.

205 Statutory Construction

A statute is a written enactment of the legislature and is reflective of the will of the people represented. There are some statutes which affect the law of torts. Where a need arises, whether due to a change in customs or usages or whether the need arises from the recognition of the necessity for a change from the old rules, the legislature, responsive to the will of the people, will enact laws which enlarge or diminish the liability imposed by the common law, or laws which will create new causes of action.

When a new statute is enacted, it will then be the task of the courts to construe it and to determine its legal effect. The courts proceed on the basic premise that a statute which is contrary to or "in derogation of" the common law will be strictly construed, and they will hold that the statute changes the common law only in the areas and to the extent that it specifically sets forth that it does. Should there be any doubt as to the meaning of the statute, it will be construed most strongly in favor of the common-law rule then in existence, the courts looking to the plain language of the statute and not to the legislative intent which inspired it.

206 The Common Law in the United States

As a result of the Revolutionary War, the Thirteen Colonies became separate sovereign states. They exercise all of the rights of sovereignty to this day, with the exception of the rights which the states specifically delegated to the federal government by means of the Constitution of the United States. One of the inherent rights of sovereignty which was not delegated to the federal government was the right of each to make its own statutes applicable within its jurisdiction, as well as the maintenance of courts for the purpose of interpreting and applying the law to matters within the same jurisdiction.

The states adopted the English common law as it existed at the time of the Revolution. The courts of each state in turn, from that time forward, developed common law in response to the prevalent customs and usages.

Thus the highest court of each state has the supreme authority to declare what constitutes the common law of the state that is applicable to all matters occurring within its borders. It is not bound by the decisions of the courts of other states as to applicable common law. The common law of one state may well differ from the common law of another. Where there is some uniformity, and a large group of states has adopted certain common-law principles as a rule of decision, this view is generally referred to as the *majority* view, as opposed to the *minority* view held by a smaller group.

The Constitution of the United States authorizes the establishment of federal courts in the various states for the purpose of hearing and determining certain matters within their jurisdiction. In matters not involving federal law, the federal district courts apply the common law of the state in which they sit, so that it is quite possible to find one federal court (applying the common law of one state) reaching a conclusion entirely different from the decision of another federal court.

207 Judicial Authority

The common law consists of rules of law promulgated by the courts and based on the customs and usages of the people. It is clear that customs change with the passage of time and with the introduction of new inventions, as well as with advances made in science, sociology, and medicine. As customs change, the courts sometimes find that the reason for a common-law rule has ceased to exist, or that the application of an old rule would be unjust. Since the common law was originally the judicial reflection of general customs, the courts can be responsive to the changes as they occur, modifying old rules or abandoning some rules entirely.

Under our political system, the states have retained certain rights of sovereignty, one of which is the right to maintain a judiciary independent of the federal government, and independent of all other states. The supreme court of each state, therefore, has the power and the authority to decide the common law applicable in the state.

When a change in conditions is called to the attention of the supreme court of any state, and it is urged by a litigant that the change requires a modification of the common law, the supreme court will determine whether there has in fact been a change. If so, the court will determine whether the change requires a modification of the common law and the extent of the modification required. The views of each state supreme court will not always be the same, and the response to the change in conditions likewise may not be the same. Thus, we do not have a uniform system of common law in the United States. To ascertain the applicable common law in a given state, recourse must be had to the latest pronouncements of the supreme court of that state on the particular subject.

208 Choice of Law

Generally, the substantive rights of the parties are governed by the law of the place where the rights were acquired or the liabilities incurred. Substantive law is that part of the law which creates, defines, and regulates the rights of the parties. Procedural law prescribes the method of enforcing the rights so created or obtaining redress for their invasion.

Where there is no agreement to the contrary, the law of contracts is governed by the law of the place where the contract is made. The parties may agree that the rights of the parties will be governed by the law of another state, rather than the state in which the contract was actually made.

In tort cases, as a general rule, the substantive rights of the parties are determined by the law of the place where the wrongful act was committed, regardless of whether suit was actually brought and tried in another jurisdiction. There are some exceptions to this rule. (See the next section, Significant Contacts Rule.)

The procedural law of the court in which the action is brought will govern with respect to procedure. All contract and tort actions are transitory, in the sense that the action may be brought in any state where the court has jurisdiction of the parties. For example, let us assume that an automobile accident occurred in Massachusetts, involving a negligent New Jersey driver and a Massachusetts citizen. The Rules of Court of New Jersey, the place where the action is brought, will govern the procedure to be followed, but the court ordinarily will apply the substantive law of Massachusetts in determining the remedy available.

209 Significant Contacts Rule

This rule relating to the exercise of jurisdiction by a court over a transaction, event, or accident which occurred outside the borders of the state is sometimes referred to as the center-of-gravity rule.

In tort cases, the general rule is that the place of the tort is determinative of the applicable law. Actions in tort are transitory in the sense that the action may be brought in any court having jurisdiction of the parties, regardless of the situs of the accident. The law of the forum (*lex fori*) is applied to matters that are procedural only. But the law governing the rights of the parties (substantive law) as between themselves will be governed by the law applicable at the place of injury, or the *lex loci delicti*. An exception to this rule has developed where there are special circumstances, usually where the parties to the action are citizens and residents of the forum state and where the accident has occurred elsewhere. In such a case, since the forum state has a greater interest in the outcome (greater significant contacts) because it involves only its own citizens, the local law of the forum state may be applied.

The practical result of this rule is that, at the outset, the plaintiff has a choice of the law under which he will bring his action. He may proceed in the state where the accident occurred, in which case the law of that state will be applied. He may proceed in his own state of residence, in which case the law of the forum state will be applied. As a result, the plaintiff will select the jurisdiction which is more favorable to his recovery. The perceived plaintiff's advantage may refer to a variety of factors: the required quantum of proof, as in ordinary negligence states as opposed to guest statute states; or nonprivity states, as against privity states in products cases; or the amount of recovery, as in states which have a monetary limitation on recoveries for wrongful death as against those having no limitation on such recoveries. However, it must be emphasized that the rule is applicable only when those special circumstances exist and there are greater significant contacts with the parties to the litigation on the part of the forum state than those of the state of the accident. The Restatement (Second) on Conflict of Laws states:

> In an action for a personal injury, the local law of the state where the injury occurred determines the rights and liabilities of the parties, unless some other state has a more significant relationship with the occurrence and the parties as to the particular issue involved, in which event the local law of the latter state will govern.

Not all states have accepted this rule. Some have approved it, some have rejected it, and still others have not had occasion to examine it at all. We will make brief reference to the decided cases and the specific states of fact to which the rule has been either applied or found inapplicable.

In *Kilberg* v. *Northeast Airlines, Inc.* [9 N.Y. 2d 34; 172 N.E. 2d 526], the decedent, a New York resident, purchased in New York a plane ticket to Nantucket, Massachusetts, as a paying passenger on the defendant's flight originating in New York. He was killed when the plane crashed in Massachusetts. The Massachusetts wrongful death statute then limited recovery to $15,000. The deceased's administrator brought an action in New York for wrongful death and for breach of an implied contract of safe carriage arising from the purchase of the plane ticket in New York. The plaintiff contended that the death limit of $15,000 as set forth in the Massachusetts wrongful death statute was merely a procedural rule and as such was not binding on the New York court. It was also argued—since the deceased was a citizen and resident of New York, since the ticket was purchased in New York and since the flight originated in New York, and, in addition, the defendant corporation conducted some of its business in New York—that New York State had greater significant contacts with the tort than did Massachusetts, which was merely the site of the accident. It was held that the Massachusetts limitation of $15,000 was not applicable, and the New York court could apply its own law to the recovery. Since New York has no limitation in its wrongful death statute, an award of $150,000 was made, which was subsequently affirmed by the New York Court of Appeals.

In *Pearson* v. *Northeast Airlines, Inc.* [309 Fed. 2d 553], the plaintiff's decedent was killed in the same air crash which took the life of Kilberg. An action was begun, however, in the federal district court, and the constitutionality of the *Kilberg* decision was attacked on the theory that New York had failed to give full faith and credit to the statutes of the state of Massachusetts and, in so doing, had violated the federal Constitution in that regard. The court held there was no constitutional violation and awarded judgment in the sum of $160,000, applying the New York unlimited damages rule, which judgment was upheld by the

Circuit Court of Appeals. The U.S. Supreme Court denied certiorari in 372 U.S. 912, thus leaving the Court of Appeals decision in place.

Where the forum state has no significant contacts with the occurrence or the parties, the rule does not apply. For example, in *Cherokee Laboratories* v. *Rogers* [398 Pac. 2d 520], the Oklahoma Supreme Court held that in an action brought in Oklahoma for the wrongful death of a person killed in a crash of an airplane in Missouri, the substantive law of Missouri was controlling and that the statutory wrongful death limit of Missouri should be applied. The court refused to follow *Kilberg* and *Pearson* (*supra*), because there was a failure of proof that Oklahoma had any significant contact with the event.

The same result obtained in *Skahill* v. *Capital Airlines* [234 Fed. Supp. 906], where the Federal District Court for the Southern District of New York held that, in an action for wrongful death arising from an airplane crash in Virginia, the Virginia limitation on wrongful death recovery was applicable—even though such limitations are against public policy in New York, where the action was brought. The court held that a New York court can refuse to apply the law of the state where the accident occurred only if New York has some interest in or contact with the transaction. Here neither the deceased nor his dependents were residents of New York nor was the flight scheduled to pass through New York.

While there are other classes of cases that could be discussed, the few examples cited should suggest that the choice of law area is characterized by myriad fact situations and subtle legal distinctions between substantive and procedural law.

Obviously, many conflicts between the laws of various jurisdictions are spawned by the interstate automobile and commercial vehicle travel that is characteristic of our society. In *McDaniel* v. *Sinn* [400 Pac. 2d 1018], the Kansas Supreme Court, taking a position contrary to the New York courts in *Kilberg*, refused to apply the substantive law of Kansas to an automobile accident occurring in Missouri and involving Kansas citizens. The court noted that some states have decided that, where all the parties are residents of one state, the substantive law of that state could be applied to accidents occurring in another jurisdiction. The court cited *Richards* v. *United States* [369 U.S. 1] in which the headnote states:

> The general conflict of laws rule followed by a vast majority of the states is to apply the law of the place of injury to the substantive rights of the parties, but the recent tendency of some states has been to depart from this rule in order to take into account the interests of the state having significant contact with the parties to the litigation.

The court also noted the Annotation in 15 ALR 2d 762 as follows:

> The great weight of judicial authority is inclined to view that questions as to the measure and amount of damages recoverable or a limitation on that amount are just as much questions of substantive law and therefore governed by the law of the place where the fatal injury was inflicted as the right generally to recover for the wrongful death.

The court also referred to a later Annotation in 92 ALR 2d 1180 and cited the following:

> It is the general rule, subject to some exceptions . . . that questions as to the measure, extent or amount of damages recoverable in wrongful death actions are to be determined by the law of the place where the wrong causing the death occurred, this rule being founded upon the view that the measure, extent or amount of damages for wrongful death pertains to a matter of substance of the right to recovery, which should be governed by the law of the place wherein the cause of action arose.

The above quotations, while they may not greatly clarify, at least illustrate the complexities that arise when courts, relying not only on judicial precedents, but on their views of public policy, seek to adjust conflicting laws of different jurisdictions.

210 Jurisdiction, Venue, and Forum Shopping

Where there are significant contacts with more than one state the plaintiff, as noted above, will attempt to file his or her lawsuit in the most advantageous place. This is known as ''forum shopping.'' State A may have a body of law, or a supreme court, perceived to be more liberal than State B in allowing broad scope for plaintiffs' recoveries. The plaintiff may even seek to file suit in a particular county in State A. For example, in County Y of State A, the population of potential jurors may be perceived as strongly proplaintiff and antibusiness —particularly where a local plaintiff is suing a large, out-of-state corporation.

In order for the lawsuit to proceed, the court must have *personal jurisdiction* and *subject-matter jurisdiction* over the parties. These terms refer to the persons about whom and the subject matter about which a court has the power to make legally binding decisions. For example, in the case of the out-of-state corporate defendant, the court may examine whether the corporate defendant has persons (such as agents, sales representatives, or other employees) operating in the state, or things (such as financial assets, places of business, property) located in the state, over which the courts of that state can exercise jurisdiction. The corporate defendant—if it has few if any contacts with State A—may challenge the court's jurisdiction. Even if there is no question of jurisdiction, the defendant may challenge the plaintiff's forum-shopping scheme on the basis of *forum non conveniens* (inconvenient court). Thus, the defendant may seek a judicial ruling that the lawsuit should be brought in State B rather than State A for reasons of fairness or convenience of the parties. Because of such factors as distance, location of witnesses, etc., it may be unreasonable to hear the case in State A. For similar reasons of fairness or convenience, the defendant (even if it acquiesces to trial in State A) may seek a change of venue from one county (or judicial district) within the state to another. In the alternative, the defendant may seek to have the case removed from the courts of State A to federal district court on the basis of *diversity of citizenship*, because the plaintiff and the corporate defendant live in (or have their base of operations in) two different states. The corporate defendant, for example, may ask a federal court to invoke its *diversity jurisdiction* to hear the case, because it thinks the judge and/or the jury in federal court will be more impartial than the judge and/or the jury in the state courts.

211 Restatement of the Law

As we have seen, the common law consists of the sum total of all the decided cases. Some leaders of the legal profession have determined that there should be an orderly statement of the common law, and that this would be preferable to continuing to rely on the "growing indigestible mass of decisions." It was for this purpose that the American Law Institute was formed in 1923. Its membership included outstanding lawyers, judges, and law professors. Its purpose was to make a statement of the law based on the mass of decisions which constituted the common law. The result of their labors is called the *Restatement of the Law*. It deals with various branches of the law, notably Agency, Conflict of Laws, Contracts, Restitution, and Torts.

The common law applicable in each state is what the supreme court of that state says it is. We took the English common law and added to it our own decisions. These were made by the various state courts, and the decisions are not all consistent. In some areas there is a hopeless conflict. Therefore, in such situations, the *Restatement* recommends a rule to be applied. While the *Restatement* is not binding on any court, many of them have been persuaded to adopt the *Restatement* rule as their own, or to accept the *Restatement* rule with some exceptions. Others have rejected certain *Restatement* rules. Therefore, we can regard the *Restatement* as being persuasive of what the American Law Institute, and a number of courts, think the law should be.

212 Origin of Equity

The English common-law courts had the power only to award money damages or to deny them. They could not avert a threatened injury, nor could they compel the performance of a contract. They could not look behind a written contract to determine if it represented the agreement of the parties, or whether the contract was induced through fraud. They could and did award money damages after the injury had been sustained or the contract had been breached.

In a large number of cases, the award of money damages was a satisfactory solution. But there were some cases where the award of money damages was inadequate and others where the award of damages would be unjust. For example, if a person maintained a nuisance in the form of a slaughterhouse in a residential neighborhood and the noxious fumes permeated the home of a neighbor, endangering his health and impairing his enjoyment of his property, the common law gave him a right to bring an action for damages against the slaughterhouse operator for each intrusion of noxious fumes. Clearly, the award of damages would not enable the neighbor to enjoy his home, and for that reason the common-law remedy was inadequate.

Because of such cases the practice arose of appealing to the English monarch for the relief which the common-law courts were unable to give. If the king determined that the common-law remedy was inadequate, he would hear the evidence and take whatever action his conscience dictated. He might command the slaughterhouse operator to cease and discontinue his operations *(injunction)*; he might order that a contract be rewritten so as to conform to the agreement of the parties *(reformation)*; or he might command that a contract be delivered up and destroyed *(rescission)*. It should be emphasized that the king had no desire to impair the authority of his courts, and he would act only in those instances where there was no adequate remedy at law available.

As cases became more numerous, the king delegated the decision-making authority to the chancellor. Since all of the cases were appeals to the king's conscience, it seemed fitting to turn over this duty to the chancellor, who was known as the "keeper of the king's conscience." The chancellor soon established other courts presided over by his vice-chancellors, and these courts came to be known as *chancery* or *equity* courts. Their jurisdiction was confined to cases in which there was no adequate remedy at law.

The chancery or equity courts functioned as a separate system, independent of the common-law courts, until the last century. By degrees, almost every state in this country has consolidated the functions of the law and equity courts into one legal system, accomplishing this result either by constitutional amendment or by legislation.

213 Equitable Remedies

The remedies which the king delegated to the chancellor consisted of those types of cases wherein there was no adequate remedy at law, and even though the courts of equity could award damages under certain circumstances, the remedies with which we will be concerned consist of the following:

1. Injunction. An injunction may forbid the defendant (or his agents or servants) to do some act, which he is threatening or attempting to commit, or it may restrain him in the continuance of such an act. For example, a man operates a dog kennel in a residential neighborhood, and the residents are disturbed by the barking of the dogs at night. The court could issue an injunction, or order, compelling the kennel owner to cease his operations and to remove the dogs from the neighborhood. In such a case, it is clear that a judgment for money damages would not be an adequate remedy because the neighbors want to be free from the disturbing noise, rather than to receive money in payment for the continued inconvenience.

2. Reformation. This is the power of a court of equity to reform or rewrite a contract to conform to the intent of the parties. It is a remedy afforded by the courts of equity—to parties to a written instrument which imports a legal obligation—to reform or rectify such an instrument whenever it fails through fraud or mutual mistake to express the real intention of the parties. For example, a man's house is partially destroyed by fire on March 10. He has no insurance, but his loss convinces him of the necessity for fire insurance. He promptly applies for such insurance on March 11 and an insurance contract is issued. Through a mistake, the inception date of the policy was incorrectly noted as March 1 instead of March 11 as agreed. The man makes a claim for the fire damage which occurred on March 10. The insurance company may petition a court of equity to reform the policy so as to reflect the intentions of the parties: that the inception date of the policy was to be March 11 and not March 1 as written.

3. Rescission. This refers to the power of a court of equity to abrogate, annul, void, or cancel a contract upon a showing of fraud, either in the inducement or making of the contract. For example, an adjuster induces a claimant to sign a general release on the representation that, in spite of the language of the document, it is only a partial release and that other and further payments would be made to him. On those facts, the court of equity could set aside the release, voiding the document. This is an example of *fraud in the inducement*, in that the claimant was induced to sign the release solely as a result of the adjuster's fraudulent statements.

214 Appellate Courts

In America, each colony had a judicial system comparable to that of England. With the coming of independence, each colony established a Supreme Court, as the highest judicial authority in the state. The Constitution of the United States created the Supreme Court of the United States and empowered Congress to create the federal judicial system. This system includes both trial and appellate courts.

A party who is dissatisfied with a judgment rendered at the trial level by a federal district court has a right to appeal to the U.S. Court of Appeals for the federal judicial circuit in which the district court is located. Each of the thirteen circuits encompasses an area of the country. A party who is dissatisfied with a judgment of the U.S. Court of Appeals (or even the highest court of a state) may want to appeal to the U.S. Supreme Court. However, except for a few unusual situations, a party has no right to require the Supreme Court to hear its case. It may petition for a *writ of certiorari*, stating the arguments that it believes should persuade the Court to hear its case. Of the many petitions presented to the Court, very few are granted.

215 Federal Jurisdiction and Authority—the Federal Judiciary

The Constitution provides that the judicial power of the United States shall be vested in one Supreme Court, and in such inferior courts as Congress may establish. By the Judiciary Act of 1789, Congress established federal district courts and circuit courts of appeals. Federal district courts have been established throughout the country.

Most suits are filed in state courts. The federal courts cannot hear every type of case. The Constitution defines the jurisdiction of the federal courts as follows:

> The judicial Power shall extend to all Cases, in Law and Equity, arising under this Constitution, the Laws of the United States, and Treaties made, or which shall be made, under their Authority;—to all Cases affecting Ambassadors, other public Ministers and Consuls;—to all Cases of Admiralty and maritime Jurisdiction;—to Controversies to which the United States shall be a Party;—to Controversies between two or more States;—between a State and Citizens of another State;—between Citizens of different States;—between Citizens of the same State claiming Lands under Grants of different States, and between a State, or the Citizens thereof, and foreign States, Citizens, or Subjects.

The federal jurisdiction with which we are concerned most frequently is the jurisdiction over controversies between citizens of different states—that is, diversity jurisdiction. In that area, the present rules passed by Congress limit this jurisdiction to cases involving $50,000 or more, exclusive of interest and costs. Therefore, to invoke federal jurisdiction at the present time, there must be diversity of citizenship between the plaintiff and the defendant, and the amount in controversy must be more than $50,000 exclusive of interest and costs. In absence of either of these elements, the federal courts do not have jurisdiction.

In diversity cases involving citizens of different states, the federal courts apply the common law and statutes of the state in which they sit or in which the cause of action arose. Under this system, it is possible to find inconsistent decisions among the judgments of the various federal courts. The reason usually is that, in each instance, the court is applying the law of the state in which it is located or the law of the state which is applicable to the cause of action. Where the laws of the various states differ, so will the decisions of the federal courts.

This system produces yet another problem. In some cases the federal court is called upon to interpret the law of the state, but the supreme court of the state has never passed on the question. Since the federal court must dispose of the litigation, it has to "guess" what the law of the state is. These cases frequently arise where the state legislature has passed a new statute and the federal court is required to interpret the statute even before the legal issues involved have been determined by the supreme court of the state. In any case, the supreme court of the state is not bound to follow the decision of the federal court and may come to the opposite conclusion. When the supreme court of the state has determined the law applicable, the federal courts interpreting the law of that state are bound to follow the latest decisions of that court.

This may be a little confusing, but our initial premise must be that the common law of the state is what the supreme court of that state says it is. Therefore, when a federal court decision is cited as the authority for the law of a particular state, it merely means that the decision represents the federal court's guess as to the applicable law of the state and it is subject to being confirmed or overruled by the state supreme court if and when a similar case is presented to that court.

216 Preemptive Statutes

The powers granted to Congress by the Constitution can be exercised only by legislation. Where Congress has not legislated in any particular area, the rule is that the states may exercise that power until it is displaced by Congressional legislation. Where Congress has legislated, the rule is that Congress has "preempted" the field, or occupied the area, and states thereafter cannot exercise the power. For example, Congress has passed the Federal Employers Liability Act, which provides a remedy for personal injuries sustained by employees of interstate carriers by railroad. No state, therefore, can exercise that power with respect to interstate railroad employees. However, Congress has never legislated with respect to personal injuries sustained by other employees engaged in interstate commerce, such as interstate bus drivers and truck drivers. Therefore, as to this class of employee, the state may exercise jurisdiction, and such employees come within the jurisdiction of state workers' compensation laws.

Congress has exercised the powers granted to it by the Constitution in many fields. Under the interstate commerce power, Congress has regulated in such areas as railroads, aircraft, food and drugs, television, and radio. The statutes passed by Congress are contained in the United States Code. This is a set of volumes numbered in sequence. References, therefore, are made to the United States Code (abbreviated USC) or the United States Code Annotated (abbreviated USCA). Sections of the code may be identified by the title or volume number and the name of the series (USCA), followed by the section number. Therefore, 46 USCA 688 would refer to volume 46, section 688.

217 Code of Federal Regulations

Congress has from time to time established various federal agencies and delegated to them, and to some of the executive departments, certain lawmaking power. Such agencies are authorized, by enabling legislation, to make rules and regulations with reference to their particular responsibilities. The rules thus made have the same force and effect of a law passed by Congress. The rules promulgated by these various agencies are collected in a series of volumes called the

Code of Federal Regulations (abbreviated CFR), and the volumes are numbered consecutively in exactly the same way as any other series of law books. When reference is made to the code, the applicable volume number is cited first, then the code initials, and finally the section number. For example, section 250 of volume 21 of the code would be cited as 21 CFR 250.

A partial list of the agencies likely to be encountered by the claim representative is as follows: Federal Aviation Administration; Interstate Commerce Commission; Food and Drug Administration; Department of Health and Human Services.

Federal Aviation Act. This act created a federal aviation agency headed by an administrator who was empowered by a later act of Congress to promote the safety of aircraft flight by prescribing such reasonable rules and regulations for the operation of aircraft as may be necessary. The civil air regulations thus promulgated do not determine legal liability, but they do impose duties and responsibilities which specify the standards of care which must be observed. Applying common-law principles, the courts have held that a failure to comply with the regulations is evidence of negligence.

Interstate Commerce Commission Act. This act created the Interstate Commerce Commission, whose function it is to supervise the interstate transportation of passengers and freight by land and by water. The commission was also given the power to make rules and regulations governing such transportation. Among the numerous rules promulgated by the commission are those relating to safety of operation by the carriers. The commission also may require carriers to obtain liability and cargo insurance on vehicles. Since the claim representative will frequently encounter accidents involving interstate motor carriers, he or she should be familiar with the sources of these regulations.

Federal Food, Drug, and Cosmetic Act. This act regulates hundreds of commodities that move in interstate commerce, including all varieties of food stuffs and all types of drugs, together with cosmetics, as to their ingredients. Violation of the act is negligence per se.

Federal Food Additives Act. This act gives authority to the Secretary of Health and Human Services to regulate the ingredients which may be added to food as a preservative. It is the Secretary's function to determine and regulate the safe products which can be added, and to prohibit the addition of any toxic substances. Since this act is an exercise of the interstate commerce power, the act and its regulations apply only to food products in interstate commerce.

Federal Hazardous Substances Labeling Act. The act authorizes regulation of household chemical products, requiring certain precautionary labeling. The purpose of the regulations is to safeguard the consumer against dangerous household products by placing a duty upon the manufacturer to adequately warn those who will probably come in contact with the product as to its latent and inherent dangers. The regulations set forth the manner of labeling and the requirement that the label contain first aid instructions and antidotes.

PROCEDURE IN A CIVIL SUIT

218 Trial Preparation Generally

Trial preparation begins with the original investigation. In a case which qualifies for investigation, the claim representatives have no way of anticipating whether the case will be settled or whether it will result in litigation. Therefore, they will investigate the claim as if it were being prepared for trial. They will evaluate the witnesses, including the claimant and the insured. They will arrange with all favorable witnesses some means of communicating with them so that, should their presence be required at the trial, they can be reached easily. This might in some cases consist of obtaining, for example, the names and addresses of relatives who will always know where they are, or the name and address of some close friend who will always be in touch with them.

219 The Summons

A lawsuit is begun by the service of a summons. It is a writ issued by the clerk of the court and directed to the sheriff or other proper officer, requiring the sheriff to notify the person named that an action has been commenced against him, and to appear on a day named to answer the complaint in that action. The purpose of the summons is twofold. The court does not have jurisdiction of the defendant unless and until the summons is served. Its second purpose is to notify the defendant of the action.

Since most states follow rules similar to the Federal Rules of Civil Procedure, we will use those rules in discussing the service of process and the time limitations within which they must be served. If your state does not utilize the federal rules, it will be necessary to check your own code of civil procedure to determine if there are any differences. Under the federal rules, the summons must be served by a sheriff or other proper officer on the individual. This is done by delivering a copy of the summons and complaint to the defendant personally or by leaving a copy at the defendant's dwelling, house, or usual place of abode with some person of suitable age and discretion then residing there, or by delivering a copy of the summons and complaint to an agent authorized by appointment or by law to receive the service of process.

Service upon an infant or an incompetent person is made by serving the summons and complaint in the manner prescribed by the law of the state in which the service is made. Some states provide for the appointment of a guardian for the minor or incompetent, and then service on the guardian by the sheriff.

Service on a corporation or upon a partnership or other unincorporated association, which is subject to suit under a common name, is made by delivering a copy of the summons and complaint to an officer, a managing or general agent, or to any other agent authorized by appointment or by law to receive service of process, and, if the agent is one authorized by statute to receive service (such as the director of motor vehicles in automobile substituted service cases), and the statute so requires, by also mailing a copy to the defendant.

The form of the summons is similar in virtually every state, with some very minor differences. So that claim representatives may be familiar with this process, the form of summons used in the federal district courts is reproduced in Figure 2–1.

220 The Complaint

The federal rules and those of most states require that the complaint be served with the summons. In others, the summons may be served without the complaint, which is served within 20 days after the defendant appears. The complaint is a statement of the plaintiff's claim, setting forth the material facts

FIGURE 2–1

UNITED STATES DISTRICT COURT
FOR THE
SOUTHERN DISTRICT OF NEW YORK

Civil Action, File No.__________

John Doe Plaintiff vs. *Richard Roe* Defendant	Summons

To The Above Named Defendant:

You are hereby summoned and required to serve upon James Brown, plaintiff's attorney, whose address is 144 Main Street, City of Mineola, New York, an answer to the complaint which is herewith served upon you, within 20 days after service of this summons upon you, exclusive of the day of service. If you fail to do so, judgment by default will be taken against you for the relief demanded in the complaint.

Joseph Green
Clerk of Court

Seal of U.S. District Court

Dated: ________________1995

on which the plaintiff's case depends. Its purpose is to inform the defendant of the nature of the action and the amount of the damages (*ad damnum*) claimed.

Federal district courts do not have jurisdiction in actions between individuals unless there is a diversity of citizenship (plaintiff and defendant are citizens of different states) and the amount in controversy exceeds $50,000, exclusive of interest and costs. Therefore, the complaint will allege both of these facts for jurisdictional purposes. In the first of the two accompanying complaints (Figure 2–2, a simple pedestrian knockdown case which does not require much information to set forth the cause of action), these facts are alleged in paragraph 1. The second complaint (Figure 2–3) alleges that the plaintiff sustained injuries as a consequence of slipping on snow and ice.

FIGURE 2–2

UNITED STATES DISTRICT COURT
FOR THE
SOUTHERN DISTRICT OF NEW YORK

Civil Action, File No.__________

John Doe
Plaintiff
vs.
Richard Roe
Defendant

COMPLAINT

1. Plaintiff is a citizen of the State of New Jersey and defendant is a citizen of the State of New York. The matter in controversy exceeds, exclusive of interest and costs, the sum of fifty thousand dollars.
2. On May 1, 1994, on public highway called William Street in the City of New York, New York, the defendant negligently drove a motor vehicle against plaintiff who was then crossing said highway.
3. As a result, plaintiff was thrown down and had his leg broken and was otherwise injured, was prevented from transacting his business, suffered great pain of body and mind, and incurred expenses for medical attention and hospitalization in the sum of three thousand dollars.

   Wherefore, plaintiff demands judgment against defendant in the sum of one hundred thousand dollars and costs.

James Brown
Attorney for Plaintiff
Office and Post Office Address
144 Main Street
Mineola, New York

FIGURE 2–3

UNITED STATES DISTRICT COURT
FOR THE
SOUTHERN DISTRICT OF NEW YORK

[Title of Action]

1. [Allegation of jurisdiction]
2. Plaintiff is a tenant of the defendant and resides in an apartment house project known as ''Kent Village.'' Kent Village consists of various separate units connected by interior sidewalks, which are owned and maintained by the defendant for the use of their tenants and guests.
3. On March 1, 1994, plaintiff, after shopping in the American Store on the property of the defendant, was pushing her baby stroller over an interior walkway owned and maintained by the defendant. This walkway was the most direct route to the apartment occupied by her. The walkway was covered by a heavy coating of slippery ice, which had been on the walkway for a lengthy period of time and which defendant had negligently failed to remove or failed to treat in such a manner as to make the same safe for pedestrians.
4. As a result of defendant's negligence, plaintiff in traversing this walkway, slipped on the ice and fell to the ground.
5. As a result, plaintiff's coccyx bone and lower sacrum were seriously and permanently injured, and she was otherwise injured. Plaintiff was, and will be, prevented from carrying on her duties as a housewife, suffered great pain of mind and body, and incurred medical attention and hospitalization in the sum of $15,000. Wherefore, plaintiff demands judgment against defendant in the sum of $100,000 and costs.

221 Duties of the Insured Receiving Process

All liability policies contain the following type of condition with respect to the action which must be taken by the insured when process is served on him: ''If claim is made or suit is brought against the insured, he shall *immediately* forward to the company every demand, notice, summons or other process received by him or his representative.'' The purpose of this condition is to give the company adequate opportunity to perform its obligation under the policy contract. Since the company is obligated to defend any suit or other proceeding brought against the insured arising out of the hazards insured against, it is apparent that the company must have the process which was served in time to appear and answer or to take whatever other legal proceedings are appropriate. Therefore, the company has included in its contract, as a condition of its responsibility, the requirement that the insured forward the process to the company immediately. This requirement does not mean that the insured will satisfy the condition by merely notifying the company of the suit. It means that the actual process served must be forwarded to the company at once. Failure on the part of the insured to comply strictly with this condition may release the company from its obligations under the contract.

There has been considerable litigation over what ''immediately'' means in connection with this contract. Most companies construe it to mean that, if the process is received in time to appear and answer within the 20 days, or whatever period of time is applicable, the insured has met the obligation of forwarding the process to the company immediately. Courts, however, may construe the condition more leniently in favor of the insured.

222 Duties of the Claim Representative Receiving Process

When the summons and complaint are received by the company—whether delivered by the insured personally, or by mail, or by the insured's agent—the claim representative's first duty is to ascertain the date and the manner of service. The date on the summons merely indicates the date on which the clerk issued the process, not when it was served—the sheriff may have had the process in his office for a week before service was effected. The insured can advise of the actual date he received it and whether it was served on him personally (and if not, upon whom it was served).

When the date of service has been ascertained, the defendant has 20 days, exclusive of the day of service, within which to appear and answer. If he fails to take this action within the time limits, the plaintiff may apply for and receive a judgment by default. This latter situation is to be avoided. In some states, it is extremely difficult to set aside a default judgment without conclusive evidence of a meritorious defense being offered in support of the application. In others it is not so serious a situation; but in any case it calls for more legal work than would be necessary if the case were handled expeditiously.

If the case is one for trial, then the papers should be transmitted to defense counsel as soon as possible. The more time counsel has to prepare an answer and consider the defenses available, the better. It is recommended that papers should be transmitted to counsel the same day as they are received. In any case, where the process is received within the 20-day period, defense counsel must have them in time to appear and answer before the 20 days expires.

223 Stipulation to Extend Time for Answer or Otherwise Plead

In most circumstances, the plaintiff's attorney, upon request, will probably agree to extend the 20 days for an additional period of time. In most jurisdictions this can be done by a stipulation which the plaintiff's attorney will draw and send to the company, or merely by a letter on the attorney's stationery, extending the time within which the defendant must appear and answer. The claim representative will have to be familar with the rules of court in the particular jurisdiction as to the periods of time which can be the subject of extensions. Local defense counsel should be consulted as to the procedures to be followed in these matters.

In any case, the use of the extenion of time is helpful in reducing legal costs and, if a case can be settled, even with an extension of time, the plaintiff can discontinue the cause of action and the company will have incurred no legal fees whatever.

224 Tender of an Overdue Process

An insured, who forwards a process to the company which has been served more than 20 days before, has breached the policy condition. Should the company accept the process with knowledge of the breach of condition, such action might constitute a waiver of the breach. Therefore, in an instance where the process was not forwarded in time, the claim representative must immediately notify the insured that the company may not be bound by the insurance contract because of the insured's breach of condition.

The insured must be informed that any prejudice to the defense of the suit resulting from the delay will cause the insurer to deny coverage. The claim representative must immediately determine whether there has been any prejudice, such as a default judgment. Failure by the claim representative to notify the insured of a potential coverage problem may result in waiver of the insurance company's rights.

225 The Answer

The answer is a pleading served on the plaintiff by which the defendant responds to the plaintiff's demand by an allegation of facts, either denying the allegations of the plaintiff's complaint or confessing them and alleging new matters in avoidance, which the defendant alleges should prevent recovery on the facts alleged by the plaintiff. The complaint is the statement of the claim by the claimant, and the answer is the statement of the defendant's defense. The answer may deny some allegations of the complaint and may admit others. As to the allegations admitted, the plaintiff does not have to offer proof.

For example, in the pedestrian knockdown complaint (cited above) the defendant could admit the first part of paragraph 1, where the plaintiff alleges the diversity of citizenship between plaintiff and defendant, and could deny that the controversy exceeds $50,000 exclusive of interest and costs. His answer might read "The defendant admits the allegations of paragraph 1, except that he denies that the matter in controversy exceeds the amount of fifty thousand dollars exclusive of interest and costs." Then the plaintiff would not be required to offer any proof of the diversity of citizenship between plaintiff and defendant, since this is admitted, but would have to sustain the burden of proof that the matter in controversy exceeds the amount of $50,000 exclusive of interest and costs.

The rule of pleading is that any allegation of the plaintiff's complaint that is not denied is deemed admitted. Therefore, if the answer was silent as to the allegations of paragraph 1, the plaintiff's allegations are admitted and no proof of the allegation is required.

New matter may be alleged in the answer as an affirmative defense. Let us assume that the claim representative has settled the case and taken a release in return for the payment. Later a suit is brought, and the complaint does not mention anything about the release or the settlement. The answer would set up as an affirmative defense the allegation that the claim had been released.

Pleadings and other legal proceedings must be handled by counsel, and the claim representative must be guided by counsel as to what is required in that regard. However, this does not preclude the claim representative from having some familiarity with the general objective of pleadings and the purposes they serve.

226 Discovery Proceedings

Generally speaking, a party to an action may take the testimony of any person, including a party, by deposition upon oral examination or written interrogatories, for the purpose of discovery or for use as evidence in the action, or for both purposes.

In most states, the witness, either by deposition or interrogatory, may be examined regarding any matter, not privileged, which is relevant to the subject matter in the pending action, whether it relates to the claim or defense of the examining party or to the claim or defense of any other party, including the existence, description, nature, custody, condition, and location of any books, documents, or other tangible things, and the identity and locations of persons having knowledge of relevant facts. A party may require the adverse party to disclose the names and addresses of proposed expert witnesses on whom the party will rely. Discovery may not reach the work product (e.g., notes reflecting thought processes) of the attorney for either party, or any communications passing between attorney and client.

Oral depositions consist of taking the witness's testimony under oath, before a notary or other person authorized to administer oaths, and with a question and answer record being taken by a court reporter. Interrogatories, on the other hand, consist of the submission of written questions to the witness and the return of them with the answers. This procedure is usually used where the oral deposition is deemed unnecessary, either because of the cost factor or because written interrogatories will serve the same purpose. It is clear that the taking of oral depositions is a costly undertaking. The party demanding the depositions must defray the costs, which will include the services of the reporter and the transcription of the testimony taken. If the same result can be obtained by the use of written interrogatories, which are served on the adverse party by mail and returned by the same means, the procedure is less costly. Figure 2–4 illustrates a written interrogatory used in a personal injury action by the defendant.

FIGURE 2–4

CAPTION

The defendant demands of the plaintiff the following particulars in accordance with the cause of action set forth in the complaint.

1. Full name, address, and place of birth.
2. Date, approximate time and condition of weather at the time of accident.
3. Detailed description of the nature, extent, and duration of any and all injuries.
4. Detailed description of injury or condition claimed to be permanent together with all present complaints.
5. If confined to hospital, state name and address of same, date of admission and discharge therefrom.
6. If X rays were taken, state the name and address of the place where they were taken, the name and address of the person who took them, the date on which each was taken, and what is disclosed.
7. If treated by doctors, state name and present address of each doctor, the dates and places where treatments were received and the date of last treatment.
8. If still being treated, state the name of the address of each doctor rendering treatment, when and how often treatment is received, and the nature thereof.
9. If a previous injury, disease, illness, or condition is claimed to have been aggravated, accelerated, or exacerbated, specify in detail the nature of each and the name and present address of each doctor, if any, who rendered treatment for said condition.
10. If employed at the time of accident, state:
    a. Name and address of the employer.
    b. Position held and nature of work performed.
    c. Average weekly wages for the past year.
    d. Period of time lost from employment, giving dates.
    e. Amount of wages lost, if any.
11. If other loss of income, profit, or earnings is claimed:
    a. State total amount of said loss.
    b. Give complete detailed computations of said loss.
    c. State nature and source of loss of such income, profit, and earnings, and the date of deprivation thereof.
12. If there has been a return to employment or occupation, state:
    a. Name and address of present employer.
    b. Position held and nature of work performed.
    c. Present weekly wage, earnings, income, or profit.
13. Itemize in complete detail any and all monies expended or expenses incurred for hospitals, doctors, nurses, X rays, medicines, care, and appliances and state name and address of each payee and the amount paid or owed each payee.
14. Itemize any and all other losses or expenses incurred not otherwise set forth.
15. State the names and addresses of all persons who have knowledge of any relevant facts relating to the case.
16. State names and addresses of any and all proposed expert witnesses.

It can be seen that the answers, either to the depositions or the interrogatories, will open many avenues of investigation to the claim representative. They will also disclose the extent of the injuries claimed and the special damages. Specific questions can be designed for special cases and can be added to the interrogatories or asked at the time the deposition is taken. In some states, the rules of discovery permit an inquiry and disclosure of insurance, and the policy limits, even though such evidence is not admissible in the trial of the case. The rationale of this procedure is that, where the plaintiff knows exactly the extent of the insurance coverage, there is a greater likelihood of settlement than where the plaintiff is in the dark and cannot know that his demand is in excess of the policy limits.

Discovery proceedings include medical examinations of the claimant, and the defendant may compel the plaintiff to submit to a medical examination, which may include the taking of X rays, blood samples, and other tests where appropriate. These are all matters of evidence to which the defendant is entitled prior to trial.

Liberal discovery rules have the potential for abuse, particularly with regard to demands for document production. One defense lawyer concisely identified the sorts of problems defendants and their attorneys may face:

> Plaintiffs' attorneys are also attempting to bury the unwary defendant in broad discovery requests that ask for every document in the possession or knowledge of the defendant. Failure to produce every conceivable item then creates a "discovery fraud" issue which becomes the centerpiece of the plaintiff's presentation to the jury. Complete and thorough review and preparation of documents on the part of "discovery counsel" can allow the trial attorney to concentrate on defending the facts of the case, not the preparation. [Schoemaker, *Document Collection, Review and Production*, 37 *For the Defense* 9 (January 1995).]

Procedural rules and sanctions exist to control such abuse of discovery, but judges sometimes are reluctant to enforce the rules firmly or to impose appropriate sanctions on attorneys and litigants. Discovery abuse wastes time, creates needless expense, and is often used as a club to coerce settlements.

227 Motions

A motion is an application to the court for a ruling or for an order, made by counsel. There are many kinds of motions, depending upon the ruling sought. They may be made in advance of trial, during, or after trial. In advance of trial, the defendant may make a motion, for example, to compel the plaintiff to answer interrogatories—where the plaintiff has failed or neglected to do so when the proper demand was made. If the motion is granted, the court will issue an order directed to the plaintiff to answer the interrogatories.

During the trial, the attorney for the defendant, for example, may move to dismiss the complaint and, if this motion is granted, it ends the trial right at that point; the court will direct a verdict for the defendant. After trial, the defendant, for example, may move for a new trial on the grounds that the verdict is against the weight of evidence or that the amount of damages awarded is so excessive as to shock the conscience of the court. If either of these motions is granted, the verdict will be set aside and a new trial ordered. (These are merely examples of motions which can—and must in appropriate circumstances—be made by counsel.)

228 Subpoenas

A subpoena (Latin *sub*, under; *poena*, penalty) is a process to cause a witness to appear and give testimony, before a particular court or magistrate, at a particular time. It is a writ issued either by the clerk of the court, or the attorney as an officer of the court, directed to the witness. It is served on him personally, either by the sheriff or other officer so authorized, or, in some jurisdictions, by any person over the age of 21. The process will also state on its face that, for failure to attend and testify, the person will be held in contempt and subject to penalties. In addition, a fee must be tendered to the witness covering his expenses in coming to and going from the court. This amount is usually fixed by the court and in an amount applicable to all cases, with additional mileage being allowed where the witness has to travel some distance.

A straight subpoena merely calls for the presence of the witness and nothing more. Where the witness is required to bring with him and produce books of account, records, or other items, documentary or otherwise, a process called a *subpoena duces tecum* is utilized. This process commands the witness—who has in his possession or control some document or paper or other thing which is pertinent to the issues of a pending controversy—to produce it at the trial. The most common use of this type of process is to obtain the production of hospital records of the claimant, by serving the custodian of the records and having him or her appear and identify the records. It is also used to compel the attending physician to appear and bring along all office records, records of tests, X-ray plates, and other information in his or her possession relating to the treatment of the patient.

229 Functions of the Judge and Jury

The fundamental principle is that the judge decides the law and the jury determines the facts. For example, the judge decides the applicable law in a situation where the defendant had been operating his motor vehicle in excess of the speed limit, and that damages should be awarded if the defendant was in fact speeding and his excessive speed was the proximate cause of the accident. Assume that the defendant contends that he was going 20 m.p.h. in a 25 m.p.h. zone and that the proximate cause of the accident was the plaintiff's negligence in failing to take reasonable precautions for his own safety. Assume that the plaintiff contends that the defendant was going 50 m.p.h. in a 25 m.p.h. zone and that the proximate cause of the accident was the defendant's excessive speed.

It is clear that both of these contentions cannot coexist; at least one has to be wrong. The jury will decide which contention it will believe. If it believes the defendant, and so finds, the judge will instruct them to return a verdict for the defendant. Conversely, if it believes the plaintiff, the verdict will go the other way.

The jury, therefore, has two questions of fact to decide. The first is the speed of the defendant. If they find that the speed of the defendant exceeded the speed limit, then they have to decide, from the facts, if the excessive speed was the proximate cause of the accident. The judge will decide, as a matter of law, what evidence is admissible and what is not. The judge will exclude evidence which he or she decides is not admissible.

The most frequent question of fact submitted to the jury is the application of the "reasonably prudent person" standard to a set of circumstances. The evidence will indicate certain facts. As to disputed facts, the jury will decide the ones that it will believe. Having decided the believable facts, it will then decide whether such conduct approximated what the reasonably prudent person would do under the same or similar circumstances. The law of the situation, as given to the jury by the judge, would be that if the defendant's conduct was that of a reasonably prudent person, then the defendant would not be negligent, whereas if it was not, the defendant could be found negligent.

230 Waiver of a Jury

The rules of court in most states require that the litigant who desires a jury trial make a demand for a jury in his suit papers. If he fails to do so, the right to a jury trial is waived, in which case the judge decides both questions of fact and questions of law. However, if either party demands a jury, the case is tried by a jury irrespective of the desires of the opposing side.

231 Selection of the Jury

Jurors are selected from a panel and are usually subject to a process of questioning. This is called the *voir dire*: "to speak the truth." It refers to this preliminary examination which is made of the prospective jurors, either by the court or by the counsel for each side. The purpose of the examination is to determine their fitness to serve as jurors, and the questions are intended to bring out whether they have any interest whatsoever in the case, are related to any of the litigants or witnesses (or counsel for either side), have any knowledge of the case or have formed an opinion as to its merits. The questions are likewise used to elicit any mental reservations that the prospective juror may have as to his ability to render a true verdict under the facts of the case.

Either party may challenge a juror. This means that the party objects to the person serving as a juror in the case. Challenges or objections to prospective jurors are of two kinds, peremptory and for cause. In a peremptory challenge, the party making the objection is not required to give any reason whatsoever for the objection. Because extensive use of this challenge could delay the trial, in civil cases most jurisdictions limit the number of peremptory challenges. Challenges for cause are unlimited. They relate, for example, to prospective jurors who are related to either party, have an interest in the outcome of the case, or are employed by either party. Such persons are challenged for cause, because it is clear that they could not render a fair verdict under the circumstances.

232 Opening Statements

After the jury has been selected and sworn, both sides are permitted to make opening statements. These serve as an introduction for the jury to the nature of the case and the evidence which will be presented. Since the plaintiff has the burden of proof, plaintiff's counsel will open the case by making a statement as to the claims alleged and the evidence to be produced. Then the defendant makes an opening statement, admitting whatever facts will not be controverted and outlining the theory of defense, as well as the evidence to be produced to support it.

It should be noted that neither side is *bound* to state the evidence on which it relies but, as a practical matter, attorneys seldom forego the opportunity to acquaint the jury with the facts they intend to prove. Most attorneys feel that this gives the jury the "feel" of the case and makes the evidence more understandable as it is presented.

233 The Trial

The plaintiff introduces his or her evidence first. Witnesses are sworn and testify on direct examination by the plaintiff's attorney. Each then may be cross-examined by the defense. Physical exhibits, such as plats, photographs, diagrams, X-ray plates, etc., are identified and offered in evidence. At the close of evidence, the plaintiff rests.

The evidence offered by the plaintiff must establish the allegations of the complaint. The plaintiff has the burden of persuasion as to the existence of the facts relied upon, including the fact of the damages suffered and their monetary value. In negligence claims, for example, the plaintiff must establish:

1. A wrongful act or omission on the part of the defendant.
2. The wrongful act or omission as the proximate cause of the injury to the plaintiff.
3. Damages as a result of the wrongful act or omission.

The sum total of these three requirements constitutes a prima facie case. The failure of the plaintiff to establish all three requirements, or a prima facie case, will compel a dismissal of the action, because the plaintiff will not have sustained the burden of proof which the law requires. The defendant does not have to prove anything. The law does not require that the defense produce any evidence or testify in its own behalf. The law *does* require the plaintiff to meet the burden of proof.

At the close of the plaintiff's case, the defendant may, at its option, introduce evidence in contradiction of the plaintiff's evidence, as well as evidence sustaining any affirmative defenses which may have been interposed. For example, in certain jurisdictions contributory negligence of the plaintiff is a defense to be alleged and proved by the defense. The defendant may establish this fact by evidence of its own, or by the cross-examination of the plaintiff. The same is true with respect to assumption of risk as a defense. The statute of limitations is an affirmative defense, as is the fact that the claim has been released. These may be alleged and proved by the defendant.

Where the defendant offers evidence, the plaintiff is permitted to introduce rebuttal evidence, contradicting the defendant's evidence. He may recall his prior witnesses in order to accomplish this. If rebuttal evidence is offered, the defendant likewise has an opportunity to offer further evidence in contradiction to the rebuttal evidence. If no rebuttal evidence is offered, once both sides have rested there is no further right, by either party, to introduce further evidence.

At the close of both the plaintiff's case and the defendant's case, there are certain motions or requests for rulings which may be made to the court, relating to a dismissal of the complaint, a directed verdict, or a mistrial. Both sides are then given an opportunity to sum up in an effort to persuade the jury as to the merits of their respective cases.

234 The Court's Charge and the Verdict

When both sides have rested, the court will outline to the jury the questions which it must decide and will instruct them as to how they are to do it. After the charge, the jury retires to its deliberations. This process takes place in the jury room, where they are completely alone, and each juror acts independently and voluntarily in forming his or her conclusions. Votes are taken by the foreman of the jury at intervals to determine if they are in agreement. When an agreement is reached, they return to the court and deliver their decision. This is called their verdict.

In some jurisdictions the verdict must be unanimous: all the jurors must agree. In others, a 5/6th verdict is acceptable; this means that if ten of the twelve (or five of the six) jurors agree, that will be the verdict of the jury. When the jury fails to agree, it is called a "hung" jury. At the discretion of the court, such a jury may be discharged and a new trial ordered.

235 Motions After Verdict

After verdict, either side may make a motion to set the verdict aside or for judgment notwithstanding the verdict. Usually the basis of the motion is that the verdict is against the weight of evidence, excessive, or contrary to the evidence. The motion may be granted, or denied, in the discretion of the court.

The general rule is that the court will deny the motion unless the verdict is so inadequate, or excessive, or so contrary to the evidence that it ''shocks the conscience'' of the court. The fact that the amount awarded is less than the plaintiff demanded, or in excess of what the defendant thinks it should have been, is not enough. The verdict must be so far out of proportion to the evidence that the court itself will term it disproportionate. If the motion is granted, the court may then grant a new trial.

236 Responsibilities of the Claim Representative with Respect to Litigation

Every claim in litigation can be settled by the simple expedient of paying the plaintiff what he or she wants in settlement. It is the claim representative's duty to decide how far the company should go in meeting the demand of the plaintiff. He or she will determine largely which cases will be tried and which will be settled, either prior to or during trial. He or she will weigh the evidence and will estimate the evidence favorable to each side. He or she will obtain the opinion of counsel as soon as the case goes into litigation and will compare counsel's opinion with his or her own as to the possibilities of a successful defense, the possibilities of a lesser verdict than the plaintiff's demand, and the possibilities of an adverse verdict.

While it is counsel's reponsibility to recommend, the final decision as to trial or settlement rests with the claim representative. If he or she decides that it is a case to try, and it eventually comes to trial, the claim representative will keep in touch with the progress of the case, the evidence offered by the plaintiff, and the recommendations of counsel at the close of the plaintiff's case. The claim representative will take advantage of a settlement opportunity even during the trial if it is to the advantage of the company to do so. In major cases, it is not uncommon for the claim representative to sit at the counsel table during the trial, so that if the evidence is against the defense, a settlement can be arranged before submitting the case to the jury. In any case, it is the claim representative's duty to make the final decision as to whether the case is to be submitted or settled.

237 Responsibilities of the Claim Representative with Respect to Trial Preparation

Generally the responsibilities of the claim representative in this respect are to place in the hands of defense counsel a fully investigated case and to see that the witnesses upon whom the defense will rely are available to testify at the time and place of trial. This will undoubtedly mean that they all will have to be recontacted, and in some cases relocated. He or she will, in addition, conduct such additional investigation as is recommended by counsel.

When the date of trial is reached, the claim representative will arrange for the presence of the witnesses when needed, arranging for their transportation and their reimbursement for the time they have lost in appearing at the trial. He or she will also serve subpoenas when necessary and, in general, see that counsel is provided with all the evidence that it is possible to produce in support of the defenses which are being urged.

238 Alternative Dispute Resolution

No discussion of civil litigation would be complete without some mention of *alternatives* to civil litigation. *Alternative dispute resolution* (often referred to as ADR) is a generic term encompassing various methods of resolving disputes, short of litigation.

Certain ADR techniques are used in various state courts and in varous federal district courts around the country. The programs using these techniques are referred to as court-annexed programs, because they are administered under the jurisdiction of courts and overseen by the courts. Some of these techniques were described as follows, in *Court Based Dispute Resolution Programs* (1991), published by the Federal Judicial Center.

Early Neutral Evaluation. Early in the case, the litigants meet with an outside neutral expert in the subject area to discuss all aspects of the case. Its major purposes are to enhance communication, narrow issues, structure the discovery process, and promote settlement.

Judge or Magistrate Hosted Settlement Conferences. The litigants meet with a judicial officer other than the trial judge to discuss settlement. The purposes are to increase the chances of settlement or to narrow the issues for trial. If held relatively early in the pretrial process, such conferences may also promote earlier settlement of cases likely to settle anyway.

Mediation. The litigants meet with an outside neutral, appointed by the court or selected by the litigants, for in-depth settlement discussions. Often, the mediators are experts in the subject matter. Mediators facilitate discussions among the litigants to assist them in identifying the underlying issues and in developing creative and responsive settlement packages. The purposes are to increase the chances of settlement, help the litigants devise better settlements, and improve the relationships among litigants.

Nonbinding Arbitration. The litigants briefly present their cases to an outside neutral or panel of neutrals who then give the litigants their opinion of the judgment value of the case. Its purpose is the same as case valuation except that it offers parties the opportunity for an advisory adjudication of their case.

Nonbinding Summary Jury Trials. The litigants briefly present their cases to a jury which returns an advisory verdict. The purpose is to use the assessment of typical jurors as a spur for settling cases that are poised for a lengthy trial.

The reader should note that some of these techniques, especially mediation and nonbinding arbitration, are offered by ADR providers in the private sector, and are used by parties who seek to resolve disputes without recourse to the judicial system at all. In addition, there are other dispute-resolution methods that are widely used in the private sector.

For example, in *binding arbitration*, the parties present evidence to a single arbitrator (or a panel of arbitrators) who render a decision. The arbitrator can make a monetary award for the claimant. Mechanisms exist to transform the award into an enforceable judgment under the Uniform Arbitration Act (a uniform law which is applicable in most states). Another example of dispute resolution that is popular in the private sector is the *minitrial*. This is a technique often used in business disputes. Executives of the companies engaged in the dispute may conduct a hearing at which the conflicting positions of the parties are presented in abbreviated form. The executives then try to resolve the case.

Some of the above-noted methods have been described as *assisted negotiation*, where a *third party neutral* helps the parties to work out a resolution. Other methods involve a decision and imposition of a judgment.

The methods of ADR are developing continually and being used in new ways, as alternatives to costly and time-consuming litigation.

Chapter 3

Law of Torts

TORTS AND NEGLIGENCE

TORT LAW—AN OVERVIEW

300 Tort Defined

301 Classification of Torts

NEGLIGENCE

302 Negligence Defined and Described

303 Negligence Per Se

304 Degrees of Care

305 Gross Negligence

306 Proximate Cause

307 Intervening Cause

308 Foreseeability

APPICATIONS OF NEGLIGENCE

FORESEEABILITY

309 Foreseeability as Applied to Motor Vehicles

310 Foreseeability as Applied to Premises

311 Foreseeability as Applied to Products

312 Rescue Doctrine

OWNERS AND POSSESSORS OF PROPERTY

313 Duties of the Possessor of Land

314 Trespassers

315 Licensees

316 Social Guests

317 Invitees

318 Area of Invitation or License

319 Revocation of Invitation or License

320 Police Officers and Fire Fighters in the Line of Duty

321 Modifications of Occupiers' Liability

322 Landlord and Tenant

323 ''Attractive Nuisance'' Doctrine

EMOTIONAL DISTRESS

324 Negligent Infliction of Emotional Distress

TORTS AND NEGLIGENCE

TORT LAW—AN OVERVIEW

300 Tort Defined

While a completely satisfactory definition of a tort is yet to be devised, we may define the term for the purposes of our work as follows:

> A tort is a wrongful act or omission—arising in the course of social relationships other than contracts—which violates a person's legally protected right, and for which the law provides a remedy in the form of an action for damages.

This definition contemplates that for an act or omission to constitute a tort, all three of the following elements must be present:

1. A legally protected right (other than those arising from contracts).
2. A wrongful invasion of that right.
3. Damages as a proximate result of that invasion.

1. The Existence of a Legally Protected Right. The English common law recognized certain rights which were legally protected, such as the right of the individual to: liberty; security of person, property, and reputation; and the services of a wife and an unemancipated child. Under our present system, these rights are still legally protected, but we have added others, either by statute or by further development of the common law. Among the added rights are the right of privacy, the right to vote, the right to earn a living, and the right to an education. In some states the common-law rights have been extended to include matters which were never contemplated before. As an example, some states recognize that the members of the family have a ''property'' right in the body of a deceased member and allow recovery for the mishandling or the mutilation of the body.

Not all rights are legally protected, and those which are not will not form the basis of tort liability. For example, a customer offers to buy a certain article from a store owner and tenders the purchase price. The owner refuses to sell. The right to purchase is not a legally protected right, and therefore there is no tort liability involved.

2. A Wrongful Invasion of that Right. This contemplates not only acts which are either intentional or negligent, but also acts which subject the actor to liability even though they are neither intentional nor negligent. This latter classification includes the possession and maintenance of dangerous instrumentalities as well as the conducting of ultrahazardous operations, both of which expose others to unreasonable risks of harm.

The invasion must be wrongful. Merely because a legally protected right is invaded does not in and of itself create tort liability. For example, the right to liberty is a legally protected right. If a police officer with a warrant arrests an individual, the right to liberty has been invaded. The invasion, however, is legal and not wrongful. On the other hand, if the police officer made the arrest without having reasonable and probable cause for believing that the individual had committed a crime, or without a warrant, then the invasion would be wrongful and the police officer would be answerable in damages.

3. Damages as a Proximate Result. Theoretically, if the first two elements are established, a tort has been committed, but, in the absence of actual damages sustained as a proximate result, the plaintiff would be entitled only to nominal damages. Where damages are alleged, it must be established that they were sustained as a direct result of the tort committed and that there is a direct chain of causation running from the tortious act to the injury claimed.

The person charged with the commission of the tort is referred to as the *wrongdoer* or the *tort-feasor*. Where two or more persons commit the tort, they are sometimes referred to as joint tort-feasors.

Tort and Contract Distinguished. Liability in tort arises out of social relationships. Members of society are entitled to rights and are subject to liability solely because of their status as members of the community. The rights and liabilities of the members of the community are imposed by law. No member can waive his rights or avoid his responsibilities. On the other hand, the obligations of contract are voluntarily assumed as a consequence of an agreement. A person can avoid the obligations of a contract by not making one.

Tort and Crime Distinguished. The common law required that each member of the community regulate his or her conduct in such a way that none of his acts were offensive to the community at large. If an act offensive to the community was committed, the person would, upon conviction, be subject to criminal liability. Such acts would include assault and battery, larceny, burglary, mayhem, and homocide. Criminal liability would subject the person to punishment in the form of a fine, imprisonment, or, in extreme cases, execution. This criminal liability is often referred to as the "public consequences" of his act. Penal statutes have been enacted which define the elements of these crimes and, in some states, fix the amount of punishment to be imposed.

The same act may have "private consequences" as well, and in such a case the injured person will have the right to bring a civil action for damages. For example, *A* assaults *B* with a deadly weapon, causing serious injuries. *A* is indicted, tried, and convicted of assault with a deadly weapon, and is sentenced to a term of imprisonment. These are the "public consequences" of his act. However, *B* has sustained injuries, which are "private consequences" and *A* may be subject to civil liability for the injuries which his action has caused. Thus, *A* may be subject to criminal liability for his act, and civil liability as well.

301 Classification of Torts

Torts may be divided into three groups, according to their nature and origin, as to whether they involve:

1. Intention.
2. Negligence.
3. Liability without fault.

1. Intention. An intentional tort is an act done with the intention of bringing about injury to the person or property of another. It contemplates a state of mind, either prior to or concurrent with the commission of the act, where the tortfeasor deliberately determines to do the act which produces the injury. This state of mind can usually be established by the nature of the act itself.

Thus, if a man strikes another with his fist, inflicting physical injury, that action is deemed a battery. Since a man is deemed to have intended the reasonable consequences of his acts, mere proof of the occurrence will be sufficient to create an inference of the tort-feasor's intent. But the words spoken immediately preceding the act and the surrounding circumstances may change the character of the act. If *A* and *B* decide to engage in a boxing bout and, during the encounter, *A* strikes *B*, no tort has been committed. *B* gave up his right to the security of his person and voluntarily assumed the risk of injury which would arise as a result of the boxing bout. Therefore *A* has not invaded the right of *B*. However, *B* relinquished his right to security of person only for the limited purpose of boxing, and he assumed only the risk of being struck by the boxing gloves on *A*'s hands. If, during the bout, *A* became infuriated and struck *B* with an axe which was near at hand, this would be a tortious act and would subject *A* to liability. The intended victim is not the only person who can claim damages for an intentional tort. Suppose *A* discharges a pistol into a crowd of people, intending to injure *B*. His aim is poor and the bullet hits *C*. Although *A* had no intention of injuring *C*, the law will transfer his intent to injure *B* to *C*, making *A* liable for an assault and battery on *C*. This is called the doctrine of *transferred intent*. In addition to assault and battery, which we have considered, intentional torts include *malicious prosecution* (prosecution begun with evil intent and without probable cause to believe the charges can be sustained), *malicious abuse of legal process* (willfully misapplying court process to obtain an object not intended by law), *false imprisonment* (wrongfully depriving a person of his right to liberty), *defamation,* including *libel* and *slander* (injuring a person's character, fame, or reputation by false and malicious statements), and *conversion* (the wrongful taking of the property of another).

2. Negligence. Negligent torts refer to those which arise as a result of the failure to meet the duty to exercise care. The invasion of a legally protected right may come about with no intention of so doing, but because of carelessness, neglect, or indifference. The person who fails to exercise due care so as to avoid invading the rights of others, is answerable for any injury or damage caused by his negligence, or lack of due care.

3. Liability without Fault. These torts refer to situations where a person is held to a standard of liability which is usually referred to as strict liability. Such a form of liability (also sometimes called absolute liability) may be imposed regardless of any negligent act, fault, or intent. These torts can be divided into two classes as to their origin: (1) those created by the common law and (2) those created by statute.

Torts Created by the Common Law. The common-law rule applicable in most jurisdictions is that, where the owner or occupier of property makes such unnatural or abnormal use of his property as to expose the community to a greater risk of harm than normal, he is absolutely liable for any injury or loss occasioned by his unnatural use. The abnormal use might consist of the storage of explosives or inflammable liquids, or the unnatural collection of water in a dangerous place, or the keeping of wild animals dangerous to man, such as lions or tigers. Abnormal activities on the land which will subject the community to an unreasonable risk of harm are also within the purview of these torts. Such activities could consist of blasting, fumigating a building with cyanide gas, or the digging of a dangerous excavation which removes the lateral support from adjoining land.

Torts Created by Statute. The legislature has the power to enact statutes that impose absolute liability regardless of any negligent act, fault, or intent, and they have done so in a number of areas. For example, under the Uniform Aeronautics Law, adopted in some of the states, absolute liability is imposed upon the owner of an aircraft for injuries to persons or property on land caused by the ascent, descent, or flight of the aircraft, or the dropping or falling of any object from it. This means that, regardless of fault, mere proof of the happening of the event will be sufficient to impose liability upon the owner, even though the event occurred as a consequence of what is sometimes called an "act of God," or from a cause which human foresight could not have anticipated or prevented.

At common law an employee could recover from the employer for bodily injury only where the injuries were sustained as a result of the negligence of the employer. By the enactment of workers' compensation laws, the common law rule of liability has been eliminated, and an employer generally is liable, regardless of negligence, if an employee is injured in an accident which arises out of and in the course of employment.

NEGLIGENCE

302 Negligence Defined and Described

Negligence is the failure to exercise that degree of care which the law requires to protect others from an unreasonable risk of harm. This contemplates a legally protected right, a duty owed to the person possessing the right, conduct which falls below the standard required by law to meet that duty, and injury as a result of the failure to meet that standard. In a tort cause of action based on negligence, the following elements must be established by the person asserting the claim in order for that person to recover damages:

1. A legal duty owed.
2. Failure to comply with the standard required by law to meet the duty.
3. A causal relationship between the failure to meet the standard and the resulting injury.
4. Damages as a proximate result.

1. A Legal Duty Owed. A duty is an obligation recognized by law to conform to a certain standard of conduct for the protection of others. It arises from the social relationships of the parties and, in the absence of such a social relationship, which creates the duty, there is no obligation. For example, the owner of a motor vehicle is required to maintain his vehicle in reasonably safe condition for the protection of others using the highway, but his car has faulty brakes.

It is stolen by a thief who is injured in an accident caused by the failure of the brakes to function. There is no social relationship between the car owner and the thief from which a duty of care on the part of the owner could arise for the benefit of the thief.

The same rule traditionally has applied where a burglar or trespasser made illegal use of an owner's premises and was injured because of negligent maintenance. No duty of care is owed to either by the owner. An old English case sums up the relationship of duty and negligence as follows: "The question of liability for negligence cannot arise at all until it is established that the man who has been negligent owed some duty to the person who seeks to make him liable for his negligence. . . . A man is entitled to be as negligent as he pleases toward the whole world if he owes no duty to them."

The duties which the law recognizes as arising out of social relationships have their origin in one of the following three sources:

1. The common law.
2. A statute.
3. A voluntary act.

1. The Common Law. Among the duties recognized by the common law is the duty of the owner or occupier of land to maintain his premises in a reasonably safe condition for the safety of those who are lawfully on the premises by invitation or license. The duty is owed only to those persons who are within the class designated, namely, those who are lawfully on the premises by invitation or license. The duty does not exist in relation to anyone not in the designated class. An automobile driver has a duty of reasonable care in the maintenance of his vehicle and in its operation. He owes this duty of care for the safety of the person and property of others lawfully using the highway or situated at or near the highway. Thus the driver owes this duty to his own passengers, the drivers and passengers in other cars, pedestrians, the owner of property lawfully on the highway, and the owner of property adjoining or adjacent to the highway.

2. A Statute. Not all statutes or ordinances create duties. There are some which require that an act be done, or an act not be done, for the safety of certain classes of persons. When a statute sets up a requirement for the safety of a certain class of persons, a duty arises, but only to that particular class of persons.

For example, where a statute required that every three-story apartment house have either fire escapes directly accessible to each apartment, or two independent stairways not adjacent to each other, the owner of the apartment house was held liable for the deaths of tenants when a fire broke out in the hallway and prevented the tenants from escaping because of the absence of either fire escapes or two independent stairways.

On the other hand, if the person injured is not within the class of persons for whose safety the statute was enacted, there is no duty owing to that person. For example, a local ordinance prohibited the washing of cars on a public street. The statute was enacted for the traveling public for the purpose of expediting travel.

A washes his car on the street in violation of the statute. The water he used for washing his car collects in the gutter and freezes during the night. The next morning *B* slips on the ice thus formed and breaks his leg. *A* is not liable to *B* by virtue of the statute. The purpose of the ordinance was to expedite travel and not to prevent the water from collecting in the gutter or freezing. The class of persons for whose benefit the statute was passed was the class traveling on the highway. *B* was not within the class of persons for whose benefit the statute was passed, and therefore the statute created no duty on the part of *A* to *B*.

3. A Voluntary Act. The law does not require anyone to aid another person in distress. This is true even though a man is a physician and he sees another person in dire need of medical treatment. In no case is there any duty imposed by law to give aid and assistance to an injured person, even though common decency would seem to require it. Where one does come to the aid of a person in distress, he has assumed a duty of reasonable care in the performance of the assistance, and he will be answerable in damages if he fails to exercise due care and the victim sustains further injury as a result.

For example, a man is trapped in a burning automobile. His rescuer, in the course of removing him from the vehicle, carelessly drops him to the ground. The rescuer may be held answerable in damages for the injury sustained as a result of the fall to the ground. This is true even though the victim might have been burned to death had the rescuer not intervened.

The same concept has been applied to situations where no emergency existed but where there was a voluntary assumption of a duty not required by law. For example, a railroad might have no duty to station a signal at a grade crossing, but it does so. The signal is present for a long period of time, and the public has become accustomed to relying on the warning every time a train approached. Should the railroad fail to maintain the signal, the railroad could be held responsible for any accident which might occur because of the absence of the signal. Having assumed the duty of supplying a signal, the railroad has a duty to exercise reasonable care in its operation.

2. Failure to Comply with the Standard. The courts require, where there is a duty owed, that the person owing the duty exercise reasonable or due care in performing the duty. Clearly, the amount of care which must be exercised will vary with the circumstances and the degree of danger involved. Therefore, the common-law courts applied the *reasonably prudent person standard*, which means that the defendant's conduct will be judged by comparing it with what the reasonably prudent person would or would not do under similar circumstances. If the conduct of the defendant falls below the standard thus invoked, the defendant is liable for negligence.

The conduct of the defendant may involve an act or a failure to act. If an act is one which the reasonably prudent person would not have done, then the act is one of *commission* and constitutes negligence. If the duty required the doing of an act which the reasonably prudent person would have done in the exercise of due care, and the defendant failed to act, then the failure to act is referred to as an *omission*, and is also negligence.

For example, the reasonably prudent person will obey the traffic regulations with respect to the use of a vehicle and will obey the rules of the road, the posted speed limits, and the traffic control signs displayed on the highway. If the defendant's conduct differed from that of the prudent person in exceeding the speed limit (an act of commission) or in failing to obey a traffic control sign (an act of omission), his conduct is negligent. The reasonably prudent person standard is applied to all persons irrespective of intellect or education, with the exception of children and, possibly, aged persons. As to children, the law requires that they exercise a degree of care and caution commensurate with their age and intelligence. This standard will vary with the age and intellectual attainments of the child.

3. Causal Relationship. In some cases, it is quite possible that there was a duty owed and that conduct fell below the required standard—but that there was no chain of causation running from the duty (and the failure to meet it) to the event which occurred. In such a case, there is no actionable negligence. For a recovery to be had, there must be a causal relationship between the duty, the failure to meet it, and the event. This is usually referred to as the requirement of *proximate cause*.

4. Damages. In a negligence cause of action, damages are never presumed. They must be pleaded and proved by the plaintiff, and it must be shown that all of the damages claimed were sustained as a direct result of the negligence of the defendant and from no other cause. (See also Section 306.)

303 Negligence Per Se

This is negligence in itself or negligence as a matter of law. It is conduct, whether an action or omission, which may be declared and treated as negligence without any argument or proof of the surrounding circumstances, because it is so palpably opposed to the dictates of common prudence that it can be said without hesitation that no careful person would have engaged in it. Whether certain actions or lack of action constitute negligence per se is a question for the court and not for the jury. Where the court decides the question affirmatively, it will direct the jury to assume the negligence has been established as a matter of law. For example, if the evidence indicated that the defendant drove his automobile at a speed of 100 miles per hour in a congested area where the posted speed limit was 20 miles per hour, reasonable minds could not differ as to whether he was negligent. Therefore, the court would rule that the defendant was chargeable with negligence as a matter of law, because there was in fact no question for the jury to decide.

Where there is a duty to the public created by a statute and the person injured is one of the class of persons intended to be protected by the statute, the majority of the courts which have passed on the question hold that the violation of the statute is negligence per se. The theory is that the legislature has fixed the standard of conduct which must be observed and the jury would have no right to overrule the legislative objective. A minority of states treat the violation of a statute as creating a presumption of negligence, which can be overcome by evidence in the form of an explanation of his conduct by the defendant. Still others hold that the violation of a statute is merely evidence of negligence and nothing more.

As to the plaintiff, the general rule is that his violation of a statute which relates to his injury constitutes contributory negligence per se and is therefore a complete defense to his cause of action in states that recognize the contributory negligence defense.

304 Degrees of Care

Some cases refer to degrees of negligence, although what they actually discuss are degrees of care. The courts sometimes characterize an act in terms of negligence rather than in terms of the amount of care which is exercised. Expressed in terms of the care which the defendant failed to exercise, the negligence terms are as follows:

1. Slight negligence: failure to exercise great care.
2. Ordinary negligence: failure to exercise reasonable care.
3. Gross negligence: failure to exercise slight care.

1. Slight Negligence. This term is relevant in cases where the defendant is under a duty to exercise a high degree of care. For example, a common carrier of passengers is under a duty to exercise a high degree of care for their safety. If it fails to exercise great care or, conversely, is chargeable with slight negligence which results in an injury to a passenger, the common carrier is answerable in damages. Also, a high degree of care is required of motorists who take some action which is contrary to the normal flow of traffic, such as making U turns or backing. The failure to exercise great care under these circumstances constitutes actionable negligence.

2. Ordinary Negligence. This refers to situations where the duty owed is one of reasonable care, as measured by the reasonably prudent person standard. If the defendant's conduct falls below the standard, he or she is chargeable with ordinary negligence.

3. Gross Negligence. This connotes a more aggravated form of carelessness than ordinary negligence. It is discussed in the following section.

305 Gross Negligence

This term is relevant in cases involving gratuitous bailments, automobile guest statutes, and comparative negligence statutes. The cases tend to agree that it means conduct more culpable than ordinary negligence, but when it comes to fixing the dividing line between ordinary and gross negligence, the cases are in hopeless confusion. At one extreme are the cases which define gross negligence as a complete lack of care, or a complete lack of regard for the safety or the rights of others, characterized as an intentional failure to perform a manifest duty in reckless disregard of the consequences. At the other extreme are the cases which hold that gross negligence is the same as ordinary negligence except that it is carelessness of a more exaggerated form, not necessarily involving recklessness. The trend of the more recent cases seems to be toward this view rather than the first extreme.

It must be recognized that, if the burden is on the plaintiff to establish the gross negligence of the defendant, the burden would be much more onerous under the first definition than the second and that there would be fewer recoveries possible under the first view than the second.

306 Proximate Cause

Proximate cause is the connecting link between the defendant's breach of a duty and the injuries sustained by the plaintiff. To prevail, the plaintiff must establish that the defendant's negligent act was responsible for the injury sustained. The mere fact that the defendant's conduct was negligent will not sustain the claim unless it can be shown that there was an unbroken chain of causation from the negligent act to the infliction of the damage. When this chain is established, it is said that the defendant's negligence is the proximate cause of the damage.

Proximate cause has been defined by the courts as that which in a natural and continuous sequence, unbroken by any efficient intervening cause, produces the injury, and without which the result would not have occurred. To determine whether the defendant's negligent act was or was not the proximate cause of the injury, the courts applied the "but for" or *sine qua non* test: Could it be said that the damage would not have been sustained *but for* the defendant's negligent act?

If the damage would have been sustained *without* the negligent act of the defendant, then the defendant's act is not the proximate cause of the damage. On the other hand, if no damage would have been sustained but for the defendant's negligent act, then the negligence of the defendant is the proximate or responsible cause of the damage. If the defendant's negligent act were to be eliminated, would there have been any damage sustained? If so, then the negligence of the defendant was not the proximate cause. However, if no damage would have been sustained but for the defendant's negligent act, then the negligence of the defendant is the proximate cause of the damage. For example, if the defendant's vehicle struck a pedestrian on the sidewalk, the proximate cause of the pedestrian's injuries would be the negligent operation of the defendant's vehicle. If the negligent operation of the vehicle was eliminated, then the pedestrian would have sustained no injury. Therefore, but for the negligent operation of the vehicle, the injury would not have been sustained.

An eighteenth century English case offers a classic example of proximate cause. The defendant threw a lighted squib, which appears to be an ancient version of our modern day firecracker, into a crowded marketplace. In the instinct of self-preservation, several persons in the crowd successively took the squib and threw it away from themselves. It ultimately exploded and caused injury to the plaintiff. Clearly the original act of the defendant in throwing the lighted squib into the marketplace was wrongful, but the question before the court was whether this act was the proximate cause of the plaintiff's injury. The defendant contended that if the squib had exploded at the place where he threw it originally, some distance from where the plaintiff was standing, the plaintiff would not have been injured, and therefore the negligent or intentional wrongful act was not the proximate cause of the plaintiff's injuries. The court ruled that the defendant should have reasonably foreseen the action of others endangered by the lighted squib, and therefore ruled that there was an unbroken chain of causation running from the negligent act to the injury. Applying the "but for" test, the court reasoned that, if the defendant's act was eliminated, the injury would not have occurred. Therefore, the throwing of the lighted squib was the proximate cause of the plaintiff's injuries.

The application of the "but for" test was found to produce a satisfactory solution to most of the cases. But as time went on, the courts were confronted with situations where there was more difficulty in applying it. For example, automobiles driven negligently by *A* and *B* collide at an intersection, and as a result *A*'s vehicle is forced onto the sidewalk where it hits *C*, a pedestrian. It is clear that both drivers are to blame for *C*'s injuries, but the application of the "but for" rule would lead to a conclusion that the negligence of neither driver was the proximate cause. If we eliminate *A*'s negligent act, then the accident would not have happened but for the negligence of *B*; therefore, *A*'s negligence is not the proximate cause of *C*'s injuries. Applying the same reasoning to *B*'s negligence, the accident would not have happened but for the negligence of *A*, and *B*'s negligence is not the proximate cause either. With this result, *C*, the innocent party, would be without a remedy against either *A* or *B*.

To avoid such an unconscionable result, the courts adopted the *substantial factor* rule as being applicable to situations of this kind. The rule is that the defendant's conduct is a proximate cause of the event if it was a "material element and a substantial factor in bringing it about." Applying this test to the preceding situation, the proximate cause of *C*'s injuries was the negligence of *both A* and *B*, and both are answerable. The negligence of either *A* or *B*, when examined separately, was a material element and substantial factor in the causation of the event.

The rule of proximate cause applies not only to the happening of the event but also the events which follow as a natural consequence of the event itself. For example, if *A*'s automobile, negligently driven, damages a fence belonging to *B*, with the result that *B*'s cattle wander off, *A* is liable not only for the damage to the fence but also for the expense of rounding up the cattle—as well as any damage which might be caused by the escape of the cattle. To cite another example, *A* negligently stalls the passenger bus he is driving on a railroad crossing. A train is approaching at a fast rate of speed. *B*, a passenger on the bus, jumps through the window and fractures his ankle. *A*'s negligence is the proximate cause of *B*'s injury. This is true even though *A* is able to get the bus started and clears the track before the train arrives.

Proximate cause has also been applied to complications and events following the infliction of a bodily injury. Three situations may be involved.

1. Complications of the injury itself.
2. Complications as a result of the medical treatment.
3. Consequential injuries.

1. The Injury Itself. The tort-feasor is answerable for the injury he or she inflicted, together with any other physical conditions which unavoidably arise from the injury. Therefore, if the injured person sustains lacerations which subsequently become infected, even though prompt and proper medical treatment is instituted, the tort-feasor is answerable not only for the lacerations but for the results of the infection as well.

Another such example is that of a claimant suffering from a preexisting heart condition who, as a result of the accident and injuries she sustains, requires an immediate operation to save her life. During the operation, the claimant dies as a result of surgical shock superimposed upon an already weakened heart. The tort-feasor is liable for the claimant's death; there is a direct chain of causation from the infliction of the injury to the death of the claimant. Were it not for the accident, the operation would not have been required. And since the operation was required solely as a result of the injury, the tort-feasor is liable for the result of the operation, whatever it may be.

Where the injured person refuses medication, refuses to follow the advice of his physician, or removes a bandage or a plaster cast, all with the result that his injury is aggravated or his disability prolonged, the proximate cause of his increased disability is not the injury but his own acts. The tort-feasor therefore is not responsible for the increase in disability or any medical costs incurred as a result of the injured claimant's own failure to cure and relieve himself.

2. Complications as a Result of the Medical Treatment. The tort-feasor is answerable for any normal complications which could result from the treatment rendered by a physician chosen with reasonable care by the injured person. If, for example, the person is allergic to tetanus antitoxin and this fact is unknown to the injured person or his physician, and the patient suffers a severe reaction when such antitoxin is administered in the course of treatment, the tort-feasor is answerable for this result.

Where the complications are the result of the malpractice of the physician, the tort-feasor is still liable for the entire damage, since this is a foreseeable risk of harm to which the tort-feasor's negligent act exposed the victim. The physician is himself responsible as a joint tort-feasor for his malpractice and may be joined as a codefendant by the injured person, but the physician is liable only for the effects of his malpractice and not for the entire injury. In no case will the malpractice of a physician insulate the tort-feasor from liability for the entire injury, since the risk of improper diagnosis or negligent treatment is a risk inherent in all medical service.

When an event which is entirely unrelated to the original accident takes place in the course of treatment, the tort-feasor is not answerable for the result. For example, if, while in the hospital recovering from his injuries, *A* makes an improper advance to a nurse and she hits him on the head with a chair, causing severe head injuries, the original tort-feasor is not liable for those injuries.

3. Consequential Injuries. The rule of proximate cause has been applied to subsequent injuries alleged to have been sustained as a result of the original injury. If there is an unbroken chain of causation from the original injury to the second injury, recovery will be allowed; otherwise not. For example, *A* sustains a badly fractured leg as a result of *B*'s negligence. While in the hospital, *A* is supplied with a walking caliper and is told to begin weight- bearing. While she is trying to walk, *A*'s leg gives way, and she sustains a fracture of the other leg. *B* is liable for both fractures.

Now let us assume the same facts, but add that *A* has been discharged from the hospital and given a prescription for medications she must take. On the way to the pharmacy *A* slips on the ice, or is struck by an automobile, sustaining a fracture of the other leg. *B* is not liable for the second fracture, even though the trip to the pharmacy was required as a result of the original injury. The second occurrence was too remote from the chain of causation to be a part of it.

307 Intervening Cause

There are situations where another act or cause comes in between the original negligent act of the tort-feasor and the resulting injury. If this act or cause is in concert with the original wrongful act, it does not break the chain of causation and does not absolve the original wrongdoer from liability.

Again, we apply the "but for" rule; if it can be said that but for the intervening cause the accident would not have happened, then the intervening cause becomes a superseding, independent cause and a proximate cause of the injury. For example, assume that a driver is operating an automobile at a speed of 80 miles per hour, in excess of the speed limit and an excessive speed under the driving conditions, and a passenger grabs the wheel to turn the car away from an oncoming vehicle with the result that the car goes out of control and rolls over, injuring the passenger and the driver. The original act of negligence —driving at an excessive speed—has been superseded by another cause, the action of the passenger. It cannot be established that the excessive speed would have caused an accident; the driver could have slowed down or could have controlled the vehicle so as to have avoided an accident. Therefore, there is no evidence that an accident would have happened had the passenger not intervened. The action of the passenger relieved the driver of the responsibility arising from the excessive speed. The condition created by the driver was merely a circumstance of the accident and not its proximate cause.

The negligence of the operator of a motor vehicle in obstructing the highway may be a proximate cause of an injury to others, even though the negligence of the operator of another vehicle is an active and later cause in contributing to the final result. One cannot excuse himself from liability arising from his own negligent conduct merely because the later negligence of another concurs to cause an injury, if the later act was legally foreseeable. A later event, or second act, will break the chain of causation only where the later act of negligence could not have been reasonably foreseen.

If an automobile breaks down on the traveled portion of the highway, and the owner does not remove it, or does not provide for some means of warning oncoming traffic of the obstruction, either by flares, lanterns, flags, or other devices, the conduct of the owner is negligent. It is reasonably foreseeable that oncoming traffic might not be able to avoid the obstruction where no warning of its presence has been given. But if a car carrying passengers runs into the disabled vehicle, it could be claimed that the negligence of the driver of the oncoming car, in not having it under control, was the proximate cause of the accident; the circumstances do not absolve the second driver from responsibility to his passengers. It may well be that the negligence of the driver, as between himself and the owner of the disabled vehicle, would be considered contributory negligence, defeating the driver's recovery. The passengers are not chargeable with their own driver's negligence, and since the negligence of their driver was foreseeable by the owner of the disabled vehicle, both the owner and the driver may be liable to the passengers as joint tort-feasors. The negligence of both were material elements and substantial factors in causing injuries to the passengers.

The theory of intervening cause can also be applied to the injuries sustained. The action of a patient in interfering with the work of the physician by removing bandages or plaster casts is an intervening cause, in the sense that it is itself the proximate cause of any disability occasioned by the patient's removal. But a more perplexing question is presented where the injured person commits suicide during the period of medical treatment. For example, assume the evidence establishes that the injured person suffered such excruciating pain that it affected his mind to the extent that it drove him to suicide; or that it was established that the injured person had been told that he would never work again, or that his lifespan had been shortened by the injury, and he destroyed himself rather than become a burden on his family or on society. Then it appears that a direct chain of causation could be established running from the injury to the suicide, and the act of the injured person would not be an independent, intervening cause of his death. On the other hand, if the evidence establishes that the injured person had other personal motives for the commission of the act, such as a death in his family or a divorce, and his injury had nothing to do with the motive for suicide, then his act of destruction is an intervening cause of his death which relieves the tortfeasor from liability.

308 Foreseeability

The prudent person will reasonably anticipate the risks of harm or injury to which others will be exposed as a consequence of his or her action or lack of action in a given situation. He or she will therefore govern conduct accordingly and avoid injury to others, when the injury can be reasonably anticipated. The failure on the part of an actor to conform to this standard is negligence.

The doctrine of foreseeability is applied to provide a limitation on the application of the reasonably prudent person standard. The actor is answerable for any injuries that occur to others which should be reasonably anticipated. He or she is not answerable for injuries which could not be reasonably anticipated.

For example, *A*, driving his automobile, negligently collides with a plainly marked truck containing explosives. The truck carries a red flag and signs indicating the purpose for which it is being used. In the ensuing explosion, *C*, the driver of the truck, is seriously injured. *D*, a pedestrian on the sidewalk near the point of impact, is injured, and *E*, who is sitting at a desk in his office one block away, is injured by falling glass which shattered as a result of the explosion.

A is liable to *C, D,* and *E*. *A* should have reasonably anticipated the risk of injury to which all persons would be exposed as a result of his collision with a truck which he knew contained explosives.

Let us use the same facts but assume that the truck was not marked at all and that there was no way that *A* could anticipate that the truck was carrying explosives. Under these circumstances, *A* would still be liable to *C* and *D*, but he would not be liable to *E*. Even if the unmarked truck did not contain explosives, *A* would be bound to reasonably anticipate injury to *C*, the driver, and also the possibility of injury to *D*, the pedestrian near the scene of the collision. *A* did not know that the truck contained explosives, and therefore he could not have reasonably anticipated any risk of injury to which *E* might be exposed. For this reason, *A* is not liable to *E; E* was not within the "foreseeable orbit of danger."

In the famous *Palsgraf* case [*Palsgraf* v. *Long Island Railroad*, 248 N.Y. 339], a subway guard in the defendant's employ roughly shoved a passenger onto the platform of a moving train in such a way as to knock out of the passenger's hand a small package. The plain covered package, unknown to the guard, contained fireworks. They set off an explosion which injured the plaintiff, approximately 25 feet away. The court held that the guard had no reason to foresee, as a result of carelessly jostling the passenger's arm, any substantial risk of injury to Mrs. Palsgraf 25 feet away on the station platform.

Before there can be negligence, there must be a rational duty of care owed by the defendant to the plaintiff. The risk reasonably to be perceived defines the duty to be obeyed, and the duty runs only to those persons who are within the foreseeable zone of danger. Here a recovery was denied for the reason that the guard could not anticipate injury to a person at that distance from the scene of the act. Some courts have criticized the *Palsgraf* decision, and cases decided since that time are indicative of a growing trend toward permitting a recovery in all cases where the defendant's conduct is a *substantial factor* in causing injury, whether the injured person could qualify as a foreseeable victim or not. The majority of the courts adhere to the application of the doctrine of foreseeability as laid down in the *Palsgraf* case. But in many instances even these courts allow a recovery, finding some facts in the evidence on which to base a conclusion that the injured person was within the orbit of foreseeability.

A driver passes a large cardboard box which is lying in the left lane of the road. She can see that the box is empty. On her return trip the box is still there, but unknown to the driver, a small child is inside the box. The driver, thinking the box is still empty, and since it is in her line of travel, runs over the box, causing injury to the child.

On those facts, the question to be decided is whether the driver should have anticipated the presence of the child in the box, especially bearing in mind that, a short time before, she had actual knowledge that the box was empty. There is a difference of opinion as to the applicability of the doctrine of foreseeability to such a situation. However, we add just one additional fact: as the driver was passing the box, she noticed a large number of children playing in the immediate vicinity. A strong argument could be made that, with this additional fact, the driver should have anticipated the possibility of children playing inside the box, and therefore she would be answerable for injuries sustained as a consequence of an accident.

APPLICATIONS OF NEGLIGENCE

FORESEEABILITY

309 Foreseeability as Applied to Motor Vehicles

A person who owns or operates a motor vehicle is bound to anticipate the risks of harm to which others will be exposed as a consequence of its operation. Persons within this foreseeable zone of danger would include others using the highway, operators and passengers of other vehicles, pedestrians, and the owners of property on the highway, such as traffic stanchions, road dividers, and traffic signals. He is also bound to anticipate the risks of harm to others who are near the highway, such as pedestrians on the sidewalk, people on private property abutting the highway, and owners of property along the highway, such as owners of telephone poles, street lights, fences, advertising signs, and buildings. If the owner or operator of the motor vehicle fails to exercise due care for the safety of these persons, he is guilty of negligence.

Due care will consist of the careful operation of the motor vehicle, including obedience to traffic signs, speed laws, maintenance of a careful and proper lookout, and the maintenance of control of the vehicle. Due care would also include the proper maintenance of the operating parts of the vehicle, and the owner is bound to foresee the risks of harm to others should he or she operate the vehicle with improper brakes, improper lights, or improper tires.

The owner of a motor vehicle is also charged with the duty of reasonable anticipation with respect to the risk of harm to others which would be occasioned by the use of his or her vehicle by an incompetent operator. Therefore, if the owner entrusts his vehicle knowingly to an unlicensed driver, an intoxicated person, or a driver who has a reputation for recklessness, the owner may be responsible for resulting damages sustained by others. The owner is bound to anticipate the risks of harm which will accrue to other persons as a result of his permitting such a driver to operate his or her vehicle.

310 Foreseeability as Applied to Premises

With respect to the ownership and maintenance of public premises, the owner or lessee is bound to maintain the premises in a reasonably safe condition, to make periodic inspections, and to remove dirt, debris, and other foreign substances which may accumulate as a result of the use to which the premises are put. The maintainer of the premises is bound to anticipate or foresee all possible risks of injury to persons invited to make use of the premises. This duty would consist of a warning to the public of any unsafe or hidden defect, unusual construction, or repairs.

The extent of the warning will differ with the circumstances; it might merely require a sign or a barricade, or the nature of the condition might require the posting of an employee at the site of the defective repairs for the purpose of orally warning all people passing that point. If the condition is of an extremely dangerous nature, it might consist of closing off that portion of the premises entirely.

The duty of inspection and removal of dirt and debris will differ with the type of premises involved. The inspection must be reasonable and at reasonable intervals of time, although these intervals will differ, depending on the circumstances. For example, in a vegetable store where vegetables fall with frequency —where lettuce leaves, beet tops, and other debris are likely to find their way to the floor used by the customers—the duty of inspection and cleaning would require that this be done at much more frequent intervals than would be required in a dry goods store.

As to private premises, the owner is required to maintain them in a reasonably safe condition and to warn persons entering the premises with respect to any hidden defects of which he has knowledge and which are not open and apparent. The owner is required to reasonably anticipate the risk of harm to which persons lawfully on the premises will be exposed.

311 Foreseeability as Applied to Products

In the area of food, the rule of strict liability is imposed upon the manufacturer, grower, processor, canner, or baker, if the product is not fit for human consumption. This liability is imposed irrespective of negligence. He or she must reasonably foresee that all food products are bought for eating purposes, and the manufacture and sale of products which are not fit for human consumption is negligence per se.

With respect to products other than articles of food, the manufacturer must foresee the risks of injury to which purchasers of the article will be exposed. This means that the manufacturer must design the product with reasonable care, give detailed and proper instructions as to its use, and further warn the purchaser as to any inherent dangers which are not open and apparent. This warning must be adequate. The manufacturer is held to a high degree of scientific knowledge with respect to the ingredients, design, and purity of the product.

In the application of this knowledge, the manufacturer is also required to anticipate the risks of harm which may arise, not only from the use to which the product is normally put but also any attendant hazards which may exist in connection with such use. For example, a man applied an ointment to his chest in the course of treatment for a cold. While the product was so applied, and while the man was attempting to light a cigarette, the head of the match came off and fell on the man's chest. The product ignited, causing severe burns. The court, in upholding a verdict for the plaintiff, took the position that the manufacturer was charged with the knowledge of the flammable nature of its product, and its failure to warn the user of this hazard constituted negligence. [*Morton* v. *Bengay*, 130 Atl. 2d 863 (New Jersey).]

312 Rescue Doctrine

This is an extension of the doctrine of foreseeability. The defendant must foresee that, if his negligent act places an injured person in a perilous position or imminent danger, it is reasonable to expect that others will come to the aid of the injured person. It is likewise reasonable to expect that, if any of the rescuers are injured in the process of giving such aid, the injury to the rescuers could be considered as consequential in the sense that the defendant's negligence was the proximate cause not only of the victim's injuries but also of the injuries to the rescuers.

Among the foreseeable consequences of negligently endangering one person is the likelihood of injury to an intervening rescuer. Therefore, the rescuer is also entitled to maintain an action for damages against the person whose negligence placed the victim in the dangerous position. In order to sustain such a cause of action, the rescuer, in addition to proving his damages and injuries, must prove the following elements:

1. The negligence of the defendant as the proximate cause of the victim's position.
2. The imminent danger to which the victim is exposed. This element is *not* present when the victim has already been injured and no longer faces danger.
3. The justifiable exposure by the rescuer to danger in aiding the victim. The voluntary exposure by the rescuer to a known danger does not constitute contributory negligence if the rescue attempt has a reasonable chance of success and, further, if the attempt is one that the reasonably prudent person would make under the circumstances.

OWNERS AND POSSESSORS OF PROPERTY

313 Duties of the Possessor of Land

The possessor of land, for the purposes of determining the duties owed, is the person in control of the premises. He could be the owner of the property or he could be a tenant. A lease could involve the entire premises, leased to one tenant, or several tenants, or it could involve a transfer of part of the premises to one or more tenants with the owner reserving some part of the premises to himself. In either case, the responsible party will be the one who has the right of occupancy and control of that portion of the premises from which the duty of care arises.

The owner or occupier of land must exercise reasonable care in the maintenance and use of his premises so as to avoid any interference with the rights of others, as well as to avoid exposing others to unreasonable risks of harm. The persons to whom he owes these duties will come within one of two classes:

1. Those outside the premises.
2. Those on the premises.

1. Those outside the Premises. These will include all who are in the vicinity, either neighbors or those using the public streets and sidewalks. To his neighbors the owner owes the duty of making reasonable use of his premises so as not to interfere with the neighbors' property and their peaceful enjoyment of it. He or she may not change the natural drainage of his land so as to deposit excess water on his neighbor's land. He or she must exercise reasonable care in the erection of buildings and other structures on his land (as well as in the digging of excavations) so as not to interfere with the neighbor's use of his or her property or the neighbor's right to lateral support for his land and buildings. Also, the possessor of land is required to exercise reasonable care in the inspection of his premises and to keep them in repair so that no part of the buildings will collapse and injure the neighbor or his property.

He or she has no common-law duty of care with respect to natural conditions on his land, either to his neighbor or anyone else. Thus he or she is not required to remedy a swampy condition, fence in a lake or pond, or prevent weeds from spreading to the neighborhood. Local ordinances may create a duty with respect to these conditions but, in the absence of such statutes, the owner has no responsibility to others for natural conditions.

As to the public streets and sidewalks, the abutting owner has no responsibility for their maintenance, but he or she is liable for any conditions which he creates, such as the deposit of excess water on the street which collects in a pool and freezes, or damage to the street or sidewalk caused by his or her actions. He or she is also responsible for the safe maintenance of such things as sidewalk elevators within his control, and objects overhanging the street and sidewalk from his property. He or she is not responsible for the accumulation of snow and ice or water on the street and sidewalk, which are natural incidents and not ones he or she worsened or created. (See Section 516.) He or she is, however, responsible for the safe maintenance of objects on the premises which can be seen from the highway and which are attractive to children of tender years. (See Section 323.)

2. Those on the Premises. To those who are on the premises, by invitation or license, the owner has a duty of maintaining the premises in a reasonably safe condition, the extent of the duty depending upon the relationship of the parties. In addition, there are some duties arising out of the presence of a person on the premises without either invitation or license. The persons mentioned above are classified as trespassers, licensees, social guests, and business invitees. The general rules concerning the responsibilities of the owner as to each class will be discussed in the following paragraphs.

314 Trespassers

The owner or occupier of land has a legally protected right to the exclusive use of his property, and no one may enter on his premises without his consent. A trespasser is a person who is on the premises without the consent of the owner and therefore is invading a legally protected right. The trespasser is liable to the owner for any damage which his unlawful use of the property may cause.

The owner owes no duty of care to the trespasser either as to the maintenance of the premises or his or her own activities on them. He or she is under no duty to inspect the premises to discover the presence of a trespasser, but if the owner has knowledge of the trespasser's presence on his or her premises, he or she may not take action which is designed to injure him, beyond the use of such force as is necessary to expel the trespasser from the premises. The owner may not set traps or other devices calculated solely to injure the trespasser. This duty of refraining from committing an assault on the trespasser, and from maintaining traps and other devices designed only to injure him, is sometimes referred to as the duty of *slight care*.

315 Licensees

A licensee is a person who enters or remains on the premises with the owner's or occupier's consent, express or implied, for the licensee's own personal benefit, convenience, or pleasure. To the licensee, the owner or occupier owes practically no duty at all. The general rule is that the licensee voluntarily exposes herself to the same conditions and the same dangers to which the owner or occupier herself is exposed. Thus the licensee takes the premises as she finds them, and the licensee may not expect that the owner or occupier will take any steps to prepare for her coming, or any inspection of the premises to discover the presence of unsafe conditions. The owner or occupier is required to warn the licensee of any unsafe condition which is not open and apparent but, once the licensee has knowledge of the unsafe condition, there is no duty to repeat the warning. This duty to warn is limited in that it applies only to those portions of the premises which the owner or occupier may reasonably expect the licensee to use.

Both the licensee and the trespasser enter the premises for their own purposes and not for the purpose of conferring any benefit on the owner, but the distinction between the two lies in the presence or absence of the owner's consent, which may be manifested in several ways. She may expressly invite the person to enter the premises or, in the absence of any notice, her consent may be implied from local customs and usages. Thus, in a community where it is customary to issue licenses to door-to-door salesmen, canvassers, and solicitors of charitable contributions, the owner will be held to have given her implied consent to the custom in the absence of a fence or sign excluding such persons. Where it is a local custom for persons to take a shortcut across the owner's land, and the owner has made no effort to exclude them and has not erected any signs, fences, or other barriers, her consent will be implied from her lack of protest and lack of action.

The failure of the owner to exclude these people, by fences, barriers, or signs, is generally construed as an implied consent. The same is true with reference to persons who enter the premises for the purpose of visiting the owner's employees. Consent to their presence will be implied from the absence of rules enforced by the owner forbidding such visits.

316 Social Guests

The traditional view of social guests is that they are licensees. According to this view, the duty of the owner to them is the same as to any other licensees. This is true no matter how cordial the invitation is and no matter how formal the party to which they are invited happens to be. The common-law view is that the social guest comes as a quasi-family member, that he takes the premises as he finds them, and is subject to the same conditions as other members of the family.

It should be noted that a number of courts have been troubled by the common-law categorization of social guests as licensees. Some have expanded the scope of invitee status, and a few courts now classify all social guests as invitees. Other courts (and legislatures) have done away with the traditional categories of entrants upon land, or have modified the licensee/invitee distinction. (See Section 321 for further discussion.)

317 Invitees

An invitee is a business visitor whose presence on the premises is encouraged either by the use to which the premises are put or by an express or implied invitation. The business which is the subject matter of his visit must be for the advantage of the owner, even though it might be to the advantage of the business visitor as well. This characteristic distinguishes the invitee from the licensee. To the invitee, the owner owes the following duties. He or she must:

1. Exercise reasonable care in the maintenance of the premises for his safety.
2. Warn the visitor of any dangerous conditions which are not open and obvious, and of which the owner has knowledge.
3. Make reasonable inspections of the premises and remedy any dangerous conditions which the inspection reveals.

The duties owed to an invitee are the same as those owed to a licensee, but there is an additional duty of inspection and repair, and whether the inspection is made or not, the owner is chargeable with the knowledge which a reasonable inspection would have revealed. What would constitute a reasonable inspection will depend upon the type of premises involved and the use to which they are put.

For example, if the owner is operating a fruit and vegetable store where water and vegetable debris will accumulate on the floor, the exercise of reasonable inspections and the correction of unsafe conditions might require an inspection every 30 minutes during the business day. If the owner is conducting a millinery store, reasonable inspections might consist of one inspection per day.

The courts have been extremely liberal as to the qualifications which create the legal status of invitee. The general requirement is that there be some business advantage to the owner of the premises, but this has been extended to matters where the advantage is extremely obscure. For example, friends who visit the guests of a hotel are invitees with relation to the hotel; people who meet incoming passengers at a railroad depot are invitees in relation to the railroad; persons attending free public lectures or church services are all invitees as to the owners of such premises. With respect to federal, state, and municipal services, those who utilize public parks, playgrounds, libraries, toilet facilities, and community centers are invitees as to the authority operating these services.

With respect to stores open to the public, any customer, prospective or otherwise, who enters that portion of the store which is devoted to the sale of the owner's goods is an invitee regardless of whether the customer actually makes a purchase. Persons who use the store as a shortcut to somewhere else and persons who come in out of the weather, both without protest from the owner, have been held to be invitees on the theory that there was always a possibility that such persons might be attracted by the merchandise and make a purchase, thus supplying the business advantage element to the status.

Sales people and solicitors who enter the premises without special invitation are licensees, but where the owner specifically invites them to demonstrate a particular product, or to estimate the cost of repairs, they become invitees, because they are business visitors for the business advantage of the owner.

Applicants for employment who appear looking for work without invitation are usually licensees. However, where they appear in response to an advertisement inviting applications for employment, they are invitees. Also, in industries where the customs are such that there is a continuing need for employees and applications are accepted on a daily basis, such applicants are business invitees on the theory that the owner impliedly invites such persons to make application because of the custom and usage of the particular business in which he or she is engaged.

An owner maintaining a private home is considered to be in the "business" of maintaining a place of abode. Persons who enter the premises for the purpose of rendering some service in connection with the business of living in the home are invitees. Thus, this category would include delivery people of all kinds, meter readers employed by utility companies, and public employees such as letter carriers, safety or sanitary inspectors, garbage collectors, and even tax appraisers and collectors.

318 Area of Invitation or License

It is possible for a person to be a licensee or an invitee as to one portion of the premises and a trespasser as to another. It is also possible for a person to be a licensee or an invitee at one time of the day and a trespasser at another. The extent of the license or invitation given by the owner will determine the limitations of his consent. For example, a meter reader is normally an invitee, but only as to those portions of the owner's premises which must be traversed in order to read the meter. Should the meter reader go into the backyard and use the owner's swimming pool, he is a trespasser. In addition, such invitation is limited to those times during the day when the meter can conveniently be read. If the meter reader called in the early hours of the morning, he would be a trespasser on the premises. Therefore, the question for the jury may turn on circumstances of time or place.

319 Revocation of Invitation or License

The owner or occupier of the land is not required to extend the invitation or license indefinitely. He may revoke the invitation or license at any time. He may ask the person to leave the premises, and the person must leave. If that person remains, he or she is a trespasser from that point forward.

A person may enter the premises as an invitee or a licensee, but because of his conduct, which amounts to a breach of the peace, become a trespasser *ab initio* (from the beginning). This is an ancient rule of the common law.

320 Police Officers and Fire Fighters in the Line of Duty

Police officers and fire fighters do not readily fit the categories of licensees or invitees. They are in a special class. Both licensee and invitee enter upon the premises with the consent of the owner; one is tolerated and the other solicited. In the case of the police and fire fighters, the owner's consent is irrelevant. It makes no difference if their entrance is permitted or invited since, if conditions calling for their entry exist, they enter the premises as a matter of right. The landowner is not free to give or to withhold his consent, nor are policemen and firemen in a position to make a choice as to whether they will enter or refrain from entering the premises. They act neither by permission nor invitation but by command of the government authority by whom they are employed.

Since the consent of the owner is not required, the owner cannot revoke or rescind an invitation or license. The owner has no right to bar their entry or in any way to impede them in the performance of their duties. Fire fighters may enter the premises and extinguish the fire, or do whatever else is necessary, in the line of their duty. A police officer may enter upon any portion of the owner's property for the purpose of apprehending a criminal. This includes any room in the house, the roof, the outbuildings, or any part of the premises. The owner may not impede the police in the execution of their duty.

As to fire fighters and police, the owner is obligated to use reasonable care in keeping in a safe condition those portions of the premises utilized as the ordinary means of access for all persons entering. The owner is not required to keep all portions of his premises in a safe condition, but only those portions ordinarily used for access. For example, if a police officer is chasing a fugitive and in such pursuit he finds it necessary to climb the owner's fence, which gives way under the officer's weight, the owner has no liability, because he or she is under no duty to keep the fence in such repair so as to withstand the weight of anyone who decides to climb over it. As a matter of fact, the purpose of a fence is to prevent access. The owner has no duty to safeguard those parts of his or her property not ordinarily utilized for passage through the premises or to make any inspection in order to discover potential dangers.

In some cities, there are municipal ordinances which require that certain precautions be taken by the owner for the safety of fire fighters in their duties. For example, in New York City the owner of the premises is required to mark by appropriate signs any windows which enter into a shaftway. The purpose of the statute is to give notice to fire fighters who might enter the premises through these windows that there is no floor on the other side of the window. If the owner failed in his duty and a fire fighter were injured as a consequence of the failure, the owner would be required to respond in damages, since his failure to comply with the ordinance enacted for the safety of firemen resulted in injury. The same rule would apply where the ordinance required the erection and maintenance of fire doors, sprinkler systems, and other appliances designed to control the fire and prevent injury to fire personnel.

As to fires caused by the negligence of the owner, either by specific negligent act or failure to maintain the premises in condition to prevent the inception of a fire, most jurisdictions hold that if a fire fighter is injured in fighting such a fire there is no liability to him on the part of the owner. This would be true even though the owner himself turned in the alarm and was responsible for the presence of the fire fighter on the premises. The theory on which this view is based is that the fire fighter, by his or her calling, assumes all the risks incidental to fighting a fire, irrespective of the cause.

It might be added that in the case of a negligent fire the liability of the owner of the premises to his neighbor (should the neighbor's premises or business suffer as a result of a fire) is the common-law responsibility of ordinary care. The owner is liable to the neighbor for damages as a result of a negligent fire, whereas the owner would not have a similar responsibility toward the fire fighters attempting to extinguish the fire.

There are some exceptions to the general rule with respect to the owner's liability to fire fighters on account of injury sustained in fighting a negligent fire. A fireman who is employed by private persons, or who responds to such a call as a volunteer, has been held to be an invitee or business visitor to whom the landowner owed a duty of reasonable care to keep the premises safe. Courts in California and a few other states have imposed the duty of reasonable care in the maintenance of the premises upon the landowner with respect to injuries to municipally employed fire fighters resulting from an attempt to extinguish a fire on the premises. The court specifically held that the fire fighter was in the category of a business invitee on the theory that the benefit to the landowner was the decisive factor. Therefore, the landowner was held to a high degree of care as to the fire fighter, and responsible for any condition which could have been reasonably foreseen as a cause of fire or of injury.

321 Modifications of Occupiers' Liability

In 1968, the California Supreme Court was called upon to reexamine the status of a social guest and the liability of the host toward him. In *Rowland* v. *Christian* (70 Cal. Rptr. 97), the plaintiff, a guest, was injured when the defective knob of a bathroom faucet broke in his hand and he sustained very serious lacerations. Ordinarily, the guest would take the premises as he finds them and there would be no liability on the part of the host, but in this case the court decided that there was no legal justification for the exceptions from liability on the part of the social guest or even a trespasser. The court said that: "Everyone is responsible for an injury occasioned to another by his want of ordinary care or skill in the management of his property." The court refused to follow the rigid classifications of licensee, invitee, and trespasser, and substituted instead the following: "The proper test to be applied to the liability of the possessor of land . . . is whether in the management of his property he has acted as a reasonable man in view of the probability of injury to others, and although the plaintiff's status as a trespasser, or as a licensee or invitee may in the light of the facts giving rise to such status have some bearing on the question of liability, the status is not decisive."

In 1975, the Supreme Court of Rhode Island in *Mariorenzi* v. *Joseph DiPonte, Inc.* (333 Atl. 2d 127) decided to follow the reasoning of the California court. The case involved an infant trespasser. In abandoning the classifications of trespasser, licensee, and invitee, the court determined that the real issue is whether the owner has used reasonable care for the safety of all persons reasonably expected to be upon his premises.

Both of these cases apparently have reference to the status of a trespasser, even though the latter case refers to an infant trespasser attracted to the premises. In applying the rule enunciated by both cases, the occupier must exercise care for the safety of all persons reasonably expected to be on the premises. As to invitees and licensees, it is easy to apply, but in the case of a trespasser it is difficult to imagine a situation where the presence of a trespasser on the premises is to be "reasonably expected." Cases in other jurisdictions, which in some aspects follow the *Rowland* case, restrict the application of the rule of reasonable care to all lawful entrants. A number of states, by court decision or statute, have abolished the distinction between invitee and licensee and have adopted the rule of reasonable care.

With the exception of California and a few other jurisdictions, the duty owed to a trespasser would seem to remain the same. The trespasser is making illegal use of the occupier's premises and therefore the only duty of care which is imposed on the occupier is a negative one in that he need only refrain from willful, wanton, and intentional misconduct which is calculated to injure the trespasser.

Some prominent commentators have summarized the status of the law in this area as follows. Within 10 or 12 years of the *Rowland* decision, "eight other jurisdictions followed suit, abolishing all distinctions between entrants on land, and five other jurisdictions discarded the distinctions between licensees and invitees but retained the traditional duty limitations toward trespassing adults." [Prosser & Keeton, *Torts* §62 (1984, 1988 Supp.)] However, since about 1979, most of the decisions have applied the traditional classifications. Prosser and Keeton surmise "that the courts are gaining a renewed appreciation for the considerations behind the traditional duty limitations toward trespassing adults and . . . a healthy skepticism toward invitations to jettison years of developed jurisprudence in favor of a beguiling legal panacea.''

322 Landlord and Tenant

The owner of real property may transfer to another all of the incidents of ownership and use of the property, or of a part of it, for a period of time in return for a consideration called *rent*. The contract by means of which this transfer is accomplished is the *lease*. Like any other contract, the rights of the parties may be modified, limited, or extended by the insertion of various terms in the contract. Therefore, the consideration of any claims arising in connection with the relationship of landlord and tenant must begin with an examination of the lease.

Under a ''bare'' lease which contemplates only the transfer of possession and the incidents of ownership to the tenant for a term of years, the general rule is that the landlord is under no obligation to keep the premises in repair, nor is he or she responsible either to the tenant or others for conditions which develop after the transfer of possession, whether arising from the premises themselves or from the activities conducted by the tenant. The general rule also is that the tenant takes the premises as he or she finds them and assumes the responsibility for any damages which may arise from dangerous conditions on the premises, whether they are open and obvious or hidden and concealed. This rule has been modified to the extent that the landlord is obligated to reveal to the tenant any hidden dangerous conditions of which he has actual knowledge, and is responsible for his failure to do so.

In the absence of an agreement to the contrary in the lease, the tenant generally is responsible for the condition of the premises and is required to make necessary repairs to keep them in reasonably safe condition. The rule has been modified by statute in a number of states by requiring the landlord to maintain in safe condition certain types of premises, such as multiple dwellings and apartment houses, and creating a liability on his part for his failure to do so.

The cases have developed another exception to the general rule with respect to premises which are leased for the purpose of admitting the general public, such as stores, theatres, amusement parks, beaches, hotels, and stadium grandstands. In those cases, the landlord is under a duty to inspect and to repair any dangerous conditions existing prior to the transfer of possession, and agreement by the tenant to make these repairs will not relieve the landlord of his duty to do so. Clearly, the obligation of the landlord would be limited to those portions of the premises which would normally be open to the public and would also be limited to the persons who would normally be invited to use the premises for the purposes for which they are leased.

The tenant is liable to his invitee for injuries sustained on the premises as a result of a failure to maintain them in a reasonably safe condition. If the condition which caused an injury existed at the time of the transfer of possession, the invitee will have an additional cause of action against the landlord, which he may or may not assert, at his election. Where he does not, the rules of court in most states will allow the tenant to bring the landlord in as an additional defendant on the theory that the tenant is entitled to indemnity from the landlord. Adding the landlord as an additional defendant in the same action will obviate the necessity of another suit covering substantially the same subject matter.

In many cases, the landlord will transfer possession of only part of the premises to the tenant, retaining part of the building himself. This condition is usually met in cases of multiple dwellings, such as apartment houses and duplexes. The landlord will retain the common access ways, the elevators, stairways, and other parts of the building, and will transfer possession to the tenant of an apartment. As to the apartment, the tenant has the same rights and is subject to the same rules of responsibility as would be the case if the entire building were in his possession. He is responsible for repairs and is liable to others if he fails to keep his apartment in a reasonably safe condition.

Usually, the landlord has no right to enter the leased portion of the premises during the period of the lease without the consent of the tenant. As to the portions of the premises reserved to himself, the landlord is under a duty to maintain them in a reasonably safe condition, and he is liable for his failure to do so. The parts of the premises reserved include not only the access ways mentioned above but also such parts of the premises as the tenant is invited to use, such as a laundry room, a recreation room—or an outside swimming pool or recreational area. In addition, the landlord is responsible for the safe maintenance of other parts of the premises, reserved but not physically accessible to the tenant, such as the roof, water pipes, gas and electric conduits, sewer pipes, and heating vents. Failure to maintain these parts of the premises in reasonably safe condition, which results in injury to the tenant, will require the landlord to respond in damages.

As to the portions of the premises retained by the landlord, the relationship of the tenant to the landlord is that of an invitee. Her presence on the premises is to the business advantage of the landlord, and therefore the tenant is entitled to all of the rights of an invitee. This relationship also applies to the members of the tenant's family, her employees, her social guests, and her business invitees. All of these people are invitees as to the landlord, because they produce a business advantage to the landlord in the sense that she would not be able to rent his premises if she excluded them.

The tenant is required to maintain the premises of which she has possession in a reasonably safe condition. Therefore, she is liable to those entering her premises in the same manner and to the same extent as any other landowner. Her social guests are licensees as to her, and her employees and business visitors are invitees as to him. The parties to the lease can alter or vary the general responsibilities required by these rules, or create obligations of indemnity or contribution, by inserting appropriate clauses in the contract. Such variations, unless they violate public policy, will be given effect.

323 "Attractive Nuisance" Doctrine

The rule is that a person who has an instrumentality, agency, or condition upon his premises, or who creates such conditions on the premises of another, or in a public place, which may reasonably be apprehended to be a source of danger to children, is under the duty to take precautions. These are the precautions that a reasonably prudent person would take to prevent injury to children of tender years whom he knows are accustomed to be there, or who may, by reason of something there which may be expected to attract them, come to play. It does not apply to natural conditions or common dangers existing in the order of nature; it applies in favor of children of tender years—too young to appreciate danger.

The doctrine had one of its origins in the famous *Turntable* case [*Sioux City R.R.* v. *Stout*, 17 Wall. (U.S.) 657], decided in 1873. The court upheld a recovery by a six-year-old trespassing boy, who lost his foot playing on the defendant's turntable. The rationale of the case was that the defendant knew or should have known that the turntable was dangerous to children and, further, that children played in the vicinity. The turntable was clearly visible from the place where the children normally played. The defendant was further charged with the knowledge that children, unable to appreciate the extent of the danger, would be attracted to the turntable. The defendant, therefore, was under a duty to protect the children from an unreasonable risk of harm created by the presence of the turntable. The railroad's failure to fence in the area, to erect warning signs, or, if necessary, to post a watchman to prevent access by children constituted negligence on its part for which it was answerable in damages.

The original theory was that the defendant was liable because the child was enticed upon the premises by the condition created by the defendant. Conversely, there was no liability if the child had not been attracted to the premises by the condition. From these decisions the rule of liability to children acquired the name of "attractive nuisance." This theory has now been generally rejected, and the more generally accepted rule is that the owner of premises has a duty of reasonable care not to maintain a dangerous condition on the land, the use of which could result in foreseeable harm to another; or, where such a dangerous condition does exist, the owner has a special duty to trespassing children where he knows, or in the exercise of reasonable care should know, that they are likely to trespass on his premises. The fact that the child is a trespasser may be a fact to be considered, but the responsibility arises when the owner knows that children are likely to trespass. Therefore, the owner is under a duty to prevent the foreseeable harm to a child against which the child cannot be expected to protect herself.

The *Restatement of the Law of Torts, Second,* Section 339, states the rule as follows:

> A possessor of land is subject to liability for physical harm to children trespassing thereon caused by an artificial condition upon the land if
>
> *(a)* the place where the condition exists is one upon which the possessor knows or has reason to know that children are likely to trespass, and
>
> *(b)* the condition is one of which the possessor knows or has reason to know and which he realizes or should realize will involve an unreasonable risk of death or serious bodily harm to children, and
>
> *(c)* the children because of their youth do not discover the condition or realize the risk involved in intermeddling with it or coming within the area made dangerous by it, and
>
> *(d)* the utility to the possessor of maintaining the condition and the burden of eliminating the danger are slight as compared with the risk to children involved, and
>
> *(e)* the possessor fails to exercise reasonable care to eliminate the danger or otherwise protect the children.
>
> The doctrine contemplates the existence of two basic elements: (1) a dangerous, artificial condition which involves an unreasonable risk of harm to trespassing children, and (2) the nature of children who, because of youth, are unable to recognize the existence of the peril.

1. Dangerous Condition. Any structure or artificial condition on land could under certain circumstances present a danger to children, but the dangerous condition to which the rule refers is one which has a hidden peril not open and obvious to children. When a child is permitted to roam, it is contemplated that he or she is aware of certain hazards inherent in his or her activities, such as the danger presented by height, water, or fire. Comment (j) which followed the Restatement Rule makes the following observations:

> There are many dangers, such as those of fire and water or falling from a height, which under ordinary conditions may reasonably be expected to be fully understood and appreciated by any child of an age to be allowed at large. To such conditions the rule stated in this Section ordinarily has no application, in absence of some other factor creating a special risk that the child will not avoid the danger, such as the fact that the condition is so hidden as not to be readily visible, or a distracting influence which makes it likely that the child will not discover and appreciate it.
>
> Where, however, the possessor knows that children too young to appreciate such dangers are likely to trespass on his land, he may still be subject to liability to such children under the rule stated.

Thus, the decided cases turn on the question of whether the peril was one which the child could and should apprehend or one which children were likely to overlook. In *Senders* v. *Baird* [112 S.W. 2d 966 (Arkansas)], the court said:

> If every instrumentality that is attractive to a venturesome boy and, also, has an element of danger about it constitutes an attractive nuisance then there is no limit to its

> application. Perils or dangers, such as exist from climbing, are obviously known to children who are old enough to be unattended and capable of venturesome conduct. Any child capable of climbing knows that if he falls from a fence, a tree or any elevated structure injury can result.

The majority of cases dealing with drowning in areas where there is an artificial accumulation of water, whether because of the construction of a swimming pool or otherwise, without any additional circumstances creating a greater duty, have been held not to involve the attractive nuisance doctrine.

In the case of natural bodies of water on the land, the same rule of nonliability applies, except in cases where the landowner has created a greater hazard because of his or her activities on the land. If the landowner does nothing more than to merely allow the condition to remain in its natural state, he or she is under no duty to anyone, including children, to take any precautions for their safety.

Where in addition to the water hazard there is another condition created by the landowner which is dangerous to children, there may arise a special duty on the part of the landowner, which would compel the court to invoke the attractive nuisance doctrine. For example, in *Allen* v. *Wm. P. McDonald Corp.* [42 So. 2d 706 (Florida)], the defendant constructed spoil banks of white sand which sloped down to the water. A two-and-one-half-year-old child slid down the bank into the water and was drowned. The court held that the sand banks were not only an attractive nuisance but also were the proximate cause of the child's death, causing him to fall into the water.

The same rules and the same court decisions applicable to water accidents apply equally to climbing accidents where the child is injured because of fall from a height. Children who are allowed to roam are generally aware of the dangers posed by the possibility of a fall from a height. Therefore, the landowner, who merely maintains a structure, tower, pole, scaffold, or a construction activity on his premises is under no duty to prevent children from climbing them, even though he is aware that trespassing children are likely to intrude on his premises. For example, in *Pardue* v. *City of Sweetwater* [390 S.W. 2d 683 (Tennessee),] the court held that a city was not liable for the injuries sustained by an 11-year-old boy who fell while climbing on the city's water tank. The doctrine of attractive nuisance did not apply, since the only danger present was that of falling, which was a danger easily recognizable by the child.

Conversely, the child is not expected to appreciate a danger presented or exaggerated by a defect in the structure or other peculiar circumstance, which is hidden from the child or which the child would fail to appreciate because of immaturity. For example, in *Diglio* v. *Jersey Central Power & Light Co.* [120 Atl. 2d 650 (New Jersey)], the defendant erected a high woven-wire fence around its premises. It was topped with sharp spikes projecting upward, and suspended above the spikes were three strands of barbed wire. Horizontal crossbars between sections of the fence were so placed as to resemble a ladder. In spite of this fence, the defendant permitted children to play on its premises without warning or even chasing them away. The plaintiff, a nine-year-old girl, while climbing the fence on the ladderlike crossbar, slipped and impulsively grasped the sharply barbed wire. The court held that the condition was an attractive nuisance and that the defendant was liable for the reason that it maintained a dangerous condition which exposed the child to an unreasonable risk of harm.

2. The Nature of Children. The age and mentality of the child are among the determining factors in deciding whether a particular condition is one which exposes the child to an unreasonable risk of harm. A condition dangerous to a child of 6 years because she or he is unable to appreciate the danger, might not be a dangerous condition to a 14-year-old. Therefore, as the child grows older, the number of conditions which could be regarded as dangerous will decline. It is for this reason that courts seldom apply the rule to children over the age of 14 unless the hazard posed by the instrumentality is so hidden that even a 14-year-old could not be expected to realize the danger.

Creation of the Dangerous Condition by Other than the Property Owner. It is possible in some instances for a dangerous condition to be created by one other than the property owner. If the owner tolerates the condition, he will be liable to the child just as if he had created the condition himself. In other cases, where the condition is created and maintained by one other than the property owner, then he could be held liable together with the property owner as joint tort-feasors. This situation usually comes about in connection with the maintenance of streets and highways where a contractor is allowed to store supplies, etc., on the shoulder or some other part of the public land.

EMOTIONAL DISTRESS

324 Negligent Infliction of Emotional Distress

The original common-law rule was that without physical impact there can be no recovery for injuries, physical or mental, incurred by fright or emotional distress negligently inflicted. This is contrary to the fundamental principle of the common law that a wrongdoer is responsible for the natural and proximate consequences of his conduct. The courts felt that it was necessary to establish this rule of nonliability on the grounds of public policy.

Most states follow this rule and do not permit recoveries for fright unless there is some impact upon the claimant's person. This impact may be very slight and one which, in the nature of things, would not in and of itself be the entire cause of the claimant's mental apprehension. The reasoning seems to be that there is a recovery for fright or emotional distress if such is the natural and probable consequence of a wrongful act, but that public policy demands that there be some impact before a recovery will be allowed.

In 1961, New York specifically reversed the common-law rule in sustaining a complaint which alleged that the claimant was negligently caused to suffer severe emotional and neurological disturbances with residual physical manifestations. The complaint alleged that the infant plaintiff was placed in a chair lift at a state-operated ski center by a state employee who failed to secure and properly lock the belt intended to protect the occupant; that as a result of this negligent act the infant plaintiff became frightened and hysterical upon descent, with consequential injuries. The court said: "It is our opinion that [the common-law rule] should be overruled. It is undisputed that a rigorous application of its rule would be unjust, as well as opposed to experience and logic. On the other hand, resort to the somewhat inconsistent exceptions would merely add further confusion to a legal situation which presently lacks that coherence which precedent should possess." In disposing of the public policy theory of the common-law rule, the court remarked that the possibility of fraud, extra litigation, and speculative damages "is no reason for a court to eschew a measure of its jurisdiction"; that even if "a flood of litigation were realized by abolition of the exception, it is the duty of the courts to willingly accept the opportunity to settle these disputes."

The court rested its decision on two grounds, namely (1) that the reason for the rule no longer existed, and (2) the advances in medical technology were such that fraudulent claims can now be easily detected.

The courts in some states have specifically reversed the impact rule by clear-cut decisions. The majority of states adhere to the impact requirement and deny recovery where it is not met. A minority of states, like New York, have expressly repudiated the impact requirement where the plaintiff was within the zone of danger.

Most of the cases that have abandoned the impact requirement have relied on the *zone of danger* theory. The emotional shock or fright was produced by apprehension of injury by a person who suffered the mental shock brought on by fear for his or her own safety, and, in each case, the person was in a position where injury could have resulted.

There is another class of case involving emotional shock brought on not by fear for the person's own safety but from fear of harm or peril to another, such as the shock sustained by a mother who witnessed the death of her child under the wheels of a truck. The general rule is that no recovery is allowed in such cases, even though it cannot be denied that the mother under those circumstances has suffered a mental trauma from which she might never recover. The rationale of the decision denying recovery is that, while the driver of a vehicle has a duty of care which extends to others on the highway who may be injured by his negligent operation of the automobile, he owes no duty to others who are not themselves endangered by his use of the vehicle. Other reasons given for the decision are lack of foreseeability, proximate cause, and the lack of fear by the mother for her own safety. For example, in *Waube* v. *Warrington* (216 W. 603), the court said: "The answer cannot be reached by logic . . . it must be reached by balancing the social interests involved in order to ascertain how far the defendant's duty and the plaintiff's right may justly and expediently be extended."

Another reason given for denying recovery, which has been discussed in several cases, is the matter of public policy in the sense that, if a recovery were allowed it would place an unreasonable burden on the users of the highway, and furthermore, if a recovery were allowed in the case of a mother, could not the same right of recovery be extended to the father, sister, brother, grandparents, a baby-sitter who had charge of the deceased infant, the next-door neighbor, or even a stranger? As one court put it, allowing a recovery would "enter a field that has no sensible or just stopping point."

A further phase of this problem is posed by the situation where the mother did not actually see the accident but suffered an emotional shock when told about the details of the accident and later viewed the body of her deceased child. Recoveries have also been denied in such cases.

In *Dillon* v. *Legg* [69 Cal. Rptr. 72 (1968)], the California Supreme Court by a split decision (4–3) reversed the existing common law and held that a mother who witnessed the negligently caused death of her daughter, and as a consequence suffered emotional shock and physical injury, could recover from the tortfeasor, even though at the time of the accident she was in a place of safety and not within the zone of danger. In *Archibald* v. *Braverman* [79 Cal. Rptr. 723 (1969)], the California Court of Appeals reversed a summary judgment for the defendant in the case of a mother who was not an eyewitness to the accident involving her child, but who had come upon the scene almost immediately and had seen the child's injured condition. The California Supreme Court denied review so that this will represent the California law on the subject. In these two cases, California has allowed recoveries not only where the mother was an eyewitness to the accident, but also to a mother who was not.

There is evidence that some courts are departing from the common-law rule in the area of food cases. Recoveries have been allowed for emotional disturbance caused by the sight of particularly revolting substances in food, such as cockroaches, dead mice, and the like. Obviously, if the plaintiff had eaten any of the food, there would have been physical contact and a recovery would be allowed. The cases in which the courts have departed from the rule are those in which a particularly offensive sight is the cause of the disturbance. This appears to be a growing trend, and at the present time the rule followed in the majority of states seems to be that, where a causal connection can be established between the particularly offensive sight in food and the emotional disturbance, a recovery will be allowed.

In some isolated cases, recoveries have been allowed for emotional disturbance caused by an unauthorized autopsy on the body of a close relative, mishandling of dead bodies of deceased relatives, and the burial of the wrong body in a grave.

Chapter 4

Law of Torts, Continued

INTENTIONAL TORTS

400 Assault and Battery

401 Defamation: Libel and Slander

402 Right of Privacy

403 Conversion

404 Trespass

405 False Imprisonment

406 Malicious Prosecution

407 Wrongful Civil Proceedings

408 Nuisance as a Basis of Tort Liability

409 Dram Shop Acts

410 Intentional Infliction of Emotional Distress

STRICT OR ABSOLUTE LIABILITY

411 Dangerous Instrumentality Doctrine

412 Animals as Dangerous Instrumentalities

413 Ultrahazardous Operations Doctrine

WRONGFUL DEATH AND SURVIVAL

414 Survival Actions

415 Death by Wrongful Act

DEFENSES

416 Contributory Negligence

417 Comparative Negligence

418 Assumption of Risk

419 Unavoidable Accident

420 Act of God

421 Statute of Limitations

INTENTIONAL TORTS

400 Assault and Battery

Assault and battery are two separate intentional torts. Even though they are usually referred to as connected, one can exist without the other. Simply stated, an assault consists of placing a person in fear of bodily harm, and a battery is the infliction of bodily harm (including physical violence or constraint). In both cases, the *intention* to harm is an essential element.

The wrongful physical violence, as noted in the definition of battery, has been construed to mean the slightest touching of another, of his or her clothes, or anything else attached to one's person—even a dog on a leash—if done in a rude, insolent, and angry manner.

An assault may be committed without a battery, as where a person is placed in fear and apprehension of bodily harm but his or her person is never touched, either because the directed force missed or was never exerted. Damages, however, may be recoverable for the mental disturbance caused by the apprehension.

A battery may be accomplished without an assault, as where a sleeping person is subjected to physical violence or where a surgical operation is performed upon an anesthetized person without consent. Damages may be recoverable for the physical injury thus inflicted.

Where an assault *and* a battery are committed, damages may be claimed for the mental apprehension caused by the assault and for the physical injury inflicted as a result of the battery.

401 Defamation: Libel and Slander

Defamation, which may consist of either libel or slander, is the wrongful invasion of the legally protected right of security of reputation. Originally, libel consisted of anything of a defamatory nature which was written or published by a printing or other process which had some degree of permanence, whereas slander consisted of defamation of an oral nature, conveyed and published only by speech. The distinction today seems to be that slander is defamation which is conveyed by speech and is heard, whereas libel is defamation conveyed by sight. Thus, in addition to printed text, libel could consist of pictures, cartoons, moving pictures, signs, and statues. In any case, libel traditionally has been regarded as the greater offense because the damage sustained was potentially greater: printed or other visual material may be seen by many, whereas slanderous speech (at least before the advent of mass electronic communication) could be heard by only a few.

The elements of defamation, whether libel or slander are:

1. A false statement tending to hold the plaintiff up to public disgrace.
2. Publication of the statement.
3. Damage.

1. A False Statement. This is defined as an untrue statement which, if believed, would hold the plaintiff up to hatred, contempt, or ridicule, or cause him or her to be shunned and avoided. Malice, or evil intent, is inferred from its utterance. Thus it may be defamatory to say that a man will not pay his just debts, is immoral, a coward, a crook, a bastard, or that he has committed an act which is morally reprehensible or dishonorable. On the other hand, it is not defamatory to say that a man is tight with his money, does not go to church, is not a member of any church, or that he has taken advantage of his legal rights. None of these things, even if believed, would necessarily hold the man up to public disgrace or ridicule.

2. Publication. The statement must be published, made known intentionally or negligently, to someone other than the person defamed. Publication is the act of making the defamatory matter known publicly, or communicating it to one or more persons.

3. Damages. In most cases, damages must be alleged and proved by the person asserting the cause of action. Some states consider libel as defamatory per se, and actionable without proof of damages, on the theory that the permanence of the writing and its potential widespread harm justifies the rule. Other states require proof of actual damages. As to slander, some aggravated forms are actionable without proof of actual damages, and in states requiring proof of damages in libel actions, the same rule applies. The following may be actionable without proof of actual damages:

1. Imputation of serious crimes.
2. Imputation of a loathsome disease, such as venereal disease.
3. Imputation adversely affecting the plaintiff in his business, trade, or profession, such as calling an attorney a shyster or a crook.

(In some states there is an additional category, the imputation of unchastity to a person. Some states restrict this to women and others apply it to both sexes.)

The defenses to actions for libel or slander are *truth* and *privilege*.

1. Truth. It is clear that if the statement is true, there is no cause of action, because the cause of action is founded upon the falsity of the statement.

2. Privilege. Utterances or writings which are privileged fall into two classes, *absolute* and *qualified* or *conditional*.

Absolute privilege refers to statements made in judicial proceedings, legislative proceedings, executive communications between the chief executive and his officials of the executive departments, and husband and wife. Statements made in the course of any of these proceedings or relationships, even if untrue and damaging, are not actionable.

Qualified or conditional privilege exists with reference to publication made by a person in the discharge of some public or private duty, whether legal or moral, or in the conduct of his or her own affairs, in matters where his or her interest is concerned. Even in those situations, the privilege is lost if the person making the statement goes beyond that which is necessary to protect his interest or meet his duty, or if he communicates the information to another person who has no connection with the business and is in no position to give any assistance with the problem.

402 Right of Privacy

The right of privacy has been defined as the right of an individual to be let alone, to live a life of seclusion, or to be free from unwarranted publicity. A wrongful invasion of that right may give rise to an action in tort for damages.

It is difficult, however, to define such a right. The right to privacy perhaps can be most readily understood by reference to the wrongs that may give rise to a cause of action.

Unwanted publicity is the key to two areas. For example, one person may cause publicity to be directed toward some private fact about another. This conduct may give rise to liability, if the fact publicized would be highly offensive to a reasonable person and is not a matter of legitimate public interest. Or a person may cause publicity to be shed upon another concerning a matter that places the latter person before the public in a false light. The offending person may be liable provided that the false light would be highly offensive to a reasonable person and the offender had knowledge of (or acted in reckless disregard of) the falsity of the matter and the false light created.

The rights and wrongs mentioned in the preceding paragraph are set forth in the *Restatement (Second) Torts* §§ 625D and 625E. If the facts disclosed are true, then such disclosure ordinarily is not actionable. The facts are considered matters of public knowledge, or at least available for public knowledge. Disclosure of such matters may be personally embarrassing to the offended party but, at the same time, they may be *news*—matters of legitimate public interest.

It would be difficult to establish that public figures—such as politicians, athletes, and entertainers—have any right to privacy at all. Virtually any fact about them may be a matter of legitimate public interest.

The First Amendment to the United States Constitution, and court decisions interpreting it, accord great respect to freedom of speech and freedom of the press. Courts are likely to weigh First Amendment freedoms in the balance against claims for wrongful invasion of various asserted rights of privacy.

Another aspect of privacy relates perhaps less to unwanted publicity but more to physical or electronic *intrusion* upon a person's privacy. *Restatement* § 652B provides that a person may be liable for intrusion upon the solitude, seclusion, or private life and affairs of another, provided the intrusion would be highly offensive to a reasonable person. Examples might include trespassing on a person's property; interference with personal mail or telephone calls; "stalking" or similar forms of annoying, threatening or "harassing" conduct; "Peeping Tom" or eavesdropping activity.

Some such forms of offensive conduct (as well as such activities as searches and seizures) may be engaged in by law enforcement officers or other governmental officials. Some courts will recognize a right to freedom from unreasonable governmental intrusions, and may consider various provisions of the civil rights statutes supportive of such a right.

Casualty claims sometimes may involve the issue of intrusion upon the solitude, seclusion, or private life and affairs of another. When a person makes a claim for bodily injury or property damage, it is reasonable to expect that the defendant or his insurer will make some inquiry to determine the truth or falsity of the claim. In some cases, it is not uncommon for insurance companies to employ the services of a private detective to make activity checks to determine the claimant's physical ability to perform some type of work. This could involve the taking of motion pictures or placing the claimant under surveillance. Where the investigation is unobtrusive and within reasonable limits, there is no invasion of the plaintiff's privacy. [*Forster* v. *Manchester,* 189 Atl. 2d 147 (Pennsylvania).] The right of privacy is invaded where the investigation exceeds reasonable bounds, such as subjecting the claimant to obtrusive surveillance for a long period of time, coming on the premises at night, eavesdropping on conversations in the claimant's home, telephoning the claimant under various pretexts at all hours of the day, and other activities amounting to harassment of the claimant. In *Pinkerton National Detective Agency, Inc.* v. *Stevens* [132 S.E. 2d 119 (Georgia)], the court said: "The right of privacy may be implicitly waived, and is waived by one who files an action for injuries from a tort to the extent of the defendant's intervening right to investigate and ascertain for himself the true state of injury. However, this includes only a waiver of that reasonably unobstrusive type of investigation which would be to the best interests of the defendant in preparing its case."

Electronic eavesdropping and wiretapping have both been held to be an unreasonable invasion of privacy and actionable, even though the purpose of each was to obtain information in the defense of a lawsuit which had already been filed. For example, in *McDaniel* v. *Atlanta Coca-Cola Bottling Co.* [2 S.E. 2d 810 (Georgia)], the plaintiff claimed to have swallowed a piece of glass from the defendant's bottle. The defendant secretly placed a microphone in the plaintiff's hospital room and overheard conversations that went on. These actions were held to constitute an invasion of the plaintiff's privacy and she was awarded damages.

403 Conversion

Conversion consists of the wrongful assumption of ownership over items of personal property. The owner is entitled to the possession and use of his property. Any wrongful interference with this right of ownership, possession, or use is a conversion, and the wrongdoer is subject to liability. Conversion may also be defined as an unauthorized assumption and exercise of the right of ownership over goods or personal chattels belonging to another, to the alteration of their condition or the exclusion of the owner's rights.

The possession by the other party may have been lawful in the first instance, but his use of the property for his own purposes may constitute a conversion. For example, an automobile owner leaves his car at a garage for repairs and, without the owner's permission, the garageman takes the car for his personal use. This is a conversion, even though the car is not damaged, and the garageman is liable to the automobile owner for the value of the use of the car. Moreover, if the car is damaged, the garageman is liable not only for the unlawful use, but also for the damages.

404 Trespass

At common law, trespass consisted of any unlawful entry on the lands of another. The ownership of land includes the right of exclusive possession. Anyone, who, without the permission of the owner, express or implied, enters upon the land of another is making illegal use of the property. He is liable in damages to the owner for any loss or damage to the property including shrubbery, or perennial or annual crops. The owner may adopt reasonable means to exclude trespassers, such as the erection of fences and walls as well as the ownership of a watchdog. Likewise, the owner may use reasonable force to exclude a trespass where the intrusion occurs in the owner's presence. What is ''reasonable force'' will depend upon the facts and circumstances of the intrusion and in most cases will be a jury question.

The wrongful entry upon the land of another does not necessarily have to be made by the trespasser himself. For example, if he allows his cattle to roam and to intrude upon the land of another, he is guilty of trespass.

The same rule would apply in cases where the defendant in the course of blasting operations on his own land caused rocks, rubbish, and other debris to be thrown upon the plaintiff's land. Also where the defendant felled a tree on his own land which fell on the plaintiff's land, the defendant is strictly liable for the damage. Likewise, where the defendant dammed a stream, operated an automobile, bus, or streetcar on his own property or on the public way, and his act resulted in the stream or the vehicles going directly on the land of the plaintiff, he would be liable for the consequences.

The common-law view was that the owner of real property owned not only the surface property, but also the airspace above to the heavens and below to the center of the earth. This rule has given way to the circumstances of modern living and the use of aircraft. Judicial modifications of the common-law view have established two zones above the owner's land, the first being that which he has reduced to possession by erecting a building and also the space needed for the enjoyment of his property. The space above that zone is considered as being in the public domain and, therefore, available for use by anyone. However, one may not string wires across the owner's land without permission or shoot across the land, even though the bullets do not fall on the land. Also, where an adjacent building encroaches upon the property, either at the foundation or by an extension above which extends over the other's land, this is a trespass.

As to the ownership of the area beneath the land, the common-law rule seems to be applied. It is a trespass to mine under another's land, construct a tunnel or to invade it by a projecting foundation.

A problem arises where the personal property of the owner is on the land of another, and the personal property owner claims the right to enter on the land in order to remove it. Generally, the rule is that, where the personal property was placed on the land through no negligence or intention on the part of the owner of the personal property, he may enter to remove it and is not required to secure the permission of the landowner. This situation would arise where the personal property is brought to the land by the forces of nature, such as a windstorm or tornado. In addition, where the personal property was originally owned by the landowner and was sold to a buyer, the buyer, upon the payment of the purchase price, has the right to enter the land and remove it.

405 False Imprisonment

Everyone has the right of safety of person, which, as we have seen, includes liberty and freedom of movement. Any wrongful interference with this right is an actionable tort. *Imprisonment* does not necessarily refer to confinement within the walls of a state prison, although this could be included, but it does consist of the use of any force which completely restricts the person's right of movement. Imprisonment also consists of any confinement in a house, or a store, or by forcibly detaining a person on the streets against his will.

A person may be confined by the retention of his property. For example, a store detective retains a woman's purse and refuses to return it. Under those circumstances, the woman is confined. The same thing would be true where a woman's luggage was dumped from a train at a place other than at her station. The fact that the person voluntarily left the train to reclaim her luggage does not change the situation. She has been confined, because her movements have been restricted by the action of the conductor or train crew.

False arrest is another form of imprisonment in that the person is deprived of freedom of movement. While a private citizen may arrest another where a crime is committed in his presence, he or she may not deprive another of liberty without probable cause. On the other hand, a police officer may arrest a person without a warrant if the crime is committed in his presence, or if a crime has been committed and the officer has reasonable cause for believing that the person arrested has committed the crime. The officer is protected from liability where he executes a warrant valid on its face, even though it might have been issued by an official who was without jurisdiction.

406 Malicious Prosecution

As an element of the right of safety of person, the individual has a right to be protected from the institution of criminal charges brought without probable cause for believing that the individual has committed the crime. Malicious prosecution is an action begun with the intention of injuring a person, and as a result, that person has a cause of action against the person bringing the charges.

The elements of an action for malicious prosecution are as follows:

1. A criminal proceeding instituted by the defendant accusing the plaintiff of a specific crime.
2. Absence of probable cause for believing that the plaintiff had committed the crime.
3. Termination of the proceeding in favor of the plaintiff.
4. Malice, or evil intent, which may be defined as the intentional doing of a wrongful act without just cause or excuse, with the intent to inflict an injury, or under circumstances from which the law would imply evil intent.

1. Institution of Criminal Proceedings. The proceedings must be instituted. The fact that a complaint has been filed with the proper authorities, where no official action has been taken, is not sufficient. On the other hand, where a warrant has been issued for the arrest of the plaintiff and it has been served, that is sufficient evidence of the beginning of criminal proceedings.

2. Absence of Probable Cause. It is the duty of each citizen to bring to the attention of the authorities any person who is reasonably suspected of having committed a crime. Probable cause has been defined as "a reasonable ground of suspicion supported by circumstances sufficient to warrant an ordinarily prudent man in believing the party is guilty of the offense." In each case the facts and circumstances will determine whether this test is met.

3. Termination in Favor of the Accused. This means that the proceedings must be terminated in favor of the accused. It does not mean that the proceedings have been terminated by the accused, where he agrees to a compromise into which he entered voluntarily.

4. Malice. In an action for malicious prosecution, the plaintiff has the burden of proving that the defendant acted with an evil purpose. Malice may be found where the defendant uses the prosecution to extort money from the plaintiff, to collect a debt, to recover property or to compel the performance of a contract. The existence of these facts will spell out a bad motive or an evil intent. It should be noted that prosecuting attorneys who merely conduct the proceedings on complaints sworn to by others are in a quasi-judicial position and, as such, they are protected by absolute privilege and are immune from suit for malicious prosecution. Also, the police officer who serves the warrant of arrest is similarly protected.

Damages. The damages recoverable cover a variety of losses, which may include damage to a person's reputation (analogous to libel or slander), business, or credit standing. In addition, the plaintiff may recover for the expenses to which he has been put in defending himself, the securing of witnesses, the humiliation following arrest and incarceration, as well as those damages sustained by being deprived of the society of his or her family during this period.

407 Wrongful Civil Proceedings

Most jurisdictions allow recovery for wrongful civil proceedings (sometimes called *malicious use of process*). When a defendant is sued, he or she can be expected to expend the money necessary for a successful defense. This includes fees paid attorneys, costs of depositions and subpoenas, and fees for expert witnesses. In addition, where property has been attached and the property is needed for the continued operation of the defendant's business, the cost of the bond to release the attachment may add another cost to the defendant. Included as well may be the expenses incurred in defending a garnishment, replevin, injunctions, or proceedings in bankruptcy or for the dissolution of a partnership

The English common law limited the successful litigant to the recovery of costs, and some of our states have adopted that rule. However, in the United States (in contrast to English practice), the costs to the successful litigant are fixed by statute and generally the litigant is not entitled to the amount of his expenses, legal and otherwise, nor to damages which he or she has sustained as a result of the interruption of his or her business.

In other states, this rule has been abrogated and the general rules applicable to malicious prosecution have been adopted and, under the following circumstances, the bringing of wrongful legal proceedings has been considered a tort. To establish a tort, the plaintiff in the present action must show that the action was begun without probable cause, that the action was terminated in his or her favor, that the defendant was actuated by malicious motives or evil intent, and that specific damages were sustained. The damages could consist of the expenses incurred in defending the original suit, compensation for seizure of or interference with property and the resulting financial loss to a business, as well as injury to credit or reputation. In any case, the plaintiff must establish the amount of his or her damages. Thus far, this remedy has been limited to situations where the original lawsuit affected the person, property, or reputation of the plaintiff.

408 Nuisance as a Basis of Tort Liability

A nuisance is defined as anything dangerous to health, indecent or offensive to the senses, or an obstruction to the free use of property, so as to interfere with the comfortable enjoyment of life or property, or anything which unlawfully obstructs the free passage, or use in the customary manner, of any lake, river, square, street, or highway.

The question of whether a condition is a nuisance is determined by whether it will produce such a state of things as, in the judgment of reasonable persons, would naturally cause actual physical discomfort to persons of ordinary sensibilities, tastes, and habits. It arises from the unreasonable, unwarranted, or unlawful use by a person of his or her property, either real or personal, or from his or her own improper, indecent, or unlawful personal conduct, working an obstruction of or injury to the right of another, or of the public, and producing such material annoyance, inconvenience, discomfort, or injury that the law will presume resulting damages. The creator and maintainor of the nuisance is liable in tort to anyone injured as a result of its existence. The nuisance might consist of an unreasonable use of the public street or sidewalk so as to prevent others from using the street or sidewalk. Or it might consist of the production of noxious fumes which permeate the neighborhood and cause illness to persons or animals, destruction of growing crops, or otherwise interfere with the comfortable enjoyment of property.

The creator and the maintainor of the nuisance need not be the same person. The creator may be held liable after he has disposed of the premises, and the new owner may be held liable also for continuing to maintain the nuisance after he has acquired the premises. This liability will attach to both individuals, irrespective of when the accident or injury occurs.

The difference between the tort of negligence and that of nuisance is that, in nuisance, contributory negligence is not a defense. Proof that the nuisance exists, plus the injuries sustained as a result of it, will make out a prima facie case. In a negligence action, it will be necessary to show that there was a duty on the part of the defendant, a breach of that duty, and damages as a proximate result of the breach. To this the defendant may be able to interpose the defense of contributory negligence. To an action for nuisance, there are only two general defenses: that the condition complained of is not a nuisance, or that the defendant did not create or maintain it.

409 Dram Shop Acts

At common law a third person who was injured as a result of the intoxication of one who had imbibed liquor at a tavern had no cause of action against the tavern keeper, regardless of the amount of liquor or the circumstances under which it was sold. To create such a cause of action, most states have passed legislation known as *dram shop* or *civil damage* laws. While there are variations, the language of a Minnesota statute is typical:

> Every wife, husband, child, parent, guardian, employer, or other persons who are injured in person or property, or means of support, by an intoxicated person, or by the intoxication of any person, has a right of action in his own name against any person who, by illegally selling, bartering or giving intoxicating liquors, causes the intoxication of such person for all damages sustained.

Dram shop acts are only applicable to illegal sales of liquor. Other laws must be consulted to determine which sales are illegal. The laws of all states relating to the operation of establishments licensed to sell intoxicating beverages forbid the sale of intoxicating liquor to a minor (states differ as to the age requirement) or to an obviously intoxicated person. Therefore, any sale in violation of these regulations would be an "illegal" sale. Likewise, the sale of an excessive amount of liquor consumed on the premises would be an illegal sale, because at some point it would be a sale to an intoxicated person.

In some states which do not have dram shop legislation, the courts have imposed what might be termed a common-law dram shop rule. For example, in *Rappaport* v. *Nichols* [156 Atl. 2d 1 (New Jersey)], three tavern owners sold and served alcoholic beverages to a minor (an illegal sale under the New Jersey statute and regulation). Thereafter, while in an intoxicated condition, the minor drove his car and collided with a car driven by the plaintiff's intestate. The court held all three tavern owners liable on the theory that, when alcoholic beverages are sold by a tavern keeper to a minor or an intoxicated person, the unreasonable risk of harm not only to the minor or the intoxicated person but also to members of the traveling public may be readily recognized and foreseen. This is particularly evident under modern conditions when traveling by car to and from a tavern is so commonplace and accidents resulting from drinking are so frequent.

Generally, dram shop laws are only applicable to taverns and other holders of liquor licenses. However, the common-law dram shop liability has been applied in some states to individuals who supplied whiskey or other alcoholic beverages to a person who was involved in an accident while intoxicated. For example, in *Williams* v. *Klemesrud* [197 N.W. 2d 614 (Iowa)], there was a successful tort action brought against a college student who purchased vodka for a minor driver. The driver drank the vodka, became intoxicated and was involved in an accident which resulted in injuries to the plaintiff. Inasmuch as the Dram Shop Act imposed strict liability without negligence on the defendant, the court found there was no reason why the same rule should not apply to an individual defendant. The court further held that the defense of contributory negligence is not available to the defendant under these circumstances.

Some states have expanded their dram shop rules to impose liability upon a social host for serving liquor to guests; some of these states restrict such liability to cases of serving to minors.

410 Intentional Infliction of Emotional Distress

The intentional infliction of mental anguish and mental suffering is actionable only where the conduct of the defendant was extreme and outrageous. In other cases, mere insulting words and conduct which do not amount to such extreme action, even though they cause some mental distress, are not actionable. In *Alsteen* v. *Gehl* [124 N.W. 2d 312 (Wisconsin)], the court held that the following elements must be established to effect a recovery for intentional infliction of mental distress. There must be:

1. Intentional misconduct by the defendant.
2. Defendant's conduct must be extreme and outrageous, exceeding the bounds of decency.

3. Defendant's misconduct must be a cause-in-fact of the plaintiff's emotional distress.
4. The plaintiff must have suffered "an extreme emotional response" to the defendant's conduct.

For example, in *Zayre of Atlanta, Inc.* v. *Sharpton* [139 S.E. 2d 339 (Georgia)], a floorwalker in a department store loudly accused the plaintiff of larceny and shoplifting. Plaintiff recovered a judgment, based upon her humiliation and emotional distress, against the corporate defendant.

Section 46, *Restatement of Torts, Second,* states the rule as follows:

Outrageous Conduct Causing Severe Emotional Distress

(1) One who by extreme and outrageous conduct intentionally or recklessly causes severe emotional distress to another is subject to liability for such emotional distress, and if bodily harm to the other results from it, for such bodily harm.
(2) Where such conduct is directed at a third person, the actor is subject to liability if he intentionally or recklessly causes severe emotional distress
    (a) to a member of such person's immediate family who is present at the time, whether or not such distress results in bodily harm, or
    (b) to any other person who is present at the time if such distress results in bodily harm.

The comments following this section point out that the rule is intended to apply only to conduct of such outrageous character that it exceeds the bounds of decency. It will not be enough that the defendant acted with a malicious intent or that he or she intended to inflict emotional distress. Moreover, the rule does not extend to mere insults, threats, indignities, or other annoyances, because the law is not required to intervene in every case where the plaintiff's feelings are hurt.

In some cases, the circumstances under which the defendant's action is taken will have some bearing on the question of whether the conduct is outrageous or not. For example, *A* is in the hospital suffering from heart disease. *B,* an insurance adjuster, calls on *A* in an effort to settle a claim which *A* has. Due to the adjuster's harassment and boisterous attitude, *A* suffers from emotional distress and has a heart attack. If *B* was aware of *A*'s heart condition, his conduct could be deemed "outrageous." On the other hand, if *B* did not know of *A*'s heart condition, and could not reasonably have known, his conduct will not be so classified. This example follows the comment in the *Restatement.*

However, in *Crisci* v. *Security Insurance Co. of New Haven* [426 Pac. 2d 173 (California)], it was claimed that the insurance carrier's wrongful refusal to settle a case within the policy limits, where there was an opportunity to do so, was the proximate cause of the plaintiff's mental suffering and suicide attempts. An excess award had stripped the plaintiff of all of her property and caused her to be dependent upon the charity of her grandchildren. The court held that the insurance carrier was guilty of tortious conduct under the circumstances and awarded damages not only to compensate her, but also for mental distress. The *Crisci* decision was based on the special relationship and duties between an insurer and its insured, *not* on the *Restatement* rule.

STRICT OR ABSOLUTE LIABILITY

411 Dangerous Instrumentality Doctrine

This doctrine contemplates the application of a rule of strict liability. Anyone who possesses, stores, maintains, or transports a dangerous instrumentality is strictly liable for any injury or damage caused by the instrumentality, regardless of the presence or absence of due care. The reasoning behind this rule is that the person in possession of the dangerous instrumentality has exposed the community to an unreasonable risk of injury or damage and, therefore, should be responsible for such injury or damage regardless of fault. The members of the community are required to guard against all ordinary, foreseeable risks of harm to their persons and property. They are not required to anticipate extraordinary risks of harm which the presence of a dangerous instrumentality will create. Consequently, where a dangerous instrumentality is involved, the defense of contributory negligence will not be available. The dangerous instrumentality may consist of the possession, storage, or use of commodities such as dynamite, gasoline, explosives, and firearms. With respect to explosives, the possessor is absolutely liable to any member of the community for any injury or damage caused by an explosion. The community is not required to take any precautions with respect to a possible explosion, such as boarding up windows. There is, therefore, no defense on the grounds of contributory negligence if the community fails to take any of these precautions.

Strict liability is imposed upon the owner of land who uses explosives for the purpose of blasting and excavation. This duty of care is nondelegable. Strict liability is imposed upon the owner of the land even though he or she has delegated the blasting operation to an independent contractor and has used reasonable care in the selection of a competent contractor. The owner is still strictly liable for any damage caused by the use of explosives on his or her land.

The rule of strict liability also applies with respect to the use of firearms. A person who entrusts firearms to another person, unfamiliar with their use, creates a dangerous instrumentality situation. The firearm in the hands of an incompetent person then becomes a dangerous instrumentality, and the owner is strictly liable to anyone injured as a result. Likewise, a parent who carelessly leaves firearms in places where they are accessible to children becomes strictly liable to anyone injured as a result of the use of the firearms by the children. Again, the firearm in the hands of a child becomes a dangerous instrumentality. While it is true that a parent ordinarily is not responsible for the torts of a child, liability is imposed, not because of the act of the child, but because of the neglect of the parent in creating an extraordinary risk to others. The parent is liable for his own tortious act of leaving a dangerous instrumentality in a place where it was easily accessible to others unfamiliar with its use or irresponsible with respect to its use.

If the individual who took the firearm is injured, he will have assumed such a risk and, as to him, the other has no responsibility. Should others be injured as a result of the use of the firearm by the one in possession of it, the owner would be responsible to them. The same is true with respect to explosives.

The rule of strict liability generally does not apply to municipalities, counties, and other arms of government. The use of dynamite for blasting in the construction of roads, clearing of land, and other governmental activities, is quite common. They are, however, answerable where the injury or damage is caused by their own *negligence* or carelessness in the handling of the blasting operation.

412 Animals as Dangerous Instrumentalities

For the purposes of determining the duties and responsibilities of the owner or harborer of an animal, the law divides animals into two classes—domestic and wild. A domestic animal is defined as an animal which is in the service of mankind, such as dogs, cats, horses, sheep, pigs, cattle, chickens, turkeys, and even bees. On the other hand, wild animals are those which are not domesticated, and would include such creatures as bears, lions, tigers, snakes, and elephants.

Wild Animals. The rule is that wild animals are dangerous instrumentalities and the mere ownership thereof imposes liability upon the owner where damage or injury occurs. The theory is that the owner, in bringing the animal into the neighborhood, subjects his neighbors to an abnormal risk of harm, and regardless of whether the animal escapes as a result of the owner's negligence or not, the mere ownership or possession of such an animal imposes liability upon the owner for any injury or damage which the animal may inflict.

An exception to the imposition of the rule of strict liability concerns persons who exercise possession of the wild animal in response to a public duty. Such persons are liable only for negligence in the exercise of possession in allowing the animal to escape or otherwise injure others. Possessors in this category would include a municipality maintaining a city zoo and its employees engaged in such operations, as well as common carriers (such as a railroad or an express company) which are required by law to transport wild animals.

The doctrine of strict liability with respect to the actions of wild animals has been applied to persons other than the owners or possessors of the animal (such as the operator of a theater or arena), who stood in some relationship of responsibility to the injured person.

Domestic Animals. These are generally regarded as harmless, and the owner is not liable for their actions unless the injury or damage is caused by animals which fall into one of the following three classes:

1. Livestock—animals which because of their size or habits are known to cause damage when they intrude on another's property.
2. Animals in which dangerous propensities are normal.
3. Abnormally dangerous animals.

1. Livestock. The law defines livestock as those kinds of domestic animals and fowls normally susceptible of confinement within boundaries without seriously impairing their utility, and the intrusion of which upon the land of others normally causes harm to the land or crops. Thus, the term includes horses, cattle, pigs, and sheep as well as poultry—unless by custom in the area poultry are permitted to run at large.

The English common-law rule, which has been adopted in the majority of American states, is that the intrusion of livestock upon the land of another is a trespass and that the owner of the livestock is strictly liable for the damage so caused. It has been said that "the owner trespasses with his cattle." The damages recoverable include not only the damage to the land itself but all consequential damages, such as bodily injuries sustained by the owner of the land in attempting to exclude the animals, injuries to the property owner's cattle sustained as a result of fights with the intruding animals, the communication of a disease to the property owner's cattle, and any other damage in which a causal connection with the trespass can be established.

A minority of states, especially those in the western part of the United States, did not accept the English common-law rule, but promulgated one of their own which permitted cattle to roam on the open range at will and required the owner of land to fence in his property (including a railroad right of way) in order to keep the cattle out.

2. Animals in Which Dangerous Propensities Are Normal. These are certain species of domestic animals in which dangerous or vicious propensities are normal and are known to exist. A bull, a stallion, and Brahma cattle are all regarded as being vicious and dangerous, and these characteristics are inherent in the nature of the animal. The owner of such animals is not subject to the rule of strict liability as in the case of trespassing livestock, but he is liable to anyone who is injured as a result of his failure to exercise that degree of care for the safety of others which is commensurate with the nature of the animal.

3. Abnormally Dangerous Animals. This division refers to animals normally regarded as harmless, such as dogs and cats. The rule is that the owner of such an animal is not responsible for the property damage or injury sustained as a result of the animal's activities. The amount of property damage which a dog or cat could do to the premises of another is inconsequential, and injury that they could cause would be considered as negligible when these things are balanced against the owner's right to possess such an animal. However, if the owner has knowledge of a particular characteristic or vicious tendency on the part of the animal, the existence of which exposes others to a risk of injury, the rule of strict liability will be applied. The liability is imposed on the owner of such a dog, not because of his failure to exercise care in confining the dog, but in possessing the dog at all, since he has knowledge of dangerous characteristics which expose others to the risk of injury. The dangerous characteristics referred to include not only vicious traits which the animal may have exhibited but also habits which (while not vicious in themselves) are likely to cause injury. For example, where an owner of a large dog knows of the animal's habit of jumping at people in an overabundance of affection, the owner is liable regardless of the dog's intent.

Watchdogs. An owner has the right to maintain a watchdog for the purpose of excluding unwelcome strangers from his premises. He is subject to the same rules which govern his liability, if any, to trespassers. He is not required to maintain his premises in reasonably safe condition for the safety of a trespasser, but he is under a duty to refrain from maintaining any mechanical device or vicious dog on the premises, both of which are utilized solely for the purpose of injuring trespassers. In the case of a vicious watchdog, notice of the presence of the dog by signs or otherwise will subject the trespasser to the defense of either assumption of risk or contributory negligence, where it is established that such notice has been brought to the attention of the trespasser. As to others—licensees and business invitees—the right to possess a watchdog does not relieve the owner of his duty to maintain the premises in reasonably safe condition for the safety of those who are present on the premises by invitation or license

Dogs—Statutory Modifications. Some states have enacted legislation modifying the common-law rule by making the owner or harborer of a dog liable for bodily injury caused by the dog, regardless of whether the owner knew of any habits or vicious tendencies on the part of the dog. The provisions of such statutes vary from state to state. It should be emphasized that the statute does not change the common-law rule, but it does add another cause of action in favor of the victim. The injured victim may bring his action at common law or under an applicable statute.

Many municipalities have leash laws that require dogs to be on a leash at all times. The dog's owner thereby becomes liable for any damage caused by failure to keep his dog on a leash.

413 Ultrahazardous Operations Doctrine

This doctrine is related to the dangerous instrumentality doctrine and is based on the same duty of care which the owner of land owes to the community with respect to making reasonable use of his property. If he should conduct an operation which involves an abnormal risk of harm to the neighborhood, he will be held strictly liable for any damage which occurs as a result, irrespective of whether the ultrahazardous or inherently dangerous operation was conducted with due care. The general reasoning is that, by conducting such operations and making abnormal use of his land, the owner has subjected the community to an unusual risk of harm, and, having done so, the risk should be his and not that of the community. Nor is the community contributorily negligent if it fails to protect itself against the threatened harm. Thus, if a blasting operation were to be conducted, neighboring landowners are not required to live in the basement and board up their windows as protection against the effects of the operation.

The duty of the landowner making abnormal use of his property is to protect the rest of the community from all harm resulting from the abnormal use. This is a nondelegable duty, and he may not shift the responsibility to a contractor to whom he has assigned the task, even though the contractor was selected with due care and even though the owner has no control over the work of the contractor.

What usually happens when an independent contractor is employed is that the contract for the work contains a *hold harmless agreement,* whereby the contractor agrees to indemnify and hold the owner harmless from any liability imposed upon him as a result of the operation. The existence of such an agreement does not affect the landowner's liability and duty to his neighbors, but merely provides a means of reimbursement to him should he be required to respond in damages to any member of the community.

Clearly, if the contractor does not conduct the operations with due care, he is responsible for his own negligent acts, and he may be held answerable in damages. In such a case, the injured person may sue either the contractor, or the owner, or both. The *quantum* of proof necessary to hold the owner responsible will be less than that required for the contractor. The elements of proof necessary, as against the owner, will be (1) proof of the abnormal use of the property, and (2) damages. Against the contractor, proof would have to show (1) the nature of the operation, (2) his negligent act or acts, and (3) damages.

WRONGFUL DEATH AND SURVIVAL

414 Survival Actions

The common law is that a person's earthly activity ceases at death. Therefore, a dead person could neither sue nor be sued, and if he had begun the action in his lifetime, or an action had been begun against him, his death ended or abated the action. Thus the common law gave no consideration to the possibility of having the personal representative of the deceased, such as an administrator or executor of his estate, appear for or in behalf of the deceased.

Under this system, if a claimant received serious injuries, suffered excruciating pain, suffered a loss of earning capacity, and incurred medical and hospital expense, and he died before the case proceeded to judgment, there were no legal means by which his estate could recover damages or even the out-of-pocket expenses from the wrongdoer. This was true even though the payment of heavy medical expenses and other losses would diminish his estate and leave that much less to be divided among his heirs.

As to the defendant, if he should die prior to judgment, his estate would not be liable to the injured person, no matter how serious the injuries were and no matter how culpable the defendant's conduct was in causing them, and his estate would be divided among his heirs without regard to any obligation, moral or otherwise, which he may have had toward the seriously injured person.

To correct this situation, some of the states have enacted legislation relating to *survival actions,* and in others the courts have given recognition to a right of survival of the cause of action in favor of the estate of the deceased. The statutes provide that the cause of action shall not abate by the death of the plaintiff, whether his death was caused by the injury or not, but shall survive for the benefit of his heirs, and that the action may be brought by his personal representative. This refers only to the cause of action which the deceased had in his lifetime, and the damages recoverable are those which he himself could have recovered had he lived.

The recoverable items of damage include medical expense, loss of earnings, and other out-of-pocket expenses as well as an amount reasonably calculated to compensate for the deceased's physical and mental distress. They do not include his funeral expenses, for the reason that the deceased never owned a cause of action against the tort-feasor in his lifetime which would contemplate the payment of his funeral expenses. The claim that can now be asserted by the personal representative of the deceased is the claim that the deceased could have made had he lived. This means that the action will be based upon damages suffered from the date of the accident to the date of the deceased's death and not thereafter.

In the case of the death of the tort-feasor, the statutes provide that the action shall not abate but will survive against his estate. This means that the defendant's personal representative must pay the defendant's obligations before distribution of the estate among the heirs. The action may be brought or continued against the defendant's personal representative.

In either case, if the lawsuit were settled and releases given, there would be no cause of action to survive. If the deceased had settled his case with the defendant and extinguished the cause of action by the receipt of a payment in settlement (giving back a release in exchange) even if the injured person died as a result of the injuries received, he had no cause of action against the defendant as of the date of his death. Therefore there was no cause of action to survive to his personal representative. The same thing would be true in a case that was settled before the defendant's death. Since there was no cause of action in existence as of the date of the defendant's death, there was no cause of action that would survive against his estate.

415 Death by Wrongful Act

In the normal course of events, when a person reaches the end of a natural life span, his or her worldly assets are distributed, either by will or by operation of law. Also, when a person lives out a normal life span, he or she will have contributed gifts, support, or other things of value to the natural objects of his or her bounty, usually family members and close relatives.

Where, however, a person's life has been shortened by an accidental death which occurs through the negligence of another, it is clear that the survivors have sustained a loss.

The common law did not recognize that these beneficiaries had any legal rights against the tort-feasor, nor did the common law recognize that this class of persons had sustained damage as a result of the death of their possible benefactor. Where an injured person survives, the personal injury claim is his and his alone. He may bring the action, and the damages recoverable belong solely to him. This is true even though his dependents or close relatives may have suffered some deprivation because of his injury and may have been required to perform some services for him during his illness. The common law does not recognize damages sustained by relatives as actionable where the injured person survives, and, therefore, since they were strangers to the claimant's cause of action in his lifetime, there was no reason why the death of the claimant should change their status.

In England, social conditions dictated the necessity for legislative change. When the breadwinner of the family lost his life, the family more often than not was left destitute, and, since they had no remedy when the death was caused by wrongful act, they joined other destitute persons on the public charity rolls. The cases became so numerous that public sentiment caused Parliament to pass the Fatal Accidents Act of 1846, which is more commonly known as Lord Campbell's Act.

The act created a new cause of action which could be brought for and in behalf of the dependents of the deceased against the tort-feasor where death was caused by the wrongful act, neglect, or default of the defendant. The underlying purpose of the act was to create a means whereby the persons who normally would be supported by the deceased could recover an amount which would be the same as they would have received had the deceased lived, thereby preventing them from becoming objects of charity. Therefore, the measure of damages was the pecuniary loss suffered by these people as a result of the death. There was no recovery allowed for mental anguish and bereavement, since these were not pecuniary in nature.

The majority of the American states have enacted wrongful death statutes, similar to Lord Campbell's Act, limiting the recoverable damages to the value of the deceased's future contributions to the beneficiaries. The other states have enacted three general types of statutes to cover the situation: (1) punitive statutes, which base the measure of damages on the culpability of the defendant's conduct, (2) statutes which base damages on the loss to the estate, and (3) combined death and survival statutes, by means of which one action can be brought for both the survival claim and the claim for wrongful death.

Beneficiaries. In most states the action for wrongful death is brought by the executor or administrator of the estate of the deceased for the benefit of a class of persons which includes the husband, wife, children or, if none of these, for the benefit of the mother and father of the deceased. In other states the action may be brought by the persons immediately concerned. It might be added parenthetically that the terms ''husband'' and ''wife'' refer to a legal relationship. Because most states do not recognize a common-law relationship as legal, the so-called common-law wife and husband have no status under the wrongful death statutes and therefore cannot recover.

If any of the beneficiaries should die before the action is begun, or even if they would die after the commencement of the action, the claim dies with them and does not inure to the benefit of their estates. Of course, if there are other beneficiaries, the death of one of their number would not have any effect on their rights. Obviously, if all of the beneficiaries should die prior to judgment, the action will fail. As one of the elements of the cause of action, the plaintiff must establish that the claim was one which the deceased could have maintained had he lived.

Most states have a statute of limitations which requires that actions for personal injury must be brought within a certain period of time from the date that the cause of action accrued. For example, let us assume that the statute of limitation is two years from the date of the accident. If we assume that no action was brought, and at the time of the decedent's death more than two years had passed from the date of the accident, then it is clear that the injured person could not have maintained an action for his injuries if death had not ensued. His cause of action is already outlawed by the passage of time and by the expiration of the period of limitation. Under those circumstances there could be no qualification under the provisions of the statute. However, if the injured person died within the two years from the date of the accident, then an action for wrongful death under this statute could be brought at any time within two years from the date that the cause of action accrued.

On the other hand, if the deceased had settled the claim during his lifetime, or brought an action which proceeded to judgment, he could not have maintained a further action had he lived. Under those circumstances, the general rule is that the beneficiaries do not qualify under the statute to bring a wrongful death action. The majority of American courts follow this rule.

Damages. The original concept of Lord Campbell's Act was to provide a means by which the beneficiaries would recover as damages an amount which would reasonably compensate them for the monetary support they would have received from the deceased had he lived. The recovery was therefore limited to the pecuniary loss which these beneficiaries would have sustained because of the death. The majority of American states which have enacted statutes similar to Lord Campbell's Act have the same restriction as to damages. Some states have a limitation on the amount of damages which may be recovered. Some other states have added other and further elements of damages in addition to the pecuniary losses. These states may specify that damages include, for example: funeral and burial expenses; damages for injury or loss including loss of support, services, society, prospective inheritance and mental anguish; spouse's loss of consortium; children's grief; parents' grief; loss of companionship; and, in a proper case, punitive damages. Because these statutes vary widely from state to state and are subject to change by the legislature, it is recommended that, if the claim representative is confronted by claims of this type, reference be made to the current statute.

Death of a Minor Child. At one time a minor child was an economic asset in that he or she could be sent to work at a very early age and the wages were contributed to the family maintenance. With the coming of child labor laws, this is not possible today. Therefore, even today, a minor child's contribution to family maintenance would hardly balance the cost of raising and educating the child, so that in most cases the child is an economic liability rather than an asset. In states where the wrongful death statute is similar to the original Lord Campbell's Act, the only element of damages recoverable would be the child's funeral expenses. However, sometimes a jury will award much more than the funeral expenses, and such an award will not be set aside by the court. In such cases, the court is giving tacit recognition to mental anguish suffered by the parents. In states where the statute provides for a recovery for mental anguish and bereavement, such awards are customarily made. For a case discarding the ''wage-profit'' formula (the expected earnings of the child less the cost of raising him), see *Wycko* v. *Gnodtke* [105 N.W. 2d 118 (Michigan)]. This case valued the life of the child in connection with his relationship with the family as part of the family unit. See also *Currie* v. *Fitting* [134 N.W. 2d 611 (Michigan)] and *Fussner* v. *Andert* [113 N.W. 2d 355 (Minnesota)].

Defenses. In order to recover, the beneficiaries must establish that the injuries to the deceased were caused by the ''wrongful act, neglect, or default'' on the part of the defendant and that the injuries were causally related to the death which ensued. The defendant may interpose any defense which he may have had against the deceased had he lived. This means that the defendant has available the defenses of contributory negligence, assumption of risk, or consent to the defendant's conduct. In addition, in most states, the defendant may interpose the defense that the claim has been released or has proceeded to verdict. In addition, the defense of the statute of limitations can be pleaded in an appropriate case.

DEFENSES

416 Contributory Negligence

The common-law rule is that if the conduct of the injured person falls below the standard of care which he or she is required to exercise for his or her own safety, and if such conduct was a contributing cause of the event, the injured person may not recover. Therefore, if the injured person's lack of care for his or her own safety contributed in the slightest degree to the happening of the event, the verdict must be for the defendant. This is true even though the negligence of the defendant is great and that of the injured person is slight. Contributory negligence on the part of the injured person is a common-law defense against all causes of action based on negligence. It should be emphasized that contributory negligence is not a defense against actions where the conduct of the defendant is intentional or reckless. (See Sections 400–410 for discussion of intentional torts.)

The individual is required to exercise reasonable care for his or her own safety. Conduct will be measured by the *reasonably prudent person standard*, sometimes known as the *reasonable man* or *reasonably prudent man* standard and, if it falls below that standard, it will be characterized as negligent. The standard is a variable one and will depend upon the surrounding circumstances. For example, the reasonably prudent person would not run in front of a speeding train, but might feel compelled to do so if it was necessary to save the life of a child who was in the path of the train. It might be contributory negligence to run in front of the train with no other surrounding circumstances, but where it is necessary to do so to save a child, the chances are that the jury would view the same act as not constituting contributory negligence. The standard by which the injured person's conduct is judged is what the reasonably prudent person would have done—or would not have done—under the same or similar circumstances.

In cases involving a claim for damages arising out of the intentional infliction of injuries, or reckless misconduct amounting to an intentional infliction of injuries, contributory negligence is not a defense. Thus, if a woman walked down a dark street in the dead of night and was assaulted, the fact that a reasonably prudent person might not have walked on that street at that hour is not a defense to an action brought against the wrongdoer for damages arising out of the bodily injuries sustained.

Imputed Contributory Negligence. Just as in negligence, contributory negligence may be imputed from one person to another where there is a relationship between them which makes one responsible for the acts of the other. This situation usually comes about where there is a right of control on the part of the one over the actions of the other, as in the relationship of principal and agent and master and servant. Thus, where the agent or servant of the owner of a motor vehicle is involved in an accident caused by the joint negligence of the servant and another person, the contributory negligence of the servant is imputed to the owner and may be interposed as a defense to his action against the other person for the damage to the owner's vehicle. This is sometimes known as the "both ways" rule in the sense that the negligence of the driver-agent is imputed to the principal-owner, regardless of whether the action is one by the other person for damages or an action by the owner-principal for the damage to his vehicle or to his person.

On the other hand, the contributory negligence of a bailee-driver is not imputed to the bailor-owner, since the element of control is lacking in a bailment relationship. It is only where the owner has the right to control, whether he exercises it or not, that the negligence of the driver is imputed to him.

The doctrine of last clear chance (discussed below) is a modification of some of the harsher consequences of contributory negligence. It really has more to do with proximate cause than with contributory negligence. As the rule is often expressed, if the defendant had the last clear chance to avoid harm, the plaintiff's negligence is no longer a proximate cause, or the defendant's later-occurring fault is somehow worse than the plaintiff's negligence.

Last Clear Chance. The law imposes a duty on the part of every person to exercise due care for the safety of others. This means that the individual is under a duty to avoid injury to another if it is possible to do so. This duty continues even though the contributory negligence of the other has placed him or her in a position of peril. Where a party has the *last clear chance* of avoiding injury to another, he or she is under the duty of avoiding the accident, and failure to do so may result in liability. This is true even though the negligence of the other party has placed the individual in a position of peril. The theory here is that the negligence of the party having the last opportunity of avoiding the accident is the sole proximate cause of the injury. Manifestly, the defendant must have had actual knowledge of the plaintiff's perilous position or, in the exercise of ordinary care, should have known of it. In addition, there must have been an opportunity available to the defendant to avoid the accident. Where these elements appear and an accident occurs, the plaintiff is absolved of contributory negligence, and a recovery is allowed against the defendant.

If the defendant by the exercise of reasonable care could not have discovered the peril of the plaintiff, or if there was no opportunity afforded to the defendant of avoiding the accident, the doctrine does not apply.

The classic example of last clear chance involves a man who drives a negligently maintained vehicle onto the tracks of a railroad at a time when signals are flashing, warning of an approaching train. The vehicle stalls on the tracks, and the driver has no means of extricating himself from the vehicle. The engineer of the approaching train has an unobstructed view of the vehicle and could bring the train to a stop within the range of his vision and before striking the stalled vehicle. If he fails to do so, his negligence is the proximate cause of the accident, and the railroad is liable.

For the defendant to have had an opportunity of avoiding the accident, it is clear that the plaintiff's contributory negligence must have occurred some time prior to the happening of the accident. If the plaintiff's contributorily negligent act occurred simultaneously with the occurrence of the accident, it is obvious that the defendant could not have had an opportunity of avoiding the accident. In other words, there would have to be some interval of time within which the defendant could take some action which would avoid the accident.

Thus, the doctrine of last clear chance is an exception to the general rule that the contributory negligence of the plaintiff defeats recovery.

417 Comparative Negligence

Comparative negligence applies the rule that the contributory negligence of the plaintiff will not defeat his recovery, but will be taken into account by the jury in reducing the amount of his recovery. The theory of comparative negligence is not new to the law. It had its genesis in admiralty and is traditionally applied in all cases of admiralty and maritime jurisdiction. The common law never accepted it, adhering to the rule that the contributory negligence of the plaintiff, no matter how slight, will defeat his recovery.

The comparative negligence rule has been adopted in several federal statutes, such as the Federal Employers Liability Act, applying to injuries sustained by employees of an interstate carrier by railroad, the Jones Act, applying to injury or death of seamen, and Death on the High Seas by Wrongful Act, applying to death sustained on American vessels on the high seas.

Most states have adopted the comparative negligence rule either by statute or judicial determination. States are not uniform in their approach to the rule. The result is that we have three distinctly different rules applicable. These rules take the form of (1) pure, (2) modified, and (3) slight versus gross.

1. Pure Form. Under this form, the plaintiff is entitled to recover, regardless of the amount of contributory negligence applicable to him, provided that the defendant was in some degree negligent. Theoretically, the plaintiff would recover if he or she was 99 percent negligent and the defendant 1 percent. The amount of the plaintiff's recovery would be reduced by the percentage of negligence of which he is guilty. Thus, if the plaintiff sustained $10,000 in damages and was 75 percent contributorily negligent, he would be entitled to recover only 25 percent of his damages ($2,500). Likewise, the defendant could counterclaim for his damages and he would be entitled to a 75 percent recovery, since his contributory negligence amounted to only 25 percent. Obviously, where the defendant had sustained no damages, the only recovery involved would be by the plaintiff.

A minority of the states that have adopted comparative negligence adhere to the so-called pure form.

2. Modified Form. This type of comparative negligence allows a recovery by the plaintiff if her negligence did not exceed that of the defendant. There are, however, two variations of this type of statute. The first requires that the plaintiff's contributory negligence be less than the negligence of the defendant. Thus, the plaintiff can be up to 49 percent negligent and still recover, because the plaintiff's negligence is less than the defendant's. For example, the plaintiff with $10,000 damages would have his award reduced by his 49 percent negligence, but would still recover $5,100. However, if the plaintiff's contributory negligence equals or exceeds that of the defendant, there will be no recovery.

The second variation of the modified form allows a recovery by the plaintiff if her contributory negligence equals or is less than that of the defendant. Under this type of statute, the plaintiff could be 50 percent negligent and still recover $5,000 of her $10,000 damages.

3. Slight versus Gross Negligence. A very few states by statute apply the rule of comparative negligence only where the court finds that the plaintiff's contributory negligence as compared with defendant's negligence is slight. If the plaintiff's negligence is more than slight, contributory negligence rules control and the plaintiff is barred from recovery.

It should be noted that most comparative negligence states do not permit the plaintiff's contributory negligence to reduce his or her recovery where the defendant's conduct was intentional. Most permit such a reduction where the conduct was reckless.

418 Assumption of Risk

A person who knowingly exposes himself to the danger of injury is said to have assumed the risk of such injury. This means that, under the circumstances, the injured person cannot recover, even though the injuries were sustained through no fault of his own but through the fault of someone else.

In order to invoke the defense of assumption of risk, two elements must be present:

1. Knowledge or awareness of the existence of the risk, with a corresponding appreciation of the extent of the danger.
2. A voluntary exposure to the danger.

Suppose *A* has a learner's permit. B, knowing this, agrees to teach *A* how to drive an automobile, and therefore in entering the car assumes all risks incident to riding in a car operated by such a driver. If an accident should occur as a result of a lack of skill on the part of *A*, and *B* is injured, *B* cannot recover. Both of the necessary elements of assumption of risk are present. *B* knew that *A* was inexperienced and knowingly exposed herself to the risk of *A*'s inexperience. Therefore, she cannot recover.

Suppose *A* has a learner's permit, or no license at all, but assures *B* that he has a driver's license and that he is an experienced driver. *B*, unaware of *A*'s lack of driving experience, enters the car and is injured as a result of *A*'s incompetent driving. *B* may recover from *A*, because both elements of assumption of risk are lacking in this case. *B* did not know of the risk to which she was being exposed in riding with *A*; therefore *B* could not possibly have voluntarily assumed a risk of which she was not aware.

When spectators at baseball games sit in areas without a protective screen they voluntarily assume the risk of being struck by batted balls. The risk is open and obvious, and if the spectator does not wish to assume such a risk, he or she can secure a seat behind a protective screen or refrain from going to the ball game altogether. In the case of injury in the open area, the defense of assumption of risk can be successfully interposed. The spectator is charged with the knowledge of the danger, and in sitting in an unprotected area voluntarily exposes himself or herself to the danger. If a spectator secures a seat behind a protective screen, he or she has assumed no risk at all as far as batted balls are concerned. Should a ball go through the protective screen and strike the plaintiff, the plaintiff would be entitled to recover.

The patron of a theater assumes the risk of injury occasioned as a result of darkness within the theater and other conditions which the patron normally expects to find and to which he voluntarily exposes himself. The theater owner has the duty of maintaining the premises in a safe condition and the duty of maintaining order in the establishment. The patron does not assume the risk of injury as a result of the breach of either of these duties by the theater owner.

The same rules apply to patrons of an amusement park and those who participate in the use of amusement devices. The patron will be considered to have assumed the risk of injury in any situation where the risk is open, obvious, and foreseeable. The owner of the amusement device is responsible for its proper maintenance and is required to take all possible measures for the safety of those using the device.

The preceding discussion relates primarily to express assumption of risk, where the plaintiff in some way affirmatively demonstrates a choice to assume a risk and relieve the defendant of his legal duty toward the plaintiff. This should be distinguished from implied assumption of risk, where the defendant engages in unreasonable conduct that seems to be very much like contributory negligence. "Many courts have held that the contributory negligence form of assumption of risk—probably the most common form in which the doctrine appears—should be absorbed into the mainstream of comparative fault, thereby serving only to reduce the plaintiff's damages, not to bar them altogether." [Prosser and Keeton, *Torts*, § 68 at 497 (1988, Supp. 1991).]

Thus, the growing influence of comparative negligence has resulted in a decline in the significance of implied assumption of risk. Some legislatures, as well as courts, have determined that comparative negligence requires the modification or abolition of the assumption of risk rule, or its blending or merger into the developing body of comparative negligence law.

419 Unavoidable Accident

This has been defined as an inevitable accident, or one that could not have been foreseen or prevented by using ordinary diligence, and resulting without fault. Therefore, it is an accident that could not be prevented by the exercise of ordinary care and prudence.

For example, an automobile driver who had no prior knowledge or history of heart disease suffers a fatal heart attack while driving her automobile, and as a result her car crashes into another, causing personal injuries and property damage. Here the driver had no notice of her heart condition. This is an unavoidable accident, and no recovery can be had against the estate of the deceased automobile driver.

Let us add one fact to the previous situation; let us assume that the automobile driver had been physically examined, had been told that she had a serious heart ailment, and had been warned not to subject herself to any stress or strain, including the driving of an automobile. Despite this warning she drove the car, with the same unfortunate result. The accident could not be considered unavoidable, and certainly the exercise of reasonable prudence could have prevented it. Therefore, it is not an unavoidable accident and recovery may be had.

The defense is sometimes offered that an insect, usually a bee or a wasp, entered the automobile and stung, bit, or otherwise deprived the driver of the ability to control the vehicle. Since the presence of the insect is not something that reasonable prudence could have prevented, the accident then is unavoidable. Since this defense can be easily fabricated, a great deal will depend upon whether the fact can be established by clear and convincing evidence. This is a question of fact for the jury to decide. If the jury finds that the insect so distracted or deprived the driver of the ability to control the vehicle, they can find that the accident was unavoidable.

An unavoidable accident defense may be used in a case where an irresponsible party is actually guilty of a wrongful act. Infants of tender years are not chargeable with negligence, nor are people of unsound minds. If one of these individuals dashes into the street in the path of an oncoming automobile and is struck by the automobile, without any negligent act on the part of the driver, this occurrence is termed an unavoidable accident. The fault, if there was any, is on the person who dashed into the street. Legally, fault cannot be ascribed to the injured person, and therefore the accident is deemed to be unavoidable.

The defense of inevitable accident is frequently interposed in automobile cases where, without any previous notice of the condition, a car is suddenly enveloped in smoke from a railroad train or a nearby fire, or an unanticipated fog, or where the driver is confronted with an unanticipated patch of ice or water on the highway. If the driver were driving the car at a proper speed, maintaining control and his or her ability to stop within the range of vision, he or she cannot be charged with negligence if one of these unusual and unforeseeable conditions arises and the vehicle strikes another car or object.

Some courts take the position that the defense of unavoidable accident is simply a denial of negligence and proximate causation. These courts may refuse to give such an instruction as to unavoidable accident except in the clearest cases (such as the heart attack suffered by a driver noted above).

420 Act of God

This is defined as any accident, misadventure, or casualty that happens by the direct, immediate, and exclusive operation of the forces of nature, uncontrolled or uninfluenced by human power, and without human intervention. Such an occurrence will be of such a character that it could not have been prevented or avoided by any amount of foresight or prudence, or by any reasonable degree of care or diligence, or by the aid of any appliances which might reasonably be required. Where damage occurs solely as a consequence of an act of God, no liability is imposed upon anyone; however, if human agency or negligence concurs *with* an act of God, the person injured or suffering damage because of the occurrence may recover.

The classic example of the application of these principles involves a case where the owner of land constructs a dam across a stream running through his property. The dam will withstand the normal pressure exerted against it by the water as well as the extra pressure created by an ordinary rainfall. An unprecedented cloudburst occurs, however, which so increases the pressure against the dam that it crumbles under the impact and the water thus released inundates the land of his neighbor. This is an act of God, and the dam owner is not liable to his neighbor for the damage caused by the water. Nor is the owner of the dam bound to anticipate and guard against all of the possibilities of damage that the forces of nature might create. But he is bound to anticipate the ordinary course of nature. Therefore, under these circumstances, the owner of the dam would be responsible if the dam crumbled under the impact of ordinary rainfall.

In another case, the owner of a business establishment suspends a large electric sign on the outside of her premises. The sign is so anchored that it will withstand ordinary rainfall and the pressure of ordinary wind. A tornado strikes the area, and the sign is torn loose from its moorings and crashes into a building, causing property damage and personal injuries to the persons inside. This again is an act of God, and the owner of the sign is not answerable for the damage or for the personal injuries. On the other hand, if the sign should fall as a result of the impact of wind ordinarily present in the neighborhood at certain times, the owner of the sign is liable for any resulting loss or damage.

The application of these principles poses questions of fact for the jury. The jury will decide, as a matter of fact, whether the cloudburst is unprecedented, whether the wind is unusual, and whether the owner of the dam or the sign should have anticipated the possibilities of injury from the forces of nature. In deciding the question of fact, the jury may be guided by evidence of weather conditions of previous years, the testimony of persons who have lived in the area for a long period of time, as well as by evidence with respect to other damage in the vicinity caused as a consequence of the same forces of nature.

421 Statute of Limitations

In the public interest, the legislatures of the various states have decided that there must be some time at which the threat of possible litigation must cease. Therefore, they have enacted statutes which prescribe the periods of time within which actions may be brought upon certain claims, and declare that no suit shall be maintained on such causes of action unless brought within the period of time specified. A statute setting forth the limitations of time within which certain causes of action must be brought is called a statute of limitations. Failure to bring suit within the period of time prescribed deprives the plaintiff of his right to enforce his claim.

There are different periods of time prescribed for different forms of action. The period of time referable to personal injury actions is different from the period for property damage actions, and the limitation applicable to tort claims is generally a shorter period of time than that applicable to contract actions. Reference must be had to the specific state statute applicable to the cause of action to determine the limitation of time applicable.

Because the statute of limitations is a substantive rule, the law of the place where the cause of action arose determines the period of limitation applicable, irrespective of where the action is tried. For example, assume that an accident causing personal injuries occurred in New Jersey, which has a two-year period of limitation within which the action must be brought; suit is brought in New York, which has a three-year period applicable to personal injury claims, two years and three months after the accident. The cause of action would be barred by the New Jersey statute of limitations (which would be applicable to the claim) even though the action was brought in New York which grants a longer period of time.

The statutes usually provide that the limitation will not run against an infant during the period of his infancy and that the infant, upon attaining his majority, has an additional period of time within which the action must be brought before it is barred. There are other provisions, with regard to incompetent persons, which toll (suspend) the running of the statute during the period of incompetence or during the period in which the person is without a guardian to protect his or her interests.

Were it not for these statutes, the potential defendant would have to be prepared to defend a lawsuit at any time, no matter when it was brought. This would place upon the potential defendant the burden of perpetuating all evidence, if it were possible to do so. In cases where vital evidence could be destroyed by the passage of time, the defendant would be at a decided disadvantage. In addition, life is short and human memory faulty, so that the defendant may be deprived of a defense by the death of an important witness or the failure of other witnesses to recall the event with absolute clarity.

Technically, the statute of limitations does not destroy the claim; it merely makes it unenforceable. Therefore, the defendant may waive the statute or fail to interpose it as a defense, in which case the claim can be prosecuted to judgment even though the statute of limitations has run.

The time period of the statute of limitations begins to run from the date the cause of action accrues. In tort cases, this would mean that the statute begins to run from the date of the accident, or the date the tortious act was committed. In addition, most statutes provide that any period during which the defendant is absent from the state or secretes himself within the state is deducted from the period of limitation.

Medical malpractice cases and others of similar nature pose a special problem where the negligent act cannot be discovered until some time after it has occurred. For example, a surgeon leaves a surgical instrument or a sponge in the patient's body at the time of the operation. The patient is unaware of this, and after he has suffered some pain for a period of time, it is finally discovered. It is possible that by the time that the discovery is made, the statute of limitations has run against the claim. In other words, the statute could run against the patient's claim even before he knows that he has a claim. To correct this, some states have amended their statutes to provide that the period of limitation is to be computed from the date when the facts were discovered, or from the time when the facts could have been discovered by the exercise of due diligence. In other states, the courts have accomplished the same result without the aid of the legislature.

Chapter 5

Tort Parties and Immunities

PARTIES

500 Consortium

501 Prenatal Injuries

502 Minors and Insane Persons

JOINT TORT–FEASORS

503 Joint and Several Liability

504 Release-of-One Rule

505 Contribution and Indemnity

506 Joint Tort–Feasors Contribution Law

VICARIOUS LIABILITY

507 Vicarious Liability or Imputed Negligence

508 Employer–Employee

509 Owner and Independent Contractor

510 Parent–Child

511 Husband–Wife

IMMUNITIES

512 Family Immunity

513 Federal Tort Claims Act

514 Governmental Immunity: Federal

515 Governmental Immunity: State

516 Governmental Immunity: Municipal

517 Governmental Immunity: Effect of Insurance

518 Charitable Immunity

PARTIES

500 Consortium

At common law, a husband was entitled to the services of his wife. He was required to pay her medical bills in the case of illness or injury. Where the wife was injured, only the husband could bring an action, which consisted of two counts: one was for the personal injury to his wife, including her physical and mental distress; the other was for his own loss of services, for his medical expenses, and related damages. A married woman was under a legal disability and could not sue in her own name. Suit could be brought only by her husband for and in her behalf.

At common law the wife was considered as a sort of superior servant, who as a consequence of the marriage contract owed certain duties to her husband. These duties collectively are called *consortium*. They consist of sex, society, and services. ''Sex'' means the right of the husband to have sexual relations with his wife. ''Society'' means that the husband is entitled to the companionship of his wife. ''Services'' consist of routine household chores, such as keeping the home in proper condition, cooking meals, and other duties necessary for the maintenance of the home. Any injury to the wife which impaired her ability to perform these duties and deprived the husband of his right to have them performed gave rise to a cause of action by the husband against the wrongdoer who caused the wife's injuries.

With the emancipation of married women from this common-law disability, the same two causes of action remained, but now the injured wife may sue in her own name for the injuries she has sustained, including her physical and mental distress. The husband still has his cause of action for loss of services and medical expenses which he can assert in his own name. Thus, under present conditions, where a married woman is injured, both the husband and the wife may have causes of action arising out of the same event, which can be prosecuted jointly or separately. A release by the wife alone would not extinguish the husband's cause of action and, conversely, a release by the husband alone would not extinguish his wife's cause of action.

At common law, when the husband himself was injured, only he had a right of action against the wrongdoer, and the release by him of his cause of action would extinguish the entire claim. Whether any right on the part of the wife to the services of her husband existed is obscure. Possibly one reason, at least, why such a right was never recognized was that the wife could not assert such a right even if she had one, since she was under a legal disability and could not enforce such a cause of action.

In *Hitaffer* v. *Argonne Products* [183 Fed. 2d 811; certiorari denied in 340 U.S. 852], the Circuit Court of Appeals for the District of Columbia, recognizing the irrationality of denying the wife a remedy available to her husband, modified the common law of the District of Columbia and held that the wife had an assertable cause of action for her loss of consortium where her husband had been injured by the tortious act of the defendant. The court reasoned that the husband had a cause of action for loss of his wife's services where she was injured; the wife, therefore, in the case of injury to her husband, had sustained similar damage.

The wife, being under a legal disability at common law, could not assert this cause of action. Since married women now by statute have been emancipated from the legal disability imposed by the common law, the court said that the wife now could assert such a cause of action and recover. Therefore, under the ruling of the case, where a husband is injured, a cause of action arises on the part of the wife for damages for the loss of her husband's services.

At first the *Hitaffer* decision was generally rejected, but at the present time there seems to be a trend toward a reexamination of the question, with the result that a majority of states have now adopted the *Hitaffer* rule. Some of the contrary decisions are quite old, and, even though the courts in some states have not adopted the rule, there is no guarantee that they will not reconsider the adoption of the rule in an appropriate case. It undoubtedly will be argued that, in view of the opinion in the majority of states which have adopted the *Hitaffer* rule, the continued rejection of the rule denies to women equal protection of the laws. Therefore no reliance should be placed on decisions to the contrary.

In states where the *Hitaffer* rule has been adopted, two causes of action arise in cases where the husband is injured—one by the husband for his own injuries, pain and suffering, and medical expense and one by the wife for her loss of consortium. A release of one cause of action will not extinguish the other. Therefore, it is recommended, in all cases where the injured person (man or woman) is married, that releases be taken from both husband and wife. This procedure is recommended even in those states which have specifically rejected the *Hitaffer* rule.

501 Prenatal Injuries

The common-law rule is that an injury to an unborn child is solely an injury to the mother. The reasoning is that an unborn child is not a person endowed with legal rights until actually born. A fetus is considered to be part of the mother's anatomy until birth. Therefore, any injury to the fetus prior to birth is considered to be an injury to the mother only. This rule is applied even though the infant is born later with some physical or mental defect which can be directly traced to the injury sustained by the mother. Under those circumstances, settlement by the mother of her claim for personal injuries will extinguish the entire cause of action.

Some courts felt that the application of this common-law rule was entirely unjust, especially in cases where the child was forced to go through life with a physical or mental impairment which was visited upon it as a result of the wrongdoing of another. Therefore, these courts changed the rule and permitted recoveries in actions brought by such children whose injuries could be traced to the injury to the mother. This sounds like a fairly simple rule to apply, but the decisions of the courts are in hopeless confusion as to the situations in which they will apply the rule.

A number of states allow recoveries for personal injury sustained by a viable child prior to birth. Other states in which the question has been presented, and where the viability rule has been rejected, make no distinction in cases of personal injury as to whether the injury was sustained by a viable or nonviable fetus.

In cases involving the death of the injured fetus, either prior to birth or immediately thereafter, we find still more diversity of opinion among the courts. We will simply mention death cases within three categories: infants born alive, stillborn infants, and nonviable fetuses.

Some states have allowed recoveries in cases where the viable infant sustained injuries and survived birth, but then died as a result of the injuries. Some jurisdictions have allowed—while others have denied—recovery for prenatal injuries where the viable infant was stillborn. In a few states recoveries have been allowed for prenatal injuries in the case of death of a nonviable fetus. Recent years have seen dramatic advances in medical science—particularly in the field of neonatology—as well as growing concern for the legal rights of unborn children. As a result, the questions of when an unborn child is viable and what degree of legal protection should be afforded to an unborn child are in a state of flux. Some of the states which considered the problem of the death or destruction of a nonviable fetus have regarded this as part of the injury to the mother and have denied recoveries for and in behalf of the unborn child.

These differences of opinion among the courts pose a real problem for the claim representative who is faced with a claim for personal injuries by a pregnant woman. In cases where there is a possibility of an injury to the unborn child, settlement with the injured mother will not necessarily extinguish a possible claim for and in behalf of the infant who is later born with a physical or mental disability due to the accident.

502 Minors and Insane Persons

The law refers to anyone under the age of majority as an *infant*. An infant is liable for his own torts and may be sued, through a guardian, in exactly the same manner as an adult. The parents of the infant, in the absence of a statute, are not liable for the torts of the child, nor is the negligence of the child imputed to his parents. The parents, however, are liable for their own negligence, as in a case where the parents make firearms available to an infant who is unfamiliar with their use.

At common law, a child under the age of seven is conclusively presumed to be incapable of committing a crime, forming a malicious intent, or being guilty of negligence. Thus, as to intentional torts, where a malicious intent is one of the elements which must be established, the conclusive presumption will prevent the court from receiving evidence of malicious intent. The same thing would be true with respect to negligence. The child under the age of seven is incapable of negligence and, since this is a conclusive presumption, no evidence is admissible to establish the child's negligence or contributory negligence.

As to torts committed by infants over the age of seven, the question of the infant's responsibility will turn on her actual age and her mental capacity for apprehending whether her action is wrongful. The intelligence of the infant will be taken into account in determining whether the infant was capable of exercising due care. These considerations apply equally to contributory and comparative negligence. An infant under the age of seven who is incapable of being negligent, could not be guilty of contributory negligence in failing to exercise due care for her own safety. An infant over the age of seven will be chargeable with negligence only if her age and intelligence are such that she should have been able to apprehend the danger and then failed to take reasonable precautions for her own safety.

There are few cases reported concerning insane or mentally ill persons—either as to the duties owed to them by others or the duties owed by them. In the few cases available, the general rule seems to be that insane or mentally ill persons are held to the same duty of care which would be required of sane persons, whether that duty of care is owed to others or required for their own safety.

JOINT TORT–FEASORS

503 Joint and Several Liability

Where two or more persons owe a duty to another and, by their common neglect, the other is injured, they are joint tort-feasors. All tort-feasors are responsible for the legal consequences of their wrongful acts, but where the causation of the injury is complicated by the introduction of other wrongful acts in the chain of causation, the extent to which the individual tort-feasor is answerable will depend upon the relationship which his particular wrongful act bears to the causation and result. His negligent act will partake of one of the following causative qualities:

1. Concurrent.
2. Successive.
3. A combination of both.

1. Concurrent. Where the negligent acts of two or more persons, although independent of each other, combine to produce a single event or a single injury, they are classified as concurrent, and the tort-feasors are jointly and severally (i.e., individually) liable to the injured person for the entire damage.

Paraphrasing *Restatement* § 882, joint and several liability may be described as follows. If more than one tort-feasor injures a person, that person is entitled to sue one or some or all of the responsible parties, obtain judgments against as many of them as possible, and then collect the judgments against one or some or all of othose found jointly and severally liable.

For example, two automobiles negligently driven by *A* and *B* collide at an intersection, and *B*'s car goes out of control and strikes *C*, a pedestrian on the sidewalk. *C* may recover for his entire injury from either *A*, or *B*, or both. The fact that *B*'s car struck *C*, and *A*'s did not, will not in any way alter the situation. The negligence of both *A* and *B* combined to produce the event and the injury to *C*. Nor would the fact that one driver was more culpable than the other change the situation in any way. If *A* was driving 10 miles over the speed limit and *B* was driving 30 miles over the speed limit, both are still liable for the causation of the event.

In the foregoing example, the joint negligence of *A* and *B* produced a single indivisible result, the injury to *C*. But suppose some facts were added and, with the additional facts, we were able to separate *C*'s injuries into two parts: those caused by *A* and those caused by *B*. Would these additional facts change the responsibilities of the parties? Suppose that after the initial impact, *B*'s car struck *C* first, causing a fractured leg, and immediately thereafter *A*'s car struck *C*, causing a fractured skull. Could it be said that *B* is liable only for the fractured leg and that *A* is liable only for the fractured skull? The answer to the question is in the negative. The transaction is considered a single event and under the circumstances the courts will not apportion responsibility between *A* and *B*, but will hold both jointly and severally liable for the entire damage.

C may, at his election, sue either *A* or *B*, or both, for his entire injury. Should he decide to sue one and not the other, his recovery from one will extinguish his cause of action for the reason that *C* is entitled to only one satisfaction for one injury. Therefore, the practical effect of a recovery from one will be to discharge the other. Where *C* elects to sue one of the joint tort-feasors and not the other, his motivation for so doing is not an issue, and he is not required to offer an explanation as to why he made the decision. He may have been persuaded by the fact that one is a rich man and the other poor, one is insured and the other is not, or that one is his friend and the other is not. In any case, he is not required to explain. From a tactical standpoint, however, if he sues only one and not the other, it gives the defendant an opportunity to claim that the event was caused solely by the negligence of the other who has not been joined as a defendant. The practice followed by most plaintiffs' lawyers is to include all parties who have a possible responsibility as defendants in the action.

2. Successive. Where the negligent acts of two or more tort-feasors do not combine to produce the event, but do combine to produce the injury, the general rule is that each is responsible for the effects of his own act, whether the injury sustained is a single indivisible injury or multiple injuries which can be separated. For example, *C* is injured through the negligence of *A*, and sustains a fractured right leg. While lying on the sidewalk, awaiting an ambulance, *C* is struck by an automobile negligently driven by *B* and sustains a further injury in the form of a fractured skull. *A* is liable for the fractured leg, and *B* is liable for the fractured skull; the damages are apportioned against each by the jury under instructions from the court. If we change the facts to the extent that *C* sustained a fractured right leg in the first accident, and the same leg is further damaged by the second accident, we would have a single indivisible injury. There would be no evidence as to how badly fractured the leg was prior to the second accident, or exactly what physical injury was caused by the second impact. Under those circumstances the jury would be instructed to apportion the damages between *A* and *B* on the basis of whatever evidence was produced.

C has the right to sue *A* and *B* in separate actions or to combine both claims in one action against both. If he brings separate actions, a recovery in one action will not extinguish his cause of action against the other tort-feasor. Again, the usual practice of the plaintiff's attorney would be to sue both in one action for the entire injury.

3. Combination of Both. It is possible for the negligent acts of two tort-feasors to be concurrent with respect to a part of the claimant's injuries and to be successive as to the remainder. For example, *C* is injured through the negligence of *A*, sustaining a fractured skull. While lying in the roadway, *C* is again struck by an automobile, this time negligently operated by *B*, and he sustains a fractured right leg as a result of the second impact. The negligence of *A* caused the fractured skull—and also placed *C* in a position of danger where it was reasonably foreseeable that he might be further injured by other motorists. Therefore *A* is liable for both injuries. As for *B*, his negligence did not cause the fractured skull, and he is liable only for the injuries which he did cause, namely, the fractured right leg. Therefore, as to the fractured skull, *A* alone is responsible. As to the fractured leg, *A* and *B* are concurrent joint tort-feasors and are jointly and severally liable.

In the foregoing example, the injuries are separable, and the relative responsibilities of the tort-feasors are capable of ascertainment. Complications develop in this type of situation where the injuries are of such a nature that they constitute one single indivisible result. For example, if *C* was lying in the roadway in a dying condition as a result of *A*'s negligence, and was then struck by *B*'s car, which kills him outright, what is the extent of *B*'s responsibility? If *C* was going to die anyway, it would appear that *B*'s responsibility would be limited to the value of what life *C* had left—or to the outside possibility of a recovery. The extent of *B*'s responsibility is a jury question. On the other hand, if *C* was already dead when *B* struck him, then *B* would not be liable for any bodily injury.

The same problems arise in cases where further injury is caused by the malpractice of a physician treating the case. The original tort-feasor is liable for the entire injury, including that sustained as a result of the physician's malpractice. The physician's liability is limited to the injury caused by his malpractice alone.

Where the claimant sues the original tort-feasor, who is liable for the entire injury, and recovers, such recovery extinguishes his cause of action. He has obtained complete satisfaction for his entire injury and he is entitled to no more. The effect of the recovery will be also to extinguish the liability of the successive joint tort-feasor. A recovery against the successive joint tort-feasor (*B* in the first example and the physician in the second) would exonerate the original tort-feasor from the responsibility for the second accident, but he would still remain liable for his original negligence and the damages sustained as a result. This latter situation is extremely rare and highly unlikely, since the practice would be to sue all tort-feasors in the one action, and if there is to be a choice between them, the "better" defendant would be the one who is liable for the entire injury rather than one who is liable for only a part.

504 Release-of-One Rule

The English common-law rule, to which some of our courts are still committed, is that the release of one or more joint tort-feasors releases all of them. This rule is based on the theory that there can be but one satisfaction for one injury. Most states, through legislation or court decision, have relaxed the rule at least to the extent that they hold that a release of one joint tort-feasor does not release the other unless the release was so intended or unless the consideration which was given constituted full satisfaction of the claim. Where it is held that the release constituted only partial satisfaction of the claim, the holding is that the claim is satisfied to the extent of the payment made (See Section 630.)

Some states have changed the rule by statute. For example, in New York the General Obligations Law, Section 15–108 provides (*a*) that a release given to one or more joint tort-feasors, unless specified to the contrary, releases that tort-feasor only. It also provides that a release reduces the plaintiff's recovery from the other tort-feasors by the amount of damages attributable to the released tort-feasor. (*b*) It further provides that the released tort-feasor is free from any liability to any other tort-feasor for contribution, provided that a good faith release was given by the injured party. (*c*) In any case the tort-feasor who procures his own release waives his right to contribution from any other tort-feasor. This legislation is designed to encourage settlements and, ultimately, to reduce the calendar congestion in the courts. Many states have adopted similar legislation, patterned after the Uniform Contribution Act.

Some courts still hold to the common-law rule that a release to one or more, but less than all, concurrent tort-feasors is a complete surrender of the entire cause of action, without regard to the sufficiency of the compensation so received. This rule is followed even though there is an agreement between the parties that it shall be only a partial release or the agreement is in writing and made part of the release itself. Some courts give effect to a *restrictive* release, where there is language inserted in the instrument to the effect that it is to be construed as a release of one tort-feasor only and is not intended to be a release of the entire cause of action. Other states have accomplished this same result by statute.

Even in those states where the rule is strictly applied, the courts have allowed the parties to circumvent the rule by the use of an agreement called a *covenant not to sue* in which the claim is not released at all; in consideration of the payment by one tort-feasor, the injured party agrees not to sue him, and if the injured party actually sues the tort-feasor, he agrees to make himself liable for an amount equivalent to the amount of the recovery (See Section 631.)

505 Contribution and Indemnity

Contribution refers to the right of one of the joint tort-feasors, who has paid more than his share of the settlement or judgment, to recover the excess over his proportionate share from the others equally liable. Contribution contemplates a situation where there are two or more joint tort-feasors whose combined negligence produced the accident and who are therefore equally responsible for the resulting injury. For example, *A* is a passenger in a car driven by *B*. *B* collides with a car driven by *C*, and the accident is caused by the joint negligence of *B* and *C*. *A* sues *C* and recovers a judgment of $10,000, which *C* pays. *C* is entitled to recover $5,000 from *B*, since this represents the excess over *C*'s proportionate share.

The common-law courts never recognized the right of contribution as an enforceable right. They reasoned that since both were wrongdoers, the courts would not aid one tort-feasor against another, because no one should be permitted to found a cause of action upon his own wrong. This common-law rule has been modified by statute in a number of states so as to permit claims for contribution.

Indemnity also involves joint tort-feasors, but it is implied only where the joint tort-feasors are not equally culpable, and where one joint tort-feasor is held liable because of his relationship to another.

Among the more common situations involving indemnity are the liabilities arising out of the relationship of principal and agent and that of owner and independent contractor. Consideration of both will illustrate these principles.

Principal and Agent. Let us assume that *A* is driving *B*'s car at the direction of *B* and on *B*'s business. *A* negligently injures *C*, a pedestrian. *C* recovers a judgment against *B*, whose liability is based upon the application of the doctrine of *respondeat superior*. Clearly, there was nothing that *B* could have done to have prevented the accident, and the event was due solely to the negligence of *A*. *B* is entitled to indemnity from *A*, and may recover the entire amount of the judgment. Thus, the negligent tort-feasor is compelled to assume the entire loss.

It is also quite possible that a principal may be liable to the agent on the theory of implied indemnity. For example, *B* instructs *A*, his employee, to demolish a small building which *B* believes to be located on his property. *A* does as he is instructed. Unknown to both *B* and *A*, the building is owned by *C* and is located on *C*'s property. *C* recovers a judgment against *A*. *A* is entitled to indemnity from *B*. *B*'s negligence consists of his failure to verify that the building was located on his property. *A* was not negligent at all. He was under no duty to ascertain the ownership of the building, and he was entitled to rely on *B*'s instructions.

Owner and Independent Contractor. *B*, a carpenter, installs a cornice on *A*'s house in such a negligent manner that it falls and strikes *C*, a business visitor. *C* recovers damages from *A* on the allegation that *A* was negligent in failing to maintain his premises in reasonably safe condition for his safety, and further because *A* had failed to make inspection to determine the presence of an unsafe condition. As to *C*, both *A* and *B* are joint tort-feasors in the sense that they both owed *C* a duty of care. *C* chose to sue *A*. Independent of his duty to *C*, *B* owed *A* the duty of reasonable care in the installation of the cornice as well as the duty to do the job in a workmanlike manner. As a result of the breach of *B*'s duty to him, *A* has been compelled to respond in damages to *C*, since if *B* had properly installed the cornice, *A* would not have sustained any loss. Under the common-law rule, *A* is entitled to indemnity for the entire loss from *B*.

506 Joint Tort-Feasors Contribution Law

At common law, there was no contribution among joint tort-feasors. Thus, where a cause of action was asserted against only one of several joint tort-feasors, and a judgment recovered, the defendant would be required to respond and pay all of the damages. The tort-feasor paying all of the damage would not have a cause of action, nor would he have a right to contribution from the other wrongdoers. The common-law concept was that all were wrongdoers, and therefore none had any status in court for the purpose of minimizing or in any way recouping any part of the loss which he or she sustained, partly as a consequence of his own wrongdoing. Since the injured party had elected to hold only one of several joint tort-feasors liable, the common-law courts felt no compulsion to change the situation.

Some states have felt that the common-law rule should be modified and, as a consequence, have enacted statutes creating a right of contribution from other joint tort-feasors in favor of the joint tort-feasor making the payment. The statutory language differs state by state, but the uniform law, which generally forms the basis of the statutes, reads as follows:

> The right of contribution exists among joint tort feasors.
>
> Where injury or damage is suffered by any person as a result of the wrongful act, neglect, or default of joint tort feasors, and a person so suffering injury or damage recovers a money judgment or judgments for such injuries or damage against one or more of the joint tort feasors, either in one action or in separate actions, and any one of the joint tort feasors pays such judgment in whole or in part, he shall be entitled to recover contribution from the other joint tort feasor or tort feasors for the excess so paid over his *pro rata* share; but no person shall be entitled to recover contribution under this act from any person entitled to be indemnified by him in respect to the liability for which the contribution is sought.

To be joint tort-feasors, parties must either act together in committing the wrong, or the acts, if independent of each other, must unite in causing a single injury. By this definition, the wrongful act or acts must be actively committed by the persons in order to constitute them joint tort-feasors. This will eliminate those whose liability is vicarious, such as a principal for the acts of his agent or an automobile owner for the negligence of his driver.

VICARIOUS LIABILITY

507 Vicarious Liability or Imputed Negligence

Imputed or vicarious negligence is negligence not directedly attributable to the person himself but which is the negligence of a person with whose fault he is chargeable. At common law it contemplates an actual or fictional relationship of master and servant, or principal and agent. Where the employer (or master) has control of the employee's (or servant's) behavior, he or she thus becomes responsible for the negligence of the employee in relation to third persons as if the negligence were his or her own. Imputed negligence may arise from the following relationships and situations: employer–employee (including agents, partners, and joint venturers); owner–independent contractor; parent–child; and husband–wife.

508 Employer–Employee

The negligence of a servant is imputed to the master when his negligent act is within the scope of his employment. The original concept was that, where the servant was on a frolic or a detour of his own, the master was not liable. However, this concept has been limited in its application in the more recent cases. These cases hold that, where the master could reasonably expect a deviation, he is still liable.

A joint enterprise is a situation where two or more persons engage in a joint undertaking with a common purpose and mutual rights of control. Imputed negligence is involved only with respect to the liability of the members of the joint enterprise to third persons and is not applicable to actions between the parties against each other. This is similar to a partnership, where the negligence of one partner is imputed to the other with respect to injuries sustained by a third person.

Some statutes create a vicarious liability by imputing the negligence of one person to another. For example, some motor vehicle statutes create a fictional relationship of master and servant between the owner of a motor vehicle and another person driving the car with the owner's permission. Other statutes make the owner liable for the negligence of anyone driving the car with the owner's permission, with no attempt being made to create a relationship of master and servant, fictional or otherwise.

The question of imputed negligence also arises in family relationships, such as parent and child, and husband and wife. The general rule, subject to few exceptions, is that the negligence of one in this relationship is not imputed to the other.

509 Owner and Independent Contractor

Generally the master is not responsible for the negligence of an independent contractor over whom he exercises no control, except

1. Where the work involves a duty of the master which is by law nondelegable.
2. Where the subject matter of the work involves an inherently dangerous or ultrahazardous operation.

If the master continues to control the work, the contractor is not independent and is regarded as a servant. A contractor is independent when he or she is responsible to the owner or master only for the results to be accomplished and cannot be controlled as to the methods and means of doing the work.

510 Parent–Child

The negligence of an infant has never been imputed to the parent solely because of the relationship of parent and child. The infant or minor child is responsible for his own torts, whether the negligence of the child resulted in bodily injury or property damage or both. The relationship of parent and child imposes no liability on the parent for the torts of the child. This common-law rule applies not only to natural parents but also to anyone standing *in loco parentis* (in place of a parent) to the child, such as a stepparent, adopting parent, or a guardian. The exceptions to this rule under which the parent may be liable are:

1. When the child's act is done as the parent's agent or servant.
2. Where the parent's negligence makes the injury possible.
3. Where the parent participates in the child's tortious act by consenting to it.

1. Agency. Where the parent authorizes or commands the child to act as his agent and to do a certain act, the parent will be liable for the negligence of the child within the scope of the authorization or command thus given. This liability does not arise out of the relationship of parent and child. Rather, it arises from the relationship of principal and agent and is merely an application of the fundamental principle of agency that, where a principal does an act through another under his control, he does it himself. Therefore, in this situation, the vicarious liability of the parent is based on the rules relating to principal and agent.

2. Negligence of the Parent. The majority of the cases involving exceptions to the common-law rule of nonliability on the part of parents are found in this particular area. Generally, the parent is required to exercise reasonable care in controlling the actions of his child for the safety of others. This does not mean that the parent is liable if he fails to maintain strict control over the action of the child. He must reasonably foresee the risks of harm to others which might arise under unusual circumstances, such as placing a gun in the hands of a child unfamiliar with its use or making such an instrumentality available to the child by failing to take adequate measures to store the gun out of the reach of the child. If the parent fails to take such steps as are necessary to avoid these risks of harm to others, he will be held liable for negligence.

Similarly, where the child has exhibited vicious tendencies toward other children, adults, or animals, and such characteristics were known to the parent, the parent is himself negligent if he fails to adopt reasonable means for the protection of others who may be injured as a result. The extent of the protective measures which the parent must take will be measured by the extent of the danger to others. In addition, where such characteristics are known to the parent, he or she might be under a duty to disclose the existence of these characteristics to persons who might be injured, such as a baby-sitter, private tutor, or any other person who has temporary custody of the child. It must be emphasized that the liability of the parent arises not from the negligent or tortious act of the child, but from the parent's own negligence in failing to warn the injured person of the dangerous characteristics of the child, thus failing to meet the duty which the law imposes.

Also the parent would be held liable in a case where the parent, either in violation of an ordinance or statute or in failing to foresee the risks of injury to others, provides the child with a dangerous instrumentality.

The question of whether an object is a dangerous instrumentality will depend not only upon the inherent nature of the article but also upon the age of the child to whom it is entrusted. Thus, where a parent provides an automobile for her 17-year-old son, who is a licensed driver and who has a satisfactory driving record, the parent is not negligent. However, should the parent permit a 15-year-old unlicensed driver to use the automobile, the parent is negligent. An automobile in the hands of such an immature, inexperienced driver becomes a dangerous instrumentality and exposes others to an unreasonable risk of harm. The parent thus would be answerable in damages for any injuries which may occur.

On the other hand, where the parent provides ordinary toys or sports equipment normally used by children, he or she is not accountable if the child should use the article for a purpose for which it was not intended. Thus, if a child should use a baseball bat, a hockey stick or other similar article as a weapon, the parent would not be chargeable with negligence solely because he or she provided the child with it.

3. Participation. Where a parent actively participates in the commission of a tort together with his or her child, the parent then becomes a joint tort-feasor and is liable as such. Participation may also consist of a failure to act when there is a duty to do so. For example, in one case, a mother allowed her son's practical joke to proceed, at the expense of a visitor in the home; the surprised visitor ran into a brick wall, injuring herself. The court allowed a recovery against the mother on the theory that she had participated with her son in the practical joke and derived amusement from it.

Statutory Modifications. In most of the states, statutes have been enacted which in substance provide that the parent is liable for the malicious and willful acts of his child resulting in property damage to others. These statutes are subject to a limited amount of recovery. Originally these laws were enacted at the request of the state highway departments and were intended to provide a means whereby some recovery could be made from the parents of children who removed highway signs and other directional markers from the highway. But the scope of many of these statutes has been expanded to benefit such entities as municipal corporations, counties, cities, villages, school districts, and religious organizations.

It should be emphasized that the liability created by these statutes is in addition to any other liability imposed by law. The common-law liability of the child is still in existence, and the liability of the parent for the acts of the child under certain circumstances may still be enforced. A settlement under the statute will not absolve either the child or the parent from liability in tort, although payments under the statute will be taken into account in the event of a tort judgment.

The acts of the child for which the parent is liable under the statute are those which can be characterized as "willful and malicious." This means that the child must have had an intent to do the act and also that such intent was evil and with malice. At common law, a child under the age of seven years is incapable of forming an intent. Therefore, where a child of that age or younger is involved, no evidence of willful or evil intent can be introduced. In cases of older children, the burden of proving the intention of the child is on the person asserting the claim. In most cases the facts of the case will be such that the jury can infer the intent.

511 Husband–Wife

With the emancipation of married women, the wife is considered as an individual, capable of acting independently without any coercion or direction from her husband. She can sue or be sued in her own name. She is not the agent of her husband in all matters nor is he hers. With few exceptions, the negligence of one spouse is not imputed to the other solely because of the marital relationship. The exceptions are found in some of the states where community property laws are in effect. In such states, any recovery obtained would become part of the community property owned by both husband and wife. In those states the negligence of the husband is imputed to the wife and may be an effective bar to her recovery.

IMMUNITIES

512 Family Immunity

The common-law rule is that no lawsuits based on tort liability are permissible between certain members of the family. Under this rule, a husband may not sue his wife, a wife may not sue her husband, a child may not sue his or her parent, and a parent may not sue his or her child. The reason behind this rule is that, since the family unit is one of the cornerstones of our society, the preservation of the family is a matter in which the public interest is involved. The court will not lend its aid to litigation which can only have a disruptive influence on family life and could completely destroy the peace and harmony of the home. Regardless of the severity of an injury or the complete absence of care where reasonable care should have been exercised, a person standing within the relationships noted above may not maintain a cause of action against the negligent defendant.

From a practical standpoint, except for the presence of insurance, there would be no particular incentive for suits of this character where the family relationship is a continuing one. The payment of the judgment from one to the other would merely result in a realignment of the ownership of family assets. Attorneys' fees and court costs would be involved, and the actual result would be some impairment of the family resources with no particular advantage being gained by the successful litigant.

Husband and Wife. The original common-law concept of the unity of marriage merged the legal personality of the wife into that of her husband. She could sue or be sued only in her husband's name, with him acting as her "guardian." With the coming of the Married Women's Acts, which in essence emancipated married women from the common-law disability and allowed them to sue or be sued in their own names without the involvement of their husbands, the courts reexamined the question of whether a married woman could sue her husband in tort. The majority concluded that the family immunity doctrine constituted a bar to the maintenance of any action based on tort liability. Conversely, it was held that the family immunity doctrine also barred the husband from maintaining an action against his wife. A minority of courts took the position that the Married Women's Act abrogated the family immunity doctrine insofar as it related to actions between husband and wife. They reasoned that, if the legislatures intended that suits between husband and wife were not included within the scope of the act, they could have said so.

As to torts committed by the husband or wife prior to marriage, and where the cause of action is asserted after the marriage has taken place, there are only a few cases at common law reported. Most jurisdictions which have considered the problem have concluded that such a suit would impair the peace and harmony of the marriage; and, even though the tort was committed prior to the inception of the relationship of husband and wife, as long as the relationship continued, the injured spouse would be prevented from asserting a tort cause of action against the other. Most of these cases are quite old, and, in view of the latest pronouncements of some of the same courts on the subject of interspousal immunity, it is doubtful whether the same cases would be decided the same way if they were presented now.

Effect of Divorce or Separation. There are few cases on this subject, but it would seem that, where there has been a divorce and the marital relationship has terminated, there would be no peace and harmony of the home which could be disrupted. Therefore, the injured spouse would not be precluded from bringing an action in tort for bodily injury, even though the injury occurred during the period of the marriage. It would seem that the same reasoning should apply where the parties are permanently separated.

Wife versus Husband's Employer. It sometimes happens that, when the husband is acting in the course and scope of his employment, he negligently injures his wife. Because of the common law family immunity doctrine, the wife is precluded from maintaining an action against her husband. However, there is no impediment to an action against the employer based upon the employer's vicarious liability for the negligent acts of his or her agents.

Effect of Death of Either Spouse. As between husband and wife, the death of either ends the family relationship, and, since there is no possiblity of the litigation having any effect upon the peace and tranquility of the home, the family immunity doctrine does not apply. Thus, if a husband or wife suffers bodily injuries in an accident caused by the negligence of the other spouse, who is killed in the accident, there is no legal impediment to the bringing of suit against the legal representative of the deceased spouse. Likewise, where both husband and wife are killed in the accident caused by the negligent driving of the husband, an action for the wrongful death of the wife may be maintained. See for example, *Mosier* v. *Carney* [138 N.W. 2d 343 (Michigan)] (widow's recovery from the estate of her deceased husband allowed); *Poepping* v. *Linderman* [127 N.W. 2d 512 (Minnesota)] (surviving spouse may maintain a negligence action against the deceased spouse's estate for injuries caused during the marriage by the decedent's negligence).

Rejection of the Interspousal Immunity Doctrine. The courts in about half the states have reexamined the interspousal immunity doctrine and decided that it should be abolished. No doubt some consideration was given to the availability of insurance in our modern society as well as the changed status of the wife under present concepts. Many other states have eroded the immunity by clearly and explicitly recognizing certain exceptions. One such exception applies to suits brought after the marriage has been terminated. Another applies to suits against persons vicariously liable for the tort committed by the spouse.

Yet another exception relates to intentional torts. In *Bogen* v. *Bogen* [12 S.E. 649 (1941)], the Supreme Court of North Carolina refused to apply the interspousal immunity doctrine to an intentional tort. The court said: "Whether a man has laid open his wife's head with a bludgeon, put out her eye, broken her arm, or poisoned her body, he is no longer exempt from liability to her on the ground that he vowed at the altar to 'love, cherish, and protect' her. We have progressed that far in civilization and justice." While the interspousal immunity doctrine originally may have been applied to all torts involving husband and wife, the later cases that accept it seem to apply the doctrine only to "nonwillful" torts. Therefore, it can be concluded that even states which still recognize the doctrine will not apply it to intentional torts.

For some years, legal text writers have urged the abolition of the interspousal immunity doctrine. The argument is advanced that neither spouse should be able to injure the other and then be immune from liability. Even though the act complained of may later be used as a grounds for divorce, the injured spouse may be without a remedy because divorce settlements contemplate only the future losses which the spouse will bear and do not compensate for injuries already sustained. In *Freehe* v. *Freehe*, [500 Pac.2d 771 (Washington)], the court said:

> A second major reason given for the disability is the notion that to allow a married person to sue his or her spouse for tort damages would be to destroy the peace and tranquility of the home. On reflection, we are convinced that this is a conclusion without basis. If a state of peace and tranquility exists between the spouses, then the situation is such that no action will be commenced or that the spouses—who are, after all,

the best guardians of their own peace and tranquility—will allow the action to continue only so long as their personal harmony is not jeopardized. If peace or tranquility is nonexistent or tenuous to begin with, then the law's imposition of a technical disability seems more likely to be a bone of contention than a harmonizing factor.

Parent and Child. The family immunity doctrine applies to actions in tort between parent and child on the theory that the barring of such suits is necessary for the preservation of family accord and parental authority. The doctrine applies to any relationship where there is an unemancipated minor child and a parent. The suit between these two parties is barred, whether brought by the child against the parent or by the parent against the child.

Where the child has attained the age of majority or has been emancipated (released from parental authority) prior to the occurrence of the accident, the reason for the rule no longer exists. Therefore, the doctrine is not applicable, and suits by such a child or suits by a parent against such a child are maintainable.

Where the child has not attained majority or has not been emancipated at the time of the accident, and suit is begun either by the child against the parent or by the parent against the child after the child has been emancipated or has attained his majority, the general rule is that such suits are not maintainable. The rule is that the rights of the parties are determined as of the date of the accident. If the plaintiff—whether the child or the parent—could not maintain the action as of the date of the accident, the subsequent change in the child's legal status does not create a cause of action where none existed before. Note, however, that in *Brown* v. *Parker* [375 S.W. 2d 594 (Missouri)], the minor was unemancipated at the time of the accident but had reached majority before the issue was joined. The court stated that an unemancipated minor child could not sue his parent for an unintentional tort and held the same rule would apply to prevent a parent from suing an unemancipated child. In each situation the basis for the rule is a "public policy which refuses to allow the family relationship to be disturbed by such action."

Child versus Parent's Employer. The same considerations and the same general rule which were applicable to cases involving a suit by the wife against the husband's employer are applicable here. The employer is vicariously liable to a minor child injured through the negligence of the father acting within the scope of his employment. Although the father-employee is immune to suits brought on behalf of his infant son, this immunity does not extend to his employer.

Effect of Death. In cases where either the child or the parent has suffered death, the immunity doctrine does not apply to a suit between the survivor and the estate of the deceased. The family relationship has been terminated by death, and the nonapplication of the rule barring suits between family members would not in any way disturb the family relationship, since it has ceased to exist. For example, in *Oliveria* v. *Oliveria* [24 N.E. 2d 766 (Massachusetts)], it was held that a parent's administrator could maintain an action against an unemancipated child for negligence in causing the death of the parent, since the reason for the application of the immunity doctrine disappears with death. A further reason advanced by some courts for not applying the immunity doctrine in death cases is that the legislature in passing the wrongful death statutes created a cause of action which could be asserted against the tort-feasor (or his or her estate) by either a living plaintiff or the administrator of the estate of a deceased person.

Emancipated Children. The rule is that, in the case of an emancipated child, either the child or the parent may sue the other in tort. A child may become emancipated (legally free from parental discipline) by attaining the age of 21, by being married, or by the consent of the parents who completely surrender the right to the care, custody, and earnings of the minor child. The mere fact that the parent continues to support the child after one of these events has happened does not change the legal status of the child. For example, in *Fitzgerald* v. *Valdez* [427 Pac. 2d 655 (New Mexico)], the parent was allowed to bring an action against the child who was over the age of 21 at the time of the accident, even though the child continued to reside in the parent's home under the parent's care, custody and control, attending school, and was completely supported by the parent. Undoubtedly there was an insurance element in this case.

Rejection of the Parent-Child Immunity Doctrine. Many states have carved out exceptions to parent-child immunity. Roughly half of our states have reexamined the application of the doctrine and have decided that, in the light of modern-day conditions, the doctrine should be modified in part or abrogated. In most cases there was some recognition of the existence of insurance particularly, in the case of automobile accidents, the existence of automobile liability insurance. These cases involve not only claims by an unemancipated child against the parent, but also actions by a parent against the unemancipated child. For example, in *Gelbman* v. *Gelbman* [245 N.E. 2d 192 (New York)], the plaintiff was a passenger in an automobile owned by her and driven by her unemancipated 16-year-old son. In affirming her right to recovery, the court said: "The parties recognize, as we must, that there is compulsory automobile insurance in New York. Such insurance effectively removes the argument favoring continued family harmony as a basis for prohibiting this suit. The present litigation is, in reality, between the parent passenger and her insurance carrier. Viewing the case in this light, we are unable to comprehend how the family harmony will be enhanced by prohibiting this suit."

Effect of Insurance. With the increasingly widespread use of liability insurance, especially automobile, suits have been brought attacking the application of the family immunity doctrine where insurance was in existence at the time of the accident. It is usually urged that, where there was insurance, there was no possible impairment of the peace and tranquility of the home. As a matter of fact, a recovery against the insured family member would provide a fund to take care of the medical and hospital expense as well as providing other funds to cover loss of wages and pain and suffering. Far from disturbing the tranquility of the home, the family purse would be increased rather than being depleted by having to assume the costs of the medical and other attention that the injured member would have to receive. Therefore, the peace and tranquility of the home would be undisturbed.

This is the line of reasoning taken by the *Gelbman* court, noted in the preceding paragraph. In opposition, it has been argued that to abrogate the immunity doctrine would open the door to fraud and collusion with the eventual result that the family integrity would be impaired. There are various types of available insurance, other than liability, which will provide payment for accidents and the medical expense incurred as a result. Some of the courts which have reexamined the rule have decided to retain it in its present form, holding that the existence of insurance would not create a recoverable cause of action where none existed before. In *Clark* v. *Ruidoso-Honda Valley Hospital* [380 Pac. 2d 168 (New Mexico)], the court said: "The question is whether the parent's suit may be maintained against the child. So far as the plaintiff is concerned, liability insurance pertains to the collection of any judgment which might be obtained, and accordingly its presence or absence is not relevant in determining whether the action lies in the first instance." In the same case, it was urged that the purchase of insurance should be construed as a waiver of immunity because, if the defendant remains immune from suit, there could be no other reason for carrying insurance. Obviously, however, liability policies cover a variety of risks, including areas in which the defendant might be immune from suit. The court held that, where the defendant is immune from suit, the mere purchase of liability insurance could not be regarded as evidence of a clear unequivocal intention to waive that immunity.

In the states that have abolished or limited the family immunity doctrine, it seems clear that some recognition, tacit or otherwise, has been given to the existence of insurance. There would hardly be much incentive for such suits unless there was an insurance fund at the end of the litigation.

513 Federal Tort Claims Act

As a sovereign, the United States may not be sued for torts committed in the exercise of its governmental functions unless it consents to be sued. By passage of the Federal Tort Claims Act (abbreviated FTCA), 28 USCA 2671, the United States has waived its sovereign immunity with respect to most torts. Furthermore, the FTCA provides that federal employees shall be immune from liability whenever the United States attorney certifies that the employee was acting within the scope of his or her employment.

The statutory procedure for making a claim under the FTCA requires that the claim be filed with the agency concerned within two years after it accrues, and requires that the claimant bring a court action within six months after the final denial of the claim. The failure of the agency to make final disposition of the claim within six months after it is filed is deemed a final denial. The action is forever barred unless the time periods above noted are observed. Specific FTCA forms are provided for use in filing a claim against the United States. They are filed with the agency against which the claim is made.

514 Governmental Immunity: Federal

Sovereign immunity is a rule we inherited from the English common law. It came into existence at a time when England was under the feudal system and when all of the powers of government were exercised only by the king. The king created, amended, or repealed the laws which he had made by his every act and deed. Therefore, all of the king's conduct was bound to be lawful, and hence the expression "The king can do no wrong."

The king, as an absolute monarch, was not accountable to his subjects and could be sued only if he gave his consent. The king was therefore immune from suit, even for damages caused by his own wrongful acts, unless he consented to be sued.

In adopting this common-law rule, we substituted for the king the various sovereign states and the federal government. These political entities cannot be sued in tort without their consent, even where the act causing the injury is in violation of the law of the state itself. The federal government occupies a similar position with respect to the citizens of this country that the king occupied with respect to his subjects. Like the king, the federal government can consent to be sued. It has done so by enacting the Federal Tort Claims Act, referred to in Section 514.

In doing so, the federal government (as well as state governments [Section 515]) has responded to criticism of sovereign immunity. Critics asserted that there was little logic to a legal system that compensated people injured as a result of the tortious conduct of others but denied relief if the tortious conduct was committed by the government or one of its political subdivisions.

Under the provisions of this Act, the federal government has waived its tort immunity for damages

> . . . caused by the negligent or wrongful act or omissions of any employee of the Government while acting within the scope of his office or employment, under circumstances where the United States, if a private person, would be liable to the claimant in accordance with the law of the place where the act or omission occurred." 28 U.S.C. §1346(b). Certain specific activities of the federal government (relating to such activities as wartime combat, mail delivery, and tax collection) are excepted from coverage of the Federal Tort Claims Act. Other exceptions include liability for intentional torts and strict tort liability. Another exception relates to discretionary acts. The federal government will not be liable for acts done in the execution of a statute or regulation or for an act or omission involved in the exercise "of a discretionary function or duty . . . whether or not the discretion be abused.

515 Governmental Immunity: State

Most states, by statute or court decision, have abolished or modified their sovereign immunity. The minority of states that still retain sovereign immunity provide statutorily for a means of making certain specified types of claims against the state.

Legislation or common law in a number of states limit liability for certain governmental functions, such as actions of the judiciary and the legislature. Thus, officials empowered to perform judicial and legislative acts, as well as those who exercise administrative discretion at a high level, continue to enjoy immunity. It is widely recognized that such officials as a state's governor, cabinet officials, heads of administrative departments, legislators, judges, and prosecutors must establish policy and make judgment calls, and should have broad discretion in the discharge of their duties. As was noted in the discussion of federal governmental immunity and liability (Section 514), immunity is preserved for "governmental" or "discretionary" actions of government officials. Similarly, immunity is preserved for the "governmental or discretionary" actions of state government officials, even in states where governmental immunity virtually has been abolished.

The distinction between "discretionary" actions and the more mundane, everyday "proprietary" (or "ministerial") actions is difficult to define. Courts have struggled with the concepts, and the terminology used by the courts will often vary from state to state. The examples given in the following section (Section 516) may help to clarify matters for the reader.

516 Governmental Immunity: Municipal

Frequently in today's complex society, the government of the state, or a political subdivision of the state, will engage in what would normally be considered a business activity. A municipality may supply gas, water, and electricity to the residents, or it may maintain a swimming pool, skating rink, athletic stadium, or theater. When the government functions in a business area, it is not performing functions reserved exclusively to the government but is in an area which could be occupied by a private corporation. When this occurs, the function is referred to as a proprietary as opposed to a governmental function, which only the government can perform.

In the case of a governmental or discretionary function, the sovereign, or a representative thereof, in the form of a political subdivision, can be sued in tort only with its consent. With respect to proprietary functions, the government is in the same status as a private individual or corporation and may be sued in exactly the same way as a private individual or corporation may be sued. There is no governmental immunity to shield the government from its liability while engaged in a proprietary function.

It is sometimes difficult to draw the line between what functions could be considered governmental, in which the immunity will attach, and those which would be considered proprietary, in which no immunity defense is available. The general rule is that, if the function undertaken by the government is one which could be performed by a private person or private corporation, then the function is proprietary. On the other hand, if the function is one only the government may perform and which cannot be performed by a private individual or corporation, then the function is governmental and the immunity defense will be available.

For example, the planning of a municipal sewer system is a governmental function. Only the government can plan and lay out the details of a sewer system which will utilize city property and provide for the disposal of waste. Government officials must make judgment calls and must be able to exercise broad discretion. The actual construction of the sewer is a proprietary function if done by the city, since a private contractor could build it just as well. For that reason, the city then is in a business (or proprietary) area when it builds a sewer, and in a governmental (or discretionary) area when it plans the sewer.

As a further illustration: The regulation of traffic is a governmental function, and no private corporation can exercise this function. The city can and does erect traffic controls in the form of traffic lights and other devices for the regulation of traffic. But the maintenance of the traffic light or the stop sign is a function which can be performed by a private individual or corporation. Therefore, if the municipality or the state undertakes this duty it is operating in a business area, and this is construed to be a proprietary function. The same rules would apply to streets and sidewalks. Only the governmental unit can plan the location of streets and sidewalks. Once planned, a private corporation can build and maintain them. Therefore, the building and maintenance of streets and sidewalks is a proprietary function when performed by a governmental entity.

There are some cases in which the performance of one act will represent concurrently the exercise of both a governmental function and a proprietary one. If this is the case, the courts generally require that the government respond in damages because of the proprietary aspect of the act. For example, in a Texas case, the claimant was injured when she slipped on fresh paint the city had applied to the street in marking off parking meter stalls. It had failed to erect any signs warning the public of the wet paint. It was held that, while the regulation of traffic was a governmental function whose negligent performance would not expose the city to liability, the maintenance of the streets in a reasonably safe condition was an element of the proprietary function of the city. Therefore, a recovery was allowed on the basis of the failure of the city to meet its duties with respect to the maintenance of the street. [*City of Austin* v. *Daniels*, 335 S.W. 2d 753 (Texas).]

It should be emphasized that the sovereign immunity doctrine, where applied, is available only to the governmental body against whom a claim is asserted; this immunity is not necessarily a defense to an action against a public officer based upon his or her own negligence. A public officer or governmental agent often is responsible for any injury or damage caused by his or her negligence, although immunities may exist for acts within the scope of employment.

Governmental Responsibility for Riot and Mob Violence. In England, the community is answerable in damages for any injury or property damage caused by riot or mob violence, and this liability is imposed regardless of whether the local police are negligent in the performance of their duties. American courts have not adopted this rule. They have held generally that the maintenance of law and order is a governmental function and, therefore, the immunity doctrine applies to the governmental unit charged with that responsibility. Because of this view, many municipalities, counties, and states have by legislation assumed the responsibility for damages arising out of riot and mob violence. They have permitted recoveries under the statutory provisions where the state or political subdivision has failed to provide the necessary police protection. In general, in the absence of specific legislation along these lines, claims against a local government for injury or damage as a result of mob violence and riot are not actionable.

Responsibility for Streets and Sidewalks. The state has the governmental authority to plan and lay out streets and sidewalks, and also the proprietary function of maintaining them. The state may delegate all of this authority to various political subdivisions of the state, such as counties, cities, and municipalities. Where such a delegation of authority takes place, the responsibility for the maintenance of the streets and sidewalks is that of the political subdivision alone. As to roads maintained by the state, the responsibility of the state remains. Because this is a proprietary function, the state or the governmental authority responsible for the maintenance of the streets and sidewalks may be sued in the regularly constituted courts, just as any other private individual or corporation.

The governmental authority responsible for the maintenance of streets and sidewalks is required to exercise due care for the safety of all persons privileged to use them. This duty of care consists of proper maintenance, the repair of any defects and, where the defect cannot be remedied immediately, the posting of adequate warning by means of signs, lights, barricades, and other protective devices. The governmental authority is required to remedy only such defects concerning which it has knowledge or which, by the exercise of reasonable inspection, it could discover. The mere presence of a defect is not enough. It must be shown that the authority had notice of the defect or that the defect had existed for such a period of time that reasonable inspection would have revealed its presence.

It would be virtually impossible for the governmental authority to maintain its streets and sidewalks in an absolutely level condition. There is bound to be some variation due to wear and the impact of extreme temperatures. Whether a condition is one which is defective and dangerous to the users of the highway or sidewalks is a question of fact for the jury, and they will be entitled to take into account its dimensions, the amount of depression, and also whether it is a condition that is open and obvious so as to be discoverable by the users of the facility.

Where the state or the governmental unit contracts with a private contractor for the reconstruction or repair of the street or sidewalk, it is customary for the governmental unit to require a hold harmless agreement from the contractor by the terms of which the contractor agrees to protect the governmental unit from liability. The existence of this hold harmless agreement does not change the responsibility of the governmental unit, and claims may be brought against it. The hold harmless agreement simply provides the governmental unit with an indemnitor for its liability.

With respect to the private property owner, he is not responsible for the maintenance of the public street or sidewalk which abuts or adjoins his property, but he is responsible for any private walks, or driveway, or road on his own property. As to the public sidewalks and the public roads, these are responsibilities of the governmental authority. The property owner, even though aware of an existing defect, has no responsibility to others who are injured as a result of its presence.

If the property owner himself should create an unsafe condition in the street or on the sidewalks, he is responsible for any injuries that occur as a result of its presence. He is required to remedy any defects or unsafe conditions that he himself created. If the defect is of such a nature that the governmental authority had notice of it—or if it had existed for a sufficient period of time so as to spell out constructive notice on the part of the government authority—the injured person could sue both the landowner and the government authority as joint tort-feasors.

In some states and in some municipalities, there are laws or ordinances which require that a property owner keep any adjoining sidewalks in good repair. This creates a public duty and makes the property owner liable for the cost of the repair. But unless the statute specifically creates an obligation to respond in damages to a third person who may be injured as a result of the property owner's failure to repair a defect, there is no such obligation.

This is an exception to the usual rule that violation of a statute or ordinance is negligence per se. The exception is justified by the courts by reasoning that ordinances of this kind are designed to aid the government in the performance of its duty to maintain public walkways, not to confer rights on those who use the walkways. Therefore, when handling a case of this kind where there is a claim made against the abutting landowner by a traveler on the public sidewalk, the claim representative would be well advised to study the statute or ordinance (if there is one applicable) to ascertain whether it does specifically create a cause of action on behalf of the traveler against the abutting property owner. If it does not, then there is no liability.

Responsibility for Snow and Ice. The rules with respect to the proper maintenance and regard for the safety of those using the streets and sidewalks also apply to the hazards created by the presence of snow and ice. The governmental authority is required to use reasonable care to keep the streets and sidewalks in a safe condition. The matter of what would constitute reasonable care depends to a great extent upon the particular circumstances (for example, the severity of the storm) as well as the question of whether the governmental authority had any notice of a particularly unsafe condition and failed to correct it. The authority cannot be required to keep all of the streets within its limits entirely free from snow and ice in cases where they are present in the entire area.

Any recovery against the governmental authority would have to be based upon negligence. The governmental authority is not an insurer of the safety of the traveling public privileged to use the streets or sidewalks. In order to make out a cause of action, the plaintiff would have to show that the failure of the authority to remove the ice amounted to actionable negligence. This would not mean that the authority had any duty to combat a general condition, but that it is under a duty to remedy unsafe conditions which, for example, might result from the overflow of sewers, or the accumulation of an unusual amount of water, or the failure of other drainage facilities to carry off the excess. The question of whether the streets or sidewalks were in a defective or dangerous condition because of the accumulation of snow and ice is generally a question of fact for the jury.

As in the matter of the maintenance of the public sidewalk, we find statutes or ordinances in some states which require that the abutting owner remove the snow and ice from the public sidewalk and, if he fails to do so, that the municipality may do so at the expense of the owner. This does not create a cause of action on the part of an injured person against the property owner where the owner has failed to remove the snow. The reasoning is similar to situations involving repair and maintenance of sidewalks.

517 Governmental Immunity: Effect of Insurance

It sometimes happens that a governmental unit will purchase liability insurance, either voluntarily or under the authorization or compulsion of a statute. The problem in all cases is whether the governmental unit, by the purchase of insurance, has waived its immunity. There are five variations of circumstances under which the insurance may be purchased, and the answer to the question whether immunity has been waived depends upon which of the five categories is involved. The classifications are set forth below.

1. Voluntary Purchase. It is the general rule in the majority of states that voluntary procurement of liability insurance by a governmental subdivision does not waive that unit's immunity from suit. As it is generally stated, the power to waive such immunity lies with the legislature of each state, not with the department or the department head.

2. Authorized Purchase. Where there is simply a statute that authorizes the purchase of insurance in the discretion of the governmental unit, the cases hold that there is a continuation of immunity notwithstanding the authorization and the actual purchase of insurance.

3. Authorized Purchase with No Express Waiver. This category might seem to overlap number 2. In each of the situations, the courts seem to focus on the fact that the legislation did not contain an express waiver, and, under those circumstances, hold that the procurement of insurance against tort liability as authorized by the statute did not require the unit's immunity from liability to be abrogated.

4. Waiver to the Extent of Insurance Purchased. Cases in this category hold that, where the governmental unit is authorized to purchase insurance, the otherwise existing immunity of that unit is removed to the extent that the liability insurance protects the unit. This is the conclusion reached by an expanding line of authority. In the other categories, as far as the performance of a governmental function is concerned, the governmental unit had no liability because of its immunity, and therefore the insurance so purchased would seem to be of doubtful value.

5. Mandatory Purchase of Insurance. Some states have required by statute that certain governmental units carry liability insurance with certain stated limits. The units usually are school districts operating school buses, and units providing other types of service where the risk of injury is high. The problem then posed is whether the requirement that insurance be carried is indicative of the legislative intent to abrogate the governmental immunity as to that particular unit, where there is no express waiver of immunity in the statute. The general rule is that, where the statute requires that insurance be carried, the immunity has been waived at least to the extent of the limits of insurance.

Statutory Immunity. There are situations in states where the courts have rejected the common-law doctrine of governmental immunity and where the legislature has reinstated the immunity defense by a specific statute. In such a case, regardless of whether insurance is carried, the statute will control, and the defense of immunity may be interposed as a complete bar to liability.

518 Charitable Immunity

A charity is an institution, corporation, organization, or association which freely and voluntarily administers to the needs of those financially unable to help themselves. This category includes schools, hospitals, churches, rescue missions, industries, and organizations of like kind and character, which are supported almost entirely by gifts in the form of donations from the public or bequests by will.

At common law, all charitable organizations enjoyed complete immunity from liability in tort. There were two reasons given for the establishment of this doctrine: the *trust fund theory*, and the *quasi-governmental theory*.

Under the trust fund theory, the courts reasoned that, where a gift or bequest by will was made to the charity, the donor or the testator directed by implication that the gift was made on the condition that the money so donated would be devoted entirely to the charitable purpose. Therefore, the charity held all such money received in trust, and the money could be expended only for the charitable purpose. The courts reasoned that, since the charity had no funds other than those received as a consequence of gifts, it had no right to use the gifts to pay claims. Should the money be used to pay claims, the charity would be guilty of a breach of trust and answerable to the donor of the gift.

The quasi-governmental theory is that in supplying the needs of indigent or poor people, the charity is actually assuming some of the responsibilities of government. Having done so with the consent of the government, the same immunity which would be available to the government, if it undertook this duty, would likewise be available to the charity.

As liability insurance became available, some courts reasoned that the payment of premiums for liability insurance would not be a breach of trust and that such an expenditure could reasonably be considered as being made in furtherance of a charitable purpose. Therefore, these courts have specifically repudiated the charitable immunity doctrine.

The courts in other states have taken the position that the charitable immunity doctrine will be applied to all cases where a cause of action is asserted by a beneficiary of the charity, but hold the charitable organization responsible for tort liability arising from the injury or damage to the person or property of a nonbeneficiary. Still other courts make a distinction between nonpaying and paying beneficiaries of the charity. This distinction usually is found in the cases of hospitals, where certain patients are treated through the social service division of the hospital as charity cases, in which no payment is demanded or received, as opposed to patients who pay for the accommodations received in the very same hospital. As to the charitable beneficiaries, the charitable immunity doctrine is applied, but not as between the paying patient and the hospital.

Even in states which subscribe at least in part to the charitable immunity doctrine, the cases generally hold that the charity is not entitled to immunity when engaged in any noncharitable function. The charity must respond in those cases in exactly the same manner as any other person or corporation conducting a business enterprise. Immunity does not extend to such enterprises as the operation of a store or a commercial building (even though the proceeds might be devoted to a charitable purpose).

Almost all states today reject complete charitable immunity. In those few states that retain the doctrine, it is ameliorated by statutory measures providing a mechanism to reach liability insurance funds covering the charity. Today's legal climate is reflected in *Restatement* §895E, which states that charities are entitled to no immunity simply because of their charitable status. [Prosser & Keeton, *Torts* §133.]

Chapter 6

Law of Contracts, Agency, and Bailments

CONTRACTS

CONTRACTS—ELEMENTS OF CONTRACTS

600 The Elements
601 Offer
602 Duration of Offer
603 Offer to an Attorney or Agent
604 Offer through an Authorized Agent
605 Termination of Offer
606 Acceptance
607 Consideration
608 Capacity to Contract

DEFENSES TO CONTRACTS

609 Void and Voidable Contracts
610 Mistake of Fact
611 Fraud
612 Parol Evidence Rule

INTERPRETATION OF CONTRACTS

613 Representations
614 Warranties
615 Conditions
616 Waiver and Estoppel
617 Nonwaiver and Reservation of Rights
618 Ambiguities
619 Assignments
620 Law Governing Contracts

SOME TYPES OF CONTRACTS

621 Contracts to Compound a Crime
622 Contracts to Procure Evidence
623 Attorney's Contingent Fee Contracts
624 Exculpatory Contracts
625 Hold Harmless Agreements
626 Arbitration Agreements
627 Beneficiary Contracts
628 Leases
629 Accord and Satisfaction
630 Releases
631 Covenant Not to Sue

AGENCY

TYPES OF AGENCY RELATIONSHIPS

632 Agency Defined
633 Types of Agents
634 Specific Agency Relationships
635 Appointment of Subagents
636 Agency by Emergency
637 Special and General Employees
638 Attorneys as Limited Agents
639 Fiduciary Agents
640 Trustees
641 Independent Contractors

LIABILITIES IN AGENCY RELATIONSHIPS

642 *Respondeat Superior*
643 Scope of Agency
644 Deviation from the Scope of Agency
645 Direct Liability of the Principal

646 Liability of Agent to Principal
647 Liability of Agent to Third Persons
648 Liability of Principal to Agent
649 Ratification or Adoption of Unauthorized Acts

BAILMENTS

NATURE OF BAILMENTS
650 Bailments Defined

LIABILITIES IN BAILMENT SITUATIONS
651 Kinds of Bailments
652 Degrees of Care Required
653 Liability, Bailor to Bailee
654 Liability, Bailee to Third Persons
655 Liability, Bailor to Third Persons
656 Liability, Third Person to Bailee
657 Liability, Third Person to Bailor
658 Limitation of Liability
659 Conversion or Unauthorized Use by the Bailee
660 Exculpatory Contracts as Applied to Bailments
661 Innkeepers' Liability
662 Liability of Common Carriers
663 Exculpatory Contracts, Common Carriers
664 Private Carriers

CONTRACTS

CONTRACTS—ELEMENTS OF CONTRACTS

600 The Elements

For the most part, claim representatives will be concerned with contracts already in existence. These include, among others, insurance contracts, leases, hold harmless agreements, and arbitration agreements. Claim representatives will be involved in the formulation of only a few. These are contracts of release, covenants not to sue, nonwaiver agreements, and instruments of similar character. Throughout this chapter, references will be made to contracts in the context of claims and settlements.

A contract may be defined as an agreement related to a legal subject matter between two or more persons, having the capacity to contract, whereby for a valuable consideration one or more become entitled to acts or forebearance to act on the part of the other or others. The element which distinguishes a contract from a mere unenforceable agreement is the consideration. (Consideration, called *quid pro quo*, means ''something for something.'') For example, *A* has the right to bring a personal injury action in tort against *B*. *B* agrees to pay, and *A* agrees to accept $100 to settle his case. The consideration running from *B* to *A* is $100, and the consideration running from *A* to *B* is *A*'s forebearance of the right to sue. Therefore, this is a contract and, as such, enforceable at law.

A contract comes into existence as a result of two preliminary steps: (1) an offer by one and (2) an acceptance by the other. When both of these preliminary steps have been taken, and where both are supported by a valuable consideration, there is a contract.

601 Offer

An offer is a proposal to make a contract. It must be made by the person who is to make the promise or that person's agent, and it must be made to the person to whom the promise is made or to that person's agent. It may be made either orally or in writing, either personally or by messenger. But in whatever way it is made, it is not in law an offer until it comes to the knowledge of the person to whom it is made.

The insurance industry uses two terms to differentiate between an offer of settlement made by the company and an offer of settlement made by the claimant. These terms are *offer* and *demand*. An offer refers to the amount which the company has already transmitted to the claimant as the amount that it will pay in full settlement of the claim. A demand is the amount that the claimant has submitted to the company for which he will settle his claim. Under contract law, both are offers or proposals to enter into a settlement contract. In both instances, no contract will result until the amount so offered or demanded, as the case may be, is accepted by the opposite party.

The person making the offer, the offeror, has the right to decrease, increase, vary, or withdraw the offer at any time before it is accepted. Any such change in the offer is not legally effective until it is brought to the attention of the person to whom the original offer was made, the offeree. If the original offer is accepted prior to the time that the offeror's intention to change the offer has been received by the offeree, then there is a contract based on the original offer.

Once an offer has been made, the offeree can bring a legal contract into existence by an act of acceptance. There is no further step which the offeror can take, once the offer is made, in order to bring a contract into existence. The initiative is with the offeree. He can, at his option, bring a contract into existence or refuse to enter into a contract.

602 Duration of Offer

The period of time within which the offer will remain open, and during which the offeree may accept, can be specifically stated by the offeror at the time of making the offer. Then, if the offer is not accepted within the time so limited, the offer will terminate by its own terms. If no time is stated at the time the offer is made, in the absence of any withdrawal of the offer by the offeror, the offer is considered to remain open for a reasonable time. What would constitute a reasonable time would depend upon the facts and circumstances of the situation.

What would be a reasonable time in one case might be an unreasonable time in another. For example, if an offer were made to a claimant who was still under medical treatment, and the facts indicated that he expected to be discharged by his doctor within the next two weeks, under such circumstances it would be reasonable to expect that the claimant would not be in a position to accept the offer or reject it until such time as his medical treatment had terminated. In the absence of any change or withdrawal of the offer during that period of time, the acceptance of the offer at any time within the two-week period, or perhaps even one week beyond the termination of treatment, might not be an unreasonable length of time. Therefore, it would be considered that the offer remained open at least until the termination of the claimant's treatment, and then perhaps for a short time longer.

If the claimant waited six months after the termination of his treatment before deciding to accept the offer, the offeror could treat the offer as having expired by the passage of time and regard the claimant's acceptance as an offer itself. It is not required that an offer remain open indefinitely. Where a reasonable time has expired between the time of the offer and the time of the attempted acceptance, the offeror can treat the offer as no longer in existence.

To take another example, let us assume that during the course of the trial of a personal injury action, the defendant's attorney offered to settle the case for a stated amount. Even if no other words were spoken, it would be contemplated under the circumstances of the offer that an immediate acceptance was required and that the offer would terminate if not immediately accepted. Clearly, the plaintiff could not regard the offer as continuing until after verdict. The circumstances under which the offer was made indicate that the offer was made in order to avoid submitting the matter to the jury, and that a reasonable time within which the offer must be accepted would be a matter of minutes rather than a longer period of time.

603 Offer to an Attorney or Agent

An attorney is a special or limited agent of his client. He has no authority to release his client's claim unless and until the client authorizes him to do so. Anyone dealing with an attorney is on notice of the fact that he is dealing with a limited agent who cannot bind his client to a settlement without his client's consent. An offer to an attorney is then an offer to an agent or messenger of the offeree. Unless there is a time limit expressed in the offer, or it is revoked before acceptance, the offer will be considered to remain open for a reasonable period of time. Since the offeror knows that the offer must be communicated to the client, a reasonable period of time would be of at least sufficient duration to give the attorney an opportunity to communicate with his client and receive a reply.

When an offer is made to an attorney, he or she will sometimes venture an opinion whether the offer will be acceptable to the client. This expression of opinion is in no way binding on the client. The attorney may say that the amount offered is too small and that she doubts that her client will accept it but, if she is successful in securing the client's consent to a slightly higher figure, she inquires as to whether the company will pay it. The objective is to obtain an increase in the offer before making any sort of a demand.

For example, if an offer of $500 were made, the attorney might say that she knows that her client will not accept it, but she will communicate it anyway. She might venture the opinion that she is sure her client would be interested in a settlement of $750, and she then might inquire whether the company would be willing to pay $750, provided that she can induce her client to accept that amount. If the company agrees that it will pay $750 under those circumstances, it has actually increased its offer to $750. The mere fact that this increased offer is made on the condition that the client accepts it doesn't change its character from an offer into something else; it is still an offer of $750. If the company intended to stand on its original offer of $500 it should have said so, and it should have advised the attorney that if, her client wishes to submit a counteroffer of $750, or any other figure, the client may do so, and the company will give due consideration to any such counteroffer.

While the attorney is a limited agent of the client, it is possible for the client to give the attorney authority to settle the claim. This happens most frequently where the client is absent from the state or from the country. Under those circumstances, an agreement by the attorney to settle at a certain figure is binding on the client, and where the attorney warrants that he or she has such authority, the claim representative may deal on that basis.

Whether the attorney has actually warranted his or her authority to so act will be determined by the words which were said and the conditions under which they were spoken. If the attorney were to say, ''You can deal with me because my client will take whatever I tell him is reasonable,'' the attorney has not warranted the authority to settle the claim for the client. She has merely expressed an opinion as to how the client will react to the attorney's recommendations and nothing more. To be a warranty of authority, the words spoken must clearly communicate the fact that the authority has already been delegated to the attorney and that the attorney can bind the client to a contract of release. Anything less than this will not be construed as a warranty of authority. For these reasons, the claim representative should exercise extreme care in deciding whether a warranty has been given. If there is any doubt whether the attorney is giving a warranty as to authority to settle, a letter or other writing from the attorney spelling out the authority should be secured. This writing can be relied upon, since attorneys will not put themselves on record as having authority unless they actually have it.

In addition to the authority to settle the claim for the client, the attorney may be given the power to execute a release or other document extinguishing the claim. Where such is the case, the claim representative may accept such a document, executed by the attorney only, but should also obtain a verified copy of the document granting such authority (usually a power of attorney).

When dealing with an agent of the claimant, other than an attorney, the claim representative is likewise on notice that the agent has no greater authority than that granted by the claimant. Inquiry should be directed to the authority and to the basis on which the agent is purporting to act, and copies of the documents granting the authority should be secured. Dealings with the agent can be had but only to the extent of the authority set forth in the documents submitted.

The situation may arise where a husband is in military service and has executed a power of attorney to his wife by which she can act in his place and stead during this time. Where the wife has been injured through the negligence of another, she can, by means of his power, execute a release extinguishing the husband's cause of action for loss of consortium and medical expense. She could also release any other claim the husband may have for his own personal injuries. A verified or photostatic copy of the power of attorney should be obtained and filed in support of the release executed.

604 Offer through an Authorized Agent

The offer does not have to be made directly by the person, firm, or corporation making the offer, but can be made through an agent selected and authorized for that purpose. The agent selected for the purpose of communicating the offer may be a telegraph company, a telephone operator, an attorney, or an employee. When an offer is made through an agent, the offeror is bound by the mistakes of the agent in transmitting or communicating the offer. If this were not so, business of any kind could not be conducted with any degree of certainty or dispatch. The offeree therefore can rely on the offer as it is received, and when accepted in good faith as received, a contract will result. For example, a claimant makes a demand for $500 for the settlement of her claim. The insurance company sends a telegram offering to settle for $250. Through an error in transmission, the telegram actually received offers $350, which the claimant accepts. The company is bound to a settlement for $350.

Now let us assume that the error in transmission had to do with an additional digit and the telegram received by the claimant read $2,500, rather than the $250 intended, and the claimant accepted the $2,500. The company is not bound to a $2,500 settlement. The acceptance was not in good faith. The claimant knew, or should have known, in the face of her demand of $500, that the telegram was an obvious error, and she was therefore put on inquiry as to the exact terms of the offer.

The same principles apply where the offeror has selected other agents for the purpose of transmitting an offer. Suppose that an adjuster was authorized to settle for $250 a case in which there was a $500 demand. By mistake the adjuster offers $350, which the claimant accepts. The company is bound to the $350 settlement. On the other hand, let us assume that the claimant authorized her attorney to make a demand of $500 and by mistake the attorney makes a demand of $350, which the company accepts. The claimant is bound to a settlement of $350. The attorney's authority to make the offer of settlement came directly from the client, and a demand or offer of settlement was actually made on the strength of that authority. If the attorney merely gives his or her opinion as to the amount that the client should receive for the injury, the attorney has not made a demand or transmitted an offer of settlement from the client to the company. In such a case, the client would not be bound by the attorney's own opinion as to value.

Where an offer is made by an agent outside the scope of his or her agency, or without authorization to do so by the principal, the law of agency will be applied in determining whether the principal is or is not bound to a contract created by the acceptance of such an offer. Where the agent has made a mistake in transmitting the offer, or where the agent exceeds his or her authority in making the offer, the rights and liabilities of the parties as between themselves are governed by the principles of the law of agency.

605 Termination of Offer

An offer of settlement may be terminated by any one of the following:

1. Rejection by the offeree.
2. Lapse of time.
3. Death of the offeree.
4. Revocation by the offeror.

Rejection. A rejection by the offeree immediately terminates the offer. This is true even though the offeror indicated by the terms of the offer that it would remain open for a certain period of time. For example, if *A* makes an offer of settlement to *B* with the understanding that the offer would remain open for the next 14 days, and if *B* rejects the offer the very next day, the offer is terminated as of the time of rejection.

A counteroffer by the offeree is a rejection of the original offer. The original offer does not necessarily have to be rejected specifically. The making of a counteroffer by the offeree indicates his unwillingness to accept the original offer as made and, as such, terminates it.

Lapse of Time. An offer not accepted within a reasonable time will terminate. An acceptance after a reasonable time has passed is regarded as an offer itself, since there is no outstanding offer which can be acccepted.

Death of Offeree. The death of the offeree prior to acceptance of the offer terminates it. The offeree is an essential person in the making of a contract, and his or her death terminates the offer and likewise terminates any unfinished negotiations.

Revocation by Offeror. Prior to acceptance, the offeror may withdraw or revoke the offer he has given. This termination of the offer is effective only when brought to the attention of the offeree. If the information is communicated to the offeree prior to acceptance, the offer terminates, and an acceptance after receipt of this information will not result in a contract.

606 Acceptance

The *acceptance* of an offer is an expression of assent made by the offeree to the terms of the offeror. This assent must comply exactly with the terms and conditions of the offer. If there are any variations in the terms of the acceptance, as compared with the terms of the offer, it is not an acceptance but a counteroffer. However, with respect to contracts for the sale of goods, the law allows an acceptance that alters immaterial terms.

The acceptance may be made by the offeree or by someone in his behalf authorized by him to do so. Therefore, the offeree may authorize his or her attorney to accept the offer for him or her, or authorize an agent to perform the same function. However, where an offer is made to an offeree and, before acceptance the offeree dies, acceptance by the offeree's personal representative or executor will not constitute a contract. The offer expires as of the time of the offeree's death, and therefore the act of the executor cannot bring a contract into existence.

The silence of the offeree, or lack of response to an offer, does not constitute an acceptance. This is true even though the offer stipulated that a failure to reply would be construed as an acceptance. For example, if a claim representative wrote to the claimant, offering her $100 in full settlement of her claim, further advising that if the claim representative did not hear from the claimant by a certain date, he would assume that the $100 is acceptable, the lack of response by the claimant under those circumstances would not constitute an acceptance and there would be no contract.

If a person accepts and uses goods or merchandise forwarded to him on an unsolicited basis, his use of the goods implies an *acceptance by conduct* of an offer to sell, and also implies an obligation to pay for the goods. The same principle would apply to a situation where the adjuster sends the claimant a release form draft stating that the payment constitutes a full and complete settlement of any cause of action which the claimant may have against the insured. The acceptance and deposit of such a draft under those circumstances would constitute an acceptance of the offer. The claimant is precluded from claiming that he did not accept an offer of settlement. He could not claim that he accepted the check as part payment, since the terms of the tender of the draft contemplated a settlement in full.

607 Consideration

Even though there is an offer and an acceptance, one additional element is necessary to give the resulting agreement the binding force of a contract. The agreement must be supported by adequate consideration. Consideration for a promise is either an act or a forebearance. It is that which is bargained for in exchange for the other party's promise.

For example, in the giving of a release of a personal injury claim, the consideration for the claimant's promise to relinquish her right to bring suit is the amount of money paid to her. The agreement by the insurance carrier to pay an amount of money it is not legally required to pay until the claimant has secured a judgment, represents a legal detriment to the insurance carrier. The forebearance by the claimant from asserting her legal rights is a legal detriment to her. Neither of the parties is obligated to do either act. Therefore, there is some benefit moving from each party to the other. This benefit to one, and legal detriment to the other, is called consideration. Consideration is sometimes described as the doing of something which a person is not legally obligated to do, such as the payment of money or the waiver of some legal right.

The courts generally will not inquire into the relative value of the consideration moving from one party to the other, taking the position that the parties may enter into any type of agreement they please and that it is no part of the court's function to determine whether the value of the consideration moving from one party to the other is commensurate with the value of the consideration moving from the other. Under this theory, where only a nominal consideration is expressed, $1, the courts generally will not inquire whether the action of the other party has the value of $1 or something in excess of that amount. Generally, the courts will consider the question of the adequacy or value of the consideration only where there is a promise of goods for goods or money for money, or where the consideration is so inadequate as to be unconscionable. For example, it has been held that a consideration of $1 would be insufficient to support the payment of $5,000 by the other party.

In the casualty claims context, where there is a claim of misrepresentation, fraud, or mutual mistake of fact, and an attempt is made to set aside or vacate the release, the amount paid as the consideration will have some bearing on the issues. For example, a payment far below the value of a claim might be evidence that it was accepted as part payment and that the release was signed on the representation that it was a receipt for such payment. On the other hand, a large payment, or one which, when viewed in comparison with the injuries suffered, was entirely adequate, would be evidence against a claim that it was accepted as a partial payment.

608 Capacity to Contract

According to the traditional common-law rule, there are some classes of persons who are either totally or partially incapacitated when it comes to making a binding contract. These are infants and persons of unsound mind. We will consider each in their relationship to the making of a contract.

1. Infants. An infant or minor is a person who has not attained the age of majority and, for that reason, receives special protection from the law. The age at which a person attains full majority and the right to exercise full legal capacity to contract is fixed by the state law. Most states fix the age of majority at 18. Some states grant full capacity to contract to infants who are married. An infant may be emancipated prior to attaining majority. This merely means that he is no longer subject to parental control and, as a result, he may retain his own earnings. This does not affect his legal capacity to contract.

A contract entered into by an infant is voidable, not void. At any time prior to attaining his legal age, and for a period of time thereafter as fixed by law (usually one year), an infant may disaffirm a contract which he has made, and there is no further liability on his part under the contract. He is required to return to the other party any advantage that he may have gained under the contract.

A guardian may act for an infant and may enter into a binding contract for and in behalf of the infant within the statutory limitations provided for in the state of his appointment. In most states, a contract releasing a claim arising out of bodily injuries sustained by the infant must be submitted to a court of competent jurisdiction for review and approval before the contract will be binding on the infant and effectively extinguish the claim. The rules of court in the particular jurisdiction involved will determine the type of proceeding necessary to bring the matter to the attention of the court.

2. Persons of Unsound Mind. A person may have little or no mental capacity. Therefore, he or she cannot form an intent to enter a contract and, consequently, any contract entered into by an such a person of unsound mind is a nullity and is void.

The contract of a person of unsound mind, who has not been judicially declared insane, is voidable not void. A person of unsound mind occupies the same position as an infant, and may disaffirm the contract through a guardian after he or she has been declared to be incompetent, or may disaffirm should he or she regain sanity. The burden of proving that a person was of unsound mind at the time the contract was made is on the party seeking to disaffirm. In the case of persons who are mentally incompetent due to senility, the burden of proof is less onerous than in other cases, since the opposite party is charged with the knowledge of the person's age and apparent mental capacity as of the time of the contract.

Where a person has been judicially declared to be insane, and has been committed as an insane person, he or she no longer has the capacity to enter into a contract. A contract with such a person is void. In dealing with cases involving bodily injuries sustained by such a person, the settlement may be concluded with the guardian of his or her property, or the conservator of the insane person's assets. The settlement and the release of the claim must be submitted to and have the approval of the court having jurisdiction of the incompetent.

If it can be established that, at the time of contract, a person was so intoxicated that he or she was unable to understand the nature of the transaction, the contract is voidable. The person may disaffirm it when sobriety is regained. Failure to disaffirm the contract upon regaining sobriety (with knowledge of its existence) will extinguish the right to avoid it. If a case were settled with a person under those conditions and, upon regaining sobriety, the person spent the money paid under the contract of release with knowledge of its source, such action would be construed as a ratification of the contract and would extinguish the right of avoidance.

DEFENSES TO CONTRACTS

609 Void and Voidable Contracts

An agreement may have all of the elements of a contract, such as offer, acceptance, and a valuable consideration. The parties may have intended to enter into a legal contract. But the contract may not be recognized by the courts either because it contemplated the doing of an illegal act, because it is against public policy, because there was fraud in the execution of the instrument, or because of a mutual mistake as to the subject matter. These contracts, if they are contracts at all, are void *ab initio* (from the beginning), and no rights, duties, or obligations arise because of their existence. No action is required on the part of either party to declare it to be a void contract, since it is void and unenforceable from the very beginning.

There are some contracts which may be disaffirmed by one of the parties, because he was an infant or under some other legal disability when he entered into it, or because there was fraud in the inducement, or because of a mistake on his part caused or induced by the other party. Such a contract is treated as valid until the party who has the right to disaffirm it has manifested the election to do so. If he or she does not do so, it is a valid and enforceable contract. During the time he or she still has the right of disaffirmance, it is called a *voidable* contract.

610 Mistake of Fact

A mistake of fact may be *mutual* (by both parties) or *unilateral* (by only one party). A mutual mistake of fact as to the existence of the subject matter, its quantity, quality, nature, or the law relating to the situation will usually prevent the formation of a contract.

For example, *A* has what she believes to be a diamond ring. She agrees to sell the ring to *B*, who also believes the ring to be a diamond, for $1,000; but the stone is glass and not a diamond. There is no contract because there was a mutual mistake of fact. *A* thought she was selling a diamond ring and *B* thought he was buying a diamond ring. The nature of the subject matter was such that they were both mistaken as to its nature and quality.

In another example, *A* sustained injuries to his leg which were described by his doctor as lacerations and contusions. Both *A* and *B* (the claim representative) relied on these statements as being an accurate description of the injury. Under those circumstances, a release of the claim by *A* for $250 and the payment of that amount by the adjuster would constitute a full and complete release of the claim. However, suppose that, unknown to both *A* and *B*, *A* was suffering from a thrombosis which ultimately set up an occlusion, as a result of which the leg was subsequently amputated. At the time that the contract of release was made, neither *A* nor *B* was aware of the existence of this other condition. Therefore, there was a mistake on the part of both parties as to the nature and extent of *A*'s injuries. *A* thought he was settling a case which involved only lacerations and contusions of his leg, and *B* thought she was settling a case involving those same injuries. Both parties were mistaken as to a material fact, and both were mistaken as to the same fact; the extent of *A*'s injuries. The contract did not contemplate the release of any claim except one involving lacerations and contusions of the leg. The case involved a much more serious injury; a contract entered into under such a mutual mistake as to a material fact is no contract at all.

With respect to a unilateral mistake of fact, the general rule is that there is a binding contract unless the mistake on the part of the one party was caused or induced by the opposite party. Therefore, if a case were settled by a claim representative with the claimant, where no reliance was placed upon any medical reports and where there was no assumption as to the extent of the injuries, the release is binding and enforceable even though the injuries prove to be more serious than the claimant anticipated at the time the release was given.

611 Fraud

A contract may be avoided or may never come into existence at all because of the fraud of one of the parties. The fraud may be in the *factum* (the making) or in the *inducement*. In the first instance, there is no contract at all, and in the second instance, the contract may be avoided by the party defrauded. For our purposes, fraud normally will consist of the following elements: (1) A party lied. (2) He knew he lied. (3) He lied with the intent that the other party should rely on his statement. (4) The other party did rely. (5) The other party sustained damage as a result.

Let us assume that the claimant is unable to read and write and that she signs a contract of release, using a mark which is properly witnessed. She is told that the paper she is signing is merely a receipt for the draft being delivered to her, or is an acknowledgment of the fact that the claim representative called on her. This is an example of fraud in the factum (in the making). The claimant never intended to give a general release and was misled into believing that she was signing some other type of instrument. There is no contract.

Assume that the claim representative represents to the claimant that—even though the language of the instrument that she is signing does have the appearance of a general release—the instrument will be regarded by the company as merely a partial release. This is fraud in the inducement. There is a contract, but it may be disaffirmed or avoided by the claimant if she so elects. On the other hand, if the claimant is satisfied with the contract, she may accept it, and it is a perfectly legal instrument. It should be emphasized that the claimant alone has the option and can bind or discharge the company as she sees fit.

612 Parol Evidence Rule

Where a written instrument is complete on its face, the general rule is that oral testimony may not be received to alter or vary any of its terms. This is called the parol evidence rule. Like other rules of law, this rule is subject to certain exceptions. Oral testimony is admissible for the following purposes:

1. To explain the meaning of ambiguous words in the instrument.
2. To prove facts rendering the agreement void or voidable for illegality, fraud, mistake, or insufficiency of consideration.
3. To prove facts in a suit for rescission of the written agreement, showing such mistake as affords grounds for such a remedy.
4. To prove facts in a suit for a specific performance, showing such mistake, oppression, or unfairness as affords grounds for denying that remedy.
5. To provide essential terms to an obviously incomplete agreement.
6. To show that a condition precedent to the operation of the contract has not occurred.

These exceptions give a party to the contract the means of showing outside facts which will establish fraud in the factum, fraud in the inducement, and mistake of fact (be it mutual or unilateral), or the means of explaining any words in the contract which cannot be interpreted by the average person.

INTERPRETATION OF CONTRACTS

613 Representations

Any statement made by either party to the contract, prior to its making or concurrently with its making, is either a *representation*, or a *warranty*. A representation, if untrue, will not entitle the opposite party to rescind or avoid the contract unless the representation is material to the contract itself. A warranty, if untrue, goes to the heart of the contract and prevents the formation of a contract. A representation, in order to have any influence on the contract, must be in relation to a material fact and be untrue. If the representation is material and untrue, it will enable the party to whom the representation is made to avoid the contract at his or her option.

In relation to an insurance contract, the same distinction is made between a representation and a warranty. Representations, which precede the contract of insurance and are no part of it, need only be materially true. Warranties are part of the contract and must be exactly and literally fulfilled, or else the contract is broken and inoperative.

In most insurance applications, statements are required from the proposed insured with respect to some of the conditions of the risks to be assumed by the insurance company. These are representations and not warranties. They are statements made by the proposed insurance carrier before or at the time of the making of the contract in regard to some past or existing fact, circumstance, or state of fact pertinent to the contract, which is influential in bringing about the agreement. To avoid the contract once it is made, the insurance company will have to show not only that the representations were untrue, but that they were material to the risk in that—if the insurance carrier had known of the existence of the fact misrepresented—it would not have entered into the contract. The question of whether a misrepresentation is material is a question of fact for the jury.

The same fact may be material in one situation and immaterial in another. For example, if a prospective insured represented that his name was John Smith, and in truth and in fact his name was originally John Brown, and he decided to change it for no reason at all, this might be considered a misrepresentation; but it certainly would not be material to the risk, since the insurance carrier intended to contract with this particular person, irrespective of his name. However, let us assume the same set of facts, but add to them other facts. Under the name of John Brown, the prospective insured had been convicted of automobile homicide and had a long record of traffic violations and accidents. The prospective insured's representation would be material to the risk. If the insurance carrier had known that the person requesting insurance had the driving record of John Brown, it would not have entered into the contract in the first place. The insurance carrier can avoid this contract. There was a misrepresentation, and such misrepresentation was material to the risk.

614 Warranties

The *intention* of the parties determines whether a statement is a representation or a warranty. If no intention is expressed, then the statement is considered to be a representation. To be a warranty, there must be some evidence that the parties to the contract intended that the statement be a warranty. This intention may be evidenced by the fact that the warranty is contained in the contract itself, or the warranty may be implied by law from the nature of the transaction.

For example, where an agent contracts with another for her principal, the agent by that act impliedly warrants to the third person that she has the authority to bind her principal by making a contract for him. In a contract of sale, the seller impliedly warrants that the product sold is of merchantable quality. These warranties arise from the nature of the transaction and are not expressed. They are regarded as implied warranties.

Where the warranty is untrue, this is referred to in law as a breach of warranty. Where that happens, the aggrieved party has a choice of remedies. She may regard the contract as void, or no contract at all, and she may refuse to perform her part of the bargain. She may sue the other party for any damages which may arise as a result of the breach of warranty.

For example, in a sales transaction where the product is not of merchantable quality, the buyer may return the article to the seller and rescind the contract. If the buyer had used the product and was injured because of some defect in the product, the buyer can maintain a cause of action against the seller for any damages which she incurred as a result of the defect in the product.

615 Conditions

A condition is a qualifying agreement in the contract which describes the circumstances under which the contract is to operate. Its object is to modify, suspend, or rescind the principal obligation. For example, in a contract of sale, the buyer agrees to pay the purchase price prior to delivery, and the seller agrees to deliver upon receipt of the purchase price. The principal obligation of the seller is to deliver, but this obligation is conditioned upon the prior payment of the purchase price. The failure of the buyer to make the payment relieves the seller of his principal obligation.

All liability insurance policies require, as a circumstance of the performance of the principal obligation by the insurance carrier, that the insured report all accidents as soon as practicable. This is a condition, since it describes the circumstances under which the contract of insurance is to operate. The failure of the insured to meet this condition will relieve the insurance carrier of its principal obligations, which are to defend and to indemnify the insured.

There is a difference in the two examples given. In the first, the failure of the buyer to tender the purchase price within a reasonable time will not only relieve the seller of the obligation to deliver but will nullify or rescind the contract entirely. In the second, the failure of the insured to meet the condition merely suspends the carrier's principal obligation as to that particular event; namely, the accident which was not reported as soon as practicable. As to future events or as to past events, if the condition is met, the policy of insurance is still operable. Therefore, should the insured fail to report a particular accident "as soon as practicable" the principal obligation of the insurance carrier is rescinded only as to that particular event. The breach of condition does not, as in the first example, bring the contract to an end, or nullify the entire contract. The contract continues as to other events with the same obligations and subject to the same conditions.

Conditions are classified by the times at which they are to be performed, such as conditions precedent (before the other party's obligation), conditions subsequent (after the other party's obligation), and conditions concurrent (simultaneous with the other party's obligation).

616 Waiver and Estoppel

A waiver is the intentional or voluntary relinquishment of a known legal right. Estoppel is the legal result of a waiver, or of conduct from which a waiver can be implied. It prevents the party from asserting his original right. In insurance practice, we meet this situation most frequently when there has been a breach of a condition of the policy contract. Where such a breach occurs, the insurer may consider the breach as having the effect of relieving it of its obligation to perform, or may forgive the breach and treat the contract as being in full force and effect. In the latter case, the insurer will have voluntarily relinquished any rights which it may have acquired as a result of the breach. This voluntary relinquishment constitutes a waiver.

A waiver may be express or implied. An express waiver, as the term suggests, is an oral or written statement specifically relinquishing the rights which accrued as a result of the breach. A waiver is implied where one party has pursued such a course of conduct with reference to the other party as to evidence an intention to waive his or her rights. To make out a case of implied waiver of a legal right, there must be a clear, unequivocal, and decisive act of the party showing such a purpose, or an act amounting to an estoppel on his or her part.

For example, in a liability insurance contract situation where the insured has failed to make a report of an accident to the insurer as soon as practicable after it has occurred, the insurer has the choice of either waiving the breach of condition and accepting the claim, or of considering the breach as relieving it of its obligation and rejecting the claim. If it decides to waive the breach, then it has relinquished its right to disclaim responsibility, and it must perform all the obligations of the contract as if there had been no breach. If it decides to consider the breach of condition as relieving it of the responsibility to perform, it must give notice to the insured of its position, and may not thereafter take any action or pursue any conduct which is inconsistent with that position.

For example, the insurance contract gives the insurer the right to investigate, settle, or defend any claims made against its insured within the coverage afforded by the policy. If a claim is made that is not within the coverage of the policy—either because it does not arise out of the hazards insured against, or because of a breach of a condition of the contract by the insured—the insurer has no right to investigate, settle, or defend. Where there has been a breach of a condition of the policy, and the insurer has given notice of the fact that it considers the breach as relieving it of its contractual obligations, it may not later exercise rights granted to it only with respect to claims within its coverage. If it should investigate, settle, or defend the claim, such action would constitute an implied waiver of the breach of condition.

The aggrieved party must have knowledge of the breach of condition before its actions can be construed as a waiver. However, immediately upon the acquisition of knowledge of the breach of condition, the aggrieved party must make its decision. If it continued with a course of conduct which would be inconsistent with a denial of liability under the contract, such action would constitute a waiver.

For example, let us assume that the insured has made an untruthful statement with regard to the facts of the accident to the insurance carrier. This is in violation of the cooperation clause of the insurance contract. The insurance carrier is not aware of the untruthful statement and does not acquire this knowledge until the insured admits under oath in the trial of the case that the statement is untrue, or, in the alternative, testifies to an entirely different version of the accident. At that moment the insurance carrier acquires knowledge of the fact that there has been a breach of condition and that the insured has not cooperated. It is at that time that the insurance carrier must give notice of its election to treat its obligations under the policy as nonexistent.

It is quite true that up until that point, in the history of the case, the insurance carrier did exercise its rights under the contract, but it did so under the mistaken apprehension that the insured had made a truthful statement to it concerning the accident. As soon as the aggrieved party acquires knowledge of the breach of a condition, it must retire from the case and take no further action that would be inconsistent with a denial of liability under the contract.

In many instances it is the duty of the aggrieved party to give notice to the other party that he has decided to disclaim any responsibility under the contract because of the breach of condition. Failure to give notice in some cases might amount to a waiver. For example, if an insured gave a delayed notice to his insurance carrier, the insurance carrier could treat the condition as breached and refuse to carry out its obligations under the contract. However, the insurance carrier must notify the insured of its position. If it does not, the insured would be perfectly within his rights in assuming that the insurance company was performing in accordance with its contract. For that reason, the insured would take no steps toward protecting himself by making his own investigation and arranging for either settlement or defense, as the case might be. Therefore, the failure of the insurance carrier to notify the insured so that he could take steps to protect himself could constitute a waiver in and of itself.

The courts of the various states have not been consistent in the use of the terms waiver and estoppel. Some do not refer to an implied waiver, as defined above, but consider such a situation merely as an estoppel by conduct or an equitable estoppel, and not a waiver at all. They consider only an affirmative, overt act as a waiver. Still others do not refer to estoppel at all. When they decide that there is a waiver, it abrogates any defense which may be interposed on the theory of a breach of condition. Whatever terms are used, the result is usually the same.

617 Nonwaiver and Reservation of Rights

Where there has been a breach of a condition by the insured, the insurance carrier, for a variety of reasons, sometimes desires to investigate the case and defend the insured without waiving its rights under the contract.

It may accomplish this by a notice of reservation of rights, a nonwaiver agreement, or a reservation-of-rights agreement. The most generally used method is for the insurer to give its insured notice of reservation of rights, by which the insurer reserves its rights to later deny coverage under the policy.

618 Ambiguities

In a written instrument, an ambiguity is defined as indistinctness or uncertainty of meaning. In the law of contracts the rule is that, where there is any doubt as to the meaning of any particular clause in the contract, or where the clause is amenable to more than one interpretation, the language will be construed against the maker of the contract and most strongly in favor of the other party. The person who wrote the contract had the opportunity to make his meaning clear. If he did not do so, and his language is subject to more than one interpretation, the court will adopt the interpretation most favorable to the party who did not write the contract.

The insurance policy contract is constructed by and offered by the insurance carrier. If any of the terms or conditions of the policy contain any ambiguities, in the sense that they are susceptible to more than one meaning, the meaning most favorable to the insured will be adopted. In construing insurance contracts we can expect that the courts will, if possible, find there is insurance coverage unless there is clearly an intent, expressed in the language of the policy, to exclude or limit the amount of coverage afforded.

619 Assignments

All contracts, with the exception of contracts for personal services, are assignable unless there is an express provision in the contract preventing assignment. In all casualty insurance policies, the contract by its terms provides for an assignment on the condition that the assignment be approved by the company and evidence thereof be attached to the policy in the form of an approval from an officer of the company authorized to do so. The policy can be assigned only with the consent of the insurance carrier.

620 Law Governing Contracts

The general rule is that, unless there is a contrary intent expressed in the contract itself, the place where the contract is made is determinative of the law governing the contract. The theory is that in making the contract at that particular place, both parties entered into the agreement in contemplation of the law of the state which was applicable at the place of contract. This has no reference whatsoever to the place where the contract is to be performed.

Contracts come into existence as a result of an offer and an acceptance. If we assume that the offeror is located in one state, and he sends his offer to the other party in a second state, the contract will come into existence as soon as the second party accepts the offer. Therefore, the contract is made in the state where the offer is accepted. If the offeror had intended that the law of the state in which he was located should govern the rights of the parties, he could easily have included that stipulation in his offer. Then acceptance of the offer with that stipulation attached would establish that the parties intended that the law of a place other than the place where the contract was made should govern the rights of the parties.

This same rule applies to contracts of insurance. The law of the place where the contract is made will govern the rights of the parties to the insurance contract, namely, the insured and the insurance company. In automobile liability contracts it is quite possible that the performance of the contract by the insurance company might take place in a state other than the state in which the contract was made. The fact that performance is required in another state will not in any way alter the rights of the parties insofar as the contract of insurance is concerned. The place where the contract is made will still govern the rights of the parties.

In the law of torts, the place of the happening of the event will determine the substantive law governing the rights of the parties involved. Under those circumstances, where insurance is involved, it is possible to have two different jurisdictions concerned with the handling of the claim. If the place of the contract is a state different from the one where the tort was committed, the laws of that state which is the place of the contract will govern the rights of the parties to the insurance contract, and will measure the responsibility of the insurance company to its insured. The tort law of the place of accident will govern the rights of the parties involved in the accident and will be determinative of whether there is any liability imposed upon the insured by law.

For example, if an automobile liability insurance policy were entered into in the state of Louisiana, the rights of the parties under the contract of insurance would be determined by the state law of Louisiana. If an accident occurred in the state of Texas, the law which would be applicable to the rights and liabilities of the parties to the accident would be the law of Texas.

SOME TYPES OF CONTRACTS

621 Contracts to Compound a Crime

Any contract whose purpose is to conceal a crime or to hamper the prosecution of a crime, or to refrain from making a criminal complaint, is void as against public policy. In some states, the mere entering into of such a contract will constitute a crime in itself as to both parties. The theory behind this reasoning is that, where such contracts are made, the criminal is free to continue his nefarious conduct, to the detriment of the public. The public good, or public policy, demands that where a crime has been committed, the perpetrator be tried and convicted if the evidence warrants.

This type of contract should not be confused with an agreement between the wrongdoer and the person injured for the return of his property or the payment of damages caused by the wrong. Where a criminal prosecution is pending, it would be to the defendant's advantage in mitigation of sentence to be able to show that full restitution had been made to the injured party.

622 Contracts to Procure Evidence

It is perfectly legal to employ an investigator to procure evidence in connection with any claim or lawsuit, provided that the agreement for payment has reference to the actual work performed and is not conditioned upon the outcome or the amount of recovery obtained. Such latter contracts are void and are against public policy, because they place a premium upon the manufacture of evidence and subornation of perjury. In any case, the existence of the contract could be brought out in the trial of a main case in order to reflect upon the credibility and reliability of the evidence so procured.

A contract with an expert witness conditioned upon the amount of recovery is also void. For example, in *Laffin* v. *Billington* (86 N.Y. Supp. 267), it was held that a contract with a physician for expert testimony in a personal injury action, in which his fee was contingent upon the amount of the verdict, was contrary to public policy and therefore void.

623 Attorney's Contingent Fee Contracts

A contract of retainer between an attorney and his client—whereby the attorney's fee is conditioned upon a recovery and is based on a percentage of the amount so recovered—is a valid contract, provided that the amount of compensation agreed upon is fair and reasonable. These contracts are recognized on the theory that they are a social necessity. To require a retainer fee be paid in advance, and the full fee be paid irrespective of the outcome of the lawsuit, would work a serious injustice to poor people who could not afford counsel under those circumstances.

As between the attorney and client, the percentage of the recovery to be paid must be fair and reasonable and not extortionate. This is a matter which is solely between the attorney and the client, and even though the amount of compensation paid to the attorney will have a considerable influence upon the amount demanded in settlement, the defendant cannot complain. Also, the defendant cannot complain even though this type of arrangement makes the attorney a coproprietor of the personal injury cause of action.

In some jurisdictions, contingent fee percentages are regulated by statute or court rule. In some states, the rules of court require that all such contingent fee contracts be filed with the clerk of the court having jurisdiction in the area in which the attorney maintains his office. The retainers thus filed become public records and in most instances are available to the public for inspection.

624 Exculpatory Contracts

The public has an interest in the maintenance of conditions conducive to the preservation of wealth, property, and human life. Therefore, contracts which exculpate or relieve a tort-feasor from the consequences of his own negligence are void if the public interest is involved. On the other hand, if the only persons affected by the contract are the immediate parties and there is no danger of involvement of the public interest, then such contracts have been upheld.

Let us assume that an employer inserted a clause in the contract of employment whereby the employer was exonerated in advance from any liability arising out of injuries to the employee, either caused by the negligence of the employer, or occurring under such circumstances as to permit a recovery under the workers' compensation law.

The public policy of the state, as expressed by the workers' compensation law, would be defeated if such a clause were upheld. Therefore, the public interest would demand that the clause be considered void as against public policy. Another reason for rejecting the contract would be that, if such a contract were allowed to stand, the employer would be under no duty to maintain his premises in a safe and satisfactory condition, or to provide the proper tools, machinery, and safeguards.

Generally, the burden of proof as to the public interest involved in a contract of this sort is on the party asserting such a defense. The contracts are upheld unless there is evidence that the public interest is involved. For example, a clause in a lease of a private dwelling providing that the landlord shall not be responsible for damage from leakage, whether due to the negligence of the landlord or not, is a valid condition of the lease and, since there is no public interest involved, the clause will be given legal effect. Here, both the landlord and the tenant bargained on equal terms in the sense that neither had to enter into contractual relations with the other, and therefore it is a matter in which the parties were free either to accept or reject the clause as they saw fit.

In an action for damages for injuries sustained in a fall at the edge of a swimming pool, arising out of the alleged negligence of the defendant health club, it appeared that in becoming a "member" or patron of the health club, the plaintiff signed a membership contract containing an agreement to assume full responsibility for any injuries which occur in and about the gymnasium premises "including, but without limitation, any claims for personal injuries resulting from or arising out of the negligence of" the defendant. The court held that the clause was valid, and in considering the legal relationship between the contracting parties and the possible public interest involved, the court said:

> Here there is no special legal relationship and no overriding public interest which demand that this contract provision, voluntarily entered into by competent parties, should be rendered ineffectual. Defendant, a private corporation, was under no obligation or legal duty to accept the plaintiff as a member or patron. Having consented to do so, it had the right to insist upon such terms as it deemed appropriate. Plaintiff, on the other hand, was not required to assent to unacceptable terms, or to give up a valuable legal right, as a condition precedent to obtaining employment or being able to make use of the services rendered by a public carrier or utility. She voluntarily applied for membership in a private corporation, and agreed to the terms upon which this membership was bestowed. She may not repudiate them now. [*Ciafalo* v. *Vic Tanny Gyms, Inc.*, 214 N.Y.S. 2d 99.]

Here again, there was a private agreement between two contracting parties, and one in which the public had no interest whatsoever.

In the preceding case, the contract set forth an intent to absolve the defendant from all liability arising out of the particular transaction. Because the intention of the parties was clear, the court gave effect to the agreement. On the other hand, if the intention to absolve the defendant from liability for negligence is not clear, the courts will not construe the agreement as exculpating the defendant from liability. For example, in *Hertzog* v. *Harrison Island Shores, Inc.* [251 N.Y.S. 2d 164], the plaintiff's membership application stated that the member agreed to ''waive claim for any loss to personal property, or for any other personal injury while a member of the said club.'' The court held that the language did not possess the clarity or explicitness necessary in an exculpatory agreement to express the intention of the parties to absolve one of them from liability for negligence. This case enunciates the general rule that an exculpatory clause or agreement will be strictly construed against the party it favors.

Exculpatory agreements are frequently encountered in the recreation area where the operators of the facility seek to avoid liability for their own negligence by this means. The cases can be divided into two groups: (1) those involving signed agreements and (2) those involving unsigned agreements where the agreement is contained on the back of a ticket or there is a notice posted to that effect

1. Signed Agreements. When an exculpatory agreement with an amusement operator is signed by an adult, whether he read it or not, the courts hold that the adult is bound by the agreement. For example, in *Moss* v. *Fortune* [340 S.W. 2d 902 (Tennessee)], the court held that the plaintiff—by signing a written agreement that he exonerated the defendant from liability and that he assumed the risk of injury to which he would be exposed in hiring and riding a horse from the defendant's riding academy—could not recover for bodily injuries sustained as a result of the defendant's negligence. The court specifically stated that the parties could agree between themselves that one would not be liable to the other.

In *Broderson* v. *Rainier National Park Co.* [60 Pac. 2d 234 (Washington)], the plaintiff signed a printed slip which contained an assumption-of-risk clause on the part of patrons using the defendant's toboggan course. The court held that the signing of the agreement absolved the defendant from liability, even though the plaintiff claimed that he had not read it and he was unaware of its terms.

2. Unsigned Agreements. Attempts have been made by the operators of amusement devices and other recreational areas to create an exculpatory contract by printing an agreement on the reverse side of the ticket, which states that the use of the device would constitute an acceptance of the exculpatory clause.

If it can be shown that the customer was aware of the agreement and consented to its terms, then the customer is bound by it, and the defendant is exculpated from liability for his own negligence. The difficulty is that the operator seldom is able to establish that the customer actually read the agreement or used the device with any awareness of the existence of operator's lack of liability. In the absence of being able to establish notice to the customer and the customer's assent to the agreement, the courts will not release the operator. In many of the cases, the agreement is printed in fine print on a small ticket, which the customer holds only momentarily until it is collected, or torn in half (with the customer retaining only the stub).

Many amusement operators post signs on the premises which read ''Use at your own risk.'' While these signs might have the effect of discouraging small claims, they are not exculpatory in nature and do not absolve the operator from liability for negligence.

Effect of Infancy. An infant who signs an exculpatory contract has the same right of disaffirmance as he has in respect to any other contract. In *Cunningham* v. *State* [32 N.Y.S. 2d 275 (New York)], the court held that a minor was not bound by a waiver of liability which she had signed, since she had disaffirmed the contract. Because of the minor's right of disaffirmance, some operators of summer camps and other similar facilities require that the parent or guardian of the child sign a release-of-liability form of contract, exculpating the operators from liability for their own negligence. There are few cases on the subject, and it may well be that the contract may have the effect of discouraging litigation. In *Fedor* v. *Mauwehu Council, Boy Scouts of America, Inc.* [143 Atl. 2d 466 (Connecticut)], the infant-plaintiff's father signed a contract, which included a clause containing a waiver of all claims for damages in the event of injury. The court based its decision on the matter of public policy, holding that it would not confer immunity, because of the unequal bargaining positions of the parties. But the court also stated that it was doubtful whether a parent had the authority to waive the rights of his child against the defendant, for the defendant's negligent acts.

625 Hold Harmless Agreements

It frequently happens that, as a condition of a business contract, one party agrees to hold harmless or to indemnify the other party from certain liabilities, which may be imposed upon him by law, that arise out of the subject matter of the contract. The terms and the responsibility assumed differ with the agreement, and may range from the assumption of all liability arising out of the premises or the operation—irrespective of whether the liability arises because of the negligence of his own employees or the negligence of the other contracting party and his employees—to merely the assumption of liability for the negligence of his own employees.

For example, under the ultrahazardous operations doctrine, the owner of land is held to a strict liability for any accidents or injuries which are sustained as a result of the operations, whether they are under the control of the owner or an independent contractor. Let us assume that the owner hires an independent contractor to do the work, but insists that he, the owner, be held harmless from any liability which may be imposed upon him by law arising out of the ultrahazardous operations. The contractor may execute a hold harmless agreement which will so indemnify the owner in respect to all liability which may be imposed, irrespective of whether the accident occurred as a result of the negligence of the contractor's employees, the employees of the owner, or the owner himself. The hold harmless agreement also may be restricted to the liability imposed on the owner which arises out of the negligence of the contractor's employees only.

Hold harmless agreements must be distinguished from an exculpatory contract. Under an exculpatory clause the agreement exonerates the tort-feasor from liability arising from his own negligence. Under a hold harmless agreement the tort-feasor is not absolved from liability. He still remains liable to the injured person for his negligence, but when his liability is established, the hold harmless agreement may require someone else to respond for him or to reimburse him for the damages which he has paid.

There are two general forms of hold harmless agreements: (1) an agreement to hold the indemnitee harmless, which may be imposed by law, because of the negligence of the indemnitor, and the indemnitor's servants, agents, or employees, and (2) an agreement which not only indemnifies the indemnitee for the acts of the indemnitor's servants, agents, and employees, but also agrees to hold the indemnitee harmless from any liability imposed because of the negligence of the indemnitee's own employees, servants, or agents.

1. Liability for the Acts of the Indemnitor. In most cases an agreement of this type is not against public policy and is valid. An exception arises where there is a disparity in the bargaining power of the parties and the stronger party has taken advantage of the weaker party, in which case the agreement is void.

2. Liability for the Acts of the Indemnitee. Ordinarily a contract whereby one party assumes the liability of the other, for the negligent acts of the other and his employees, is not invalid as being against public policy. However, in a number of states, legislation has been enacted which prohibits, voids, or modifies the use of such hold harmless agreements on construction contracts. Other hold harmless agreements which assume the liability of the promisee generally are not affected. This latter category would include the standard sidetrack agreements executed in favor of the railroad, whereby the person for whose benefit the sidetrack is built assumes all the liability of the railroad, including liability for the negligent acts of the servants, agents, and employees of the railroad.

These agreements are of importance to the claim representative because, if the person indemnified is the insured, he can call on the other party to perform under the contract. Should the insurance carrier be compelled to pay the claim, it will succeed to the insured's rights and can subrogate against the indemnitor.

Liability assumed under a contract or hold harmless agreement can be the subject of insurance, so that the claim representative may be called upon to represent the indemnitor in such cases.

626 Arbitration Agreements

There are many insurance policies containing an agreement to arbitrate differences in evaluation, or liability, which may arise between the parties to the contract, namely, the insurance carrier and the insured. These are contracts to arbitrate future disputes. The common-law rule is that such contracts are unenforceable and are voidable at the will of either party. The reasoning behind the rule is that private persons cannot, by a contract to arbitrate, oust the jurisdiction of the courts. As to disputes which are in existence, the parties then may waive their rights to a trial by jury, and dispose of the dispute in any manner they see fit, be it by negotiation, arbitration, or recourse to the courts. The prohibition is not against arbitration as such, but is against an agreement which obligates the parties to submit disputes, which have not now arisen but which may arise in the future, to arbitration.

Therefore, in those states which adhered to the common-law rule, the policy provisions with regard to arbitration were not enforceable, and neither the insured nor the insurance carrier could compel the other to submit the dispute to arbitration, notwithstanding the policy provisions. The vast majority of states, recognizing the advantages of arbitration as an alternative to litigation, have passed statutes modifying the common-law rule by making contracts to arbitrate future disputes valid, enforceable, and irrevocable.

627 Beneficiary Contracts

It is possible for two parties to enter into a contract which is for the benefit of a third person who is not a party to the contract. Upon the happening of the event, or the payment, or performance which is provided by the contract, the third-party beneficiary acquires legal rights under the contract which are enforceable at law. The most common form of a beneficiary contract is a life insurance policy. The insured pays the premium to an insurance company, which agrees to pay a stated sum to the beneficiary upon the happening of the death of the insured. When the event takes place, the beneficiary, although not a party to the contract, may bring legal action against the life insurance company if it does not perform within the terms of its contract.

The medical payments provision of various liability insurance policies is also a beneficiary contract. It does not name a specific beneficiary by name but does designate the beneficiaries by class. When any member of this class or group of persons qualifies as a beneficiary by sustaining injury in the automobile or on the insured premises, the right of such a beneficiary comes into existence. Should the company fail to make the payments required under its contract, the beneficiary may enforce his or her claim by bringing suit for damages for breach of contract directly against the company.

628 Leases

A lease is a contract by which, for a consideration called the rent, the owner of real property transfers possession for a period of time to the other party, called the tenant. A lease merely transfers temporary possession of real property. The tenant is obligated to return the premises to the owner in the same condition as he received them, subject only to ordinary wear and tear. In the case of any deterioration or damage to the premises, the tenant has the obligation of making repairs, since he has a responsibility to return the premises to the owner in substantially the same condition as he received them.

As in any other agreement, the parties may insert any legal terms and conditions, either imposing greater liability upon one party or the other, or relieving one party or the other from the normal lease obligations. Therefore, one of the most important steps in the investigation of accidents due to defects in the premises, where such premises are occupied by a tenant, is to secure a copy of the lease to determine exactly what obligations were assumed by each party.

Under the terms of a lease, the landlord may transfer possession of an entire building and the grounds around it, or part of a structure (retaining some parts of it for his own use); or he may lease a number of parts or apartments to various tenants, reserving to himself the grounds, access ways, and other parts of the building, some of which he makes available to the tenants for their own use. As to the parts of the property which the landlord reserved to himself or for the use of the tenants, the landlord is ordinarily responsible for their condition and will be answerable in damages should he fail to exercise reasonable care in maintaining them. This would refer to the elevators, stairways, lobby, the laundry room, and private sidewalk to the building. In addition, the landlord retains to himself the electric conduits in the walls, water pipes, sewer pipes, the roof, the heating facility, and the like. He is liable to the tenant if he fails to maintain these in safe condition and they cause injury to the tenant. The parties to the contract of lease can vary, diminish, or enlarge these responsibilities. Likewise, the tenant could exculpate the landlord from all liability for his own negligence. In addition, some leases contain hold harmless agreements whereby the tenant agrees to indemnify the landlord for any liability imposed upon the landlord as a result of an injury to a social guest of the tenant.

Unless the lease so stipulates, the landlord may not enter the leased premises during the term of the lease. Some leases permit the landlord to enter at certain reasonable times for the purposes of inspection or repair. Some leases obligate the landlord to make necessary repairs and contain a clause allowing him to re-enter the premises for that purpose. Should the tenant notify the landlord of the need for repairs, and the landlord makes an inspection which confirms the tenant's opinion, and the landlord promises to make the necessary repairs, the failure of the landlord to make those repairs does not subject him to liability to someone who is injured as a result of the condition. If the landlord is obligated to make repairs under the lease, and fails to do so within a reasonable time after he has notice of the necessity of repairs, the tenant's only remedy is to have the repairs made himself at the expense of the landlord. This is contrary to the popular notion that where this condition exists, the tenant may expose himself to the unsafe condition, with the landlord held strictly liable in case of injury. The defense of contributory negligence would generally be available to the landlord.

Where the landlord does make the repairs, whether the lease obligates him to do so or not, he is liable if the repairs are made in an unsafe or negligent manner, with the result that the tenant, his family, or social guests are injured.

629 Accord and Satisfaction

A disputed claim of any kind may be settled by the agreement of the parties. This agreement may involve the extinguishment of the claim by one party in return for a payment of money by the other. The agreement by the parties to settle the disputed claim, and the terms of the agreement, is called an *accord*. This is merely an agreement to settle and is executory, because it contemplates that something more must be done to complete the transaction. *Satisfaction* is the payment required by the accord. When the payment is made and received, the contract is executed and complete. Both sides are bound by the transaction and the disputed claim is extinguished. Therefore, to have a completed transaction, the two necessary steps are (1) the agreement to settle (accord), and (2) performance by payment under the agreement (satisfaction).

An accord is a contract in and of itself. It comes into existence as a result of an offer from one party and the acceptance by the other, both supported by adequate consideration. The consideration moving from the party offering the satisfaction is the payment of a sum of money to settle a disputed claim which the party has a legal right to resist. The consideration moving from the opposite party is the agreement to forego pressing a claim for a larger amount. When either party fails to perform his or her promise under the agreement, the contract is breached. If the party who is to make the payment fails to do so, the opposite party has the option of considering the contract rescinded by the nonperformance of the other, thereby releasing his or her obligations under the contract; or he or she may stand on the contract and sue the party for the payment which the contract demands. Therefore, where an agreement was made with a claimant to settle her case for a certain amount, for which she signed a release, and the company thereafter declined to make the payment, the claimant has the option of regarding the contract of release as rescinded. This would release her from her obligations and permit her to sue on the original claim; or she may sue the company for damages for breach of contract, the damages being the amount that she should have received under the accord (the release), together with the cost of the action.

Conversely, after she has signed the release, thereby evidencing an intention to settle the claim, the claimant may have a change of mind and return the draft uncashed. If there is a period of time between the execution of the release and the delivery of the draft and she refuses the draft when tendered, the majority rule, in the absence of fraud and deceit, and in the absence of a statute modifying the rule, is that the accord is a contract and the claimant is bound. In *Reynard* v. *Bradshaw* [196 Kansas 97], the claimant signed a release for $2,500 which was delivered to the claim representative representing the insurance company. The claim representative was employed by an independent firm and did not have draft authority, so that no payment of money was made to the claimant at the time of the execution of the release. The day after the release was signed, an attorney representing the claimant notified the adjuster that the sum of $2,500 would not be acceptable in settlement, and demanded the return of the release. The insurance company, in the meantime, had mailed its check in the sum of $2,500 to the claimant some four days after the date of the release. The claimant thereafter brought suit against the tort-feasor; an affirmative defense that the claim had been released was interposed. The plaintiff admitted the release but claimed that, since the consideration was not accepted by her, the release was nothing more than an offer to settle as opposed to a binding contract. In upholding the defense, the court said:

> As a matter of law it would make no difference who made the offer and who made the acceptance. What is essential is that there was a definite proposition accepted by both parties. In other words, the release shows a mutual meeting of the minds of the parties resulting in mutual promises and we think the release on its face shows it was so intended by them. The compromise of a disputed claim furnishes good consideration for a contract. . . . Here there are all the elements of a valid contract and we have no doubt either of the parties could have enforced it. The law favors contracts in settlement of disputed matters and the avoidance of litigation and it ought not to circumscribe the means of carrying such settlements into effect.

630 Releases

A release is a formal document providing for the relinquishment, concession, or giving up of a right or claim by the person in whom it exists (or to whom it accrues) to the person against whom it may be demanded or enforced. It is a contract, supported by a good and valuable consideration. A release may be (1) general, or (2) partial or *restrictive*. (See also Section 504.)

1. General As its designation implies, a general release extinguishes all claims which the releasor may have against the releasee. The releasor clearly cannot release a claim he does not own, either because he never had it or because he has assigned it to another. Thus an injured wife in most jurisdictions can release her claim for her injuries, but a release from her will not be a bar to others who may have a claim arising out of her injuries or out of the same accident. Her release will not affect her husband's claim for loss of consortium, since this claim is owned by the husband and the husband alone. Conversely, a release from the husband will not release the wife's claim for her injuries. His release will effectively release any claims which he might have, such as a claim for loss of consortium, and his own injuries if he were involved in the same accident. It is generally advisable, in the case of an injury to a married person, to obtain a release from each spouse.

Since the releasor cannot release a claim which he does not own, it follows that if he has assigned any part of the claim, he can release only that part which he retains. Where he has assigned part of the claim, and he executes a general release, the question of whether the release so given affects the rights of the assignee will depend upon the circumstances. If the releasee settles the case and takes back the release with knowledge or notice of the assignment, then the rights of the assignee are not affected by the release. But where the releasee having no knowledge, or not chargeable with knowledge of the assignment nor any notice of it, settles the case (believing that he was extinguishing the entire claim), the assignee may be estopped from enforcing his claim.

This situation usually arises where there is collision coverage on the claimant's car, and payment less the deductible has been made by the collision carrier. If the releasee has knowledge of the collision carrier's rights, he cannot obtain a full release from the claimant, because the claimant no longer owns part of the property damage claim. He does own that part of it which is represented by the deductible, and a general release from him will include the deductible but will not extinguish the collision carrier's claim for the balance. Some companies will add language to the release indicating that it covers only the property damage represented by the deductible, stating the exact amount of the deductible.

In all cases, the properly drafted and executed release will effectively extinguish any claim which the releasor has against the releasee. Whether it also releases the claims which the releasor may have against others who stand in the relationship of tort-feasor depends upon the applicable law.

In cases where the insured has a possible cause of action against the releasor and the insurance carrier seeks to avoid the possibility of the release being pleaded in bar to the insured's cause of action, some companies have inserted a condition in the release, which reads substantially as follows:

It is understood and agreed between the releasor and the releasee that this release and settlement is not construed as an admission of liability on the part of the releasee, by whom liability is expressly denied. It is further understood and agreed that this release and settlement shall not be available as a defense by the releasor or anyone on his behalf, or as an estoppel, in any action which is now pending, or which hereafter may be brought by the releasee, or anyone in his behalf against the releasor.

2. Partial or Restrictive. It is possible for a releasor to release part of the claim and retain the balance. This can be done by appropriate language in the instrument itself. It is seldom used in insurance matters where the part retained can be asserted against the insured. Some states still adhere to the common-law rule that the release of one of the tort-feasors releases all. But many states, by statute or court decision, have altered the traditional rule and give effect to restrictive words in the release, which limit the surrender of the releasor's legal right to merely a release to the releasee and no one else. Some of these even give effect to an oral agreement which accompanies the release.

631 Covenant Not to Sue

A solution was sought to the problem presented where a plaintiff desired to release one of the tort-feasors, but not all, without extinguishing his or her entire claim. In states where the common-law rule is rigidly imposed, a release would not accomplish the desired result. A covenant not to sue was the device adopted for the purpose of avoiding the consequences of a release and also of accomplishing the result. A covenant not to sue is an agreement by one who has a right of action at the time of making it against another person, by which he agrees not to sue to enforce such right of action forever in return for the payment of a consideration.

Technically, the person giving such a covenant does not extinguish his claim. The claim is still in existence, but he has given up his right to bring legal action in order to enforce it. Since no other means of enforcement are available, the practical result is that the person giving the covenant is prevented from recovering on his claim against the other person. Should the person giving the covenant attempt to bring action on his claim, the defendant could counterclaim for damages arising out of the breach of the covenant. The damage recoverable for the breach would be exactly the same amount which the plaintiff was claiming to be due to him. The result would be that any judgment obtained by the plaintiff would be offset by a judgment on the counterclaim for exactly the same amount. In order to avoid such a circuity of action, most courts regard the covenant as a bar to the action, and will render judgment for the defendant accordingly. Some courts, however, deny or restrict the validity or effect of such covenants.

AGENCY

TYPES OF AGENCY RELATIONSHIPS

632 Agency Defined

The fundamental principle of the law of agency is that, when a person does an act through an agent under his or her control, it is that person who performs the act. Because one is answerable for the legal consequences of his or her own acts, that person is likewise answerable for the acts of an agent. The person for whom the act is done is called the *principal*.

The word *agent* has various connotations in our everyday language and may mean different things under numerous circumstances. There are, for example real estate agents, insurance agents, and theatrical agents. But we are concerned with agents in the legal sense, and whether any of the persons described will qualify as *legal agents* depends on their relationship with an employer or principal. An agent is defined as one who is authorized to do certain acts for or in relation to the rights and property of another at his or her request, instruction, or command. The two elements which distinguish an agency relationship from other types of relationships are (1) authority to act for the principal, and (2) control by the principal.

1. Authority to Act. For the agency relationship to exist, the principal must delegate some authority to the agent to do some act, for and in behalf of the principal. If a person has no authority to act for the principal, he is not an agent, and his acts are not the acts of the principal. For example, an individual is in the real estate business, and she fraudulently represents to another that she is my agent for the purpose of selling my house. She has never received any authority from me. She executes a contract of sale with the other, and when the purchase price is tendered, it is refused. The principal is not bound to the contract because the purported agent had no authority.

2. Control by the Principal. Merely because an act is done for and in behalf of a person does not make the person doing the act the agent of the beneficiary of the act, unless the act was done under the control of the beneficiary as to the methods and means of accomplishment. For example, *A* takes a suit to the dry cleaner to have it cleaned and pressed. *A* gives the dry cleaner the authority to clean the suit, but *A* does not exercise control and supervision over the methods and means employed by the dry cleaner to accomplish the result. Since there is no control by *A*, the dry cleaner is not her agent.

An agent may devote full time to the business of the principal, as in the relationship of employer and employee, or may merely represent the principal in one or more isolated transactions. The acts done for the principal may be of both a business and a social nature, and they may also be done for a fee, or for a salary, or gratuitously. For example, the principal asks his neighbor to drive the principal's car to a garage, or to take the principal's car and drive his wife to the store. The neighbor is the agent of the principal while engaged in driving the principal's car for these purposes.

An independent contractor is not an agent, and the acts of an independent contractor are not the responsibility of the principal who employs him. An independent contractor is defined as one who works for another as to the result to be accomplished, but who is not subject to the other as to the methods and means of doing the work. Thus, if the principal employs a painter to paint her house for an agreed price, even though the principal chooses the color of the paint and directs the painter as to where the paint is to be applied, under those circumstances the painter is an independent contractor. On the other hand, if the principal furnished the paint, the ladders, brushes, etc., and fixed the hours of employment and directed the means of doing the work, paying for the job on a fixed daily rate, then the painter would be an employee and the agent of the principal. The question of whether an individual is an independent contractor always turns on the question of control. If there is no control exercised, there is no agency.

The agency relationship is created by the mutual agreement of the parties. The principal must offer to delegate some authority to the agent to be exercised under the control of the principal. The agent must accept the delegation of authority and the terms on which it is offered. Both mutual agreement and delegation of authority must be present for the relationship of principal and agent to arise. If either element is lacking, there is no agency.

633 Types of Agents

Agents are generally classified by the nature and extent of the authority given to them by the principal. These classifications include *universal*, *general*, *limited*, *implied*, or *apparent agents*.

A *universal agent* is one who is appointed to do all the acts which the principal can personally do, and which he or she may lawfully delegate the power to another to do. Agents of this type are extremely rare. Since the occasion for the delegation of such complete authority comes about only in extreme cases of necessity, the law presumes that the agent is not a universal agent unless there is clear and convincing evidence of the principal's intent to create that type of agent.

A *general agent* is one to whom the principal confides his whole business, or all transactions or functions of a designated class. In the insurance business, a general agent is one who exercises complete underwriting authority in the territory to which the principal assigns him. The acts of a general agent of an insurance company are the acts of the company. This is true even though the company may have placed some limitations upon his authority. Unless the limitations of the authority of the general agent are actually brought to the attention of the third person dealing with the general agent, the third person has a right to assume that (because this person is held out to the public as a general agent) he or she has all of the powers normally delegated to a general agent.

A *limited agent* is one who is an agent for the principal within a certain area, limited either by contract or by the usage in the particular trade or occupation in which he is engaged. For example, a grocery clerk is an agent of the owner of the grocery store. He has authority to sell groceries at retail to customers and to collect the purchase price. His authority is limited to this particular function. He could not, without additional specific authority, undertake to sell the entire grocery store, including the stock, the fixtures, the building, and the goodwill. A person dealing with the grocery clerk would be bound to recognize that grocery clerks by the usage of the business are not clothed with the authority to sell the business. Likewise, a truck driver employed to drive a truck from one place to another would not have authority to sell the truck or to pledge it as security for a loan on behalf of his principal without actual authority so to do. He would have authority, however, to have the truck repaired should it break down, and the principal would be liable for the repair bill.

An *implied* or *apparent agent* is one whom the principal, either intentionally or by want of ordinary care, constitutes his agent, though the agent is not clothed with any specific authority by the principal. This situation is also classified as one involving an ostensible agent or an agent by estoppel.

For example, if a grocer leaves a person in charge of her store, with directions merely to watch the store and do nothing further, the limitation of this person's authority would be known only to the grocer and the person she placed in charge of the premises. If this person undertook to sell some of the groceries to retail customers, the grocer as principal would be bound by the transaction. This is true, even though the grocer may have expressly instructed the person in charge that this was not to be done.

As to the third person's dealings with the agent in charge of the store, becuase she had no knowledge of the limitation of the authority of the agent, and because the principal had created a situation wherein third persons would assume that the person in charge had authority to act, the grocer is estopped from denying the authority of her agent. She is bound by the unauthorized transactions which the agent undertook on her behalf.

An *insurance broker* is a limited agent. He or she is the agent for the insured only. His or her agency is limited to the procuring of insurance coverage for the principal. Therefore, acts within the scope of the agency are the acts of the principal, or the person for whom the insurance is being procured, and not the acts of the insurance companies with whom he or she deals. He or she differs from an insurance agent who is employed by an insurance company for the purpose of selling insurance, or a subagent employed by the general agent for the purpose of selling insurance, in that the broker is the representative of the insured. The other two types of agents are agents of the insurance company.

634 Specific Agency Relationships

1. Employment. The most common form of agency relationship is that of employer and employee. It is also referred to as a relationship of master and servant. An employee is defined as anyone who, for a lawful consideration, undertakes to perform a lawful pursuit at his or her employer's direction. This contemplates a contract of hire between employer and employee, and control by the employer, not only of the result to be accomplished, but the methods and means of performing the work. It also contemplates that the employer or employee shall have the right to terminate the agreement at any time.

An employee is a limited agent and may act for the employer in all matters within the scope of the employment. As stated above, the key factor distinguishing employees from independent contractors is control. An employer has the right to control the methods and means of work of an employee, but can only determine an end result to be produced by an independent contractor. Other tests as to whether an employer-employee relationship exists include the following:

1. Does the employer fix the hours of work?
2. Does the employer supply the tools, equipment, and protective industrial clothing for the person hired?
3. Does the person hired receive pay in accordance with stated periods of time, and/or stated units of work; or is he or she paid an agreed price for the entire job?
4. Does the employer withhold income taxes from the person's salary, provide unemployment insurance, provide compensation benefits, and pay social security tax?

If the answers to all of these questions are in the affirmative, and the answer to 3 is that the pay is in accordance with stated periods of time or stated units of work, then the employer-employee relationship exists. If it does, the negligence of the employee acting in the scope of employment will be imputed to the employer, and, in addition, any acts performed by the employee within the scope of employment are binding upon the employer under the doctrine of *respondeat superior*.

A corporation is a legal person created by statute. It can function only through agents. An individual operating a business as such can exercise all the powers incidental to the management of the business. In the case of a corporation, the management of the business is placed in the hands of a board of directors. These directors exercise all of the powers of management and may specifically delegate powers to officers of the corporation or other employees. Therefore, in those cases of administrative management where the authority has been specifically delegated in advance, the corporation is bound by and responsible for the acts of such designated employees within the scope of the authority thus given.

For example, the secretary of a corporation normally is given the authority to sign legal documents in behalf of the corporation. This authority may be on a blanket basis or it may be limited specifically to a certain kind or class of legal documents. If the secretary of the corporation is authorized to compromise claims which the corporation may have and is further authorized to execute a release for and in behalf of the corporation, then the claim representative may deal with the secretary. On the other hand, such authority may have been delegated by the board of directors to some other officer. In either case, the claim representative would have no way of knowing the exact authority of the officer executing the release. In the absence of an actual examination of the minutes of the board of directors' meetings, the claim representative may rely upon a sworn statement attached to the release signed by an appropriate officer who has knowledge of the directors' action, indicating that the officer executing the release has been specifically authorized to do so by action of the board of directors.

As to purely ministerial functions, all executive officers, and all employees, are authorized to act for the corporation within the scope of their authority or employment. Torts committed or contracts executed within this area of employment then become the responsibility of the corporation.

2. Partnership. A partnership is a form of business enterprise created by a voluntary contract between two or more competent persons wherein they agree to commit their money, efforts, labor, and skill to a lawful business, with the understanding that there shall be a proportional sharing of the profits and losses between them. Each partner is an agent of the partnership, and, because of the nature of the business, he or she represents all of the individuals who make up the partnership, including himself or herself.

Partners are jointly and severally liable for the obligations incurred by the partnership in the course of the partnership enterprise. This means that a person having a cause of action against the partnership could sue one partner, some of the partners, or all of the partners. Partnerships, like any other business enterprise, can have employees who are not partners. The liability of the partnership for the negligence of its employees would be the same as that of any other employer.

3. Joint enterprise. A joint enterprise is an undertaking somewhat similar to that of the partnership. It does not connote a permanent arrangement, but refers to an association formulated to accomplish some specific purpose. To be a joint enterprise, all of the persons engaged in the common purpose must have an equal right to control, or at least have a voice in, the management. A joint enterprise therefore can be defined as the joint prosecution of a common purpose under such circumstances that each has authority, express or implied, to act for all in respect to control, means, or agencies employed to execute such a common purpose. The existence of a joint enterprise, sometimes referred to as a joint venture or common purpose, depends entirely upon the right of joint control. Even though people having the same objective are involved, there is no joint enterprise unless each of the people so engaged has a voice in the control of the methods and means utilized in order to accomplish the common purpose.

Suppose *A* and *B* decide to go on a vacation and they jointly rent an automobile for that purpose. It is understood that both will drive the car on occasions, both will be responsible to the renting agency for the return of the vehicle, and both will be responsible for the charges incurred in connection with the use of the vehicle. Here there is a joint right of control, and there is a joint enterprise.

Joint enterprise has importance only on the issue of liability. Where there is a joint enterprise, all joint venturers are liable to third persons, and the negligence of one member of the joint enterprise is imputable to the others. Just as in a partnership, the injured third person may sue one of the joint venturers, some, or all. The injured party is not required to join all joint venturers.

With regard to the liability among themselves, the same rules are applicable to joint venturers as are applicable to members of a partnership. Where a joint venturer or a partner is injured through the negligence of another joint venturer or partner, the negligence of the person causing the injury is not imputed to the partner or joint venturer who is injured so as to prevent a recovery by the injured partner against the negligent partner. Imputed negligence occurs only where a third person, or a stranger to the joint enterprise or partnership, is injured. It does not apply as between partners or joint venturers.

635 Appointment of Subagents

An agent normally does not have the authority to delegate any part of his or her duty to someone else unless specifically authorized to do so by the principal, or where custom or usage in the particular trade in which they are engaged normally gives the agent that authority. If an agent does employ the services of another where the agent has no authority to do so, and where the custom or usage in the trade or business does not authorize such employment, the person so employed is not a subagent of the principal and cannot bind the principal in contract, nor can this person's negligent act be imputed to the principal.

For example, the *X* Insurance Company appoints *A* as its general agent for the state of *Y* with the understanding that *A* will maintain offices in several parts of the state. *A* is authorized to employ subagents who will have authority to bind the *X* Insurance Company, even though there is no specific agreement between *A* and the *X* Insurance Company that *A* was authorized to appoint subagents. The custom and usage of the business, together with the area to be covered, imply the employment of subagents.

636 Agency by Emergency

Normally an agent performing a purely ministerial function does not have the authority to delegate any part of the work to another. However, there are situations where an emergency arises and where efforts to communicate with the principal or employer have failed. In such a case, the agent or employee would have the implied authority to make whatever arrangements the facts of the situation demanded.

For example, if a truck driver who suffered an illness while on his route, unsuccessfully attempted to communicate with his employer and was unable to continue with the truck, and where his load consisted of a perishable commodity, the driver would have the implied authority under those circumstances to employ another driver to complete the trip at the expense of his employer. In such a case, even though the employer had no knowledge of the employment of the other driver, should an accident occur, the other driver's negligence would be imputed to the principal, or employer.

Therefore, in all cases involving an agency by emergency, a meticulous investigation is required to determine whether an emergency was in existence, whether the truck driver had actual authority to employ the services of others, or whether such authority could be implied from the facts of the particular situation.

To constitute an agency by emergency, three elements must be present:

1. There must be an emergency requiring immediate action.
2. Efforts to contact the principal for instructions must have failed.
3. There must be an actual contract of hire made with the subagent.

637 Special and General Employees

This concept of agency is sometimes referred to as the *borrowed servant rule*, or the rule of the loaned employee. It comes about where the employee's regular or general employer, with the consent of the employee, temporarily lends the services of the employee to another, called a *special employer*, for the purpose of doing some specific task. The employee still remains in the employ of the general employer, and there usually is some arrangement by which the special employer will reimburse the general employer for the salary earned by the employee while absent from his regular job. The question is whether by such an arrangement the employee becomes at least temporarily an employee and/or agent of the special employer. The answer to the question will turn on the matter of control. If the general employer retains entire control over the employee, then the employee is an agent of the general employer and not of the person for whom he or she is working. On the other hand, if the general employer relinquishes the entire control of the employee's actions to the special employer, then the employee becomes an employee or agent of the special employer while under such control and direction, even though the employee still remains on the payroll of the general employer.

Therefore, the question of whether the employee becomes a temporary employee of the special employer, or remains a regular employee of his or her general employer, will almost always be determined by which employer has the right to control and direct the employee's activities in the performance of the act, and whose work is being performed. The negligence of the loaned employee or "loaned servant" (as such an employee is sometimes called) will be imputed to the employer who has the right of control and direction at the time of the accident.

638 Attorneys as Limited Agents

An attorney engaged for the purpose of bringing an action at law against a defendant is a limited or special agent of the client who employs her. Her agency is limited to the cause of action for which she is engaged, and she may act for the client only in connection with legal representation in that case and no other. Within the scope of her authority, she may do the following acts without consultation with her client, and the action so taken will be binding upon the client. She may: admit facts, waive a jury, consolidate actions, waive rights of appeal, dismiss an action, submit a matter to arbitration or some other form of dispute resolution, and engage experts at the client's expense if the fee is reasonable.

She may *not* release the cause of action without her client's consent. She is bound to transmit to her client all offers of settlement so that the client may accept or reject them. This is a duty that she has only to her client. Her failure to do so, which results in damage to the client, will subject her to liability to the client alone. She does not owe this duty to any other party to the action.

Unless the attorney warrants that she has specific authority to do so, an agreement on the part of the attorney to settle a certain case at a specific figure will not be binding on her client. If the attorney warrants that she has such authority and she does not, the client still is not bound by the agreement, but the attorney does expose herself to liability for damages arising from the breach of this warranty of authority.

639 Fiduciary Agents

An agent is said to act in a fiduciary capacity, or to receive money or contract a debt in such capacity, when the business which she transacts, or the money or property which she handles, is not her own or for her own benefit, but for the benefit of another person as to whom she stands in a relation implying and necessitating great confidence and trust on one part and a high degree of good faith on the other. A fiduciary agent, therefore, is one who performs not just ministerial functions but is entrusted with the title to or custody of the property of another, concerning which the agent has undertaken the responsibility of performing some function. Examples of this type of relationship include trustees, under a technical or express trust; executors, under a last will and testament; attorney-at-law; guardian; broker; director of a corporation; public officer.

All of these are held to a high degree of care in the faithful performance of the duties that they have undertaken. All of these agents receive money or contract a debt in a fiduciary capacity. The business which the agent transacts or the money or property which he handles is not his own, nor are the transactions which he makes for his own benefit, but for the benefit of another person or persons as to whom he stands in a relationship implying and necessitating great confidence and trust.

Out of such a relationship the law raises the rule that neither party may exert influence or pressure upon the other, take selfish advantage of the trust, or deal with the subject matter of the trust in such a way as to procure it for himself or to prejudice the other. Business shrewdness, hard bargaining, and astuteness to take advantage of the forgetfulness or the negligence of another is totally prohibited between persons standing in such a relation to each other. A fiduciary agent may not deal with the principal's property in his hands in any other way except for the advantage of the principal. The agent may not exercise any self-interest in dealing with the property in his hands. The law presumes that a person cannot serve two masters.

Where an agent does deal with the property in her possession and buys the property for her own account, or sells property of her own to the principal, on the principal's account, then the law *conclusively* presumes the transaction to be fraudulent. This means that, even though the agent dealt with the property fairly, and paid more than the market price, the agent is precluded from presenting this evidence. A conclusive presumption is one which cannot be overcome by any evidence, and the court will not receive any evidence with respect to it. In other words, a fiduciary agent must act solely for her principal and cannot, in the exercise of this agency, deal with herself personally in any way.

A claim representative is a fiduciary agent of the company which he represents, at least in certain phases of his activities. He is an agent who is given the authority to contract a debt or to receive property for and in behalf of his principal. The claim representative is required in the performance of his duties to inform his principal of any facts coming to his knowledge which will have any influence upon the contracting of the debt or the disposition of the property.

640 Trustees

There are fiduciaries who are in possession and control of property for the benefit of others, whose relationship comes about as a result of an appointment by the court. They are responsible to the court for the faithful performance of their duties and are not under the control of the parties for whose benefit they act. Therefore, they are not agents, although acting in a fiduciary capacity. In this classification we find *receivers*, *executors*, or *administrators* of the last will and testament of a deceased, and *guardians* of infants or incompetents.

A *receiver* is a fiduciary and has the power to bind the organization of which he is the receiver to contract and tort liability. He is not appointed by the organization or, necessarily, with its consent. He is a representative of the court, and he acts only under the court's direction. The persons for whose benefit he is appointed, be they stockholders or creditors, have no right of control over his actions. His actions are his own.

Executors and *administrators* under a last will and testament are fiduciaries, but they are not the agents of the beneficiaries under the will. Like the receiver, they are responsible to and under the direction of the court which appointed them. They may bind the estate in contract or expose the estate to liability in tort. However, the negligence of the executor or administrator is not imputed to the ultimate beneficiaries of the estate.

Guardians of infants and incompetents are the same type of fiduciaries. They are appointed by the court, subject to its control and direction, and are personally responsible for their acts in connection with the administration of the trust. They are not the agents of the infant or the incompetent.

The same rule applies to fiduciaries of this character as to fiduciary agents. Trustees may not deal with the property in their hands for their own benefit, nor may they sell property of their own to the estate or organization that they represent. Such acts are conclusively presumed to be fraudulent, irrespective of the nature or character of the act.

641 Independent Contractors

An independent contractor is defined as one who exercises an independent employment and contracts to do a piece of work according to his or her own judgment and methods, and without being subject to the employer except as to the results of the work. An independent contractor has the right to employ and direct the action of the workers independent of the employer, and is free from any superior authority in the employer to say how the specified work shall be done or what the laborers shall do as it progresses. It is very generally held that the right of control as to the mode and method of doing the work is the principal consideration in determining whether one employed is an independent contractor or a servant. Therefore, one who works for another with respect to the result to be obtained but not with respect to the methods and means of accomplishing that result is an independent contractor.

An independent contractor is not the agent of the principal. An independent contractor is liable for his or her own tortious acts, and negligence in the performance of the work is not imputed to the principal.

The employment of an independent contractor does not always insulate the principal from liability for the negligent acts of the contractor. There are certain duties which the principal, as an owner of land or as an operator of a business, is bound to perform with respect to the risk of harm to third persons. The duty of care in certain areas cannot be delegated to an independent contractor. The principal is liable for any failure to meet the duties imposed by law in the following situations:

1. Where the principal has failed to exercise due care in the selection of a reasonably competent contractor.
2. Where the work to be done by the independent contractor is by its nature inherently dangerous.
3. Where the negligent act or omission involves a violation of a duty imposed upon the principal either by the common law or by statute.
4. Where the work to be done by the independent contractor is forbidden by law.

Where any one of these conditions prevails, the negligence of the contractor is the negligence of the principal.

The owner's liability to the members of the public who may be injured as a consequence of these conditions remains, irrespective of any of the terms of the contract which may be made between the owner and the contractor. It is customary in such situations for the contractor to agree to indemnify the owner for any liability arising out of the operations of the contract. This is referred to as a "hold harmless agreement." All that a hold harmless agreement does is to provide for a means of protection or reimbursement to the owner after the liability has been imposed upon the owner. As between the owner and the injured member of the public, the duties and responsibilities remain exactly the same, and the existence of the hold harmless agreement does not in any way alter the responsibilities of the owner towards the public. (See also Section 414.)

As to the duties and responsibilities which can be delegated to the independent contractor, the contractor is liable for his own negligent act committed by him, his agents, servants, or employees. As to nondelegable duties imposed upon the owner, both the owner and the independent contractor are liable in damages to a person injured. In the delegable duty area, only the independent contractor is liable for his own negligence. If the subject matter of the contract is one where it is within the contemplation of the parties that some part of the work be subcontracted to others, such subcontractor is liable for his own negligence and the negligence of his agents, servants, or employees.

The contractor who has the contract with the owner of the property, and who subcontracts some portion of the work, is referred to as the *general* or *prime contractor*. As such, he has the responsibility to the owner for the completion of the job as well as responsibility for the direction of the work. He is responsible for the general housekeeping on the job, the maintenance of fences, barricades, lights, and other warning devices. These latter duties are owed not only to the members of the public but to the employees of subcontractors who may be injured as a consequence of the failure to meet such responsibilities. The general contractor has the duty of maintaining the premises on which the work is in progress in a reasonably safe condition, and is liable to employees of the subcontractor or other persons legally on the premises, if they are injured as a result of the failure to meet this duty.

The subcontractor is liable for any injuries occasioned by his negligence or the negligence of his servants, employees, or agents. This responsibility extends not only to the general public and persons legally on the premises, but also to employees of the general contractor and employees of other subcontractors as well.

The existence of these various responsibilities on the part of the general contractor and the subcontractor sometimes poses a very difficult problem of investigation, especially on a large construction project where a number of subcontractors are involved. For example, if a brick falls from the building during the course of construction and injures a member of the public, how can the offending subcontractor be identified? The mere fact that the falling object was a brick would not necessarily point to the bricklayer, unless the bricklayer was the only subcontractor working on the job at that particular time. A subcontractor or his employees will seldom admit that they dislodged the brick, and therefore a claimant would have a problem of proof. The contractors against whom claims are asserted likewise would have a problem of defense.

Some insurance companies have met this problem by refusing to insure any large construction project unless the general contractor and all of the subcontractors take out liability insurance coverage with them, either on a general or specific job basis. This avoids any controversy among insurance carriers and leaves the management and control of the defense of any action arising on the job with the one insurance carrier. Where this situation obtains, it is extremely important that the claim representative check the insurance coverage.

LIABILITIES IN AGENCY RELATIONSHIPS

642 Respondeat Superior

Where a principal does an act through an agent, and the agent is negligent in the performance of that act to the extent that some third person sustains injury, the negligence of the agent is imputed to the principal. The principal is answerable in damages to the injured person, even though the principal himself did not participate in the event.

This response for the actions of another which the law imposes on the principal is called vicarious liability. The doctrine under which it is imposed is called the doctrine of *respondeat superior* (let the master answer). The doctrine applies only where there was a relationship of principal and agent in existence at the time the event occurred, and in respect to the very transaction from which it arose. The doctrine is inapplicable when the agent is acting outside the scope of his or her authority.

643 Scope of Agency

In the performance of the principal's business, all of the acts of the agent are within the scope of his agency. When the agent is performing acts solely for his own purposes, he is not within the scope of his agency. In applying these rules, we should make a distinction between agents regularly employed by the principal and those agents employed for some specific purpose. As to employees, all acts performed in the course of employment designed to further the interests of the principal are within the scope of the agency. This is because, during the hours of employment and with respect to the work itself, the agent-employee is under the control of the principal-employer. Acts done by employees for their personal convenience, or for some private purpose entirely disassociated from the business of the employer, are outside the scope of the agency.

Agents employed for a specific purpose are within the scope of the agency only when they are acting for the principal within the area of their particular employment. All other acts, preliminary to or subsequent to action within the specific purpose, are outside the scope of the agency.

As to intentional torts committed while acting for the principal, the general rule is that if the intentional act is committed while serving the interest of the principal, however much of a mistake in judgment it might be, the doctrine of *respondeat superior* applies, and the principal is answerable. On the other hand, if the intentional act was neither intended to serve nor did serve the master's interest, then it is a deviation from the scope of the agency, and the principal is not answerable.

644 Deviation from the Scope of Agency

The fundamental rule under which the negligence of an agent is imputed to the principal is that, where a person does an act through another under his control, he does it himself and is responsible for the result. As long as the agent is performing his duties under the control of the principal, the agent is within the scope of his agency. When the agent performs an act for his own purposes, the element of the principal's control is lacking and therefore, until the agent returns to the control of the principal, his acts in the interim are his own. The negligence of an agent in the performance of personal acts is not attributable to the principal.

These seem fairly simple rules to apply when the personal act of the agent is entirely disassociated from the business of the principal. A difficulty arises where there is the combination of both. Let us assume that a truck driver is instructed to take a load from New York City to Albany, New York. There is no question that if the truck driver takes a reasonably direct route to Albany, all of his acts in connection therewith would be solely for the benefit of his principal, under the control of the principal, and therefore within the scope of his agency. Should an accident occur under these circumstances, the negligence of the agent would be imputed to his principal. However, let us assume that for some reason personal to himself, the truck driver decides that instead of going directly to Albany he will stop off at Stamford, in Connecticut, to attend to some of his own business and then proceed from that point to Albany. If the truck driver commits a wrongful act while en route from New York to Stamford, the cases hold that, while on this leg of the journey, the employee had abandoned his employment and was not under the control of the principal. Therefore, the risks of the highway are his own and not those of the principal.

If a negligent act is committed between Stamford and Albany, the courts are divided as to whether the principal's liability is involved. The more liberal view is that once the truck driver's personal business has been completed, at that moment, in proceeding toward Albany, he has resumed his employment. Therefore, as to any negligent act occurring between Stamford and Albany, the negligence of the agent would be imputed to the principal.

Other states have held that, until such time as the truck driver is actually back on what could be considered a direct route to Albany from New York, his deviation from the employment was still in progress.

645 Direct Liability of the Principal

The principal has been held liable for the acts of his agents to persons to whom the principal owes a duty of protection even when the agent acts outside the scope of his agency. For example, a conductor on a railroad assaults a female passenger. The railroad is required to respond in damages for the injuries to the passenger. It is clear that the act of the conductor in assaulting the passenger is outside the scope of his agency. Certainly, the railroad did not authorize or approve of the action of the conductor. However, the railroad owes a high degree of care to its passengers. It is for that reason that the railroad is responsible for the injuries. In cases where there is a special duty of protection, this liability is imposed upon the principal where the principal knew, or by the exercise of reasonable care should have known, that such conduct on the part of its agents was likely to occur.

In other cases, where the principal is under no specific duty of protection to the person injured, the principal will be liable only when he is negligent in the selection or retention of his agents. For example, a landlord employs a janitor for his apartment house. The janitor is given master keys and has the means of access to all portions of the building. The janitor has a clear employment record and has never been accused of or convicted of a criminal act of any sort. The janitor enters the apartment of a tenant and assaults a woman tenant. The landlord is not liable for the injuries to the tenant.

On the other hand, let us add to the same factual situation one additional item. Assume that the janitor had been discharged from his previous employment because of complaints by tenants that his conduct consisted of entering their apartments without authorization and attempting to molest female tenants. This fact was not known to the landlord at the time that he hired the janitor, but could have been ascertained by making reasonable inquiries. Under those circumstances, the landlord would be liable to the female tenant assaulted by the janitor. The liability is based upon the landlord's negligence in employing a janitor of this character and his failure to exercise reasonable care in the selection of such an employee.

646 Liability of Agent to Principal

The agent is liable to the principal for any damages sustained by the principal as a result of the acts of the agent amounting to (1) negligence or (2) misrepresentation, concealment, and nondisclosure.

It is fundamental in the law of torts that the tort-feasor is answerable for the legal consequences of his or her own acts. The fact that another may be vicariously liable for the acts will not absolve the tort-feasor from responsibility. Therefore, where the principal is required to respond in damages because of the negligent act of the agent, the principal is entitled to a recovery from the agent for the damages so sustained.

As between the agent and the principal, the negligence of the agent is not imputed to the principal, and the principal may recover damages from the agent for any injuries sustained by the principal as a result of the agent's negligence. The damages sustained by the principal might be bodily injury or property damage, or they might consist of business losses sustained by reason of the agent's negligent performance of his or her duty.

In all actions against the agent based on negligence, the usual defenses to negligence actions are available to the agent, such as contributory negligence of the principal and assumption of risk.

Where the agent supplies information to the principal which he or she either knows is false or has reason to believe is false, and the principal acts in reliance, the agent is liable to the principal for any losses sustained as a result. This is an intentional tort, and the rule of strict liability is imposed. The defense of contributory negligence or assumption of risk is not available. The same result will obtain where the agent is under a duty to report, and he or she conceals or fails to disclose information obtained in the course of the employment as agent.

647 Liability of Agent to Third Persons

An agent is answerable for his or her own acts to third persons just as if there were no relationship of principal and agent in existence. Merely because the injured person has a cause of action against the principal, based on vicarious liability, it does not protect or insulate the agent from responsibility. The injured person may elect to hold the agent responsible and waive any rights which she may have against the principal. She may elect to hold the principal and waive her rights against the agent, and, finally, she may (and usually does) proceed against both the agent and the principal.

An agent, in acting for the principal in dealings with third persons, impliedly warrants that he or she has the authority to act for the principal. If it should occur that the agent did not have the authority, the agent is liable to the third person for any loss sustained as a result of the reliance by the third person on the agent's warranty of authority.

648 Liability of Principal to Agent

The principal is answerable in damages for the consequence of all his or her tortious acts. The fact that the injured person is an agent of the principal will have no influence upon the principal's responsibility. The extent of the response by the principal for his or her own acts might be altered by the state workers' compensation act, in the case of agents who are employees, but, in any case, the legal requirement that the principal be answerable for his or her own tortious acts is not in any way altered or changed because of the existence of the relationship of principal and agent.

649 Ratification or Adoption of Unauthorized Acts

Sometimes agents act outside the scope of their authority. Where this happens, the principal may repudiate the transaction, or ratify or adopt the agent's action. In the first case, the principal is not bound by the acts of the agent. Where the principal has adopted or ratified the act of the agent, the principal in effect has waived any defect in the agent's authority and is therefore bound by the act of the agent just as if the agent had actual authority to so act.

For example, an insurance company and an insurance agency terminate their contract of agency by mutual consent. Therefore, the insurance agent has no further authority to represent this particular insurance company. However, the agent does issue an insurance policy for the company, collects the premium, and remits the premium to the company. The acceptance and retention of the premium payment by the company will amount to a ratification or adoption of the agent's act in issuing the policy. Therefore, the company is estopped from denying the agent's authority to issue the policy. The agent had apparent authority to issue the policy, even though he or she had no actual authority to do so. On the other hand, if the company had immediately returned the premium and notified both the agent and prospective insured of the lack of authority on the part of the agent, then no contract of insurance would result, and there would be no ratification.

BAILMENTS

NATURE OF BAILMENTS

650 Bailments Defined

A *bailment* is the delivery of personal property by the owner to another for some specific purpose, on an express or implied contract. There is an understanding that, after the purpose has been fulfilled the property will be returned to the owner, or otherwise dealt with according to the specific purpose to be accomplished. It contemplates situations where title and ownership of the property will be retained by the owner. The owner who transfers possession is called the *bailor*, and the person to whom the possession is transferred is called the *bailee*. While the subject matter of a bailment can be any type of tangible personal property, the claim representative will be concerned for the most part with automobiles and other property which may be involved in accidents while in the hands of a bailee.

To constitute a bailment, there must be (1) a voluntary transfer of possession by the owner to another person, and (2) an acceptance of possession by the other person. For example, if a woman entered a restaurant and hung her coat on a hook provided for that purpose and, while she was eating, the coat disappeared, the action would not constitute a bailment. The owner had not transferred possession of her coat to the restaurant keeper, and the restaurant keeper did not accept possession.

Let us use the same facts again but add that, when the woman entered the restaurant, she handed her coat to a waiter, asking him to check it for her. Upon finishing her meal and requesting her coat, she was informed by the waiter that it was missing from the hook where the waiter had hung it. The delivery of the coat to the waiter constituted a bailment because it involved a transfer of possession of the coat. The difference between the first situation and this one is that in the first case, irrespective of the intention of the owner of the coat, there was no actual transfer of possession from the owner to the restaurant keeper. Furthermore, there was no acceptance of possession by the restaurant keeper. Thus, the two necessary elements of a bailment were lacking. In the second case, there was an actual transfer of possession as well as an acceptance of possession by the waiter, and, therefore, the requirements of a bailment were fulfilled.

Where there is a bailment, the bailee is required to return the property to the bailor, and he is liable in damages if he fails to do so. Where there is no bailment, clearly no liability to respond in damages can arise.

1. Bailment as Distinguished from a Sale or Exchange. One of the essential elements of a bailment contract is that it contemplates that the identical property in the same or in an appropriately altered state be returned to the owner. Fungible goods, such as grain delivered to a warehouse or grain elevator, are the exceptions to this situation. When the grain is so deposited, it is not contemplated by the contract or custom that the bailee shall return the identical grain stored, but only an equal amount of grain of the same kind and grade from the comixed mass. The contract is still a bailment. In all other cases, to constitute a bailment, the contract must contemplate the return of the identical property.

2. Bailment as Distinguished from Custody. The employer provides tools to be used by his employee in the course of the employment. As to these tools, the employee is not a bailee. He has mere custody of his employer's property while acting as the agent of the employer in the course and scope of his employment. Possession by an agent within the scope of his agency is the possession of the principal. Therefore, the possession of the tools never was transferred by the owner or employer. For that reason the transaction is not a bailment.

3. Bailment as Distinguished from Rental of Space. This subject will come up most frequently with respect to automobile parking lots. If the owner of an automobile transfers possession of his vehicle to the operator of an automobile parking lot, by giving him the keys to the vehicle, or permitting him to move the vehicle from place to place while it is on the parking lot, the transaction is a bailment.

On the other hand, some parking lot operators seek to escape the liability of a bailee with respect to parked automobiles by merely renting the parking space to the automobile owner. In these cases, the automobile owner parks and locks his car himself, and retains the keys. The parking lot operator does not have any control over the vehicle while it is in the rental space, and, under those circumstances, there is no bailment.

4. Bailment as Distinguished from Theft or Conversion. The relationship of bailor and bailee can never exist between the owner of the property and a thief. The essential element missing from such a transaction is the voluntary relinquishment of possession of the property by the owner. The owner is entitled to the return of the property irrespective of the person who has possession of it and irrespective of the circumstances under which that person received the property. Let us assume that a thief stole a valuable diamond ring from the owner. The thief pledged it to a pawnbroker. The owner of the ring is entitled to possession of the ring and is not required to reimburse the pawnbroker for the amount of money which she had advanced to the thief on the security of the ring.

The taking of a chattel from the owner without legal justification, and with the intention of exercising dominion or ownership over it, is a *conversion*. The wrongful taking or wrongful use of a chattel, without the consent of the owner, amounts to a tort and will subject the tort-feasor to liability for damages. To constitute a conversion, the chattel does not have to be taken from the owner's actual possession. (See also Section 403.)

For example, an employee is given a company-owned car to be used solely on company business. If the employee should use the car for personal errands, such an act would constitute a conversion. The mere fact that the employee returns the automobile to her employer, or that she uses the automobile in an authorized manner after her personal errand has been accomplished, will not in any way change the nature of the transaction.

In this example, the person converting the property to her own use is liable to the true owner for the full value of the use of it, for any damage which may have occurred to the chattel, and for any diminution in value which might have occurred as a result of such use. To recover, the owner would not have to show a negligent act or lack of due care. The owner's case would be established merely by showing that the chattel was used in an unauthorized manner and that he or she had sustained damage as a consequence. In contrast, the bailee is liable to the bailor only when damage occurs to the bailed property through his or her negligence.

LIABILITIES IN BAILMENT SITUATIONS

651 Kinds of Bailments

Bailments are classified according to the purpose for which they arise, and the obligations between the parties are governed by the class in which the bailment falls. The classifications are as follows:

1. Bailments for the sole benefit of the bailor.
2. Bailments for the sole benefit of the bailee.
3. Bailments for the benefit of both bailor and bailee.

The average person in the course of a lifetime is involved in many contracts of bailment. If she permits a friend to park his automobile in her driveway or backyard, or to leave some property in her possession for storage, with no charge for this service, this would be an example of a bailment for the sole benefit of the bailor. On the other hand, if the woman borrows her neighbor's lawn mower, tools, or other appliances for temporary use for her own benefit, a bailment would be implied while such articles are in her possession. This is an example of a bailment for the sole benefit of the bailee or borrower. It is contemplated that the same article will be returned in the same condition as it is received.

If the woman took her clothing to a dry cleaner for the purpose of having it cleaned and pressed, this would be a bailment. It is contemplated that the property will be returned in an altered state but that the same property will be returned. For a price, the bailee agrees to exercise his skill in accomplishing the objective of cleaning. This is an example of a bailment for the benefit of both bailee and bailor. It is also referred to as a *mutual benefit bailment* for the reason that both parties profit from the arrangement.

652 Degrees of Care Required

The classification into which the bailment falls will determine the degree of care required of the bailee. These classifications are as follows:

1. For the Sole Benefit of the Bailor. In this class the bailee receives no compensation for the deposit of the goods on his or her property, and therefore owes to the bailor a slight degree of care. This has been defined as the duty of refraining from the commission of any act which would damage the property. The bailee is responsible only for his own wrongdoing, and, if he commits any act which does damage to the property while it is on his premises, this will impose a liability. The bailee, however, is not liable for failure to act. He is under no duty to protect the property from the weather or to perform any other act for its preservation. He is liable only if his own active wrongdoing results in damage to the bailed property.

2. For the Sole Benefit of the Bailee. In this class of bailments, the bailee owes a high degree of care to the bailor and is liable for any loss caused by slight negligence on his or her part.

This, however, does not mean that the bailee is responsible under all circumstances where the property is damaged or lost. He is liable only if his lack of care played some part in the loss or damage to the property. If he meets his obligation and, in spite of the exercise of a high degree of care, the property is damaged or lost, the bailee is not responsible. Should the property be stolen or taken away without any negligence or lack of the high degree of care imposed, the bailee will not be liable for the loss or damage. A borrower of property is not an insurer of it, even when it is gratuitously lent.

3. Those for the Benefit of Both Bailor and Bailee. The bailee is required to exercise ordinary care, which means such care as the ordinary, prudent person would exercise in caring for his or her own property under like circumstances.

653 Liability, Bailor to Bailee

The bailor is not an insurer or guarantor of the safety of the bailed property. He or she likewise is not liable for injuries from known risks assumed by the bailee. The bailor is answerable in damages only where he or she has knowledge of a defect which constitutes an unreasonable risk of harm and fails to disclose the existence of such defect to the bailee, or where by the exercise of reasonable care, in the form of inspection, the bailor would and should have discovered a harmful defect but did not ascertain its existence.

654 Liability, Bailee to Third Persons

The liability of the bailee arising out of the maintenance or use of a bailed article, be it an automobile, a horse, or machinery, is the same as if the bailee were the actual owner of the property. The bailor's liability to third persons would rest in tort, and the bailee would be responsible for his or her own negligence in operating or using the particular article. Liability would be the same whether it was a gratuitous bailment or one for hire. While it is true that the bailee may have an action over against the bailor for the bailor's failure to supply an article without defects, or for the failure of the bailor to warn the bailee of defects of which the bailor had knowledge, this would not in any way affect the bailee's responsibility to third persons.

655 Liability, Bailor to Third Persons

In the case of gratuitous bailments, the few available cases hold that there is no greater obligation on the part of the bailor toward a third person than there would be to his or her immediate bailee. Therefore, when there is a borrowed or lent article, and no compensation is paid for the use thereof, the bailor has no duty to the bailee with respect to warning of known defects or to inspection of the appliance.

This duty is no greater when a third person, other than the bailee, is injured. Therefore, in cases involving gratuitous bailments, it can be said that the bailor has no liability to a third person who is injured as a consequence of the use of the article by the gratuitous bailee.

The law of torts teaches us that, where one person places a dangerous instrumentality in the hands of another who is unfamiliar with its use or incapable of exercising care in its use, he or she is liable to anyone injured as a result of the use of the dangerous article. (See also Section 411.) For example, if a person gives a gun to a child, who is obviously incompetent in the use of firearms, the person supplying the gun would be liable to anyone suffering injury as a consequence of its use. This responsibility, however, does not arise out of the contract of bailment. It arises because of the duty on the part of the owner of the gun to use reasonable care in its use, and this duty runs to anyone injured as a result of the use of the firearm.

Along the same lines, a gratuitous bailor of an automobile has been held liable where he or she knowingly entrusted the use of the vehicle to an inexperienced, intoxicated, or habitually careless driver and the accident, involving an injury to a third person, was proximately caused by the negligence of such a driver. Also, a gratuitous bailor will be liable if he or she knowingly transfers the possession and use of a vehicle which is unfit to drive because it has no brakes or is otherwise seriously defective. This liability will extend to third persons injured as a result of the use of such a vehicle.

A bailor for hire is subject to these same responsibilities; in addition he or she has a duty of making reasonable inspection of the vehicle, not only for the safety of third persons but also for the safety of the bailee.

656 Liability, Third Person to Bailee

One of the quirks of the common law, based on an early case, is that where the chattel is wrongfully damaged while in the possession of a bailee, only the bailee may sue and recover from the wrongdoer, not only for the value of his interest but also for the entire loss. The bailee, whose interest is usually very small in contrast to that of the bailor, may sue without the knowledge or consent of the bailor for the full value of the damages to the bailed property caused by the tort-feasor.

A recovery by the bailee for the full value of the damage will preclude another and further suit by the bailor for any damages whatsoever, since, from the standpoint of the tort-feasor, he "cannot be vexed twice for the same wrong."

In any case where the claim representative is faced with a claim by the bailee, he or she should first ascertain whether the bailee has a right to the possession of the chattel, and also check whatever contractual limitations there may be on the right to recovery.

657 Liability, Third Person to Bailor

The common-law rule, as noted above, applies to the person who has the immediate right of possession. If the bailor has a right to demand possession at once, then the bailor, and not the bailee, may maintain an action for damages against the tort-feasor.

In an action brought by the bailee against the tort-feasor, the defense of contributory negligence of the bailee may be interposed, and, if it is sustained, it is a complete defense at common law to the action by the bailee. However, in an action by the bailor against the tort-feasor, the contributory negligence of the bailee generally is not imputed to the bailor, and the defense of the bailee's contributory negligence may not be interposed against the bailor. Some states have modified the common-law rule by statute, permitting the contributory negligence of the bailee to be interposed as a proper and valid defense to an action brought by the bailor.

Some states have statutes which impose vicarious liability on the owner of a motor vehicle where the vehicle is being used by another with the owner's consent, express or implied. These statutes impute the negligence of the driver to the owner.

658 Limitation of Liability

In the absence of an agreement to the contrary, with respect to the liability of the bailee for damage to the goods while in his or her possession, the bailee is liable to the bailor for any loss or damage caused by his or her negligence. The parties may enter into any contract they desire, and such a contract can provide for a maximum amount for which the bailee would be responsible in the event of damage or loss. This must be the subject matter of a contract, and both parties must have knowledge of and agree to such terms.

It frequently happens that a bailee, operating an automobile parking lot, a checkroom, or a dry cleaning establishment will attempt to limit his liability by the posting of notices on the premises to the effect that he is not responsible for goods left over 30 days, or that in the event of loss the maximum liability shall be $50, or similar types of limitation.

It is fundamental in the law of contracts that, for the limitations to be an effective element of the contract, both parties must mutually assent to the terms. Where notices are posted, the limitation of liability will not be effective unless it is shown that the bailor had actual knowledge of the limitation and delivered his property to the bailee upon the terms of limitation. In the absence of knowledge on the part of the bailor and his or her agreement to the terms, the notices, however conspicuously posted, will not effectively limit the liability of the bailee.

659 Conversion or Unauthorized Use by the Bailee

The contract of bailment requires that the bailee perform in accordance with its terms. If the contract contemplates storage of the goods at a certain place, the bailee is bound to store the goods at that place. If the contract contemplates that the bailee will exercise some process in connection with the goods, she may exercise that process and no other. She may not use the goods for her own purposes, nor may she use any different process than that which was agreed upon. If she performs any of these unauthorized acts, her action amounts to a conversion, and she is responsible to the bailor for any loss or damage.

660 Exculpatory Contracts as Applied to Bailments

The general rule in contract is that the parties to the contract may include within its term any agreements to which they are mutually agreed. While the parties may make any contract they desire, any provisions which violate public policy will have no legal effect. Therefore, it would seem that a bailor and bailee could agree in the contract of bailment that, in the event of loss due to the bailee's negligence, the bailor waives in advance any cause of action that he or she may have to recover for such damage.

Unfortunately, the courts are not in agreement with respect to this legal proposition. Some take the position that it is against public policy for one party to contract away liability for his or her own negligence, and others take the position that, if the parties involved are private parties and the general public is not involved, they may make any contract they wish, providing that both parties to the contract bargain on equal terms.

For example, if a public utility, having the exclusive franchise in a given locality to supply gas for heating, rented heating appliances to its customers and had a provision in the rental contract absolving the public utility from liability arising out of the negligent acts of its agents or servants, all courts would agree that such a provision is void as being against public policy. The public utility is a business which is affected with the public interest. The customer could deal only with the public utility in order to obtain the required service, and could not obtain the same service from any other source. The parties did not bargain on equal terms, and the public utility, because of the nature of its public duty, is precluded from contracting away its liability for negligence.

On the other hand, two private parties might agree that the bailment contract was merely one of storage, and that the bailee was relieved of any liability arising out of the loss or damage to the goods due to freezing, water damage, or any other specific peril, whether the bailee was negligent or not. This would seem to be a proper provision of the contract, and the public interest would not be involved in any way. In this case, the bailee will be absolved of liability because of the terms of the contract.

661 Innkeepers' Liability

In feudal times there was little or no police protection afforded to travelers on the highway. Outlaws were numerous, and the traveler and his property were in jeopardy when on the open highway. They therefore traveled in groups or caravans in order to afford mutual self-protection. At nightfall, the travelers sought protection and lodging at an inn. The inn was required not only to furnish accommodations for the traveler himself, but also stable room and provender for the traveler's horses or cattle. The primary purpose of travel in those days was to bring products to market, which might consist of grain or animals. Therefore, the traveler often carried with him a certain amount of valuable personal property. It would be easy for the innkeeper to conspire with outlaws to relieve the guest of his property during the nighttime hours.

To meet this contingency, the courts imposed the rule of strict liability upon the innkeeper with respect to the guest's property. This rule made the innkeeper an insurer of the guest's property while the relationship of innkeeper and guest continued. This means that if the guest's property was lost or damaged, from any cause whatsoever, the innkeeper was liable. This has no reference to the negligence of the innkeeper, and his liability attached whether he had anything to do with the loss or damage to the property or not.

There were three situations in which the innkeeper would be relieved of this responsibility: (1) an act of God, (2) an act of the public enemy, and (3) negligence of the guest, his servant, or companion.

It is clear that the innkeeper could not provide protection against an act of God, such as a hurricane, storm, flood, or lightning. Likewise, he could not provide protection for the guest from the actions of another nation with whom his nation is at war. It is also clear that the innkeeper should not be responsible for any loss or damage occasioned by the guest's own neglect of his property or the act of the guest's servants or companions.

An inn has been defined as a house where a traveler is furnished with everything the traveler needs while on his or her way. It is a house where all who conduct themselves properly and who are able and ready to pay their entertainment are received if there are accommodations for them, and who, without any stipulated engagements as to the duration of their stay, or as to the rate of compensation are, while there, supplied at a reasonable charge with their meals, their lodging, and such services and attention as are necessarily incident to the use of the house as a temporary home. An inn is synonymous with hotel, motel, or a place for the entertainment of travelers, where all their wants as travelers can be supplied. A restaurant where meals only are furnished is not an inn.

The innkeeper's liability as an insurer of the property of guests has been modified in some states by statute. The statutes usually provide that where the inn maintains a safe on the premises for the deposit of certain valuables, such as jewelry, precious stones, negotiable instruments, money, and certificates, and the availability of the safe is brought to the attention of the guest (either by printed notice in each room or a printed notice placed in a conspicuous place in the public rooms of the inn), the liability of the innkeeper for the loss of articles of this type, not deposited in the safe, is limited to a certain sum of money, such as $500. This means merely that where the articles mentioned in the statute are actually deposited in the safe, the innkeeper's liability as an insurer remains.

662 Liability of Common Carriers

Common carriers are defined as those who hold themselves out or undertake to carry persons or goods of any and all persons who choose to employ them.

Common carriers of passengers are those that undertake to carry all persons who may apply for passage, so long as there is room, and there is no legal excuse for a refusal. In this classification we would include airlines, railroads, public buses, taxicabs, subways, and trolley cars. Also included within the classification of common carriers of passengers would be elevators in buildings open to the public, escalators, and even a roller coaster in an amusement park.

Common carriers of property include airfreight lines, railroads, trucking companies, elevators, and express companies.

A common carrier of property is an insurer of the property it carries. It is liable if the property is damaged in any way while in transit or is delivered in a damaged condition at the point of destination. This liability as an insurer is subject to only five exceptions: (1) an act of God, (2) an act of the public enemy, (3) the inherent vice of the goods, (4) an act of a public authority, or (5) neglect on the part of the shipper.

An act of God would include a tornado, hurricane, earthquake, lightning, and the like. To absolve the common carrier from liability, the loss of the goods or the damage to the goods must be occasioned entirely by an act of God, and without any concurrent act on the part of the common carrier. The act of a public enemy would refer to belligerent action by a nation with whom we are at war. The third exception refers to the nature of the goods carried, in the sense that they are perishable or explosive, and such fact was not made known to the carrier by the shipper.

The common carrier may limit the amount of its liability in the event of loss or damage. This can be accomplished by a specific agreement made prior to acceptance of the shipment. However, the carrier cannot by agreement escape liability as an insurer of the goods while in its possession.

With respect to common carriers of passengers, the carrier owes a high degree of care for the safety of its passengers. A high degree of care is not the legal equivalent of ordinary care. It means something involving care and caution in excess of what would be exercised by the ordinary prudent person under the same or similar circumstances. It has been defined as that degree of care which a very cautious, careful, and prudent person would exercise. It is for the jury to decide, in a proper case, whether the carrier has exercised that degree of care which the law imposes upon it in the exercise of its business.

663 Exculpatory Contracts, Common Carriers

It frequently happens that a common carrier, usually a railroad, will issue a gratuitous pass to employees and/or their families, clergymen, and others upon the express agreement that the carrier will have no responsibility to the passenger in accidents caused by its negligence. The courts, generally, have upheld agreements of this sort, some on the theory that, where a gratuitous passage is given, the relationship of the common carrier and passenger does not exist, and others on the theory that since there was a gift or a reduced rate allowed, the donor could affix to the gift any conditions that it chose. Normally, courts will not uphold exculpatory contracts where one of the parties is at a bargaining disadvantage. But here, arguably, the parties bargained on equal terms. The passenger could pay full fare for this transportation and the relationship of common carrier, with its attendant liabilities, would ensue. Taking advantage of the gift, the passenger must accept the terms on which it is offered.

664 Private Carriers

A private carrier is one which does not hold itself out to the general public as a carrier for all who may employ it. It does transportation work only for such private individuals, firms, or corporations with whom it has made a contract. A private carrier is not bound to accept all contracts of carriage that are offered, and it may refuse employment if it does not regard the contract as being desirable. The liability of the private carrier is governed by the rules of ordinary negligence, both as to persons and property. A private carrier may, however, assume greater liability by means of a contract, but in the absence of any contractual assumption of liability, it is responsible only for personal injuries or property damage caused by ordinary negligence on its part.

It is possible for a common carrier to become a private carrier in certain specific instances, as a consequence of a private carrier contract made with a specific person, firm, or corporation. For example, a bus normally used for public transportation can be chartered by a private individual, firm, corporation, club, or other group for one specific purpose.

Chapter 7

Law of Products

700 Products Liability Generally
701 Early Concepts
702 Elimination of the Privity Requirement
703 Effect of the Elimination of Privity
704 Liability of the Retailer for Negligence
705 Liability of the Retailer for Breach of Warranty
706 Liability of the Manufacturer or Distributor for Breach of Warranty
707 Duties of the Manufacturer
708 Duty of Safe Design
709 Duty to Warn
710 Identification of Manufacturer
711 Strict Liability for Retailers and Manufacturers
712 A Seller Engaged in the Business
713 Defective Condition
714 An Unreasonable Danger
715 User or Consumer
716 Physical Harm
717 Defenses: Use of Product for Unintended Purpose
718 Defenses: Contributory Negligence
719 Defenses: Allergy and Susceptibility
720 Defenses: Third Party's Conduct
721 Defenses: State of the Art
722 Defenses: Government Specifications
723 Defenses: Disclaimers
724 Defenses: Statute of Limitations
725 Indemnity and Contribution
726 Long-Arm Statutes
727 Products Liability Investigation
728 Plan of Investigation

700 Products Liability Generally

Products liability refers to the responsibility arising out of the manufacture, distribution, and sale of allegedly defective or dangerous products and the alleged failure of the manufacturer, distributor, or retailer to meet the duties which the law imposes with respect to the particular product.

Caveat emptor, "Let the buyer beware," was the original rule of the marketplace. In the distant past, the merchandise offered for sale consisted primarily of the natural products of the soil or simple manufactured products. The buyer could and did inspect the articles, and in that way he could gain as much knowledge of the products as the seller himself had. The buyer did not rely on the expertise of the seller, but entirely upon what his own inspection of the article revealed. He saw what he bought and he bought what he saw. If he bought a defective product, he had only himself to blame. Should the buyer seek to hold the seller responsible for selling the defective article, he could be confronted with the defense of contributory negligence, because the buyer had as much opportunity to ascertain the defective condition as did the seller. Thus, in the beginning, the common-law courts applied the rule of *caveat emptor* to virtually all sales.

As products became more complicated, it was possible for the seller, by packaging or coloring, to deceive the buyer by offering an inferior and defective product in place of one of merchantable quality. In such situations, the courts permitted the buyer to bring a tort action based on the seller's deceit, taking the position that the seller was under a duty to offer a product of merchantable quality (that is, one that would compare favorably with other products of like kind found on the market). While most of the early actions were based on tort liability, some courts referred to this duty of the seller as a ''warranty'' of merchantability, using a term which is usually referable to contracts in describing a tort action.

This chapter offers a fairly detailed discussion of the law of products liability and how it developed to its present stages. At the outset, a brief overview of this dynamic area of the law may be helpful to the reader.

Through the first half of this century, only a handful of cases in the courts involved questions of products liability. Today, these suits number many thousands per year. Products liability has become and continues to be one of the most expansive and most litigated areas of tort law. The courts today commonly assume that manufacturers and sellers of products are in the best position to absorb the costs of product-related injuries.

There are several extra-legal reasons for this increase in products liability claims and lawsuits:

1. Modern technology has placed (and will continue to place) an ever-increasing number and variety of products on the market.
2. The public is becoming more conscious of its opportunity to sue if damages are suffered because of a product-connected accident.
3. A social philosophy favoring the consumer, which also favors expansion of tort remedies.

Evidence of this changing social philosophy is found in the expansion of legal theories: (1) the defense of ''lack of privity,'' the rule which requires a special contractual relation between the parties, has been scaled back and limited to a few special situations; (2) disclaimers of liability have been severely restricted in application, as the courts and legislatures impose liability by law, rather than permitting its apportionment by agreement between contracting parties; (3) courts have widely espoused the theory of strict liability of the manufacturer for defects in his products regardless of how careful he has been or whether he could have avoided such defects by the exercise of reasonable care; (4) jurisdiction of the state courts has been extended by ''long-arm'' statutes, often allowing plaintiffs to choose the most advantageous and sympathetic legal forum.

The organized plaintiffs' bar supports the movement to expand theories of products liability recovery. Their motto, "sue for safety," is predicated on the theory that lawsuits will promote safer products. They urge courts and legislatures to recognize the social responsibility of the manufacturer to pay regardless of fault, and the social responsibility of courts to impose liability on manufacturers as a form of financial pressure, rather than on the basis of responsibility for negligent conduct.

All of the factors mentioned above lead to greater operating costs to the manufacturer and higher prices to the consumer. The manufacturer's loss costs, including insurance premiums, have increased tremendously during the past few years. Increased jury verdicts, higher medical costs, and expanded concepts of tort liability have transformed products liability claims cost from a minor administrative item into a major factor requiring executive attention. The cost of liability for injuries involving manufactured products is reflected ultimately in the cost of those products. The domestic manufacturer may find itself at a competitive disadvantage with respect to foreign manufacturers. The foreign competitor may, to some degree, be able to avoid jurisdiction of local courts and compliance with safety regulations and standards to which the domestic producer is subject.

In response to these trends, many states in recent years have enacted products liability tort reform legislation. These laws are designed to counter the pro-plaintiff "tilt" that has become characteristic of the common law of products liability. The general thrust of this legislation—as well as federal legislation which has been considered (but not passed) by Congress—is to enhance stability and predictability in the law and to lighten the legal burdens of product manufacturers and sellers.

Liability in products cases usually results from the application of the legal doctrines of negligence, breach of warranty, or strict liability in tort.

There are essentially two different theories under which a manufacturer may be liable for negligence: (1) design of the product, and (2) its manufacture. A product may fail because it was not properly designed. On the other hand, although it is designed properly, it may cause harm because it is constructed of inferior materials or improperly assembled.

Under strict liability theories in products cases, the plaintiff need not prove negligence or establish privity of contract. Imposition of strict liability, in effect, extends liability to cover the sale of any product which, if defective, may be expected to cause harm to the ultimate consumer or user or to his property.

Two legal theories have been used by the courts to enforce strict liability: warranty and tort. A warranty is a representation, expressed or implied, referring to the character or quality of an item sold. A warranty arises primarily out of a contract of sale and entitles the buyer to obtain relief from the seller. In any action based upon warranty, it is necessary to prove the existence of the warranty, that the warranty was breached, and that the breach was the proximate cause of the injury sustained. The tort rule of strict liability requires the claimant to prove that the product was in a defective condition (unreasonably dangerous to the consumer or user) when it left the seller's control and that the defect caused the claimant's injury while it was being properly used for a purpose reasonably foreseeable by the seller.

701 Early Concepts

The early cases turned on the relationship of the parties as being determinative of whether any duty existed. Unless the parties had some relationship to the transaction, or were in privity with each other, the courts declined to recognize an existing duty. One of the earliest cases, *Winterbottom* v. *Wright* [10 Meeson & Welsby 109], decided in 1842, is illustrative of this concept. In that case an action was brought by a mail-coach driver against a contractor who had contracted with the postmaster-general to provide and keep in repair the mail coach. It was claimed that the contractor so disregarded his duties as to place an unsafe coach on the road, which overturned and injured the plaintiff. In holding that the plaintiff's complaint did not state a maintainable cause of action, the court said:

> There is no privity of contract between these parties; and if the plaintiff can sue, every passenger, or even any person passing along the road, who was injured by the upsetting of the coach, might bring a similar action. Unless we confine the operation of such contracts as this to the parties who entered into them, the most absurd and outrageous consequences, to which I can see no limit, would ensue.

In the landmark case of *MacPherson* v. *Buick Motor Co.* [217 N.Y. 382; 111 N.E. 105 (New York Court of Appeals)], the plaintiff was injured when a spoke wheel on the automobile crumbled while the automobile was being operated. The automobile was bought from a dealer, and there was no privity of contract between the plaintiff and the manufacturer. The court held that an automobile defectively made was an *inherently dangerous instrumentality* and this fact justified an exception to the privity requirement.

It might be noted that one of the defenses urged by the defendant was that it had not manufactured the wheel, but had purchased it from a reputable and competent manufacturer. The court held that the manufacturer of the finished product is under a duty of inspection, and if it put a finished product on the market which is defective, it is liable even though some component part not manufactured by it is negligently made.

In summary, the early cases established the rule that, if there was privity of contract between the parties, the injured plaintiff could bring an action in tort based upon negligence or deceit, or bring an action for breach of contract based upon the failure of the seller to meet the contract specifications. If there was no privity of contract between the parties, the injured party could not maintain a cause of action unless the facts of the case brought it within either of the following two exceptions:

1. The product involved imminent danger to the lives of others if it were negligently labeled (for example, poison or explosives), or became hazardous if defectively made (for example, automobiles).
2. The product was dangerous to the life and limb of anyone who may use it, and the manufacturer or supplier, having knowledge of this danger, failed to give notice of the danger.

702 Elimination of the Privity Requirement

In recent years many of our courts have had occasion to reexamine the privity requirement set down in the *Winterbottom* case as well as the exceptions to that requirement in cases where the product was ''inherently dangerous'' to life and limb. The majority of the states which have considered the problem, either by legislation or court decisions, have eliminated the privity requirement as an element of a cause of action against the manufacturer, distributor, or retailer arising out of the sale of a defective product.

703 Effect of the Elimination of Privity

It should be emphasized that the elimination of the privity requirement merely gives a broader class of plaintiff the legal capacity to sue the manufacturer. In order to recover, or even to have the claim submitted to a jury, the plaintiff must make out a prima facie case either of negligence, breach of warranty, or strict liability. In other words, the plaintiff's obligation is to present sufficient evidence to raise a presumption in favor of the plaintiff's position, unless or until rebutted by the defense.

704 Liability of the Retailer for Negligence

Since the retailer is in privity of contract with the buyer, there is no impediment in the way of the buyer maintaining an action against the retailer for damages sustained as a result of the retailer's negligence. If the retailer is to be charged with negligence, it must be because of his or her failure to meet some duty owed to the buyer. The duties are few, since the retailer is merely the conduit through which the product finds its way from the manufacturer to the consumer. Unless the nature of the product or the duties assumed by the retailer require that the retailer exercise care, he or she is under no duty to do so. Retailers have been held liable for negligence in the following categories:

1. Failure to inspect or test the product.
2. Failure to warn of the dangers of the product.
3. Failure to properly assemble the product.

4. Negligent sales.
5. Sales in violation of a statute.

1. Failure to Inspect or Test the Product. Ordinarily the retailer is under no duty to inspect or test the product. This is especially true in the cases of a product sold in a sealed container, such as tin cans, bottles, and other types of containers. It is clear that it would be unreasonable to expect the retailer to open and test each sealed container, and it is obvious, because of the buying habits of the public, that the retailer would have difficulty in selling any product which had been subjected to such testing. There is one exception referable to the automobile business, which includes automobile agencies as well as used car dealers. Such retailers have been held liable for their failure to test and inspect their products before sale when subsequent facts revealed that defects were present which a reasonable inspection would have uncovered. With respect to other products, the cases generally hold that the retailer who purchases the article from a reputable manufacturer is under no duty to inspect it, and is not liable even in cases where an inspection might have revealed a defect. There is also a line of cases holding that the retailer is under no duty to inspect and test for the purpose of discovering latent defects.

Where the retailer sells a reconditioned product and guarantees that it "is as good as new" or that it is "safe to use," such a retailer is under a duty to inspect. If the retailer fails to do so, and a defective condition causes an accident, the seller is negligent and consequently liable to the purchaser.

2. Failure to Warn of the Dangers of the Product. Whether there is a duty to warn on the part of the retailer depends upon the nature of the product and the retailer's knowledge of the danger. If the product is one which as a matter of common knowledge is dangerous, then the retailer has no more information than does the buyer, and consequently the retailer may have no duty to warn the buyer. It is only where the retailer has knowledge of the danger and has reason to believe that the purchaser will not discover the danger that the retailer has a duty to warn. This duty can normally be met by adequate labeling.

The age and intelligence of the buyer will have some influence upon whether there is a duty to warn. If the retailer knows or has reason to know that, because of his or her age or intelligence the buyer is not aware of the dangers of the product and the retailer had such knowledge, the retailer must warn of the danger.

Where it is established that there is a duty to warn, the question of the retailer's liability will turn on the question of whether the warning was adequate or not. If no warning was given, then the retailer is liable for any injuries sustained as a consequence of failure to do so. If the warning was given but it was inadequate in the sense that it was not conspicuously placed on the package, was not large enough, or was not readable, or was not adequate to warn of the nature of the hazard, the retailer is likewise liable. For example, in *Tampa Drug Co.* v. *Wait* [103 So. 2d 603 (Florida)], the label warned that the vapor of the carbon tetrachloride purchased was harmful and that prolonged breathing of it or repeated contact with the skin should be avoided and that the product should be used with adequate ventilation. The purchaser used the product to clean the floors of his home. Several days later he died of carbon tetrachloride poisoning. The court held the defendant liable on the theory that, since the warning did not call attention to the deadly effects or the potentially fatal consequences which might follow the use of the product, the warning was inadequate. On the other hand, a warning ''Caution: do not use near fire or flame'' and a further warning, ''Use in a well-ventilated area. Do not smoke, extinguish all pilot lights'' was held to be adequate for the purpose of warning the purchaser of the danger of using an adhesive product. *Moschkau* v. *Sears, Roebuck & Co.* [282 Fed. 2d 878 (7th Cir.)].

3. Failure to Properly Assemble the Product. Where the retailer assembles, or assembles and installs the product, he is under a duty to the purchaser to exercise care in so doing. This would mean that he would have to follow the manufacturer's assembly instructions or installation instructions, but, more important, he would have to test and inspect the completed article.

4. Negligent Sales. Where the retailer delivers a dangerous product in place of a comparatively safe product, which was ordered, and the substitution cannot be detected upon reasonable inspection, the retailer will be liable for the resulting damage. Many of the cases in this category involve pharmacists who failed to deliver the product called for in a prescription and substituted some other ingredient, which the pharmacist knew or should have known was dangerous to the purchaser. Also in this category, we can include sales made to persons who, because of their age or condition, are not in a position to appreciate the dangers of the product sold. Thus, where the retailer sold gasoline to a child [*Clark* v. *Ticehurst,* 271 Pac. 2d 295 (Kansas)] and where a retailer-druggist sold carbolic acid to a man in such a state of intoxication that he could not appreciate the danger and died as a result of drinking it [*Bennet Drug Stores, Inc.*, 20 S.E. 2d 208 (Georgia)], the retailers were held liable for the resulting injuries.

5. Sales in Violation of a Statute. Generally, a sale made in violation of a statute or ordinance is negligence per se, and the retailer is liable if the person injured is within the class of persons the statute or ordinance was designed to protect. The majority of the cases in this category arise under pure food laws where the vendor has sold contaminated food which was unfit for human consumption and thus was in violation of the statute.

Most states have either statutes or regulations of an alcohol beverage control commission, which have the force of law, making the sale of intoxicants to a minor or a visibly intoxicated person unlawful. Such a sale is negligence per se, and the purchaser may recover for injuries received as a consequence of the unlawful sale. (As to the retailer's liability to persons not purchasers, see Section 409, Dram Shop Acts, above.)

705 Liability of the Retailer for Breach of Warranty

The parties to a contract of sale, like the parties to any other type of contracts, may mutually agree to any terms and conditions they desire. The party who breaches the contract may have to respond in damages to the other. In the early cases involving sales where there was no express warranty or guarantee in the contract itself, the rule of *caveat emptor* was applied with no warranty or guarantee implied from the nature of the transaction. Later, as commercial transactions multiplied, the courts recognized that the seller had superior knowledge of the ingredients of the article, and the quality of the article with respect to its salability and its fitness for the particular purpose for which it was bought. Therefore, where there was a contract of sale, the courts imposed the obligation on the seller to warrant or guarantee certain things about the article sold which were implied from the nature of the transaction, even without any specific agreement between the parties with reference to it. The implied warranties are (1) warranty of title, (2) warranty of merchantability, and (3) warranty of fitness for a particular purpose. These are described as follows:

1. Warranty of Title. When an article is offered for sale, the seller guarantees that he has title and ownership, or that he has been authorized by the owner to pass good and sufficient title. The purchaser is not required to trace the chain of ownership from the manufacturer to the seller, but may rely on this implied warranty.

2. Warranty of Merchantability. This has come to mean a guarantee that the goods are of such quality as to meet the description specified in the agreement, and are reasonably fit for the ordinary uses to which such goods are put. Courts equate merchantability with "salability." If goods do not meet the ordinary tests of the marketplace for goods of similar kind, they would be unmarketable and not within the scope of the unexpressed intention of both parties.

3. Warranty of Fitness for a Particular Purpose. This implied warranty came in logical sequence to the preceding warranty, and means generally that "if a person sold a commodity for a particular purpose, he must be understood to warrant it reasonably fit for such purpose." To obtain the benefit of this warranty, the purchaser must show that the seller was aware of the purpose for which the commodity was bought.

706 Liability of the Manufacturer or Distributor for Breach of Warranty

Generally, the manufacturer and distributor are not in privity of contract with the ultimate consumer and therefore, in the absence of statute, there are no implied warranties arising out of the relationship among the manufacturer and distributor and ultimate consumer of the product. However, the manufacturer or distributor or both may make express warranties to the ultimate consumer as an inducement to buy the product, in which case the manufacturer or distributor will have to respond in damages if the express warranty is untrue and results in injury to the purchaser.

As between the retailer and the distributor, they are in privity of contract, with the retailer being the purchaser and the distributor the seller. Should the retailer be required to respond in damages to the ultimate consumer because of a breach of warranty, the retailer could then sue the distributor on the same warranty theory. Clearly, there were implied warranties in the contract of sale between the distributor and the retailer, and if the retailer sustains damages as a result of the breach of any of these implied warranties, the retailer is entitled to damages from the distributor. The same situation obtains as between the manufacturer and the distributor, with the manufacturer in the position of the seller and the distributor in the role of the purchaser. Therefore, the manufacturer would be liable to the distributor on the same theory as the recovery first obtained against the distributor by the retailer. Thus, by means of these multiple actions, the manufacturer would be the one ultimately to pay the claim originally asserted by the ultimate consumer. However, where there is a privity requirement, the ultimate consumer has no cause of action directly against the manufacturer or distributor.

In view of all the varying decisions, customs, and practices dealing with commercial transaction and sales, it was deemed desirable that the existing law be codified in one statute and that each state enact the same statute. In this way, commercial transactions would be treated on a uniform basis for the benefit of business and the general public. This challenge was addressed by the National Conference of Commissioners on Uniform State Laws. This organization was formed for the purpose of promulgating proposed laws in certain general areas which would be submitted to the various state legislatures with a recommendation that they be accepted and passed. Since the same laws would be submitted to each state, they were called uniform laws. In the area of products, the first such law was the Uniform Sales Act. This was a codification of the common law and in some ways patterned after the English Sale of Goods Act. From the time of its first submission in 1906, 36 states accepted it as part of their law. In 1958, it was deemed desirable to recodify the law and to combine into one statute the Uniform Sales Act and other uniform laws covering somewhat the same area. The recodification is called the Uniform Commercial Code, and at the present writing it has been accepted and enacted into law in 49 of the 50 states,

Louisiana being the sole exception. It has also been enacted in the District of Columbia.

This chapter contains several references to the Uniform Commercial Code (or UCC). An in-depth analysis of the UCC would be far beyond the scope of this work. The UCC, among many other issues, codifies the law relating to such matters as: express warranties; implied warranties of quality, merchantability, and fitness for a particular purpose; sales contracts; disclaimers; and damages. Suffice it to say, at this point, that the claim representative should be aware of the UCC's general scope and purpose, and that it can have an impact on cases involving products liability issues.

707 Duties of the Manufacturer

Generally, the manufacturer is required to exercise reasonable care in the design, production, and assembly of the product, the degree of care being governed by the risk of harm to which the consumer is exposed. The *Restatement, Second, Law of Torts*, states the following rule:

> 395 Negligent Manufacture of Chattel Dangerous Unless Carefully Made
>
> A manufacturer who fails to exercise reasonable care in the manufacture of a chattel which, unless carefully made, he should recognize as involving an unreasonable risk of causing physical harm to those who use it for a purpose for which the manufacturer should expect it to be used and to those whom he should expect to be endangered by its probable use, is subject to liability for physical harm caused to them by its lawful use in a manner and for a purpose for which it is supplied.

This *Restatement* rule states the law as it generally has been adopted. It contemplates the duty of the manufacturer to the general public, arising out of the purchase of the product by the ultimate consumer. Since the manufacturer made the product, it supposedly knows more about it than the consumer. It knows what raw materials or ingredients were used. It knows the properties of those materials and is charged with the knowledge of the possible harm to others which may come about if proper care is not exercised. Finally, by placing the article on the market, the manufacturer represents that it can be safely used. Since the manufacturer derives an economic benefit from placing the article in the stream of commerce, liability is imposed for failure to exercise reasonable care in its manufacture.

It should be noted that the rule creates a liability to "those who use" the article, which means that the rule is not only for the benefit of the buyer, but also all others who reasonably may be anticipated to use it. In addition, liability also is imposed upon the manufacturer for injuries suffered by "those whom he should expect to be endangered by its probable use." This could encompass a large number of people who are not directly or indirectly involved in the sale or use of the product. For example, let us assume that an automobile manufacturer placed a defective automobile on the market, the defect consisting of ineffective braking power when the brakes are suddenly applied. Under this rule, passengers, other motorists, and pedestrians would come within the definition of those whom the manufacturer ''should expect to be endangered by'' the probable use of the automobile.

The ''manufacturer'' of the article is the one that makes or assembles the article and places it on the market under its name. The mere fact that the manufacturer purchased raw material or a component part from another supplier will not insulate it from liability, even if the material or the component part is the cause of the defect. Because the manufacturer is the one who had the duty to inspect the article for defects prior to its release to the market, the person injured does not have to go any farther back in the chain than that manufacturer.

What will constitute reasonable care in the manufacture of an article generally will be commensurate with the foreseeable danger in its use if defective. This is a relative term and the greater the danger imposed by the article the greater the duty of care. Conversely, if the article is one which poses little or no danger of anything more than trivial risk, then the duty of care is that much less.

708 Duty of Safe Design

The manufacturer is bound to exercise reasonable care in designing the product, and is bound to foresee the possible risks of harm to which others will be exposed because of unsafe design. If a person suffers injury as a result of the unsafe design of the product, the manufacturer is liable. For example, in *Greenman* v. *Yuba Power Products, Inc.* [377 Pac. 2d 897 (California)], the defendant designed and marketed a power tool, called a Shopsmith, which contained an inadequate set of screws which would sometimes allow the tailstock of the lathe to move away from the piece of wood and thus cause the piece to fly out of the machine. The court held that strict liability might be imposed because there was a defect in design which made the Shopsmith unsafe for its intended use. The court pointed out that the duty of the manufacturer was not to design a product which was perfectly safe or foolproof, but that the product in this case was not reasonably safe; and, furthermore, it was not safe for its intended purpose.

1. Automobiles. There is no question that, if the design of an automobile was such that it was the cause of the accident, the manufacturer may be liable. For example, in *Carpini* v. *Pittsburgh & Weirton Bus Company* [216 Fed. 2d 404 (West Virginia)], the court permitted a recovery against the manufacturer because of a defectively designed petcock in the undercarriage of a bus which became dislodged by an obstruction in the road, causing the brakes to fail. Likewise, if the design causes an injury, or exposes the person to a greater injury, the manufacturer may be liable.

However, in *Evans* v. *General Motors Corporation* [359 Fed. 2d 825], the deceased was driving a Chevrolet station wagon, designed with an X-frame chassis, when it was struck on the left side by another automobile at an intersection.

The plaintiff contended that the manufacturer was negligent in designing a vehicle with an X-frame rather than a perimeter frame, because the X-frame provided insufficient protection to an occupant in the event of a collision. In holding that the manufacturer was under no duty to design an automobile which would be safe in the event of a collision, the court said:

> The intended purpose of an automobile does not include its participation in collisions with other objects, despite the manufacturer's ability to foresee the possibility that such collisions may occur. As defendant argues, the defendant also knows that its automobiles may be driven into bodies of water, but it is not suggested that defendant has a duty to equip them with pontoons.

2. Roadworthiness versus Crashworthiness. In spite of *Evans* v. *General Motors, supra,* there is a continuing dispute between consumer advocates and the automobile manufacturers as to the extent of the duty of safe design on the part of the manufacturer. Consumer advocates feel that, because the automobile manufacturers can reasonably foresee the risk of injury to passengers arising from a collision with another vehicle or another object, the duty of safe design should include a duty to design a vehicle that would reasonably protect the users of the automobile from the consequences of a collision. The manufacturers, on the other hand, contend that their design duty consists merely of supplying a product that will provide reasonably safe transportation. The manufacturers claim that they are not under any obligation to design a vehicle that would be safe under all circumstances, whether the vehicle was misused or not. Thus, it is the position of the manufacturers that they have the obligation of designing a vehicle which is roadworthy, but not necessarily crashworthy or crashproof.

3. Second Collision or Enhanced Injury. Where the design of the automobile is such that, in the event of a collision the driver and passengers are exposed to an unreasonable risk of harm, a number of cases hold that the manufacturer is liable. For example, in *Larsen* v. *General Motors Corporation* [391 Fed. 2d 495 (8th Cir.)], the plaintiff was involved in a head-on collision with another vehicle while driving a Corvair automobile. The plaintiff alleged that the automobile was defectively designed in that the steering shaft was so constructed as to produce a rearward displacement in a head-on collision. In finding for the plaintiff, the court said:

> While automobiles are not made for the purpose of colliding with each other, a frequent and inevitable contingency of normal automobile use will result in collisions and injury producing impacts. . . . Where the injuries or enhanced injuries are due to the manufacturer's failure to use reasonable care to avoid subjecting the user of its products to an unreasonable risk of injury, general negligence principles should be applicable. The sole function of an automobile is not just to provide a means of transportation, it is to provide a means of safe transportation or as safe as is reasonably possible under the present state of the art.

4. National Traffic and Motor Vehicle Safety Act. In 1966, Congress passed the National Traffic and Motor Vehicle Safety Act (15 USCA 1381). The act created a National Traffic Safety Agency, to create standards of motor vehicle design under the following four categories:

1. Engineering design which reduces the risk of accidents.
2. Engineering design which reduces the risk of injury when accidents occur.
3. Engineering design which provides greater tolerance for pedestrians on impact.
4. Engineering design which protects persons from injury while the vehicle is not in operation.

Whether the manufacturer complied with the standards will not determine his common-law liability for unsafe design. It will, however, be evidence of his lack of due care where he did not comply.

In addition, mere compliance with the standards created will not insulate the manufacturer from liability for unsafe design if there are other areas in which the manufacturer has failed to exercise due care in creating the design. The statute (15 USCA 1397) provides that "compliance with any Federal motor vehicle safety standard issued under this Title does not exempt any person from any liability under common law." This is generally true of other statutes which Congress has passed, regulating the manufacture and sale of certain types of products. Examples are: The Pure Food, Drug, and Cosmetic Act; the Federal Hazardous Substances Act; the Federal Flammable Fabrics Act; and (one of the most significant) the Consumer Product Safety Act.

5. Consumer Product Safety Act. This act was passed by Congress in 1972 and is found in 15 USCA 205 et seq. The primary purpose of the act is to reduce the unreasonable risk of injuries to consumers caused by consumer products. It creates a commission known as the Consumer Product Safety Commission, whose duty it is to determine the products which contain a defect which would create a "substantial products hazard." When this is determined, the Commission could take certain actions for the protection of the consumer, such as promulgating standards for consumer products, issuing consumer product safety rules, and banning allegedly hazardous products.

In addition, where the Commission has set some safety standards, the fact that the product which is the cause of the accident did not meet these safety standards may be evidence of negligence on the part of the manufacturer.

709 Duty to Warn

The manufacturer who places a product in the stream of commerce is held to possess a high degree of scientific and technical knowledge with respect to that product. The manufacturer is bound to anticipate the uses to which the product will be put, and, if there are any dangers in connection with such use, the manufacturer is under a duty to warn the ultimate user of any dangerous propensities inherent in the product.

A product design must take into consideration anticipated uses of a product, even though they arguably may be unexpected or unintended from the manufacturer's perspective. The manufacturer may be expected by a court to have anticipated the human frailties of users, and thus the possibility of misuse and accidents, as well as the nature of potential misuse of a product. It must anticipate the environment in which the product will be used, such as: home, factory, construction site, or jet airliner cockpit. It may also be expected to anticipate whether the product will be used by a child, a skilled industrial worker, an unskilled farm worker (who cannot speak or read English), an airline pilot, or a hospital employee.

It may not be possible for a manufacturer to design away all product hazards or to incorporate guards or safety features to prevent all possibility of accidents. A legal duty to anticipate "reasonably foreseeable" uses may be imposed. It may be necessary to provide warnings and instructions concerning the use of a product and possible hazards. If warnings are provided, they should be as clear and complete as possible. A warning must be sufficiently conspicuous and sufficiently intense to warn a user adequately of the possible hazard.

Different methods of presenting instruction or warnings (such as user manuals, labels, stamped metal plates) will be appropriate for different products. They should be as permanent as reasonably possible. Again, the manufacturer may be expected to anticipate risks which may arise not only from normal and intended use of a product, but also risks arising from abnormal use or misuse.

Most litigation involving the duty to warn or instruct relates to the adequacy of, rather than the complete absence of, a warning. The plaintiff may allege that the warning given was diluted or overly broad, and thus did not precisely identify the risk of harm involved in the injury-producing event.

A disregard of specific instructions supplied by the manufacturer or seller has been found to be a legitimate defense in a products case. A lawnmower user, contrary to "easily readable" instructions, attempted to mow a steep slope in an improper manner. He was injured when his foot slipped under the blade housing. The court rejected the plaintiff's allegation that the manufacturer violated its duty to warn. The danger was not only open and obvious, but the peculiar use made of the product was neither intended nor within the reasonably foreseeable use of the product. The court, citing numerous informative examples, found that the clear fact situation dictated its conclusion:

> We also reject cases that demand that a manufacturer warn against uses which were neither intended by the manufacturer nor within the reasonably foreseeable uses of the product. [The court cited decisions in which a perfume manufacturer was held liable for burns to teenage girls who used a cologne to scent a lit candle and in which a manufacturer in a failure-to-warn case was held liable when a child drank furniture polish.] These decisions fail to recognize that individual consumers have certain responsibilities. Manufacturers cannot foresee and warn of all absurd and dangerous uses of their

products. . . . The duty to warn is concomitant with the general duty of the manufacturer, which "is limited to foreseeing the probable results of the normal use of the product or a use that can reasonably be anticipated." [*Thibault* v. *Sears, Roebuck & Co.*, 395 A.2d 843 (N.H. 1978)].

An "adequate" warning, while difficult to define concisely, has been well described by several courts. For example:

> (1) it must be in such form that it could reasonably be expected to catch the attention of the reasonably prudent man in the circumstances of its use; (2) the content of the warning must be of such nature as to be comprehensible to the average user and to convey a fair indication of the nature and extent of the danger to the mind of a reasonably prudent person. . . . The question of whether or not a given warning is legally sufficient depends upon the language used and the impression that such language is calculated to make upon the mind of the average user of the product. Implicit in the duty to warn is the duty to warn with a degree of intensity that would cause a reasonable person to exercise the caution commensurate with the potential danger. . . . A clear cautionary statement setting forth the exact nature of the dangers involved would be necessary to fully protect the seller. . . . [*Bristol-Myers Co.* v. *Gonzales,* 548 S.W.2d 416 (Tex.Civ.App. 1977)].

Another court described an "adequate warning" as follows: "A notice . . . reasonably readable, that apprises a consumer exercising reasonable care under the circumstances, of the existence and seriousness of the danger, sufficient to enable the consumer to protect himself against it, and sufficient to accomplish the purpose intended by the seller in the light of present conditions." [*Michael* v. *Warner-Chilcott,* 579 P.2d 183 (N.M. App. 1978).

There are products which are unavoidably unsafe, especially in the field of pharmaceutical drugs, but the manufacturer is absolved of liability, provided that adequate warnings are given. The law recognizes that, although the use of certain drugs may be attended by side effects, their utility outweighs their risks. The question of whether the warning given (usually to the physician) is adequate is a question for the jury. For example, in *Yarrow* v. *Sterling Drug Co.* [263 Fed. Supp. 159, affirmed in 408 Fed. 2d 987 (South Dakota)], the plaintiff was given Aralen as treatment for an arthritic condition. The drug was known to the manufacturer to have some risks of ocular complications and the plaintiff's doctor received instructions to that effect. As a result of the daily administration of the drug, the plaintiff became 80 percent blind. The court found that, although the drug was not defective, liability should be imposed because of the defendant's failure to adequately warn the plaintiff's doctor of the possible side effects of the use of the drug. The court further held that the treatment by the doctor did not insulate the manufacturer from liability.

On the other hand, where the dangers attendant with the use of the product are open and obvious, there generally is no duty on the part of the manufacturer to warn. He can assume that most individuals are aware of the dangers of gasoline, kerosene, acids, natural gas, electricity, and other commodities and, unless a duty is imposed by government statute or regulation, there may be no duty to warn involved. Also, there is no duty to warn of the dangerous propensities of knives, hammers, hatchets, and other implements of like kind.

The duty to warn also may be conditioned by the type of individual using the product. For example, in *Lockett* v. *General Electric Company* (375 Fed. Supp. 1201), the plaintiff was employed by the Sun Shipbuilding and Dry Dock Company. He was seriously injured when caught in the gears of a drive shaft of a vessel being constructed by his employer. He sued the manufacturer of the gears, General Electric, alleging that it should have warned of the need to guard the gears and that it should have supplied the needed guards. The court held that:

> . . . even assuming that the condition was not readily observable to a person without special experience, it certainly can be assumed that Sun Ship has special experience in the assembly and construction of vessels, and G.E. had reason to believe that those in Sun Ship's employ, working in the vicinity of the gears, would be able to perceive the danger. . . . there is ordinarily no duty to give a warning to members of a profession against dangers generally known to that profession. . . . Where a dangerous condition is equally within the technical knowledge of the supplier and the employer, there is no duty on the part of the supplier to warn the employer of the danger.

710 Identification of Manufacturer

The person who has suffered bodily injury or property damage as a result of the use of a product, and brings an action against the alleged manufacturer, has the burden of proving that the product which caused the injury or property damage was in fact a product made by the manufacturer sought to be charged. The person injured must establish that the particular product, which allegedly was defective or harmful, was actually produced by the manufacturer who is alleged to be liable.

For example, let us assume that a farmer bought a certain fungicide, produced under a trade name, and used this product for dusting his own crops. If the product is defective, and causes damage not only to his own crops but also to the crops of his neighbor, both the farmer and his neighbor would have a cause of action in tort against the manufacturer for the damage caused by the product to both crops. In order to recover, however, both the farmer and his neighbor would have to show that the damage was caused by the use of the particular product, that it was used in accordance with the instructions, and that no other product was used to mix with it.

It frequently happens that, because of the usages of the trade, a distributor or retailer will market a product under its own brand name or label, which product is produced by someone else. This is especially true in the canning industry, and it is not unusual to find one cannery labeling the same product for three or four different distributors under three or four different brand names. Under those circumstances, the distributor (by the use of its own trade name) has adopted the product as his own and will be charged with liability in the case of a defective product just as if he had made it himself. Having used its own trade name, or brand, or label on the product, the distributor may not interpose the defense that the product was processed or manufactured by someone else. It is true that, as between the canner and the distributor, there may be a hold harmless agreement, or the distributor may have a cause of action against the canner for breach of warranty, but the existence of either the agreement or the cause of action will not in any way affect the action brought by the injured person against the distributor.

A product identification problem also has arisen with regard to generic drug products. In the ordinary case where a drug is prescribed for a patient, most adverse effects will manifest themselves within a short time after taking the drug. In most cases, the patient will have no difficulty in identifying the manufacturer. In other cases, the effects of the drug may not be apparent for long periods of time—and in some cases, for years. For example, DES (diethylstilbestrol) at one time was prescribed for pregnant women in order to prevent miscarriages. This drug had been prescribed since the early 1940s and 1950s. In 1971, it was discovered that a number of the daughters of women who had received DES during pregnancy were developing vaginal and cervical cancer. Because of the passage of time, none of the mothers could establish which pharmaceutical manufacturer made the drug they had taken.

In *Sindell* v. *Abbott Laboratories,* [426 Cal. 3d 588 (California Supreme Court, 1980)], the plaintiff was the daughter of a mother who had taken DES during pregnancy to prevent miscarriages. It was claimed that taking the drug caused cancer in the daughter. Large quantities of DES were packaged and sold by entities other than the manufacturers. That is, it generally was sold as a generic drug. Since the plaintiff could not identify the manufacturer of the particular product her mother took, she sued a number of manufacturers who produced drugs under the same formula. In reaching its decision, the court created the *market share theory of liability,* holding that the defendants were liable to the plaintiff in proportion to their share of the product market, unless they could show that they could not have marketed the product taken by the mother. In addition, where all manufacturers were not joined by the plaintiff, they could cross-complain against the others and join them in the lawsuit. Inferentially, the court pointed out that the manufacturers were better able to bear the cost of injury resulting from the manufacture of a defective product, the rationale being that the manufacturers could recover their losses by increasing the price of the product, whereas the plaintiff had no other source of recovery.

A few other states have adopted some form of market share liability. Still more states have rejected the doctrine because of the strong likelihood that it would impose liability upon a manufacturer for a product it did not produce.

711 Strict Liability for Retailers and Manufacturers

Most courts now recognize and apply a form of strict liability to products which, if defectively made, are dangerous to the consumer. There are two theories in support of this conclusion. The first to be enunciated was the *war-*

ranty theory and the second was the *tort* theory. The warranty theory holds that the manufacturer's warranty or guarantee (that the goods are not defective and are fit for the purpose for which they are sold) runs with the product for the benefit of the ultimate consumer, thus eliminating the necessity for privity of contract. Thus, if the warranty were breached, the consumer could recover from the manufacturer without any evidence of negligence on the manufacturer's part. This created the imposition of liability without fault on the sellers of defective products.

Later, some courts felt that the warranty theory was too confusing, especially since the word ''warranty'' was closely associated with the law of contracts. The later cases have largely discarded the warranty theory and adopted the strict liability in tort doctrine. The American Law Institute, in the *Restatement of the Law of Torts, Second*, recommends the following rule as enunciating the strict liability in tort doctrine:

> 402A. Special Liability of Seller of Product for Physical Harm to User or Consumer.
> (1) One who sells any product in a defective condition unreasonably dangerous to the user or consumer or to his property is subject to liability for physical harm thereby caused to the ultimate user or consumer, or to his property, if
> (a) The seller is engaged in the business of selling such a product, and
> (b) It is expected to and does reach the user or consumer without substantial change in the condition in which it is sold.
> (2) The rule stated in Subsection (1) applies although
> (a) The seller has exercised all possible care in the preparation and sale of his product, and
> (b) The user or consumer has not bought the product from or entered into any contractual relation with the seller.

The Comment which follows the rule makes it clear that this special liability of the seller is an imposition of liability without fault where a defective product is involved, and, regardless of whether the court follows the warranty theory or the tort theory, the result is the same. The application of the rule contemplates the existence of a number of elements, which must be considered. These are (1) the seller of the product engaged in the business, (2) a defective condition, (3) an unreasonable danger, (4) a user or consumer, and (5) physical harm to the user or consumer or his property.

712 A Seller Engaged in the Business

The comment which follows the rule defines the seller as the one who markets the product for the use and consumption of the general public. The seller then is the one who places the product in the stream of commerce, or the one who manufactures it or assembles it into one complete unit. The term ''seller'' has been interpreted to include manufacturers, component suppliers, distributors, retailers, bailors, and even builders of housing developments.

1. Manufacturers. Most of the cases involve suits between the consumer and the manufacturer, and, where the manufacturer has placed a defective product in the stream of commerce and it has not been subjected to alteration from the time it left the manufacturer until it reached the consumer, the rule has been applied to impose liability.

2. Component Suppliers. There has been some question as to the application of the rule to a supplier of component parts who supplies them to the manufacturer to be made into the finished product. It would appear that the supplier had delegated the duty of inspection to the manufacturer and that the primary responsibility for placing the finished product on the market rests with the manufacturer. This may account for the scarcity of cases wherein the ultimate consumer seeks to hold the supplier of a component part liable for the injury, although it is clear that strict liability is applicable.

3. Distributors. There are few cases involving the application of the strict liability rule to distributors, although the distributors would come within the *Restatement* definition of sellers of products. One of the reasons for the lack of cases may be that the same rule of liability would be applicable to the manufacturer so that it would be just as easy to sue the manufacturer as it would be to sue the distributor. Also the relative size and wealth and public profile of the defendant-manufacturer may be greater than that of the distributor, so that it generally would be to the plaintiff's advantage to sue the manufacturer.

4. Retailers. The rule has been applied to retailers although a few states have retained the sealed container exception holding that, where the retailer sold the product in a sealed container, liability would not be imposed upon him if the product proved to be defective and dangerous.

Hospitals and other medical institutions have for years taken the position that the supplying of blood for transfusions—as well as the incidental use of other products in the course of medical treatment—constituted a service rather than the sale of a product. Therefore, they argued, the rule of strict liability was not applicable. However, in *MacNeal Memorial Hospital* v. *Cunningham,* [266 N.E. 2d 785], the Illinois Supreme Court held that the furnishing of blood for transfusions constituted a sale, and therefore the rule of strict liability would apply. In that case, the blood which was furnished was infected with serum hepatitis, and even though the hospital had no means of testing the blood to determine its purity, the transaction amouted to a sale of impure blood and thus was subject to the rule of strict liability.

As a result of this case, hospitals were reluctant to give transfusions unless the patient released them from liability in advance. This was unfortunate since, in many cases, the patient was in no physical condition either to give the release or to understand its terms.

The Illinois legislature responded to this situation by passing a declaration of public policy, followed by a statute limiting the liability of any person, firm, or corporation furnishing human blood. The declaration follows:

> *Declaration of Public Policy.* The availability of scientific knowledge, skills, and materials for the purpose of injecting, transfusing or transplanting human whole blood, plasma, blood products, blood derivatives and products, corneas, bones or organs or other human tissue is important to the health and welfare of the people of this state. The imposition of legal liability without fault upon the persons and organizations engaged in such scientific procedures inhibits the exercise of sound medical judgment and restricts the availability of important scientific knowledge, skills and materials. It is therefore the public policy of this State to promote the health and welfare of the people by limiting the legal liability arising out of such scientific procedures to instances of negligence or willful misconduct. (Ill. Rev. Stat. Ch. 91, Sec. 181.)

The statute enacted in furtherance of this declaration—similar to statutes that have been enacted in many other states—reads as follows:

> *Limitation of Liability.* The procuring, furnishing, donating, processing, distributing, or using human whole blood, plasma, blood products, blood derivatives and products, corneas, bones or organs or other human tissue for the purpose of injecting, transfusing or transplanting any of them in the human body is declared for the purposes of liability in tort or contract to be the rendition of a service by every person, firm or corporation participating therein, whether or not any remuneration is paid therefor, and is declared not to be a sale of any such items and no warranties of any kind of description nor strict tort liability shall be applicable thereto. . . . (Ill. Rev. Stat. Ch. 91, Sec. 182.)

713 Defective Condition

Even though the rule imposes strict liability, it is still necessary that the plaintiff meet the burden of proving that the product was defective. He may do this by invoking the rule of *res ipsa loquitur* (''the thing speaks for itself'') in appropriate cases, but in virtually every case the plaintiff must establish that the product was defective when it left the hands of the manufacturer and that the product was in the same defective condition when the accident happened. Failure on the part of the plaintiff to establish these elements will deny him the application of the rule. The drafters of Section 402A intended that a product cannot be in a defective condition if (after it left the seller's control) it was misused or altered in a way that rendered the product harmful.

Generally, anything that would be grounds for a negligence action, such as improper design, assembly, or warnings, would also qualify (in the view of many courts) as a ''defective condition'' in a strict liability action. Section 402A was originally intended by its drafters to apply only to miscarriages in the manufacturing process and not to design defects. However, some courts have ignored this limitation and have decided that strict liability applies, whether the plaintiff attacks the concept (design) of the product or the manner in which the design is carried out in the manufacturing process.

714 An Unreasonable Danger

Not only must the plaintiff establish that there was a defect in the product, but also that the defect was unreasonably dangerous to the user or consumer. For example, a manufacturer produces a needle that has neither an eye nor a point. The product is defective, but the defect is not of such a nature that it is dangerous to the user.

715 User or Consumer

Within this definition would come the purchaser, of course, but the terms have been held to include the following: members of the purchaser's family; guests, employees, lessees, and donees of a purchaser; vehicle and airplane passengers; beauty shop customers or hospital patients treated or injected with a product; prospective purchasers testing product.

Bystanders. The American Law Institute, in promulgating Rule 402A, refused to express any opinion as to whether a bystander per se would come within the rule.

In spite of several decisions to the contrary, there are several cases which do apply the doctrine of strict liability in favor of a bystander. In the California case of *Elmore* v. *American Motors* [451 Pac. 2d 84], the facts indicated that Mrs. Elmore—because of an alleged defect in the automobile manufactured by the defendant—swerved to the wrong side of the road and collided with the car of plaintiff Waters. Both she and Waters sued the retailer and the manufacturer. The court held that Waters, the bystander, was entitled to the benefit of the strict liability doctrine if there was a defect. The question of the existence of the defect was for the jury. The court stated that the purpose of imposing strict liability upon the manufacturer is to shift the costs from the injured persons who are "powerless to protect themselves" to the maker of the offending instrumentality. The court also pointed out that the bystander was in an inferior position as compared to the consumer—the purchaser had an opportunity to inspect the product, whereas the bystander did not.

The Indiana case of *Sills* v. *Massey-Ferguson* [296 Fed. Supp 776], is a federal court decision in which the court was called upon to determine the Indiana law on the subject of the recovery by a bystander. Unfortunately there were no Indiana cases on the subject, but the court did what federal courts sitting in a particular state sometimes do when interpreting the law of that state. It decided that the "direction of the law in Indiana was clear." It then decided to adopt a rule protecting the bystander.

Therefore, while the question of the application of the doctrine of strict liability in tort to injuries sustained by bystanders is still an open one in many states, there may be a general trend toward utilizing the doctrine for the protection of an injured bystander, thus including him or her within the definitions of a "user or consumer."

716 Physical Harm

The plaintiff must establish that, as a user or consumer, he or his property have suffered physical harm proximately caused by the defect. Merely to establish that physical harm has occurred is not enough. The causal relationship between the defect claimed and the physical harm is an essential element of the plaintiff's proof. For example, in *State Stove Mfg. Co.* v. *Hodges* [189 So. 2d 113 (Mississippi)], a water heater which was equipped with defective thermostats exploded and completely demolished a new home. In the suit against the manufacturer of the heater, the evidence indicated that the building contractors had failed to install a temperature relief valve on the heater in accordance with the manufacturer's instructions. The jury found that the negligence of the building contractor in failing to follow instructions was the proximate cause of the explosion and exonerated the manufacturer from liability.

717 Defenses: Use of Product for Unintended Purpose

The traditional rule is that the seller is not bound to foresee that the consumer or user will make abnormal use of the product or will use it for a purpose not intended. Thus the manufacturer traditionally was not bound to anticipate that an automobile will be negligently driven, or an airplane negligently flown. He is not required to produce an automobile or plane that is incapable of an accident. Similarly, where a tire manufacturer produces a tire which is safe for ordinary driving, he is not liable to a consumer who uses the tire on a racing car and sustains injury when the tire blows out in the course of a race.

The failure to use the product in accordance with the directions which accompany it also has been regarded as an abnormal use for which the manufacturer is not liable. For example, hair dye preparations have frequently warned of the danger of using the product without first conducting a ''patch'' test to determine whether the user is allergic to the product. The failure of the user—whether a professional hairdresser or the actual consumer—to conduct the patch test may be an abnormal use of the product which may provide a defense to the cause of action.

On the other hand, there are unusual uses to which the product may be put and which the manufacturer is bound to anticipate. Failure to warn of these possibilities may subject the manufacturer to liability. Strict liability has been imposed on the manufacturers of the following products: a chair that collapsed while the user was standing on it [*Phillips* v. *Ogle Aluminum Furniture Co.*, 235 Pac. 2d 857 (California)]; a cocktail robe that caught fire when worn in close proximity to the flame of a kitchen stove [*Ringstad* v. *I. Magnin & Co.*, 239 Pac. 2d 848 (Washington)]; and flammable hair spray used without warning of its properties near a candle [*Hardman* v. *Helene Curtis Indus., Inc.*, 198 N.E. 2d 681 (Illinois)]. Whether the use was expected, ordinary, or normal will be determined by the particular facts and circumstances of a given case. The manufacturer's or seller's subjective determination of the product's intended use may be relevant, but will not be the sole test.

Where the manufacturer may reasonably anticipate that the product can come into the hands of children, it is held to strict liability if it fails to take all means at its command to label and otherwise warn of the dangers to children which might come about from its use. See *Spruill* v. *Boyle-Midway, Inc.*, [308 Fed. 2d 79] (furniture polish drunk by child).

Of course, the defendant may be able to raise the defense that the plaintiff's use of the product was contrary to warnings or instructions. This would require the jury to consider (1) whether the warning was adequate and (2) whether the conduct was actually in disregard of the warning. If these questions are answered affirmatively, it would appear that the defense rests on use with knowledge of danger.

In *Blunk* v. *Allis-Chalmers Mfg. Co.*, [242 N.E. 2d 122 (Indiana App.)] a farmer brought suit for injuries sustained when his leg became caught in the moving parts of a corn picking machine. He alleged design negligence on the part of the defendant for not guarding those parts. The evidence showed that the plaintiff left the power take-off from his tractor to the picker running when he dismounted his tractor to clean the picking device. When he had finished, he chose to remount the tractor from the front of the picker by placing his foot on the fender of the machine. The fender was wet with moisture and his foot slipped into the moving parts of the machine. The court held that his conduct—in using a product in the face of a known danger—amounted to contributory negligence as a matter of law. This is the type of contributory negligence that is often characterized by the term ''assumption of risk.''

The defense of ''use of a product for an unintended purpose,'' like other defenses to be discussed, relates to the plaintiff's own conduct in the use of the product. A somewhat closely related defense is ''use with knowledge of defect or danger.'' This defense is well illustrated by some case examples.

Hunt v. *Firestone Tire & Rubber Co.*, [448 Pac. 2d 1018 (Oklahoma)] clearly exemplifies the use of a product with knowledge of a defect—one might even say ''expert'' knowledge based on extensive experience. The plaintiff was injured when a tire on his 2 1/2-month old car blew out. Evidence showed that the plaintiff was aware that the tire was defective when the car was delivered to him, because there were cuts in its sidewall. Despite many years of experience as a truck driver and his concern about the tire, he did not substitute the spare but drove on the defective tire for 8,000 miles until the blowout. The court found that, through his conduct, he assumed the risk of the accident.

When a defense based upon use with knowledge of a defect or danger is involved, it raises a question of fact as to what the plaintiff knew or should have known. Clearly, though, in certain cases, the plaintiff's conduct may be in such obvious disregard of his or her own safety that contributory negligence or assumption of risk may be found as a matter of law.

718 Defenses: Contributory Negligence

The defense of contributory negligence as well as the defense of assumption of risk generally may be interposed to an action based upon the rule imposing strict liability. In products cases there does not appear to be any appreciable distinction between the two defenses, the main difference being in the nomenclature favored by the courts of various jurisdictions.

Generally, the cases hold that the plaintiff is under no duty to discover the existence of a defect in the product, and the defense of contributory negligence under those circumstances has not been sustained. Therefore, if the plaintiff drives on a defective tire without any knowledge of the defect even though it could have been discovered, he or she is not charged with contributory negligence. On the other hand, if the plaintiff is aware of the defect and voluntarily and unreasonably continues to use the product with knowledge of the defect, he or she is chargeable (in the language of the *Restatement*) with "the form of contributory negligence that commonly passes under the name of assumption of risk." For example, in *Saeter* v. *Harley Davidson Motor Co.* [21 Auto Cas. (CCH) 2d 643 (California)], the plaintiff continued to operate a motorcycle after he had discovered a defective damper that caused the front wheel to wobble. He was denied recovery because he was guilty of contributory negligence in so doing. Also in *Stevens* v. *Allis-Chalmers Mfg. Co.* [100 Pac. 2d 723 (Kansas)], the manufacturer failed to provide a cover for the takeoff shaft, and because the farmer who used it was well aware of the defect and the danger, he was denied recovery because his continued use of the harvester constituted contributory negligence.

In the jurisdictions that have adopted comparative negligence, the question arises whether the doctrine should be applied to cases involving strict liability in tort. Some courts have taken the position that strict liability in tort is a form of negligence per se and thus subject to application of comparative negligence. [See, e.g., *Dippel* v. *Sciano,* 155 N.W.2d 55 (Wis. 1967).]

In a case involving a snowmobile accident, the defendant contended that the plaintiff was negligent in racing the vehicle and in failing to maintain it properly. The court held that a manufacturer is entitled to offer evidence on the general misuse of its product. Once the misuse is established, the principles of comparative negligence will apply. [*Butaud* v. *Suburban Marine,* 555 P.2d 42 (Alaska)]. A contrary view was adopted in *Kinard* v. *Coates* [553 P.2d 835 (Colo.App.)], holding that comparative negligence is not applicable to strict liability in tort.

719 Defenses: Allergy and Susceptibility

This defense is involved in the use of drugs, cosmetics, and other products for intimate body use. The general rule is that the manufacturer is not an insurer against rare and unforeseeable allergies and susceptibilities which might exist in a particular person. These are sometimes referred to as "idiosyncratic reactions." The manufacturer has a right to assume that the product will be used in a normal manner by persons who have normal reactions.

However, where the manufacturer knows, or in the exercise of care should know, that a large number of persons would be likely to be affected by the use of the product, it is liable if it should fail to warn them. Thus in *Sterling Drug, Inc.* v. *Cornish* [370 Fed. 2d 82 (Kansas)], the court held that if the manufacturer knew or should have known that a group of users of its drug would suffer side effects, particularly retinal damage, it had the duty to warn the medical profession of the susceptibility of such a group even though their numbers might be small. Other cases hold that there is no liability on the part of the manufacturer in absence of proof that the use of the product will affect a "substantial" number of persons. [See *Magee* v. *Wyeth Laboratories, Inc.*, 29 Cal. Rptr. 466.]

720 Defenses: Third Party's Conduct

If the defendant can establish that the conduct of some third party was actually the proximate cause of the plaintiff's damages, this may be the basis of a successful defense. This involves proof that a third party's negligence, rather than any defect in the product, was the proximate cause of the injury or damage. For example, in *Magee* v. *Wyeth Laboratories, Inc.*, it was found from the evidence presented that a doctor's negligence in failing to follow instructions which accompanied a drug—and not the drug itself—was the cause of the patient's death. The drug company was absolved of liability.

Similarly, when the conduct of a third person causes an otherwise safe product to become dangerous or defective, the conduct of the third party generally will insulate the manufacturer of the product from liability. A common instance of such a defense arises when a third person renders inoperable a safety device accompanying a machine. Either the device is completely removed or the machine is rigged to operate while the safety device does not. In *Santiago* v. *Package Machinery Co.* [260 N.E. 2d 89 (Illinois)], for example, an inspection of a machine after the plaintiff was injured revealed that a switch, installed by a third party, allowed the machine to be operated without a safety gate in place. This, and the fact that the plaintiff's employer did not properly maintain the machine and safety equipment, absolved the manufacturer of liability.

These cases illustrate the need for defense counsel to determine who, other than the plaintiff, was involved with the use, control, or maintenance of the product. A postaccident investigation and inspection of the product is also imperative to determine what changes, if any, may have been made after the product left the manufacturer's control.

If a manufacturer puts a defective product in the stream of commerce, it will be held strictly liable even though some intermediate party should have discovered the defect and remedied it. In such a case, the intermediate party (such as a distributor, wholesaler, or retailer) who should have discovered the defect can be brought in as a joint tort-feasor, and if there was a duty owing from the intermediate party to the manufacturer, there is always the possibility of a claim for contribution. For example, in *Duckworth* v. *Ford Motor Co.* [320 Fed. 2d 130 (Pennsylvania)], the injuries were sustained when the steering mechanism on a new car failed. The manufacturer brought in the dealer as a third party defendant. The court found that the manufacturer and the dealer were joint tort-feasors, even though their negligent acts were not simultaneous. The manufacturer was negligent in failing to properly assemble the steering mechanism at the factory and the dealer was negligent in failing to repair the steering mechanism properly after the defect had been called to his attention by the buyer. Under the circumstances the manufacturer was entitled to contribution from the dealer.

In *Vandermark* v. *Ford Motor Co.* [391 Pac. 2d 168 (California)], the defendant sought to escape liability for injuries sustained as a result of defective brakes on a new car on the theory that it was the duty of its dealer to service the car before delivery. Therefore, the defect in the brakes was caused by something the dealer "did or failed to do" in connection with its servicing duty. In reviewing the applicable law and holding that the manufacturer cannot delegate its duty to place a nondefective product in the stream of commerce, the court, citing a landmark strict liability case, said:

> In *Greenman* v. *Yuba Power Products,* 59 Cal. 2d 57, we held that "A manufacturer is strictly liable in tort when an article he places on the market, knowing that it is to be used without inspection for defects, proves to have a defect that causes injury to a human being." Since the liability is strict it encompasses defects regardless of their source, and therefore a manufacturer of a completed product cannot escape liability by tracing the defect to a component part supplied by another. . . . Moreover, even before such strict liability was recognized, the manufacturer of a completed product was subject to vicarious liability for the negligence of his suppliers or subcontractors that resulted in defects in the completed product. . . . These rules focus responsibility for defects, whether negligently or nonnegligently caused, on the manufacturer of the completed product, and they apply regardless of what part of the manufacturing process the manufacturer chooses to delegate to third parties. It appears in the present case that Ford delegates the final steps in that process to its authorized dealers. It does not deliver cars to its dealers that are ready to be driven away by the ultimate purchasers but relies on its dealers to make the final inspections, corrections and adjustments necessary to make the cars ready for use. Since Ford, as the manufacturer of the completed product, cannot delegate its duty to have its cars delivered to the ultimate purchaser free from dangerous defects, it cannot escape liability on the ground that the defect in Vandermark's car may have been caused by something one of its authorized dealers did or failed to do.

On the other hand, where the product leaves the manufacturer free of defects, or where the user or consumer cannot sustain the burden of proving that the product causing the injury was in the same condition at the time of accident as it was when it left the manufacturer, the manufacturer cannot be held liable. Such a situation might come about where the intermediate parties modified a machine or failed to exercise care in a product's preservation, as for example in the case of frozen foods which the intermediate parties failed to keep under refrigeration.

721 Defenses: State of the Art

The ''state of the art'' defense often is urged as a defense in products liability cases. The argument may be stated as follows: where the design or method of manufacture of a product was in conformity with the state of the art (or with prevailing industry standards) at the time the product was designed or manufactured, it should not be considered defective.

Plaintiffs, especially through the use of expert testimony, often seek to persuade juries to apply the current state of the art (or today's current design, manufacturing, or testing standards) to a product manufactured years earlier. Defendants counter that it is quite reasonable to use a design or method of manufacture that is in customary use in an industry, even though other possible designs or methods could be conceived which, theoretically, could be safer or, in the future, could prove practicable. The court in *Day* v. *Barber-Colman Co.,* 135 N.E. 2d 231 (Ill. 1956), agreed with this defense argument. Most courts would agree that a manufacturer has a duty to comply with the existing state of the art and standards prevailing in the industry, and that such compliance is reasonable and constitutes a viable defense to claims of strict liability or negligence.

722 Defenses: Government Specifications

There are many instances in which violations of governmental standards regulations, rules, or specifications have resulted in liability. If violation of governmentally imposed norms can be used as a basis of liability, it appears reasonable that compliance with them should constitute a defense. There is little case law support for this common-sense proposition. However, some interesting developments have taken place recently with regard to the related issue of preemption. In *Papas* v. *Upjohn Co.,* 985 F.2d 516 (11th Cir. 1993), the court held that the Federal Insecticide, Fungicide and Rodenticide Act (FIFRA) preempts (or bars) state common-law tort claims for inadequate labeling. The court determined that ''if a pesticide manufacturer places EPA-approved warnings on the labeling and packaging of its product, its duty to warn is satisfied, and the inadequate warning issue ends.'' The court based on its decision on the recent U.S. Supreme Court decision in *Cipollone* v. *Liggett Group Inc.,* 112 S.Ct.2608 (1992). The court examined the effect of the Federal Cigarette Labeling and Advertising Act, which specifies the warning for all cigarette packages. The court held that some state common-law claims under a failure to warn theory were preempted or barred. These recent developments in the law are of great significance to manufacturers of products that carry warnings mandated by federal law. They signify that courts will be less inclined to hold that an ''inadequate'' warning renders a product defective, when that exact warning is mandated by law. It can be expected that the preemption defense will be advanced in many more cases in the near future.

723 Defenses: Disclaimers

In a contract of sale, just as any other contract in which the parties bargain on equal terms, the parties can agree upon any terms or conditions that they see fit. Thus, where the goods are sold "as is" without any warranty or guarantee as to their quality, and the buyer is willing to make the purchase under those circumstances, it was once upon a time generally accepted that the seller or manufacturer assumed no responsibility to the user or consumer for any defects which cause injury. This situation was most frequently found in the sale of second-hand or used goods, or goods sold as "factory seconds."

The courts have been quick to recognize that the application of this contractual principle in most cases would result in injustice to the user or consumer. Section 2–316 of the Uniform Commercial Code sets forth the general rules that apply to disclaimers. In any consumer transaction, they will be subject to very strict interpretation. Properly utilized, disclaimers may be effective in commercial loss cases. They will be worthless in any attempt to avoid liability for personal injury caused to a consumer by a product.

724 Defenses: Statute of Limitations

The applicable statute of limitations in a given jurisdiction may form the basis of a defense to a products liability action.

The claim representative or lawyer must consider (1) which statute (tort or contract) is applicable and (2) when the cause of action arises and when the time period begins to run.

With respect to the first question, in the case of a products liability personal injury action, the courts of most jurisdictions will hold that their personal injury, or tort, statute will apply. This is generally the rule whether the action is based upon negligence, strict liability in tort, or breach of warranty. The jurisdiction's contract statute of limitations (often codified in a form similar to Section 2–725 of the Uniform Commercial Code) may apply to a commercial loss case involving a breach of warranty. Generally, tort statutes of limitations are shorter than contract statutes of limitations.

With regard to the second question, it must be determined when the cause of action accrues and the time to bring an action begins to run. Most products liability cases deal with injury caused by a clearly defined incident involving a product. "Disease" cases—often alleging disease caused by exposure to a "toxic" substance such as asbestos or a chemical compound—are becoming more frequent. These can present much more complex statute of limitations questions. Different courts apply different rules. The court in one state may determine, for example, that the cause of action arises or accrues and the statute begins to run at the time of first exposure to the substance. The courts in another state may consider the critical time to be the time at which the disease is or should have been discovered.

If the time for filing of a products liability action has expired, the action will be barred. However, the interpretation of a state's statutes of limitation can be a complex process.

725 Indemnity and Contribution

The terminology of buyer and seller is not necessarily restricted to a retailer and its customer, but in the chain of distribution from the manufacturer to the retailer the product may pass through several hands, and each of these (including the manufacturer) could occupy the position of buyer or seller with relation to the other. As between the retailer and the manufacturer, the retailer is the buyer and the manufacturer is the seller. The retailer in that case would be entitled to all the rights of a buyer as against the manufacturer. Consequently, when a retailer, acting as a seller, has been forced to settle a claim brought against it by its buyer, it has suffered damage as a result of the sale made by the manufacturer. Therefore in that case, the retailer as the buyer from the manufacturer can assert a cause of action against the manufacturer. The retailer then may be entitled to indemnity from the manufacturer, and the measure of such indemnity will be the damages which the retailer has suffered. This may include the settlement made and any other expenses which have been imposed, such as legal fees, court costs, and the like. Also, if the retailer can show that it has suffered a deprivation of business, loss of goodwill, or damage to its reputation, it may be entitled to a recovery for these items as well. Where the retailer or other person in the chain of distribution is sued, the Uniform Commercial Code provides for the vouching in of the responsible party as an additional defendant. Section 2–607 provides as follows:

> (5) Where the buyer is sued for breach of warranty or other obligation for which his seller is answerable over
>
> a) he may give his seller written notice of the litigation. If the notice states that the seller may come in and defend and that if the seller does not do so he will be bound in any action against him by his buyer by any determination of fact common to the two litigations, then unless the seller after seasonable receipt of the notice does come in and defend, he is so bound.

Under this section, if the retailer were sued for breach of warranty of merchantability in that the product was defective, notice to the seller or manufacturer to come in and defend will require the manufacturer to do so; otherwise the manufacturer would be bound by any determination of fact reached in the litigation, such as the existence of the defect, and in a subsequent suit against the manufacturer it could not relitigate the issue of whether or not there was a defect.

As to contribution, at common law there was no contribution between joint tort-feasors. Some states have passed Joint Tortfeasors Contribution Laws, which enable one joint tort-feasor that has paid more than its proportionate share of the judgment to recover the excess from the other. In products cases this might come about where the manufacturer produced a defective article which in turn was improperly assembled by the retailer who failed to discover the defect, in which case both the retailer and the manufacturer are joint tort-feasors.

726 Long-Arm Statutes

Where the manufacturer is located outside of the state of the plaintiff's domicile and is not subject to the service of process within the state, some states, for the protection of their citizens, have enacted so-called long-arm statutes. These are designed to enable the plaintiff to obtain personal jurisdiction over nonresidents who otherwise would not be subject to the service of process within the confines of the state.

There is no uniformity among these state statutes. Some "borrow" from their nonresident motorist acts, and require, in addition to notice to the defendants, that the service of process be made upon some state official. Others merely require that service be made upon the nonresident defendant. Usually these statutes base their jurisdiction, as in the nonresident motorist acts, upon the doing of some act within the state. For example, North Carolina confers jurisdiction on the North Carolina courts with respect to any cause of action arising "out of the production, manufacture or distribution of goods by such corporation with the reasonable expectation that such goods are to be used or consumed in the state and are so used or consumed, regardless of how or where the goods were produced, manufactured, marketed or sold or whether or not through the medium of independent contractors or dealers."

Illustrative of the problems in this type of jurisdictional proceeding is the case of *Gray* v. *American Radiator and Standard Sanitary Corp.* [176 N.E. 2d 761 (Illinois)], wherein the defendant manufactured a safety valve in Ohio and sold it to an independent dealer outside of Illinois. The valve was later attached to a water heater in Pennsylvania and then sold to an Illinois consumer. While being used in Illinois, the valve exploded, injuring the plaintiff. The defendant was served with process in Ohio. The Supreme Court of Illinois held that a "tortious act" within the meaning of the Illinois long-arm statute, had been committed in Illinois and upheld the recovery.

The Nevada long-arm statute provides: "Any company . . . which manufactures, produces, makes, markets or otherwise supplies directly or indirectly any product for distribution, sale or use in this state may be lawfully served with any legal process in any action to recover damages for injury to person or property resulting from such distribution, sale or use in this state."

In *Metal-Matic, Inc.* v. *The Eighth Judicial District* [415 Pac. 2d 617], the injuries were allegedly caused by a defective boat railing, manufactured by *D* Corporation, a Minnesota corporation. *D* Corporation contended that it never directly or indirectly solicited or conducted any business in Nevada. *D* Corporation was the manufacturer of a component part of the boat, the railing, and the final product was assembled by a different manufacturer who then shipped it to a distributor in Nevada. The boat was purchased from a retail dealer. While the boat was being used by the purchaser, a passenger leaned against the railing, which gave way, and he fell into the water and was drowned. In sustaining Nevada jurisdiction, the court said:

> In our case, a manufacturer of a component part of a boat can presume or reasonably foresee that its potential market would be Lake Mead or Lake Tahoe, in Nevada, as well as the lake areas of Minnesota, Wisconsin, Michigan or any other part of the United States where navigable lakes or waters are located. It should not matter that the purchase was made from an independent middleman or that someone other than the defendant shipped the product into this state. . . . Our statute says directly what the Illinois and New York courts had to interpret. . . . Where it is reasonably foreseeable that a product will enter the flow of commerce, the manufacturer of that product can expect to be sued in any state where the product is alleged to have caused an injury. This is without regard to how many hands have touched the product from its production to the time of injury.

Therefore, whether or not jurisdiction will be assumed will depend upon the type of statute and the extent to which it will apply to a given situation.

727 Products Liability Investigation

The investigation of a products liability claim requires a certain amount of resourcefulness and imagination. The factual situations are so varied that it is impossible to forecast exactly what will confront the claim representative. It is best to start out with the initial premise that, for the claimant to recover, it must be established that the product was defective. If the claimant cannot establish a defect, either in the product itself or from the lack of warning or the lack of adequate instructions for its use, the claimant cannot recover.

Therefore, the first inquiry made in the products liability investigation will be directed toward ascertaining the defect, if any, that is the basis of the claim. In serious cases involving bodily injury, the allegations should be established in a signed statement from the person making the claim. The statement should establish that there was a sale of the product, what instructions, if any, accompanied the product, what warnings, if any, were attached to the label, and exactly how the product was used.

Among the defenses to products claims are those discussed in Sections 717–724 above.

The claim representative should determine what theories of liability the claimant seems to be relying upon and what defenses potentially seem to be available.

The claim representative's initial consideration will include identification of other possible parties. Conduct on the part of retailers, suppliers, distributors, manufacturers of component parts, or the claimant's employer may have been the cause of the injury. The possibility of cross-claims or third-party actions, therefore, must be considered. On the other hand, such other entities may be allies and sources of information for preparation of the defense. If there possibly can be cooperation between these potential adversaries, the defendant will usually find such cooperation helpful.

The plaintiff's background should be investigated at an early date. Neighbors and fellow employees should be interviewed regarding the claimant's prior injuries, work habits, and use of the product. A retail credit report can sometimes be developed that will include such information, as well as information about prior litigation and the claimant's financial situation. An insurance index report should be obtained as a reference to prior claims.

If the claimant was injured on the job, the workers' compensation file available from the state industrial commission will be useful. The workers' compensation carrier's file ordinarily will include a complete investigation with statements, photographs, and even expert opinions; the file normally should be accessible, if a good relationship exists with the carrier. Indeed, many product liability claims first appear as subrogation actions from compensation insurers.

The claimant's employer often will be a useful source of information. The claimant's supervisor and fellow workers may be able to describe exactly how and why the plaintiff was injured; records may be available to prove such statements.

The claim representative should make immediate personal contact with the insured manufacturer, seeking out and establishing, as the primary contact in the company, a person who can truly assist in the preparation of the case (and perhaps even testify for the company in a future trial). This person should occupy a reasonably high position in the company. At the same time, he or she should be technically qualified as an expert and capable of becoming thoroughly conversant with the details, legal issues, and technical problems involved in the case. A practical engineer who learned the business the hard way, from the ground up, may make the most helpful and effective technical adviser.

The product itself eventually may be on trial. The claim representative should become thoroughly familiar with it. In the case of a worker injured by a product manufactured by the insured, the particular product that injured the plaintiff will usually be available—in the hands of either the employer or the claimant. If so, whatever legal proceedings are necessary to produce the product for inspection by the defense will need to be initiated.

It is important to have all of the insured's records available. This would include descriptive material pertaining to the product involved and how it was manufactured and what purpose it was intended to serve, as well as all instructions, warnings, and other material which accompanied the product. Most companies have detailed records, keyed to serial numbers and descriptive model numbers, which will identify the time of production and sale and the procedures used in manufacturing the particular product. Quality control records also may be utilized. Such evidence may be used to nullify the claim that there was a defect in the product.

There are a number of industry trade associations and other organizations which have promulgated safety standards for many types of products. These include the American National Standards Association and the Underwriters Laboratories. Certain products are certified. The National Safety Council is also active in this area. If the product meets the average safety standard and has been certified by one of these organizations, it is some evidence that the product is not defectively designed. Inquiry should be made through the insured and, in appropriate cases, through the organization having the duty of setting such standards. In addition, there are governmental agencies at both the federal and state level which establish either by statute or regulation the standards of certain products which must be met.

The claim representative must continually impress upon the insured that *all* of the company's records and documentation must be made available and that company personnel should not attempt to prejudge the relevance of materials.

Obviously, the accomplishment of the aforementioned tasks may require input from more than just the claim representative. In serious cases, an important priority is to assemble a defense team that will develop the defense in the pretrial stages—with the long-range view of defending the product at trial if the claim is not settled. The team will include: representatives of the insured manufacturer or seller; representatives of the insurer; one or more attorneys (in-house and/or from the defendant's law firm). The team should meet at an early stage and agree upon what needs to be done, when, how, and by whom.

To summarize, the highest priority of this defense team is preservation. The product must be preserved; the files must be reviewed and preserved; the claimant and the witnesses must be examined so that their testimony is preserved.

Plaintiff's Burden of Proof. It must be emphasized that, regardless of whether the action is brought under strict liability in tort or some other theory of liability, the plaintiff (in order to recover) must establish that the offending product was defective, and that the defect caused the alleged injury. The purpose of the investigation is to ascertain the facts and to determine whether the plaintiff can in fact meet the burden which is thus assumed.

728 Plan of Investigation

When an assignment is received, the investigator must determine the known facts from the accident report or other information submitted and decide what unknown facts are needed to decide the type of handling required. He or she must also decide the order in which the evidence will be obtained. It is clear that the investigator cannot see all witnesses and gather all the evidence at one and the same time. Generally, the rule is that critical evidence should be secured as promptly as possible. *Critical evidence* is evidence which is available now but may not be available after the passage of time.

For example, if the point of impact in an automobile case is important, time will obliterate skid marks, gouges, and other marks in the roadway, and the damage to the cars will be repaired. Therefore, if pictures are needed to establish the existence of these things, they must be taken immediately, and evidence by witnesses, identifying the marks made by each car, must be secured before their memory of the details fades. The same thing would be true of a products case, or a case where there is a claim of an unsafe condition on the premises. The defective product should be secured as soon as possible and tests made, or the premises must be examined for defects and photographs taken of the place of accident under conditions as nearly similar to the circumstances of the accident as possible. In each instance, the passage of time will handicap the investigation and may make the evidence unobtainable.

Another example of critical evidence is the statement of the adverse driver and the personal injury claimant. In the initial stages, it may be possible to get statements from all participants in the accident. After they have retained counsel, no direct contact can be made with them. Where there is more than one personal injury claimant, generally the most seriously injured should be seen first, and the others in order of the seriousness of their injuries.

Another factor which brings the injured party or parties within the realm of critical evidence is the fact that part of the investigation will refer to the injuries sustained, the treatment rendered, and the diagnosis made. Since doctors and hospitals are reluctant to release medical information without an authorization from the patient, medical authorizations can be obtained from the injured party at the time of the first contact. Later may be too late, especially if the information is refused or the injured person is represented by counsel. Therefore, contact with the injured person will result in securing two things: his or her version of the accident and the subsequent medical treatment received, and the authorization to obtain detailed medical information from the doctor and the hospital where the treatment was rendered.

Less critical but of great importance is the evidence of other fact witnesses who saw the accident, or some part of it, but who are not interested in the result because they were not involved. Such witnesses should receive the same priority as that given to parties to the event. Secondary fact witnesses who can contribute to the delineation of the event are the police officer who investigated the case, the tow truck driver who towed the wrecked automobiles away, and the paramedic and ambulance driver. All of these can testify to the scene of the accident when they arrived, the condition of the injured parties, the location of the cars when they came to rest, skid marks, gouges in the roadway, debris on the road, blood, glass, etc., and their relationship to the center line. These witnesses are given less priority than the others, but there is always the possibility of the opposing side getting its statements first. Therefore, while the gathering of critical evidence will occupy the investigator's initial efforts, it is important to contact these secondary witnesses as soon as possible after the happening of the accident.

The plan of investigation might include attendance at the coroner's inquest in death cases, attendance at traffic court hearings, or the securing of school reports, weather reports, the adverse driver's license (and record of whether the license required the wearing of glasses, and whether there have been any refusals, suspensions, or revocations of the license). It also may be necessary to secure the official documents referring to the event, such as the police report, motor vehicle accident reports, and, if a public utility is involved, reports to the government authority. This latter would include reports to the public service commission by transit companies and electric light and power companies, reports to the CAB by airlines, and reports to the local transit authority by taxicab companies.

Hazardous Products. In cases involving these products, a certain amount of investigation is required to determine the theory of defense, if there is one. (See Sections 717–724, above.) An accident involving a consumer product such as a tool, appliance, or toy usually takes place at a clearly defined time. The investigation may be relatively simple and straightforward. However, in many of these cases, the public is exposed to a product hazard over a period of time, and the first manifestation of an injury or a disease does not occur immediately but after a period of years. For example, asbestosis is a lung condition caused by the inhalation of asbestos fibers over a period of years, and the diagnosis is not made until a long time after initial exposure. The same thing is true with regard to the ingestion of some drugs. The results may not be apparent until a long time after the drug was first ingested.

In making an investigation of a claim for exposure to a hazardous substance, the areas of inquiry include: (1) coverage; (2) liability; and (3) possible additional defendants.

1. Coverage. The first inquiry must be directed to the insured's records to determine when the manufacture of the deleterious material began and when it was released to the general public or discharged into a waste disposal area. If the release began after the termination of the insurer's policy, there would be no coverage applicable. On the other hand, if the same insurer was on the risk during the period when the hazardous material was first released and still on the risk when the claims were made, the insurer's coverage would be involved. If the release produced effects which were unintended or unexpected, the transaction could be considered as an ''occurrence'' within the terms of the Commercial General Liability policy (CGL)—formerly called the Comprehensive General Liability policy—which is the type of coverage purchased by companies engaged in industrial or commercial enterprises.

A more difficult problem arises when there are one or more insurers on the risk during the period of exposure, but another on the risk at the time of the first manifestation of injury or disease. The court then would have the problem of deciding which insurer was liable under its policy for the injury or damage. The courts have been struggling with this problem for quite some time. The decisions are not in agreement; some courts hold that the insurer on the risk at the first manifestation of the condition is liable, whereas others take the position that all insurers who were on the risk during the period of exposure are jointly liable. Thus, we have decisions based principally (although several other theories exist) on the (*a*) ''Manifestation Theory'' or (*b*) ''Exposure Theory,'' as follows:

a. Manifestation Theory. This theory was first announced in a case involving the liability of the manufacturer of DES, which the plaintiff ingested. The court held that the insurer on the risk at the time that the cervical cancer was discovered was liable. The case is *American Motorists Insurance Co.* v. *E. R. Squibb & Sons, Inc.*, [406 N.Y.S. 2d 658]. DES (diethylstilbestrol), a synthetic estrogen, was advertised as preventing miscarriages. In holding the insurer liable, the court pointed out that "coverage is predicated not on the act which might give rise to ultimate liability, but upon the result."

See also *Eagle-Pitcher Industries, Inc.* v. *Liberty Mutual Insurance Co.* [682 Fed. 2d 12 (1st Cir., Mass.)]. Here, the circuit court defined "manifestation" as being the time when the disease "becomes reasonably capable of medical diagnosis" rather than the date of the actual diagnosis. This case involved over 5,000 asbestos-related injuries.

It should be noted that, in a number of workers' compensation statutes, the occupational disease section provides that in such cases the date of disability is regarded as the "date of the accident" in determining the insurer who is liable.

b. The Exposure Theory. In determining the liability of the insurers of a particular risk, the courts have held that all insurers who were on the risk during the period of exposure were jointly liable. For example, *Insurance Company of North America* v. *Forty-Eight Insulations, Inc.* [657 Fed. 2d 814, certiorari denied in 454 U.S. 1109)], involved the liability of the defendant for the manufacture of products containing asbestos during the period from 1923 to 1970. During this period of time the defendant was insured by many different insurers at different periods of time. The federal district court in Michigan adopted the exposure theory, holding that all insurers were jointly liable. Since there was no evidence of insurance prior to 1955, the asbestos manufacturer was deemed to be a self-insurer for that period of time. This brief discussion can only hint at the difficulty of these coverage issues in this rapidly changing area of the law; the full complexities are beyond the scope of this chapter.

2. Liability. The investigation should include an inquiry as to the kind and nature of the product which is alleged to have been deleterious, either to human beings, animals, or the environment. The claimant must be able to allege the nature of the product and how the exposure was created, as well as establishing that there was causal relationship between the alleged exposure and the subsequent medical condition. The investigation should be directed toward ascertaining these facts, or the absence of such facts, in a particular case.

3. Possible Additional Defendants. The investigation should also include others who may have contributed to the exposure, and, while in some cases the manufacturer or creator of the hazard may be insulated from liability, there are situations where such additional defendants may be jointly liable. The prime example is the Love Canal situation where several defendants are involved. The history of Love Canal goes back almost 100 years. In 1892, William T. Love started to construct a canal between the upper and lower levels of the Niagara River in order to develop a means of creating hydroelectric power. The project was abandoned in the latter part of the 1890s, and there remained only a partially dug canal in the southeast corner of the city of Niagara Falls. There was no housing in the area and children used to travel to the site and use it as a swimming hole. In the 1920s the canal became a disposal site for many chemical companies, including the Hooker Chemical and Plastics Co. Subsequently, the land was sold to developers in the 1950s and the land was covered over with earth, houses were built, and a school opened. On August 2, 1978, the New York Health Commissioner declared that a health emergency existed in the Love Canal area, recommending that families with pregnant women near the canal temporarily move from the area as soon as possible, and that the residents avoid using their basements. Within months, the two elementary schools were closed and the state agencies purchased hundreds of residential homes. Over 600 lawsuits were instituted against Hooker Chemical, the city of Niagara Falls, the Niagara Falls Board of Education, and the County of Niagara. The insurers of the defendants disclaimed liability. However, in *Niagara County* v. *Utica Mutual Insurance Co.* [427 N.Y.S. 2d 171], the lower court held the pollution exclusion on which the insurer relied did not apply, holding in favor of the plaintiff. This decision was unanimously affirmed by the Appellate Division [439 N.Y.S. 2d 538]. The court said:

> The complaints in the underlying actions, besides charging the various defendants collectively with dumping and abandoning chemicals, waste products, etc., further allege that Niagara County was negligent in failing to warn and safeguard its citizens or enforce health regulations, failing to remove chemicals and the plaintiffs from the Love Canal area and wrongfully conveying property in the area without notice of the infirmities contained and in violation of ordinances and regulations.

This situation illustrates that there can be more than one defendant involved in a particular incident. Therefore, the plan of investigation must include all possible defendants. The same type of inquiry should be made with respect to injuries. If the injured person was in normal health at the time of the accident, then the inquiry with respect to injuries would be limited to the period following the date of accident. However, if the claimant was suffering from some preexisting injury or disease, then the inquiry would have to develop the nature of the preexisting disability and whether such disability had any influence upon the injury sustained, and also, if the claimant was the adverse driver, whether that disability had any influence on the causation of the accident.

Outline of Investigation. In creating the plan of investigation, due regard should be had for the theories of defense and the necessary legal elements needed to establish it. In gathering the evidence, the investigator will determine the presence or absence of the facts necessary to make the defense available. He will also consider other and further defenses should the inquiry reveal that the elements are present. In a word, the plan of investigation should be flexible, contemplating the abandonment of certain theories of defense when inquiry shows they are untenable, and adopting other defenses if the inquiry indicates their existence.

A general plan of investigation, where the insurance coverage is in order, will consist of all or some of the following elements in this sequence:

1. Critical Evidence
   a) Statement of the adverse driver (if an auto case)
   b) Statement of the claimant (or claimants in the order of the severity of the injuries)
   c) Photograph of the scene of the accident, showing skid marks and other evidence of the accident
   d) Examination and photographs of the vehicles themselves, showing the damage and point of impact
   e) The product itself or the instrumentality causing the injury
2. Fact Evidence
   a) Statements of disinterested witnesses
   b) Statement of the insured, his or her driver, or employee having knowledge of the accident, the instrumentality causing it, or the part of the premises in which the accident is alleged to have occurred
   c) Negative statements from persons who were in a position to have seen the accident or have some knowledge of its occurrence, but who deny having such knowledge
3. Official Reports
   a) Police report
   b) State motor vehicle reports filed by the parties to the accident
   c) Fire department reports
   d) Reports of state motor vehicle inspectors
   e) Traffic court proceedings
   f) Arraignment in magistrate's court
   g) Death certificates
   h) Autopsy reports
   i) Coroner's inquest transcript
   j) Birth and marriage certificates
   k) Weather reports
   l) School records
   m) Certified copies of court records showing prior convictions of crimes
   n) Transit authority reports (if a taxicab is involved)
   o) C.A.B. reports (aircraft)
   p) I.C.C. reports (interstate truckers)
   q) Coast Guard reports (boats)
4. Unofficial Reports
   a) Newspaper accounts
5. Medical Reports
   a) Hospital records
   b) Attending physician's report and records
   c) Medical or hospital reports covering preexisting injury or disease
6. Documentary Evidence
   a) Deeds of ownership of land

   b) Leases
   c) Contracts and agreements, especially contracts for construction, alteration, and repair, as well as hold harmless agreements
7. Visual Evidence
   a) Diagrams or sketches of the scene of accident
   b) Engineering plats
   c) X rays
   d) Photographs
8. Verification Evidence
   a) Employer's records to show wage loss
   b) Index bureau reports
   c) Workers' compensation claims made by injured party, arising out of the same accident
9. Expert Evidence
   a) Report of company medical examiner
   b) Automobile inspector or appraiser
   c) Engineer or chemist
   d) Actuaries
   e) Handwriting expert

In states requiring the renewal of operators' licenses on an annual basis, investigators have found it to be advantageous to obtain a copy of the claimant's application for this license whether he was driving a car at the time of the accident or not. If he was the driver, the license might reveal that it was issued on a conditional basis, requiring that he wear glasses at all times when driving, or that it has been revoked or suspended. More important, however, most applications require an answer relative to the applicant's physical condition and whether there has been any change in it during the past year. The question usually reads "Have you suffered any physical or mental injury during the past 12 months?" If the application is made after the accident and it is claimed that there were severe physical injuries suffered, a negative answer on the application could be used in evidence to controvert such a claim.

Chapter 8

Law of Automobiles

RULES OF THE ROAD

800 Rights and Duties of the Motorist

801 Rules of the Road

802 Assured Clear Distance Rule

803 Compliance with Traffic Signs

804 Failure to See Traffic Warning Signs

805 Vehicles Traveling in the Same Direction

806 Vehicles Traveling in Opposite Directions

807 Vehicles Traveling at Right Angles

808 Violating Rules of the Road in an Emergency

809 Stop Signs

810 Vehicles Entering the Highway from Private Way

SPECIAL SITUATIONS

811 Railroad Crossings

812 School Buses

813 Emergency Vehicles

814 Motorcycles and Bicycles

815 Parked Vehicles

816 Disabled Vehicles

817 Commercial Vehicles

818 No-Contact Cases

819 Seat Belt Defense

OWNER AND VICARIOUS LIABILITY

820 Vicarious Liability of the Owner

821 Family Purpose Doctrine

822 Statutory Liability of the Owner

823 Vicarious Liability of Person Other than Owner

PASSENGERS AND PEDESTRIANS

824 Rights and Duties of Passengers

825 Automobile Guest Statutes

826 Guest Defined

827 Driver's Negligence Not Imputed to Passengers

828 Rights and Duties of Pedestrians

829 Traffic Officers and Workers on the Roadway

STATUTORY REQUIREMENTS

830 State Licensing Regulations

831 Unregistered Vehicles

832 Financial Responsibility Acts

833 Compulsory Automobile Insurance

834 Statutory Policies of Automobile Liability Insurance

835 Service of Process on Nonresident Motorists

PERSONAL INJURY PROTECTION (PIP) NO-FAULT SYSTEMS

836 Purpose and Scope

837 Legislation

838 Insurance

839 Benefits Provided

840 Tort Exemption

841 Third-Party Claims

842 Subrogation under No-Fault Statutes

843 Arbitration under No-Fault Statutes

844 Claims Administration under No-Fault

RULES OF THE ROAD

800 Rights and Duties of the Motorist

The operator of a motor vehicle is required to exercise reasonable care for the safety of others who may be endangered by its use. The operator owes this duty of care to the operators and occupants of other vehicles on the highway, occupants of the operator's own car, and pedestrians, as well as owners of property, either on the highway or adjacent to it. *Reasonable care* is a relative term in that the extent of the care required is entirely dependent on the circumstances. It is measured by the reasonably prudent person standard. (See Section 302, above.) The question of whether the operator's conduct conformed to the standard or fell below it is usually a question of fact to be determined by the jury, unless the facts of the occurrence are so clear that reasonable minds could not differ as to the application of the standard.

The reasonably prudent person will maintain his or her vehicle in a reasonably safe condition, will obey the rules of the road, will conform to the highway regulations, will observe and obey traffic control signs and signals, will keep the car under control, and will do everything possible to avoid an accident. Clearly, the duty of care is a varying one which will be measured in each case by the circumstances and the degree of danger involved. As one court put it: "The danger to be perceived determines the duty to be obeyed."

Thus, if a motorist sees a pedestrian with a white cane crossing at an intersection, he is charged with the knowledge that the pedestrian is blind, and therefore the duty of care is greater than would be the situation if the pedestrian had no infirmity. In this case, the duty of care would require that the motorist yield the right-of-way to the blind person. Where a pedestrian has normal faculties, and is crossing in the path of the motorist, the duty of care would consist of giving the pedestrian adequate warning of the motorist's approach by sounding the horn. When the motorist is on the highway, he or she must operate the vehicle with a degree of care commensurate with existing conditions. If it is a clear day, vision unimpaired, and the roads dry, the motorist will be expected to exercise a certain degree of care. Where the weather is bad—raining, snowing, or sleeting, with vision impaired and the roads wet or slippery—a much greater degree of care is required.

The area in which the vehicle is being operated will also have some influence on the amount of care needed. A greater degree must be exercised in a congested city area as opposed to the open highway, and in dense as opposed to light traffic. A motorist passing a school or nursing home would be required to exercise more than the normal amount of care if there is notice of the presence of these institutions by means of warning signs. Likewise, if a motorist is traveling through an area in which a number of children are playing, he or she would be required to exercise more care for their safety than if traveling through a business area where there are no children.

The motorist has the right to assume that others using the highway will exercise care for the motorist's safety as well as for their own and will obey the rules of the road, the highway regulations, and the traffic controls. The motorist may rely upon this assumption until it becomes clear that the other person will not act with reasonable care. Thus, if a motorist sees a vehicle approaching on the wrong side of the road, he or she has a right to assume that the other motorist will return to the proper side before they meet. Just how long a driver can rely on this assumption is a question of fact for the jury. When it becomes clear that the other car will not return to its proper side of the road, the motorist must take some defensive action to avoid an accident if it is then possible to do so. (See also Last Clear Chance, Section 416.)

In a number of states, minors are licensed to operate a motor vehicle after they have attained a certain age. A minor, operating a vehicle under those circumstances, is required to exercise the same degree of care as is required of an adult. The minor's conduct will be judged by the reasonably prudent person standard, and if his or her actions fall below that standard, the minor can be held liable for negligence. The argument that a minor is incapable of mature judgment is not a defense. The conduct in operating the vehicle will be judged as if the minor driver were an adult.

801 Rules of the Road

The highway and traffic regulations of a state constitute the rules of the road for that particular state. They determine how travelers may use the highway, which vehicle has the right-of- way, and the conditions under which the right-of-way is acquired, as well as the rights and duties of the vehicles which do not have the superior right-of-way. They also fix the maximum speed and the conditions under which motor vehicles may be driven on the public roads. The rights granted by the rules of the road are not absolute in that they may be exercised under all circumstances; they are subject to the qualification that the motorist exercise care for the safety of others. For example, if a motorist is stopped at a controlled intersection, and the light changes to green in his favor, he must allow the traffic and the pedestrians already in the intersection to clear before he proceeds. Since they are designed to promote safety and to restrict extreme action by any individual, there is a general uniformity among the laws of the various states.

Some of the chief rules of the road are summarized in the following sections, with some brief comments on the relationship between some of these rules and the law of negligence. Some cross-references to Chapters 3, 4, and 5 (dealing with the law of torts) are provided for the reader's guidance.

802 Assured Clear Distance Rule

The application of this rule requires that the driver keep the car under such control as to be able to stop within the range of his or her sight, should such a stop be necessary in order to avoid an accident. The distance will vary according to the circumstances. At night the distance would be measured by the range of the headlights, whereas in the daylight hours visibility will depend upon weather conditions. In any case, if the driver fails to maintain such control as would enable the driver to stop within the range of vision, the driver may be liable for negligence. To be applied, the rule contemplates the existence of two elements: *visibility* and *opportunity*.

Visibility. The dangerous condition or object must be large enough or of such a nature as to be visible to an individual with average eyesight, or there must be adequate warning of its existence. Thus, if there is a slowly moving truck on the highway, a clearly marked barricade with warning signs, blinkers, lanterns or flares, construction in progress with a signaler some distance in advance of it, or signs warning of a cattle crossing, the motorist may be liable for negligence if unable to avoid the objects by reducing speed or stopping the vehicle. In each of these cases the driver saw, or should have seen, the object, or received adequate warning of their existence.

Opportunity. The driver must have had an opportunity to slow down or stop. Where the dangerous condition or object is not visible, and the driver has had no warning of its existence, the driver is not negligent if he or she does everything possible to avoid the accident when the dangerous condition is apprehended. For example, if an excavation or hole in the highway is not visible at a greater distance than five feet, and there are no warning signs, the motorist cannot be deemed to be negligent if she cannot stop or avoid it, because she had no opportunity to do so.

803 Compliance with Traffic Signs

The state highway law in most jurisdictions contains the requirement that ''No person shall fail, neglect or refuse to comply with any lawful traffic regulations displayed on any highway.'' This means that the motorist must observe and obey all regulatory signs posted along the highway, provided they are *lawful* and *displayed*.

Lawful. The authority for the erection of any traffic control sign is granted either by a state law or by an ordinance passed by a political subdivision of the state to which lawmaking power of this kind has been delegated. If the sign is erected without the authority of a state law or ordinance, it is an unlawful sign and the motorist is not bound to obey it. The same result will follow where the ordinance is illegal because it was not enacted according to law, or covers a portion of the highway outside of the jurisdiction of the body enacting it.

Displayed. This means that it must be possible for the motorist to observe the sign; it must be clearly readable and visible. If the sign has been damaged by exposure to weather so that it is not readable, or if the motorist's view of the sign is obstructed because of an overgrowth of shrubbery, weeds, bushes, or debris piled in front of it, the sign is not "displayed" and the motorist is not charged with the knowledge of the presence of the sign. And, where the sign has been damaged because of a prior accident or the action of vandals, or has been stolen, it is not being "displayed."

804 Failure to See Traffic Warning Signs

A motorist traveling on the highways has the duty of making reasonable use of his vision in order to determine whether there are any traffic control signs (erected for the driver's protection and the protection of others). The motorist cannot escape the duty imposed by the statute by stating that he or she did not see plainly visible signs, because the motorist has the duty to see what, in the exercise of reasonable care, he or she should have seen. The failure to see and comply with plainly visible traffic control signs is negligence.

805 Vehicles Traveling in the Same Direction

Where two cars are traveling in the same direction on the same road, the general rule is that the car ahead has the superior right and may maintain its position. Further rights and duties arise in situations involving (1) passing, (2) reduction in speed or stopping, (3) turns at intersections, and (4) turns between intersections.

1. Passing. The leading vehicle is under the duty to keep to the right side of the road. There is no absolute legal duty on the part of the motorist to stop his car in order to permit a faster vehicle to pass, even though, when the passing is being attempted, there might be a duty to reduce speed or come to a full stop under special circumstances where such action might prevent an accident.

In some parts of the country, especially where there are long, winding, uphill roads, it is customary for the driver of a slow-moving truck to signal those behind that it is safe to pass. The signal is usually a hand signal or the blinking of marker lights. The truck driver is under no duty to give such a signal, and does so only as a matter of courtesy. Having voluntarily assumed the duty, however, the truck driver must exercise reasonable care in the execution of it. Should the truck driver give the signal, and the following motorist rely on it with the result that an accident occurs, the truck driver may be held partially responsible as a joint tort-feasor. In any case, reliance on the signals given by the truck driver will not relieve the passing driver of the duty to exercise care.

The overtaking driver may pass only when it is safe to do so. He or she must exercise care and judgment as to when and where the passing maneuver may be accomplished, and must use proper signals. Where there is insufficient room for safe passage, it is the duty of the following driver to maintain position and wait until a place is reached where it can be done in safety.

Whether the passing motorist exercised care and judgment and gave adequate warning of intention to all vehicles concerned are questions of fact to be determined by the jury in the light of all circumstances.

Most statutes require that the passing vehicle must be to the left of the overtaken vehicle. Where the statute requires that all vehicles pass on the left, violation of the statute has been held to be negligence per se. Most states, however, hold that passing other than on the left does not in and of itself establish negligence unless such movement was the efficient cause of the accident which ensued. In some jurisdictions, ordinances prohibit the overtaking and passing of another vehicle at intersections. Violations of such statutes, where they exist, constitute negligence.

2. Reduction in Speed or Stopping. Most highway statutes require that the motorist give warning by means of a hand signal or adequate signal device of any marked reduction in speed, or stopping on the highways, to the vehicles behind, if there is an opportunity to do so. But where the forward driver is suddenly confronted by an object on the highway, such as an animal, a person, an unmarked barricade, or a defect in the roadway, and has no opportunity of signaling an intention, the driver is relieved of the obligation.

Where a motorist driving at night is suddenly confronted with glaring headlights which prevent seeing the road ahead, he or she is under a duty to slacken speed or stop, as the occasion demands. A motorist is not entitled to operate a vehicle on a public street when he or she cannot see. Thus, the blinded motorist may have two duties: to exercise care as to persons on the highway whom the motorist cannot see, and to signal the intention of markedly reducing speed or stopping to the vehicle following. If the motorist has an opportunity to signal the following vehicle, he or she must do so.

Where the following vehicle runs into the forward vehicle because of a sudden stop or slackening of speed, the defense is usually interposed that the vehicle was following the forward car too closely and therefore was contributorily negligent. What constitutes a safe following distance will depend upon the facts and circumstances of each case, with due regard being given to the density of traffic at the point of accident, the speed of the cars, and the condition of the road. What might be a safe distance in one case might be entirely unsafe in another.

3. Turns at Intersections. If a right or left turn is to be made at an intersection, the driver is required, in addition to checking traffic and signaling, to place the vehicle in the proper position and make the turn from one proper lane to the other proper lane when safe to do so. Signals for a right or left turn must be given for a distance of not less than 100 feet before turning.

4. Turns between Intersections. As to right turns into a private driveway, alley, or parking lot, the same rules referable to turns at an intersection are applicable. As to left turns, the general rule is that where the driver intends to make such a turn between intersections, he or she is under a duty to give a timely signal to the motorists who are following. The driver must exercise care and caution to be certain that the turn can be made in safety. Where the driver is on notice that the car immediately behind intends to pass, most states require that the driver allow it to pass, and then make the turn in safety.

806 Vehicles Traveling in Opposite Directions

The rules of the road require that all vehicles be driven on the right-hand side of the road. This means that vehicles must be driven on the extreme right side of the road, or to the right of the center line, except when overtaking and passing a vehicle ahead, or when a highway having more than one lane in each direction becomes congested with traffic to the extent that vehicles must be driven in all lanes so provided. Specific situations involving vehicles traveling in opposite directions will arise in the following situations: (1) passing, (2) left turns at intersections, and (3) left turns between intersections.

1. Passing. When two vehicles traveling in opposite directions meet, each is required to keep to the right of the center line. When a collision occurs on the wrong side of the road, a presumption of negligence ordinarily arises against the driver of the vehicle who is on the wrong side. The presumption can be overcome by an explanation of the facts and circumstances of the accident, which may absolve the driver of negligence or the lack of due care. For example, if it could be shown that the driver operating a vehicle with due care was hit by a negligent motorist—and his vehicle was forced onto the wrong side of the road, with another accident ensuing—the explanation, if believed, will overcome the presumption.

2. Left Turns at Intersections. Where a left turn is being attempted at an uncontrolled intersection, or a controlled intersection not having left turn directional signals, the general rule is that the oncoming vehicle has the superior right-of-way and that the left-turning vehicle shall yield the right-of-way to the oncoming vehicle. In making a left turn or crossing the line of traffic, the driver must exercise due caution to see that the way is clear so that it is safe to cross traffic which is coming in the opposite direction.

3. Left Turns between Intersections. When driving between intersections, the driver has a right to assume that approaching vehicles will keep to the right, and he or she has no reason to anticipate that a left turn will be made by an approaching vehicle. Therefore, when a left turn is to be made between intersections, the left-turning driver has a greater duty of care than would apply in the case of a left turn at an intersection.

807 Vehicles Traveling at Right Angles

It is clear that a motorist approaching an intersection is on notice that others (either motorists or pedestrians) will use the intersection by crossing that motorist's lane of travel. Therefore, the motorist is charged with a greater duty of care and vigilance than would be the situation while driving on the open road.

1. Controlled Intersections. The motorist is under a duty to obey the traffic directional signals at a controlled intersection and to yield the right-of-way to other vehicles where required, and to pedestrians on a crosswalk with a green light. The mere fact that the motorist has the right-of-way because the traffic signal is in his or her favor does not confer the right to proceed without the exercise of due care. This duty continues even though another driver may negligently operate a vehicle in the intersection.

2. Uncontrolled Intersections. The general rule is that the motorist who first enters an uncontrolled intersection has the right-of-way over vehicles approaching the intersection. As in the case of the controlled intersection, the fact that the driver has the right-of-way does not give that driver the right to proceed without the exercise of due care; nor would the fact that another driver is operating a vehicle negligently in the intersection excuse all other drivers from their duty of exercising due care. Most highway rules further provide that, when two cars approach the intersection simultaneously, the car on the right has the right-of-way and the other must yield.

808 Violating Rules of the Road in an Emergency

The application of the foregoing rules may be affected by an emergency. A motorist confronted with an emergency is not required to give detached reflection as to what course of action is the most desirable, but is required to take such action as a reasonably prudent person would take in order to avoid injury to herself and others, even though this action may involve a violation of the rules of the road. Each such act will be judged by the circumstances confronting the motorist, and the amount of time available within which to decide what to do. A violation of the rules of the road will not constitute negligence if the following evidence is available: (1) the violation of the rules was justifiable under the circumstances; (2) the motorist's own failure to exercise due care did not create the emergency; (3) the motorist exercised reasonable care in facing the emergency.

It should be emphasized that the emergency rule applies only in favor of the innocent motorist whose conduct did not create the emergency. If the motorist was negligent and created the emergency, she is responsible for the consequences of her own acts, and the emergency rule is inapplicable.

809 Stop Signs

A motorist approaching a stop sign is required to come to a full stop. After stopping, he or she may proceed with caution and, at that point, has the same right of use of the highway as any other car. The same duties and the same rights applicable to uncontrolled intersections apply equally here. The stop sign merely obligates the motorist to come to a full stop and make an observation. A motorist who has done that has done all that the law requires, as far as the stop sign is concerned.

The fact that a motorist did not stop at a stop sign is not in and of itself evidence of negligence unless it can be shown that the failure to stop was the proximate cause (see Section 306, above) of the accident. If it had no influence on the causation of the accident, it is regarded as an excusable violation.

810 Vehicles Entering the Highway from Private Way

A motorist entering the highway from a private driveway, alley, or garage is required to exercise that degree of care and caution that the hazards of the situation demand. If the entrance to the driveway is obscured from the vision of motorists already on the highway because of foliage or other obstructions to vision, the care to be exercised is that much greater. The motorist already on the highway is not bound to anticipate that vehicles will enter the highway between intersections. He or she is required to exercise the usual care in having the vehicle under control as to speed and stopping ability. The driver is not held to the same degree of care as would be the case when approaching an intersection. The entering motorist's conduct will be judged by the facts and circumstances of the occurrence, the weather conditions, the density of traffic, and the kind and type of driveway involved.

SPECIAL SITUATIONS

811 Railroad Crossings

In spite of the fact that, at many grade crossings, the railroads still maintain signs directing people using the crossing to "stop, look, and listen," this slogan does not define the duty of the motorist. The rule is that motorists approaching a railroad crossing must reduce their speed to a safe limit after passing the warning sign, usually required to be erected 300 feet from the crossing. The motorist then is required to proceed cautiously and carefully, with the vehicle under complete control.

Most statutes require that certain vehicles make a full stop at railroad crossings at all times. These vehicles include buses with a capacity of more than six passengers, school buses, vehicles transporting explosives, and certain types of construction vehicles. Drivers in following vehicles, in the exercise of due care, are bound to anticipate such stops and to govern their conduct and driving accordingly.

812 School Buses

Under most statutes, the driver of a vehicle approaching or overtaking a school bus, displaying proper school bus signs at front and rear and stopped to pick up or discharge a school child, is required to stop his or her vehicle not less than 10 feet from the bus and remain stationary until the child has entered the bus or has alighted and reached the side of the highway. A few exceptions are usually provided to prevent unnecessary traffic delays when the safety of school children is not affected. The identification and equipment of the school bus will differ state by state, although most require the bus to be of yellow color and carry plain markings. Certain flashing stoplights, front and rear, are required, and in some states a gate is required to be extended from the left side of the bus when it is in a stopped position.

813 Emergency Vehicles

The emergency vehicles with which we will be concerned for the most part are ambulances, fire apparatus, and police cars.

Ambulances. In the absence of a statute granting a preferential use of the highways, ambulances are subject to the same traffic rules as any other vehicle. They must obey the speed laws, traffic signals, and traffic control signs. Where statutes confer preferential rights and privileges to ambulances, these rights may be exercised only when the ambulance complies with the statute as to the use of a siren, flashing lights, and other signals as may be prescribed, and only when the ambulance is responding to an emergency. When used for any other purpose or driven at any other time, the ambulance has no rights superior to those of any other motor vehicle. However, even when responding to an emergency, the driver of the ambulance is charged with the duty of exercising that degree of care commensurate with the hazards involved.

Where it is claimed that the ambulance was responding to an emergency, it should be established that an emergency existed and its character was such as to justify the speed at which the ambulance was being driven. If there was no emergency or the call for assistance was such that speed was not essential, the duty of exercising due care would be the same as that imposed on other drivers. Where there is an emergency, and the ambulance has given the warning required, the ambulance driver has a right to rely on the assumption that all vehicles in the vicinity will yield the right-of-way. Where the statute requires that the motorist turn out of the way of an ambulance, the motorist who fails to do so, after receiving warning of the approach of the ambulance, is chargeable with contributory negligence (see Section 500, above) if an accident should ensue.

Fire Apparatus. The same rules that apply to ambulances govern the operation of fire apparatus on the highways. When responding to an alarm, the driver of the fire apparatus must exercise the care required under the circumstances by sounding the proper warning and affording other vehicles on the highway an opportunity to move out of the way.

Police Cars. Police cars are privileged to exceed the speed limit and otherwise disregard traffic controls when engaged in pursuing a fleeing criminal. This privilege is granted only for the limited purpose of police duty and, even while it is being utilized, the driver must exercise whatever due care the hazards of the situation require. Should the privilege be abused, the officer is answerable.

814 Motorcycles and Bicycles

The riders of motorcycles and bicycles using the highway are subject to the same rights and the same duties as motor vehicles. Because of the slow speed of bicycles, there are several additional rules which are applicable. The statutes usually provide that every person operating a bicycle upon a roadway shall ride as near to the right side of the roadway as practicable, and exercise due care when passing a standing vehicle or one proceeding in the same direction. Bicycles are required to have brakes that will enable the operator to make the braked wheels skid on dry, level, clean pavement. When in use in the nighttime, the bicycle must be equipped with proper lights and reflectors. The bicycle must be equipped with a bell or other device capable of a signal audible for a distance of at least 100 feet. Local statutes and ordinances may increase or diminish these duties, and these should be consulted in each case.

The equipment required of a motorcycle is practically the same as any other motor vehicle as to lights, brakes, signals, and horn.

The driver of a motor vehicle owes the same degree of care to the rider of a motorcycle or bicycle as he is required to exercise toward operators of other motor vehicles.

815 Parked Vehicles

A vehicle is parked when it is stopped, whether the driver is behind the wheel or not, except when it is stopped in obedience to a traffic officer, sign or signal, or taking on or letting off passengers or merchandise. The highway statutes and local ordinances specify how and where a vehicle may be legally parked. In cities and populated areas, the usual rule is that a vehicle may be parked on the right-hand side of the road, parallel to and within 6 inches of the curb and headed in the direction of traffic. Parking on the left side of one-way streets or angle parking constitute exceptions to the rule.

Generally, parking is prohibited in the following places:

1. Within an intersection, including the T-end type.
2. On a crosswalk.
3. Within 25 feet of an intersection.
4. Between or within 20 feet of a curb and an opposite safety zone.
5. Alongside or opposite any street excavation or obstruction where parking would obstruct traffic.
6. Alongside another vehicle parked at the curb (double parking).
7. Upon a bridge or elevated highway or within a highway tunnel or underpass.
8. In any officially marked ''No Parking'' space.

A motorist is negligently parked in violation of the parking rules, but is liable in damages only if such parking is the proximate cause of an accident. The motorist is likewise negligent if he or she parks the vehicle in such a way that a part of it projects onto the traveled portion of the highway, rendering travel unsafe for passing motorists. A motorist who parks a vehicle in a prohibited area may also become liable to others where the accident was caused by an obstruction to vision created by the improperly parked vehicle. The mere fact that the vehicle was illegally parked will not in and of itself impose liability. It must be shown that the fact of illegal parking was the cause or a contributing cause of the accident.

816 Disabled Vehicles

Where a vehicle is improperly parked on the highway, the law raises a presumption of negligence from this fact against the operator of the vehicle. The burden of overcoming the presumption by explanation is placed upon the defendant. If it can be shown that the parking was the result of an emergency, such as a mechanical failure or collision with another object or another motor vehicle, and that the driver of the vehicle exercised due care under the circumstances for the safety of others, the jury can find that the illegal parking was an excusable violation of the statute. We will consider, therefore, emergency and due care.

Emergency. The condition of the vehicle must be such that it cannot be removed from the traveled portion of the highway. If it can be so moved, the driver is under an obligation to move it to the shoulder. The burden of establishing the impossibility of moving the vehicle is imposed upon the driver of the vehicle.

Due Care. The statutes usually require—when in case of accident or emergency it becomes necessary to leave a vehicle on the highway at night—that a light be conspicuously displayed and that the owner or operator of the disabled vehicle notify, by the quickest means of communication, the nearest police authority. Where there is an opportunity to do so, it would appear that the minimum requirement of due care would be compliance with the statute.

Where a vehicle is stopped on the traveled portion of the highway for the purpose of emergency repairs, and an accident occurs, a number of fact questions are involved. Again, in this situation, whether the operator exercised the degree of care commensurate with the danger is a question for the jury.

817 Commercial Vehicles

The statutes prohibit loading or operating a loaded vehicle in such a way that the contents may be scattered or dropped on the highway. Thus, where part of the load falls to the pavement in the path of a following vehicle, and is the proximate cause of an accident, the persons injured have a cause of action against the operator or the person responsible for the loading, or both. In addition, where vehicles are carrying a projecting load, the statutes require that a red flag in the daytime and a red light at night be attached to the end of the projecting material.

818 No-Contact Cases

It is fundamental that, where negligence of the motorist is the proximate cause (see Section 306, above) of an accident, the motorist is answerable. This is true whether there is any contact between the offending vehicle and the injured pedestrian or not. For example, if a motorist drives the car on the sidewalk, and, to avoid being struck, a pedestrian jumps out of the way and is injured in so doing, the proximate cause of the injury is the negligence of the motorist in driving on the sidewalk. While there was no actual contact between the offending vehicle and the pedestrian, nevertheless the motorist is answerable in damages.

In another case, let us assume that the offending motorist ran through a red traffic light into the path of another vehicle proceeding on the green. The vehicle stops short and there is no contact with the offending vehicle. Because of the sudden stop, vehicles behind are unable to stop and crash into the stopped vehicle. The proximate cause of the accident is the negligence of the motorist who ran through the red light. He or she is liable for all the damage caused by his or her negligence, whether to the vehicle into whose path the motorist drove or to the other vehicles which were following. The motorist who stopped suddenly in order to avoid an accident is not to blame for the accident which followed; the responsibility is entirely that of the motorist who ran the red light.

The difficulties attending these no-contact cases do not lie in the direction of the law governing the situation, but in the matter of proof. What usually happens is that the motorist who caused the accident escapes and is unidentified. When it is alleged that the motorist who stopped suddenly was negligent, he or she can be absolved of negligence only by showing the necessity for the action.

If there was no other vehicle involved, then a sudden stop without warning could be considered a negligent act. The plaintiff is interested in establishing that there was no other car involved because the plaintiff then can recover from the defendant. Otherwise, if the defendant was not negligent, and the accident was caused by the other car, which is unidentified, the plaintiff will have to find and identify the other driver before a recovery can be had. Where a defense such as this is interposed, plaintiffs like to refer to the unidentified vehicle as the "phantom car," which tends to raise some question as to its existence.

819 Seat Belt Defense

For a number of years, federal law has mandated that passenger automobiles be equipped with safety belts (often referred to as seat belts). More than 30 states have enacted statutes requiring the use of available seat belts.

The legal problem presented by the use of seat belts involves the question of whether the driver or passenger of an automobile equipped with seat belts is contributorily negligent and is barred from recovery because of failure to use them. In addition, it has been urged that the failure of the injured person to use an available seat belt constitutes the failure to mitigate damages and, therefore, the defendant is not responsible on the theory that the defendant is not liable for the avoidable consequences of the accident. In opposition, it has been argued that the failure to use seat belts has nothing to do with the causation of most accidents and, further, that the plaintiff's duty to mitigate damages or to take such steps as to eliminate the avoidable consequences of the accident is a duty which arises not before but after the accident has occurred.

Some courts have recognized what has come to be known as "the seat belt defense." The defendant may be allowed to introduce evidence of the plaintiff's failure to wear seat belts. This may be considered as evidence of plaintiff's failure to mitigate damages. The point of allowing such evidence is that plaintiff would not have been injured as severely if he or she had been wearing a seat belt, and any damages should be reduced accordingly. As an alternative, some states allow evidence that the plaintiff's failure to wear a seat belt is contributory negligence and bars recovery or, in a comparative negligence state, affects apportionment of fault.

Closely related to the seat belt defense is the safety helmet defense which can be urged against motorcycle riders. Many states have statutes which require that operators and passengers of motorcycles wear safety helmets. The failure of the plaintiff to obey the safety statute has been held to be contributory negligence as a matter of law, or at least evidence of contributory negligence in some states.

In *Spier* v. *Barker* [323 N.E. 2d 164 1974)], the New York Court of Appeals considered for the first time the seat belt defense and the effect of the failure of the plaintiff to use a selt belt, even though the automobile in which she was riding was so equipped. The facts indicated that she was involved in an intersection accident with a tractor-trailer and, as a result of the impact, she was ejected from her automobile, which then ran over her legs. She was not wearing the seat belt. The jury found that she was contributorily negligent, and it returned a verdict for the defendant. The Appellate Division affirmed the verdict on appeal. Upon further appeal to the Court of Appeals, the court considered three theories in support of the seat belt defense: (1) nonuse of a seat belt constitutes negligence per se, precluding the plaintiff's recovery; (2) nonuse is the failure of the plaintiff to act as a reasonable person and the plaintiff may be found to be contributorily negligent; and (3) nonuse may, in particular circumstances, mean that the plaintiff acted unreasonably and should not be permitted to recover damages for injuries which a seat belt would have prevented. The court adopted the third proposition, holding that the seat belt offers an automobile occupant the opportunity, prior to the accident, to minimize damages. The court said that there is no doubt of seat belt effectiveness in preventing injuries and juries should be able to separate injuries caused by the initial impact from those caused by the plaintiff's nonuse of a seat belt. Thus, injuries which can be directly traceable to the nonuse of the seat belt will be classified as avoidable consequences for which no recovery can be had.

A majority of states, even though they require seat belt use by statute, do not recognize nonuse as negligence per se and do not even allow evidence of nonuse to bar recovery or to reduce damages. However, in any auto accident case, the use or nonuse of available seat belts is certainly a pertinent point for investigation by the claim representative.

OWNER AND VICARIOUS LIABILITY

820 Vicarious Liability of the Owner

Ordinarily, the owner of a motor vehicle who entrusts the use of the vehicle to another person possessing competence to drive is not answerable for the driver's negligence unless, at the time of the accident, the driver was acting as agent for the owner. In the latter case, the basic principles of agency apply, and the principal is liable for the acts of his or her agent within the scope of that agency under the doctrine of *respondeat superior* (see Section 642, above). In the absence of agency, the owner is not vicariously liable for the negligent acts of the driver.

Where the owner of an automobile is riding in the car driven by another, a presumption arises that the driver is the agent of the owner and is under his control. This presumption was once regarded as irrebuttable, but the present tendency of the courts is to allow evidence to be submitted for the purpose of showing that no agency did in fact exist. For example, in *Greyhound Lines* v. *Caster* [216 Atl. 2d 689 (Delaware)], the evidence indicated that the owner-passenger was asleep at the time of the accident. The court held that he had relinquished control and that the driver's negligence was not imputable to him.

Imputed Contributory Negligence. In many cases it has been urged that, because the negligence of the agent is the negligence of the principal where a third party is seeking damages, the same rule of responsibility should apply where the principal is seeking damages from a third party for injuries sustained to person or property. The courts generally adopted this rule, and it came to be known as the "both ways" rule. Under this rule of imputed contributory negligence (see Section 416, above), the principal is charged with the negligence of the agent regardless of whether a third party is seeking damages from the principal or the principal is seeking to recover damages from the third party. Thus, if the master is riding in his own car driven by his servant, and is injured through the joint negligence of the servant and a third party, he is charged with the contributory negligence of his servant in his action against the third party, even though the master personally is entirely blameless and had no means at his command whereby he could have avoided the accident. It is true that the master has a cause of action against his servant to recover any damages which he may have sustained as a result of the negligence of the servant, and the master in that situation would not be charged with contributory negligence or the negligence of the servant. The contributory negligence of the servant is imputed to the master only for the benefit of other parties. The practical result here is that the servant could be held entirely responsible for the damage and the third party, although a joint tort-feasor, would escape liability.

The rule has been under attack for many years by legal scholars and courts, who question its logic as well as its justice. It is pointed out that the application of the rule deprives a faultless plaintiff of the right to recovery solely because he or she stood in some relationship to one of the parties.

In the adoption of the new *Restatement, Torts, Second*, imputed contributory negligence was abandoned as to many of the relationships to which it originally applied. It now reads: "Sec. 485: Except as stated in 486, 491, and 494, a plaintiff is not barred from recovery by the negligent act or omission of a third person." In the Comment, which accompanied this change in the rule, we find the following:

> The rule stated in this Section rejects except as indicated by the reference to other Sections, the doctrine of "imputed contributory negligence" under which the plaintiff is barred from recovery against the defendant because the negligence of a third person, with whom the plaintiff stands in some relation, has contributed to his harm.

The Comment further notes that, in many of the cases involving imputed contributory negligence, the decision was based on a fictitious agency relationship and should no longer be recognized as valid.

The doctrine of imputed negligence is now applied only in a limited number of situations. These are as follows:

1. The negligence of a servant acting within the scope of his employment is imputed to bar the recovery of his master.

2. In a small number of jurisdictions which have the law of community property, the negligence of one spouse is still imputed to bar recovery by the other.
3. The negligence of one member of a joint enterprise is imputed to bar recovery by the others.
4. In an action for death or loss of services, the negligence of the person who is injured bars recovery by the person who has been deprived of the relation.

In bailments, the element of control by the owner is lacking. The applicable common-law rule is that the contributory negligence of the bailee is not imputed to the bailor and, therefore, it cannot be interposed as a defense to the bailor's action against the negligent third party to recover damages. This common-law rule has been modified by statute in some states.

Negligent Entrustment. It is possible for the owner to be held liable for his or her own act of negligence if the owner knowingly entrusts the use of the vehicle to a person who is intoxicated, incompetent, reckless, or irresponsible with respect to the use of an automobile, and an accident occurs as a result. The liability thus imposed is not based on the negligence of the driver in causing the accident; it is based on the owner's own negligent act in making the vehicle available to such a person. In order to hold the owner responsible, it must be established that the owner knew, or by the exercise of reasonable care should have known, of the incompetence of the driver, and that the owner consented to the use of the vehicle by such a person. Both elements must be established or the action against the owner must fail.

821 Family Purpose Doctrine

This doctrine creates a fictional relationship of principal and agent with regard to the use of a family automobile, whereby the member of the family driving the car is considered to be the agent of the owner, whether there is any agency in fact or not. If an automobile devoted to family purposes is purchased, then any member of the family driving the automobile with the owner's consent is acting as the agent of the owner.

This doctrine is applied even where the member of the family is driving the car solely for his or her own purposes. The doctrine is a rule of expediency since it is applied solely for the purpose of permitting an action against a financially responsible person (the owner) rather than limiting the plaintiff to a recourse against another member of the family who may not be able to respond in damages.

Only about half of the states which have considered the doctrine have adopted it, either by specific statute or by judicial determination. The others have specifically rejected the doctrine and refuse to apply it.

The purpose of the family purpose doctrine is achieved through compulsory insurance laws, discussed later in this chapter. (See Section 833.) In states having compulsory insurance laws, it is questionable whether the family purpose doctrine any longer serves a useful purpose.

822 Statutory Liability of the Owner

A few states have by statute imposed liability upon the owner of a motor vehicle where the vehicle is being driven by another with the owner's consent, express or implied. Some create an irrebuttable presumption of agency, and others merely impose the liability from the fact of ownership, with no attempt being made to create an agency relationship. Some have limitations as to the amount for which the owner is responsible under the statute, while others have no limitation whatsoever. Recourse must be had to the specific statute to determine the exact liability imposed and the limitations, if any. States providing for owner liability whenever the owner has consented to the vehicle's use are a small minority. In the vast majority of states, the owner is only liable when the driver is his or her agent or when the owner is at fault for negligent entrustment.

In states where an operator's license is granted to a minor of the age of 16 and upwards, some statutes require that the minor be sponsored by an adult, who will assume responsibility for all damages arising out of the operation of a motor vehicle by the minor.

823 Vicarious Liability of Person Other than Owner

In order to become vicariously liable for damages arising out of the operation of a motor vehicle, a person does not necessarily have to be the owner of the vehicle. Under the basic principles of agency, the person, firm, or corporation—on whose business and for whose benefit the vehicle is being operated by a driver under their control—is liable under the doctrine of *respondeat superior*. It makes no difference whether the vehicle is owned by the driver or by someone else. If the vehicle is being operated by an agent, servant, employee, or someone under the control of the principal, and on the principal's business, the principal is liable for the acts of such driver. Thus, if an employee is driving her own personal car, or one owned by someone else, on the business of her employer, the employer is vicariously liable for damages arising out of the employee's negligence in operating the vehicle.

PASSENGERS AND PEDESTRIANS

824 Rights and Duties of Passengers

The driver of a motor vehicle is required to exercise reasonable care for the safety of all passengers. This duty of reasonable care (see Section 302, above) extends not only to the operation of the vehicle but to its maintenance as well. For example, a driver knowingly operating a vehicle with faulty brakes, lights, or tires is liable to a passenger who may be injured as a result of an accident occurring because of the defect. Where there is a defect in the vehicle and the defect is unknown to the driver but could have been discovered upon reasonable inspection, some cases make a distinction between a gratuitous passenger or guest and one who is riding in the car for the business advantage of the driver. They use the analogy of licensee and business invitee in holding that the duty of reasonable inspection is imposed only in the case of the business passenger and not in the case of the gratuitous passenger or guest.

The passenger is required to exercise reasonable care for his or her own safety, and failure to do so will bar recovery in the case of an accident. The defenses interposed are assumption of risk and contributory negligence. (See also Sections 416 and 418, above).

Where a passenger knowingly entrusts his or her safety to an incompetent driver, whether such incompetence is due to illness, intoxication, or the lack of driving experience, the passenger will have assumed all the risks that arise out of the driver's incompetence. The defense is based on the existence of two elements: (1) knowledge of the risk and (2) voluntary exposure to it.

Thus, if the passenger enters a car driven by a person with only a learner's permit, and the passenger has knowledge of the driver's lack of experience, she will have assumed all the risks arising out of the driver's lack of driving experience. But if the vehicle has faulty brakes, which fact is unknown to the passenger, and the accident occurs because of this condition, the passenger has not assumed this risk. If the driver has only a learner's permit, or is intoxicated, or ill, and these facts are unknown and could not be ascertained by the passenger by the exercise of reasonable care, she will not be held to have assumed any risk of injury arising out of these conditions.

The passenger is required to exercise reasonable care for his or her own safety. A passenger may not interfere with the operation of the vehicle, distract the driver's attention, attempt to get out of the car while it is in motion, or do any other act which will involve a risk of injury. The passenger is entitled to rely on the driver when it comes to the operation of the vehicle and is not required to watch the road and warn the driver of impending dangers. As a matter of fact, the passenger may even go to sleep, provided that in so doing he or she is not in a position that interferes with the safe operation of the vehicle.

825 Automobile Guest Statutes

In a number of states, it was determined that, as a matter of legislative policy, some modification should be made in the common-law rule imposing liability upon the host-driver for ordinary negligence where the injured person was given transportation without payment of any kind. Some states decided that the host should be exposed to liability only where his or her conduct exceeded certain limitations set forth in the statute. Others decided that the statutes were necessary, where insurance was involved, to discourage collusive actions of both host and guest. Collusive actions would have an adverse effect upon insurance rates, and it was felt that automobile guest statutes were necessary in order to protect the insurance-buying public. In any case, whatever the motivation, these states enacted statutes which limited the liability of the host-driver insofar as it related to a gratuitous guest. Each of these states has fixed its own standards of responsibility to which the host is subject, but in each instance something more than ordinary negligence must be established.

Many states have repealed their guest statutes. In the cases of repeal, the guest statute will be applicable only to accidents which occurred prior to the effective date of the repeal. In states that do not have guest statutes, the rule of ordinary negligence will be applied to the conduct of the host, and the guest may recover if the host is chargeable with ordinary negligence.

The constitutionality of guest statutes has been under continuous attack. The Supreme Court of the United States upheld the statutes, holding that they were not violative of the Constitution of the United States [*Silver* v. *Silver*, 280 U.S. 117 (1929)]. Since that time guest statutes have been considered by the state courts, and many have invalidated their guest statutes by declaring them to be violative of the state constitutions.

In *Thompson* v. *Hagan* [523 Pac. 2d 1370], the Supreme Court of Idaho, while recognizing that the law was intended to prevent collusive lawsuits, took the position that, by denying recovery to all guests, the guest statute is all-inclusive in its sweep and bars all actions. In that respect, the court found, the law is invalid because it denies to the guest equal protection of the laws.

Conversely, the Delaware Supreme Court upheld the state's guest statute in *Justice* v. *Gatchell* [325 Atl. 2d 97]. The court said:

> . . . on the basis of the record before us, even on the basis of information of which we might take judicial notice, we are unable to say that there are no longer any evils to be corrected, or permissible objectives to be accomplished by the Guest Statute. Whether the concept of hospitality-protection or collusion-prevention has been so eroded by changing conditions, as to have disappeared as acceptable justification for the Guest Statutes is a problem more appropriate for legislative solution than for judicial determination. The General Assembly has access to relevant information bearing upon these matters more significant than any afforded this Court, bound as it is by the limitations of this judicial proceeding.

Only a minority of states still have guest statutes in force. In many states which had previously enacted guest statutes, they have been struck down by court decision, principally on grounds that they are unconstitutional or that they, in some way, invidiously discriminate against certain claimants. Although the trend in recent years has been against guest statutes, they are still in force in a significant minority of states.

826 Guest Defined

A guest in an automobile has been defined as a person who takes a ride in an automobile driven by another person merely for his or her own pleasure or personal business, and without making any return or conferring any benefit on the automobile driver.

Where the passenger pays for the transportation in an amount which approximates its cost, there is no question that he or she is not a guest. Where a passenger is given transportation gratuitously and during the course of the trip pays for a meal, or for some gasoline—payments not intended to be payment for transportation and not received as such—the mere payment of such small amounts will not change the status as a guest. Between these two extremes will fall a certain group of cases where there is a doubt as to whether the payment was intended and received as payment for transportation, and which are decided on the basis of their own particular facts and circumstances. The general rule is that the occupant of a motor vehicle is not a guest where the ride is intended to further the business interests of the driver or owner, or where it is to promote the mutual business interests of both the host and the occupant.

The courts are divided on the question of whether an infant can attain the status of a guest in a vehicle so as to come within the provisions of the guest statute. To achieve the status of a guest, the decisions all agree that there must be an invitation, expressed or implied, and an acceptance, formal or informal. The courts further agree that an infant of tender years is incapable legally of accepting the invitation. The courts, however, part company on the question of whether the parent or guardian can accept the invitation for the infant so as to make such acceptance binding on the infant to the extent of making it subject to the guest statute.

827 Driver's Negligence not Imputed to Passengers

In the absence of an agency relationship between the passenger and the driver, the negligence of the driver is not imputed to the passenger. The passenger or guest has no control over the operation of the vehicle or the actions of the driver, and therefore is not chargeable with or responsible for the lack of care on the part of the driver. This same rule applies even where there is some family relationship between the passenger and the driver, such as husband and wife, parent and child, and the like.

Where there is an agency relationship between the driver and the passenger, as where the owner is riding in his own car driven by his chauffeur, the general rule of agency (see Section 633, above) is usually applied in that the negligence of the agent is imputed to the principal.

828 Rights and Duties of Pedestrians

The pedestrian has certain rights and duties when (1) on the sidewalk, (2) crossing the street at a controlled intersection, (3) crossing at an uncontrolled intersection, (4) crossing between intersections, and (5) walking on the highway.

1. Sidewalks. The pedestrian has a clear statutory right-of-way on the sidewalk, and the motorist must yield to this superior right. When a pedestrian on the sidewalk is injured as a result of being struck by any part of a motor vehicle, a presumption of negligence on the part of the operator of the motor vehicle arises. The driver may overcome the presumption by a showing that he or she was operating the vehicle with reasonable care, but was forced onto the sidewalk by the negligent act of another motorist.

2. Controlled Intersections. The pedestrian has a clear substantial right-of-way over any motorist when crossing on a crosswalk with a green light in the pedestrian's favor. The pedestrian has a right to assume that the motorist will obey the law and meet the duties imposed. On the other hand, the pedestrian must exercise reasonable care for his or her own safety, and, failing in this, can be charged with contributory negligence.

3. Uncontrolled Intersections. The extent of the vigilance and care which the pedestrian must exercise for his or her own safety is greater at uncontrolled intersections than at an intersection controlled by a traffic officer or traffic lights. When crossing at an uncontrolled intersection, the pedestrian is on notice of the possible danger, and must meet the duty of observation which requires looking before crossing. Failure to do so is usually contributory negligence as a matter of law.

The motorist approaching the intersection must have the car under control, and if he or she sees a pedestrian, or clear vision of the intersection is obscured by foliage, parked cars, or other objects, the motorist is under a duty to warn of his or her approach by sounding the horn or other means. Under most statutes, the pedestrian has the right-of-way at unguarded and unlighted crosswalk intersections, as well as at those which are well lighted and guarded by stop signs or other warning signs.

4. Between Intersections. In the absence of a statute or ordinance which prohibits jaywalking, the pedestrian is not negligent merely because he or she crosses the street between intersections and not at a place set aside for a pedestrian crossing, but is required to exercise a greater degree of care and caution. Whether the conduct of the pedestrian was negligent is generally a question of fact for the jury applying the reasonably prudent person standard. If there is a statute or ordinance which forbids crossing between intersections, the pedestrian is contributorily negligent as a matter of law if he or she does so.

5. Walking on the Highway. In the absence of statute or ordinance, the basic rule is that both the pedestrian and the motorist have an equal right to use the highway for the purpose of travel. Upon approaching a pedestrian on the highway, the motorist has a duty to slow down and give proper warning of approach. The generally accepted warning signal, and one required by most statutes, is the sounding of the horn.

The pedestrian is under a duty of exercising reasonable care for his or her own safety. The extent of the care that must be exercised is determined by the facts and circumstances of each case, such as the density of traffic, width of the road, obstructions to the motorist's vision, and the extent of the warning signals given by the motorist.

Statutes and ordinances have altered the rights and duties of pedestrians. In most cases, they have increased the duties and decreased the rights. For example, the statutes of most states provide that the pedestrian must walk on the sidewalk where one is provided and may cross the streets only at intersections. On the open highway pedestrians are required to walk on the left side of the roadway and face oncoming traffic. If the failure on the part of the pedestrian to obey the statute is the proximate or a contributing cause of the accident, the pedestrian will be charged with contributory negligence.

829 Traffic Officers and Workers on the Roadway

A traffic officer must exercise reasonable care for his or her own safety and avoid being struck by a vehicle if it is possible to do so. Because of the nature of the work, however, the officer is not held to the same degree of care required of a pedestrian crossing the street, and, of necessity, must rely to a greater degree upon the care and caution of motorists. Where the officer is directing traffic on the open road, the motorist normally has no reason to anticipate the officer's presence unless he or she receives some advance notice. Usually this is done by warning signs, or by flashing lights at night. Where an accident occurs at such a place, there is almost always a question of fact for the jury whether there was sufficient notice given of the presence of the officer, or whether the motorist should have reasonably anticipated that an officer would be there.

The same rules are applicable to a worker on the road. A worker is not held to the same degree of care and caution as is imposed upon the pedestrian, for reasons of necessity: the worker would never get the work done if he or she spent all the time watching for traffic. On the other hand, the worker must exercise some care. He or she must stay within the work area and may not carelessly step out into a lane of traffic without making a reasonable observation as to whether it is safe to do so. The worker is required to avoid any known danger.

The motorist, observing a worker in the road or noticing the existence of road repairs by means of warning signs or devices, is required to slow down, and to stop if necessary. In any case, the motorist must guide the vehicle in such a way as to avoid any possibility of accident. A motorist knows that the worker cannot exercise the same degree of care and caution as a pedestrian would, and therefore the motorist has a duty to exercise a higher degree of care for the safety of the worker than would be required in the case of a pedestrian.

STATUTORY REQUIREMENTS

830 State Licensing Regulations

The license to drive a motor vehicle on the public highways of the state is a privilege and not a right. The distinction between the two is that a right is an element of citizenship which belongs to each individual citizen. A privilege is a license granted by the state permitting the performance of certain acts. With respect to motor vehicles, the regulations usually require that the operator pass a driving test as well as meet certain physical standards. Thus, the state may grant the privilege to those who qualify and deny it to those who do not. The state may also attach to the granting of the privilege certain conditions with respect to its exercise and its duration. It may provide for a renewal of the privilege at certain intervals, and it may revoke the privilege at any time.

The fact that the driver of a vehicle involved in an accident did not have a driver's license is not evidence of negligence. It is evidence of the fact that the operator has failed to comply with the statute, and, in operating a motor vehicle, has committed an act that may subject him or her to criminal liability and the penalties imposed for such an offense. But the true test of whether the operator is chargeable with negligence is how he or she operated the car under the circumstances of the accident; the fact that the motorist did or did not have a valid driver's license at the time of the accident has no bearing whatsoever on the issue of negligence.

Evidence of lack of a driver's license is admissible on the issue of credibility. Because the jury is required to determine which witnesses it will believe and which it will not, any evidence that will assist in this determination is admissible. The jury is entitled to know that the driver operated the motor vehicle in violation of the law so that they can determine whether they will believe the driver's version of the accident.

831 Unregistered Vehicles

The fact that the driver of a vehicle involved in an accident did not display license plates as required by law is not evidence of negligence on the part of the owner or operator. The ordinary rules of negligence will apply, and the facts of the accident will be determinative of the liability of the driver or owner.

Obviously, the owner or driver of such a vehicle is making illegal use of the highway and will be answerable to the public authority for the infraction. The fact that the vehicle was being used in violation of the state law is a fact admissible in evidence, not as evidence of negligence, but as a fact to be taken into consideration by the jury in deciding upon the credibility of the driver.

832 Financial Responsibility Acts

As one of the conditions of the granting of the privilege to operate a motor vehicle, most states have imposed the provisions of a financial responsibility law. These acts generally provide that, where the motorist has been involved in an accident for which he is responsible, and for which he is unable to respond in damages, his license to operate a motor vehicle may be revoked unless he can furnish proof of future financial responsibility. This proof can take the form of an insurance policy containing the liability limits required by law, or he can qualify as a self-insurer by a deposit of security with the state. When an insurance policy is certified as proof of financial security, the insurance carrier must agree to abide by the conditions of the act as to cancellation and disclaimer. Some acts provide that, if the motorist presents to the state proof that the claim against him has been settled by him, the provisions of the act are not applicable, and he is not required to file proof of future financial responsibility.

As a means of enforcement, some states require that all drivers submit proof of insurance either concurrently with or within a short time after filing the state motor vehicle report of accident. Forms for this purpose are supplied (usually called SR 21's), and the insurance carrier certifies by submission of this form to the state that insurance is carried. This system is the means by which the state can ascertain who is subject to financial responsibility and who is not. If the insurance form is not submitted within the time required by the act, the state assumes that no insurance is carried and that the operator is therefore subject to financial responsibility. The fact that insurance is carried is an indication that the operator can respond in damages if they are awarded, and thus he or she is not subject to the act.

833 Compulsory Automobile Insurance

Some states determined that the problem of the financially irresponsible motorist could be solved by compelling all motorists to carry automobile liability insurance with certain minimum limits. Therefore, compulsory insurance laws were passed requiring, as a condition precedent to the renewal of a license, that the motorist present proof of insurance in the form of a policy or certificate from an insurance carrier. Clearly, this type of legislation would require insurance on all cars licensed within the state, but it falls short of the objective of having insurance available in every case involving an automobile accident. Insurance would not necessarily be available in the case of a stolen car, an out-of-state vehicle, or an unregistered vehicle.

834 Statutory Policies of Automobile Liability Insurance

Most state laws require, as a condition precedent to the license to operate on the streets and highways, that common carriers (passenger buses, freight carriers, and taxicabs) file with the state a certified copy of a liability insurance policy, with minimum limits as prescribed in the law and subject to the conditions of the law. Interstate carriers, licensed by the Interstate Commerce Commission, are required to carry the amount of insurance prescribed by the commission. The policies must be filed with the Commission and conform to its rules and regulations as to cancellation and disclaimer.

835 Service of Process on Nonresident Motorists

A state may grant the privilege of operating a motor vehicle on its highways to drivers licensed in other states. This is done as a matter of reciprocity, since the foreign state grants the same privilege. As with its own citizens, the state may affix conditions to the granting of this privilege. The condition attached to the grant of the use of the highways is that the foreign motorist constitutes some state official (usually the Secretary of State or Director of Motor Vehicles) as his agent upon whom service of process may be made in an action arising out of any accident which occurs within the state while the foreign motorist is using the highways.

This is sometimes referred to as ''substituted service,'' and is a statute enacted for the protection of the citizens of the state whose highways are being used by the foreign motorist. Were it not for legislation of this type, the offending motorist could return to his home state and escape a lawsuit in the state where the accident happened. The injured person would then have to bear the financial burden of bringing his action in the defendant's home state.

PERSONAL INJURY PROTECTION (PIP) NO-FAULT SYSTEMS

836 Purpose and Scope

When the automobile first appeared on the American scene, the courts had no difficulty in applying common-law principles which were formerly utilized in determining liability in cases involving horse-drawn vehicles. Statutes implementing the common-law rules were enacted, and the courts adopted certain doctrines which were especially applicable to automobiles.

Almost from the beginning, some legal scholars and others expressed the view that the application of horse-and-buggy rules to the operation of automobiles was unfair. They pointed to the potential for personal injury which the automobile brought with it and recommended that some other legal system should be created which would provide for compensation for each person injured as a result of an automobile accident, regardless of who was at fault. They pointed to the automobile as the offending instrumentality and argued that some method of redress should be available to all persons injured as a result of automobile accidents. Although earlier studies advocated various compensation schemes, it was the 1965 plan by Professors Keeton and O'Connell that had the greatest impact on the problem. Their "Basic Protection for the Accident Victim" plan came to the attention of many of the state legislatures and was seriously considered. In view of this, other plans were suggested by the American Insurance Association and by the insurance commissioner of Connecticut. The basic concept of all these plans is that the automobile accident victim is entitled to recover for economic losses, regardless of fault. This would include not only the automobile driver and passengers, but pedestrians as well. The only test for recovery would be whether the injured person sustained the injuries in an automobile accident. Borrowing from the workers' compensation concept, the plans provided that there would be no recovery or payment for noneconomic losses, such as pain and suffering, disfigurement, or impairment to the future enjoyment of life. Many states have enacted legislation to modify the tort system. The traditional system of compensating automobile-related injuries and property damage has been modified in favor of a statutory automobile reparations system (no-fault).

It should also be noted that, in recent years, we have seen the widespread availability of coverages designed to remedy certain problems that have afflicted the automobile tort compensation system. Examples of such problems are lack of medical benefits for people injured in auto-related accidents, and lack of recourse for people injured by uninsured motorists. The insurance industry has devised various coverages to alleviate the shortcomings of the tort system that left some injured people with little effective recourse against negligent drivers. Such coverages include Medical Payments, Uninsured Motorist, and Underinsured Motorist. These are commonly referred to as first-party coverages (although the latter two are "hybrid" rather than true first-party coverages). These are "first party" in the sense that the insured driver purchases these coverages to protect the "first party"—himself or herself—as well as family, passengers, etc., from injury. Many states (by statute or insurance department regulation) make such coverages mandatory—or at least make it mandatory that insurers offer them to their insureds.

The general availability of such coverages to the insurance-buying public has (in the majority of states that still retain the tort system) taken some of the edge off the demand for replacing the tort compensation system with a true ''no-fault'' reparations system.

837 Legislation

The legislatures of most states, as well as the federal government, have considered the enactment of ''no-fault'' statutes. Some states have passed such laws and others have not. All no-fault statutes that have been passed are modifications of the plans that have been offered. They differ as to the extent of the benefits to be paid and the maximum liabilty for each of the scheduled benefits. Thus, the benefits to be paid will differ from state to state, and it is to be expected that the amount of benefits may be reexamined by the legislatures and appropriate changes effected by amended legislation.

Approximately half of the states have enacted ''no-fault'' in some form. Some of these plans have broad application and impose some type of exemption from tort liability. Generally, this is a partial exemption that applies unless a ''threshold'' of damages is exceeded. Some of them (as noted in Section 836) simply provide for expanded first-party coverages for bodily injury expenses. These, in effect, are added onto existing policies with their liability and first-party coverages, and do not restrict the availability of tort remedies.

The ''no-fault'' legislative acts requiring PIP benefits are either (1) mandatory or (2) optional.

Under the mandatory form of legislation, the insurance carrier must provide the coverage set forth in the legislation, and the insured must accept and pay a premium for it. The states are not uniform in setting forth the kind and types of automobiles affected by the legislation, nor are they in agreement as to the cases coming within the tort exemption.

In states favoring the optional form, the legislation requires some form of first-party or no-fault benefits to be offered to the insured. In most cases, the insured can reject these benefits.

838 Insurance

The plans require that added coverage be provided in automobile liability policies, which will pay all of the PIP benefits to the named insured and family members residing in his or her household who sustain bodily injury as a result of an accident involving an automobile. Benefits are also extended to other persons sustaining bodily injury while occupying the insured automobile, or while using such automobile with the permission of the named insured, and to pedestrians who sustain bodily injury caused by the named insured's automobile, or by being struck by an object propelled by or from the automobile. Some plans cover all motor vehicles, commercial and private, including motorcycles. Others restrict the operation of the plan to private passenger automobiles and exclude motorcycles. Under most of these plans, insurance is mandatory and the insured must purchase it.

839 Benefits Provided

The personal injury protection (PIP) plans generally provide for payment of the following types of benefits: economic loss, consisting of (1) medical expense benefits; (2) income continuation benefits; (3) essential services benefits; (4) survivor benefits; and (5) funeral expenses.

1. Medical Expense Benefits. The general plan is that "medical expenses" means expenses for medical treatment, surgical treatment, dental treatment, professional nursing services, hospital services, rehabilitation services, prosthetic devices, ambulance services, medication, and other reasonable and necessary expenses resulting from treatment prescribed by persons licensed to practice medicine and surgery or dentistry. Some plans include treatment by a chiropractor and nonmedical remedial treatment rendered in accordance with a recognized religious method of healing.

Medical expenses also includes hospital services consisting of: (1) the cost of a semiprivate room, based on rates customarily charged; (2) the cost of board, meals, and dietary services; (3) the cost of other hospital services, such as operating room, medicines, drugs, anesthetics, treatments with X ray, radium, and other radioactive substances, laboratory tests, surgical dressings and supplies, and other medical care and treatment rendered by the hospital; (4) the cost of treatment by a physiotherapist; (5) the cost of medical supplies, such as prescribed drugs and medicines, blood and blood plasma, artificial limbs and eyes, surgical dressings, casts, splints, trusses, braces, crutches, rental of wheelchair or hospital bed, and oxygen and rental of equipment for its administration.

2. Income Continuation Benefits. This is intended to pay for the economic loss suffered by the victim arising from the inability to work, and to compensate the victim for loss of earnings. This would be recoverable regardless of whether the employer continued the salary.

3. Essential Services Benefits. Payment of this benefit is designed to pay for the necessary and reasonable expenses incurred for a substitute who performs the essential services ordinarily performed by the injured person for herself and her family. This covers such things as cleaning, cooking, shopping, and laundry. This type of payment usually comes into play where a homemaker, who has no income, is injured and the family requires someone to perform the services.

4. Survivor Benefits. In the event of the death of an income producer as a result of injuries sustained in an accident which would entitle such person to income continuation benefits, the maximum provided for income continuation should be paid to the surviving spouse, or, if there is no surviving spouse, to the surviving children, or to the estate of the deceased. In the case of the death of one performing essential services, the maximum amount provided will be paid to the person incurring the expense of providing such essential services.

5. Funeral Expenses. These benefits consist of the payments of funeral, burial, and cremation expense. As in all other benefits, these amounts will be subject to a maximum amount.

840 Tort Exemption

One of the objectives of these plans is to reduce litigation and to substitute in its place a sure method of recovery. Therefore, they exempt from tort liability all persons who are required to have PIP benefits insurance, with some exceptions. Thus, the injured person will recover the PIP benefits from his or her own insurance carrier and is deprived of common-law rights against the person responsible for the injury. In place of the right to file a lawsuit, the injured person is entitled to the immediate payment of benefits without regard to liability. The proponents of these plans argue that such a plan is superior to the system of tort litigation with its attendant delays and the uncertainty of the outcome. This parallels the situation that obtained in the matter of workers' compensation, wherein the common-law rights of employees against the master were abrogated and a system of periodic payments of compensation substituted for those rights.

Unlike workers' compensation the plans provide, in cases involving a certain severity, that the injured person may, at his or her option, assert common-law rights. In such a cause of action the injured person may recover for such noneconomic losses as pain and suffering and future enjoyment of life. The cases in which the injured person retains common-law rights are usually defined as those in which the medical treatment exceeds a certain sum (the "threshold" amount), or the injury causes extensive temporary disability or disfigurement or permanent injury. Thus, if the results of the injury do not reach the "threshold" as set forth in the plan, the injured person's recovery is limited to the PIP benefits. If the injury goes over the threshold, then the injured person has the option to bring an action against the third party responsible for the injury. The PIP insurance carrier is entitled to subrogation against the carrier of the responsible party, but in most instances this right of recovery can be asserted only by arbitration.

It should be added that no plan has been suggested nor has any state legislated what could be considered a "true" no-fault system of automobile reparations.

Such a plan would eliminate entirely all tort litigation arising out of automobile accidents and substitute in its place personal injury protection benefits alone. This would utilize the workers' compensation approach.

841 Third-Party Claims

Until the injured person has met the ''threshold'' fixed by the no-fault statute, he or she has no actionable claim against the third-party tort-feasor. However, when the insurer of the tort-feasor receives a report of accident, there is no reason in serious cases that an investigation should not begin immediately and, in most cases, all the information can be supplied by the PIP carrier. From that point on, a decision can be made as to the quantum of investigation which will be required in order to meet the claim if it is made.

Even though the claimant has exceeded the threshold, there is nothing in the no-fault statutes that obligates the claimant to begin suit against the tort-feasor. The claimant can continue to receive and accept PIP benefits. The third-party carrier, of course, can expect a subrogation claim from the PIP carrier.

In serious cases, especially where the liability is clear, it can be expected that the existence of no-fault statutes will have some effect on jury verdicts.

Therefore, in appropriate cases there is no reason why the third-party insurer should not initiate settlement negotiations even before suit is started.

842 Subrogation under No-Fault Statutes

The general rule adopted in all states is that a personal tort, including personal injury actions, may not be assigned either in whole or in part. This rule can be amended by statute (as in the case of some workers' compensation laws) which will set forth the nature of the permitted assignment and the extent of such permission. The no-fault statutes are no exception. Some laws permit an assignment of the injured person's cause of action to the PIP insurance carrier where benefits have been paid and set forth the circumstances under which such assignment may be enforced through a subrogation action. Other statutes do not allow an assignment at all.

843 Arbitration under No-Fault Statutes

Some statutes require that the PIP insurers submit their claims for reimbursement against the insurer of the tort-feasor to arbitration. In some states this is a mandatory requirement, providing the only means by which the PIP insurer may recover, and in other states it is an optional remedy which can be utilized or not as the PIP insurer sees fit. In order to comply with the requirements of the statutes, the insurance companies, through their representatives, have subscribed to an intercompany arbitration agreement dealing with the subject of arbitration under no-fault statutes.

The companies have bound themselves to arbitrate all intercompany disputes arising from their pursuit of subrogation claims created by their payment of claims or benefits to insureds or third parties. This intercompany arbitration agreement is designed to apply to all states having a mandatory or optional provision covering subrogation by arbitration, with the exception of Massachusetts, in which there is a special arbitration agreement.

The subscribing companies have agreed to a comprehensive set of rules governing applicability of arbitration, and matters of jurisdiction and procedure. The procedure contemplated by this agreement is that the cases will be submitted on evidence consisting of the claim files of the applicant company and the respondents, together with any other documents which may have some probative value in the decision-making process. Ordinarily, witnesses are not presented before the arbitrator, but there is a provision in the agreement that permits this—with the understanding that sufficient notice is given to the adverse party so that opposing witnesses may be presented.

The burden of proof is on the applicant company. If its file does not present a prima facie case of negligence, the decision must be in favor of the respondent. In the latter case no reference whatever is made to the respondent's file. Therefore, the claim representative for the applicant company must be satisfied that the file establishes a prima facie case of negligence on the part of the respondent's insured before application is made for arbitration.

844 Claims Administration under No-Fault

Claim handling under no-fault represents something of a change in the normal approach to disposing of automobile bodily injury claims. Under no-fault the benefits are required to be paid by the automobile liability insurer covering the automobile which the injured person was occupying at the time of the accident, as well as pedestrians who sustain bodily injury caused by the automobile. The concept of the automobile liability carrier being liable for first-party benefits is not new. For a number of years, medical payments coverage has been in existence; this coverage requires the payment of medical expenses incurred within a period of time, typically one year. What is newer is the requirement that the income continuation benefits, the essential services benefits, the survivor benefits, and the funeral expenses are payable as first-party claims by the automobile liability insurance carrier. (See discussion at Section 836.)

To recover any of these benefits, it must be established that the disability or death suffered by the claimant is causally related to the injury received in the automobile or by being struck by the automobile. When that is established, the payments will continue only as long as the causally related disability continues. If the claimant is suffering from an unrelated condition, whether traumatic or not, which did not come about as a result of the accident, no benefits are payable.

Most states have provisions which exclude from the operation of the law intentional injuries; injuries due to intoxication or while under the influence of drugs; injuries sustained in the commission of a crime, in avoiding arrest, or in a stolen car; injuries received in a race or speed test. An analysis of the benefits to which a qualified claimant might be entitled is presented below.

1. Medical Expenses Benefits. Under most statutes, the claimant is entitled to reimbursement for medical expense incurred as a result of the accident. The amount is conditioned on the fact that it must be reasonable. What is reasonable and what is not is a question which imposes some difficulty. Some states have promulgated a medical fee schedule which sets forth the reasonable fees that may be charged in these cases. In other states, the question may be resolved by recourse to the usual charges made by the profession in the locality in which the medical treatment is rendered. In the event of a dispute, the burden of proof will be on the claimant to establish that the charges claimed are reasonable. The amount of medical expense will be further limited by the maximum, if any, provided in the act.

The statute usually provides for reimbursement to the claimant for the amount of medical expenses incurred. There is no relationship between the insurance carrier and the doctor rendering the treatment, and there is no obligation on the part of the carrier to guarantee the payment of medical or hospital bills. The doctor might, as is done in some workers' compensation cases, request that the insurance carrier authorize an operation and the hospital bills which will be incurred. The insurance carrier is under no obligation to do so.

In some states the amount of no-fault benefits is reduced by the collectible benefits under workers' compensation, disability benefits laws, and social security disability payments. In some cases the entire amount of the medical expense is collectible from these other sources, in which case no benefits are available under no-fault.

The insurance carrier is also granted the right to require periodic medical examinations to determine the reasonableness of the medical treatment that is being rendered. In order to obtain the medical information from the attending physician, a medical authorization form should be obtained from the claimant. An example is shown in Figure 8–1. The usual medical authorization form may be used unless the state has other prescribed forms.

Some states have regulations prescribing the forms to be used for medical reports. Others do not. When no form has been created for this purpose, it would seem that the standard workers' compensation form with appropriate additions could be used.

In order for the claimant to be reimbursed for the medical expenses, it must appear that the treatment rendered was causally related to the automobile injury received. If the treatment covers any other condition, it is not reimbursable.

2. Income Continuation Benefits. In order to recover for this benefit, two elements must be present. There must be (1) medical proof of disability and (2) evidence that the claimant did not in fact work and earn a salary during this period of time. The medical evidence can be in the form of the medical report from the attending physician or a medical examination conducted by the insurance carrier. In addition, there must be evidence from the claimant's employer that he did not work. If either element is missing, there is no recoverable claim for this benefit. In order to obtain the information from the employer, it is customary to obtain an authorization from the claimant. See Figure 8–2.

FIGURE 8–1

AUTHORIZATION FOR RELEASE OF HEALTH SERVICE OR TREATMENT INFORMATION

This authorization, or a photocopy thereof, will authorize you to furnish all information you may have regarding my condition while under your observation or treatment, including history obtained, X-ray and physical findings, diagnosis and prognosis. You are authorized to provide this information in accordance with the ____(state)____ Automobile Reparations Act (no-fault law).

____
Name (print or type)

Date ______________________

____
Signature

(If a minor, parent or guardian shall sign and indicate capacity and relationship.)

FIGURE 8–2

AUTHORIZATION FOR RELEASE OF WORK AND OTHER INFORMATION

This authorization or a photocopy thereof, will authorize you to furnish all information you may have regarding my wages, salary or other loss while employed by you. You are authorized to provide this information in accordance with the ____(state)____ Automobile Reparations Act (no-fault).

____
Name (print or type)

____
Signature

Social Security No.________________ Date ______________________

The authorization together with a letter requesting the work record of the claimant is then sent to the employer. The information usually required consists of answers, for example, to the types of questions shown in Figure 8–3

Where the claimant is self-employed, statements can be obtained (where necessary) from his or her employees. The books of account also may be examined.

3. Essential Services Benefits. The payment of these benefits will be made only where there is medical proof of disability. If the claimant is not disabled and continues to incur these expenses, there is no obligation on the part of the insurer to pay them. In any event, the amount of payment to be made under this benefit is limited to the amounts set forth in the statute, governed either by a time limit or a maximum dollar amount.

4. Survivor Benefits and Funeral Expenses. When death of the income producer is caused by the accident under such circumstances as would have entitled the deceased to income continuation benefits had he or she lived, the survivor benefits as set forth in the particular statute are paid, usually to the surviving spouse or children or the estate of the deceased. As to funeral expenses, some states have no provision whatsoever, and others provide for limited expenses.

Workers' Compensation Deduction. Most states provide that, where the injured person is also entitled to workers' compensation, the compensation amount to which he or she is entitled will be deducted from the no-fault benefits. This

FIGURE 8–3

1. Employee's occupation:
2. Dates of employment: from: ______________ to ______________
3. Gross earnings during 52 week period prior to the accident:

   $______________________________

   Wages or salary as of the date of the accident:

   $____________ Hourly _____Weekly _____Monthly_____
4. Dates absent from work following the accident:

   From ____________ to ____________
5. Has employee filed a claim for benefits under any Workers' Compensation Law as a result of this accident?

   If "yes," name and address of workers' compensation Insurer:
6. Has employee received, or is he receiving or is he entitled to receive benefits under any Workers' Compensation Law as a result of this accident?
7. Is employee receiving, or is he entitled to receive any federal Social Security Disability benefits?

Date ____________ Signed______________________________________ would include disability compensation and also the medical expense. Some states also require that social security disability and public assistance benefits be deducted. At least one state has provided that, if the injured person is entitled to workers' compensation, he or she is not eligible for PIP benefits.

Payment and Penalties. Most states require that payment of PIP benefits be made within 30 days after the filing of a proper proof of loss. Penalties of from 10 to 15 percent are assessed for late payments. The proof may be filed at any time after the injured person becomes entitled to some payment, and further proofs may be submitted from time to time. Most states have specific forms which are utilized as a proof of loss or application for benefits.

Settlement of Claims and Disputes. If the claim is not paid within 30 days after submission of the proofs of loss and supporting papers, the claimant may bring an action in contract under the policy, alleging that the insurer is guilty of a breach of its obligation to pay no-fault benefits. If a judgment is rendered, the court will automatically add whatever penalties the law allows. In some states the claimant has the option of bringing suit on the policy or submitting the dispute to arbitration.

Where the claim is denied, the insurer can expect that some of the claimants will file a complaint with the Insurance Department of the state on the theory that the insurer has failed to meet the obligations of its contract.

As a postscript to this discussion, it should be noted that these no-fault automobile statutes are under constant review by the various state legislatures. The claim representative should be aware of the latest legislative amendment. Proposed no-fault statutes also may be the subject of debate in states where legislation is being newly considered.

Chapter 9

Law of Evidence

REQUIREMENTS FOR EVIDENCE

900 Nature of Evidence

901 Admissibility of Evidence

902 Weight of Evidence

903 Qualifications of Witnesses

904 Expert Testimony

SUBSTITUTES FOR EVIDENCE

905 Presumptions and Inferences

906 Irrebuttable Presumptions

907 *Res Ipsa Loquitur*

908 Judicial Notice

THE HEARSAY RULE AND ITS EXCEPTIONS

909 The Hearsay Rule

910 *Res Gestae* Statements

911 Declarations of Pain and Suffering

912 Admissions against Interest

913 Testimony in Prior Proceedings

914 Prior Contradictory Statements

915 Book Entries in the Regular Course of Business

RULES OF EVIDENCE IN CERTAIN SITUATIONS

916 Plea of Guilty at a Motor Vehicle Hearing

917 Conviction in Traffic Court

918 Conviction of Prior Crimes

919 Admissions by Conduct

920 Admissions by an Agent

921 Deception Tests

922 Subsequent Precautions to Prevent Harm

923 Offers to Compromise and Similar Conduct

924 Liability Insurance

PRIVILEGES

925 Privileged Communications

926 Husband and Wife

927 Attorney and Client

928 Physician and Patient

929 Priest and Penitent

DEMONSTRATIVE EVIDENCE

930 Photographs

931 Videos

932 X Rays

PUBLIC RECORDS

933 Admissibility of Public Records

934 Motor Vehicle Accident Reports

935 Intoxication Tests

936 Police Records

937 Traffic Court Hearings

938 Weather Reports

939 Autopsy Reports

940 Public Service Commission Accident Reports

941 Civil Aeronautics Reports

942 Federal Income Tax Returns

943 Veterans Administration Records

944 Selective Service Records

945 Social Security Records

946 Unemployment Compensation Records

947 Workers' Compensation Records

948 Vital Statistics: Birth, Marriage, Death

949 Court Records: Divorce or Prior Proceedings

950 Interstate Commerce Commission Records

REQUIREMENTS FOR EVIDENCE

900 Nature of Evidence

The trial of the lawsuit is a process which has for its objective the discovery of truth. The court and jury are the parties charged with the responsibility of performing this function. Since the court and jury have no means of investigating the case before them, they must rely upon data furnished by the interested parties. These data are called *evidence*. They consist of any species of proof, or probative matter, legally presented by the act of the parties and may consist of witnesses, records, documents, and concrete objects. Both parties to the action present evidence for the purpose of inducing belief in the minds of the court or jury of the validity of the claim asserted by the party producing the evidence.

There are generally three kinds of evidence: oral, documentary, and demonstrative.

Oral evidence consists of the testimony of witnesses testifying to the facts within their knowledge which are germane to the case. Oral evidence also includes the testimony of expert witnesses (see Section 904, below) who express opinions, the validity of which depends upon specialized knowledge and experience in the area in which the opinion is expressed.

Documentary evidence, as the name implies, consists of evidence in the form of books, papers, reports, public records, and private records.

Demonstrative evidence refers to matters of a visual nature, such as photographs, motion pictures, scale models, X rays, as well as actual courtroom exhibitions of various scientific instruments such as a colorimeter, spectrograph, microscope, and X-ray shadow box. It could also include the offending instrumentality itself, such as an allegedly defective heater, motor, bottle, can, food item, or automobile.

The subject of evidence is of importance to claim representatives who must know what evidence is admissible, the kinds and types of witnesses necessary in order to establish certain facts, and the inferences or presumptions which can be derived from them.

901 Admissibility of Evidence

It was recognized early in the development of the law that there had to be some limitation with respect to the evidence that could be received in a given case. If this were not so, either side could prolong the trial indefinitely by producing an interminable procession of witnesses to testify to almost anything under the sun. In such a situation, the ends of justice would not be served. Therefore, as an initial premise, the courts decided that the only evidence which would be received would be evidence that was relevant, material, and competent. If the evidence did not contain these three qualities, the evidence was objectionable and was excluded.

Relevant evidence means evidence that has a connection with the case. It must have some application or relation to the matter.

Material evidence is evidence that goes to the substance of the matter in dispute and has a legitimate or effective influence or bearing on the decision in the case. It must tend to prove or disprove a fact which is in issue in the case.

Competent evidence refers to the source or the type of evidence offered. It means that the evidence must be by means of testimony of a person who had the ability to see, hear, or recall the event which is the subject matter of the lawsuit.

Some examples will probably be helpful in illustrating these three qualities. Let us suppose that there is a negligence action pending which arose as a result of an automobile accident. Evidence is offered that the driver of the offending vehicle was wearing a blue serge suit at the time of the accident. This fact would be relevant because it had some relation to the matter. If it were offered by a person who was in a position to see and to judge the type of clothing worn by the driver, the evidence would then be competent. However, the fact that the driver was wearing a blue suit would not in any way enable the court or the jury to determine the negligence of the driver.

The matter before the court for determination was whether the driver operated his car in a careless or negligent manner. The fact that he was wearing clothing of a certain color would not in any way enable the court and jury to decide this question. Therefore, while the evidence did meet two of the requirements, relevancy and competency, the evidence is immaterial, and therefore objectionable.

Let us assume that there is a blind man who was present at an intersection where an accident occurred. He offers to testify as to exactly how the accident happened. His testimony might have some relation to the matter and his testimony could be material to the issue. However, a blind man who does not have the facility of sight is incompetent to testify as to the circumstances of the accident because, even though he was present at the time and place of the occurrence, he did not have the physical ability to observe the happening of the accident. His testimony is incompetent and inadmissible. He could testify to the sounds that he heard at the time that the accident occurred and to what was said by certain voices, but unless he had prior knowledge of the person speaking, he could not identify the person who spoke the words he heard.

902 Weight of Evidence

In civil cases, the plaintiff, in order to prevail, must establish a claim by a preponderance of evidence; he or she must produce the greater weight of evidence, or evidence that is more credible and convincing. It must be evidence which, when fairly considered, produces the stronger impression, has the greater weight, and is more convincing than the evidence in opposition. Preponderance of evidence is not to be determined by the number of witnesses but by the greater weight of all evidence. This does not necessarily mean the greater number of witnesses, but means that the opportunity for knowledge, the information possessed, and the manner of testifying determine the weight of testimony. The plaintiff will have sustained the burden of proof if his or her evidence outweighs that of the defendant. If the weight of evidence is equal on both sides the defendant must prevail, because the plaintiff has the burden of proof. And, if the defendant's evidence is more believable, the defendant likewise must win.

In criminal cases, the guilt of the accused must be established beyond a reasonable doubt. This is a much greater weight of evidence than the ''preponderance'' required in civil cases. ''Beyond a reasonable doubt'' means that the jury is entirely convinced and satisfied to a moral certainty. The phrase is the equivalent of clear, precise, and indubitable. If there is any reasonable question in the minds of the jury, they must acquit. The rule in the criminal law is that it is better that ten criminals escape punishment than one innocent man be convicted. It is for this reason that the prosecution must establish that the accused committed the crime, and the evidence must establish this beyond a reasonable doubt.

903 Qualifications of Witnesses

A witness is defined as a person who is possessed of knowledge of the matter pending before the court. He or she is not disqualified from being a witness because of race, color, relationship to any of the parties, infancy, interest in the outcome of the litigation, mental derangement, conviction of a crime, or self-confessed moral turpitude. With the exception of race and color, all of the other matters mentioned, while not disqualifying the person from being a witness, can be taken into consideration by the jury in determining the weight to be given to the testimony.

Is the testimony of an infant six years of age to be given more, or less, consideration than opposing testimony given by an adult? Is the testimony of a person who had led a previous exemplary existence to be given more, or less, consideration than that of a person who has been convicted of a crime? What is the relative weight to be given to the testimony of a person with a mental disability as opposed to testimony by a person of sound mind? If the judge admits the testimony, the weight to be given it is a matter that the jury will be called upon to decide. They decide the quality or believableness of the testimony rather than the qualification of the witness to testify.

A witness must be capable of expressing himself or herself concerning the matter of the testimony so as to be understood by the judge and jury either directly or through interpretation by one who can understand the witness. The fact that a witness speaks a foreign tongue does not disqualify a person. He or she may testify through an interpreter, and, if otherwise capable of adequately being understood in the foreign tongue, the person can be a witness. The same thing would be true with respect to a person who is deaf or dumb, or both. This witness can testify through an interpreter who is capable of communicating with the witness by means of a sign language. An insane person, a person with a mental disability, or an infant may not be capable of making himself or herself understood or expressing the circumstances in understandable terms. If this is the case, such a witness is not qualified to testify.

A witness is disqualified from testifying if he or she does not understand the nature of an oath, does not regard the taking of an oath as binding on conscience, or does not understand the duty of a witness to tell the truth.

In some states an atheist, as well as a person who has conscientious scruples against taking an oath, is prevented from testifying. The reasoning behind this view is that testimony given under oath is more likely to be truthful and honest than testimony that is not. Some states have departed from the strict application of this rule and have permitted testimony by such witnesses provided the witness would recognize the duty to tell the truth and regard the testimony as being binding on conscience. The taking of an oath in such cases has been waived.

904 Expert Testimony

The results of civil litigation today often turn on expert testimony. This is particularly true in high-visibility, high-damages cases such as those involving products liability, medical malpractice, and toxic torts, where complex medical and scientific issues make it necessary for the parties to rely upon the testimony of experts to help to explain the case to the jury.

Experts will be called upon in virtually every case involving substantial damages and any degree of complexity. Claim representatives, as well as lawyers for both plaintiffs and defendants, may retain experts as consultants to help them to understand and prepare cases. Further, the lawyers will call those consultants (and/or other experts) as witnesses at trial.

At every step of the way—finding experts, consulting with them informally, consulting in preparation for trial, pretrial discovery of experts' opinions, direct and cross-examination of experts at trial—many problems, both of a legal nature and of a practical nature, must be addressed and solved.

There is a large body of statutory law, procedural rules, and case law defining the use of expert testimony. In recent years the enormously influential Federal Rules of Evidence (and state codes in most jurisdictions modeled on the federal rules) have greatly changed the way cases are tried. These rules relaxed traditional restrictions on expert testimony and enhanced the importance of experts in civil litigation.

Need for Expert Testimony. Illustrative of the need for and efficacy of expert witnesses is that even causation must be proved by expert testimony when the pertinent issue is not one within the common knowledge of lay people. In a case involving such an issue, expert testimony will be needed to create a jury question.

In an actual medical malpractice case, the plaintiff failed to call an expert witness. The court, because of the lack of expert testimony, directed a verdict for the defendant. The plaintiff had undergone neck surgery to remove an imbedded piece of glass, which had been identified by his family doctor through his reading of X rays he had taken. The first surgeon the plaintiff consulted could not find the glass because he never bothered to look at the original X rays. Five months later, the plaintiff consulted another surgeon, who took a second set of X rays and found that the glass had migrated upward. The second surgeon was able to remove the glass in a 10-minute outpatient surgical procedure under local anesthesia. The trial court directed a verdict for the defendant (the first surgeon), because the plaintiff had failed to provide expert testimony. The appellate court, in *Harvey* v. *Fridley Medical Center* [315 N.W.2d 225 (Minn. 1982)], stated that the surgeon's failure to examine the X rays was the direct cause of his failing to remove the glass. Although causation must have seemed fairly obvious to the plaintiff, the court found that the cause of the injury was not within the realm of common knowledge of laypersons. Expert testimony was required concerning the standard of care. The court held that, "causation in a medical malpractice case must be proved by expert testimony when the issue is not within the common knowledge of laymen."

In a case involving this type of issue, the trial judge should not allow the jury to consider the case without the guidance of expert testimony. This is the type of case, in effect, where expert testimony *must* be used.

In such cases, the jury clearly will not have the education, training, or experience to arrive at sound conclusions from facts presented to them at trial, unless they are assisted by an expert stating his or her opinion. The expert is equipped by education, training, or experience to draw sound conclusions and to assist the jury.

In a case involving bodily injuries caused by an auto accident, the jury may be perfectly capable of listening to witnesses testify about the facts of the accident and then deciding how the accident happened and who was at fault. But there may be a question of permanent disability. The nature, degree, and consequences of such injuries may be beyond their experience. They must have the guidance of a medical expert, and possibly one or more experts in such fields as rehabilitation, economics or actuarial science, and vocational guidance.

Expert testimony generally *may* be used where it will help the jury, even though it may not be strictly necessary, that is, where persons without specialized knowledge are not likely to be able to form a correct judgment without the assistance of a specialist. "A reasonable test to be applied is whether the members of the jury . . . would be aided in the consideration of the issue by the offered testimony." [*Clark* v. *Rental Equipment Co.* 300 Minn. 420, 220 N.W.2d 407, 512 (1974)].

The need for expert witnesses in litigation may be expressed in terms of getting to the jury, convincing a jury, and holding a jury verdict. When the subject matter of a case is not within the common knowledge of laypersons, a plaintiff whose contentions are unsupported by qualified expert testimony should not be allowed by the trial judge to have a jury decide his or her case. Competent expert testimony may lend credibility and support to an otherwise weak and questionable case: the judge (who otherwise might grant a summary judgment or direct a verdict) may let the jury hear everything and give the expert testimony whatever weight they wish. Even if it has been possible for a party to motivate a jury to render a verdict on the basis of tenuous expert testimony (or none at all), many appellate decisions have focused on whether the expert testimony was adequate to sustain the verdict or even to have allowed the jury to consider the case.

The use—and possibly abuse—of expert witnesses has been one of the most visible and significant characteristics of civil litigation in recent years. Myriad articles in scholarly publications and the popular press have focused attention on the civil litigation explosion and the blockbuster verdicts which have triggered liability insurance crises. The perceived problems with the tort reparations mechanism and our system of civil justice have fueled the heated controversy over tort reform. The tort reparations system as we know it today would be hard to imagine without extensive use of expert testimony.

Depending upon one's perspective, the burgeoning volume of products liability and medical liability litigation can be seen as either the glory or the bane of the civil justice system in the years between 1960 and today. The ingenious and efficacious use of expert testimony in civil litigation has helped immeasurably in securing larger awards for plaintiffs.

Products liability litigation must figure prominently in any discussion of the preeminent role of the expert witness in today's litigation. It is useful, therefore, to review a few examples of cases in which counsel and the courts have looked to expert testimony for appropriate guidance in the resolution of issues.

In a products liability case involving permanent disability, a party may seek to introduce testimony of a vocational guidance expert and an actuary who will project the present value of the future loss of earning capacity. A party in a case involving an eye injury caused by an ejected champagne bottle cork may seek to rely upon the testimony of a Ph.D. in fluid mechanics and heat transfer with experience in design of pressurized containers. Parties in cases involving a wide range of products (from automobiles to garage door openers to propane lanterns to cosmetics) may seek to rely upon expert testimony that it was (or was not) technologically possible and economically feasible to design and manufacture a safer product at the time the product was actually designed and manufactured. [See, e.g., *Hagans* v. *Oliver Mach. Co.*, 576 F.2d 96 (5th Cir. 1978); *Garst* v. *General Motors*, 484 P.2d 47 (Kan. 1971).]

The Basis for Expert Testimony. In recent years, the ground rules of expert testimony have changed drastically enough to provide a basis for strong criticism of the role and power of the expert in determining the outcome of litigation.

One such change is reflected in the emergence of the expert whose alleged expertise cuts across various technical disciplines. Examples include the safety engineer and the human factors or ergonomics expert. The human factors engineer professes to be able to homogenize principles of engineering science and psychology into a statement of an opinion. The opinion may be that—in light of such factors as fatigue, familiarity, distraction, stress, depth perceptions, and others—an accident was statistically inevitable, or a condition was unreasonably dangerous or unsafe.

Another such change in the ground rules of expert testimony has occurred which is almost contemporaneous with the advent of new and esoteric types of experts. That change was the promulgation of Rule 704 of the Federal Rules of Evidence. Rule 704(a) provides:

> Except as provided in subdivision (b), testimony in the form of an opinion or inference otherwise admissible is not objectionable because it embraces an ultimate issue to be decided by the trier of fact.

Under Rule 704, more than ever before, the expert can shape the decision of the jury. Opinions stated by the expert can thus become a form of argument to the jury in midstream of the trial.

This is permissible by virtue of Rule 703 of the Federal Rules of Evidence. Rule 703 states:

> The facts or data in the particular case upon which an expert bases an opinion or inference may be those perceived by or made known to him at or before the hearing. If of a type reasonably relied upon by experts in the particular field in forming opinions or inferences upon the subject, the facts or data need not be admissible in evidence.

The expert, in a sense, becomes the conduit through which material not received in evidence, and often not admissible in evidence, nonetheless may be offered to the jury for its consideration. The Rule offers an opportunity for a dialogue between the direct examiner and his expert witness amounting to an exposition of the expert's ultimate opinion and the explanation of its basis.

As noted above, Rules 703 and 704 make it easier to get an issue before a jury. Moreover, the expert may state the basis for his or her opinion, and that opinion may be based upon facts or data made known to the expert of a type reasonably relied upon by experts in that field. Thus, even though the facts or data have not been received in evidence, and regardless of their admissibility, the issue is joined and can be decided by the jury. The effect of the expert's opinion is ordinarily as great as or as small as the jury, in its discretion, may want it to be. The opinion may be accepted. The opinion may be rejected because the jury feels it is outweighed by other evidence. It may be rejected also because the jury decides that the expert is unqualified or that the opinion is unreasoned. The Federal Jury Instruction Guide tells the jury:

> If you should decide that the opinion of an expert witness is not based upon sufficient education and experience, or if you should conclude that the reasons given in support

of the opinion are not sound, or that the opinion is outweighed by other evidence, you may disregard the opinion entirely.

In *Daubert* v. *Merrell-Dow Pharmaceuticals, Inc.* [113 S.Ct. 2786 (1993)], the U.S. Supreme Court required federal district courts to assume a ''gatekeeper'' role—assessing the qualifications of experts, the relevance of their testimony, and the scientific soundness of their methodology—before allowing the experts to testify. This recent landmark decision has caused a strong impact on the use of expert testimony in federal courts.

SUBSTITUTES FOR EVIDENCE

905 Presumptions and Inferences

There are certain facts that the law will accept as true without any proof whatsoever. For example, it is presumed that everyone regulates his or her conduct in such a way so as to obey the law. In criminal cases, this is referred to as the presumption of innocence. Before any testimony whatsoever is offered to the court, the defendant, accused of the crime, is presumed innocent. This may be overcome by the introduction of testimony that in truth and in fact the defendant is not innocent and did not regulate his or her conduct in accordance with the law, but actually followed a course contrary to the conduct expressly required by the law.

A somewhat similar type of presumption applies to civil cases. A person is presumed to have driven an automobile in accordance with the statutes regulating its use; he or she is presumed to have utilized personal property with due care and regard for the rights of neighbors, and is presumed to have kept his or her premises in proper repair. The same presumption applies in fatal cases, and the deceased is presumed to have obeyed the law and exercised due care.

These facts can be overcome only by evidence to show that the defendant did not operate a motor vehicle in accordance with the statute; did not maintain his or her premises and use them with due regard for the rights of neighbors, and did not keep his or her premises in the condition of repair which the law requires. The burden of proof is upon the person asserting that the defendant did not act in obedience to the law. These presumptions arise by operation of law and are rebuttable by the adverse party. This means that the presumptive fact may be shown to be incorrect by the testimony offered by the opposing party.

The proof of one basic fact may give rise to the assumption, as a matter of logic, that a second fact exists. For example, proof of possession gives rise to a presumption of ownership. The fact that repairs to the premises have been made gives rise to a presumption or inference that the person making such repairs has control of the property. These presumptions arise as a matter of common experience. Most of the time, property possessed by a person is owned by that person. People do not make repairs on premises they do not control nor repair premises they are not obligated to repair. The registration of a motor vehicle in the name of a person gives rise to a presumption that that person is the owner. In order to prove ownership of a motor vehicle, therefore, mere proof of the fact that the motor vehicle is registered in the name of a certain person will be sufficient to establish ownership, as well as control. The mere fact that proof is offered of the registration of the motor vehicle will be sufficient to establish ownership.

In all these cases, the presumption is rebuttable, and each can be overcome by specific testimony contradicting the presumed fact. Where there is no evidence justifying a finding contrary to the presumed fact, the jury will be instructed that the presumed fact must be taken as true. If there is evidence justifying the finding contrary to the presumed fact, the jury then is at liberty to find the existence or nonexistence of the presumed fact upon all of the evidence exactly as if the presumption had never been in existence.

There is an additional presumption with respect to official records. Where official records of birth, marriage, divorce, and death are produced and identified by the official custodian of the records, there arises a presumption that the information contained in the official records is true, even though the custodian identifying the records has no specific knowledge with regard to the event set forth in the documents produced.

There is a presumption that a status, once established, is a continuing one. Proof that an unsafe condition existed on a certain date will give rise to a presumption that the unsafe condition continued. This can be overcome by evidence that the condition was repaired or altered at a certain time, but in absence of such proof the presumption is that the unsafe condition, once established, was a continuing one and remained in existence.

In cases where the conduct of a deceased person is in issue, the presumption is that the deceased exercised due care. It makes no difference whether the action is one brought on account of the injuries suffered by the deceased under the survival statute, or for the deceased's wrongful death, or an action brought against the deceased's estate for his or her negligence in causing the injury of another person. The presumption is applied in all cases, irrespective of whether it grants an advantage to plaintiff or defendant. The presumption may be overcome by evidence to the contrary.

906 Irrebuttable Presumptions

The presumptions we have considered in the preceding section may be overcome by contrary evidence. There are some situations, however, in which, once the presumption is established, the court will not receive evidence in rebuttal. There is a common-law presumption that a child under the age of seven is incapable of negligence. Once the age of the child is established, a conclusive presumption arises that the child is not negligent. No evidence will be received to establish that the child's conduct was negligent in any way. The presumption is irrebuttable.

There is an irrebuttable presumption at common law that everyone knows the law. Therefore, ignorance of the law cannot be interposed as a defense to an action based upon a legal infraction. If a woman drives her car at a speed of 60 miles per hour in a 25-mile zone, and an accident occurs as a consequence of her excessive speed, she will be charged with knowledge of the law which restricted the speed to 25 miles an hour, whether she knew of the law or not.

There are presumptions which are only partially rebuttable in the sense that they can be overcome by testimony or evidence in a very restricted area. Evidence that a person has been missing from his or her usual place of abode for more than seven years, plus evidence that the person has not communicated with his or her spouse, relatives, close friends, and people with whom the person normally would maintain close contact, gives rise to a presumption of death. The presumption can be overcome only by evidence of someone who saw the person alive within the seven-year period. It cannot be overcome with any other evidence. Therefore, evidence of the person's age, state of health, life expectancy, and similar matters will not destroy the presumption. In the absence of direct evidence that the person was alive during the seven-year period, the presumption is irrebuttable.

907 *Res Ipsa Loquitur*

Back in 1863, there was a case in which a barrel of flour rolled out of the second-story window of a warehouse and struck a passing pedestrian. The facts of the occurrence were produced in evidence but there was no proof of any specific act of negligence on the part of the warehouse owner. In sustaining a recovery for the plaintiff, the court said that the thing speaks for itself and that the circumstances of the accident were such that mere proof of the occurrence was sufficient to warrant an inference of negligence. The court, in making the point that the thing speaks for itself, used the Latin equivalent, *res ipsa loquitur*. This has been repeated thousands of times and we still have the phrase with us.

The court thought that this was the type of accident that normally would not have occurred had due care been exercised by the warehouser. If there was an explanation for the occurrence, and if it did take place in spite of the exercise of due care, the defendant warehouser was in the better position to explain how the accident occurred and that the exercise of due care could not have prevented it. This the defendant did not do, and, in the absence of specific evidence as to the actual causation of the occurrence, proof by the plaintiff of the facts of the accident was sufficient to raise an inference of negligence on the part of the defendant.

The mere fact that an accident occurred does not compel the application of *res ipsa loquitur*. To invoke the doctrine, the following elements must be present:

1. The instrumentality which caused the accident must be in the exclusive control of the defendant.

2. The accident must be one which does not happen in the ordinary course of things if those who have control exercise proper care.
3. The accident must not have been due to any voluntary contribution (contributory negligence) on the part of the plaintiff.

This is a rule of circumstantial evidence for the benefit of the plaintiff and relieves the plaintiff of the obligation of proving specific acts of negligence by the defendant. As a defense, the defendant must offer an explanation of the occurrence which will absolve him or her from responsibility. For example, if an automobile jumped the curb and struck a pedestrian on the sidewalk, *res ipsa loquitur* would compel the inference that the driver of the automobile was negligent. All three elements of the doctrine would be present. The instrumentality causing the accident was within the exclusive control of the driver. The accident is one which normally would not have occurred but for the negligence of the driver. Lastly, the pedestrian who was on the sidewalk, a place where he or she had a right to be, was not contributorily negligent. In the absence of any other evidence, the plaintiff pedestrian should prevail.

Suppose that the automobile driver was suffering from a latent heart condition of which she had no prior knowledge. While driving her automobile, she suffered a heart attack of such severity that she was unable to control the vehicle. The accident occurred while the driver was in the throes of this heart attack. Evidence of the heart attack, if believed by the jury, would overcome the presumption of *res ipsa loquitur* and would negate any conclusion that the accident occurred because of a lack of due care on the part of the automobile driver.

Technical situations in which *res ipsa loquitur* has been applied include: an action against the beauty shop proprietor for the loss of a patron's hair; action against an airline by a passenger for injuries sustained in an airplane crash; injuries sustained as a result of a collapsing counter stool in a hotel restaurant; injuries sustained when bricks or window panes fell from the defendant's premises; falling elevators; the collapse of structures; explosion of boilers; injuries to passengers for causes within the control of the railroad, such as derailment or defective equipment; and automobile accidents where the automobile ran into a stationary object.

Thus the application of the rule of *res ipsa loquitur* gives the plaintiff a legal advantage. It correspondingly places the defendant in the disadvantageous position of having to explain the details of the accident and to show that due care on the part of the defendant would not have prevented the accident from occurring. Its application has been justified, most often, on the theory that, because the dangerous instrumentality causing the injury is in the control of the defendant, the defendant has greater access to the facts of the occurrence than the plaintiff. One of the elements of the doctrine is that the offending instrumentality must be within the exclusive control of the defendant.

It frequently happens that a specific act of negligence occurs while the offending instrumentality is in the hands of the defendant, but the accident occurred after the defendant had relinquished possession. This situation usually arises in cases of defectively manufactured products. The doctrine of *res ipsa loquitur* has been applied to such cases, and the requirement that the instrumentality causing the injury be under exclusive control of the defendant is overcome by one of several theories. Some courts take the position that, once the negligent act has occurred, the duty of the defendant is a continuing one and therefore, at least constructively or theoretically, the defendant has possession and control of the article until the defective condition is remedied, even though the defective article passes out of the possession of the defendant. Other cases merely hold that the requirement is met if it is shown that the negligent act occurred while the offending instrumentality was in the control of the defendant. In either of these cases the result is the same, and the doctrine of *res ipsa loquitur* is applied.

Illustrative of this type of situation would be a case where a manufacturer produced a loaf of bread with glass baked inside it. The bread was sold to the plaintiff in a sealed package. The *res ipsa loquitur* doctrine could be applied to any injury sustained by the plaintiff, even though this particular loaf of bread had passed from the possession of the manufacturer. Obviously, the manufacturer or packer of food products is charged with the knowledge that the item will be used for human consumption. Therefore, he or she must exercise a high degree of care to assure the purity of the product manufactured or prepared. The mere presence of deleterious substances in the product, glass in this case, would be sufficient to give rise to an inference that there was a failure on the part of the manufacturer to exercise the requisite amount of care.

The same principle has been applied in ''exploding bottle'' cases and in cases involving products other than food products, such as defectively manufactured appliances which burst into flame upon use, explode, leak illuminating gas, or collapse when subjected to the use for which the appliance was intended. It is sufficent that the negligent act in the form of defective workmanship occurred while the product was in the possession of the defendant.

908 Judicial Notice

It is axiomatic that the law does not require that to be proved which is apparent to the court. To demand otherwise would be wasteful of time and contrary to common sense. It follows that there are certain matters the court would deem to be proved, either on its own initiative or whenever its attention is directed to them. This process by which the court dispenses with proof is called *judicial notice*.

The court will take judicial notice in matters of common and general knowledge, such as the time and the setting of the sun at a given place on a certain date, or the direction in which a river within the jurisdiction flows. Proof would not be required to establish that the United States is in North America, that North

America is in the western hemisphere, or that the Atlantic Ocean is on the east coast of the United States. These are matters of geographical certainty, and it would be absurd for the court to demand proof of them or to receive evidence to prove that any of these conditions did not exist. As to the existence of statutes, the court is required to give notice judicially to all statutes of general application in its jurisdiction, the federal statutes of general application, and the Constitution and treaties of the United States.

The court will give judicial notice to physical traits such as average bodily dimensions. The court will also give judical notice to matters of common knowledge with respect to the effect of certain things on the human body. For example, if the plaintiff testified that he was struck in the eye and that he later had a black eye, it would not be necessary for the plaintiff to produce medical evidence indicating in detail the exact physiological process which occurred following the blow in order to produce the black eye. On the other hand, the court would not take judicial notice of the remote and unusual effects of physical injury, such as cancer or tuberculosis, which would call for more than the average person's knowledge of cause and effect.

Generally speaking, therefore, the court will take judicial notice of facts which are within the knowledge of the average person as well as authoritative record books, such as Lloyd's Register of Ships, telephone directories, municipal directories, and the like. The court can inform itself with respect to the contents of volumes of this character by making reference to the book itself. The following is a general list of specific matters which the courts will judicially notice:

1. Facts within the common knowledge of the average person.
2. Matters of governmental record and concern.
3. The course and laws of nature.
4. Qualities and properties of matter within the common knowledge of the average person.
5. Time, days, and dates of the calendar.
6. Scientific facts within the knowledge of the average person.
7. Geographical facts: location of principal rivers, boundaries, and municipalities.
8. Location of the 50 states and the boundaries of each, together with mountain ranges, lakes, and streams of national importance.
9. Historical facts concerning the nation as a whole and the state in which the court sits.
10. The United States census.
11. Mortality tables.

The court will likewise take judicial notice of physical facts produced in evidence which make it impossible for the alleged accident to have occurred. This type of reasoning is sometimes referred to as the doctrine of *incontrovertible physical facts*.

THE HEARSAY RULE AND ITS EXCEPTIONS

909 The Hearsay Rule

The rule is that evidence of any statement made out of court—no matter by whom, or who was present, or where it was made—if offered to prove the truth of what is contained in the statement, is hearsay and incompetent. A witness may testify only to information concerning which he or she has personal knowledge. A witness may not testify to what someone told him or her in order to establish the truth or falsity of the condition or event that is the subject matter of the statement. Any information the witness might have that came from a secondary source would not prove that a particular event happened or a particular set of facts was actually in existence at a specific time and place. As we all know from common experience, versions of a story become garbled when repeated. Therefore, any evidence which a witness could offer on this basis would be unreliable. In addition, since the witness is not testifying as to facts within personal knowledge, he or she could not be cross-examined in order to elicit further facts or to enlarge upon the facts already given. The only question on which the witness could be examined would be the accuracy of the recollection of the statement heard.

In slander cases, evidence by a witness of statements which he or she heard is admissible. This is not because the evidence tends to establish the truth of the statement made, or the truth of the facts or circumstances within the statement itself, but because it tends to establish that a statement was made. The basis of the cause of action for slander rests upon the oral publication of defamatory or untruthful statements concerning an individual. Therefore, the question before the court is whether the statement was in fact made, and not whether the statement itself established the truth or falsity of an event or a fact. For example, if a witness testified that she heard *A* say to *B* that *C* is a thief, the witness's testimony is not hearsay evidence. It is evidence that the particular statement was made.

W testifies that *X* said, "I saw Jones strike Smith." If *W*'s testimony is offered to prove only what *X* said, *W*'s statement is not hearsay. However, if it is offered to prove either that *X* saw Jones strike Smith, or that Jones did strike Smith, the statement is a hearsay declaration and *W*'s testimony is hearsay evidence. For reasons of logic and sometimes for matters of pure necessity, the law permits certain evidence to be admitted as exceptions to the hearsay rule. The exceptions with which we are concerned are as follows:

1. *Res gestae* statements.
2. Declarations of pain and suffering.
3. Admissions against interest; plea of guilty at motor vehicle hearing.
4. Conviction in traffic court.
5. Conviction of prior crimes.
6. Testimony in prior proceedings.

7. Prior self-contradictory statements.
8. Book entries in the regular course of business.
9. Admissions by conduct.
10. Admissions by an agent.
11. Admissions by a joint tort-feasor.

910 *Res Gestae* Statements

One of the exceptions to the hearsay rule is the spontaneous utterance made during the happening of the event and made by the declarant as explanatory of the event. Included in this exception are things said, things written, things done simultaneously with the happening of the event before there has been an opportunity for reflection. Evidence is not limited to those things that are done by the parties to the action alone, but also things said, written, and done, even by a stranger. This evidence is admitted as a matter of necessity and the truth of the thing is based upon spontaneity. The statement must be simultaneous with the event and made before there was any opportunity for conscious, deliberate thought.

For example, if immediately after the accident between two automobiles the driver of one got out and stated, "I was going too fast," or "My brakes didn't work," or "I didn't see your car," evidence by persons who heard these statements would be admissible against the person who made them. The reliability or truthfulness of the statement is based on the fact that it was made immediately after the event and is explanatory of the event.

Normally, to be a *res gestae* statement, the spontaneous utterance must be made simultaneously with the event or immediately thereafter. However, statements have been admitted in evidence where they were made by a person who was still acting under the nervous excitement of what he or she had seen. There is no specific rule as to the maximum period of time involved in such a situation. The evidence must show that the person is still acting under this nervous excitement and strain. An example is that of an individual who was knocked unconscious at the time of the accident and stayed in an unconscious state for several hours. Upon regaining consciousness, he made a statement. Obviously, he had no opportunity for reflection or fabrication. This is considered a *res gestae* statement.

The *res gestae* statement does not have to be made by a party to the action or event. Evidence is admissible if the court finds that the hearsay statement was made: (*a*) while the declarant was perceiving the event or condition which the statement narrates, describes, or explains, or immediately thereafter; or (*b*) while the declarant was under the stress of a nervous excitement caused by the perception of the event or condition which the statement narrates, describes, or explains.

911 Declarations of Pain and Suffering

The usual manifestation of pain is by oral expression. Since such expression is solely within the control of the person manifesting it, only those expressions of pain made to others, which are involuntary, are admissible in evidence. This refers to evidence given by those who heard the declaration. The injured person may testify to the pain he or she suffered as a fact, and upon this fact may be cross-examined.

Declarations of pain and suffering can be admissible in evidence as a spontaneous utterance if made immediately after an accident occurred. This evidence is received on the same basis as other *res gestae* statements on the theory that it is made close to the happening of the event, without any opportunity for reflection and fabrication, and for that reason is believed to be truthful.

In only two situations are declarations of pain and suffering admissible in evidence. They are: (1) voluntary statements of pain communicated to a physician who was consulted for the purpose of treatment, which are admitted on the theory that such statements are motivated by an urge to be truthful; (2) voluntary statements of pain made by a person, since deceased, where the nature and cause of the injury are in issue, which statements are received on the theory that the necessity of the case demands it.

Where the patient is being examined by a physician employed by the defendant, statements as to the pain previously suffered are not admissible in evidence (as an exception to the hearsay rule). But declarations as to the patient's then existing state of mind, pain, and suffering, are admissible in evidence and the examining physician may so testify.

912 Admissions against Interest

An admission is any statement made, any act done, or any course of conduct pursued by which a party to the litigation has indicated a contrary attitude to the one which he or she is taking at the trial. Such prior contrary attitudes tend to throw suspicion on the claim at the trial and are used as independent evidence against the person. Unlike the spontaneous utterance, an admission may be made at any time prior to the trial.

Declarations against interest are defined by the Model Code of Evidence as follows:

> A declaration is against the interest of a declarant if the judge finds that the fact asserted in the declaration was at the time of the declaration so far contrary to the declarant's pecuniary or proprietary interest, or so far subjected him to civil or criminal liability or so far rendered invalid a claim by him against another, or created such a risk of making him an object of hatred, ridicule, or social disapproval in the community that a reasonable man in his position would not have made the declaration unless he believed it to be true.

The admission against interest does not necessarily have to be made by a party to the litigation. For example, in an action between *P* and *D* for damages for personal injuries, *W* offers to testify for *D* that *X* said, "I carelessly drove over *P*; I understand he is now suing *D* for the damage." This is an admission against the pecuniary interest of *X* and is therefore admissible in order to show that *X* was responsible for the accident and not *D*.

913 Testimony in Prior Proceedings

A witness's testimony in prior proceedings is not admissible in evidence unless the witness takes the stand in the subsequent proceedings. Then the prior testimony may be identified and used on cross-examination for the purpose of impeaching the witness and raising an issue as to his or her credibility, should the present testimony be contrary to the previous testimony on the same issue. This is permissible on the theory that the jury has a right to know whether the witness has testified under oath to a different version, and also a right to such testimony to help them decide whether they will believe the witness.

This is often a significant factor in the courtroom cross-examination of expert witnesses (see Section 904). A lawyer will seek information about testimony given by an opposing expert in previous trials or pretrial depositions. He or she also will review that expert's writings in scholarly books or specialized journals. A knowledge of such prior testimony or writing—which may contradict present testimony—can provide counsel with a basis for calling the witness's credibility into question or impeaching his or her testimony.

The prior testimony of a party to the action is always admissible in evidence, whether he or she testifies or not, as an admission against interest (see Section 912).

914 Prior Contradictory Statements

Oral statements made in public, which are inconsistent with the testimony offered by the witness, may be established by the testimony of other witnesses who were present at the time and place the statement was made. Limitation on this type of evidence is within the sound discretion of the court, and the extent to which the adverse party may go in introducing evidence along these lines is fixed by the court. The oral statements may include communications given to a police officer investigating the case at some time subsequent to the occurrence of an accident, or oral statements given to an insurance claim representative. Should the person who allegedly made the statements deny having made them, then a question of fact is presented to the jury. It will decide which witness is telling the truth and which is not.

Written statements verified by the witness carry much more weight and are documentary evidence of the statements made. Denial is more difficult. These could consist of written statements given to an insurance claim representative and signed by the witness, a motor vehicle report of the accident submitted to the state and signed by the witness, a written report of the accident signed by the witness and submitted to an insurance company, or a written statement or written claim for compensation for injuries arising out of the same accident. In this same category would be claims arising out of the same event for accident and health insurance coverage.

915 Book Entries in the Regular Course of Business

A party to litigation may offer, under certain circumstances, the books kept and prepared by him or her or by others as proof of the facts they contain. If the books are prepared by the litigant, they are not only hearsay but also self-serving; whereas if they are prepared by another, they are purely hearsay. Nevertheless, for reasons of necessity, regular book entries have been admitted as exceptions to the hearsay rule upon the fulfillment of certain requirements to verify their accuracy.

Entries made in the regular course of business, prepared by record clerks and persons other than the litigants, are admissible. The preliminary proof required for the introduction of such books into evidence is as follows: it must appear that (*a*) the books are the regular books of entry; (*b*) the entries were made in the regular course of business at about the time of the transaction involved; (*c*) the person making the entry had personal knowledge of the transaction or was informed of it by one who had such knowledge and who was under a duty to communicate it to him or her.

There can be difficulty involved in producing evidence of this character, especially where bookkeeping systems are intricate and where the turnover in help is large—with discharged employees having no inclination to be helpful even if they were able to remember something of a given transaction. Therefore, many states have enacted statutes by means of which the mere identification of the books as the regular books of account of the corporation is sufficient to admit them into evidence.

RULES OF EVIDENCE IN CERTAIN SITUATIONS

916 Plea of Guilty at a Motor Vehicle Hearing

Should a party to the litigation allege that he or she was operating a motor vehicle within the traffic regulations, any action taken by the person subsequent to the event, which would be inconsistent with this position, can be admissible in evidence against the person. Such an act could consist of entering a plea of guilty to a charge of traffic violation arising out of the same event. Evidence of such a plea is received in evidence against the person as an admission.

The courts recognize that in some cases one charged with a traffic violation will plead guilty, even though believing himself or herself innocent, in order to avoid the expenditure of time and money which would be involved if guilt were denied and the charge contested. However, the courts do allow evidence of the plea of guilty to be introduced and will allow the defendant to give an explanation and the reasons for so pleading. It is then for the jury to evaluate this testimony and decide whether the plea is entitled to any weight as an admission.

Where the defendant does not appear and plead in the traffic court, and merely suffers a forfeiture of the bail bond or a fine, this lack of action is not considered an admission and evidence thereof is not admissible. It is only where some action is taken by the person, which action is inconsistent with the position at the trial, that such evidence is admissible.

917 Conviction in Traffic Court

Evidence of a conviction as a consequence of a motor vehicle hearing, in which the defendant entered a plea of not guilty, generally cannot be received in evidence as an admission or for any other purpose. The fact that another court has made a decision with respect to one phase of the case is neither binding upon nor persuasive to the court before which the present action is being tried. It would be prejudicial to the defendant's chances of a fair trial before this court if any reference were made to an action taken by another court on the same or similar evidence.

From another point of view, evidence of conviction in traffic court is pure hearsay. The conclusion reached by the court on the traffic violation is likewise hearsay. In addition, if the traffic court conviction were given any weight whatsoever, the result would be that a superior court would be bound by the findings of a lower court of limited jurisdiction.

Some states have departed from this general rule and have by statute permitted evidence of a conviction in traffic court to be received in evidence. In other states, only the conviction of a felony such as manslaughter, arson, and crimes of like quality can be received in evidence. Traffic violations, coming under the classification of minor offenses or misdemeanors, are not affected by this latter rule.

918 Conviction of Prior Crimes

There are two phases to this subject. The first is the problem of the admissibility of evidence of the conviction of a crime arising out of the same subject matter as the pending action, such evidence being offered for the purpose of proving the liability of the defendant. The second phase of the problem refers to the admissibility of evidence of the conviction of a prior crime, totally unrelated to the action pending before the court, but offered for the purpose of affecting the credibility of any witness in the action, whether the witness is a party to the action or not.

The majority view is that conviction of any crime arising out of the same event as the action pending before the court is not admissible for the purpose of establishing the liability of the defendant. Our courts have tenaciously adhered to this principle, even though in many cases an inconsistent result was obtained.

For example, *A* is convicted of arson in the third degree. This crime consists of the intentional burning of his own building with intent to defraud or prejudice an insurer. While serving his sentence, *A* brings an action against his fire insurance company, under a policy covering the building which he intentionally burned. The evidence of *A*'s conviction of the crime is excluded. Under those circumstances, where the jury is ignorant of *A*'s conviction, it is quite possible for the jury to bring in a verdict for *A* and against the fire insurance company. We then would have a situation where *A* is serving a sentence for arson, but is allowed to recover a money judgment as a consequence of his own criminal act. The inconsistency is immediately apparent. *A* has profited from the commission of his own crime, while at the same time being punished for it.

Public policy demands that there be no profit derived from the commission of a criminal act. Therefore, some states have enacted statutes modifying this rule and permitting evidence of such convictions to be received, especially in cases of arson, or other serious felony. In the above example, the evidence of *A*'s criminal conviction would be admissible in a subsequent civil trial. Under the statutes, evidence of the conviction of the crime would be admissible in evidence whether the party so convicted testified or not. The statute permits the introduction of the evidence not to affect the party's credibility as a witness, but to prove the facts recited in the judgment of conviction.

When a party to a lawsuit puts any witness on the stand, including himself, he impliedly warrants that the witness is a truth-teller. Frequently the version as told by one witness will be entirely contradictory to the version given by another. The jury has the task of deciding which version is correct. To assist it in reaching a decision, the jury has an opportunity of observing the witness and noting his or her demeanor while on the stand, as well as the cross-examination. In making their evaluation, the jury is entitled to know that the witness has been convicted of a crime involving moral turpitude, if such be the fact. Evidence of prior crimes which involve acts contrary to justice, honesty, modesty, or good morals may be shown if the witness has in fact been convicted of committing them. A convicted thief is more likely to offer perjured testimony than a person who has no such record. In deciding the relative weight to be given to the testimony of witnesses, the fact that one witness is a convicted thief will weigh heavily against the jury's acceptance of his story.

To be admissible, the conviction must be for a crime involving moral turpitude. Included in this category would be such acts as larceny, embezzlement, rape, and murder. Convictions of crimes not involving moral turpitude are not admissible. Suppose that a woman was convicted of automobile homicide. This means that she operated her motor vehicle in a willful, wanton, and reckless manner. Evidence of such conviction would not in any way indicate that she was a person who was not to be believed. That she operated her motor vehicle in a culpably negligent manner is not any indication of her character as an honest woman. The same thing would be true if the witness were convicted of violating city ordinances by failing to remove the snow from her sidewalks or failing to keep her garbage cans covered. These matters likewise do not involve any moral issue and conviction of such crimes would not be received in evidence to affect her credibility.

It should be emphasized, however, that only evidence of a conviction may be received. If the witness was accused of a crime involving moral turpitude by indictment of the grand jury or an information filed by the district attorney, and he or she was acquitted after trial or the charges were dropped, evidence of these prior proceedings is not admissible for any purpose whatsoever.

919 Admissions by Conduct

Evidence of conduct on the part of one party, which could be indicative of the fact that he himself felt that he had a poor case, is admissible against him. Such an act might consist of an attempt to bribe a witness to give false testimony in his favor. Although collateral to the issues, it is competent as an admission by act and conduct that his case is weak and his evidence dishonest. It is not conclusive, even when believed by the jury, because the party may think that he has a poor case when in fact he has a good one. The evidence tends to discredit his witnesses and to cast some doubt upon his position. It is for the consideration of the jury, after ample opportunity for explanation and denial under proper instructions to prevent them from giving undue attention to the collateral matter to the detriment of the main issue.

In one such case, a party offered testimony by a person retained as an investigator. He was employed to "look up" and "see to" witnesses for the defendant so as to enable it to defeat the plaintiff's claim. He was to find witnesses, if possible, who would swear to such a state of facts as would prevent a recovery against the defendant. The method of doing this was left to his judgment and discretion. In order to promote its interest, he saw fit to use the power entrusted to him by trying to bribe witnesses for the plaintiff to testify falsely in favor of the defendant. He was to procure evidence, the method not being specified, and he tried to get it by an unlawful method. The court concluded that, if this evidence would have been admissible against an individual defendant who had employed the agent as he was employed, it was admissible against a corporate defendant. If an honest man by mistake employs a dishonest one to look up witnesses for him, and the latter through excess of zeal resorts to bribery, although it was never thought of by his employer, it is preferable (for cleanliness and purity in the administration of justice) that the fact should be shown (with the fullest opportunity for explanation) than to exclude the evidence.

920 Admissions by an Agent

Normally an agent has no authority to make any admissions which are binding on his or her principal. There is one exception, and that is where the agent makes an admission while acting within the scope of agency and within the scope of his or her authority. For example, if an agent is driving her principal's motor vehicle and, after an accident has occurred, the agent admits that she was at fault, such an admission is binding on her principal. An attorney, as agent for a client, has no authority to make any admissions on behalf of the client. However, an admission made by the attorney in open court, when such admissions are made as a necessary incident of the handling of the client's case, are binding on the client.

921 Deception Tests

The so-called *lie-detector* tests are not admissible in evidence in civil cases. They are of no value in preparing a case for trial.

There are presently three types of lie-detector tests, as follows.

Systolic Blood Pressure Test. The blood pressure of the individual is measured in much the same way as in the electrocardiogram. The principle on which this test is based is that an untrue answer to a question will cause a measurable increase in the subject's blood pressure.

Association-Reaction Test. The subject concentrates on a list of words that has been given, some of which may evoke a guilty sensation and indicate the subject's untruthfulness.

Respiratory Test. This is based on the theory that the breathing of a subject varies perceptibly upon telling a falsehood.

People who specialize in giving these tests have recommended their use as a tool by claim representatives in their investigation. It is argued that, in cases where there is sharp conflict between the versions given by the insured and the claimant, the claim representative could ascertain the amount of reliance that can be placed upon the insured's version by giving the insured one of these tests. This contention is of dubious value and could easily produce an irritating strain on the relations between the company and its insured. In addition, no company would seriously contend that the insured was in violation of the cooperation clause of his policy if he refused to submit to the test.

922 Subsequent Precautions to Prevent Harm

Where an accident has occurred, the owner of the premises may make repairs or alterations in order to prevent a recurrence of the accident. He or she may adopt other means, such as the employment of security guards or an increase in the number of security guards. Evidence of these precautions to prevent future harm ordinarily is not admissible against the owner to prove that his or her failure to take such precautions to prevent the previous accident was negligent. If such evidence were admissible, the owner would make alterations or repairs or plans to prevent future harm only at his or her peril. The policy of the law is to the contrary and it encourages the prevention of future accidents, especially where experience has indicated that some precautions are necessary.

While evidence of subsequent repairs or alterations is not admissible in order to establish the negligence of the owner, such evidence is admissible in order to show ownership and control of the premises, but then only when the owner denies such control. In absence of a denial of control, evidence of subsequent repairs generally is not admissible.

923 Offers to Compromise and Similar Conduct

The law encourages the compromise of disputed claims. It recognizes that very often defendants will seek to avoid litigation and buy peace by the payment of money—even though they do not believe themselves to be responsible for the accident or the occurrence. Therefore evidence of offers to compromise (settlement negotiations as well as the plaintiff's demand in settlement) is excluded. Were it otherwise, the defendant would never be persuaded to make any offer of settlement, since to do so would be construed as an admission of liability. This would discourage compromises and prolong litigation.

Likewise, evidence that the defendant called a doctor for the injured plaintiff or took the plaintiff to the hospital is not admissible as an admission of liability. Here again, the law encourages acts of human decency and compassion. Nor is the defendant penalized for acts of kindness to the injured person. Testimony that the defendant called on the injured person, sent flowers, fruit, or other gifts, paid for the doctor's services in rendering first aid, or paid all of the injured person's medical bills would not be received in evidence as an admission of liability. It is clear that the defendant may have been motivated by a charitable impulse, and his or her good deeds alone should not subject the defendant to liability. The law recognizes this by excluding such evidence.

924 Liability Insurance

Evidence that the defendant was protected by a policy of liability insurance at the time of the accident is not admissible in proving the defendant was negligent. The mere fact that a person had the foresight to purchase insurance does not support such an allegation, and the existence of such insurance does not imply a disregard of due care because a personal financial response in the case of an accident had been precluded.

The matter of liability insurance is likewise inadmissible in order to indicate the defendant's capacity to pay. The general rule is that any reference to liability insurance by the plaintiff is ground for a mistrial. The theory is that the defendant is not accorded a fair trial where the jury has knowledge of the fact that the defendant is insured. The jury may be more likely to find against the defendant where they had knowledge that an insurance company, and not the defendant, would be required to respond in damages. Even in states where automobile liability insurance is compulsory, evidence of insurance is still excluded, although most juries will proceed on the assumption that there is insurance.

Some states have modified this rule of evidence by a statute which enables the plaintiff to join the insurance carrier as an additional defendant—or have provided for a direct action against the insurance carrier. In such states, the existence of insurance is admissible as a matter of statute; however, details of the coverage (such as the policy limits) are not admissible for any purpose.

PRIVILEGES

925 Privileged Communications

There are certain classes of communications passing between persons who stand in a confidential or fiduciary relationship to each other, or who, on account of their relative situations are under a special duty of secrecy and fidelity. The law will not permit these communications to be divulged or inquired into, even in a court of justice and for the sake of public policy and the good order of society. Examples of such privileged relations are those of husband and wife, and attorney and client.

The holder of the privilege, or the person for whose benefit the secrecy is imposed, may waive the privilege and permit the other party to testify concerning matters in the privileged area. In most instances, the waiver must be made in open court and without qualification.

926 Husband and Wife

The general rule is that a husband or wife shall not be compelled, without the consent of the other (if living), to disclose a confidential communication made by one to the other during marriage. This rule is based on principles which are deemed important to preserve the marriage relation as one of full confidence and affection. Public welfare demands that domestic peace be placed above the necessities of a lawsuit or even a criminal proceeding.

This privilege is seldom involved in personal injury cases and, where it is, the privilege is waived by the holder when he or she presents a spouse as a witness in his or her behalf.

It is important to note that this privilege extends only to confidential communications between husband and wife which arise out of the marital relation. A wife or husband, as the case might be, is a competent witness as to all other evidence and may be compelled to testify in behalf of either party of the lawsuit. For example, the wife is a passenger in a vehicle driven by her husband. The husband sues for his personal injuries resulting from an accident. The wife may be compelled to testify if called as a witness by either her husband or the defendant. Her knowledge of the facts of the accident is not knowledge gained as a consequence of the marital relation, and is not privileged.

927 Attorney and Client

The rule is that an attorney or counselor-at-law may not disclose a communication made by a client in the course of professional employment, or any advice given in that regard. And no employee of the lawyer—stenographer, clerk, or other person—is allowed to disclose any such communication. The rule is statutory in most states and, in others, it is considered to be a common-law rule.

The reason for the rule is a matter of necessity because expert legal advice, to be effective, can be given only by a consideration of all of the facts. Clients would be reluctant to make a full disclosure of all the facts if there was any possibility that the attorney could be compelled to testify against them. The client is the holder of the privilege and only the client may waive it.

The privilege is limited to situations where the relationship of attorney and client exists and where the communication is made as a result of such relationship. An attorney is competent and may be compelled to testify concerning other facts which were not gained from a confidential communication.

Obviously, if the relationship of attorney and client does not exist there can be no confidential communications, and an attorney, by reason of his or her profession, does not acquire a status that differs in any way from that of an ordinary witness. An attorney is competent and may be compelled to testify to any matter other than a confidential communication made by a client in the course of the attorney's professional employment.

928 Physician and Patient

Necessity demands that, if medical treatment is to be effective, the physician must have all the facts leading up the patient's present condition. This includes a personal history of previous illnesses, treatment, and exposures to disease. It also includes information gained by a physical examination, treatment, reactions to medication, and diagnostic aids such as X rays, blood tests and similar tests, and exploratory operations. As to these matters, a privilege arises in favor of the patient. This privilege is also binding on all employees of the physician, such as secretary, stenographer, office nurse, X-ray technician, and physiotherapist. The privilege also binds registered nurses, technicians who make various physical tests, and the employees of a hospital or other medical institution in which the patient may be confined.

The privilege does not extend to examining physicians of an insurance company. There is no relationship of physician and patient in these situations, and, as a result, such a physician is competent and may be compelled to testify concerning the history received and the findings.

Privileged communications arising from the doctor-patient relationship consist of all communications made by the patient to the doctor relating to the patient's physical condition and, in addition, all information which the doctor obtained as a consequence of the examination and treatment of the patient. The doctor, of course, is at liberty to disclose information thus obtained to other doctors, or to a hospital, concurrently engaged in treating the same case. It should be emphasized that the privilege attaches only to communications made to the physician for the purpose of treatment, or information gained as a consequence of examination and treatment.

As to communications which do not arise out of the relationship of doctor and patient, there is no privilege. The mere fact that the witness is a doctor does not disqualify that witness from testifying to other matters within his or her knowledge obtained from other sources. In personal injury cases, the plaintiff puts his or her physical condition in issue by the pleadings and by the presentation of witnesses as to the extent of the injuries. Under those circumstances, a number of states hold that the privilege has been waived. The physician may be required to testify as to all communications received in connection with the treatment of the case, as well as to submit any notes or memoranda that he or she may have made as to the progress of the patient.

The doctor-patient privilege did not exist at common law; it is the result of various statutes passed in different states, and they are variously interpreted. Some states go so far as to impose a legal liability upon the physician who discloses any information with regard to the patient's physical condition, whether in court or elsewhere. As a result, the medical profession is extremely hesitant to divulge medical information with respect to patients. Where a statute such as a workers' compensation law compels the physician to make reports, the physician must comply. As to other matters, the claim representative will find that the physician will rarely give any medical information without a specific written authorization signed by the patient. Since the patient is the holder of the privilege, only the patient may waive it. The doctor may not.

The patient, as the holder of the privilege, may waive the privilege and permit the doctor or registered nurse to testify to information thus obtained. In the case of death, this waiver can be given only by the personal representative of the deceased.

929 Priest and Penitent

This is another privilege which never existed at common law. It was never recognized, probably, because cases in which clergymen were called upon to testify to confidential communications (in the form of confessions and other information of like quality) were extremely rare.

Today, the majority of states have enacted statutes providing for this very privilege. They define ''priest'' as a priest, clergyman, minister of the gospel, or other officer of a church or religious denomination or organization, who, in the course of its discipline or practice, is authorized or accustomed to hear, and has a duty to keep secret, penitential communications made by members of the church, denomination, or organization. ''Penitent'' means a member of the church, religious denomination, or organization who has made penitential communication to a clergyman. The ''penitential communication'' usually means a confession of culpable conduct made secretly and in confidence by a penitent to a clergyman in the course of the discipline or practice of the church, religious denomination, or organization of which the penitent is a member. Statutes provide that the privilege is in favor of both the clergyman and the penitent. For the information to be admissible, both clergyman and penitent must waive the privilege. A waiver by one is not binding on the other.

DEMONSTRATIVE EVIDENCE

930 Photographs

Photographs are used to support the testimony of witnesses and to illustrate the existence of certain conditions. In order for the photograph to be admissible, there must be testimony either from the photographer or other witnesses that the photograph fairly and accurately represents the object or the place as it existed at the time of the accident. Thus, when the object of the photograph is to show the road conditions at the time of the accident, the sooner the photograph is taken after the accident the better. Clearly, if the accident occurred in the wintertime with snow on the ground, a photograph taken the following summer would not accurately depict the circumstances and surrounding conditions at the time of the accident. Likewise, a photograph may be inadmissible if there has been a substantial change in the conditions since the accident. For example, if it is claimed that a field was so overgrown with weeds and other foliage that a stop sign was obscured, a photograph taken after the field had been cleared and mowed would not depict the circumstances under which the accident took place. It is within the court's discretion to admit photographs that were taken in black and white, where the negative has been retouched. Where the retouching does not distort or impair the picture's accuracy, such photographs have generally been admitted. Likewise, in the case of enlarged photographs, these have been generally admissible at the court's discretion.

931 Videos

The admissibility of videos is also within the court's discretion. Videos, when offered, must be relevant to the issue and, where it is claimed that the pictures reveal activities on the part of the plaintiff, the pictures must be clear enough for the plaintiff to be identifiable. The general foundation which must be submitted in order to offer videos into evidence consists of the following:

1. Evidence of the circumstances surrounding the taking of the film, the photographer's competence, the camera type, the lens type and lens adjustments, weather conditions, lighting, and camera speed.
2. Manner and circumstances surrounding the film's developing.
3. Evidence as to how the film was stored and how it was protected.
4. Testimony by a person present when the pictures were taken that the pictures accurately depict the events as he or she saw them.

The fact that the film has been edited, spliced, or cut does not render the film inadmissible, as long as the remaining film remains accurate. Where the photographer is unavailable, it is still possible to establish the admissibility of the pictures if there is a witness who was present at the time that the pictures were taken and who can testify as to the type of camera used, the speed of the film, and the subject matter of the pictures.

932 X Rays

X rays present a peculiar problem. The only witness who can identify the person or object used to produce the X ray is the radiologist or the technician who took the X ray. No other witness, whether a physician or technician, can testify with certainty as to the object depicted in the X rays. Therefore, for an X ray to be received in evidence, the person who took the X ray must testify to the following facts:

1. Identification of the subject matter and proof that the X ray is of the person, the anatomical part, or the object lodged in the anatomy.
2. Absence of significant change in the subject and proof that the person's X ray or his or her condition when the X ray was taken is the same as at the time of the occurrence complained of.
3. Proof that the X-ray machine was dependable and was properly operated when the picture was taken.
4. Proof that the operator was qualified.
5. Evidence as to how the X ray was taken.

X rays are not *pictures* even though the term is commonly used in referring to them. Actually, they consist of the shadow produced by placing the person or object between the X-ray tube and the photographic material. Solids, such as bones, show up white whereas tissue shows up dark. In addition, it should be noted that the rays emitted by the X-ray tube descend in umbrellalike fashion. The area where the tube is directly overhead will be sharp in contrast whereas other parts not directly under the tube will show some distortion. In other words, the greater the angle of the rays, the greater the distortion.

PUBLIC RECORDS

933 Admissibility of Public Records

In the course of investigation, public records very often can be utilized as a means of proving the existence of a fact, establishing admissions against interest made by one of the parties, and also providing a source of information upon which further investigation can be based.

Public records, when properly identified by their custodian, are usually admissible in evidence where there is no statutory restriction of such use. The custodian of the record does not necessarily have to be the maker of the record, and records of this sort come within the exception to the hearsay rule in much the same manner as do business entries in books of account kept in the regular course of business. Police records covering an automobile accident are particularly helpful and, in those states where such records are not available, an interview with the police officer who investigated the case often will provide the same information.

A partial list of public records, their extent, availability, and sources from which they are obtained follows.

934 Motor Vehicle Accident Reports

Privileged Reports. The Uniform Act (regulating the operation of vehicles on highways), adopted in many states, requires the filing of an accident report, without prejudice to the individual making it and solely for the confidential use of the bureau of motor vehicles. The written report is by statute privileged and not admissible in or to be used in a civil action arising out of the facts upon which the report is based. Therefore, reports under this type of statute are not available in the investigation of claims. This type of statute has been adopted in some form in most states.

Nonprivileged Reports. Some states take the opposite view, requiring, for example, the filing of a written report with the commissioner of motor vehicles within 48 hours where any person is killed or injured, or where damage to the property of any one person exceeds a certain amount. Copies of these reports are kept on file for a period of three years after the accident and are available to interested persons upon the payment of a fee. Such reports are admissible in evidence as admissions.

935 Intoxication Tests

Some states have statutes which provide that a certain percentage (such as .05 percent) of alcohol by weight in the blood of a person is *relevant* evidence of that person being under the influence of intoxicants, and that a higher percentage is prima facie evidence of intoxication. Where the results of a blood test are desired by an adverse party, and the information is not privileged by statute, the chemist or technician who made the test, together with the result, is subject to subpoena. The statute provides that the result of the test must be made available to the person tested upon his or her request. Such records are admissible in evidence by the person tested as public documents and by the adverse party (as an exception to the hearsay rule) as an admission against interest.

936 Police Records

Police reports are normally available upon request or by offer of a stipulated fee. In states where the record can be reached only by subpoena, the investigating officer may be interviewed and, if cooperative, his conclusions reported to the file. If the officer was not a witness, the report is usually based on hearsay and some physical facts. Thus, the report may be admissible, as a business record, but the contents of the report will usually consist of inadmissible hearsay.

937 Traffic Court Hearings

Minutes of traffic court proceedings (if a court of record) are available upon the payment of the requisite fee, usually based upon a price per page. If possible, in a case warranting such treatment, the claim representative should be present at the time of hearing and make notes of the testimony, the witnesses produced, and the verdict. From these notes a determination may be made as to whether the expense of ordering the minutes is justified. The claim representative will also have an opportunity to observe the witnesses on the stand and to evalute them as to appearance, credibility, and knowledge of the accident.

938 Weather Reports

Weather information for a particular date and locality may be obtained from the nearest weather bureau office or from the Superintendent of Documents, Washington, D.C. Hourly precipitation, meteorological, and other data also may be obtained for a fee. These reports are admissible in evidence, most states having specific statutes dealing with their admissibility. When certified by the government meteorologist, they constitute prima facie evidence of the facts and circumstances stated in the report.

939 Autopsy Reports

Many states, counties, and municipalities require that an autopsy be performed where the deceased person was not under the care of a physician, or was not so attended within the 24-hour period immediately preceding his or her demise. Such autopsies are mandatory and the consent of the next of kin is not required. These reports may be obtained upon payment of the requisite fee from the appropriate medical examiner's office.

940 Public Service Commission Accident Reports

In most states a public service law provides that all proceedings of the commission and all documents and records in its possession shall be public records. However, in some states there is a distinction between accident reports filed by railroad and bus companies and those filed by gas and electric corporations.

For example, a railroad or other mass transit company may be required to give immediate notice to the public service commission of any accidents of a serious nature. However, the law may provide that such notice shall not be admitted as evidence, or used for any purpose, against the common carrier or railroad corporation giving the notice, in any suit or accident for damages growing out of any matter mentioned in the notice.

Gas and electric companies are also required to make reports of accidents to the public service commission, but no such restriction applies to these accident reports, and application may be made for a certified copy of the company's report of accident. It may be offered in evidence.

941 Civil Aeronautics Reports

In every accident involving a commercial airline, there are at least three possible defendants. The airline that owned and operated the plane may be held liable for negligent operation; the United States may be sued because commercial carriers are subject to various governmental regulations at or near the control towers and in landing and taking off; or the manufacturer may be involved because of alleged negligence in designing, manufacturing, or servicing the plane, or in failing to reveal a condition discovered on subsequent investigation and not corrected.

The Civil Aeronautics Board, created by the Federal Aviation Act of 1958, is required under the statute to assume the following duties in the case of accident (49 USCA 144): "It shall be the duty of the Board (2) to investigate such accidents and report the facts, conditions, and circumstances relating to each accident and the probable cause thereof: . . . (4) make such reports public in such form and manner as may be deemed by it to be in the public interest."

In furtherance of this duty the board may conduct accident investigation hearings, the objective of which is to determine the probable cause, and to prepare safety recommendations to prevent the occurrence of similar accidents in the future.

All factual information contained in an accident investigation report, and supporting papers, may be obtained from the C.A.B.'s regional or Washington office upon the request of any person at any stage of the accident investigation, except that the board shall not make available that portion of the file containing any opinion, suggestion, or recommendation of any employee of the Civil Aeronautics Administration when acting on behalf of the board. The regulation governing disclosure applies regardless of whether an action for wrongful death is involved and regardless of whether the United States is a party to the suit. The Federal Aviation Act of 1958 provides ". . . That no part of any report or reports of the Board relating to any accident, or the investigation thereof, shall be admitted as evidence or used in any suit or action for damages growing out of any matter mentioned in such report or reports."

While the report itself may not be admitted in evidence, it can be used for purposes of cross-examination and impeachment; and, in addition, the C.A.B. investigator's factual report, exclusive of opinions, could be admissible as a past recollection recorded in connection with his or her deposition.

942 Federal Income Tax Returns

Federal income tax returns of individuals, while matters of public record, are open to public inspection only under rules and regulations prescribed by the Secretary of the Treasury and approved by the President. The rules approved provide that the return of an individual shall be open to inspection by the individual for whom the return was made, or by the duly constituted attorney in fact of that person.

However, in court proceedings where the plaintiff's income is in issue, the courts have generally compelled the plaintiff to obtain copies of his income tax return at the expense of the defendant when proper application was made for such a procedure. Also, there is no reason why claim representatives could not ask to see the claimant's copy of the return, obtaining all the information necessary from that source and making a copy if necessary.

943 Veterans Administration Records

All files, records, reports, and other papers and documents pertaining to any claim under any of the laws administered by the Veterans Administration are confidential and privileged, and no disclosure can be made except: "To a claimant or his duly authorized agent or representative as to matters concerning himself alone when, in the judgment of the administrator, such disclosure would not be injurious to the physical or mental health of the claimant.''

Veterans Administration regulations provide that an authorization can be executed by the veteran; it should be dated, addressed to the Veterans Administration, contain the name and address of the person about whom information is to be released, and specify the purpose for which it is to be used. The authorization should be signed by the veteran. A form is available at the Veterans Administration for this purpose, but its use is for convenience only and is not required.

944 Selective Service Records

The present regulations provide that information contained in the records of a registrant's file may be disclosed, or furnished to, or examined by, the registrant or any person having written authority signed by the registrant.

Dependency information in the selective service files is expressly made nonconfidential. The regulations provide that the fact that dependency has been claimed, and the names and addresses of the claimed dependents, shall not be confidential and may be disclosed or furnished.

945 Social Security Records

These records by statute are made confidential and may be disclosed only to the individual involved—or after his or her death to a surviving relative or representative of the individual's estate. Under certain circumstances, information may be released to an employer or former employer of an individual as to the individual's Social Security account number, or as to the coverage of services rendered by him or her for the employer, or as to any information originally supplied by the employer. Disclosure of the records may be made to others only upon written authorization by the claimant or a duly authorized representative.

Therefore, it would seem that, if Social Security records are important in the investigation of the case, they can be secured when the request is accompanied by written authorization. This regulation, however, does not apply to medical information which, under the present regulations, can be disclosed only to the individual's physician or to a medical institution at which he is or she is a patient.

946 Unemployment Compensation Records

In most states, where an injury is responsible for the initial disability, in order to qualify for unemployment compensation, the applicant must show that he or she is physically capable and available for work. This eliminates those who are receiving or claiming workers' compensation benefits. The applicant shows her physical capacity by means of a physician's certificate that the disability occasioned by the accident has terminated. Records of the unemployment compensation board are public records and in most states they can be inspected. In all states they can be reached for production in court by a *subpoena duces tecum*.

947 Workers' Compensation Records

In states having a workers' compensation board or similar body, the claims filed, heard, and determined are public records, and as such are available for inspection in accordance with the rules of the compensation authority. They can be reached by a *subpoena duces tecum* and may be offered in evidence in the trial of a claim against a third party. Where the claimant has elected to proceed against the third party and to defer a claim for compensation, it will be found that the state file contains very little information beyond the employee's claim and his election. The compensation insurance carrier's file will be more complete since it will accumulate the medical reports even where the claimant is not actively seeking compensation. In some cases the compensation carrier will be cooperative and will make its file available. Where inspection of the file is refused, the file still can be reached in the event of trial by means of a *subpoena duces tecum*.

948 Vital Statistics: Birth, Marriage, Death

Vital statistics are public records and can be inspected by anyone complying with the rules of the custodian. Usually when such information is required, a photocopy of the records (duly authenticated) is necessary. The bureau having custody of the records will make a charge for the search of its records and for the certified copy. To facilitate the search the investigator should supply the custodian with the date of the birth, marriage, or death concerning which information is requested. If the date is unknown, the custodian usually makes a charge for each year that is searched.

949 Court Records: Divorce or Prior Proceedings

Court records are public records and may be inspected in accordance with the rules of the court. While a case is pending, the records are usually in the custody of the clerk of the court and may be inspected through the clerk's office. When the case has been closed, the papers are filed in the archives of the court or in the clerk's vault, where they may be located and inspected. Certified copies of papers are available upon the payment of the requisite fee.

Where information is required with respect to a divorce, or to prior proceedings of any kind, the investigator will have to know the court in which these proceedings were held and, if possible, the approximate date. In addition, the court usually assigns a docket or index number to the case and files it under that number. Therefore, if the investigator can ascertain the case number, he or she will be able to locate the file much more readily.

950 Interstate Commerce Commission Records

The rules of the Interstate Commerce Commission require motor carriers subject to its jurisdiction to report to it all accidents involving personal injury or death, as well as those involving property damage exceeding a certain amount. Such reports, however, are for the information of the commission and are not open to public inspection. Therefore, the reports are confidential and may not be reached. However, the motor carrier is required to keep an accident register at its principal place of business. These records are subject to subpoena, or may be inspected if the carrier decides to make them available.

Chapter 10

Principles of Investigation

ESSENTIALS OF INVESTIGATION

1000 Nature of Investigation
1001 Purpose of Investigation
1002 Scope of Investigation
1003 Theory of Defense
1004 Outline of Investigation
1005 Critical Evidence

WITNESSES

1006 Witnesses—Defined
1007 Classification of Witnesses
1008 Finding the Witness
1009 Interviewing the Witness
1010 Evaluation of Witnesses

STATEMENTS

1011 Structure of Statements
1012 The Signed Statement
1013 Recorded Statements
1014 Statements: Form and Substance
1015 Automobile Statements
1016 General Liability Statements
1017 Workers' Compensation Statements

STATEMENTS IN SPECIAL SITUATIONS

1018 Statements Taken in Hospitals
1019 Statements: Serious Injury and Death Claims
1020 Statements of Illiterates
1021 Statements through Interpreters
1022 Statements of Persons with a Physical or Mental Disability
1023 Statements of Children
1024 Negative Statements
1025 Multiple Statements

PHYSICAL AND DEMONSTRATIVE EVIDENCE

1026 Physical Facts
1027 Photographs
1028 Diagrams

VERIFICATION

1029 Verification Generally
1030 Verification by Experts
1031 Verification by Medical Examination
1032 Verification of Disability
1033 Verification through the Index Bureau

ESSENTIALS OF INVESTIGATION

1000 Nature of Investigation

Unless the claim representative actually witnessed the accident or the occurrence, he or she will have no knowledge of the details of how it happened and will of necessity have to rely upon secondary sources of information as to the details of the event. The process by which these secondary sources are discovered and utilized is called investigation. It is a step-by-step inquiry into the facts, which has for its objective the development and accumulation of evidence upon which an informed judgment can be made as to the believable details of the event. The components of an investigation are (1) inquiry, (2) verification, and (3) comparison.

1. Inquiry. Every claim will begin with some known facts. These come with the first notice of the occurrence, in the form of a report from the insured or a claim made directly to the company by the injured person. The inquiry is directed toward obtaining the required unknown facts. For example, the insured reports that she struck a parked car, that there was property damage to the car, that the car was occupied at the time, and that there is a claim for both property damage and bodily injuries. The known facts are the insured's version of the accident and her understanding as to the claims which are being or will be asserted. This does not mean that the insured's version is a true account of what happened. Whether it is or it isn't will be the subject of further inquiry.

The unknown facts are the claimant's version of the accident, the extent of the property damage, the cost of repairs, the nature and extent of the bodily injuries, and the amount of the special damages in the form of medical bills, loss of earning capacity, and other out-of-pocket expenses. The inquiry may establish that the claimant's vehicle was *not* parked; that she was in the act of pulling out from a parked position into the insured's lane of travel when the accident occurred. It may also develop that the property damage was inconsequential and that there are no bodily injuries at all.

In another case the insured may deny that any accident happened, or may contend that he was stopped for a traffic light when he was struck in the rear by the other vehicle. The claimant, to the contrary, says that the insured hit his parked vehicle or that the insured stopped short on the traveled highway where there was no traffic control whatever. Clearly, both of these versions cannot be correct, and the inquiry would be directed toward obtaining the unknown facts which will support one version or the other. This means that other witnesses, if any, must be contacted, a police report obtained, a copy of the motor vehicle report secured, and an examination made of the scene of the accident to establish the existence or nonexistence of traffic controls.

2. Verification. As the facts are obtained, they should be subjected to a check as to accuracy. This may be accomplished by obtaining statements from other witnesses who were present at the scene and saw the accident, checking the police report, obtaining the motor vehicle report filed by the witness, and checking physical facts (such as traffic controls, obstructions to vision, skid marks, gouges on the road, location of debris, and the like) at the scene of the accident. In general liability cases, such verification would consist of an examination of the scene of the accident to determine the accuracy of statements as to hidden traps, absence of lighting, proper maintenance, or adequate warning of an unsafe condition.

The interest of the witness in the outcome of the claim should be taken into account in determining the weight that should be given his or her version and the extent of verification required. Such a witness often gives a statement which is colored by self-interest, and a version of the accident which is most favorable to his or her recovery, placing responsibility for the occurrence on the shoulders of someone else.

This is especially true in automobile cases. The driver of the vehicle characteristically will give a version which is self-exonerating. He or she will find some reason for the accident which involves lack of care on the part of the other driver or the pedestrian, as the case may be, and completely justifies the driver's own actions. Verification in the form of a check of the statements the driver made to the police at the scene, statements he or she made in the presence of others, and statements made in the motor vehicle report—as well as verification of the physical facts and an examination of the damage to the vehicles involved with respect to the point of impact—will establish the amount of reliance which should be placed upon the driver's version.

The same treatment should be given to verification of the amount of the damages claimed, including damage to the vehicle, wages lost, medical bills, the kind and quality of medical treatment received, the length of time under treatment, and the nature and extent of the injury. Damage to the vehicle can be verified by examination and an estimate of the cost of repairs. Wages can be verified by obtaining a copy of the payroll from the employer, by an examination of the books if he or she is self-employed, or by a check with customers if the driver claims he or she was unable to perform work contracted for and not completed. As to the medical aspects, these can be verified by hospital records, the records of the attending physician, X-ray reports, and a physical examination of the claimant by the company doctor.

3. Comparison. During the investigation, comparison should be made among evidence as it is obtained, statements as they are made, facts as they are gathered, and the already known facts. This may establish the need for further information or further supporting facts. The objective of an investigation is to establish credible evidence. When contradictory "facts" appear, an effort must be made to determine which are more believable and which are false and unsupportable, whether given by the insured or by the adverse party.

Throughout the investigation, comparison is a continuing process. As each new fact is developed, it should be compared with what is already known or alleged. As conflicts appear, an effort should be made to reconcile them or, where contrary facts appear, to ascertain which of the two facts is more believable and which conforms more closely to the physical facts. This very often may change the direction of the investigation and impose a further requirement of inquiry and verification.

When the investigator has exhausted every means of ascertaining the facts, he or she may still wind up with two conflicting, contrary versions. The investigator's report should show both versions, the verification which was made of each, and the supporting evidence in connection with them. He or she should give a fair evaluation of the evidence gathered and should comment on the strengths and weaknesses of each version. The investigator should not fall into the trap of regarding favorable evidence as truthful and unfavorable evidence as unbelievable. An opinion must be based on an estimate of the evidence and the reliability of the testimony of the witnesses, regardless of whether they support the investigator's theory of defense.

1001 Purpose of Investigation

Whenever a claim is presented, the company must make a decision as to its disposition. Will it be accepted, rejected, or compromised? Investigation is the vehicle by means of which evidence is secured and preserved and upon which the answer to the question may be based. It is undertaken by an insurance company because of the right to do so granted by the insurance contract and the duty to the insured correspondingly imposed. The investigation seeks to determine from the testimony of witnesses and the physical facts the answers to the questions of *who*, *what*, *where*, *when*, and *why*. These can be broken down as follows:

Who	The person involved.
What	What happened, or the elements of the claim and whether it is covered by the policy.
Where	Where the accident occurred and where the sources of information concerning it are.
When	The time when the investigation should be conducted (promptly) and the time of the accident and conditions (weather, etc.) prevailing at the location at the time of the accident.
Why	Why the accident occurred and whether the proximate cause of the accident involves the insured's negligence.

1002 Scope of Investigation

In the investigation of insurance claims, three elements must be considered: (1) coverage, (2) liability, and (3) damages.

1. Coverage. This refers to the insurance contract. For coverage to exist, there must be an accident or an occurrence which arises out of the hazards assumed by the insurance carrier within the period of time covered by the policy contract. If there is none, there is no coverage. For example, if the insured reports that a social guest fell on her private sidewalk, and the insured carried a policy of liability insurance covering the hazards arising out of the ownership, maintenance, and use of an automobile, clearly there is no coverage applicable to the accident. Or there may be situations where the contract covers the accident or occurrence but, because of the insured's failure to comply with the terms and conditions of the policy, the insurance contract is inapplicable. This could come about because of the insured's failure to report the accident "as soon as practicable" or her failure to cooperate with the insurer. In any case, investigation is required to establish the facts.

2. Liability. This refers to the merits of the claim against the insured. The problem concerns whether the insured was responsible for a negligent act of omission or commission, whether the claimant was contributorily negligent, whether he or she assumed the risk of injury, and whether, because of the relationship of the parties, the claim is actionable or not. It amounts to establishing the existence of the legal responsibility, if any, of the insured, and the possibilities of a successful defense.

3. Damages. This refers to the amount of the loss sustained by the claimant, and occasioned, it is claimed, by the accident or occurrence for which the insured is answerable. It may refer to bodily injuries, mental and physical distress, medical and hospital expenses, and the loss of earning capacity as a consequence. Or it may refer to property damage and consequent loss of use. The claim might even be based upon damages sustained as a result of the loss of the services of the injured person. The function of investigation in these matters is to determine whether the damages were sustained as a proximate result of the accident and, if so, their reasonable value.

Investigation may be made by (1) mail, (2) telephone, or (3) personal contact. The first two methods have their limitations and generally are used only in smaller cases where there is no justification for incurring expense and where the essential information can be obtained by either method. Personal contact is the essential method of choice in larger cases.

1003 Theory of Defense

An investigation must have some direction, and the investigator must have some theory of what he or she is seeking to establish. The development of a theory of defense will point the way and will determine the course the investigation will take. When the first notice of the accident is received and reviewed, certain defenses will automatically suggest themselves to the experienced investigator, and the inquiry will be directed toward developing information and evidence which will support one or more of these defenses. As the investigation progresses, evidence may be obtained that will indicate that some of the theories cannot be supported and should be abandoned. Also, evidence may be uncovered which will suggest other and further defenses. The theory of defense suggests the areas to be investigated, but the investigation will determine whether the theory has any merit.

The theories advanced can apply to one or all of the three elements of a claim: coverage, liability, or damages. On the coverage phase, can it be established that there is no policy coverage because the facts do not bring the case within the terms of the insurance contract? Did the insured fail to comply with the terms and conditions of the contract so as to relieve the insurer of its obligation? If the failure of the insured refers to lack of notice of the accident "as soon as practicable," did such failure result in material damage to the insurer so as to prejudice its rights with respect to the preparation of an adequate defense? If the defense is based on the failure of the insured to cooperate, the investigation must establish how and to what extent the insured so failed.

On the issue of liability, it is usually alleged that the accident occurred through the negligence of the insured. To such an allegation the defense might be interposed that there was no act of commission or omission on the part of the insured, that the accident occurred through the sole negligence of the claimant, that the claimant's lack of care contributed to the happening of the accident, or that the accident was due to an act of God. It might also be urged that the claimant assumed the risk of injury or that the injury was sustained through an unavoidable accident. Investigation is the means through which evidence can be obtained to support these defenses.

On the issue of damages, it might be established that the claimant has sustained no injury and consequently there are no damages, or that the claimant has an injury which preexisted and was not aggravated by the accident, or that he or she has a condition which bears no causal relationship to the accident. It might also be urged that the amount of damages is inflated and does not represent the reasonable value of the items claimed. An investigation and verification of these same items will resolve the question of reasonableness.

1004 Outline of Investigation

In creating the plan of investigation, due regard should be had for the theories of defense and the necessary legal elements needed to establish them. In gathering the evidence, the investigator will determine the presence or absence of the facts necessary to make the defense available. He or she also will consider other and further defenses should the inquiry reveal that the elements are present. In a word, the plan of investigation should be flexible, contemplating the abandonment of certain theories of defense when inquiry shows they are untenable, and adopting other defenses if the inquiry indicates their existence.

A general plan of investigation, where the insurance coverage is in order, will consist of all or some of the following elements in this sequence:

1. Critical Evidence
   a) Statement of the adverse driver (if an auto case)
   b) Statement of the claimant (or claimants in the order of the severity of the injuries)

c) Photographs of the scene of the accident, showing skid marks and other evidence of the accident
d) Examination and photographs of the vehicles themselves, showing the damage and point of impact
e) The product itself or the instrumentality causing the injury

2. Fact Evidence
    a) Statements of disinterested witnesses
    b) Statement of the insured, his or her driver or employee having knowledge of the accident, the instrumentality causing it, or the part of the premises in which the accident is alleged to have occurred
    c) Negative statements from persons who were in a position to have seen the accident or have some knowledge of its occurrence, but who deny having such knowledge
3. Official Reports
    a) Police report
    b) State motor vehicle reports filed by the parties to the accident
    c) Fire department reports
    d) Reports of state motor vehicle inspectors
    e) Traffic court proceedings
    f) Arraignment in magistrate's court
    g) Death certificates
    h) Autopsy reports
    i) Coroner's inquest transcript
    j) Birth and marriage certificates
    k) Weather reports
    l) School records
    m) Certified copies of court records showing prior convictions of crimes
    n) Transit authority reports (if a taxicab is involved)
    o) C.A.B. reports (aircraft)
    p) I.C.C. reports (interstate truckers)
    q) Coast Guard reports (boats)
4. Unofficial Reports
    a) Newspaper accounts
5. Medical Reports
    a) Hospital records
    b) Attending physician's report and records
    c) Medical or hospital reports covering preexisting injury or disease
6. Documentary Evidence
    a) Deeds of ownership of land
    b) Leases
    c) Contracts and agreements, especially contracts for construction, alteration and repair, as well as hold harmless agreements
7. Visual Evidence
    a) Diagrams or sketches of the scene of accident
    b) Engineering plats

c) X rays
d) Photographs

8. Verification Evidence
   a) Employer's records to show wage loss
   b) Index bureau reports
   c) Workers' compensation claims made by injured party, arising out of the same accident
9. Expert Evidence
   a) Report of company medical examiner
   b) Automobile inspector or appraiser
   c) Engineer or chemist
   d) Actuaries
   e) Handwriting expert

In states requiring the renewal of operators' licenses on an annual basis, investigators have found it to be advantageous to obtain a photostat of the claimant's application for this license regardless of whether he was driving a car at the time of the accident. If he was the driver, the license might reveal that it was issued on a conditional basis, requiring that he wear glasses at all times when driving, or that it has been revoked or suspended. More important, however, most applications require an answer relative to the applicant's physical condition and whether there has been any change in it during the past year. The question usually reads ''Have you suffered any physical or mental injury during the past 12 months?'' If the application is made after the accident and it is claimed that there were severe physical injuries suffered, a negative answer on the application could be used in evidence to controvert such a claim.

1005 Critical Evidence

When an assignment is received, the investigator must determine the known facts from the accident report or other information submitted and decide what unknown facts are needed in order to decide the type of handling required. He or she must also decide the order in which the evidence will be obtained. It is clear that the investigator cannot see all witnesses and gather all the evidence at one and the same time. Generally, the rule is that critical evidence should be secured as promptly as possible. *Critical evidence* is evidence which is available now but may not be available after the passage of time.

For example, if the point of impact in an automobile case is important, time will obliterate skid marks, gouges, and other marks in the roadway, and the damage to the cars will be repaired. Therefore, if pictures are needed to establish the existence of these things, they must be taken immediately, and evidence by witnesses, identifying the marks made by each car, must be secured before their memories of the details fade. The same thing would be true of a products case, or a case where there is a claim of an unsafe condition on the premises. The defective product should be secured as soon as possible and tests made, or the premises must be examined for defects and photographs taken of the place of accident under conditions as nearly similar to the circumstances of the accident as possible. In each instance, the passage of time will handicap the investigation, and may make the evidence unobtainable.

Another example of critical evidence is the statement of the adverse driver and the personal injury claimant. In the initial stages, it may be possible to get statements from all participants in the accident. After they have retained counsel, no direct contact can be made with them. Where there is more than one personal injury claimant, generally the most seriously injured should be seen first, and the others in order of the seriousness of their injuries.

Another factor which brings the injured party or parties within the realm of critical evidence is the fact that part of the investigation will refer to the injuries sustained, the treatment rendered, and the diagnosis made. Since doctors and hospitals are reluctant to release medical information without an authorization from the patient, medical authorizations can be obtained from the injured party at the time of the first contact. Later may be too late, especially if the information is refused or the injured person is represented by counsel. Therefore, contact with the injured person will result in securing two things: his or her version of the accident and the subsequent medical treatment received; and the authorization to obtain detailed medical information from the doctor and the hospital where the treatment was rendered.

Less critical but equally important is the evidence of other fact witnesses who saw the accident, or some part of it, but who are not interested in the result because they were not involved. Such witnesses should receive the same priority as that given to parties to the event. Secondary fact witnesses who can contribute to the delineation of the event are the police officer who investigated the case, the tow truck driver who towed the wrecked automobiles away, and the paramedic and ambulance driver. All of these can testify to the scene of the accident when they arrived, the condition of the injured parties, the location of the cars when they came to rest, skid marks, gouges in the roadway, debris on the road, blood, glass, and so forth, and the relationship of such evidence to the center line. These witnesses are given less priority than the others, but there is always the possibility of the opposing side getting its statements first. Therefore, while the gathering of critical evidence will occupy the investigator's initial efforts, it is important to contact these secondary witnesses as soon as possible after the happening of the accident.

WITNESSES

1006 Witnesses—Defined

A witness is defined as a person who testifies as to what he or she has seen, heard, or otherwise observed. This definition includes the parties to the accident as well as others who have acquired some knowledge of the facts. The witness may testify to the facts acquired through the use of one or more of his or her five senses. What the witness saw, heard, smelled, felt, or tasted can be the subject of testimony. An ordinary witness is confined in testimony to the facts within the witness's knowledge and usually may not testify to an opinion, judgment, or conclusion except within a very limited area. The witness may be allowed to express an opinion, for example as to:

1. The speed of moving objects.
2. His or her own intention of doing or omitting to do an act.
3. The excited or emotional state of another person.
4. The drunk or sober condition of another person.
5. The value of objects or services with which the witness is familiar (for example, value of parts and services by garageman).
6. Identity of a person by appearance or voice (telephone conversations, for example), provided that the witness is familiar with the appearance or voice of the person.
7. Handwriting, provided that the witness is familiar with the person's handwriting.
8. Color of an object, provided that the witness has the facility of sight and is not color-blind.
9. Character and reputation of another person, providing that the witness is familiar with both by actual knowledge and experience.

An expert witness (see Section 904, above) is one who is skilled in some art, science, profession, or business, which skill or knowledge is not common to ordinary people and which has come to that person by reason of special study and experience in that art, science, profession, or business. Such witnesses may testify to opinions or conclusions drawn from the facts presented, because their special training qualifies them to do so. For example, a physician may give an opinion as to whether a certain injury or disease was caused by a certain accident (causal relation). A physician may also testify as to what, in his or her opinion, the future course of the injury or disease will be (prognosis). He or she may testify to what X-ray studies reveal and what diagnosis can be drawn from a physical examination using X-ray and other diagnostic tests.

1007 Classification of Witnesses

Witnesses may be classified generally as *friendly* or *unfriendly*. A friendly witness is one who cooperates and gives assistance to the investigator, whereas an unfriendly witness is one who does not. The friendly witness may not necessarily support the defense, but is one who makes his or her evidence accessible to the investigator and freely cooperates in giving all the information which he or she has. The witness may be a close friend of the insured, but may feel compelled to testify to a version of the accident directly opposed to the interests of the insured. Therefore, while a friendly witness in the sense of being cooperative, he or she is an *adverse* witness whose testimony may be used as evidence by the opposing side.

The unfriendly witness may acquire a noncooperative attitude because of reluctance to "get involved" in the case or aversion to testifying in court. His or her version of the accident may be favorable to the insured. In that sense the witness would be classified as an unfriendly but *supporting* witness. On the other hand, the claimant may be a friendly witness by exhibiting a cooperative spirit, even though his or her interests are adverse to those of the insured. Such a witness will usually give a version of the occurrence unfavorable to the insured and favorable to himself or herself.

A *hostile* witness is more than unfriendly and adverse. Such a witness is one who exhibits definite bias or prejudice against the insured, which has no basis in fact. The motivation may be an aversion to certain races, nationalities, occupations, or positions of affluence. Whatever the motivation, the hostile witness is of little benefit to either side. It is important for the investigator to recognize the hostility and, if possible, tie the witness down to a statement which will clearly indicate such hostility.

Therefore, as to attitude, we can classify witnesses as friendly or unfriendly, as to subject matter as adverse or supporting, and those exhibiting bias or prejudice as hostile.

Witnesses are also classified as to their interest or relationship to the event. A party to the accident is *interested* in the outcome of litigation arising from the event. The witness's spouse or relatives are likewise interested in the outcome, if only because they would like to see their relative recover, and for that reason they are more sympathetic to his or her side of the case. The same thing is true as to the passengers; they may feel a compulsion to help the insured in the suit. However, if they have been injured, they have their own interests to consider. In any event, all of these witnesses are interested witnesses who have an interest, either close or remote, in the outcome of the litigation.

Disinterested witnesses are those who have no interest in either party and no interest in the outcome of the litigation, who merely testify to the facts as they know them. Juries are more likely to rely on the evidence given by disinterested witnesses because there is no compelling reason why they should falsify any facts—and for the further reason that they do not stand to lose or gain by the outcome of the case. Therefore, juries are persuaded to believe that their testimony is honest and not motivated by any considerations of self-interest. The best type of evidence that an investigator can locate is the disinterested witness who will support the investigator's side of the case.

1008 Finding the Witness

Before the evidence of a witness is available, that witness must be identified and located. The insurance investigator begins with the report of the insured, who is an interested witness, and the name of the claimant, who is likewise an interested witness. In some cases, the insured has been able to supply the names of other witnesses, who may be friends, or of disinterested people he or she had the presence of mind to identify. In many cases, however, the investigator will have to use devices for the identification and location of witnesses other than the parties to the claim.

Several sources are available to locate or identify disinterested witnesses. The police report may contain the names and addresses of witnesses. A newspaper account may give some names, or the reporter who wrote the account may have interviewed some witnesses at the scene. In automobile cases, the tow truck operator, who is usually located near the scene of the accident, may have some names of witnesses. The motor vehicle report filed by the adverse party may also contain the names of witnesses.

Last, but not least important, is the neighborhood canvass. In this quest for witnesses, the investigator will call at all the homes or apartments in the vicinity of the accident and ask each person in each unit whether he or she saw the accident. This is a painstaking and painfully slow process, but it has been known to produce remarkable results. Another use of this method requires that the investigator be at the scene of the accident at exactly the same time the accident occurred. The investigator may then question people on the street, especially tradespeople, letter carriers, meter readers, and salespeople, as to whether they saw the accident or know anyone who did. Often the occurrence of an accident, especially a serious one, precipitates considerable neighborhood discussion, and while the person the investigator meets may not have seen the accident, if the person lives in the neighborhood the chances are that he or she knows someone who did. Tradespeople, such as store owners, are usually the best source of this type of information. The sooner the neighborhood canvass is undertaken, the better. As a rule, people are more willing to talk about an accident for a short time after it occurs.

1009 Interviewing the Witness

Any consideration of this problem must begin with the proposition that the witness is under no legal compulsion to grant an interview, discuss the case, or give a statement. When a lawsuit is brought, the witness may be compelled to testify and give evidence, but prior to suit no legal means are available to the investigator to force the witness even to discuss the case and his or her relation to it. This applies to all witnesses, interested or disinterested, to the claimant, and even to the insured. In the latter case, the refusal of the insured to make a statement at the request of the insurance carrier will constitute a violation of a policy condition which may relieve the insurance carrier of its obligations under the contract; but nevertheless, the insured, at his peril, may assert the right to refuse an interview.

The claimant as a rule invites the interview with the investigator on the theory that the interview will result in some kind of a settlement, and in any case the claimant is anxious to find out exactly what position the insurance carrier will maintain in reference to the claim. Interested witnesses of other types who desire to aid one party or the other will usually welcome the opportunity to assist the cause of the party in which they have an interest. As to disinterested witnesses, there is no method of forecasting what their attitudes might be, and the chances are about even that the witness may be unfriendly and uncooperative, or friendly and cooperative. The chances of finding the witness to be cooperative are better if the investigator seeks the interview early in the case or as soon after the accident as possible. Witnesses invariably are willing to talk about an event which just happened, and are likely to become annoyed when someone calls on them to discuss something which happened months ago. In addition, the investigator might be confronted with a situation where the witness states that he or she has already given one statement to the other side and is unwilling to go through the same thing again. While most witnesses are honest, psychologically they are more likely to support the cause of the party who interviews them first than the cause of the second party. Therefore, the sooner a witness is interviewed, the greater are the chances of a successful result.

Since the interview is for the purpose of obtaining information, the investigator should plan in advance the exact information he or she expects to obtain. While not knowing what information the witness may have, the investigator will consider the possible theories of defense, the elements needed to establish them, and the information already received from others. The investigator will then evolve the plan of the interview, certain of all the elements which must be discussed. Reinterviews are generally unsatisfactory, and therefore the investigator should proceed as if the present interview is the only one possible. The plan must exhaust all the information the witness has. This is especially necessary when the witness is the claimant. He or she may be represented by counsel when the investigator calls the next time, in which case no further statement can be obtained.

Properly timing the interview can sometimes be as important as the interview itself. The witness should not be interviewed when emotionally upset, fatigued, or ill. Likewise, the investigator should not insist upon conducting the interview when the witness has company or household tasks which require attention. The investigator should arrange to return at a more convenient time, when the witness can devote his or her entire time and attention to the interview.

There are two schools of thought as to whether an appointment should be made. The first school holds that no advance appointment should be made; the witness should be taken by surprise. Thus the witness has no opportunity for reflection and fabrication, and the interview is more likely to produce the truth. The other school holds that, since the interview should be conducted at the convenience of the witness, the courteous thing to do would be to make an appointment whenever it is possible to do so. This has the advantage of saving the investigator's time as well as creating an impression of fair and courteous dealing.

Generally, there is more to be gained by following the second procedure and making appointments for interviews. If the witness is going to tell a fabricated story, he or she will do so regardless of whether an appointment is made. It is therefore submitted that the most successful results will be obtained when the interview is conducted at the convenience of the witness and by an advance appointment, if this is at all possible.

Some witnesses can be interviewed at their place of business, others cannot. It depends upon the nature of the business, the position of the witness, and whether he or she can devote any time to a personal matter during business hours. It is best to inquire before calling at the place of business. When in doubt, see the witness at home.

The procedure for obtaining a written statement breaks down into four general phases: (1) Introduction and identification, (2) Discussion, (3) Summarization, and (4) Termination.

1010 Evaluation of Witnesses

Since the investigator often will be the only person connected with the defense side who sees the witnesses prior to the inception of a lawsuit, it is important that the file reflect the overall impression that the witness will create if called upon to testify. If the witness's evidence is favorable, the kind and type of witness he or she will make will determine the amount of reliance which can be placed on this evidence. If the evidence is unfavorable, the problem to be resolved will have to do with a decision as to how damaging the witness's testimony will be. So that an informed appraisal can be made of the evidence, the file should contain a general evaluation of the witness as to (1) appearance, (2) education, (3) characteristics, and (4) general impression.

1. Appearance. This has reference to the eye appeal, or the lack of it, the appearance of the witness will project. The description should include, whether the witness is tall or short, thin or fat, gray-haired or bald, and whether normally well dressed or poorly dressed. Facial characteristics should be noted, such as facial scarring, skin disease, or other similar conditions which detract from appearance. Does the witness wear glasses, and if so, are the lenses thick or thin? Extreme magnification might create some doubt in the minds of the jury as to whether the witness saw the accident clearly. Any other appliance or prosthesis which may be worn should be noted, especially a hearing aid. Where the witness is a driver of a car, whether the insured vehicle or another, the file should show the age of the driver and any physical condition which might have some effect upon the ability to drive carefully and fully control the vehicle: such as the absence of a hand, arm, foot, leg, or eye.

2. Education. The person reviewing the file may be able to come to some conclusion on this point by referring to the occupation of the witness. However, it is not uncommon to find a college student or graduate driving a truck or performing other types of manual labor, possibly on a temporary basis. In any case, it is best to comment on the education of the witness as well as his or her ability to understand and use the English language. If the witness is a foreigner and talks with an accent, some comment should be made as to whether the witness can be understood in English, or whether the testimony will have to be taken through an interpreter.

3. Characteristics. These can be the most important parts of the evaluation process; and the investigator should observe and analyze the demonstrated characteristics of the witness, when contact is first made with the witness, throughout the taking of the statement, and during any subsequent contacts the investigator may have. For the most part, the investigator will base his or her conclusions on the actions of the witness and the responses received while the statement is being taken. Is the witness talkative or timid, nervous and excitable or relaxed, opinionated and obstinate or open-minded? Does the witness have any speech defect, such as a tendency to stutter, lisp, or speak indistinctly?

4. General Impression. The investigator should record the general impression the witness made. Did the witness tell a convincing, believable story of the event? Did the story check out with the physical facts as well as with the statements of others? Finally, does the investigator believe this witness? In discussion of the case, did the witness ask to be paid for the testimony?

STATEMENTS

1011 Structure of Statements

Introduction and Identification. The interview should begin with the investigator introducing himself or herself, identifying the person or persons represented, and giving a brief statement of the purpose of the visit and why the investigator feels the witness can be of assistance. The investigator can comment on the weather, some current event, or some hobby that it is apparent the witness has, and other matters of a general nature. This is calculated to put the witness at ease and is, in reality, a "get acquainted" phase. The investigator must avoid any and all controversial issues, especially religion and politics.

If asked if he or she represents an insurance company, the investigator should freely admit it, but state that he or she is investigating the case for and in behalf of the insured. The investigator should not interview the witness under a pretext of representing the other side, or under the pretext of being a police officer, a post office inspector, or an agent of the F.B.I. or the Secret Service. Not only is such action morally wrong, but such impersonation is a crime punishable by fine or imprisonment. In addition, if the statement of the witness is of any value, the witness will be needed to testify if the case comes to trial. The investigator will experience extreme difficulty gaining the confidence and cooperation of a witness who has been interviewed under a subterfuge.

Discussion. As soon as the witness is at ease, the investigator will begin a discussion of the event. Just when to break off the introduction and begin the discussion will depend upon the circumstances. When interviewing at a witness's place of business, it is essential that the discussion take place as soon as possible, so the introduction phase will be comparatively short. In another case, the witness may be a farmer who insists that the investigator see the farm or some new equipment. In that case the introduction phase will be extended. In any case, the investigator will need to judge when the discussion of the case is to begin.

In discussing what the witness saw, the investigator will ask some questions merely to give the discussion some direction and purpose. The investigator should not argue with the conclusions expressed nor attempt to persuade the witness to change his or her version of the accident. The investigator is somewhat like a newspaper reporter, there to get the story of the witness and not to change it. Any effort to persuade a witness to testify falsely, whether for a consideration or not, is punishable as a criminal act. The investigator therefore should avoid making any suggestions as to how the accident happened, but should merely get the facts as the witness believes them to be. The investigator can be sure that the witness will probably tell the same story if called upon to testify, and for that reason the investigator should take into consideration not only the favorable facts but also the facts which are damaging. A fair appraisal of the witness's evidence must include both.

During the discussion, the investigator will bring out pad and pen so that some of the facts can be noted and a rough sketch made of the scene of the accident. This is especially helpful in automobile cases, since the witness will be able to describe what happened with reference to the diagram. If the witness can and will draw the diagram, so much the better. When the interview is over, the investigator will have the witness either initial or sign the sketch which he or she made.

Summarization. After the investigator has the story in outline and has covered all the points, he or she will proceed to summarize the witness's version by compiling a statement. The witness will be asked to read it and to make any corrections or additions which may be appropriate.

Termination. If the witness is not the insured or the claimant, then after the statement is signed, the investigator will leave as soon as possible without imposing on the witness's time any further. Should the witness ask for a copy of the statement he or she signed, the investigator should comply, but should ask the witness to acknowledge receipt of the copy by adding to the original statement a sentence acknowledging the copy and signing it. If the witness is the claimant, the investigator should also obtain signed forms authorizing access to medical and hospital records. In some areas, the doctors and the hospitals will accept photocopies of the medical authorization, in which case one copy from the claimant will be sufficient. In other areas, both the doctors and the hospitals demand originals, in which case the investigator must be careful to obtain a sufficient number of signed copies to meet the demand. It is important to bear in mind that this may be the only opportunity that the investigator has to obtain the medical authorizations. The claimant may be represented by counsel at the time of the next call and, although counsel will eventually supply the medical authorizations, it will save considerable time and trouble if the investigator obtains them at the time of the first interview

Group interviews should be avoided. The investigator will obtain the best results by interviewing witnesses one at a time, either alone or with not more than two other persons present. Where two witnesses are involved, it is better to interview them separately rather than in the presence of each other. The investigator needs the exact story of the witness and not one influenced by what some other witness supposedly saw at the same time.

1012 The Signed Statement

The purpose of the signed statement is to preserve the evidence. It is the record of the story told by the witness and signed by the witness to attest to its authenticity. It can be used by the witness before trial in order to refresh the recollection of the past event. Should he or she testify to a different version, the statement can be used to discredit the testimony.

Some witnesses shy away from the word ''statement'' since it seems to have some legal import. Some investigators find it is more satisfactory to refer to it as a ''report'' and to avoid the word ''statement'' entirely. The legal effect is the same whether the document is referred to as a statement, report, or account.

The statement should be reflective of the witness and the language used should be near to the ordinary language of the witness. The investigator should not attempt to translate what a witness says into perfect English when the witness habitually uses poor grammar. It should be borne in mind that at some future time the statement may be offered in evidence in a court proceeding, and the jury might find it hard to believe that a witness whose exposure to literature is confined to comic books could make a statement in the language of a business executive. If the statement contains language similar to that which the witness has used when testifying, it will be more believable. Let us consider two examples of a statement taken from a maintenance worker on the night shift of a factory. The first example is:

> John Smith and myself are permitted, beginning at 11:30 P.M. and ending at 11:45 P.M. to go outside of the factory for the purpose of having a smoke. This is in the nature of a break in our routine and is a privilege afforded to us for the reason that due to the fire regulations, we are forbidden to smoke within the confines of the building. While we were thus engaged, we saw a black Buick sedan come down the hill in front of the factory at an extremely high rate of speed and crash into a parked Ford on the north side of the highway. The Ford was unoccupied.

The second example is:

> Me and Jack were having a smoke. We ain't allowed to smoke in the factory so we take a smoke outside by the road. We seen a black Buick come down the hill like a bat outta hell and smash into a Ford parked on the other side of the street. There weren't nobody in the Ford.

The second example is more reflective of what the witness said, and, even though the English is poor and the grammar bad, a jury would be more inclined to believe that a maintenance worker made the second statement than the first.

It is always best to have the witness estimate speed and distance. In the two examples above, the writer purposely made the same mistake in each. In the first, it was said that the Buick came down the hill "at an extremely high rate of speed" and in the second "like a bat outta hell." Neither of these statements tells us what the witness means as to the actual speed, whether it was in excess of the speed limit, or whether it was excessive under the driving conditions. It would have been better to say that the car was being driven at a high rate of speed, approximately 75 miles per hour in a 50-mile zone, and to state how the witness could estimate the speed, for example, because he has driven many years himself, worked as a traffic officer, or the like. Distance likewise should have been covered. How far from the point of impact were the witnesses? How far from the crest of the hill was the Ford parked? For what distance did the driver have an unobstructed view of the road ahead? The distance should be estimated in feet, and terms like "near," "short distance," or "long distance" should be avoided.

The statement must be taken in ink or indelible pencil, or be typewritten. It should be done all in one paragraph so that there are no blank spaces—permitting a later claim that words or sentences were added. Likewise, there should be no blank lines, each page should be initialed at the bottom by the witness, and his or her signature should appear at the end. If corrections are made, the witness should place his or her initials next to the correction so that there will be no question that the witness was aware of and approved the corrections. As a matter of fact, some investigators purposely make mistakes in the statement so as to make corrections with the witness's approval and initials. Then if the witness should deny that he gave a statement, say that the statement is not a true account of what was told to the investigator, or that he or she did not read it but merely signed it, the corrections made at the witness's request will belie such testimony.

It is also good practice to continue a sentence from one page to another, since this is further evidence of the fact that no pages have been substituted for the original. Legal language is to be avoided, and the investigator should not use such terms as tort-feasor, tort, negligence, or contributory negligence. While some witnesses may know what they mean, the jury often does not. Therefore, the use of such terminology detracts from the believableness of the statement. A simple statement in ordinary language which describes exactly what happened and how it happened is the best form to follow.

The signature of the witness is placed at the end of the statement, and there should be no blank spaces between the last written words and the signature. The best method of securing the signature is to have the witness write: "I have read the above and it is true," followed by the signature. If the statement consists of more than one page (and most of them do), the witness should initial or sign the bottom of each page. On the last page the language above may be used, or "I have read the above four-page report and it is true." If these methods are not practical because the witness does not write well or is reluctant to write any more than his or her name, the following form can be used:

Have you read the above four-page report? ____________
Is it true and correct? ____________

____
Signature

The witness can answer the questions in the affirmative in the space provided and sign beneath. The first question should be on the line immediately below the last line of the statement, and there should be no blank lines between the questions or between the questions and the signature.

If it should be necessary to use the statement during the trial for the purpose of showing the witness has testified to something contrary to the statement, witnesses frequently will try to avoid the statement by saying they signed the paper but did not know what it was, or that they merely wrote their names at the end because the investigator told them to do so, or that they did not read the statement but answered the questions "yes" because they were told it was necessary. Therefore the first method—having the witness write the sentence stating that he has read the report and it is true—is the best method.

The signature of the witness should be witnessed by someone who was present at the time the signature was made. The person witnessing the signature does not have to know what is in the statement, and his witnessing the signature is merely evidence of the fact that he saw the document signed and nothing more. If no one else is available, the investigator can witness the signature even though, in the case of a dispute as to whether the statement was actually signed, the investigator is a less desirable witness than someone who is not an interested party. Where the statement is witnessed by a member of the family or a friend, it is best to include his or her home address, if other than that of the person giving the statement, so that he or she can be located when the case comes to trial.

At the top of the first page of the statement the investigator should note the date, time, and place the statement was taken. Since the investigator will take many statements in the course of work, he or she will not have an independent recollection as to where and when a particular statement was taken. The inclusion of the time, place, date, and cirumstances will jog the investigator's memory, and he or she will be able to testify, if necessary, exactly when, where, and under what circumstances the statement was taken.

1013 Recorded Statements

Some investigators advocate the use of certain types of dictating/recording equipment in order to obtain the voice of the witness telling the story, thus saving the time that a longhand statement would take, and to eliminate any possibility of misunderstanding as to what the witness said. It is claimed that the actual voice of the witness reproduced in court is more effective than the written statement, since it shows the inflections of the witness's voice and the emphasis given to certain words.

A foundation will have to be laid as to the time and circumstances under which the recording was made, and, more important, that it was made with the knowledge and consent of the witness. The opening statement of the investigator might take the following form:

> This is Ms. Alice Jones speaking. I am interviewing Mr. Peter Smith at his home at 450 Main Street, Anytown, Anystate, on October 1, 1994, at approximately 10:30 A.M. Do I have your permission to record this interview, Mr. Smith?

Some investigators find it helpful, as part of the foundation, to include some reference to the surroundings so that there can be no question that the interview took place in the witness's home.

The investigator should get as much of the witness's voice as possible, and questions to the witness should be short and only give direction to the interview. When interruptions occur (if there aren't too many) it is good practice to keep the equipment running, and the investigator can note the interruption by saying "Mr. Smith has just left the room to answer the door." By keeping the equipment operating, the record will have more weight as evidence of a recording of the entire interview. Where it is necessary to use a second tape, the investigator can say, "Mr. Smith, we are going to have to continue our interview on tape number two."

At the conclusion of the narrative, it is best to ask a general question which will give the witness an opportunity to give an unrestricted answer. The question could be: "Mr. Smith, do you have any other information concerning this accident and the people involved which you would like to add?" Some investigators find it helpful to ask as a final question: "Mr. Smith, has everything you have told me concerning this accident been true and correct to the best of your knowledge and belief?" Others use a form of attestation: "Mr. Smith, do you swear that the foregoing answers given by you are the truth, the whole truth and nothing but the truth, so help you God?"

At the conclusion of the interview the investigator should thank the witness for his or her cooperation and time. This may or may not be on the recording, but in any case the investigator should avoid terminating the interview so abruptly as to give the impression that the investigator has no further interest in the witness now that the recording has been made.

As to the admissibility of a recorded statement, the courts are in general agreement that it can be admitted if there is a proper foundation laid as a preliminary to the offer into evidence. This includes evidence that the recording machine was capable of recording voices clearly, that the operator of the device was competent in its use, that the recording is identified, that there have been no additions, deletions, or changes, and that the recording was preserved in such a way as to preclude any tampering. Evidence will also have to show the identity of the speakers and that the recording was made with the knowledge and consent of the witness, voluntarily and without any coercion. Recorded statements taken by telephone also are admissible in evidence, provided proper foundation is laid for the admission of such evidence.

1014 Statements: Form and Substance

The statement should be the story of the event as told by the witness. It should, as in a newspaper account, answer the questions of who, what, when, where, and why, and it should proceed, in natural sequence, with the steps leading up to the happening of the event. It should first identify the informant, the place where the event took place, how the witness came to be there, what the witness saw happen, the talk the witness heard at the time of or immediately after the event, the observations made by the witness of the scene of the accident, and the injuries. So that the statement will have the required continuity, it can be divided into five main divisions: (1) identification, (2) foundation, (3) accident, (4) injuries, and (5) additional facts or additional witnesses. In applying these divisions to the statement, we will consider how they are to be used in connection with automobile, general liability, and workers' compensation claims.

1015 Automobile Statements

1. Identification. The beginning of the statement should identify the witness as to name, address, and occupation. If the witness is disinterested, the investigator probably will need to locate him or her if the case comes to trial. Therefore, it is best to get as much information as possible in order to be able to locate the witness when the time arrives, including names and addresses of close relatives and employer, as well as the names of clubs or social organizations to which he or she belongs. If the witness is an injured party, in addition to the name and address of the employer, the statement should contain an expression of income, how long the witness has worked for the employer, whether the employment is steady or seasonal, piece or time work, and so on. The statement might read as follows:

> My name is John T. Jones and I am 25 years of age, residing at 42 John Street, Brooklyn, N.Y. (Telephone 676-7328) with my wife, Mary, and my two minor children, Joan, aged 6, and John, Jr., aged 3. My nearest relative is my sister, Dorothey Jones Maguire, who lives at 55 Fargo Street, Jersey City, N.J. I am employed by the Brook-

> lyn Edison Company at their plant at 234 Flatbush Avenue, Brooklyn, N.Y., as an electrician's helper. My foreman's name is Pete Smith.

Many other matters of identification could be included, such as social security number and driver's or chauffeur's license number. If the witness was the driver involved in an automobile accident, the driver's license number and whether it was revoked or suspended at the time of the accident or any prior time, should be included. If the statement is taken while the witness is in a hospital, a sentence to the effect that he or she is not under opiates or narcotics should be included. This can be substantiated by a short report from the nurse on duty or the attending physician.

2. Foundation. Before going into the happening of the accident the statement should describe the surrounding conditions, the site of the event, date, time of day, weather, and the like. In an automobile case the foundation might read as follows:

> U.S. Highway #1 runs in a general northerly and southerly direction, and is approximately 44 feet wide, or four lanes of traffic. It is of concrete construction and there is a painted yellow center line. State Road 119 intersects Highway #1 at right angles and is approximately 18 feet in width. It is of blacktop construction and the traffic lanes are separated by a painted white line.
>
> On October 20th, 1994, at about 5:00 P.M. I was driving my 1992 Ford sedan in a southerly direction on U.S. Highway #1 at about 50 m.p.h. The weather was clear and the road was dry. It was about dusk and I had my headlights on low beam. Riding with me at the time was James Smith, who was sitting in the right front seat, and in the rear seat were Joe Green and Pete Brown.

At this point the statement should cover where the witness had been previously and why the witness was on the road: returning from work, going home from a party or tavern, or just out for a ride, as the case may be. If there was any drinking, the statement should cover the movements of the witness from the time he or she started drinking up to the time of the accident, showing just how many drinks were consumed and over what period of time. Also at this point other pertinent information such as permissive use, agency, ownership of the vehicle, should be inserted if applicable. If the weather was rainy or snowy, then reference to the operation of the windshield wipers (whether they were working) and any impairment to visibility should be noted.

3. Accident. After conditions and surrounding circumstances, the statement should cover the happening of the accident. In an automobile case, this would include the travel prior to impact, the impact, and where both vehicles came to rest. For example:

> While so driving my car in the west lane of U.S. Highway #1 and while approximately 300 feet north of the intersection of State Road 119, I saw for the first time a 1985 Chevrolet being driven in an easterly direction about 200 feet west of the center

> of the intersection and travelling at about 35 m.p.h. I took my foot off the gas and assumed that the other car would stop for the stop sign.

The narrative should follow from this point of first observation toward the point of impact. Such details as the sounding of the horn, application of brakes, and any deviation from the path of travel by either vehicle should be covered. The narrative should continue to trace the paths of travel of both vehicles to the point of impact, which would be the point on the street where the vehicles first came in contact with each other, and also describe the point of contact with respect to the parts of the vehicles which came in contact with each other. For example:

> The left front fender of the Chevrolet struck the right front door of my automobile at a point about 9 feet east of the west edge of U.S. Highway #1 and approximately 12 feet to the south of the center line of State Road 119.

It is extremely important in many cases to fix the exact point of impact since the issue of negligence may turn on the place of impact with relation to the position of the cars on the road. Therefore, locating the point by the use of two intersecting axes, as in the example above, will pinpoint the exact spot where the impact took place. Such directions as the "center of the intersection" or "near the west shoulder of the road" should be avoided since they do not convey any idea of exactly where the point of impact was. It should again be emphasized that the statement may be used as evidence at the trial of the case, and it is the task of the investigator to tie up the details in such a way as to make them understandable to others and not subject to variation by the witness should he or she be called upon to testify.

The next point to be covered in the accident description is where the vehicles came to rest. The failure to trace the paths of the vehicles from the point of impact to the points of rest has lost many a lawsuit. The paths should be shown by describing the direction the car was facing with a two-directional orientation of one of the wheels of the vehicle. For example:

> My Ford came to rest facing in a general southeasterly direction with the right rear wheel at the east edge of the pavement and approximately 75 feet south of the center line of State Road 119. The Chevrolet came to rest facing south with both left wheels on about the center line of U.S. Highway #1 and the rear end of the automobile approximately 30 feet south of the center line of State Road 119.

Skid marks left by either of the vehicles should be described and should be located by direction of travel, and length, origin, and termination of the skid.

If anything was said by any of the parties involved, it should be recorded in the statement. The accurate relating of the first words spoken by any such party is admissible in evidence as an exception to the hearsay rule on the theory that, since they are said spontaneously and under the stress of the accident, there is no possibility of reflection and fabrication. Therefore they are part of the *res gestae* and descriptive of the facts of the accident. (See Section 910 in chapter 9.)

4. Injuries. Where the witness is not the injured person, it will be helpful to secure a layperson's description of the injuries, including any bleeding and other outward manifestations of injury which can be observed by the average person. If the witness heard the injured person make any complaints regarding the injuries, these remarks should be noted. In addition, there should be some information as to whether the injured person received treatment at the scene, how the injured person left the scene (whether by ambulance, private car, or other means), together with information as to whether he or she was able to walk or required assistance.

Where the claimant is the witness whose statement is taken, a clear description of the injuries, in the claimant's own words, is essential. It should accurately locate and describe the type of injuries sustained and should state that there were no other injuries except those described. This latter becomes very important if the claimant later asserts a claim for other and further injuries, which the claimant will say he or she forgot to mention because the statement-taker failed to inquire about them. Whenever possible the statement should eliminate injury to the head, neck, and back by negative statements of fact. Where head injuries are involved the statement should, if possible, rule out the matter of unconsciousness by a sentence that the claimant did not at any time lose consciousness, or was dazed for only a matter of seconds. It should also negate the clinical signs of skull fracture by a sentence that there was no bleeding from the nose, mouth, and ears.

The claimant's statement should also cover all prior injuries and conditions having any bearing whatsoever on the accident. Prior accidents should be covered, and a statement as to the injuries sustained in each included. If the claimant is suffering from, or under treatment for, any disease, such as diabetes or tuberculosis, the statement should indicate that fact, together with information as to whether the claimant was under treatment at the time of the accident and, if so, the name and address of the physician rendering the treatment.

The topic of injuries should also include information as to the treatment received up to the date of the statement, such as where and when first aid was given and by whom, and what treatment has been received since that time, whether given by a hospital, physician, nurse, or consisting simply of home remedies. It should include whether the claimant was confined to bed and for what period of time and, if the claimant is still disabled, some information as to the claimant's activities should be covered: whether he or she merely sat in the sun, or engaged in such activities as swimming, golfing, or bowling. These bits of information may prove important later.

When taking a statement regarding the injuries, whether from the claimant or any other witness, those occupying both vehicles who were not injured, or showed no outward signs of being injured, or said that they were not injured, should be noted.

5. Additional Facts or Additional Witnesses. Very often the investigator will find that additional facts not covered in the foundation play a material part in the fixing of responsibility. Therefore, the investigator should include at this point such additional facts as may be required: the width and construction of the shoulders of the highway, traffic warning signs, traffic control signs, and traffic controls, as well as description of all buildings or foliage on the sides of the road which might have constituted an obstruction to the view of either driver.

If the witness knows the names of others who were at the scene of the accident, the names and addresses should be noted, whether or not the witness knows they saw the accident. The mere fact that they were observed at the scene of the accident is indicative that they may have some knowledge of it, even if only an observation as to the position of the cars after the accident occurred. Having the names and addresses will open up other and further avenues of investigation which may be explored.

1016 General Liability Statements

The same format is used in taking statements on general liability claims, such as the usual slip and fall cases, either on sidewalks, premises, or in buildings open to the public. The identification paragraph is the same as that used in the automobile claim, and the same as the paragraph relating to injuries. The other sections of the statement will differ from the automobile statement, and we will consider those paragraphs in which there are differences.

Foundation. This should cover the claimant's (or witness's) entrance to the premises, why he or she was there, the weather (if a factor), and where the person was going. For example:

> On October 28th, 1994, at about 11:00 A.M., I entered the north entrance of Macy's, where I intended to purchase some housewares on the second floor. It was raining at the time, and there was water on the floor that had been tracked in by many customers. I was wearing low-heeled shoes with leather soles and heels.

This description establishes the claimant's status as a business invitee and sets forth the time and the circumstances under which she entered the premises.

From this point, the investigator should trace the claimant's travel to the point of the accident. For example:

> I proceeded to walk in a generally southerly direction down the main aisle to the ascending escalator.

The statement should show the claimant's itinerary for the day, where she had been, where she intended to go, whether she was carrying packages, whether she was in a hurry or under any emotional stress due to later appointments. A person under special stress of circumstances may be generally more accident-prone.

Accident. A complete description of the accident, how it happened, what caused it, and who came to the claimant's assistance, should follow:

> When I was two feet north of the entrance to the ascending escalator, my attention was attracted to a display of women's wear. I remember placing my right hand on the right

> moving rail and I think I attempted to enter the escalator by putting my left foot on the moving tread. My left foot was suddenly jerked from under me and I fell in a sitting position on the moving treads.

At this point the claimant should describe the place of accident. Invariably, the investigator will find that the claimant's observation of the surroundings is not good even though he or she has visited the premises numerous times. The person usually will not recall essential facts about the area. This point should therefore be incorporated in the statement:

> I don't remember if the floor was of wood or tile construction. I don't remember if the treads were covered by rubber or metal although I have been a customer at Macy's for many years.

The next item to be covered is an accurate description of the thing or things the witness claims caused the accident. The description should be the witness's own words concerning the walk, road, flooring, steps, elevator, or ramp, together with their condition. Lighting conditions, including the location of the lights and their effectiveness, as well as the condition of the handrails, rubber mats, or the presence of wax or oil on linoleum, wood, or tile flooring, should also be covered. Any signs or warning devices should be noted. With regard to ramps or steps, the level or grade, height of risers, and width and kind of tread are necessary facts. A description of any defects in these objects, or foreign substances on them—which allegedly caused or contributed to the accident—should be noted.

The next point is the matter of assistance. Usually the first person to assist the injured person after the accident is an eyewitness to its occurrence. The investigator should get the names of all persons who in any way assisted the injured person, and these persons should be interviewed and their statements taken as to the occurrence and what was said. Every effort should be made to ascertain from the claimant and the witness the exact words spoken by the claimant after the accident.

Spontaneous utterances (*res gestae*) are admissible in evidence if made so near in point of time to the accident as to be explanatory of it. A mere narrative of past events is not admissible. The usual explanation of a person under such embarrassing circumstances as a fall in a public place often makes it clear that he or she was contributorily negligent in not looking where he or she was going, ignoring warning signs, or momentarily forgetting that he or she was at the head of a stairway or a similar dangerous place. The words spoken might also be indicative of the presence of some systemic disease which caused vertigo, a fainting spell, or some other similar condition.

Additional Facts. The place of the accident must be established with certainty in the claimant's statement. If it occurred outside a private dwelling, the statement should pinpoint whether the fall took place on the premises, such as on the private driveway or walk, or on the public sidewalk. If it is a multiple dwelling, information should be obtained which will place the accident either on the premises, sidewalk, or common stairway (under the control of the landlord), or in the tenant's apartment, or on the public street or sidewalk. If it occurred in a store, the status of the injured person should be established by indicating exactly why he or she was in the store—either as an invitee, licensee, or trespasser—and it is also important to show exactly where and in what department the accident occurred. Very often it will be found that portions of the store are leased to others, that the store owner retains control only of main aisles and passageways, elevators, and stairways, and that the lessee has control of a specified area. Therefore the question of responsibility will turn on who has control of the premises where the accident occurred and who was responsible for the maintenance. In statements from the owner or lessee, the statement should cover the control of the area and should include by reference the terms of the lease, hold harmless agreements, and any other written documents referring to the duty of maintenance and repair of the site of the accident.

In all cases where the claimant's statement is taken, an inquiry should be made and recorded as to whether the claimant was in the course of employment when the accident occurred. If the claimant was employed and was on an errand for his employer or driving an automobile in connection with his work, then the inquiry should cover whether a compensation claim has been made or contemplated, whether any compensation has been paid and accepted (if so, how much), and the name of the insurance company which made the payment.

1017 Workers' Compensation Statements

In workers' compensation cases the measure of the employer's responsibility is governed by the workers' compensation law, and the test of liability is not negligence but whether the accident arose out of and in the course of employment. In spite of this difference, statements taken from the injured claimant, eyewitnesses, or witnesses to any material fact follow the same format as other statements, with additional information being sought as to items peculiar to workers' compensation. The statement from an injured claimant should cover the following information.

Identification. This paragraph will be the same as in other statements taken from an injured claimant in that it will give name, age, address, and the names of spouse and children (if any) along with the ages of the children. In states where the number of dependents is a factor in determining the compensation rate, or where the injury is so serious that there is a possibility of a fatality, it will be necessary to expand this phase of the statement to include the claimant's past marital history and that of the spouse. In the ordinary case, the marriage under consideration was the first marriage for both, and in that case a statement that will cover the situtation is: "My wife and I were married in South Bend, Indiana by Reverend Jones of the First Presbyterian Church on May 1, 1982. Neither of us had been married before.''

Where a common-law relationship is alleged or where either or both of the parties to the marriage have been married before, it will be necessary to cover when and where the common-law relationship was initiated, where they have lived since that time, whether there was any break in the continuity of the relationship, and why. Where there has been a previous marriage, it will be necessary to get all information as to when and where it took place and whether it was terminated by death or divorce, with the date and place of death of the previous spouse or (in the case of divorce) the court in which it was obtained and the date of the decree—or the fact that no divorce was obtained.

Foundation. This phase of the statement is concerned with the status of the injured person as an employee, his or her job and the amount of remuneration received, whether in actual cash, in other consideration, or both. To qualify for the benefits of the compensation law, the claimant must be an employee, and the employment must be one covered by the law—not one of the excluded classes such as domestic servants, farm laborers, casual employees, and independent contractors.

It should cover the contract of hire and the amount of the salary paid. Salary includes not only the actual money received but any additional consideration, and the statement should indicate whether the claimant reported the additional consideration on his or her income tax return. This is particularly important in those occupations where the bulk of the remuneration comes from sources other than the employer, such as tips to waiters. The statement might read as follows:

> I am employed by the ABC Company as a butcher and deliveryman, at a salary of $10 per hour for an eight-hour day, five days per week. I receive time-and-a-half for overtime and I have been averaging $400 per week. I also receive a Sunday roast once a week, which is valued at $15, and we also share the vegetables which are unsold at the end of the week. I estimate the value of the vegetables at $10 per week. I did not report the latter two items on my income tax return.

Where tips are involved, the statement should show the weekly average of salary and tips. Again, inquiry should be made as to the amount reported on income tax returns.

In states where compensation is based upon the average weekly wage over a period of time, it is best to include in the statement the period of time the claimant was employed, since these state laws provide for alternative methods of computing the average weekly wage where the injured person has not been employed for the average period prescribed in the act.

Accident. The statement should show exactly when the accident occurred, exactly what the claimant was doing at the time of the accident, and whether it was caused by the claimant's action or whether other persons were involved. If others were involved, they should be identified by name and by employer. For example:

> On September 25, 1994, at about 3:00 P.M., I was driving my employer's panel truck to the Ace Plumbing Supply Co. at 3rd Av. and 1st Street. While traveling south on 3rd Avenue, I stopped for a red light at the intersection of 5th Street. I was stopped for about 3 seconds when the truck was struck in the rear by a Chevrolet, driven by JoAnn Green, of 123 Brown St., Anytown, Anystate, and owned by the Black Sales Co., of 100 Brown Street, Anytown, Anystate. Ms. Green told me that her brakes wouldn't work and that's the reason she hit me. She said she was going to call on White's Drug Store at 3rd Avenue and 2nd Street. At the time of the accident, I was on a direct route to the plumbing supply house, and I had not stopped at any time since leaving my employer's plant, except to stop one block from the plant to get a pack of cigarettes.

In cases where an occupational disease is alleged, most states hold that the date of the accident is the date of disability for the purpose of reckoning the time for filing the claim and for coverage purposes. Therefore, it is important to go into detail as to how the condition first came to the attention of the claimant and when for the first time he or she was unable to work, even though the claimant's work record is intermittent. For example:

> I am employed by the ABC Restaurant as a dishwasher and have been so employed for the past five years. On March 1, 1994, we started to use a new detergent, called "Soapine," and on March 3rd, 1994, I noticed that both my hands were red and sore. I continued to work until March 5th, 1994, when my hands broke out in blisters and I couldn't work with them. I stayed home on March 5th and 6th, and returned to work on March 7th, 1994. I wore rubber gloves and my hands seemed to get better, but on September 15th, 1994, the same condition returned only worse. I stopped work on September 15th, 1994, and I haven't been able to work since.

In describing the accident, the claimant may use terminology which is peculiar to the particular industry. These should be defined and explained in the statement. For example, an oil well worker may refer to a "monkey board," "Christmas tree," or a "cat line." Also, where the claimant refers to another individual as the "pusher," it should be explained that he is the assistant foreman.

Injuries. A detailed description of the claimant's complaints and symptoms is an integral part of the compensation statement. It should contain an exact description of the part of the body which was injured, whether any other part of the body was affected, and whether the claimant had ever been similarly injured before. Where the effects of the injury are not immediate, a description of when and how the pain or other symptom manifested itself is important. For example:

> I lift heavy boxes as part of my work. I have been doing this for over 3 years. On September 1, 1994, I lifted a real heavy box with two other men. They let go and I had the full weight on me. It strained my arms a little, but I continued working. I did not feel a pain in any other part of my body. On the evening of September 5, 1994, when

> I was taking a bath at home, I noticed a large lump in the lower left side of my abdomen. It pained when I squeezed it. I went to Dr. Smith, 25 Orange Avenue, Anytown, Anystate, and he told me that I had a hernia and that I would have to be operated on. I never had a hernia or rupture before, and I guess that I got it when I lifted that heavy box on September 1, 1994. Until I noticed the lump on September 5, 1994, I felt fine and I did my work just as I always did.

The extent of the medical treatment rendered up to the time of the statement should be covered in detail. First, it should show whether the physician was authorized by the employer or whether he or she is the claimant's family doctor. The date of the first treatment should be noted as well as the actual treatment rendered. Second, the dates of the subsequent treatments should be shown, together with information as to the type of treatment, whether the doctor or nurse rendered the treatment, or whether the claimant treated himself or herself with the doctor's equipment. If X rays were taken, the name of the physician, together with the part or parts of the body X rayed and how many views (if the claimant remembers), should all be incorporated in the statement. All of this information will be helpful in determining whether the doctor is in a position to render an opinion as to causal relationship and, if nothing else, will be helpful in evaluating the medical bill when it is received. For example:

> I did not ask my employer for a doctor, but went to my family doctor, Dr. Sarah Green, 123 Main Street, Anytown, Anystate. She first treated me on October 4, 1994, when she examined my back and put some adhesive tape all around my back and chest. She did not take an X ray, nor did she give me any shots with a needle. She also put me under a heat lamp. She told me to come back the next day, but I didn't feel well so I didn't go. I called the doctor on Sunday, October 6, 1994, but her answering service told me that she didn't have office hours on Sunday. I next saw the doctor on Monday, October 7, 1994. She put me under the heat lamp again. She told me to come back every day that week, which I did. I did not see the doctor again until two weeks later. During this time either the nurse put me under the lamp or I did it myself because I knew what to do. I did not get any treatment on Wednesdays or Sundays because the office is closed on those days. I next saw the doctor on October 21, 1994. And she took the tape off my back and told me to continue with the lamp treatments until I felt better. I continued to get the lamp treatments until November 1, 1994, when I felt better and I quit going. During this time I only saw the doctor three times, October 4, 7, and 21.

The claimant's work record should be shown, indicating when he or she discontinued work because of the injury and when work was resumed. There also should be indications of whether the claimant returned on a partial or full-time basis, or whether he or she was able to work but that there was no work available.

Another part of the inquiry into the injuries concerns the matter of prior accidents and previous injuries. We should record the dates of prior accidents, the injuries sustained, whether the previous disability was continuing up to the time of the accident, and the names and addresses of all physicians, hospitals, or others who rendered treatment. Also recorded should be whether workers' compensation settlements or other types of settlements were made, and the name and address of the person, firm, or corporation responsible for the payment.

Additional Facts or Additional Witnesses. Where the accident is caused by a third party, the statement should show whether a claim has been made or is contemplated against the third party. In most states, the claimant has the option of claiming compensation or making a claim against the third party (if there is one), and in some states the claimant may do both. In any event, the statement should contain information as to the name and address of the third party, whether a settlement has been made (and if so how much), or whether there is a claim for compensation.

The statement should show the names of any witnesses as well as the name of the claimant's superior to whom the accident was reported. When and to whom the report of the accident was made should be set forth.

In summary, it should be said that a statement worth taking is worth taking well, and the document should exhaust the knowledge of the witness as far as the subject matter is concerned. Checklists of items to be covered are available and useful, but the most important ingredient in statement-taking is the curiosity, imagination, and resourcefulness of the investigator.

STATEMENTS IN SPECIAL SITUATIONS

1018 Statements Taken in Hospitals

When an injured claimant is a patient in a hospital and in a condition to receive visitors, a statement may be taken. So that the statement cannot later be denied on the theory that the patient was under opiates or drugs, and therefore unable to know or understand what he or she was saying or doing, it is best to obtain a statement from the attending physician or the nurse on duty that the patient was not under the influence of drugs at the time that the claimant's statement was taken. This can be done by means of a separate statement (indicating the date and the time) or by a sentence or two added to the original statement under the claimant's signature.

> Mr. (Ms.) ________________ read this report and signed it as being true and correct. He (or she) was alert and not under the influence of any drugs or other medication.
>
> ________________________ M.D. (or R.N.)

When the claimant is hospitalized and is not in a condition to receive visitors, it is clear that the investigator will not be able to see the claimant until the condition improves. It is best to then contact the claimant's family, identify oneself as the investigator for the other party, and arrange for an appointment to see the claimant as soon as his or her condition will permit. This will have the effect of maintaining control of the case and, perhaps, will give the investigator an opportunity of making a settlement if a settlement is in order. While the investigator is continuing with this task of contacting other witnesses and completing the investigation, he or she should keep in touch with the claimant's family and the hospital in order to be able to interview the claimant at the earliest possible moment.

Some states have statutes which make it unlawful for either an investigator or the claimant's own attorney to interview the claimant while he or she is in a hospital within a prescribed period (usually the first 15 days after admission) without the claimant's written consent.

Where there is a statute similar to this, the investigator still will want to make his or her presence known to the claimant. The investigator can contact the claimant's family and explain that no interview with the claimant is possible within the first 15 days unless the claimant consents to it. The investigator can give the family a letter, addressed to the claimant, explaining the situation, together with a consent form which the claimant can sign and return. They could be mailed to the claimant, but the procedure is more impressive if the investigator contacts the family and has them deliver the letters. An example is shown in Figure 10–1.

Some investigators prefer to quote the entire section of the statute at the bottom of the letter in order to promote greater understanding on the part of the claimant. The request form usually reads as shown in figure 10–2.

1019 Statements: Serious Injury and Death Claims

In cases involving serious injury which might result in death and in death claims, it is necessary to investigate the persons dependent upon the injured person for support, and their relationships to the injured person. First, the investigator should know when and where the injured person was married if he or she leaves a sur-

Figure 10–1

Date ____________________

Dear Mr. Brown:

I am making an investigation in behalf of Mr. Joseph Green in regard to the accident in which you were recently injured. I should be glad to talk with you in reference to this matter.

However, under the provisions of a state statute, I am not permitted to enter the hospital to see you within the first fifteen days after the accident except by your written request.

If you desire to see me, please sign the attached request and return it to me. In accordance with the law, I will call upon you five days after the letter is returned.

Very truly yours,

____

FIGURE 10–2

Date ______________________

REQUEST TO:
John Smith
420 Main Street
Anytown, Anystate

Dear Sir:

In accordance with Section 270-b of the Penal Law, I hereby request you to call on me for all or any of the purposes set forth therein, at the Anytown City Hospital.

Very truly yours,

____

viving spouse. For a marriage to be legal, both parties must have been free from any legal disability and free to marry. If either had a spouse living it was not a marriage at all, and, as to the spouse under the disability of a previous marriage, it is a bigamous marriage. If the first marriage was terminated by divorce, then the person was free to remarry and had the legal right to do so. However, the divorce must have been granted by a court having jurisdiction of the parties. As to children, it must be shown that they are natural or adopted children to whom the deceased owed a duty of support. The wrongful death statutes of the various states define the persons for whose benefit an action may be brought. Therefore, the investigator must determine whether the claimed dependents come within the classes of persons defined in the statute. The same thing is true with reference to workers' compensation cases in that the compensation act defines the dependents for whose benefit compensation will be paid.

From the standpoint of investigation, where there is a fatality, or a possibility of a fatality, the following information should be obtained:

1. Date and place of marriage if there is one, together with information as to whether either spouse had been married before, and if so, the date and place of the previous marriage and whether it was terminated by death or divorce.
2. If there was a previous marriage, the nature of its termination should be ascertained; if by death, then the place and date of death of the previous spouse, or, if by divorce, the name of the court and the date when the marriage was dissolved. If the person does not have the latter information, then the name and address of the attorney who handled the matter will be helpful in checking out the divorce.
3. A copy of the marriage certificate should be obtained, and birth certificates for all of the children.
4. If the wife survived, a statement should be obtained as to whether she is pregnant.

5. The investigation should show the names and ages of the children, including children by a previous marriage and other possible dependents.
6. Finally, the investigation should show the extent of the support provided to the dependents, including children of prior marriages.

1020 Statements of Illiterates

The mere fact that a witness cannot read and write does not disqualify that person as a witness, nor do these facts preclude the possibility of getting an adequate statement from the person. The statement should be recorded as described in Section 1013 on recorded statements.

1021 Statements through Interpreters

A witness is not disqualified because he or she speaks a foreign language and does not understand English. A statement can be taken through an interpreter who is qualified to speak the language of the witness as well as English. The witness can sign the statement after it is read to the witness in his or her language by the interpreter. Then a statement should be added, by the interpreter, that the statement was read to the witness in the Italian (German, Spanish, etc.) language; that the witness then acknowledged it true and correct, and signed it to so signify. Have the interpreter sign this statement and record his or her address. It may happen that the statement will be offered in evidence, and the evidence of the interpreter will be necessary to identify it as the statement taken from the witness.

1022 Statements of Persons with a Physical or Mental Disability

Statements can be taken from persons with a physical or mental disability, and the nature of the disability will determine the procedure to be followed. If the disability is such that it does not in any way impair the faculties of the witness to hear, understand, and read the statement, then the usual procedure may be used. On the other hand, if the disability impairs those faculties, other methods must be used. A blind witness obviously cannot read the statement and acknowledge it to be true and correct, and a tape recorded statement should be taken.

A person who is unable to hear and/or speak usually uses a type of sign language for the purpose of communication. If possible, the investigator should obtain the services of an "interpreter" who can use the same type of sign language. This will facilitate the taking of the statement and will provide the investigator with a witness who can testify to the statement and the circumstances under which it was taken. The sign language interpreter should witness the signature on the statement (and provide an address so that he or she can be located if needed). However, if an interpreter is not available, a statement can be obtained by writing out the question, having the hearing/speech-disabled witness write the answers, and incorporating the information into statement form. Since such persons can usually read, they can acknowledge the truth of the statement in the usual way. The latter is a time-consuming method, and it is suggested that an interpreter be secured if at all possible.

A person suffering from a mental disability is not disqualified from testifying as a witness provided that he or she has strength of mind enough to recall and describe past events. A statement can be taken and the evidence admitted even though the witness is an inmate of a mental institution. In most cases, it will be necessary to obtain a statement from the attending physician that the patient's mental illness is such that it does not interfere with the ability to recall past events. In any case, a person with a mental disability is not necessarily disqualified as a witness, but the nature of the disability undoubtedly will be taken into account by the jury in determining the weight that should be given the testimony. Such witnesses are not sources of the best evidence and are to be avoided if it is possible to establish the same facts through other means.

1023 Statements of Children

Children are not disqualified from appearing as witnesses merely because of age. If they are old enough to know the difference between right and wrong, and it is made to appear that they believe in the moral consequences of telling a lie, they may testify. The weight given to their testimony will depend upon their ability to recall and describe past events.

Statements can be taken from children irrespective of age, but some distinction will have to be made between those of tender years and teenagers. As to children in their teens, who have a near-adult level of understanding, statements can be taken in the same manner as those taken from an adult. As to those of tender years, it is good practice to take these statements by tape recording in the presence of one or both parents so that there can be no allegation that unfair advantage was taken of the child.

1024 Negative Statements

It sometimes happens that a person who was in a position to have seen the accident denies having seen it. This is especially true of persons who were employed at or near the scene of the accident. Under such circumstances the investigator should take a short statement from the person, stating that he or she was otherwise occupied at the time of the accident and did not see it occur. Such a statement will destroy the witness if he or she should testify to the contrary; the person can be confronted by the statement, taken within a short time after the accident, in which he or she denies having seen anything.

For example, if an accident occurred at an intersection where there is a service station, the chances are that the employees would have witnessed the accident. If one such employee states that he did not see the accident because he was lubricating a car, or was in the back of the station getting some oil, a short statement to that effect will protect the investigator's file.

Taking the negative statement may seem to be a waste of time, but many a case has been won solely because the statement was taken and the witness forgot all about it and tried to testify that he or she had seen the accident; or, in the alternative, the witness did see the accident but the opposing side could not use the witness for fear of being confronted with the statement. On the other hand, the experienced investigator can recount instances where a negative statement was not obtained, only to find the witness testifying for the other side at the time of trial. Therefore, when the investigator is faced with a witness who could have seen the accident because of his or her presence at the scene, the investigator should take a negative statement. The time devoted to obtaining the negative statement is time well spent.

An honest person who did not see the accident will have no hesitancy in giving a negative statement, if only to be extricated from any involvement in the case. However, where the witness denies any knowledge of the accident but refuses to give a negative statement, then some consideration should be given to the possibility that the person may have seen the accident and will testify for the other side. This fact should be taken into account when appraising the strengths and weaknesses of the case.

1025 Multiple Statements

Normally, multiple or group statements are unsatisfactory. They should be avoided and separate statements should be taken from each person if possible. It sometimes happens that no one in a group saw the accident, and all are willing to give a group statement to that effect but, because of the nature of their business or the pressure of time, cannot devote time and attention to the statement. Under those circumstances a statement such as shown in Figure 10–3 can be prepared.

This procedure is not recommended and should be used only when separate statements cannot be obtained.

PHYSICAL AND DEMONSTRATIVE EVIDENCE

1026 Physical Facts

A physical fact is one having actual existence as distinguished from a mere conception of the mind; it is visible, audible, or palpable, such as the scene of an accident, the sound of the impact, or the skid marks laid down by one of the ve-

Figure 10–3

Date ____________________

We, the undersigned, are employees of the ABC service station located on the corner of Main and First Sts., Anytown, Anystate, and we were all on duty on September 20, 1994, at 8 P.M. when an accident occurred on Main Street in front of the station. None of us saw the accident nor do we know how the accident happened or who was at fault.

John Jones
Jennifer Smith
Joe Brown

hicles. The scene of the accident includes all of the details which have any bearing on the happening of the event, such as the place near an escalator where the claimant fell, including the advertising displays which may have had some influence in distracting the claimant, and the offending device whether it is an elevator, escalator, or obstruction in the aisle.

In automobile cases, the physical facts of the scene include the position of the streets, their width, and physical construction; the obstructions to vision of the drivers such as buildings, shrubbery, trees, advertising signs; traffic controls such as warning signs, stop signs, traffic lights; the location of landmarks such as fire hydrants, telephone poles, and fire alarm boxes. The physical facts of the accident include skid marks, debris or blood on the highway, the position of the cars at impact, the position where each came to rest, and the damage to the vehicles themselves as indicating the point of impact. The audible physical facts can be described only by those who heard them, but the other physical facts can be established by photographs and diagrams.

1027 Photographs

Photographs of the scene of the accident should depict the place of accident under the same conditions as when the accident happened. This means that the sooner the photographs are taken the better. Difficulties may arise if an interval of time has elapsed, especially where there has been a change in the surrounding conditions, such as new construction, changes in weather, or where shrubbery or trees have been removed. While photographs taken after changes have taken place are not entirely valueless, nevertheless they are subject to objection that they do not faithfully represent the scene as it was at the time of the accident, and testimony must be presented to show the changes.

If obstructions to vision are alleged (in a case where high grass obscured a traffic control sign), a photograph taken showing the grass in the same condition as it was at the time of the accident will be of significant value. But if the investigator allows some time to pass, the grass may have been cut so that the sign is no longer obscured; a photograph taken after this has happened is not as effective as one taken before the grass was cut. The same is true of old buildings or new construction. Time is of the essence, and the sooner a needed photograph is taken the better. If physical marks of the accident are important, it is clear that gouges in the highway and skid marks become obliterated with time, and even if some of the marks remain it will be difficult, if not impossible, to identify them as the result of the particular accident.

Photographs also play an important part in general liability claims, especially where there is a claim of insufficient lighting or dangerous construction, or where premises are being altered by new construction. Photographs can show the conditions at the time of the accident, location of the lighting fixtures in relation to the place of accident, and the presence of handrails, barricades, warning signs, and other items which have some bearing on the issue of negligence or contributory negligence. As in automobile cases, where the condition is subject to change (new construction, etc.), the photograph must be taken as soon after the accident as possible and must reproduce the conditions in existence at the time of the accident as nearly as possible. Where the condition will not change and the insured does not contemplate any alterations, photographs may be taken at any time but, even in those cases, if photographs are needed, the best rule to follow is that the sooner they are taken the better.

In automobile cases, a practice has grown in some areas whereby professional photographers obtain information as to the occurrence of a serious accident and take pictures of the scene, the position of the cars, etc. The pictures are for sale and can be bought by either or both sides. When the pictures are purchased, the purchaser usually insists on having both the print and the negatives, together with the assurance of the photographer that no other prints have been run off. It sometimes happens that this latter statement is untrue; that other prints have been sold to the opposing side. Therefore, in cases such as this, the investigator should proceed on the assumption that the other side has seen or is in possession of prints.

1028 Diagrams

A diagram is a flat sketch of the scene of the accident and the activity that took place. It can be used to depict the scene of the accident together with the location and relationship of fixed objects, or to locate damage to objects, or to locate injuries and scarring sustained by the injured person. The type of diagram the investigator will draw most frequently will be the scene of the accident or, in automobile cases, the scene plus the activity that occurred. Certain symbols are commonly used to represent objects and vehicles, and are usually made with a template or stencil, available in most stationery stores. The illustrated symbols in Figures 10-4 and 10-5 are only a partial list of those used.

The diagram is made to explain, orient, or clarify the file so that it will reflect the occurrence of the accident and the surrounding circumstances. It is a visual aid to the investigator in transmitting to the file a picture of exactly what happened. Also, where photographs have been taken, either by the investigator or by a professional photographer, it is helpful if the position of the camera for each photograph is tied in on the diagram. This leads to a better understanding of the photographs and eliminates the need for further identification of them. (See Figures 10-6 and 10-7.)

FIGURE 10–4

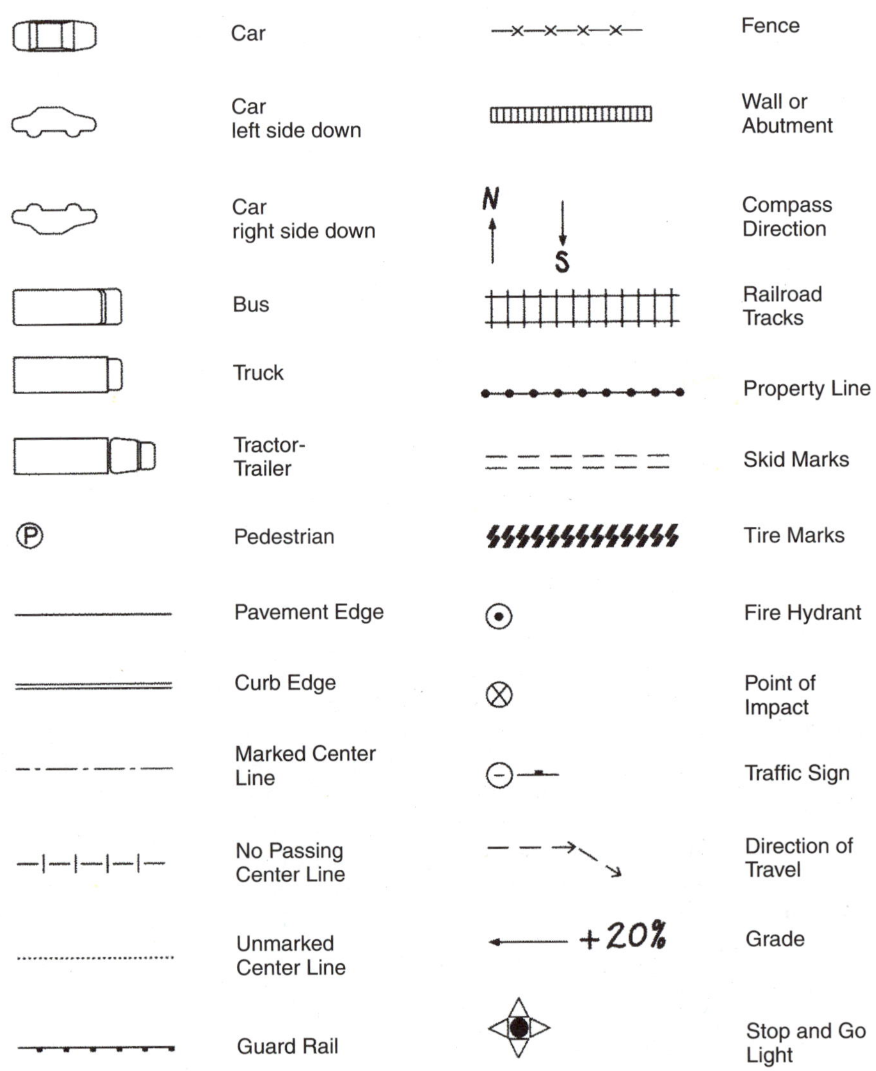

Diagrams are used most frequently in automobile cases. The minimum requirements of such a diagram are that it show the:

1. Direction of the cars involved.
2. Course of the cars immediately prior to impact.
3. Obstructions to the view of either driver.
4. Grade of the street.
5. Traffic controls.
6. Position of the cars at impact.
7. Position of the cars when they came to rest.

FIGURE 10–5

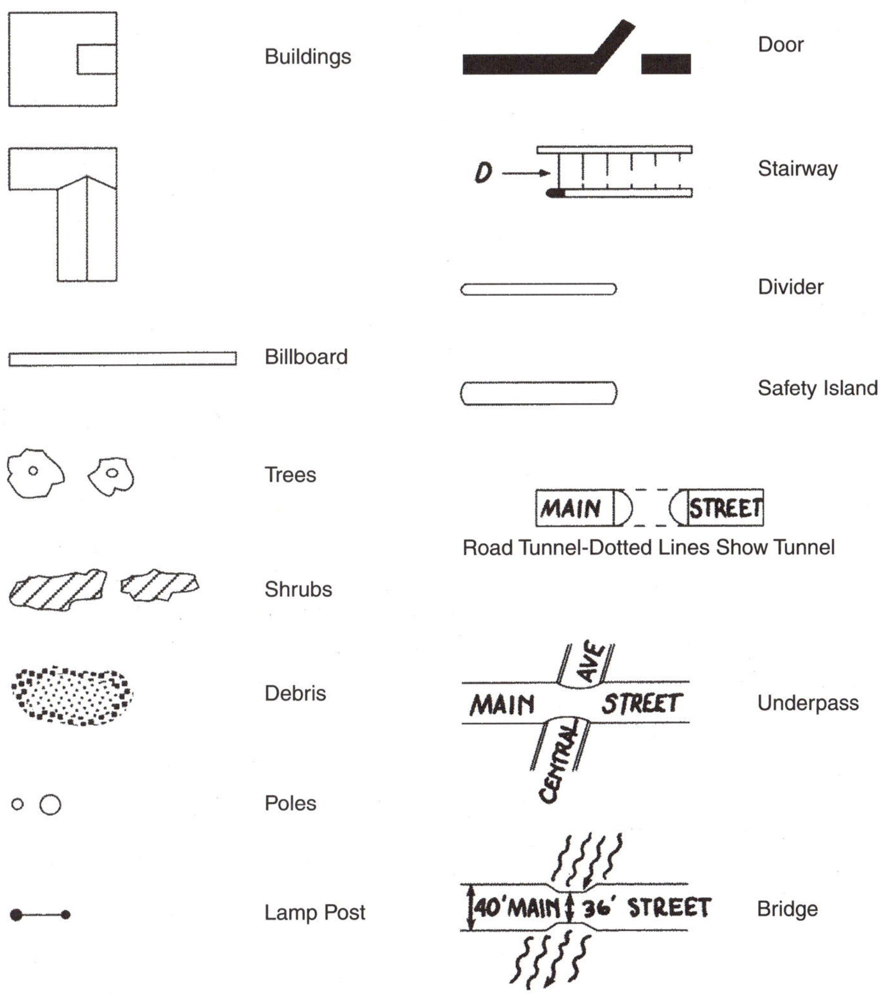

Skid marks, center lines, and gouges or debris on the highway can be located and depicted, as well as the locations of utility poles and intersecting rights-of-way, such as railroad crossings, bridges, and overpasses.

When taking a statement, it is sometimes helpful to have the witness draw a rough diagram of the intersection or place where the accident happened—and answer the investigator's questions as to the relative positions of the cars at im-

FIGURE 10–6

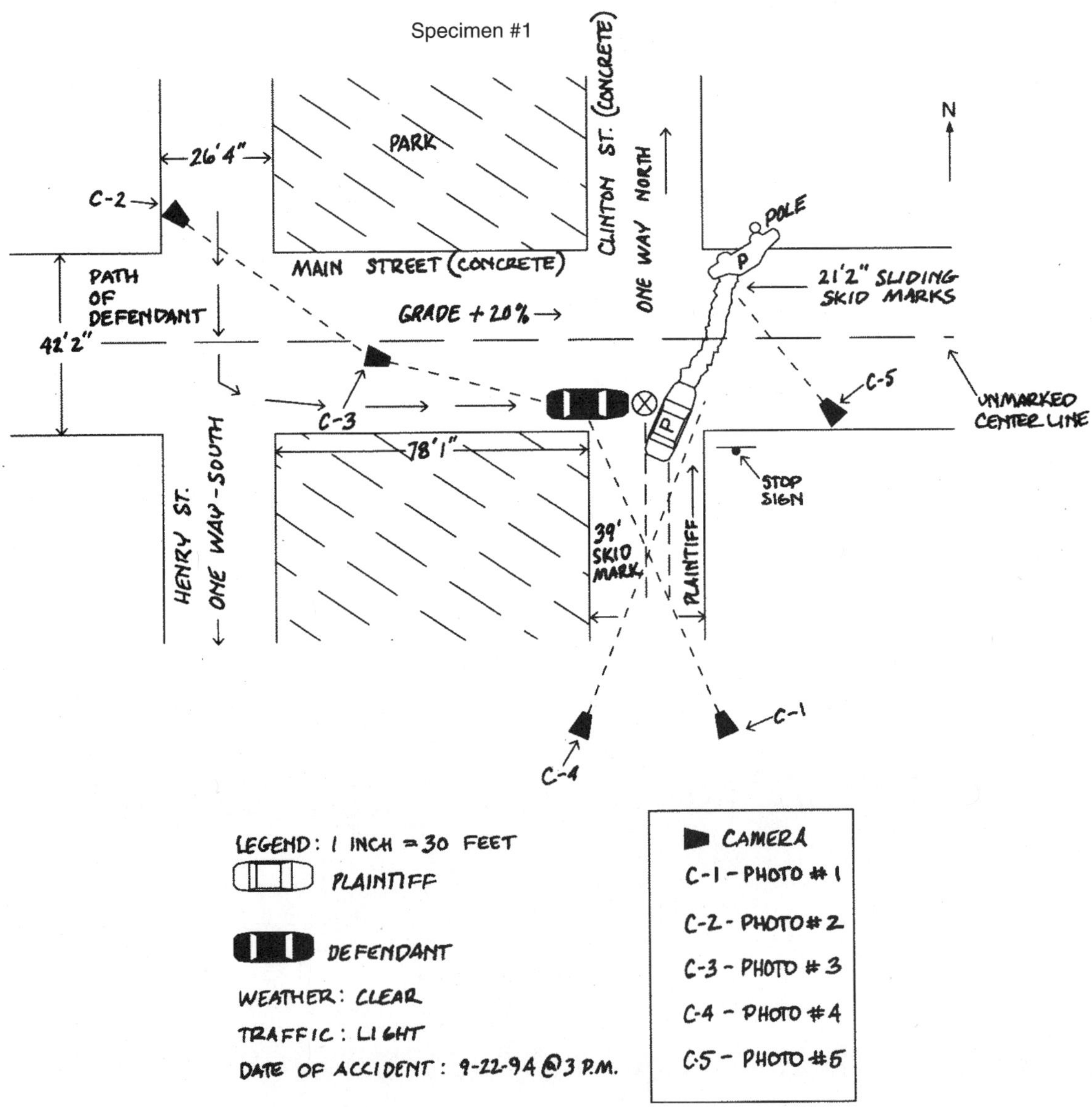

pact and when they came to rest by utilizing the diagram. Witnesses often become confused as to direction, and the corners of an intersection can be easily identifed if they are marked as NW, NE, SW, and SE. After the statement is taken, it is good practice to have the witness identify the diagram made with a statement placed on it together with the witness's signature. Then, if the witness testifies, he or she can be given the diagram, together with the statement, to aid in the witness's recollection.

FIGURE 10–7

Specimen #2

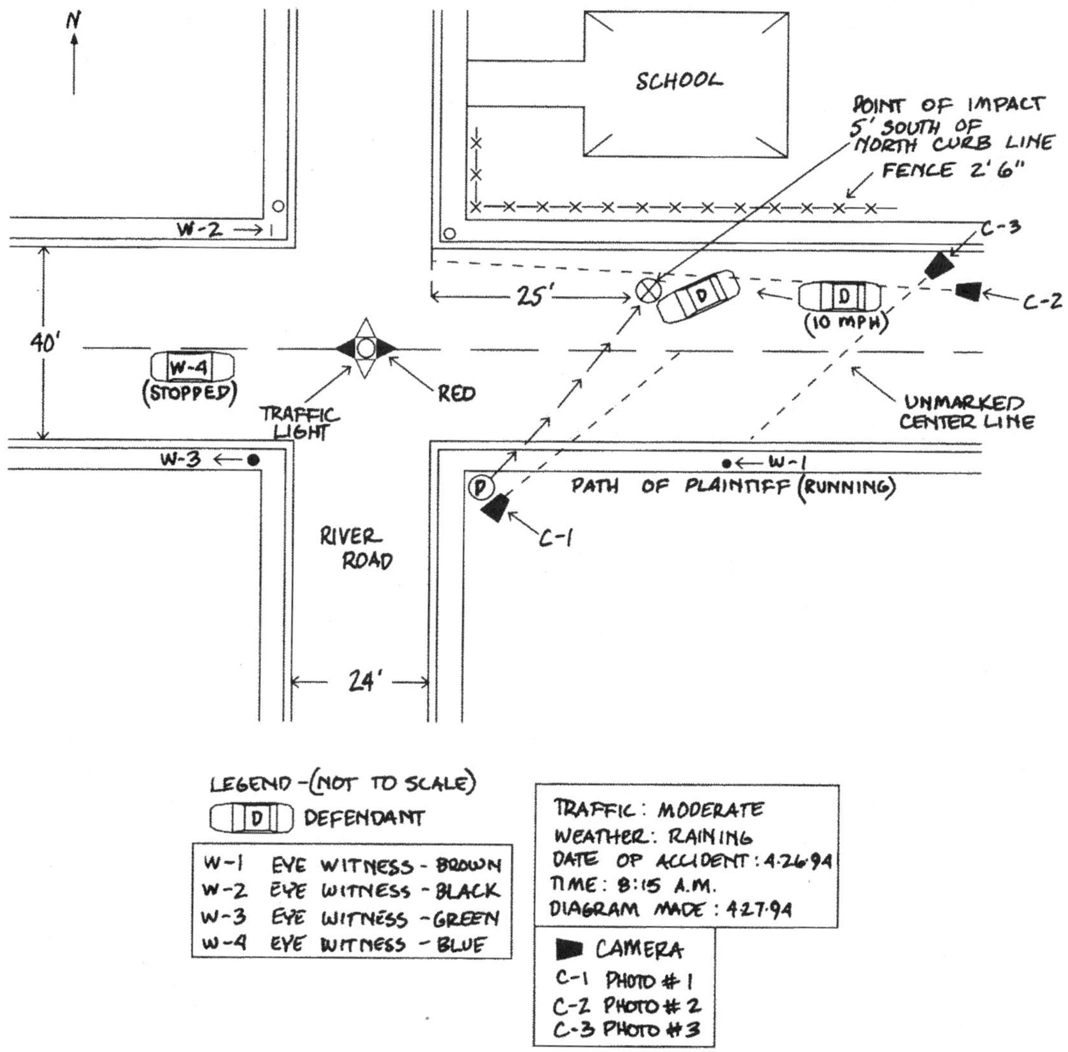

VERIFICATION

1029 Verification Generally

Verification is the process by which the investigator tests the accuracy or reliability of the evidence gathered. He or she will take each statement and decide whether it is corroborated or discredited by the statements of others. The investigator will determine whether a statement is contrary to reports made by the same witness to the police (police blotter) or to the state motor vehicle bureau, or contrary to admissions made at the scene of the accident (*res gestae*), or contrary to admissions against interest made after the event. The investigator also will test the statement with the physical facts. Can it be established that the point of impact is where the witness says it occurred? Do the tire marks, skid marks, and debris support the witness on this point?

Where the witness is friendly and favorable, it is sometimes important to visit the scene of the accident with the witness so that he or she can point out various landmarks and actually measure distances. It will be found that most people are poor judges of time and distance, and what the witness believes to be 250 feet (a favorite number) will actually turn out to be 75 feet. The witness is not to be discredited for being a poor judge, but if the witness actually steps off the distance he or she will be able not only to testify more accurately but can say he or she verified all estimates of distance after the accident happened. Or if the witness says it took 10 seconds to go to a certain distance at a certain speed, speed charts may prove this to be inaccurate. But a test at the scene of the accident may correct matters and make the witness more reliable.

1030 Verification by Experts

An expert is a skillful or experienced person who, because of education and training, has acquired special knowledge with respect to some particular art, science, trade, or profession not possessed by ordinary persons. Included within this definition would be a physician, surgeon, chemist, engineer, college professor, police officer with special training in accident reconstruction, or a mechanic. Within the limits of their respective specialties, any one of these experts can examine evidence and express an opinion which will guide the investigator. In most cases, the opinion will corroborate or refute the statement of a witness as to the happening of the accident, its causation, the speed of the vehicles, the point of impact, whether a substance is deleterious, or whether a medical condition could be caused by the trauma described by the witness. The expert will assist the investigator in determining what evidence is believable and what is not. (See Section 904, above.)

The service of an expert can be utilized in any one of three ways. The opinion can be elicited as a result of (1) a hypothetical question, (2) an examination or test of an object, and (3) an examination of the scene of the accident and measurements or tests made at the site.

Hypothetical Question. This consists of submitting the evidence to the expert in the form of assumed facts and requiring an answer as to whether or not certain conclusions can be reached on the basis of the evidence. For example, let us assume that the investigator has a claimant who says he was involved in an accident in which he twisted his back. He did not think anything of it for a period of time, continued to do his usual work (which involved manual labor), but about 30 days later felt an excruciating pain in his neck and, upon consulting a physician, had an X ray taken which indicated a compression fracture of one of the cervical vertebrae, all of which he claims was due to the accident. The investigator will immediately want to know whether it is possible for a man to sustain such a fracture and have no immediate manifestation of it, to continue to do manual labor for a period of 30 days without discomfort, and to experience the pain for the first time after that interval of time. In a case such as this, the investigator would submit the question to a surgeon specializing in orthopedics, with all the facts obtainable and, if possible, the original X-ray plates, and will ask for an opinion as to whether there could be any relationship between the accident as described and the resultant injury.

In another case, let us assume a claim that, while being used, a can of paint exploded and started a fire. The story sounds impossible, particularly where the claimant insists there are no other facts. The opinion of an expert would confirm the impossibility of this version, but would also point out circumstances under which the accident could have happened—if the paint were subjected to extreme heat, let us say. This latter opinion gives the investigator a lead as to the information to seek in contradicting the alleged version of the accident.

Examination or Test of an Object. Referring back to the previous illustration, let us assume the particular can of paint is available and can be identified as the one which exploded and burned. It could be submitted to an expert chemist to determine, by examination, what caused the can to explode and whether there is any evidence that it was exposed to extreme heat. In products cases where it is claimed that a certain item was the offending cause of an injury, the item (or a similar item) can be subjected to a chemical analysis to determine its ingredients, and an opinion can be expressed as to whether such ingredients could cause the condition of which the claimant complains.

For example, a claimant maintains she was made ill by eating a cake from the local bakery and that the ilness was caused by some unwholesome ingredient in the cake. An analysis of the cake by a chemist will determine the truth or falsity of this claim. If possible, the remaining parts of the cake should be obtained and analyzed. If that is not possible, the same type of cake, baked at the same time as the other cake and made from the same batch or mixture, should be subjected to analysis.

Examination of Scene and Tests at Site. An engineer can make an examination of the scene of the accident, prepare plats of the area, note the marks of the accident (gouges, skid marks, debris, etc.), and express an opinion as to where the accident took place with reference to the center line, the speed of the vehicles as evidenced by the damage caused, and where each came to rest. The engineer could also make tests by using the car involved in the accident, or one of similar make and model, to determine braking distance, roadability, control, and any other factors which may have been involved in the causation of the accident.

In a case where it is claimed a person contracted a disease, such as silicosis, from the inhalation of dust containing silica or other deleterious substance, the investigator will want to know whether any such substance is in the atmosphere where the person worked or visited. This can be accomplished by having an engineer make dust counts of the air, identifying the dust as to kind, size, and quantity, and expressing an opinion as to whether the dust particles can be inhaled. Identification will consist of the testimony of a witness that the test was conducted in the place where the claimant worked and under conditions which were the same or similar to those to which the claimant was exposed.

The investigator is frequently confronted with a case where it is alleged that a customer in a store slipped and fell because of an excessive amount of wax on the floor. The contention will be that wax was applied to linoleum or asphalt tile, creating an extremely slippery and unsafe condition. The fact of the matter is that the manufacturers of floor wax, especially the type used by commercial establishments, have mixed a nonskid substance in the wax and a floor treated with this wax is less slippery than it is in an unwaxed condition; the nonskid substance increases the coefficient of friction.

The investigator will have to overcome the general notion that the more wax that is applied, the more dangerous and slippery the floor becomes. To do this will require the testimony of an expert who has examined the floor and subjected it to friction tests under circumstances similar to the conditions under which the accident is alleged to have occurred.

1031 Verification by Medical Examination

A worker's claims of disability and the necessity for medical treatment can be verified by having the claimant examined by the company physician. The examining physician will verify the history of the accident, and the claimant's past medical history and present condition. He or she will express an opinion on the causal relationship between the claimant's present condition and the alleged accident, and an opinion as to whether the claimant is disabled from working (temporarily, partially, or permanently), whether any further treatment is indicated, and, if so, for how long.

Prior to litigation, the claimant is not required by law to submit to a medical examination. The claimant may however, because he or she realizes that the examination is a necessary part of the investigation which, it is hoped, will lead to a settlement. The same considerations will motivate the attorney who represents the injured person. However, the investigator should recognize that, during the period the claimant is under the treatment of a personal physician, the only evidence of his or her physical condition, and disability, will be that of the attending physician. In the absence of an examination by the company's physician, the company will have no evidence to contradict the testimony of the attending physician.

Where the claim is in litigation, the defendant is entitled to at least one physical examination as part of the discovery or disclosure proceedings. This is a matter of right, and if the claimant refuses, he or she can be compelled to submit to the examination by means of a court order. In some states, the defendant is entitled not only to an examination when the case is in the preliminary stages but also to a final examination at least 10 days prior to the trial date.

Where it is conceded that the claimant has fully recovered, and this is supported by the claimant's own statement or a certification from his or her doctor, there would be little point in conducting an examination; the company is sufficiently protected against any further claims by either of these statements. If a further claim is made, then the company can consider the advisability of an examination. Where it is conceded that the claimant has recovered and does not require further medical treatment, but has sustained some permanency, then an examination may be indicated to determine whether there is any permanent condition and, if so, the extent of it.

When it is decided that a medical examination is indicated and necessary, the following factors should receive consideration: (1) the time of examination, (2) the extent of examination, (3) the selection of the medical examiner, and (4) the report of examination.

1. Time of Examination. The first decision is the time the examination should take place. Should it be conducted immediately or be deferred to some future date, and, if so, how long should it be deferred? It is elementary that the examination should obtain information as to the claimant's physical condition. Therefore, it should take place at a time and under such circumstances as will produce the maximum information. If it is known that the claimant is in a plaster cast or in the hospital, either in traction or recovering from an operation, an immediate examination would not be revealing because the examining physician would not be permitted to remove the cast, take the claimant out of traction, or remove the bandages to examine the operative area. The examining physician could examine the X rays, hospital records, and operative report, but since these records are available any time, their immediate examination is not necessary. Therefore, in these cases, it is best to defer the examination.

As to cases where examination can be made, the answer to when it should be made will depend upon what the claim representative desires to accomplish by having it. Where there is some question as to the extent of an injury, the earlier the examination is conducted the better, because it is essential that the company have a complete picture of the injury, its extent, and potential. Also, where there is a question as to the amount of treatment required, an immediate examination can act as a deterrent to overtreatment and extended disability. It should be emphasized again that, in the absence of verification of the claimant's injury and the need for medical treatment, the statements of the attending physician stand as the only evidence on these two points. In every case, there will be an interval between the date of the accident and the examination. As to that interval, reliance will have to be placed on the report of the attending physician because no other medical evidence is available. The longer this interval is, the longer the claimant will have incontrovertible proof of disability and of the necessity for medical treatment. Because of these considerations, an early examination is a definite requirement where the matter of disability or of the necessity for medical treatment is an issue.

Where the claim representative is satisfied that the case is in good hands, and that there is no tendency on the part of the attending physician to overtreat, there would be reason to defer the examination until the treatment is concluded in order to have the examination show the final result and whether there is any permanent condition present.

The claim representative is not always restricted to having only one examination in each case. It may well be that arrangements can be made for a preliminary examination, and for a final examination at a later date. Where this is evident, it might have some influence on the claim representative's thinking as to the time of the first examination.

2. Extent of the Examination. This will vary with the type of case and the objective to be accomplished. In every case, whether the examination is made by a specialist or a general practitioner, and irrespective of the objective, the claim representative should see that the examiner is given all the information in the file as to the causation of the injury, the exact injuries claimed, whether the claimant was hospitalized, the type of treatment or operation performed, whether X rays were taken, and their results. If a copy of the hospital record has been obtained or a certificate received from the attending physician, the examiner should be furnished with a copy.

If X rays were taken, arrangements should be made with the attending physician to make the original plates available to the examiner. In appropriate cases, the examiner should be authorized to take the X rays himself, especially where the originals were positive and some time has elapsed since they were taken. In this way, he or she can give an up-to-date opinion as to the progress of the healing process. Also, where X rays are unsatisfactory, either because they were improperly taken or misinterpreted because of some defect in the plate, the examiner should have comparative X rays in order to reach a definite conclusion. Usually, the authorization for taking X rays is not given on a blanket basis, but each case is considered in light of its own particular facts and the need for new X rays, and the examiner is required to solicit authorization in each case where he or she feels there is a need for new plates. The giving of a blanket authorization not only increases the cost of the examinations, but the X rays may frequently disclose other conditions, not being claimed, as additional results of the accident. Thus, when the X rays are produced, an additional claim may be advanced. Authorization for X rays is not given unless some purpose useful to the defense can be achieved. But in any case, where there are X rays, the examiner should see the original plates rather than relying on the findings of another physician as to what they disclose.

The same criteria apply to other tests, such as blood tests, electrocardiograms, basal metabolism tests, and encephalograms. They are authorized if they will serve some purpose in producing a more complete examination or in uncovering some condition, unrelated to the accident, which may be used as a defense on the theory that the condition and not the accident is the cause of the claimant's disability.

The examination is not necessarily restricted to the findings of one physician. There can be more than one doctor participating, especially in cases where there is a multiplicity of injuries, each coming within the scope of a different specialty. For example, if the claimant is suffering from a fractured skull and claims some eye complications such as diplopia (double vision), it might be necessary to have the claimant examined by an eye specialist in addition to the general examination. The extent and number of the specialists to be called in on the case will, in each instance, depend upon the particular facts of the case and the objective to be achieved.

3. Selection of the Medical Examiner. Many doctors, otherwise competent, make poor witnesses in court. They may be inarticulate or may have a gruff and uncompromising personality or other traits which may influence the jury unfavorably. The first requisites include a pleasing personality, the ability of expression, and the facility for expressing technical medical terms in ordinary language.

The examiner must have medical knowledge sufficient to make an accurate appraisal of the injuries, the need for treatment, and the prognosis for future recovery. He or she must report the findings accurately and must not be inclined toward optimism, or to minimizing the injury, merely because he or she is examining for the defendant. Nothing is more frustrating to the claim representative than to rely on an overly optimistic report which cannot be supported by facts or testimony at the time of trial. The examiner should be capable of reporting the injuries as found, whether such findings are favorable to the defendant or not. An accurate estimate of the potential of the case cannot be made when the medical report is misleading; and, in some cases, an attractive settlement possibility will be turned down because of an inaccurate medical report.

The same considerations should influence the selection of a specialist who is needed in certain situations, but his or her qualifications also should be such that they are not open to attack by adversaries. The specialist should have hospital connections in the particular specialty and be able to support the status of specialist by demonstrating educational qualifications and experience (including Board Certification) beyond that held by the ordinary general practitioner.

4. Report of Examination. The medical report should be addressed TO WHOM IT MAY CONCERN, or some similar designation, and never addressed to the company or to the claim representative. The reason is that the report may have to be offered in evidence, and if it is addressed to the company or the claim representative, the form of the address will reveal the existence of insurance. Concealment of the existence of insurance may give the defendant a doubtful advantage, however, especially where the defendant is a large corporation or where state law requires the carrying of liability insurance. In any case, it is good practice to follow this procedure because it is difficult to predict the cases in which insurance may become an important issue. The following of this precautionary procedure assures that the risks of revealing the existence of insurance are reduced.

A satisfactory medical report will contain, as a minimum, these five items: (1) history, (2) findings, (3) causal relationship, (4) prognosis, and (5) opinion.

History. The examiner should elicit as complete a statement as possible from the claimant as to how the accident occurred, what parts of the claimant's body were injured, what pain was suffered, when the first manifestation of pain was felt—whether simultaneously with the accident or some time thereafter—whether there was loss of consciousness, when and from whom the claimant first received medical treatment, and the number and kinds of treatment received since that time. If the history differs in any way from the information supplied by the company as to the causation of the injury, the examiner should make some effort to reconcile the differences if it is possible to do so. Inquiry should also be made about X rays and other diagnostic aids which may have been used, any information developed, and when and by whom the tests were performed. The information thus gained might assist in the further investigation as well as bringing to light any questions which may exist as to the medical treatment. Some attorneys are aware of this practice involving the taking of a complete history, and insist that all examinations be made at their offices and in their presence. This limits the examiner's opportunity to explore the history thoroughly, but the examiner is entitled to inquire how the claimed injuries were incurred, and what treatment was rendered up to the time of the examination.

Findings. The actual results of the examination should be detailed, setting forth the claimant's complaints and stating whether they are substantiated by any objective signs. The report should indicate what tests were made by the examiner and the claimant's reaction to each.

Causal Relationship. The examiner should state whether all the injuries complained of could be the result of the accident as described to the examiner in the history, whether there is any evidence of preexisting injury or disease, and if so, whether in his or her opinion this condition was aggravated by the accident.

Prognosis. The examiner should state whether the claimant has fully recovered or whether further medical treatment is required. If the claimant is still disabled, some estimate of future disability should be made and, if further treatment is necessary, an estimate of the period of time needed (together with the nature and the frequency of such treatment) should be included. The examiner should also comment as to whether the injuries will produce a permanent condition and if so, the nature and extent of the permanency. If it consists of a restriction in motion of any member, the examiner should express the loss of use in terms of a percentage as compared with normal motion. Where facial scarring is involved, the report should contain a description of the scar as it now exists and an opinion as to whether it will improve by bleaching out with the passage of time and, if so, the residual result to be expected. If plastic surgery will improve the condition, he or she should express an opinion as to the possible result, the nature and extent of the surgery, and the approximate cost.

Opinion. The examiner should give an opinion as to the treatment already rendered, whether it was indicated or effective, and give recommendations as to further treatment, if necessary, whether of the same or of a different type. Where permanency is involved, the examiner should give an opinion as to what the permanent condition means in relation to the claimant's ability to continue with his or her usual work and in relation to future enjoyment of life, if the latter is involved.

1032 Verification of Disability

Disability can be verified or denied by obtaining evidence of the physical activity of the claimant. This can be secured by one or more of the following methods: (1) neighborhood check, (2) surveillance, and (3) motion pictures or videotapes.

Neighborhood Check. The claimant's activities can be checked through interviews with neighbors, storekeepers, letter carriers, newspaper deliverers, and others in the neighborhood. Inquiry should develop exactly what physical activity has been observed, such as engaging in sports, doing yard work, making repairs, sweeping the sidewalk, doing the marketing, washing the car, and other activities which involve physical exertion. Where positive information is obtainable, it should be made the subject of a signed statement. If the informant knows that the claimant has been working, an effort should be made to find out where and the kind and type of work.

Surveillance. This consists of the observation by the investigator of the claimant's activities. It might mean that the claimant's home will have to be kept under observation for long periods of time, or it might mean that the surveillance should take place at different hours on different days. The objective is to observe the claimant and to ascertain exactly what physical activity he or she is capable of doing and to what extent. Where positive information is developed, statements can be taken from others who made similar observations.

Surveillance may also reveal that the claimant is working, even though the claimant has denied the ability to do so. This is usually ascertained by observing the claimant leave at the same time each day and return at the same time each evening. Trailing the claimant to his or her place of business will establish business activity. Further investigation at that point, through the employer, will establish the date of the claimant's return to work and the regularity of attendance.

Difficulties arise when the claimant is working at more than one location, and sometimes it is necessary to continue surveillance for a period of time in order to establish that fact. In any case, the period of the surveillance and whether professionals are engaged for the task will have to depend upon the particular facts of the case.

Videotapes. These are usually taken to establish the claimant's physical ability to perform work. If he or she is working around the house, making major repairs, or painting, pictures of such activity can be used to controvert any claims that the injuries are such that the claimant is unable to perform any physical labor.

The videotapes are usually taken without the claimant's knowledge, and for that reason cannot be taken very close to the scene of the activity. Telephoto lenses are used, and the position of the camera is some distance from the claimant. In spite of these difficulties, the picture must clearly identify the claimant as the person engaging in the activity. If the pictures fail to do this, they may not be admissible in evidence. (See Sectioin 931, above.) Therefore, for the most part, videos used in connection with the trial of cases are usually taken by professionally trained persons who make a specialty of doing this type of work. There is no reason, however, why they could not be taken by a staff investigator of equal competence.

1033 Verification through the Index Bureau

The claims bureau of one of the national insurance trade associations maintains an index bureau for the purpose of accumulating records of bodily injury claims and of making this information available to its subscribers. The information is received by the index bureau by the submission on each case of an information sheet, containing the data on each bodily injury claim as it is made. When these information sheets are received, the bureau checks each case with its records, and if there is a previous record of the claimant, information is returned to the subscriber indicating the details of each previous claim, giving the injuries claimed, the date of the accident, the company involved, the company file number, and the type of claim. If further information is desired, the subscriber can contact the other company for more details.

The index bureau is nationwide in its operation and, therefore, even though the claimant is a transient, information as to prior claims may be available.

Chapter 11

Medical Aspects*

1100 Medical Knowledge in Relation to Personal Injury Claims
1101 Causation
1102 Trauma
1103 Etiology
1104 X Rays
1105 Other Diagnostic Tests
1106 Diagnostic Signs
1107 Anatomy
1108 Fractures
1109 Head Injuries
1110 Spinal or Back Injuries
1111 Traumatic Neurosis
1112 Disc Injuries
1113 Whiplash
1114 Hernia
1115 Arthritis
1116 Inflammatory Diseases
1117 Common Injuries
1118 Lengths of Disability
1119 The Eye
1120 The Heart
1121 The Blood
1122 Blood Grouping and Transfusions
1123 Compressed-Air Disease
1124 Lung Diseases
1125 Hematoma
1126 Infection
1127 Blood Tests for Intoxication
1128 Other Intoxication Tests
1129 Intoxication Tests as Evidence

1100 Medical Knowledge in Relation to Personal Injury Claims

In the evaluation and settlement of personal injury claims, the objective is to measure the extent of the injury in terms of money. To accomplish this, the claim representative must have a working knowledge of anatomy and the effects of an injury upon the human body. Clearly, the claim representative is not expected to have the knowledge of a medical practitioner, but he or she must have some familiarity with conditions caused by accidents, and what these conditions mean in terms of causation, treatment, pain and suffering, as well as disability, both temporary and permanent. The following pages are intended to give only a very limited view of the subject with reference to some of the more common terms and some of the more frequently recurring types of injury.

*This chapter was co-authored by Brian R. Hirsch, M.D.

Medical knowledge is an ever-expanding subject in the claim representative's portfolio of information. As cases are handled, the claim representative is confronted with medical reports from the claimant's physician and from specialists, and is guided by the examinations and reports made by his or her own examining physician. To properly understand and evaluate this medical information, one must know and understand all the terminology used, how and why certain tests are made, and the significance of the conclusions expressed. To understand the terms, reference must constantly be made to a medical dictionary, and in matters involving complicated injuries, consultation with the examining physician will be helpful in acquiring an understanding of the medical factors involved in the claim.

When it comes to the settlement of personal injury claims, the claim representative is a purchaser. He or she is buying the cause of action which accrued to the claimant as a result of the accident. One of the items in this purchase is the physical and mental distress suffered by the claimant. The claim representative must know the details of this distress, its extent, its effect upon the claimant in terms of pain and disability, as well as the treatment required to cure or relieve it. The buying of a commodity of this kind is no different from any other type of bargain and sale. The buyer usually insists upon examining the subject of the sale, either personally or by having an expert make the examination for him. The buyer then decides whether to make the purchase, depending upon whether the price is reasonable. Similarly, in the purchase of personal injury claims, the claim representative must know the nature of the article being bought before determining whether the price is reasonable and whether to make the purchase.

In making this determination, an adequate and detailed description of the injury is the primary step. If the physician reports that the claimant has sustained "an injury to the back" or a "traumatic condition of the spine," the description is inadequate. Both of these terms could mean various types of fractures of the spine, a strain of the muscles, a contusion in the area of the back, a herniation of the disc, spondylolisthesis. Some of the terms are indicative of a serious injury and others, such as spina bifida or spondylolysis, refer to congenital conditions not caused by an accident, and rarely aggravated by one. The value of the case and the action to be taken by the claim representative will depend upon which of these terms actually describes the injury.

In medical reports certain descriptive words are used generally to pinpoint the exact area of injury. Anatomists have divided the body by means of an imaginary line, running from the head downward at the center of the body, called the median line. The medial aspect of any bone or organ is that part which is nearest the median line. The other side of the bone or organ away from the median line is called the outer or external aspect. Lateral refers to the side, anterior to the front, and posterior to the rear. In classifying X-ray views, a side view is referred to as a lateral view. One taken from front to back is called an anterior-posterior view.

Dorsal refers to the back. For example, the dorsal surface of the hand is the back of the hand, as distinguished from the palm, which is referred to as the volar or palmar surface. The largest muscle of the back is called the latissimus dorsi which, literally translated, means "largest of the back." The bones of the arms and legs are divided into thirds for anatomical purposes. In locating a fracture or other bone condition, the report will refer to the proximal shaft (upper third) of the femur or the mid shaft (middle third) or the distal shaft (lower third).

Muscles are described by the number of "ceps" or heads they have. For example, the biceps muscle (arm) is one with two heads. The quadriceps muscle (thigh) is one with four heads.

1101 Causation

Obviously, in order to recover for an injury, the claimant must sustain the injury as a result of the accident. The claimant may be suffering from some preexisting condition which bears no relationship to the accident, in which case there should be no recovery. He or she may have a preexisting condition which has been aggravated by the accident, in which case, theoretically at least, recovery should be for the period of aggravation, and the disability should cease at the termination of that time. Unfortunately, a line as fine as this cannot be drawn, and the condition may never return to its former state. In such cases the defendant might be responsible for the entire condition.

In other situations, the claimant may have a systemic or chronic condition which delays recovery. A prime example of this is a claimant suffering from tertiary syphilis, a bloodstream disease which, in the case of injury, retards and sometimes bars full recovery. The responsibility of the defendant encompasses the entire period of disability even though, in the case of a normal person, recovery would be much more rapid. Again, the defendant would not be responsible for the cure of the syphilitic condition but would have to bear the cost of whatever treatment was required to cure the accidental injury, even though some of the treatment might be directed toward the control and care of the syphilis.

In all cases, where the defendant is alleged to be responsible, there must be a definite chain of causation leading from the accident to the ultimate injury claimed. For example, if a claimant sustained contusions and lacerations of the right hand, one would hardly assume any responsibility for a bunion on the right foot which allegedly began to cause pain right after the accident. However, if as a result of the laceration of the hand, an infection in the hand and arm or a lymphangitis (inflammation of a lymph vessel) of the arm developed, then there would be a direct chain of causation and the defendant would be responsible for the entire condition.

In determining whether this chain of causation exists, our examining doctor must have all the facts. These include the history (the facts of the accident), hospital records, reports of attending physicians, X rays, and laboratory tests. Medical diagnosis depends upon a review of all the facts and examination of the patient with special reference to objective and subjective symptoms. Objective symptoms are those that can be seen or verified by the use of X ray or other diagnostic tools. Subjective are the complaints made by the patient. The latter, of course, can easily be fabricated. In some cases, there is an interval between the trauma and the first physical manifestation of the injury or disease. It is important to cover this point in the claimant's statement, exactly indicating when he or she for the first time experienced any discomfort in the injured area. Generally, the rule is that the longer the interval of time between the trauma and the onset of symptoms, the less the likelihood of any relationship between the two. However subjective in nature these injuries to the head, neck, and back may seem, it is worth remembering that real and debilitating conditions may result, and they must not be summarily dismissed without extensive work-up and follow-through.

Therefore, when a case is referred to our examining doctor, he or she should have the benefit of all the previous medical information that you have obtained. This will consist of hospital records, X rays (if not the plates, at least a copy of the findings), past medical history, reports of doctors treating such past conditions, a concise but complete statement of how the accident occurred, the injuries complained of, the symptoms claimed (both subjective and objective), and the kind and type of disability claimed. The more information and factual data the doctor has, the more accurate will be the opinion on disability and causal relationship.

Certain injuries are so definite that they can be demonstrated by clinical examination or diagnosed by the use of X rays and other means. Head, neck, and back injuries pose a particular diagnostic problem, and it is in this area that most fraudulent or malingering claims will be found.

1102 Trauma

This is the medical word you will meet more frequently than any other. It means a blow or wound. There are internal and external traumas. An internal trauma is caused within the body by one organ exerting pressure on another. External trauma refers, as the name implies, to a blow or pressure from outside. Any condition which comes about as a result of a blow is said to be traumatic in origin. It is used to differentiate, as to origin, conditions which could be spontaneous (chronic) and those caused by external force.

1103 Etiology

The etiology of a condition refers to the causes of disease, both direct and predisposing, and their mode of operation. It does not refer specifically to the cause of the condition but generally to the causes of similar conditions, the usual progress, and the usual termination. The terminology is used in discussing a particular case with a doctor with reference to the usual cause and progress of the condition.

1104 X Rays

Contrary to the popular belief, X rays are not pictures in the sense that they are mirrorlike reflections. The X ray is made by placing an object (i.e., the part of the body) between the plate and the X-ray tube, and the shadow cast by the object is developed on the plate. X rays (or Roentgen rays) are produced by this tube, which emits the rays in an umbrellalike fashion. As a result, the object directly beneath the tube will be in sharp focus, whereas the parts of the object not under the center will show up on the plate with a certain amount of distortion. Thus, the greater the angle of the ray, the greater the distortion.

It was originally discovered that the outline of bones only would be seen on the X-ray plate; other organs would not. The problem then was to provide ways and means of making other organs radioopaque for diagnostic purposes. This was solved by introducing radioopaque material into the organ. For example, barium is introduced orally into the body and will outline the stomach and the gastrointestinal system. Lipiodol and other dyes may be introduced by injection into the body and will outline intervertebral discs and the course of the spinal fluid.

An X-ray plate is said to be negative when it demonstrates no abnormal condition, and positive when it outlines a fracture or other condition. In the skull, because of the number of bones crossing each other, a diagnosis of fracture of certain of these bones is sometimes difficult to make. Since the image produced on the plate is only a shadow, it is possible for the claimant to actually sustain a fracture of the base of the skull which is not demonstrable by X ray.

Usually, more than one view of the condition is made by X ray. These views are produced by placing the object at different angles to the X-ray tube. As noted above, a lateral view is a side view and an anterior-posterior is one taken from front to back.

More recently, the advent of nuclear medicine has allowed the development of much more sensitive imaging tests—the magnetic resonance image (MRI) and the computerized tomography scan (CT scan), which can readily detect internal organ injuries, brain and spinal lesions, and soft-tissue damage.

1105 Other Diagnostic Tests

Other means of diagnosis are available in addition to X rays. Listed below, with their definitions and use, are some of the tests encountered in claim work.

Bone conduction. A test for hearing threshold conducted by placing a tuning fork or audiometer oscillator directly against the mastoid process of the skull's temporal bone (the bump behind the ear).

Electrocardiogram (ECG, EKG). A graphic record made by an electrocardiograph of the electrical activity of the heart, taken from body surfaces. A typical normal record shows *P, Q, R, S,* and *T* waves. The *P* wave is due to excitation of the atria, *Q, R,* and *S* waves to the excitation of the ventricles; the *T* wave to repolarization of the ventricles. Any abnormality in the transmission of these waves serves as an aid in diagnosis of heart ailments (e.g., heart attacks).

Patch test. An allergy test in which material is applied to intact skin surface to demonstrate tissue sensitivity.

Snellen. Test for central vision in which the subject stands a certain distance from a standard chart and reads letters on the chart. Results are calculated by the ability of the subject to read letters of different sizes. Results are expressed by figures: 20/20 is the normal degree of visual acuity.

Weber. A hearing test in which the vibrations from a tuning fork placed on the forehead of a normal person are referred to the midline and heard equally in both ears. In unilateral middle-ear deafness, the sound is heard in the diseased ear.

1106 Diagnostic Signs

In medical reports we will note references to signs, which in the general sense are physical manifestations of disease or injury. Some of the more frequent in claims work are as follows:

Babinski. A sign for spinal cord injuries in which the response to stroking the bottom of the foot shows dorsiflexion of the great toe (flexes upward) with plantar flexion (flexes downward) and fanning of other toes. Note that this is a normal reflex for infants before their nervous system is completely developed, so a baby can be easily tested for this sign.

McBurney's. A sign for early acute appendicitis in which the area of maximum tenderness is over McBurney's point of the abdomen (which lies one-third of the way on a diagonal line from the right hip to the umbilicus).

Lasegue. A sign of sciatic nerve disease where elevation of the extended leg produces pain in the nerve trunk.

Romberg. A sign for tabes dorsalis (a disease referring to the spinal cord often associated with syphilis), in which the patient cannot maintain equilibrium when standing with feet together and eyes closed.

1107 Anatomy

Skeleton. The skeleton is a bony framework which supports the soft parts of the human body. It is composed of a number of separate bones of varying size and use.

Cranium and Face. These are the two major divisions of the skull. The cranium refers to the part of the skull that contains the brain, its membranes, and vessels. The cranium is made up of eight bones—frontal (forehead), occipital (rear of head), sphenoid (at base of skull), ethnoid (small bone with air spaces that is between the eye sockets), two parietal (forming top and side), and two temporal (forming lower part of the cranium with cavities associated with the ear).

The face is composed of 14 bones consisting of two nasal, two lacrimal, two zygomatic (zygoma), two palate, two inferior turbinate bones, two maxillas, the vomer, and the mandible. The principal bones are the nasal bones, which form the bridge of the nose; the superior maxilla, two bones which form the upper jaw; the inferior maxilla (or mandible), which forms the lower jaw, and the zygomatic bones which form the cheek.

The bones of the middle ear are commonly referred to as the anvil, stirrup, and hammer. The medical names for these bones are incus (anvil), stapes (stirrup), and malleus (hammer). They amplify the sound waves from the external to the inner ear, allowing us to hear.

Spinal Column (Vertebral Column). The spine is a flexible column composed of irregularly shaped bones called vertebrae, which protect the spinal cord. There are 26 separate bony parts: 7 cervical vertebrae (in the neck), 12 thorocic vertebrae, 5 lumbar vertebrae, a sacrum (composed of 5 fused sacral vertebrae), and a coccyx (composed of 4 fused coccygeal vertebrae). The vertebrae in each section are numbered starting at the top and are so designated. For example, the first cervical vertebrae is the topmost vertebrae of the cervical region and its designation is abbreviated to C-1. Likewise, if reference is made to the fourth lumbar vertebrae, this might be designated as L-4.

Each vertebra (except the first two cervical) is made up of two parts, a solid segment in the front and a hollow segment or arch in the back, the latter being formed by two pedicles and two laminas. The solid parts of the vertebrae are one beneath the other, and the hollow parts accommodate the spinal cord. Between each vertebra are intervertebral discs of cartilage which act as shock absorbers between the bones and permit the spine to have movement (and sometimes bulge out as disc herniations).

The Thoracic Cage. The chest, or thorax, includes the ribs, the 12 thoracic vertebrae, and the sternum. These bones form a sort of cage which protects the thoracic organs, namely the heart and lungs.

The sternum (breastbone) is in front and the first seven pairs of ribs are attached to it by cartilages which permit movement and allow the chest to expand in breathing. The upper three pairs of the lower five pairs of ribs are connected to the cartilages, but the lower two pairs are not attached at all in the front, and are therefore called "floating" ribs. All 12 pairs of ribs are attached to the spine in the back.

Clavicle and Scapula. The upper arms are joined to the body by the shoulders. Each shoulder is formed by two bones, the clavicle, or collarbone, in front, and the scapula, or shoulder blade, in the back. The inner end of each clavicle is attached to the sternum, and the outer end attaches to the scapula.

Pelvis. The pelvis is composed of the right and left hip bones, the sacrum, and the coccyx. It protects lower abdominal organs while also serving for the attachment of the legs. In women the pelvis is lighter and wider than in men.

Upper Extremities. These consist of the arm, forearm, and hand. The arm contains one bone, the humerus. The forearm is formed by two bones, the radius and ulna. The ulna is longer than the radius, and it forms part of the elbow joint.

The hand is made up of the carpal bones (wristbones), metacarpals (hand bones), and phalanges (fingers). There are eight carpal bones arranged in two rows of four each. There are five metacarpals, which form the framework of the hand from the wrist to the fingers. There are three bones per finger, designated as proximal (closest to the hand), middle, and distal (farthest from the hand).

Lower Extremities. The thigh, leg, and foot comprise the lower extremities. The upper leg (thigh) has one bone, the femur. The lower leg is formed by the tibia and fibula. The tibia is the larger of the two and is also known as the shin bone. (Note the similarity between the bony structure of the arm and the leg.)

The foot, like the hand, has three parts: the tarsus, metatarsus, and the phalanges. There are seven tarsal bones, which include the calcaneus or heel bone. There are five metatarsal bones. As in the fingers, the toe bones are called phalanges (singular is phalanx), each with three separate bones.

The patella (kneecap) is part of the knee.

Joints. A joint is formed by the articulation or junction of two or more bones. The joint is made up of smooth surfaces, one at the end of each bone, lined with a thin layer of cartilage and covered by a layer of cells which supply lubricating fluid so as to prevent friction.

Overlying some joints are small enclosed pads called bursae, containing fluid to reduce friction over the joint. These include the olecranon bursa (elbow), subdeltoid (shoulder), and prepatella (knee).

Ligaments are bands of flexible connective tissue which bind the articular surfaces of the bones together, forming a joint.

The Muscular System. Beneath the skin are muscles, masses of tissue which have specific anatomical functions. These are contractile organs affecting the movements of various organs and parts of the body. Mechanically, the muscles operate by contracting and relaxing. The muscles moving the arms, legs, and other bones of the body are attached to the bones by tendons and bring about motion by pulling the bone into a new position. Other muscles provide for the movements of the internal organs. These are the heart muscle, muscles in the walls of the digestive tract, and those in the walls of various tubular structures such as blood vessels, glandular ducts, bronchi, and the ureter. These muscles influence the flow of blood into an organ, the flow of air into the lungs, and the passage of food through the alimentary canal. Muscles are controlled by the central nervous system, which is composed of the brain and its intercommunicating mechanism, the spinal cord. Muscle movements are of two kinds: voluntary (striated muscle), subject to the will of the brain, and involuntary (unstraited), not subject to the will of the brain, such as the beating of the heart muscle.

The Nervous System. The nervous system is an extensive network of specialized cells which conduct information via impulses to control, coordinate, and regulate the function of the body. It is divided into the central nervous system (brain, brainstem, cerebellum, and spinal cord) and the peripheral nervous system (12 pairs of cranial nerves and 31 pairs of spinal nerves). The peripheral nerves transmit sensory (or afferent) impulses from the body to the central nervous system and motor (or efferent) impulses from the central nervous system to the muscles, organs, and blood vessels of the body.

The spinal cord, contained in the bony arches of the spinal vertebrae, is the connecting link between the brain and the various parts of the body, functioning not unlike an electrical wiring system by transmitting the impulses or stimuli which originate in the brain. Any damage to the cord, or interference with the transmission system, which destroys or impairs its communication function will result in partial or complete malfunction of the organs from the point of damage downward. In cases of extreme damage, partial or complete paralysis will result.

The spinal cord connects with the brainstem, which connects with the cerebellum and brain. The brain itself is contained in the cavity of the skull and consists of two hemispheres (right and left) which govern the overall control of the higher functions of the body, such as vision, hearing, thought, speech, memory, and movement. The brain is connected to the cerebellum, which controls voluntary movement, and to the brainstem, which contains three parts: the midbrain (upper), pons (middle), and medulla (lower). The brainstem is an important part of the central nervous system, containing centers for respiration, heart and blood vessel function, and other activities. It also serves as the pathway for impulses entering or leaving the brain. Injury to the brainstem is often fatal. Most of the major pathways from the brain to the spinal cord cross at the level of the brainstem so that, in general, the left hemisphere controls the right side of the body and the right hemisphere the left. Any damage to the left hemisphere might produce impairment or paralysis of the right side of the body.

Circulatory System. Oxygen (absorbed from the lungs into the bloodstream) and nutrients (absorbed from digested food in the intestines into the bloodstream) must be conveyed and deposited into cells all over the body. In return, waste products of the cells must be collected and disposed of through the lungs and kidneys. This is accomplished by various parts of the circulatory system, which is a sealed system of tubes (blood vessels) with a pump (the heart). Leading from the heart are large blood vessels, called arteries, which progressively subdivide into smaller and smaller vessels. The smallest of these vessels, almost microscopic in size, are called capillaries. These unite with each other, forming larger and larger vessels, and the largest vessels resulting from this union are the veins, which lead back to the heart.

The heart is continually pumping blood around this circuit, arteries to capillaries to veins and back to the heart. The capillaries form an extensive meshwork, surrounding all organs and throughout all the tissues in the body. A watery solution containing oxygen and nutrients leaks out of these capillary walls into the surrounding tissues, feeding the cells. Some of this fluid returns directly to the blood back through the capillary walls, and the excess filters into small tubes called the lymph vessels. These merge with one another, creating larger and larger vessels, and the largest empty into the veins. This lymphatic system acts as the sewer system of the body, collecting all the fluid and debris from the tissues in the body and draining it into the veins. It is regarded as an accessory part of the circulatory system.

One means of determining whether the circulatory system is functioning normally is by a measurement of the blood pressure. Blood pressure refers to the pressure exerted in the arterial system and is measured in millimeters by a column of mercury. Systolic pressure is the top limit reached at the end of the contraction of the heart. Diastolic pressure is the lowest pressure in the arteries when the chambers of the heart are dilated and the heart between beats or contractions (in diastole) and filling with blood. In recording pressure two figures thus are given, the first or upper figure being the systolic pressure and the second or lower representing diastolic pressure. Normal blood pressure is approximately 120 over 80. Normal heart beat rate (number of contractions) for adults is between 60 and 100 beats per minute. An abnormally rapid heart rate (over 100 per minute) is tachycardia, and abnormally low (less than 60 beats per minute) is bradycardia. A child's heart rate is normally faster than an adult's.

1108 Fractures

Some of the most frequent injuries with which claim representatives are confronted are fractures of bones. A fracture is defined as a break in the normal continuity of the bone. Fractures are classified as follows:

1. Open/closed fracture
   a) open (also known as "compound")—where at least one piece of the bone has pierced the skin
   b) closed—a bone break in which skin is intact
2. Nature of primary fracture line
   a) transverse (horizontal break line)
   b) oblique (diagonal break line)
   c) spiral (unusual twisting break line)

3. Location of fracture
   a) intra-articular (within a joint)
   b) diaphysis (shaft of the bone)
   c) epiphysis (end of the bone)
   d) metaphysis (growth zone between epiphysis and diaphysis during development of bone)
4. Bone involved (e.g., femur)
5. Comminution (fragmentation)
   a) noncomminuted (no fragments)
   b) comminuted—mild/moderate/severe
6. Displacement (out of place; at least one piece of the bone has moved to one side or another)
7. Angulation (angled out of place; at least one piece of the bone has been forced into an abnormal angle)

For example, a fracture might be classified as follows: ''Closed transverse fracture of mid-diaphysis of femur, which is noncomminuted, displaced, and angulated.''

Some other common terms relating to fractures are:

- ***Compression.*** One in which two opposite surfaces of the bone are driven together, usually found in fractures of the vertebrae of the spine.
- ***Contra-coup.*** A fracture of the skull caused by trauma with a break at a point distant from, and usually opposite, the point of trauma.
- ***Greenstick.*** An incomplete fracture of a long bone, seen in children. The bone is bent, but splintered only on the outer arc of the bend. Often heals quickly.
- ***Colles fracture.*** A fracture of the distal end of the radius, characterized by dorsal displacement of the distal fragment and radial and dorsal deviation of the wrist and hand.
- ***Depressed.*** A fracture of the skull in which the fractured part is depressed below the normal level.
- ***Impacted.*** A break in which one fragmented end wedges into the other fragmented end.
- ***Stress.*** A fracture that results from excessive physical activity, not from a specific injury. Often in metatarsals of runners. Also called ''fatigue'' fracture.
- ***Incomplete.*** A fracture which does not extend through the width of the entire bone.
- ***Multiple.*** Two or more fractures occurring in the same or different bones.
- ***Pathologic.*** One which occurs at the site of a local disease in a bone (such as carcinoma) without external violence.
- ***Sprain fracture.*** A sprain (which means tear or partial tear of ligament), usually of the ankle joint, complicated by a fracture or chipping of the bone.
- ***Stellate.*** One in which there are numerous fissures radiating from the central point of injury (''starlike'').

Incidentally, a bone within a joint may break, but when a joint is disrupted, it is called a dislocation (joint moves completely out of place with loss of normal articular surface contact) or a subluxation (if joint is only partially dislocated). Dislocations are further classified as: (1) open/closed (same as fracture description), and (2) direction of dislocation (described by where distal bone ends relative to proximal bone).

Treatment of Fractures. The correction of a fracture consists of replacing the bones in their normal positions and keeping them in that position, without any movement, until healing takes place. The correction of the position of the bones is called a reduction of the fracture. This can be accomplished by a closed reduction, which means that the bones are placed in position by manipulation. An open reduction is a surgical procedure whereby the fracture site is exposed by incision and the bone fragments are manually placed into position. Frequently, these fragments cannot be held in position without the use of surgical nails, plates, or screws, which are inserted.

Most fractures can be immobilized by the application of a plaster cast or by strapping with adhesive tape. More serious fractures may require the application of traction, which keeps the bones in place by the use of weights and pulleys.

The first stage in healing (or "union") of a fracture is one of blood clot formation between the bone ends. The next stage is the formation of fibrous tissues at the fracture site. Bone-forming cells next make their appearance and these convert the fibrous tissue into bone. This new bone at the fracture site is referred to as callus. This callus bridges the fracture completely. Where there is an inadequate callus formation, the condition is referred to as a "nonunion" or ununited fracture. Treatment of this complication might consist of grafting bone to the fracture site for the stimulation of bone growth.

Ordinarily fractures of the shaft of the long bones are not serious and seldom result in any permanency—except fractures of the shaft of the bones of the leg, femur, tibia, and fibula where there is a complete fracture with the fragments overriding each other. Such fractures can result in a bone loss and a consequent shortening of the leg. Fractures of the bones in a joint cause some restriction of motion in the joint and require treatment to restore normal motion. The result depends on the nature of the fracture and the age of the patient. In older persons, full restoration of normal motion is the exception rather than the rule, and in most cases there is a residual restriction which is permanent.

1109 Head Injuries

The head is a complex mechanism. The bony structure consists of two parts, the braincase or cranium, and the face, with upper (maxilla) and lower (mandible) jaws. The head houses the ends of the three main conduits of the body: the digestive tract, the respiratory tract, and the neural tract. The digestive tract begins as the mouth into which food is first introduced, masticated, and swallowed through the throat (oropharynx and laryngopharynx) into the esophagus and then to the stomach and on through the intestines. The respiratory tract begins with a breath of air through the nose into the nasopharynx, then down through the throat and into the trachea, through the bronchi of the lungs and their smaller divisions, down into the airsacs of the lungs (alveoli). The neural tract begins as the brain, which creates impulses that are transmitted to the rest of the body through the brainstem and the spinal cord. These impulses activate the muscles. The brain also has special senses—seeing, hearing, and smelling. The brainstem controls the involuntary muscular movements of some parts of the body, such as the beating of the heart and respiration.

Injuries in which there is a direct blow or trauma to the head may be trivial or serious, usually depending upon whether the brain is affected or not. In all cases a detailed investigation of the medical history of the claimant is essential, together with a description of the cuts, bruises, or swellings of the head which followed the trauma, and mention of any bleeding from the ears, nose, or mouth. These latter signs are usually symptomatic of a possible skull fracture. A period of unconsciousness following the injury is usually indicative of a brain concussion, a violent shaking or jarring of the brain. If the period is of short duration, then the damage to the brain may be inconsequential. Unconsciousness over a long period of time is indicative of a more serious condition, such as a severe contusion of the brain (bruise caused by violent trauma to the brain), or an epidural hemorrhage (bleeding of an artery to the brain, usually the middle meningeal), which often coincides with skull fractures and is rapidly fatal, or a subdural hemorrhage (more progressive loss of blood, usually from tearing of the bridging veins of the brain) which also is fatal unless corrected but may cause unconsciousness from within hours (sub-acute) to as late as months post trauma (chronic).

With a contusion or bruise, while there is no tearing (or laceration) of brain tissue, an area of clotted blood *does* collect. This portion of the brain swells and in some cases its function is impaired to the extent that it loses control over parts of the body. An impairment or paralysis of the vocal chords, vision, or movements is an indication of this brain condition. The swelling will usually subside in about six to eight weeks, and the claimant may gradually return to normal. If after this period of time, there is no improvement, then it can be concluded that the claimant has sustained more than a mere contusion and the condition may be due to a massive hemorrhage (bleeding) or a laceration of the brain, which generally requires surgery; these conditions can produce some permanent impairment of speech, vision, or movement.

Where it is alleged that the claimant has sustained a contusion of the brain or a shaking up of that organ producing some concussion—whether the claimant was unconscious or not—claims are frequently made for some residual condition called a postconcussion syndrome. This term merely describes a group of symptoms following a concussion or contusion of the brain. They are subjective complaints and consist of headaches and dizziness. Since there is no method whereby the existence of these conditions can be verified, the complaints are easy to claim and can be simulated.

It is sometimes claimed that an injury to the head either caused or produced epilepsy, a seizure disorder, defined as two or more unprovoked seizures (i.e., not related to specific events, such as metabolic changes, infection, fever, or trauma). Therefore, it seems appropriate to consider the condition in some detail. Epilepsy is a symptom and not a disease, just as headache, fever, chills, or dizziness are symptoms. The condition is regarded as idiopathic, or of unknown origin. Where there is a definite cause, the condition is diagnosed not as epilepsy but by the actual terms, a depressed fracture of the skull, alcoholic epilepsy, etc.

The mechanics of epilepsy consist of uncontrolled electrical discharges from nerve cells in the brain. For some unknown reason, the brain suddenly transmits maximum impulses to all parts of the body under its control, resulting in confusion not only to the motor mechanism but also to the sensory and mental centers. These recurrent episodes of convulsive seizures, impaired consciousness, abnormal behavior, and other disturbances range from several times a day to once in several years. Epilepsy is classified by the extent of the symptoms produced by these disturbances—(1) partial seizures and (2) generalized seizures.

1. *Partial seizures* have a specific onset in a certain area of the brain and may either remain confined to that area or may secondarily generalize—spread to the entire brain. They are further classified according to impairment of consciousness.

2. *Generalized seizures* have no apparent specific onset and simultaneously involve all or large parts of both cerebral hemispheres from the beginning. They are further classified according to presence or absence of particular convulsive movements.

The distinction between partial and generalized seizures is important because partial seizures are more likely to be due to a specific brain defect, such as an area of maldevelopment, an old scar, a tumor, or a vascular malformation. Thus, if identified, this defect possibly could be removed. Also, partial seizures and generalized seizures usually respond best to different medications.

The authorities seem to agree that trauma or a brain concussion from blows on the head rarely leads to epilepsy. The mechanical situation is that the brain itself must be seriously affected, and anything short of a brain laceration, produced by a fracture of the skull in which a bone fragment pierces the brain, or comparable injury, will not produce the classic symptoms of epilepsy.

1110 Spinal or Back Injuries

Fractures of the vertebrae of the spine can be serious or trivial, depending upon the portion of the bone affected. If the fracture involves one of the bony parts that protrude off the main vertebral body, such as the spinous process, a transverse process, or pedicle, it is generally not serious and usually will involve only the bone and the muscular attachments. A fracture of the neural arch or the vertebral body is usually serious, since damage to the spinal cord may follow such a fracture with subsequent impairment or paralysis of the body below that point. Impacted fractures of the vertebrae, where one vertebra is crushed against another, may have some effect on weight bearing, but usually no neurological sequelae.

Strain of the muscles of the sacroiliac region (referring to the area of the sacrum and the ilium, or hip bone), or a strain of the muscles of the sacroiliac joint, is also known as lower back strain and is quite common, especially in workers' compensation cases. It usually comes about as a consequence of lifting heavy weights. The period of disability following such an injury differs in severity according to the individual's age and muscular structure.

A subluxation is an incomplete dislocation or sprain of a joint; when vertebrae are out of alignment as a result of injury, this term is used.

Treatment of mild fractures and strains of the back consists of immobilization by means of bed rest. In more serious fractures, application of strapping (adhesive tape), plaster cast, or traction usually does the trick. Occasional severe fractures may require surgical correction.

1111 Traumatic Neurosis

This covers a situation where, as the result of trauma, it is claimed the individual has undergone mental and emotional conflicts which cannot be faced. Usually these conflicts are apprehensive in form with the claimant developing an unreasonable fear of the thing that caused the accident, such as an automobile or a machine used on the job. Another type is schizophrenia usually referred to as a change of personality. Actually, it is a psychosis characterized by a disorder in the thinking process with varied symptoms such as hallucinations, delusions, rambling speech, and unpredictable behavior, and it sometimes terminates in mental regression and total withdrawal from reality.

Many individuals are predisposed to these neuroses by their environment and mental makeup, but an accident may be a precipitating cause. If the accident aggravated the condition, this would make the insured liable for the entire condition. When claims of this type arise, a psychiatrist should be consulted and should examine the case for the claim representative at the earliest possible moment.

1112 Disc Injuries

Claims of this type are frequent. They involve a claim that the intervertebral disc (the cushioning tissues between the vertebrae) was injured in such a way as to rupture or herniate the disc outward. The most common cause is lifting heavy objects. Other causes include a sudden twisting of the back (see "whiplash," below). When this condition is diagnosed (generally by an MRI), physical therapy may help most patients, but, for many, surgery may be required.

1113 Whiplash

Often claims will be made for whiplash injury to the spine. The claim, usually arising from rear-end-collision cases, is that the force or impact caused the person's spine to go through a forward and backward motion similar to the cracking of a whip. Patently, this is not a diagnosis of the injury but more a description of how the injury was acquired. The result might be a ruptured disc, contusion of the cord, strain of the muscles, or a fracture of the vertebrae. When faced with claims of this sort, the claim representative should insist on a specific diagnosis.

1114 Hernia

A hernia is a protrusion of any structure through the muscle or tissues normally surrounding it. It commonly refers to a protrusion of the bowel through various points of weakness in the abdominal wall. Strictly speaking, there are other types of hernia, as well. The condition, normally congenital, is most frequently encountered in workers' compensation cases. The claim is one of aggravation of a preexisting condition. There are four common types of hernia: (1) is inguinal, in the groin, and either direct or indirect (herniation of the bowel through the abdominal wall of the inguinal ring of the groin). Even more common herniae types are the (2) umbilical (herniation of the bowel through the navel); (3) ventral (herniation through the forward wall of the abdomen); and (4) femoral (herniation in the region of the thigh where the femoral artery passes through a ring); protrusion may occur through this ring, and the lump will appear on the inner side of the thigh.

Strangulation occurs when the herniated organ (i.e., usually the bowel) is so pinched that it cannot function properly and may infarct, or die, from lack of blood suply. This condition usually requires immediate surgery. The inner surface of the abdomen is covered by a thin structure called the peritoneum. When an organ herniates or protrudes, it carries with it a portion of this peritoneum, which forms a sac. Old sacs are thicker than new ones, and a careful examination of the sac at the time of operation may permit the surgeon to estimate the age of the condition. Therefore, in compensation cases where the sole issue is causal relationship, the earlier the surgery is performed, the more accurate this estimate will be.

1115 Arthritis

This disease causes inflammation of a joint, which often produces redness, swelling, and pain at the site. There are several types of arthritis, but the most frequently encountered in claim work is osteoarthritis (degenerative, hypertrophic). Its cause is unknown, and it occurs most often in the elderly, characterized by degenerative changes in the joints. Osteoarthritis is sometimes aggravated by stress, and when the arthritic individual is subject to severe strain or trauma, recovery will be much less rapid. Treatment includes rest, heat, NSAIDs (non-steroidal anti-inflammatory drugs such as aspirin or ibuprofin which reduce pain and inflammation), and, if necessary, surgical replacement of a badly damaged joint.

Another type, rheumatoid (proliferative, atrophic) arthritis, is a destructive disease that characteristically begins in middle age, mostly in women. It is marked by periods of remission and exacerbation of the inflammation.

Another type is gout or gouty arthritis, a systemic disease secondary to improper metabolism of uric acid, causing uric acid to accumulate in the blood and joints, which causes pain and swelling (often in the big toe).

A final type is infectious arthritis, caused by bacterial or viral seeding of a joint. Common organisms include gonococcus, staphylococcus, streptococcus, or rubivirus (rubella).

1116 Inflammatory Diseases

Inflammation is the response of the tissues of the body to irritation or injury, characterized by pain, swelling, redness, and heat. The severity, particular characteristics, and duration of the inflammation depend on the cause, the area of the body affected, and the health of the person. The following diseases of inflammation are frequently met in claim work.

Neuritis. Inflammation of the nerve producing pain, loss of sensation, defective reflexes, and muscular atrophy (wasting of the muscles). It can result from many causes, sometimes toxic in origin, and can be considered occupational only in instances where the claimant is exposed to toxic substances. It is not the result of trauma.

Myotitis. Inflammation of a muscle or groups of muscles, most often caused by infection, parasite infestation, trauma, or degenerative muscle diseases.

Tenosynovitis and tendinitis. Inflammation of the tendon or tendon sheath. These conditions can result from strain, injury, or certain systemic conditions (i.e., gout, rheumatoid arthritis, or gonorrhea).

Bursitis. Inflammation of a bursa, which is a fluid-filled, membrane-lined sac, usually in the vicinity of joints, that lies between various structures (including tendon and bone, tendon and ligament, or other structures), serving to reduce friction, lubricate and protect these structures. It can arise by reason of direct trauma, infection, overuse, or arthritis, and is characterized by pain and limited mobility. The most common types involve the subdeltoid (shoulder), olecranon (elbow), and the prepatella (knee). Prepatella bursitis is popularly referred to as "housemaid's knee."

Osteomyelitis. An infectious inflammatory process of the bone and bone marrow. It may occur spontaneously, but it is most frequently encountered in a direct infection, in which bacteria are introduced into the bone by trauma or surgery, as in compound fractures.

Periostitis. Inflammation of the bone covering (periosteum) is usually due to infection. There is a noninfectuous type, however, in which direct trauma may activate a reaction of the periosteal tissues.

Phlebitis. Inflammation of the wall of a vein, most often occurring in the legs. Thrombosis, or blood clot, commonly develops in conjunction with phlebitis and is called thrombophlebitis. It occurs secondary to prolonged bedrest, pregnancy, surgery, and other conditions in which blood flow becomes sluggish or the blood coagulates (clots) more quickly than normal. It may also occur secondary to trauma or irritation of the vessel and infection.

Cellulitis. Infection by bacteria and a subsequent inflammation of the subcutaneous tissue below the skin. The port of entry of the bacteria is a break in the skin surface.

Lymphangitis. Inflammation of lymph channels secondary to a localized bacterial infection.

Lymphadenitis. Inflammation of the lymph nodes, secondary to local infection.

1117 Common Injuries

The following is a short list of common injury terms frequently encountered by the claim representative:

Abrasions, scratches; ***Contusions,*** bruises; ***Incisions,*** cuts of the skin; ***Lacerations,*** tears of the skin; ***Sprains,*** injuries to ligaments around a joint; ***Strains,*** muscle injuries from overuse; ***Burns*** (there are three degrees based on tissue changes—first degree, reddening and pain; second degree, blistering; and third degree, destruction of tissue); ***Dislocation,*** out of joint; and ***Amputations,*** removals.

1118 Lengths of Disability

The following is a short list of typical disability periods for common injuries:

Skull (uncomplicated fracture)	4–8 weeks
Cervical spine (fracture or dislocation)	4–6 months
Dorsal spine (compression fracture)	3–5 months
Fractures (uncomplicated):	
Clavicle (collarbone)	10–12 weeks
Humerus (upper arm)	3–4 months

Elbow	6–10 months
Head of radius (forearm)	3–5 months
Colles	3–5 months
Olecranon (elbow)	3–5 months
Forearm (one bone)	3–5 months
(both bones)	6–10 months
Carpal (wrist)	3–6 months
Metacarpal (hand)	6–10 weeks
Finger	6–10 weeks
Toe	8–12 weeks
Calcaneous (heel)	4–6 months
Hernia	6–8 weeks (following surgery)
Ruptured disc	4–6 months
Amputations:	
Finger	6–8 weeks
Major amputations (arm or leg)	4–6 months
Stump revision	3–6 weeks

1119 The Eye

The eye is the organ of vision. It occupies the anterior part of the orbit and is nearly spherical in shape. It is covered by three concentric coats: (1) the sclera and cornea, (2) the choroid, ciliary body, and iris, and (3) the retina.

The *sclera* is the white portion and outer coat of the eye, except over the colored portion of the eye, which is covered by the cornea. It contains blood vessels and serves for attachment of the muscles which move the eye.

The *choroid* is the second coat. It covers the inner surface of the sclera and its anatomical function is to serve as the principal medium for nourishment of the eyeball. It contains many blood vessels for this purpose.

The *retina* is the innermost coat. It is a light-receptive layer and the terminal expansion of the optic nerve. The structures of the eye permit the passage of light, and the parts of the eye are constructed like a camera in that there is a combination of lenses and accommodating mechanisms to produce a clear image on the retina, which in turn transmits the image through the optic nerve to the sight area of the brain.

The first mechanism to deal with light as it enters the eye is the iris. This is the colored portion of the eyeball, with a hole in the center called the pupil. Its function is similar to that of the lens-opening in a camera in that it regulates the amount of light allowed to enter the eye, prevents the introduction of excess light, and increases vision in darkness by increasing the opening. The second mechanism is the lens which operates exactly as the lens of a camera. It is operated by the tiny ciliary muscles, which are designed so that they can relax the tension that the suspensory ligament holding the lens normally maintains. The ciliary muscles cause the lens to bulge so as to increase magnification. This muscular action permits us to see close objects in more minute detail.

Where there is any interference with the transmission of light through the eye, a distorted image is produced on the retina. Thus, if any of the functions of the iris or the lens are disturbed because of either injury or the aging process, a hazy image will be produced on the retina. If the retina itself becomes detached from the optic nerve completely, then there is no transmission of the image to the brain. Where there is a disturbance in the functions of the auxiliary mechanisms, the lens and the iris, usually these defects can be corrected by wearing glasses.

The claim representative will encounter the word "vision" in many reports. Standing alone, it usually refers to central vision, or the ability of a person to see an object by focusing the eyes directly at it. Peripheral vision refers to side vision, or the sight of other objects in the same field as the object on which the eyes are focusing. Binocular vision refers to the image produced by both eyes working together. Thus if one eye is stronger, or introduces more light than the other, then the image transmitted to the brain by both eyes is distorted. This can be corrected by the use of proper glasses.

Visual acuity is the measurement of the actual vision in each eye, tested separately. The test is made by the use of a chart of letters, called a Snellen chart. A normal person 20 feet from the chart will be able to read the size and type of letters on the chart that one with perfect vision could read. Such vision is expressed as 20/20, meaning that the test was made at 20 feet and that the line read was the one near the bottom of the chart, the "20" line. Let us assume that the person could not read the bottom line but could read a line farther up which a normal person could read while sitting 30 feet away. The visual acuity then would be expressed as 20/30, meaning that the patient, sitting 20 feet from the chart, could read only the line that a normal person could read at 30 feet. This same type of measurement applies to other results from the use of the chart. Thus, if the visual acuity is said to be 20/200, this means that the patient, sitting 20 feet from the chart, could read only the line which a normal person could read at 200 feet. Eye reports also use abbreviations to designate the eye involved. OD or O-D refers to the right eye; OS or O-S means the left eye.

1120 The Heart

The heart is a pear-shaped muscular organ situated between the lungs and protected by the sternum (breastbone) and the ribs in front, and the fifth, sixth, seventh, and eighth thoracic vertebrae in the back. Its function is to act as a pump for the blood, circulating it through the lungs and to all parts of the body.

Internally, it is composed of four chambers, the right atrium and right ventricle on one side, and the left atrium and left ventricle on the other. The two sides of the heart are completely separated from each other. The function of the right atrium and right ventricle is to receive deoxygenated blood from all parts of the body, with the exception of the lungs, and to pump it through the pulmonary artery into the lungs to pick up oxygen. The blood is received in the right atrium through two large veins called the superior and inferior vena cavae. When the right atrium, which occupies the upper right quarter of the heart, becomes filled, it contracts and forces the blood into the right ventricle below.

To prevent the return of the blood into the right atrium, a heart valve, called the tricuspid, closes when the ventricle contracts. The ventricle then contracts, forcing the blood into the pulmonary artery. When the ventricle is completely empty, the pulmonary valve at the exit closes, preventing the return of the blood to the heart. The blood is then passed through the lungs where it discharges waste products in the form of carbon dioxide and picks up oxygen. The blood then is returned to the left atrium by four large pulmonary veins and forced into the left ventricle. The mitral valve lies between the left atrium and left ventricle and prevents backflow into the atrium. The left ventricle then contracts and pumps blood into the aorta. The aortic valve prevents backflow into the ventricle. The blood then is circulated throughout the body where it deposits the oxygen and picks up waste. It then returns to the right atrium of the heart via the superior and inferior cavae, and the cycle begins again.

The heart is enclosed in a sac, called the pericardium. Its inner layer is adherent to the outside of the heart, and it contains a fluid which acts as a lubricant which permits the heart to contract freely. An inflammation of the pericardium caused by infection or disease is called pericarditis.

The membrane which lines the heart chambers and heart valves is called the endocardium. It is a very thin layer of cells similar to the inner layer of other blood vessels, such as arteries and veins. Inflammation of the endocardium is called endocarditis, which is due almost entirely to infectious bacteria.

The heart muscle is called the myocardium. It differs from other muscles of the body in that it requires little or no activation from the brain, originating its contractions within itself. It does, however, respond to stimuli from other parts of the body, such as increased rate of contraction due to exercise, the need for increased blood supply after eating, or a condition such as a tumor or disease requiring increased blood supply. Because of the automatic action of the heart muscle, an injury to the brain or any part of the central nervous system seldom produces any heart condition. The heart muscle can be inflamed, usually due to an infection, such as rheumatic fever, or as a complication of another disease. This inflammation is called myocarditis.

Usually, the heart cannot be injured by accident, except in cases where there is a penetrating wound into the heart itself. It is possible to aggravate a previously diseased heart in cases where the accident produces a strain on the circulatory system or where an infection produces microorganisms which gain entrance to the bloodstream.

Some useful terms are set forth below:

1. Myocardial Infarction (MI). This is a heart attack, in which an area of heart muscle dies because of interrupted blood supply to the muscle from the coronary arteries. The arteries will have been previously narrowed by atherosclerosis (high cholesterol causes plaque build-up in artery walls, narrowing the arteries). Finally, a thrombus (blood clot) lodges in the narrowed artery, causing a complete occlusion to the artery—and death to the area of heart muscle that it serves. Typical symptoms include: crushing pain to the chest (angina) that may radiate to the arm (especially the left arm), neck, or jaw; shortness of breath; faintness; anxiety; ashen or sweaty appearance; and heart rhythm irregularities.

2. Valve Defects. When there is a defect in the valves of the heart, the blood will leak backward through the defective valve and the result might be that there is insufficient blood supply for the body's needs. Nature seeks to compensate for defects of this sort, and the heart muscle and the heart will increase in size in order to pump enough blood for the bodily needs. If the heart can continue the normal blood supply through this means, the individual is said to have a compensated heart. However, if the defect is so serious that the heart in spite of the increase in size cannot fully supply the need for blood, the patient is said to have a decompensated heart. The individual may suffer from shortness of breath upon exertion, and there may be a bluish tinge to the skin or mucous membranes from poor oxygenation of blood secondary to decreased cardiac flow through the lungs. Seldom will an injury aggravate a decompensated heart, because even a strain on circulation rarely produces any further damage to the heart, if it is of short duration.

3. Heart Failure. Inabilty of the hcart to pump enough blood to maintain normal body requirements. It can be caused by many congenital defects and many other conditions (valve defects or MI discussed previously) that overload or damage the heart muscle. Symptoms include edema (collection of fluid in the body due to poor circulation), shortness of breath, and faintness.

1121 The Blood

The majority of the cells of the body have no means of nourishment from the outside and are supplied with food solely by the blood. Also these cells have no means of distributing their own products (hormones), if any, nor a means of disposing of waste, usually in the form of carbon dioxide. The circulating blood is utilized for these purposes. It follows that, where the blood is incapable of reaching a cell because of some breakdown in the arterial system due to injury, chronic disease, or infection, the cell will die. If there is prolonged interruption of blood flow, major tissue death will occur, which is known as necrosis or gangrene. The blood itself is a watery fluid which contains many cells. These cells are distinguished as red blood cells, called erythrocytes, and white blood cells, called leukocytes. These cells and some cell fragments called platelets are referred to as formed elements and are suspended in plasma, the liquid portion of blood (made up of water and nutrients).

Red Blood Cells. The majority of the formed elements of the blood are the red blood cells, or erythrocytes. In one cubic milliliter of blood there are about 5 million red blood cells. The principal function of the red blood cell is to act as a carrier of oxygen and to assist in carrying carbon dioxide. In this task the cell utilizes one of its important chemical elements, the red pigment called hemoglobin, which combines with the oxygen and acts as its carrier in the red blood cell. Arterial blood is bright red whereas venous blood is dark red. This is because arterial blood contains oxygen, and the hemoglobin, combined with the oxygen, produces the bright red color, whereas hemoglobin without oxygen shows up as a dark red.

A red blood cell lives for about 120 days, but since the count remains constant it is clear that there is a continual process of replacement. New red blood cells are produced primarily by the bone marrow. When there is a marked reduction in the number of red blood cells, due to injury, loss of blood, or a failure on the part of the body to manufacture sufficient replacements, the person is suffering from anemia. Decreased red blood count means there is a decreased amount of hemoglobin, which means there is a lack of oxygen in the blood, that the cells of the body do not receive the oxygen needed, and thus there is a decrease in bodily efficiency.

White Blood Cells. The white blood cells, or leukocytes, are fewer in number than the red cells; there are about 5,000 to 10,000 white blood cells in one cubic milliliter of blood. The leukocytes are of several varieties and are classified into several subgroups. For our purposes we will make only one division, between mononuclear and polynuclear cells, or leukocytes with one nucleus and those with many nuclei. A condition of the blood where there is a large increase in the number of large mononuclear leukocytes (also called monocytes) is referred to as mononucleosis.

Polynuclear leukocytes have the property of being able to reach sites of infection, whether within the bloodstream or outside. They engulf and digest infectious organisms and injured or dead tissue cells. Many of them are destroyed in this process and the destroyed leukocytes and the debris of dead cells constitute pus, which is characteristic of infection.

Plasma. The liquid portion of the blood is the plasma, constituting about 55 percent of the whole blood. Plasma is composed mainly of water in which are dissolved hormones of the endocrine glands and nutrients needed for the maintenance of the cells. The plasma also picks up the waste products of the cells for elimination through the kidneys and lungs.

Coagulation of the Blood. All of us who have had a laceration of the skin are familiar with the process by which a scab is formed at the site of the wound in which liquid blood is changed into a semisolid mass, a blood clot. Platelets clump at the wound site, and chemical changes in the blood cause fibrinogen, a substance in the blood, to change from a liquid state to a solid state (known as fibrin). A meshwork of fibrin is formed and traps blood cells into a red, jellylike mass, which is recognized as a clot. As the clot shrinks and dries, a yellow liquid collects above it and is pressed out. This is called serum.

Thrombosis and Embolism. Blood does not usually clot within the body, but sometimes the wall of a blood vessel becomes weakened, due to injury or some systemic condition such as atherosclerosis, and clots form at the site of the lesion. This is a protective mechanism of the body, since the formation of clots might prevent further damage to the wall of the vessel or prevent the rupture of the wall and an ensuing escape of blood into the area, which is called a hemorrhage. Such a clot is called a thrombus. When it increases in size, so as to interfere with the normal flow of blood within the vessel, or to plug up the vessel completely, the condition is thrombosis. The complete plugging up of the blood vessel is referred to as an occlusion of the blood vessel. Sometimes a clot breaks away and is carried by the blood throughout the body until it reaches a smaller vessel through which it cannot pass. It then sets up an occlusion, or plugging of that vessel. Any foreign substance in the bloodstream, whether it is a clot as described, or a mass of bacteria, or an air bubble or oil globule, is called an embolus. Particularly urgent and of high mortality rate is a pulmonary embolus, in which an embolus blocks off the pulmonary vasculature, and thus blocks oxygen uptake from the lungs into the blood.

The cells that do not receive oxygen and nutrients because of complete cessation of the blood flow, die, and the area of dead cells so produced is referred to as an infarct. Such an occlusion in an artery to the brain results in a brain infarct or stroke (also called cerebrovascular accident or CVA) and, in an artery supplying the heart, results in a heart attack (also known as myocardial infarct or MI). In some cases, an embolus plugs up a small artery or capillary, and the blood pressure that builds up behind it may reach a point where it ruptures the wall of the blood vessel, causing a hemorrhage or flooding of the areas. This hemorrhage can be extremely serious and can cause death. Such a hemorrhage in the brain is a second way a stroke may occur. Other areas where hemorrhage can occur include the heart and lungs.

A stroke (by either occlusion or hemorrhage) results in impaired functioning of the affected area of the brain. If the area controls the patient's vocal cords, speech will be affected by a paralysis of those cords. If the area controls muscular movements of one side of the body, we can expect to find a paralysis of the muscles of that side as a result. Should the blood be absorbed and the area of the brain return to something approaching normal function, the paralysis will subside proportionately to the healing in the brain. If the stroke resulted from occlusion rather than hemorrhage, that part of the brain is dead, and little or no improvement will occur. In any case, the outward manifestation will be indicative of the condition which has arisen within the brain.

Any of these conditions can come about as a result of a chronic condition as well as traumatic injury. Where an injury is alleged, it becomes important to establish when, for the first time after the injury, the first manifestation of the condition appeared. The general rule is that the longer the interval of time between the injury and the onset of the first symptoms, the less evidence there is that the injury was the precipitating cause.

1122 Blood Grouping and Transfusions

Examination and analysis of blood revealed that red blood cells contain subtances called antigens (i.e., specific markers)—some major and some minor. The major antigens are A and B. All humans contain one or both or neither antigen (O) and inherit one antigen from each parent. Thus, people are typed as A (either AA or AO), B (BB or BO), AB (both antigens present, AB), or O (neither antigen present, OO). The most widely known minor antigen is the Rh factor and people are known as either positive (Rh factor present, the majority of people) or negative (Rh factor absent)—see below. It was also found that a person having the antigen A on his red blood cells makes an antibody against antigen B (anti-B antibody). Someone with the B antigen has anti-A antibodies. Type O people make anti-A and Anti-B antibodies, and type AB people make no antibodies to the antigens, since their red blood cells contain both antigens.

Therefore, when transfusions are performed it becomes essential that the correct type of blood be infused. As long as the blood is of the same type and is compatible, no serious results can be anticipated. To guard against the possibility of error, hospitals not only type the blood of the patient and that of the donor, but also take a blood sample from each and combine them, noting the reaction, if any, under a microscope. If there is any agglutination (or clumping due to reaction of donor red blood cells to recipient antibodies), then the donor's blood is not used. This is called cross-typing.

Rh Factor. It was found that the foregoing analysis and blood grouping was not entirely sufficient in that there were cases where the proper type blood was transfused but where agglutination took place. It was later discovered that some persons would react to an antibody created in the serum of rabbits injected with the blood of the rhesus monkey. A person who would react to this anti-Rh antibody found in the serum, had an Rh antigen in his red blood cells. An individual whose red blood cells were not agglutinated by the serum did not possess the Rh antigen. The former were classified as Rh positive and the latter as Rh negative. The Rh factor is important in obstetrics because the Rh negative mother may produce anti-Rh antibodies that cross the placenta and attack the blood cells of Rh positive babies (because of the presence of Rh antigens), causing severe, fatal anemia.

1123 Compressed-Air Disease

This disease is found where the patient has been exposed to increased external air pressure. It may develop where the patient is engaged in deep-sea diving, scuba diving, caisson work under pressure, or coffer dam work. It comes about when air bubbles form in the bloodstream following too rapid a reduction in the outside pressure. These air bubbles, or air emboli, cause symptoms of headache, dizziness, fainting spells and, in severe cases, paralysis and death.

1124 Lung Diseases

When discussing lung disease, it is important to note that there are more than 100 causes of diffuse interstitial lung disease. (Interstitium refers to the narrow tissue space between the lung blood vessels and the alveoli—the tiny air-exchanging spaces. This space greatly expands in diseased states.) These diseases can be classified according to eight different categories: infections, neoplastic (cancer), immunologic, cardiovascular, inhalational, embolic, and idiopathic.

With regard to claim practice, inhalational lung disease is probably the most important category. The inhalation of deleterious dust and fiber particles over a period of years can and does produce pneumoconiosis (lung disease caused by chronic inhalation of dust, usually due to occupation). The particles involved are infinitesimal and usually cannot be seen with the naked eye, and are of such size that they are almost weightless (and suspended in the air for certain periods of time). The most common are listed below.

Silicosis. This condition results from the inhalation of silica over a period of years. The condition comes about as a result of mining and drilling of siliceous rock and is usually found in mining operations where the process is conducted in a small space. It is believed that the wearing of respiratory masks and the use of water in the drills (Kelly trap) will reduce the risk. The silica particles lodge in the lungs, resulting in a slowly progressive fibrosis (a restrictive disease) of the lungs. There is no known cure, and silicosis predisposes the person to pulmonary tuberculosis.

Anthracosis. Similar to silicosis, caused by the inhalation of anthracite particles or other particles containing silicon dioxide and carbon. (Also referred to as black lung disease.)

Asbestosis. Caused by the inhalation of asbestos fibers over a long period of time. This condition comes about not only because of the handling or use of asbestos related products, but can also be caused by the inhalation of the fibers in any confined space where friable (crumbling) asbestos is part of the building. The asbestos fibers constitute a carcinogenic (cancer causing) substance where some form of cancer may be the ultimate result, such as mesothelioma, which is the common form found in asbestos workers.

1125 Hematoma

A hematoma is a localized mass of blood which finds its way into a small space in the body and becomes enclosed in a capsule, or encapsulated. It is caused by an injury to a blood vessel wherein blood clots are formed and are discharged into a small space. Hematomas may form on the surface of the skin where they resemble a blister with bloody fluid and are referred to by laymen as "blood blisters." They may also form in the subcutaneous layers of the skin, the belly of a muscle, and in many other spaces within the body. Hematomas represent the most serious condition when they are located either above or within the layers of matter covering the brain and the spinal cord, where they exert pressure. The more severe the pressure, the more serious the condition will be.

The brain and the spinal cord are covered by three membranes, called collectively, the meninges, which constitute three different layers. The outer membrane is the dura mater, usually referred to as the dura. The middle membrane is the arachnoid membrane, and the inner layer is the pia mater. A hematoma which occurs above the dura and exerts its pressure from that point is referred to as an epidural hematoma. One which is formed in the space between the dura and the arachnoid membrane is referred to as a subdural hematoma. Bleeding into the space between the arachnoid and the pia mater does not produce a hematoma but will cause a bloody spinal fluid.

1126 Infection

Infection is the result of the implanting of the seeds of disease in the body. These seeds of disease may be bacterial in origin or may be the result of a fungus or of a virus. The microorganisms, either bacterial, fungal, or viral, gain entry to the body usually through a wound or by ingestion. They settle in a certain place and feed on the surrounding tissue. As they grow they give off certain products which may or may not be poisonous or harmful. White blood cells are the destructive agents of microorganisms. They devour, destroy, and carry them away. The cells utilized for this purpose are called phagocytes, and the process by which they destroy organisms is called phagocytosis. This process is a battle for survival between the phagocytes and the microorganisms, and in many cases the outcome will depend upon numbers. If there are more organisms than the phagocytes can devour and carry away, the outcome of the disease may have serious consequences, even resulting in the death of the patient.

Incubation Period. The incubation period in infection is defined as the period of time within which the first manifestation of the disease becomes apparent after the entry of the infecting agent. The period is usually relatively short, in most cases about 3–5 days, so that if there is a wound which it is claimed was the port of entry of bacteria, the first symptoms of infection should be present within the period mentioned. If the symptoms present themselves at a later time, it is generally agreed that the bacteria did not enter the body at the time of the wound but gained entrance at a later time and perhaps through other means.

1127 Blood Tests for Intoxication

Intoxication is the condition which is produced by the presence of alcohol in the brain. It is characterized by a lack of coordination, a reduction in reflex action, and, in extreme cases, complete insensibility. The extent to which coordination, mental response, and reflex action are impaired will depend upon the quantity of alcohol which reaches the brain: the greater the amount of alcohol, the greater the reaction. Mechanically, what occurs is that ingested alcohol is absorbed by the blood from the stomach. The blood carries it to all parts of the body, including the brain. Since alcohol is a depressant, it reduces the activity of the brain not only as to its control over the motor senses of the body but also with regard to sensory reflexes and mental responses to the stimulation normally produced by apprehension.

Medical Standards. Medically, intoxication is classified by the objective signs which are observable by an examination of the patient's activity. These are:

1. *Acute Intoxication.* This follows the drinking of a considerable amount of liquor at once. Profound insensibility follows rapidly with irregular breathing, purplish face, frothing at the mouth, weak pulse, and increasing coma. While this form is unusual, when it does happen, immediate measures are necessary to save the patient's life.
2. *Subacute Intoxication.* This is the usual drunkenness. It can be mild or of serious nature. The mild form is usually found in persons who merely drink for the exhilaration which alcohol gives them, and who discontinue their drinking before they lose control of their faculties. The serious type refers to persons who drink until they are stupefied.
3. *Mild Intoxication.* This causes some increase in the circulation and stimulates the nervous system. In some cases, it upsets the digestive system.

Legal Standards. All states prohibit the driving of a motor vehicle while "in an intoxicated condition," "in a drunken or partly drunken condition," or "while under the influence of liquor." In considering the problem of law enforcement, the medical profession was called upon to assist in supplying scientific information. Tests indicated that there was very little variation (about 1⁄100th of 1 percent) between the alcohol content of the blood as compared to that of the brain. Therefore, based on the medical findings and its own tests, the National Safety Council promulgated standards of alcohol within the body with recommendations as to the ability to drive. These are based upon the alcohol concentration within the blood and are as follows:

0.05%	Able to drive; should not be prosecuted. (Equivalent of two ounces of whiskey or two bottles of beer.)
0.15 or less	Should not drive.
0.15 or over	Definitely drunk. (Equivalent of 6–7 ounces of whiskey or 6–7 bottles of beer.)
0.2	Dizzy and delirious.
0.3	Dazed and dejected.
0.4	Dead drunk.
0.5	Dead.

These standards have been generally accepted by the courts, and in some states they are part of the motor vehicle statute.

1128 Other Intoxication Tests

Other tests which are utilized for determining intoxication are tests of the urine, spinal fluid, and, if a sufficient sampling can be obtained, the sputum. Since there is a direct relationship between these fluids and the blood, it is claimed that by test and mathematical computation a conclusion as to the alcoholic content of the blood can be drawn.

Air or breath tests are made by the use of one of the various machines designed for that purpose, such as the Breathalyzer. The advantage of these machines is that a properly trained layman can take the sample and make an analysis, whereas in the other tests, including the blood, the sample usually must be taken by a physician and in all cases the analysis must be made by a fully qualified technician.

1129 Intoxication Tests as Evidence

When the result of an intoxication test is offered in evidence, it must be shown that the test was conducted under the above circumstances and within a short period of time after the accident so as to be indicative of the patient's condition at the time of the accident. If the sample is taken by one person and analyzed by another, the evidence must show how the sample was preserved and how it was labeled; any possibility that the sample tested was taken from anyone other than the patient must be excluded. Clearly, unless it can be established with certainty that the sample came from the patient, the patient cannot be bound by the result of the test.

In addition, evidence must exclude the possibility of any change in the patient's condition from the time of the accident to the time of the test. For example, if following the accident the patient was given a shot of whiskey, a test would show the result of all the alcohol consumed, both before and after the accident.

Chapter 12

Damages and Claims Evaluation

LAW OF DAMAGES

1200 Purpose and Scope of Claims Evaluation
1201 Nature of Damages
1202 Single Recovery Principle
1203 Time of Valuation
1204 Duty of the Claimant to Establish Damages
1205 Duty of the Claimant to Mitigate Damages
1206 Effect of a Religious Belief on Mitigation
1207 Collateral Source Rule
1208 Effect of a Preexisting Physical Disability
1209 Loss of Consortium

MEASURE OF DAMAGES

1210 Measure of Damages: Property Damage
1211 Measure of Damages: Personal Injury
1212 Measure of Damages: Permanent Disability
1213 Life Expectancy
1214 Work-Live Expectancy
1215 Present Value of Future Damages

CLAIMS EVALUATION

1216 Personal Injury: Tangible Items
1217 Personal Injury: Intangible Items
1218 Formula Methods of Evaluation
1219 The "Three Times the Medical" Formula
1220 The Unit of Time Formula
1221 Factors Increasing Settlement Valuation
1222 Factors Decreasing Settlement Valuation
1223 Survival Claims
1224 Wrongful Death
1225 Settlement Valuation of Wrongful Death

PUNITIVE DAMAGES

1226 Nature of Punitive Damages
1227 A Current Perspective on Punitive Damages

LAW OF DAMAGES

1200 Purpose and Scope of Claims Evaluation

The purpose of claims evaluation is to determine the company's position and attitude with respect to each individual claim. It consists of an objective appraisal of all of the elements of the claim, an estimate of the maximum dollar value of the company's exposure, a decision whether it would be to the company's advantage to make any payment in settlement and, if so, the maximum settlement amount. Evaluation contemplates a consideration of all of the facets of the claim which have an influence on its value. These include, among other things, the facts and circumstances of the accident, the applicable law, the nature and extent of the injuries, the measure of damages applicable to the claim, the damages claimed, the provable damages (both tangible and intangible items), and the defenses available.

The maximum settlement amount is based on the degree of danger to the company which the claim presents. It represents the amount that the company is willing to pay rather than risk the uncertainties of the trial and the possibility of an adverse verdict. It contemplates the consideration of the estimate of the company's maximum exposure, the possibilities of a plaintiff's verdict, the difficulties which will confront the plaintiff in proving the case, the possibilities of a successful defense, the difficulties (if any) of producing evidence of a defense, and imponderables such as the personalities of the parties and the effect they will have on the jury, and the ability and past performance of the plaintiff's counsel.

Some claim representatives fix the settlement valuation first by calculating the amount (if anything) the company would have to pay if the verdict of the jury was the best possible result obtainable on the basis of the facts of the case and, second by calculating the amount of the verdict on the basis of the worst possible result. An amount between the two extremes would represent the settlement value. Just how near the top figure the settlement value would come would depend upon the degree of the danger posed by the facts of the case. If the danger is minimal, then the settlement figure would approximate the amount of the best possible result, or a little more, whereas, if the danger were great, a higher settlement figure would be required.

No matter what system the claim representative uses in making these estimates, all claim representatives agree that no proper determination of the value of an individual case can be made without considering the case on the basis of its own particular facts. There are some areas which are common to most cases discussed in the succeeding paragraphs. These include the measure of damages, the items considered in settlement valuation, as well as the formula appraisals of value as used by our adversaries.

1201 Nature of Damages

Damages are defined as the monetary compensation which may be recovered by any person who has suffered loss, detriment, or injury, whether to person or property, through the unlawful act or omission or negligence of another. Compensation means that the amounts so awarded are intended to reasonably repay the injured person for the loss suffered and to place that person in the same or an equivalent position to that occupied prior to the event.

The amount to be awarded is a question of fact for the jury to decide. The court will instruct the jury as to the matters which it may take into account in computing the amount of the damages, but the actual amount to be awarded is left to the discretion of the jury. Should the jury fail to follow the court's instructions, or if the amount of the verdict is against the weight of evidence, or if the amount of the verdict is so low or so excessive that it "shocks the conscience of the Court,'' the court may, on its own motion or upon motion made by either party, set the verdict aside, dismiss the claim, or grant a new trial.

Generally, damages for breach of contract involving property rights are not difficult to determine. The jury will be instructed to take into consideration the advantages which would have accrued to the injured party had there been no breach, less the injured party's obligations under the contract. The difference will be the damages. For example, *A* agrees to sell and *B* agrees to buy a certain lot for $5,000. On the due date *A* refuses to sell. *B* can procure a similar lot in the same area for $6,000. *B*'s damage will be $1,000, or the difference between the sale price of the first lot and the price *B* is required to pay for a similar lot. On the same facts, if *B* can obtain a similar lot for $5,000 or less, and has suffered no other loss due to *A*'s breach, then *B* has suffered no damages.

Suppose *A*, a claim representative, makes an agreement with *B* to settle *B*'s claim for $5,000. *A* breaches the contract by refusing payment, after *B* has submitted a release. If *B* elects to sue on the contract, his measure of damages will be the amount which he would have obtained had there been no breach, or $5,000.

In personal injury cases, *compensatory damages* serve the same purpose. Compensatory damages are divided into *special* and *general damages*. Special damages, for the purposes of this discussion, are those specific items represented by actual out-of-pocket expenses, such as past and future loss of salary or other income, past and future medical, surgical, hospital, and nursing services, money expended to minimize the loss, funeral expenses in death cases, and repair bills for damaged property. General damages are those which do not require a specific showing of a monetary loss, but are losses which can be inferred from the evidence of injury. These include, among other things, damages for pain and suffering, loss of use or loss by amputation of a member (hand, arm, leg, eye, etc.), total or partial loss of vision, and the effect of facial or bodily scarring on the injured person's future enjoyment of life, as well as the value of the loss of ability to bear children.

Consideration is given to the position of the injured person prior to the event and his or her condition after the event has occurred. The items of damage will consist of the losses suffered up to the time of trial and, if the effects of the injury are continuing, the losses he or she will suffer in the future. Suppose *A* sustained injuries in an automobile accident caused by the negligence of *B*. *A*'s injuries consist of a strain of the muscles of the cervical region of the neck. *A* is unable to work for two weeks and loses $800 in salary. Medical bills total $750.

To reasonably compensate *A* for her injuries, consideration should be given to the actual out-of-pocket expenses she has incurred. These include her loss of salary and the cost of the medical services, and also such amount as the jury may award for her pain (if there was any), discomfort, and inconvenience. Thus by such an award of damages, *A* is now in a position comparable to that which she occupied prior to the happening of the accident.

The same principles are applicable to property damage cases. For example, *A*'s automobile is damaged by the negligence of *B*. It will cost $1500 to repair the automobile and to restore it to its condition prior to the accident. *A*'s damages are $1500. This payment will compensate *A* for the loss he has suffered. It makes no difference whether *A* uses the money to have the repairs made on his automobile or for any other purpose. *A* is entitled to the money since he has suffered the loss. *B*'s only obligation is the payment of the money. *B* is under no obligation to repair *A*'s automobile or to pay the person who repairs it. *B*'s sole obligation is to pay *A* the money damages, and when that is done *A*'s claim against *B* is extinguished.

1202 Single Recovery Principle

Our common-law system requires a single lump-sum recovery for all damages caused by negligence. This does not present any great problem when all of the items of damage have accrued prior to the trial date. The damages are known and capable of ascertainment and proof. The difficulty arises when the effects of the injury are continuing and some of the damages sought must be based upon a projection of losses to be sustained in the future. The failure of the plaintiff to seek sufficient damages, or the failure of the court to award enough money to take care of future losses will not give rise to a further cause of action to recover the deficiency. On the other hand, if the projection is inaccurate or the injuries prove to be less serious than was believed at the time of trial, there are no means available to the tort-feasor to recover the excess. Once there has been a determination of the amount of recovery, whether adequate or not, it terminates the cause of action, with the exception of the right of either party to appeal within the time limited for such action.

1203 Time of Valuation

The general rule is that the damages sustained by the plaintiff are determined as of the date of the trial. Thus everything that occurs between the time of the accident or event will be taken into account, whether it increases or diminishes the amount of damages sustained. For example, if *A* suffers what seems to be a trivial injury through the negligence of *B* but, as a consequence of the malpractice of her physician, selected with due care, *A* suffers an aggravation of the condition, *A* is entitled to recover damages from *B* for all of her injuries, including those caused by the physician's malpractice. Similarly, if *A* sustained a slight laceration and, through no neglect on *A*'s part the wound became infected, *A* would be entitled to recover not only for the laceration but for the infection as well. On the other hand, if *A* recovered a judgment against *B* for $500, which was satisfied, *A* would not be entitled to recover any further damages which she might sustain as a result of the original injury, even though the harmful effects of the injury were not manifest and were unknown at the time of trial.

In property damage cases, where the damage is measured by the value of the article at the time of its destruction, or the time the plaintiff was deprived of its use, the plaintiff is usually entitled to recover the value of the article as it was at some time prior to the trial, ordinarily the time of the accident.

1204 Duty of the Claimant to Establish Damages

The defendant is responsible for all damages proximately caused by his or her tortious act. Since the burden of proof is always placed upon the shoulders of the person asserting the claim, the plaintiff must establish exactly what damages were sustained, as well as a direct chain of causation running from the event to the injury or loss sustained. The evidence with respect to damages must clearly demonstrate the actual damages claimed. The jury is not required to imagine or speculate, and the failure of the plaintiff to produce evidence establishing damages with certainty will result in a dismissal of the claim.

For example, in *Deutsch* v. *Connecticut Co.* [119 Atl. 281 (Connecticut)], a contributorily negligent plaintiff was run over by the defendant's trolley car and further injured when the motorman negligently backed the trolley car over him. As to the first injury, the plaintiff could not recover due to his contributory negligence. As to the second injury, the defendant was liable. The plaintiff established all of his injuries, but failed to produce evidence as to the injuries which were sustained as a result of the second impact alone. Because he failed to establish the exact damage caused by the impact for which the defendant was liable, he did not meet the burden of proof required. Recovery was denied. There was no evidence on which the jury could base a conclusion as to the value of the claim because it had no information as to the extent of the injury caused by the defendant's negligence.

From this and other cases the courts have developed the *rule of certainty* as to damages. The rule of certainty requires that the plaintiff establish the exact damages without recourse to speculation or conjecture. The failure to establish damages with certainty requires a dismissal of the cause of action. However, cases which involve continuing medical treatment or continuing disability beyond the date of the trial pose special problems. It would be impossible for the plaintiff to establish such projected losses with certainty until the losses had actually been incurred. Therefore, in those cases involving projected losses, and those cases alone, the courts have relaxed the rule of certainty to the extent that the plaintiff will sustain the burden of proof if he or she can establish future losses with a reasonable degree of certainty. This means that the plaintiff's proof must show that the future losses will be sustained, and, further, the actual value of such losses. As to losses already sustained, the rule of certainty is applied.

Where a plaintiff receives regular salary or wages and the effect of the injury is such that he or she is unable to work for a period of time, evidence of medical disability and the fact that the plaintiff was employed and did not work will meet the requirements of certainty. Where the plaintiff seeks damages for a lost economic opportunity, there is some difficulty in the way of proof. The plaintiff must establish with certainty that the opportunity actually existed, that his or her condition was such that the plaintiff could not take advantage of it, and, most important, that the plaintiff would have profited by it (and the exact extent of the profit). In most cases of this type the proof will fall short of the legal requirements. Speculative testimony as to the possibilities of profit will not be sufficient. In other cases, where the plaintiff's income is derived from a business in which he or she had a monetary investment, the legal requirements are that the plaintiff must show the amount of income that is derived from his or her services as opposed to that portion which represents interest on the investment.

In addition to showing the exact damages, the plaintiff must establish that the damages were sustained as a proximate result of the defendant's act. Where medical testimony is offered, it must establish that the plaintiff's injuries were caused by the tortious act of the defendant. The plaintiff must show with certainty that there is a chain of causation running from the defendant's act to the condition from which the plaintiff is suffering. The medical testimony so offered must have some foundation in medical fact or experience. For example, if the injured person sustained severe lacerations and later developed a virulent infection even though all medical precautions were undertaken, the defendant's liability would extend not only to the lacerations but to the infection as well. It can be established with medical certainty that lacerations can become infected even though preventive measures are undertaken.

The rule of proximate cause has been applied to cases where the defendant is responsible for the original injury but where the injury has been aggravated by the malpractice of a physician, selected by the plaintiff with due care. In such a case, the defendant and the physician are joint tort-feasors as to the injuries caused by the malpractice. The defendant's tortious act is the proximate cause of the entire injury, and the malpractice of the physician is within the foreseeable orbit of danger. The malpractice is not an intervening cause which will reduce the defendant's liability or absolve the defendant from responsibility to respond in damages. The injured person may, at his or her election, hold either the defendant, or the doctor, or both, for the injuries sustained as a result of the malpractice. Clearly, the physician is not responsible for the original injury. The physician's liability is confined to the damages occasioned by the malpractice and no more.

1205 Duty of the Claimant to Mitigate Damages

The plaintiff may not recover for any damages which occur as a result of his or her own lack of care after the happening of the accident. For example, in property damage cases, the plaintiff must exercise reasonable care in protecting the property from further damage from the weather or the actions of others. Let us assume that *A*'s roof is damaged by the negligence of *B*. *A* is under the duty to make emergency repairs so as to protect his other property from weather damage. *B*'s liability is limited to the damage to the roof, and then only to such damage as was caused by his negligent act. If *A* fails to make the repairs, emergency or otherwise, and the roof is further damaged, as well as other property, *A* then would have the additional burden of showing the exact damage caused by *B*'s negligence. He could only accomplish this by showing the entire damage and showing the amount that should be deducted from the total damage because of his own lack of reasonable care.

In personal injury cases, the injured person is bound to act in good faith and to resort to such means and adopt such measures as are reasonably within reach to effect a cure. The injured person cannot neglect the injury and seek to hold the defendant responsible for the entire result. If the injured person should choose a physician who is otherwise qualified, but whose neglect of the case amounts to malpractice, he or she is not charged with a lack of reasonable care. The possibility that the attending physician might fail to exercise the proper care is a foreseeable consequence of the original tort-feasor's negligent act; and, for that reason, the malpractice is not charged against the injured person. As to the malpractice, both the tort-feasor and the physician are jointly and severally liable, occupying the legal position of joint tort-feasors. The defendant, however, is not liable for the aggravation of the injury or additional pain and suffering that is attributable to

1. The failure of the injured person to secure timely medical treatment.
2. The failure of the injured person to follow the advice or instructions of the attending physician.
3. The failure of the injured person to exercise reasonable care in the selection of the physician or surgeon.
4. The intervention of any factors that are not the natural, direct, and proximate consequences of the tort.

The rule is that the tort-feasor is not liable for the avoidable consequences of the injury brought about by the plaintiff's failure to exercise reasonable care. In addition there must be an unbroken chain of causation running from the negligent act to the injuries claimed, without any intervening factors.

Because of this duty of reasonable care imposed upon the plaintiff, the defendant is liable for the expenses incurred and the property loss or personal injuries sustained by the plaintiff in a reasonable effort to minimize the damages. These would include expenses for medical services, damage to clothing or other property as a result of an effort to extinguish a fire, or personal injuries sustained while attempting to remove or rescue people from a burning building or vehicle, or attempting to salvage valuable property endangered by the accident. These expenses are recoverable even though the attempt is unsuccessful, or proves to be unnecessary, or aggravates rather than reduces the loss. The test is whether the incurring of the expense or the exposure to injury was reasonable under the circumstances attending the event.

In a case where a surgical operation is indicated and, in the opinion of the physicians, will cure the plaintiff's condition, the plaintiff must submit to it if it does not involve any great risk. If the plaintiff fails to do so, he or she is negligent about his or her own physical condition and may not recover of the defendant any damages which are sustained as a result. On the other hand, if the evidence shows that the operation will involve great risk, and there is no guarantee of a successful result, the jury can (and usually will) find that the plaintiff is justified in a refusal to submit to the operation and that such refusal does not amount to negligence. The defendant is not liable for the avoidable consequences of the injury. If the operation will avoid further disability, the defendant is not responsible for the disability occasioned by the plaintiff's failure to take advantage of the operation. In such a case there must be convincing evidence that the operation will actually cure or reduce the disability and will not expose the plaintiff to an unreasonable risk.

1206 Effect of a Religious Belief on Mitigation

The religious belief of the plaintiff does not excuse the plaintiff from the duty of exercising reasonable care to be cured by using all medical means available. A problem is presented in cases involving members of some religions who hold to the belief that human injuries, ailments, diseases, pain, and suffering are false beliefs, illusions, or "errors" of the mind which can be erased by pointing the way to "truth." Since there is no proof that can be adduced that this belief has any basis in fact, the same rules are applicable to those who hold these beliefs as are applied to others. If the injured person allows an unreasonable period of time to elapse between the injury and the application for medical treatment, that person has not exercised the reasonable care which the law requires. This failure is regarded as an intervening cause of the injury, so as to either bar the entire claim for damages or materially reduce it. The injury so aggravated by the failure to secure timely medical treatment is an avoidable consequence of the original injury, for which the defendant is not liable. The religious belief of the plaintiff, however honestly held, will not exonerate him or her from being found negligent.

As to infants, the rule is not strictly applied. The courts recognize that infants are subject to the authority and guidance of their parents and that, where the parents are negligent, even because of a religious belief, their negligence should not be imputed to the infant. In *Lange* v. *Holt* [159 Atl. 575 (Connecticut)], an eight-year-old girl was injured through the negligence of the defendant. Her parents were Christian Scientists, and she received no proper medical treatment for a period of some 25 days, although she had the services of a Christian Science practitioner during that time. The defendant contended that her injuries were aggravated by the lack of medical attention, and further that such neglect was the proximate cause of the permanent injury which she suffered. In overruling this defense, the court said: "The test of conduct on the part of the plaintiff in promoting a recovery from injuries suffered is one of reasonable care, and cannot be made to depend on the idiosyncrasies of personal belief, no matter how honestly held. . . . A child of eight years is necessarily dependent upon her parents in regard to the steps to be taken to bring about a recovery from an injury, and, if she herself is not guilty of negligence, or improper conduct, the failure of the parents to take proper steps to that end, by a parity of reasoning, cannot be such a cause of any portion of the injuries as will defeat a recovery for all the results of the defendant's wrongdoing.''

1207 Collateral Source Rule

The general rule is that the tort-feasor is answerable for all of the damages sustained as a result of his or her wrongful act. However it frequently happens that the claimant, because of the accident, receives benefits in the form of medical payments or payments from his or her health, accident, or disability insurer. These come to the claimant from a collateral source, other than the tort-feasor, usually because of some insurance policies for which a premium was paid. The collateral source rule holds that the tort-feasor is not entitled to reduce his or her liability because of the collateral source benefits received by the claimant. In a word, the injured party can recover more than once for the same item.

It also happens that in some cases the claimant's employer will continue the payment of salary during the period of disability, so that he or she actually sustains no wage loss. The money so paid is not earned income and represents merely a gift from the employer. The tort-feasor is not entitled to credit for the money so paid, since it came to the injured person from a collateral source.

With respect to medical payments coverage, the question arises as to whether the claimant, who has received reimbursement for medical bills under the defendant's insurance coverage, can claim reimbursement for the same bills in a subsequent tort action against the defendant. The problem is whether the medical payments insurance is a ''collateral source'' so as to permit a double recovery. Courts, generally, have held that medical payments received under the defendant's insurance coverage are not collateral source payments and that a double recovery will not be permitted.

In *Tart* v. *Register* [125 S.E. 2d 754 (North Carolina)], the court decided that it was unconscionable to permit a passenger in a motor vehicle to collect under the medical payments coverage and again in an action for damages from the same company.

Workers' compensation payments are not subject to the collateral source rule. This is because under most compensation statutes the claimant has an election either to take compensation, proceed against the third-party tort-feasor, or do both. In the case of the acceptance of compensation payments or the payment of medical expenses, the insurance carrier making such payments is usually subrogated to the rights of the claimant or has a lien on the proceeds of recovery to the extent of the payments made. Such payments do not represent benefits received from a collateral source, independent of the defendant, because in most states the compensation carrier either has a lien on the claimant's cause of action or, in the alternative, is subrogated to all of the claimant's rights against the defendant. Thus, in workers' compensation cases the claimant cannot recover twice for the same item. In states where there is no right of lien or of subrogation, compensation recovered might be subject to the collateral source rule.

1208 Effect of a Preexisting Physical Disability

The law does not require that the innocent victim, who suffers personal injuries because of the negligence of another, be in perfect health in order to recover. The law recognizes the existence of disease and residual disability caused by prior injuries, as well as the infirmities of age. The presence of any of these conditions does not relieve the tort-feasor of the responsibility to respond in damages. He or she is answerable for all the injuries proximately caused by the negligent act. The fact that a person in perfect health would have sustained little disability is not taken into account in reducing the tort-feasor's liability where the injury superimposed upon a preexisting infirmity, disability, or disease produces a serious condition. The tort-feasor is answerable for whatever injuries are produced, irrespective of whether a preexisting condition contributes to the injury. In a word, the tort-feasor takes the victim as is, and is responsible for all disability causally related to the injury. Therefore, theoretically, the tort-feasor is answerable for all the effects of the injury, and, where a preexisting condition is aggravated, this responsibility attaches to the aggravation. When the effects of the aggravation have ceased, and the injured person is in the same condition as prior to the accident, the defendant's responsibility is at an end.

Sometimes it is possible to disassociate entirely the two conditions and to measure the disability and medical expense necessitated by the injury. Where the two conditions cannot be separated, the plaintiff is faced with a problem of proof. Confronted by the rule of certainty, the plaintiff must establish the exact extent of the injury caused by the accident and the expense it occasioned.

Suppose that *A* is suffering from a progressive arthritis of the spine, for which she is under treatment, prior to the accident. *A* suffers an injury to the spine which, it is claimed, aggravated the arthritic condition and accelerated its disabling effects. In this case the condition is progressive, and even if the accident had not occurred, *A*'s condition would have deteriorated with the passage of time. *A* must establish with certainty the exact injury which she sustained in the accident and must also produce evidence of the losses sustained as a result. It is clear that *A*'s condition will never return to its state prior to the accident. Therefore *A* must resort to medical testimony to show the pain and suffering she experienced as a result of the accident, the increase in medical treatment required after the accident, the differences, if any, between the treatment rendered before the accident and after, together with the increased costs of the treatment, if any.

In addition, if *A* were employed prior to the accident and after the accident could not work, the change in her earning capacity could be offered as some evidence of the effects of the injury. However, *A* is also faced with the rule of subtraction, since it is evident that her condition is not a stationary one and would possibly have prevented her from doing any work at some point in the future. *A* then would have to show the prognosis of her condition prior to injury, and the present prognosis with the injury. The difference would be the extent of the tortfeasor's liability.

Suppose *A* is blind in one eye. Through the negligence of *B*, *A* loses the sight of his good eye and is now completely blind. *B* is answerable for *A*'s blindness, and the extent of his liability is not mitigated by the fact that *A*'s previous condition contributed to the final result. Absent the accident, *A* would not have been blind. Therefore, the accident is responsible for *A*'s condition of blindness.

1209 Loss of Consortium

At common law the relationship of the wife to her husband was that of a very superior servant to the master. Any tortious act of a third person (including negligent personal injury) which interfered with the relationship and deprived the master (husband) of the services to which he was entitled gave rise to a cause of action by the master (husband) against the wrongdoer for the damages which he sustained as a consequence of the loss of such services. It should be pointed out that this is an independent cause of action which accrues to the husband because of the damages which he himself has suffered, and for which only he may recover. Under our present statutes, the wife may recover for her personal injuries, but the settlement or judgment recovered by the wife will not extinguish the husband's cause of action for loss of services. The death of the wife will not abate the husband's cause of action, but it will limit his recovery to the damages which he has sustained up to the time of her death. In the case of divorce or separation after the tort has been committed, the husband's right to the services of his wife would be limited to the period of time measured from the date of the accident up until the date of the divorce or separation.

Consortium consists of (1) sex, (2) society, and (3) services. Any injury to the wife which deprives the husband of one or more of these elements will support the husband's cause of action.

Sex refers to the marital relation of sexual intercourse and, because this item does not have a market or exchange value, the amount to be awarded is left to the discretion of the jury under instructions from the court. They may take into consideration the age and physical capacity of both husband and wife in determining the amount to be awarded.

Society refers to companionship. Again, this is an item which has no market or exchange value. The jury will decide its value. They may take into account the conditions of the home life of the husband prior to the injury and the changes that have occurred as a result of the wife's injury. If there was no home life to speak of, then there would be at the most a minimal loss. This might be shown by evidence, for example, that the wife spent very little time at home, consorted with other men, and generally neglected her family. In such a case the companionship lost by the husband would be practically nil.

Services refer to the wife's services as a homemaker. This loss could be demonstrated by the employment of a housekeeper or baby-sitter to accomplish the tasks normally undertaken by the wife. The cost of such a substitute would be the measure of damages. As to services rendered to others, as where the wife is gainfully employed, the husband has no interest. The wife's earnings are her own and, therefore, any loss of earning capacity which she might sustain must be recovered in her own action.

For the husband to have a cause of action for loss of services there must be a relationship of husband and wife at the time of the occurrence of the tort. The relationship must be a legal one. Where two people are living together as husband and wife in a state which does not recognize such a relationship as a common-law marriage, the ''husband'' does not have a cause of action for loss of services even though he has sustained a loss. The same situation would obtain where there was a bigamous marriage.

Defenses. The husband's action is based upon the liability of the tort-feasor to his wife. Therefore, as an element of his case, the husband must assert a tort cause of action based on the facts of the accident. Defenses such as contributory negligence, assumption of risk, or the statute of limitations, which could be asserted as defenses to the action by the wife, are likewise available as defenses to the husband's action. In addition, any defenses which the defendant may have against the husband personally may be asserted. For example, *H* and *W* are husband and wife. *H* is driving the automobile in which *W* is a passenger. An accident occurs in which the cars of *H* and *X* collide. The accident is due to the joint negligence of both drivers. *H*'s contributory negligence in most states is not imputed to *W*. *W* may recover. To *H*'s cause of action for loss of services, *X* can set up *H*'s contributory negligence as a defense, with the result that *H* cannot recover, or his recovery would be reduced. In states subscribing to the community purpose doctrine, the result would be that neither *H* nor *W* could recover.

As part of his marital obligation, the husband is responsible for the medical and other care needed by his wife. In personal injury cases, where the wife is injured, this obligation continues. Therefore, the husband has a cause of action against the tort-feasor for the money expended for the care of his wife. This item of damage is in addition to his claim for loss of consortium. Some few states have abandoned the theory of loss of consortium and have limited the husband's recovery only to the money expended for medical care of his wife. Most others still recognize the husband's claim for loss of consortium and make awards accordingly.

The common law never recognized a similar claim on the part of the wife for the loss of her husband's services. Therefore, when the husband was injured, only one cause of action arose—the claim of the husband. Most states have modified the common-law rule and have recognized such a right on the part of the wife. (See Section 500, above.)

A final decree of divorce terminates the marriage as of the date of the decree. The divorced husband has no further rights to consortium or the services of his divorced wife. Where the wife is divorced prior to the injury, no right of action accrues to the divorced husband for loss of services or recovery for her medical expenses, even though the award of alimony obligates him to pay for her medical expenses. Where the divorce occurs after the accident, the husband would have a cause of action for the loss of consortium from the date of the accident up to the time they separated. The same situation would obtain in the case of a separation, where husband and wife are living apart, whether by agreement or court decree.

MEASURE OF DAMAGES

1210 Measure of Damages: Property Damage

The various state courts are in agreement that the amount to be awarded to the injured party for property damage is the amount that will reasonably compensate for the loss suffered. They are not in agreement as to how this is to be accomplished. There are three different rules. Each court has adopted one of the following rules, and will allow damages based on:

1. The diminution in value. Evidence of the cost of repairs is admissible as some proof of this diminution.
2. The cost of repairs as the measure of damages, except where the repair costs exceed the value of the article before the damage. In the latter case, the value of the article is the measure of damages.
3. Either of the above rules, the damages being the difference in value of the article before and after the damage, or, at the plaintiff's election, the reasonable cost of repair, or restoration where possible, with due allowance for any difference between the original value and the value after repairs.

In the majority of cases, the application of these rules will produce the same result, since the available proof of damage will be restricted to the cost of repairs. Where there is evidence that the repaired article has suffered a diminution from the preaccident value, the application of the first rule will allow a greater recovery than the second. Also, it should be noted that, where the cost of repairs exceeds the diminution in value, the second rule will allow a greater recovery than the first, the test being the relationship between the preaccident value and the cost of repairs rather than the relationship of the diminution in value and the cost of repairs.

The third rule, which is recommended by the American Law Institute (*Restatement, Law of Torts,* Sec. 928), combines the better features of both rules and is being generally adopted by the courts. Under this rule, the difference in value is taken into account. This includes not only the diminution in the value of the repaired article, but an increase in value as well. In the latter case, the rule of subtraction would apply, and the amount of the increased value would be applied in diminishing the amount of damages recoverable.

Market Value. The value referred to in these rules is the exchange or market value. Such value is the amount that the owner would have to pay in order to replace it with property of the same kind and quality. It does not include the sentimental value or the value of the emotional distress caused by its loss. Where the article is replaceable, the damages ordinarily are limited to the replacement value.

Market value will differ as to the status of the owner in relation to it. Thus, if the owner is a consumer, the market value would be the retail price. If the owner is a retailer, the value would be the wholesale price. And if the owner is the manufacturer, the value would be the manufacturer's selling price.

Articles Having No Market Value. An item may have special value to the owner but no exchange or market value. Such items might include a family heirloom, a portrait of a deceased ancestor, or merely photographs of members of the family. The damages recoverable will be the special value to the owner, as determined by the jury, with due consideration being given to the original cost, age, and condition. Where the property consists of a work product of the owner, such as a manuscript, records of experiments, or case studies, the value may be computed on the basis of the value of the time, labor, and effort which will be required to reproduce it.

The value of an old building is not determined solely by its replacement cost or the original cost less depreciation or obsolescence. In some cases, old buildings cannot be replaced because there are no artisans available who are capable of doing the type of work necessary to reproduce it. In such cases, the value can be established by showing the use to which the building was put immediately prior to its loss, its rental value, and the present character of the neighborhood, as well as the price that a prospective purchaser would be willing to pay for the property. Of necessity, experts would be required in order to establish this type of valuation.

Loss of Use. This terminology is used by the courts to denote an element of damage arising from the injury to or destruction of certain species of tangible personal property. The term arose with the development of the law of personal property, but similar damages may be sustained as a result of the damage to real property. Consideration will be given to (1) personal property and (2) real property.

1. Personal Property. Loss of use is most frequently involved in cases of damage to motor vehicles, although there is no reason why the same principles could not be applied equally to other types of machinery used for commercial purposes, such as printing presses, computers, punch presses, and the like. Loss of use does not refer to or is not an element of damage considered in connection with the injury to or destruction of all types of personal property. For example, annual crops are personal property. In the case of the destruction of the crop, the damages will consist of the value of the crop destroyed or damaged, and, even though the owner may have planned to use the crop to feed his family and its destruction may have frustrated that purpose, there is no recovery per se for that type of damage. The payment for the crop will cover the entire damage. Similarly, loss of use is not an element of damages in the case of damage to intangible personal property, for example, the damage to an economic advantage (such as the goodwill of a business, or the impairment of an action at law).

As to tangible personal property, where the article can be repaired, most courts will allow a recovery for damages for loss of use for the period of time reasonably required to make such repairs, provided that the plaintiff can establish that damages, in fact, were sustained. Where the article is a total loss, in that the article is either completely destroyed or the cost of repairs exceeds its preaccident value, and recovery is based on the value of the article prior to the accident, most courts will not allow damages for loss of use.

Some courts do not allow damages for loss of use under any circumstances. The majority view, however, is to permit recovery in all the cases as noted in the preceding paragraph.

The amount claimed for loss of use is subject to the rule of certainty in that the plaintiff must establish with certainty the exact loss. Where there has been some inconvenience but no actual monetary loss, the plaintiff will encounter some difficulty by way of proof.

Claims for loss of use are also subject to the rule of subtraction. If a substitute vehicle is rented and the lessor provides the gas, the measure of damages would be the cost of the rental less the cost of gas. If the vehicle had not been damaged, the owner would have had to pay for the gas. Therefore, that cost does not represent any part of the damage caused by the accident and is not a recoverable item.

2. Real Property. Any wrongful intrusion onto the lands of another is a trespass and, where damages are incurred, the owner has a cause of action against the intruder to recover any loss, whether it be for permanent or temporary damage to the use of the property. The rule in real property is that the owner is entitled to the enjoyment of his or her land and the "rents, issues, and profits" arising therefrom. Any wrongful intrusion which deprives the owner of any of these is actionable, and the value of each is an element of damage. Real property includes not only the land, but the structures permanently affixed to the land, plus the perennial crops—trees, bushes, grass, etc., which are not planted annually—and in addition any other conditions on the land, whether man-made or natural, such as lakes, streams, drainage ditches, roads, fences, and swimming pools.

As has been said, the owner's enjoyment of real property includes, among other things, the rights to rents, issues, and profits. "Rents" refers to the net rents, rather than the gross receipts from the rental of the property. There are usually other expenses to be paid, such as taxes, assessments, and the normal repairs to the property, which are the responsibility of the owner, regardless of whether there was a wrongful intrusion. Issues refers to things growing on the land, such as trees, and the owner is entitled to the enjoyment of these things whether the owner planted them or whether they just grew over the years. Profits usually refer to the benefit, advantage, or pecuniary gain accruing to the owner or the occupant of the land from its actual use. This might seem to overlap the matter of rents and issues, but it is a catch-all phrase used to cover anything that was possibly not covered by the prior terms. The question then is, for how long a period of time will the loss of rents, issues, and profits be taken into account. In the case of a structure which can be replaced, the period of time would be measured by the length of time reasonably required to make the replacement or repairs.

An interest in real property can consist of something less than complete ownership. The most common example of this is where the owner divests himself or herself of the use of all or part of the property for a term of years by lease, with the right of reversion to the owner at the expiration of the term of the lease. In this sense, the tenant is the ''owner'' of the realty which is the subject matter of the lease for the period of time limited in the lease. Therefore, any damage suffered by the tenant as a result of the impairment of the right of use is recoverable by the tenant. Where the damage is not only to the tenant's occupancy but also permanently damages the realty, then the claim representative will have two claimants with whom to deal. The representative will settle with the tenant for the interference with occupancy and with the owner for the damage to the reversionary interest.

The right to engage in business is a property right, and any damage to it can be classified as property damage. An impairment of this right which results in the loss of profits as a consequence of damage to the premises or the property on which the business is conducted is actionable, and the loss of profits is an item of damage. The period of time during which this loss of profits is measurable may be the period of time necessary to repair the building, or the period of time needed to move the business to another location, depending on the circumstances.

Other Allowable Expenses. Money expended to prevent further damage to the article is also recoverable. These items could include towing charges, or temporary repairs to a building. In addition, in some jurisdictions interest is allowed from the time of the accident to the time of payment on either the diminution of value or the cost of repairs.

Settlement Value. In cases involving a repairable article the settlement value is usually the reasonable cost of repairs. No allowance is made for loss of use with respect to motor vehicles unless (1) there is a business use involved and (2) there is an actual money loss due to the rental of a substitute vehicle, or a provable loss of profit due to the lack of it. Mere discomfort or inconvenience caused by the lack of the car is not an item considered in a settlement valuation.

With respect to damage to property other than a motor vehicle, such as damage to a business building, a home, a store, or a display window, the same tests are used in determining whether a loss of use claim will be recognized. Loss of use is not considered unless (1) the property is used for business and (2) an actual business loss can be established. Mere inconvenience during a period of repair with respect to a private dwelling is not considered as an item of damage. However, where the repairs are of such a nature as to make it impossible for the owner to occupy the premises, and he or she is required to incur expense in living elsewhere or conducting business elsewhere during the repair period, such expenses as are reasonable are usually recoverable.

With respect to a completely destroyed article, or one in which the repairs will exceed the preaccident value, settlement value is usually based on the market value of the article prior to the accident, less the junk value of the salvage. No damages for loss of use are considered, nor is any consideration given to the matter of interest on the cost of repairs or diminution of value. In all cases, charges for towing or temporary repairs are given some consideration. If the expenses for these items are reasonable under the circumstances, they are allowable, even in the case of a total loss.

1211 Measure of Damages: Personal Injury

As in other claims for damages arising from the tortious act of another, the injured person is entitled to recover reasonable compensation for injuries, past, present, and future, caused by the tort. Reasonable compensation means an award of money that will repair and restore the injured person to his or her preaccident condition, and should be an amount commensurate with the extent of the injury. It is clear that in many cases the payment of money will not place the injured person in a position equivalent to the physical condition prior to injury. The payment, therefore, is to compensate the plaintiff for the pain or deterioration of the body which has been suffered and is likely to be suffered in the future.

The amount is not what a person would expect in exchange for willingly suffering the same injury, because this type of transaction is not a bargain and sale. The claimant certainly had no opportunity to decide whether to suffer the injury. Damages consist of the amount that the jury, in its discretion, decides will reasonably represent in money the value of the injuries suffered. The jury award is determined on the basis of the evidence of injury and follows the instructions of the court. The elements which the court will instruct the jury to take into consideration when deciding the question of damages are (1) out-of-pocket expenses, (2) loss of earning capacity, and (3) mental and physical distress. In appropriate cases, the jury has been instructed to take into account additional elements—such as the effect of a disfiguring scar or of the inability to bear children.

It is to be noted that the first two items are tangible in the sense that their value can be ascertained with certainty, and for that reason the rule of certainty is applied; the injured person must establish his or her exact loss. The third item is a matter of speculation. The value of the injured person's mental or physical distress is left to the discretion of the jury, and proof of this particular item is not subject to the rule of certainty. The injured person must, however, produce evidence of injury and testimony as to the pain or suffering endured or that will continue to be endured. Let us consider in detail exactly what each of these elements includes.

1. Out-of-Pocket Expenses. These involve expenditures which the injured person was compelled to make solely because of the injury. In most cases, they will consist largely of medical, surgical, hospital, and nursing costs. The injured person is entitled to recover the reasonable value of such services. In most states, he or she must establish that the amounts claimed represent not only the amount paid, but also that the amount so paid is the reasonable value of the services rendered. The injured person will also have to establish that the services so rendered were made necessary solely as a result of the injury.

If the injury is a continuing one, the injured person is entitled not only to the medical expense incurred up to the time of trial, but also to the reasonable value of medical services which will be required in the future. The need for future medical attention must be established by offering expert medical testimony as to these facts.

Other out-of-pocket expenses could include the hiring of a housekeeper, a practical nurse, or even the expense of a trip necessary for convalescence. These are allowable items if it can be shown that the necessity for the expense is causally related to the injury. Thus any expenses which would not have been incurred but for the injury are recoverable if the amount is reasonable.

2. Loss of Earning Capacity. Where the injuries are such that the injured person has been totally or partially deprived of earning capacity, damages are allowed for such disability. It makes no difference whether the injured person is unemployed or is so financially situated that he or she does not have to work at all. Damages are nevertheless recoverable for loss of earning capacity.

Where the injured person is employed at the time of injury, proof of loss of earning capacity is a comparatively easy matter. Evidence of earnings on the job, plus medical proof of disability for the period away from work, will establish this item. Difficulty is encountered when the injured person is unemployed at the time of injury, whether due to economic conditions in that particular line of work, aversion to work of any kind, or a financial situation which does not make work a necessity. Under proper instructions of the court, the jury will be allowed to determine the amount that the injured person would have been able to earn during the period of incapacity. They will take into account the person's age, education, work habits, skill, and the general condition of the labor market. In the case of a homemaker who ordinarily does not work, the measure of her loss of earning capacity could be the amount that could be earned by a person with child-care, cooking, and other homemaking skills.

Where the injured person has his or her own business, earning capacity will be measured by the value of the owner's services and not by the total profit derived from the business. The profit obtained from a business is usually due to the services rendered by the owner, the return on the capital invested, as well as profit realized from the work of others. In presenting evidence of loss of earning capacity, a business owner is subject to the rule of certainty and must establish the exact value of his or her earning capacity. The person must show the exact amount that must be subtracted from the total profit, as representing the value of the factors other than the owner's own work. This can be accomplished by showing the profit made before the owner's injury as compared to the profit made during the period of incapacity. Or, if the profit remains constant and a substitute was hired to do the owner's work, then the amounts paid to the substitute could be utilized as evidence of the value of the loss of earning capacity.

In some rare cases, evidence may be available that, immediately prior to the accident, the plaintiff's earnings were below his or her actual earning capacity. If this is the case, the jury may, with appropriate instructions from the court, determine what the true earning capacity is, based on what could have been earned and not necessarily on what was being earned at the time of the accident. While the jury is not bound to conclude that the plaintiff's earning capacity is measured by his or her prior earnings, the plaintiff is confronted with a problem of proof. It must be shown why the plaintiff was willing to accept less than full earning capacity. It must be shown, further, that the plaintiff could have earned more in another job, and why the claimant did not take the other job. Juries are not ready to accept evidence of this sort, and it is unlikely that they would agree with the plaintiff unless the proof is clear and convincing.

Where the loss of earning capacity continues up to the time of trial and is likely to continue beyond that time, damages for loss of future earning capacity are recoverable. Clearly, the claimant cannot establish such a loss with certainty. He or she must, however, establish the loss with a reasonable degree of certainty. This will require the testimony of experts as to the length of time the incapacity will continue, whether for the duration of the claimant's work life or a shorter period of time. In addition, the claimant will have to establish with a reasonable degree of certainty exactly what his or her earning capacity will be during the projected period of disability. In some occupations the ability to earn diminishes with advancing age, so that the burden is on the injured person to establish with a reasonable degree of certainty what future earnings will be, subtracting whatever amounts the future changes in earnings will require. The defendant is entitled to the reduction, and the claimant's failure to establish the amount to be subtracted could result in a failure of the requisite amount of proof necessary to sustain an award. Conversely, where the claimant's earnings could reasonably be expected to increase in the future, the claimant is entitled to recover on the basis of anticipated earnings, so that any increase must be taken into consideration if sufficient evidence of such increases is offered.

As to the evidence required to establish the loss of future earning capacity, the claimant must show (1) that the disability will continue beyond the date of trial and for how long thereafter, and (2) the effect that such disability will have on earning capacity. To meet the first requirement expert testimony, in the form of medical proof, must be submitted. The physician must testify as to the nature of the disability and the prognosis for future recovery. In addition, the physician must testify as to the extent that the disability affects the claimant's earning capacity. Having once established disability, the claimant must show that he or she had an earning capacity prior to the accident, the effect of the disability on that earning capacity, and the present value of the dollar loss suffered. Earning capacity prior to the accident is established as it would be if the disability was merely temporary. As to the projected future loss, the average weekly or yearly loss must be established. This may be shown by evidence of the average earnings of a similar person, and evidence that the injured person was either above average, average, or below average as to future earning capacity. When the average earnings are established, then the testimony of an actuary or economist must be offered to show the work-life of the claimant and the present value of the projected loss of earning capacity. We say "present value" because the judgment will be rendered on the trial date, and the defendant will be required to pay for future losses as of that date. Since payment is actually made in advance, the defendant is entitled to a discount for the advance payment.

In computing the value of loss of earning capacity, it would seem that take-home pay should be used as the basis, not gross earnings. This is because the Internal Revenue Code exempts from gross income "The amount of any damages received (whether by suit or agreement) on account of personal injuries or sickness." The actual earnings after taxes will measure the net loss and, since the recovery is not subject to tax, an award based on take-home pay would reimburse the plaintiff for what was actually lost. If gross wages were used, then the claimant would recover in tax-free damages an amount on which he or she would have had to pay taxes if the money were received in salary or other income. Therefore, the use of a gross wage figure would result in the claimant recovering more than was lost.

While a plaintiff who has recovered for the loss of earnings on a pretax basis is placed in a better position than the one occupied prior to the accident, most courts that have considered the matter follow the rule that earnings before taxes are the proper measure of damages for loss or impairment of earning capacity. There are several reasons given for this conclusion. First, some courts took the position that the inclusion of the deduction of income tax would be "too conjectural," in the sense that the jury would have to calculate the amount of the tax together with the deductions to which the plaintiff was entitled; also, they would be required to guess just what taxes would be imposed in the future. Second, some courts felt that the congressional intent was to benefit injured persons by exonerating them from paying taxes on bodily injury awards, and to reduce the award by consideration of the tax advantages would be to frustrate the congressional intent. Third, some courts utilized the collateral source rule, holding that the tax exemption was a benefit derived from a collateral source and not from the defendant; and as a result the defendant was not entitled to credit.

Not all of the courts have passed on this question, but, as noted, the majority who have considered it, have decided in favor of the injured person. However, regardless of whether the question has or has not been submitted to the courts in a particular jurisdiction, it would appear that, for settlement purposes, only the net income or the take-home pay should be the basis for the computation of loss of earning capacity.

Both out-of-pocket expenses and loss of earning capacity are tangible items in the sense that they are pecuniary losses amenable to actual proof. They are referred to as ''special damages'' since they can be so measured and represent actual money losses sustained by the injured person.

3. Mental and Physical Distress. This item of general damages is often referred to as ''pain and suffering,'' ''discomfort,'' or ''inconvenience,'' depending upon the degree of pain accompanying the injury. It is a nonpecuniary loss in the sense that the injured person has incurred no monetary deprivation because of it. It is, however, compensatory since it is designed to reimburse or repay the injured person for the pain suffered. Distress of this nature has no exchange value in the market, nor is there any guide or standard which can be used to measure it. It is a question of fact which is submitted to the sound discretion of the jury, under appropriate instructions from the court. The jury thus is the final arbiter as to the valuation of this item in terms of dollars.

The claimant is entitled to compensation for the mental and physical distress experienced up to the time of trial and, if the condition is such that it will cause pain into the future, the amount of compensation will contemplate such future suffering. In establishing such damages, the claimant will have to show by medical testimony that the pain will continue, and for how long, as well as whether the discomfort will abate in intensity, remain constant, or increase in intensity with the passage of time. Where the discomfort will persist for the rest of the claimant's life, mortality tables may be utilized to establish life expectancy.

1212 Measure of Damages: Permanent Disability

When a disability is said to be permanent, it means that the injuries are such that the claimant will never recover from them. The effects of the injury are fixed, stationary, and not subject to change. If the disability is of such a nature that it will improve with treatment or the passage of time, it has not reached a permanent stage. If it improves to the extent that there is a full recovery, then the disability is not permanent at all but merely temporary. If the improvement will not result in a full recovery, then the improved condition, when it reaches a stationary stage, is the permanent injury and is measured and evaluated as of that time.

Cases involving permanent disability may be divided into two classes: those which involve only minor disabilities, such as restrictions of motion of a finger or a toe joint, or minor amputations such as a part of a phalanx of a finger or toe (neither of which have any effect on the claimant's earning capacity); and those which involve major restrictions, such as limited motion in a hip joint, complete stiffness of a knee joint, or amputations of major members, such as a hand, foot, arm, or leg, loss of sight of an eye or of hearing of either one or both ears, which affect not only the claimant's earning capacity but also the future enjoyment of life.

As to both classes of cases, the jury will decide the amount which will reasonably compensate the claimant for the injury. In the first class, they will determine what the permanency is worth, having in mind their own experience, and the extent to which they believe the injury will inconvenience the claimant. They will hear evidence of the damage from the claimant as to the injury's effects—what the claimant can and cannot do because of it. They will hear the testimony of the claimant's physician as to his appraisal of the permanency and how it will affect the claimant. In addition they may hear the defendant's examining physician (if such testimony is offered), as to his or her view of the disability and how it will or will not restrict the claimant's activity. On the basis of the evidence, the jury will fix the amount of reasonable compensation, usually an arbitrary figure which, when added to the other provable items, will constitute the verdict.

In the second class of cases, the evidence will show the exact loss of earning capacity up to the time of trial and the effect that the permanency will have on the claimant's earning capacity. This might be for a measurable period of time or for the rest of the claimant's work-life. The evidence of future disability must establish the disability with a reasonable degree of certainty. In addition, where the permanent injury interferes with the claimant's future enjoyment of life, such as continuous pain, or the loss of the ability to engage in sports of various kinds, to drive an automobile, etc., the jury may fix an additional amount which will compensate for these lifelong losses.

Thus we have two measurements applicable to the case. First, the loss of earning capacity is measured by the period of time that someone of the claimant's age and occupation would be able to continue working. Second, the loss of enjoyment or the suffering of pain would be measured by the number of years that someone of the claimant's age would be expected to live. Clearly, the life expectancy ordinarily would exceed the work-life expectancy.

Since there is no way of predicting with absolute certainty how long a particular individual will continue working, or how long the individual will live, evidence—in the form of tables or other evidence to show the average expectancy of a large number of persons—is admissible for the purpose of assisting the jury in arriving at its verdict. The jury may accept the tables, or reject them, or use any means it desires in reaching a verdict. In any case, they are not bound by the figures produced by the tables or by the testimony of the witness who offers them. The evidence is admissible, but whether the jury uses the tables or not is a decision which is within their province to make. In the absence of other evidence, however, they usually accept the tabular figures.

Expectancy tables measure only average expectancies, whether of life or work, of average persons. If there are any unusual applicable circumstances which would place the claimant in a class either above or below the average, the jury will take these factors into account. Factors which would place the claimant in a below-average category are:

1. *State of health.* Presence of disease or injury: past medical history of illness.
2. *Heredity.* Longevity of ancestors; history of hereditary disease in parents.
3. *Occupation.* Average life, or work-life of a person similarly employed with special reference to the hazards to which persons in that occupation are particularly exposed.
4. *Habits.* Addiction to alcohol or habit-forming drugs; excessive smoking.

The jury may hear evidence on any of these points and may find that such factors have an influence on the average figures. The award will be made according to their findings. In investigating cases of this character, it is important for the claim representative to explore thoroughly the possibilities that one or more of these elements may be present in the case.

In any case, the measure of damages in permanent disability claims will be the projected value of the claimant's loss of earning capacity and the projected value of the distress, if the evidence shows that such distress will continue for the rest of the claimant's life. Loss of earning capacity will be measured by work-life expectancy, that is, the number of years that someone of that age would be able to work; distress will be measured by life expectancy because the distress will continue until death.

1213 Life Expectancy

The earliest recorded evidence of the application of actuarial science to insurance came into prominence in England in 1762 with the incorporation of a life insurance organization called the Equitable Society for the Assurance of Life and Survivorship. To establish probable cost figures and to promulgate the premium to be charged, this organization first used tables compiled by two mathematicians, in an attempt to project the number of years the average man would be expected to live. The tables, however, proved completely inadequate because they were based upon figures developed during the year 1740, the year of the Great Plague. Because the figures were computed by measuring lives during a period of unusually high mortality, the premiums thus calculated were exorbitant and not actuarially sound. Subsequent measurements were undertaken, resulting in more dependable tables.

The experience figures of various life insurance companies have been available for years. These figures are subject to the objection that they are based upon mortality among a selected group; namely, insured lives only. Since life insurance is restricted to those who are capable of meeting the health standards of the life insurance company, the experience figures are not conclusive as evidence of the average length of life that could be expected of an average group. The figures show the probable duration of life of a healthy person capable of obtaining life insurance, and nothing more. Therefore, life insurance mortality tables based upon the average life expectancies of policyholders are not ordinarily admissible as evidence of average life expectancy.

The U.S. government entered the life table field in 1936 and compiled the U.S. Life Tables from the census figures developed from 1900 to 1930. These tables are used extensively as evidence of life expectancy and are referred to as the U.S. Life Tables, or, more generally, the American Table of Mortality. Table 12–1 is a modified form of such a table; it is from *Vital Statistics of the United States*, a U.S. government publication.).

1214 Work-Life Expectancy

It is obvious that the average person does not work until the day he or she dies. A person may discontinue his or her usual occupation because of the infirmities of age, retirement, or other contingencies. Where it is necessary to estimate the working life of an individual who has suffered either permanent disability or death, we would expect to find that the period of life remaining which could be devoted to actual work would be considerably less than the same individual's life expectancy.

In calculating the present value (see Section 1215) of lost future earnings, assumptions must be made about the plaintiff's work life and retirement age. It is popularly (but inaccurately) assumed that most people in the work force certainly will work until age 65 or even 70.

Professor David D. Jones, an economist, has analyzed work-life expectancy data gathered by the U.S. Department of Labor. A person in the labor force at age 27 cannot be assumed with certainty to still be in the labor force at even age 28. Dr. Jones, writing in *For The Defense* (Defense Research Institute, January 1990, pp. 28–29) analyzed the data:

> Only (roughly) 95 percent of men in the labor force at age 27 also are in the labor force at age 28. Labor force participation declines gradually for a couple of decades after age 27, in large part reflecting normal mortality. After age 50, the likelihood of mortality or of retirement increases significantly. . . . [B]y age 65, the likelihood of a man who was in the labor force at age 27 still being active 38 years later is less than 30 percent. To assume 100 percent likelihood that he would be obviously over-states his loss from an interruption of income.
>
> • • • • •
>
> In 1963, roughly half the males alive at age 65 were retired. By 1973, at all ages 55 or over, it was less likely for a man to be active in the labor force than a decade earlier. Men age 65 in 1973 had a slightly greater than 40 percent probability of being active in the labor force. The trend toward lower labor force participation (i.e., earlier

TABLE 12–1 Expectation of Life by Race, Sex, and Age—1990

Age in 1990 (years)	Expectation of Life in Years: Total	White: Male	White: Female	Black: Male	Black: Female	Age in 1990 (years)	Expectation of Life in Years: Total	White: Male	White: Female	Black: Male	Black: Female
At birth	75.4	72.7	79.4	64.5	73.6	35	42.6	40.1	45.8	34.1	41.3
1	75.1	72.3	78.9	64.8	73.8	36	41.6	39.2	44.8	33.3	40.4
2	74.1	71.4	78.0	63.9	72.9	37	40.7	38.3	43.8	32.5	39.5
3	73.1	70.4	77.0	62.9	71.9	38	39.8	37.4	42.9	31.7	38.6
4	72.2	69.4	76.0	62.0	71.0	39	38.9	36.5	41.9	30.9	37.7
5	71.2	68.5	75.0	61.0	70.0	40	38.0	35.6	41.0	30.1	36.8
6	70.2	67.5	74.1	60.1	69.0	41	37.0	34.7	40.0	29.3	35.9
7	69.2	66.5	73.1	59.1	68.1	42	36.1	33.8	39.1	28.5	35.0
8	68.2	65.5	72.1	58.1	67.1	43	35.2	32.9	38.1	27.7	34.1
9	67.3	64.5	71.1	57.1	66.1	44	34.3	32.0	37.2	27.0	33.3
10	66.3	63.5	70.1	56.1	65.1	45	33.4	31.1	36.2	26.2	32.4
11	65.3	62.6	69.1	55.1	64.1	46	32.5	30.2	35.3	25.4	31.5
12	64.3	61.6	68.1	54.2	63.1	47	31.6	29.3	34.4	24.7	30.7
13	63.3	60.6	67.1	53.2	62.1	48	30.7	28.4	33.5	24.0	29.8
14	62.3	59.6	66.2	52.2	61.2	49	29.9	27.6	32.5	23.2	29.0
15	61.3	58.6	65.2	51.3	60.2	50	29.0	26.7	31.6	22.5	28.2
16	60.4	57.7	64.2	50.3	59.2	51	28.1	25.8	30.7	21.8	27.4
17	59.4	56.7	63.2	49.4	58.2	52	27.3	25.0	29.8	21.1	26.6
18	58.5	55.8	62.3	48.5	57.3	53	26.4	24.2	29.0	20.4	25.8
19	57.5	54.9	61.3	47.6	56.3	54	25.6	23.3	28.1	19.7	25.0
20	56.6	54.0	60.3	46.7	55.3	55	24.8	22.5	27.2	19.0	24.2
21	55.7	53.0	59.3	45.9	54.4	56	24.0	21.7	26.4	18.4	23.4
22	54.7	52.1	58.4	45.0	53.4	57	23.2	21.0	25.5	17.8	22.7
23	53.8	51.2	57.4	44.1	52.5	58	22.4	20.2	24.7	17.1	22.0
24	52.8	50.3	56.4	43.3	51.5	59	21.6	19.4	23.8	16.5	21.2
25	51.9	49.3	55.4	42.4	50.6	60	20.8	18.7	23.0	15.9	20.5
26	51.0	48.4	54.5	41.6	49.6	61	20.1	18.0	22.2	15.4	19.8
27	50.0	47.5	53.5	40.7	48.7	62	19.4	17.3	21.4	14.8	19.1
28	49.1	46.6	52.5	39.9	47.7	63	18.6	16.6	20.6	14.3	18.5
29	48.1	45.6	51.6	39.0	46.8	64	17.9	15.9	19.8	13.7	17.8
30	47.2	44.7	50.6	38.2	45.9	65	17.2	15.2	19.1	13.2	17.2
31	46.3	43.8	49.6	37.4	45.0	70	13.9	12.1	15.4	10.7	14.1
32	45.3	42.9	48.7	36.5	44.0	75	10.9	9.4	12.0	8.6	11.2
33	44.4	41.9	47.7	35.7	43.1	80	8.3	7.1	9.0	6.7	8.6
34	43.5	41.0	46.7	34.9	42.2	85 and over	6.1	5.2	6.4	5.0	6.3

Source: U.S. National Center for Health Statistics, *Vital Statistics of the United States,* 1991, p. 86; and unpublished data.

retirement) has continued unabated. In 1983, 65-year-old men had a likelihood of less than one-third of being active in the labor force.

In determining work-life expectancy for purposes of calculating damages for loss of future income, therefore, the defense attorney or insurer needs to point out the significant trend toward earlier retirement. To put it simply, a claimant cannot expect an award of lost income to age 65 or 70, because he probably won't work that long.

1215 Present Value of Future Damages

The plaintiff will recover damages which are payable as of the time of trial. As to losses sustained prior to trial, the recovery will be based upon the reimbursement due to the plaintiff; but as to losses which will occur in the future, and which have not yet been incurred, the verdict will be based upon projections of the extent of the loss as it occurs. Clearly, the defendant is being required to pay the plaintiff now for expenses or losses to be sustained in the future. Since payment is being made in advance, before the loss has occurred, the defendant is entitled to an interest discount on the amount so paid. In other words, if the plaintiff will suffer a loss of earning capacity of $20 per week for the rest of his work-life, the loss would be incurred at the end of each week of the claimant's work life. If the remaining work-life is 20 years, then the payment required now should be the present value of $20 per week for 20 years. Clearly, this is not $1,040 per year times 20 years because the defendant would lose the interest that would be earned by that money had he or she retained it and paid the plaintiff $20 each week as the loss was incurred. The rate of discount or interest to which the defendant will be entitled is based on expectancy tables, with an appropriate interest discount.

Another way of illustrating the problem is to compare it with the situation of a bank advancing mortgage money. The amount the bank advances is comparable to the defendant's payment. This amount is the equivalent of the money to be paid back over the period of years; or, in the case of the defendant, the payment is the equivalent of the losses that will be suffered over a period of years. Therefore, the award for future losses will be based upon the present value of the losses to be sustained in the future. Expectancy tables will tell us how long the claimant will live or be able to continue to work. Present value tables take into consideration the expectancy figures and project them to a present figure at a discount rate. Table 12–2, based on the American Table of Mortality, is a present value table with an interest discount of 5 percent.

The table gives the present value of $1 per year payable until death. By using it, we can readily determine present value of the claim. For example, let us assume that we have a claimant, aged 51, who has sustained a permanent injury that will cause him to suffer pain for the rest of his life. The value

TABLE 12–2 Present Value of a Lifetime Annuity of $1 (5 percent interest)

Age	*Annuity or Present Value of $1 Due at the End of Each Year during the Life of a Person of Specified Age*
10	16.50475
11	16.46076
12	16.41469
13	16.36642
14	16.31581
15	16.26274
16	16.20722
17	16.14896
18	16.08779
19	16.02372
20	15.95658
21	15.88620
22	15.81257
23	15.73552
24	15.65484
25	15.57033
26	15.48176
27	15.38910
28	15.29210
29	15.19051
30	15.08425
31	14.97307
32	14.85666
33	14.73492
34	14.60774
35	14.47479
36	14.33572
37	14.19057
38	14.03897
39	13.88092
40	13.71604
41	13.54430
42	13.36528
43	13.17891
44	12.98494
45	12.78344
46	12.57414
47	12.35728
48	12.13275
49	11.90076
50	11.66175
51	11.41594
52	11.16361
53	10.90499
54	10.64036
55	10.37017
56	10.09472
57	9.81450
58	9.52988
59	9.24127
60	8.94928
61	8.65445
62	8.35742
63	8.05876
64	7.75900
65	7.45885
66	7.15921
67	6.86074
68	6.56420
69	6.27048
70	5.98022
71	5.69422
72	5.41286
73	5.13592
74	4.86279
75	4.59264
76	4.32477
77	4.05856
78	3.79392
79	3.53109
80	3.27017
81	3.01349
82	2.76062
83	2.51052
84	2.26066
85	2.00986
86	1.76061
87	1.51750
88	1.28611
89	1.06704
90	0.85453
91	0.64497
92	0.44851
93	0.28761
94	0.13605

of the pain is estimated at $20 per week. According to the American Table of Mortality, his life expectancy is 20.20 years. Twenty dollars per week amounts to $1,040 per year. If we did not consider any discount, we would multiply $1,040 by 20.20 years, and the result would be $21,008. Using the present value table at the discount rate of 5 percent, our figures would be:

Present value of $1 per year at age 51	$ 11.41594
Yearly payment	×1040
Present or commuted value	$11,872.58

From this example it can be seen that there is a substantial difference between the value without any discount and the same amount subject to a discount figure.

In using these tables, the age figure to be taken will be the claimant's age as of the nearest birthday. If the claimant is 22 years and 8 months at the time of computation, then the figures which should be used are those applicable to age 23, the nearest birthday. If the claimant is 22 years and 4 months old at the time of computation, then the figures for age 22 should be used.

The same principles apply to discounting claims based on the loss of future earning capacity. The loss will be measured by the claimant's work-life expectancy (see Table 12–3).

As an example, let us assume that the claimant, aged 46, sustained an injury that will result in the diminution of his earning capacity by $80 per month. The computation would be as follows:

Present value of $1 per year at age 46	$ 129.00
Reduced earning capacity	×80.00
Present or commuted value	$ 10,320

Under the single recovery rule the award would cover all the damage, that already suffered and future losses. Therefore, let us add some facts to the foregoing example so as to reflect the full recovery. Assume that the case is tried or settled two years after the accident. To that date, the claimant has medical bills in the sum of $2,675, provable loss of earning capacity covering total disability of 40 weeks at $100 per week, and 64 weeks of partial loss of earning capacity of $20 per week; in addition, his future loss of earning capacity is estimated at $80 per month. The valuation then would cover the following items:

Medical	$ 2,675.00
Total disability	4,000.00
Partial disability	1,280.00
Future disability	10,320.00
Total value	$18,275.00

Let us add another fact. Let us assume that the claimant will suffer pain for the rest of his life because of the injury, and that the value of the pain is estimated at $10 per week. The pain will have no relationship to his work-life, but will continue for the rest of his life whether he works or not. Therefore we must go to the life expectancy tables for our figures. At age 46 the value of $1 paid

TABLE 12–3

Monthly Annuities for the Duration of Life at Work (present value of $1 per month while at work, at 5 percent)

Age	*Work Expectancy (years)*	*Present Value*	*Age*	*Work Expectancy (years)*	*Present Value*
18	40.11	$202.20	54	10.06	$91.40
19	39.24	200.73	55	9.32	86.11
20	38.38	199.21	56	8.58	80.67
21	37.51	197.64	57	7.85	75.08
22	36.65	196.00	58	7.13	69.34
23	35.79	194.29	59	6.42	63.45
24	34.93	192.52	60	5.71	57.30
25	34.07	190.68	61	5.10	51.96
26	33.22	188.78	62	4.44	45.86
27	32.36	186.80	63	3.76	39.39
28	31.51	184.74	64	3.08	32.57
29	30.66	182.60	65	2.39	25.32
30	29.81	180.36	66	2.82	30.07
31	28.95	178.03	67	2.56	27.47
32	28.10	175.59	68	2.26	24.37
33	27.25	173.05	69	1.92	20.81
34	26.40	170.39	70	1.62	17.48
35	25.54	167.63	71	1.94	20.88
36	24.69	164.75	72	1.92	20.69
37	23.84	161.74	73	1.90	20.50
38	22.99	158.62	74	1.87	20.58
39	22.15	155.38	75	1.85	20.05
40	21.30	152.00	76	1.83	19.81
41	20.46	148.50	77	1.80	19.54
42	19.62	144.86	78	1.78	19.29
43	18.79	141.09	79	1.75	19.00
44	17.96	137.19	80	1.70	18.59
45	17.13	133.16	81	1.66	18.11
46	16.31	129.00	82	1.61	17.62
47	15.50	124.73	83	1.52	16.74
48	14.70	120.34	84	1.46	16.12
49	13.91	115.83	85	1.27	14.08
50	13.12	111.19	86	1.17	13.03
51	12.34	106.43	87	.83	9.31
52	11.57	101.55	88	.50	5.50
53	10.81	96.55			

annually is $12.57414. Ten dollars per week is $520 per year. Therefore the computation of the value of this item is:

Present value of $1 per year at age 46	$12.57414
Annual payment	×520.00
Present or commuted value	$6,538.55

The rule is that where there is an item of loss, which loss will continue only for the period of the claimant's work-life, such as a loss of earning capacity, the tables to be used are the Work-Life Expectancy tables. Where the item of loss will continue for the claimant's life, such as pain and suffering or medical expense, the table to be used is the Life Expectancy Discount table.

When we are dealing with a matter concerning work-life expectancy, we are frequently confronted with a case where the claimant's earning capacity at the time of the accident is at a peak and where, because of the occupation, the claimant's ability to earn will diminish with advancing age. This is especially true where the occupation involves physical labor. In such cases it is necessary to establish the claimant's average wage for the remaining period of work-life.

For example, let us assume that the claimant is 46 years of age and is employed as a day-laborer. We will assume some very simple figures, for the sake of convenience. Investigation discloses that laborers of his class usually work at full wages, averaging $100 weekly, until they reach age 52, at which time they work as watchmen, earning $50 per week. At age 46 the claimant's work-life is 16.31 years. Assuming that he could work, he would have earned $5,200 per year for 6 years, and for the balance of the time, or 10.31 years, his average would have been $2,600 per year. Therefore his total wages would have been $59,006. This amount, divided by 16.31, will develop his average yearly wage, or $3,617.84. Therefore, to calculate the value of this claimant's work-life expectancy, we would use his average yearly earnings as the base on which the value is computed and not the earnings which he enjoyed at the time of the accident.

In cases where the claimant's wages are expected to increase over the period of his work-life, the same procedure may be followed. It is necessary to establish the average wages to be earned each year and, using the average, apply the present value tables to that figure.

CLAIMS EVALUATION

1216 Personal Injury: Tangible Items

The first step in the determination of the settlement value of a case—or the amount which it would be to the advantage of the company to pay in settlement—involves an estimate of the possible jury verdict in the event of trial.

The estimate is based on a comparison of the applicable measure of damages to the facts of the claim, the proof which can be offered in support of each item of damage claimed, and the anticipated jury reaction to the evidence offered. The applicable measure of damages in personal injury cases consists of both tangible and intangible items. The tangible items are the out-of-pocket expenses which are susceptible of definite proof, such as the medical, surgical, and hospital expenses incurred, and the loss of earning capacity. The intangible items include mental and emotional distress.

The initial attention is directed to the tangible items. All of the details of the items claimed must first be obtained. These include: detailed medical, surgical, or hospital bills showing the dates of the treatment; the kind and type of treatments and charge for each treatment, together with an itemization of the claimed loss of earning capacity; the period of time during which total incapacity is claimed; as well as the period of time during which it is claimed that the incapacity was partial, and the extent of the partial disability. Each item then can be evaluated as to its reasonableness by subjecting it to all three of the following tests: (1) necessity, (2) duration, and (3) verification.

(As an initial example, let us apply the tests to the claimed items of medical expense. The procedure would be as follows:)

1. Necessity. First, the exact medical diagnosis must be obtained. This can be secured from the attending physician by means of a medical report. The diagnosis must be medically descriptive of the injuries sustained and not merely descriptive of the manner of causation. For example, a "whiplash type of injury" is not a medical diagnosis and is not descriptive of the injury sustained. It refers only to the manner of causation. Second, the standard medical practice with respect to the treatment of the injury must be ascertained. This includes the method of treatment, the frequency, and the usual anticipated result. This information can be obtained by reference to standard medical textbooks or can be obtained from the company's or an independent examining physician. Third, a comparison can be made between the standard medical practice and the treatment rendered as evidenced by the itemized bills submitted. A determination can be made whether standard medical practice was followed, whether treatment was rendered with the frequency which such practice demanded, and whether the case was overtreated or undertreated.

2. Duration. While it is true that no two cases are alike, there is a certain pattern to the course of treatment which each condition will require. For the most part, recovery usually follows within the accepted period of time unless there are complications (which will have to be considered in the cases where they occur). A medical examination by the company or a consulting physician during the period of treatment will be a helpful guide in deciding whether the treatment followed the usual pattern of frequency and duration, and whether the case was overtreated.

3. Verification. There are several means of verification available. Where an inquiry has been made into the medical treatment at the time the claimant's statement was taken, the actual bill can be compared with the statement made by the claimant as to the treatment rendered, the dates of the treatment, and the type of treatment rendered up to the date of the statement. If there is any discrepancy between the two, the claim representative is immediately put on inquiry as to the validity of the other charges made. In the case of a lawsuit, the claimant can be questioned either by deposition or interrogatory as to the exact details of the medical treatment. The claimant will usually be prepared to testify to the general course of treatment received and the total amount of money expended for the treatment, but if questioned as to the exact treatment received on a week-to-week basis, what was done at the occasion of each treatment, and whether the doctor personally rendered all of the treatment or whether it was rendered by a nurse or technician, some surprising answers may be obtained.

Where there is a charge for transportation to and from the doctor's office, such as taxi fares, the receipts for such charges should be obtained and the dates compared with the dates of treatment. If the dates do not coincide with the dates of treatment on the bill, and treatment was allegedly rendered on dates for which no transportation is claimed, the claim representative is put on notice of the possibility of the medical bill being padded. On the other hand, if no treatment was rendered on the dates of any of the taxi receipts, it is clear that the transportation furnished on those dates had no reference to the medical treatment of the case. Where the claimant has been hospitalized, the nurses' notes will indicate the date and the time of the doctor's visits.

Finally, recourse may be had to the doctor's own records. An examination of the records may show that some or all of the treatment was rendered for conditions entirely unassociated with the injury, or that the dates of the entries on the records do not coincide with the dates of treatment on the bill. If it is known from the investigation that the claimant was out of town, on vacation, or in jail, a check of the dates of treatment should reflect that no treatment was rendered during these periods of time.

To explain more fully, let us examine the two bills illustrated by Figures 12–1 and 12–2 and apply the first test of reasonableness, *necessity*. Neither bill meets the test of necessity. In Figure 12–1, the standard medical practice is merely to examine, diagnose, and recommend either a truss or an operation. There is no known medical treatment of a conservative nature that will cure or relieve a hernia in the inguinal region. Therefore, even if the treatment were rendered, the value of this bill is the reasonable value of the first treatment and, at most, one subsequent office visit for the purpose of determining whether the recommended truss was properly fitted.

For the purpose of further examination, let us assume that the condition treated in Figure 12–1 required treatment for a period of time. Most doctors do not have office hours on Wednesdays and Sundays, unless there is a coming holiday. By reference to this bill it will be noted that Wednesdays are excluded from the office visits except during the last week in June (Wednesdays are June 5, 12, 19, and 26). Sundays are likewise excluded (Sundays are June 2, 9, 16, 23, and 30). Therefore, the matter of consecutive daily treatment on other days is open to some question. The bill also has a charge for June 31. June has only 30 days.

In Figure 12–2, the diagnosis is a fracture of the right clavicle. The standard medical practice is merely to immobilize the patient's arm by means of a splint and to check the case once a week for about four weeks. Since the clavicle is not a movable bone, no heat and massage will be needed to restore motion or to promote callus. Also, a patient with a fractured clavicle is ambulatory, and un-

FIGURE 12–1

STATEMENT OF DOCTOR: Joseph Green
NAME OF PHYSICIAN

Name of Injured: Guisseppe Di Angelo — Age: 30 — Date of Injury: June 3, 19 89

Name of Employer: Blank Construction Co.

First Aid Rendered by: Joseph Green, M.D. — Subsequent Aid by: ______

CODE: O—office, V—house visit, H—hospital visit, N—night visit, X—X-ray, S—operation.

Month	1	2	3	4	5	6	7	8	9	10	11	12	13	14	15	16	17	18	19	20	21	22	23	24	25	26	27	28	29	30	31
June			F							O	O		O		O		O	O		O	O	O		O	O	O	O	O	O		O
July	O	O	O			O	O																								

Total Cost First Aid Treatment		$ 35.00
Office Visits 21	@ $ 30.00 each	630.00
Home Visits	@ $ ____ each	
Hospital Visits	@ $ ____ each	
Night Visits	@ $ ____ each	
Operations	@ $ ____ each	
X-Rays	@ $ ____ each	
Other Charges must be itemized and explained fully		
Total Expense for Medical Aid		$ 665.00

DIAGNOSIS: LEFT INGUINAL HERNIA

Explain in detail special treatment, if any, giving reasons for same and of what they consisted: TRUSS

Describe Treatment: HEAT AND MASSAGE

Result: IMPROVED

Patient refused treatment on ______, 19__.

Is patient capable of doing same work as before injury? NO If not, why? HERNIA

Patient pronounced able to resume work as of July 8 19 89 Patient discharged as cured on ______ 19__

Any permanent injury? Describe fully: Hernia-Operation necessary for cure

Dated at New City (CITY), New York (STATE), this 8th day of July, 19 89

(Signed) Joseph Green M.D.

(LOCAL ADDRESS)

der such circumstances there does not appear to be any necessity for house visits. The number of X rays seems out of proportion to the injury. While a fractured clavicle can be demonstrated clinically, the usual practice is to take an X ray to verify the fracture and to rule out any further bony pathology. It might be argued that a second X ray was necessary in order to be certain of the position of the bone after the arm was immobilized. In any case, two X rays would seem to be the maximum allowable in this particular case.

Let us assume the "bill" shown in Figure 12–3 is submitted. In analyzing this bill, the first consideration is the matter of diagnosis. There is no such medi

FIGURE 12–2

STATEMENT OF DOCTOR JOSEPH GREEN
NAME OF PHYSICIAN

Name of Injured JOHN SMITH Age 24 Date of Injury 10/2, 19 89

Name of Employer CHARLES BROWN

First Aid Rendered by JOSEPH GREEN, M.D. Subsequent Aid by

CODE: O—office, V—house visit, H—hospital visit, N—night visit, X—X-ray, S—operation.

Month	1	2	3	4	5	6	7	8	9	10	11	12	13	14	15	16	17	18	19	20	21	22	23	24	25	26	27	28	29	30	31
OCTOBER		F	V	V		V		V		V		V		O		O		O		O					O			O			

Total Cost First Aid Treatment	25		$ 25
Office Visits	7	@ $ 30 each	210
Home Visits	6	@ $ 40 each	240
Hospital Visits		@ $ each	
Night Visits		@ $ each	
Operations		@ $ each	
X-Rays	10/2, 4, 10, 30	@ $ 75 each	300
Other Charges must be itemized and explained fully			
Total Expense for Medical Aid			$ 775

DIAGNOSIS FRACTURE RIGHT CLAVICLE

Explain in detail special treatment, if any, giving reasons for same and of what they consisted

Describe Treatment HEAT AND MASSAGE

Result IMPROVED

Patient refused treatment on , 19 .

Is patient capable of doing same work as before injury? YES If not, why?

Patient pronounced able to resume work as of 10/31 19 89 Patient discharged as cured on 10/28 19

Any permanent injury? Describe fully

Dated at NEWARK (CITY), N.J. (STATE), this 3rd day of NOVEMBER, 19 89

(Signed) JOSEPH GREEN M.D.

(LOCAL ADDRESS)

Figure 12–3

Mary Smith, M.D.

Services rendered Elizabeth Green	
Diagnosis: Whiplash injury to the spine	
Date of injury: January 2, 1989	
First aid: January 2nd	$45.00
Strapping: January 3rd	30.00
House visits: January 3, 4, 5, 6, 8, 9, 10, 11, 12, 13, 15, 16, 17, 18, 19, 22, 23, 24, 25, 26, 29, 30, 31 February 1, 2, 5, 6. 27 @ $25.00	1215.00
Office visits: February 7, 8, 9, 10, 12, 13, 15, 16, 19, 20, 21, 23, 26, 27, 28, 29. March 1, 2, 3, 5, 6, 8, 9, 12, 13, 15, 16. 27 @ $25.00	675.00
Total	$3,198.00

cal diagnosis as "whiplash injury to the spine." It probably tells us the manner of causation, but it is not indicative of exactly what injuries were sustained. It could mean an impacted fracture of a vertebra, a fracture of a transverse process, contusion of the spinal cord, or merely a strain of the muscles of the back. In addition, the bill does not reflect exactly what treatment was rendered, except for the strapping on January 3. The frequency of the treatment appears to be out of line, especially when we check the dates of the treatment and the fact that no treatment was rendered on Sundays during the entire period. In addition, there is a charge for strapping on January 3 and also a charge for a house visit. There is a charge for February 29—in 1989 there was no Feb. 29. Finally, the bill is added incorrectly, the correct total being $1,965.

In its present form, the bill cannot be approved. Further information is needed as to diagnosis, the kind of treatment rendered, and an explanation for the daily treatments with the exception of Sundays. As to the charges for house and office visits, we should ascertain the prevailing rate in the community in which the treatment was rendered. In some states, there is a fee schedule applicable to workers' compensation cases. It may also be possible to determine usual and customary fees in the community. Such data should be utilized by the claim person as a guide, if they are available.

Loss of Earning Capacity. We can use the same criteria in deciding the claim for loss of wages or loss of earning capacity.

Necessity. Merely because the claimant chooses to take a vacation, does not have a job, or does not have a desire to work will not alone support the claim for loss of earning capacity. There must be medical proof of disability in the form of a medical report which will indicate the condition, the disability caused by the condition (whether temporary or partial), and the duration of the disability. To recover for loss of earning capacity, two elements must be established: first, that there actually was a loss of earning capacity, and second, that the loss of earning capacity was caused by the injury. The lack of either of these elements will defeat the claim.

Duration. The period of time during which it is claimed that there was a loss of earning capacity must be supported by medical proof of disability during the entire period. This means that not only must there be a medical report, but the doctor rendering the medical report must be capable of actually knowing that there was incapacity and not merely expressing an opinion.

For example, let us assume that the claimant was injured on June 1 and was treated by a doctor on June 2. This is the only medical treatment received. Let us further assume that the claim is for two months' disability running from June 1 to July 30. The claimant presents a report from the doctor that her disability, as a result of the accident, extended to July 30. Such a report could not support the period of disability. The doctor saw the case only once, and her knowledge of the claimant's condition is limited to the condition as it existed on June 2. Any opinion she may express as to how long the claimant was disabled after that date is entirely speculative and is not based on actual knowledge.

In settling such a case, the most that could be allowed would be an approximate one-week disability. It could be said that the doctor could predict that period of disability from the one treatment and examination. Anything beyond that would be pure guesswork. It is also obvious that the claimant's condition could not have been serious or she would have required more than one treatment.

Conversely, let us assume that the claimant received medical treatment during the entire two-month period, and that such treatment was necessary, but that the claimant went back to work two weeks after the accident. The medical report from the physician indicated a total disability during all of the treatment. The loss of earning capacity is limited to the period during which the claimant did not have any earning capacity, the two-week period. After that time her earnings were unimpaired, and therefore there was no demonstrable loss of earning capacity, even though medically she would have been justified in not working.

Verification. The claimant's physical condition can be verified by medical examinations by the company physician. The loss of earning capacity can be verified by the claimant's employer, by a copy of the claimant's payroll record (by the books of the business if the claimant is self-employed), as well as by a check with customers as to exactly what work the claimant did or was capable of doing during the period of alleged incapacity.

1217 Personal Injury: Intangible Items

These items refer to physical and mental distress. They are intangibles in the sense that they are not measurable by any mathematical standards and are subject to only a limited form of verification. When these items are submitted, the jury will hear the claimant's evidence as to the intensity and duration of the discomfort and inconvenience suffered, usually supported by the testimony of the attending physician or a specialist testifying in the claimant's behalf. In appropriate cases, this evidence may be controverted by the evidence of the defendant's examining physician. The jury verdict will represent the reaction of the community in which the case is tried as to the value of these items. Where the verdict is rendered in a lump sum, it would be a comparatively easy matter to subtract the provable special damages from the verdict amount in order to ascertain the amount allowed by the jury for physical or mental distress. When the claim representative is required to evaluate these items, he or she will use the same criteria: (1) intensity, (2) duration, and (3) community reaction.

1. Intensity. Consideration of this aspect begins with the claimant's description of the severity of the discomfort or inconvenience suffered and the effect that it had on all normal activities, as well as the discomfort, if any, associated with the kind and type of treatment received. The complaints will be compared with the diagnosis, the medical information available from the claimant's doctor, and the report of the company's examining physician. The latter report should indicate the complaints which were made at the time of examination, the history of the claimant's distress, and also the physician's opinion as to whether it is medically possible for the injury to have produced the discomfort of which the claimant complains. A conclusion will be reached as to whether the claimant has honestly stated the extent of the discomfort or has overstated it.

2. Duration. The duration of the distress can be checked by the claimant's medical information, the medical bills submitted in support of the medical out-of-pocket expenses, and by the examining physician's report. For example, if it is claimed that the distress was such that the claimant could not even leave the house, the medical bill might show office visits and contradict this assertion. Also, the activity checks made of the claimant during the alleged disability might reveal participation in strenuous recreational activities. In substance, the claim of the duration of distress will be compared with the available information so as to verify or deny the extent of it.

3. Community Reaction. Having established the intensity and duration of the distress, the claim representative will apply his or her experience—as well as knowledge of the amounts awarded by the jury in prior cases—and will value the distress accordingly. Clearly, community reaction to this aspect of the case will differ from community to community, some according it a higher valuation than others. Past experience as to jury awards is one of the guides to this valuation. The claim representative will utilize his or her own experience and may also have the benefit of some reporting service or contacts with local practicing attorneys in order to keep this experience up to date. No general rule can be enunciated as to which communities will be within the "high verdict" area and which will not. While the income level of the community may have some influence on jury awards, there is no substitute for current and up-to-date experience and whatever empirical data may be available.

1218 Formula Methods of Evaluation

Numerous formula methods of evaluation have made appearances from time to time. Most of them were created by the fertile imagination of various plaintiffs' counsel and were conceived solely for the purpose of inducing the insurance companies to place higher settlement values on their cases. The use of some formula method was urged as a justification for the demand which, usually, was more than the case was worth.

The formula methods have one common ingredient. They are founded on one or more arbitrary assumptions which have no basis either in law or in fact. As a result, they do not produce figures which represent a fair and realistic settlement valuation, nor do they produce figures which approximate the verdicts. Therefore, formula methods have not received general acceptance by the insurance industry.

There are apparently three schools of thought among the companies on this subject. Some are unalterably opposed to the use of any formula cvaluations whatsoever; first, because they are unsound, and second, because the use and acceptance of formula methods of any kind would lend support to the program of the plaintiffs' attorneys advocating their use. Others will value their cases by their own methods and will accept and use the formula method only where it produces a lower valuation. Still others use a formula method of some kind in the majority of their cases. In any event, no matter which view is taken by the company represented, the claim representative should be familiar with the more common methods of formula evaluation, their basic assumptions, and their inherent weaknesses. He or she will be confronted by demands which are based on them and should be prepared to meet the arguments urged in their support.

1219 The "Three Times the Medical" Formula

In seeking some means of placing a dollar value on the item of physical and mental distress, some lawyers have reasoned that there must be some relationship between the amount of the medical treatment that was rendered and the distress the claimant endured. It was reasoned that the more medical treatment required, the greater was the amount of the claimant's distress. They felt that a fair recompense for the claimant's distress would be an amount equal to twice the amount paid for the medical treatment. It is also argued that the medical bill is a reflection of the discomfort suffered: the higher the bill, the greater the discomfort.

The two basic assumptions along this line are that the amount of the medical bill measures the discomfort, and that the community response as to the value of the discomfort is an amount equal to twice the medical bill. No evidence can be adduced that either one of these assumptions is valid. Nevertheless, while recognition must be given to the inherent weakness of the reasoning which created it, the formula did produce settlement figures that were acceptable to both parties, and for that reason the formula was and still is used extensively as the basis for settlement negotiations.

In applying the formula to specific instances, let us assume that the medical bill was $100. (The figures used here, like other figures used in this chapter, are examples only, intended to illustrate a point.) The value of the claimant's discomfort would be $200, or a total of $300 for both items. For a more convenient method of figuring, the parties usually take the medical bill figure and multiply it by 3 in order to produce the value of both items. Let us further assume that X rays were taken at a cost of $50 and that the doctor required some other tests, such as a basal metabolism, blood, or culture test of some kind at a cost of $25. The claimant was disabled for a period of three weeks, during which there was a loss of earning capacity (salary) of $225, representing a weekly wage of $75. The formula evaluation of the case would work out as follows:

Medical treatment	$100.00
Distress	200.00
X rays	50.00
Tests	25.00
Wages	225.00
Total value	$600.00

Some attorneys have modified the formula and have based their demands on "three times the medical specials," which would include all the medical expense whether incurred for treatment, examinations, or tests. There is some question whether the period and amount of treatment can be used as a measure of the claimant's distress, but certainly the number of X rays and other diagnostic tests can have no relationship whatsoever to the extent of the distress. This did not prevent the making of demands on that basis and, where the insurance carrier was agreeable, a settlement on this basis would be made. Using our original case, the result would be:

Medical	$175.00
Distress	350.00
Wages	225.00
Total value	$750.00

Thus, by the simple expedient of lumping all the medical expenses together, the settlement valuation has been increased by $150. Clearly, if more X rays were taken or more tests were made, regardless of necessity, the total would go that much higher.

A further modification in the original formula comes about where the demand is based on "three times the specials," rather than limiting the basic figure to the medical or the medical treatment. As in the tests made, there is no real relationship between the amount of salary or wages earned and the claimant's distress. Following this method, the following result is produced:

Medical total	$ 175.00
Wages	225.00
	$ 400.00
	×3
Total value	$1,200.00

Thus, by changing the concept of the formula to "three times the specials" we have changed the original valuation of $600 to $1,200—for the same case. Further analysis will reveal that in the first instance, the value of the distress was fixed at $200, but the last method of computation produces a distress valuation of $800—in a case involving only three weeks' disability. Comparing the amount claimed for distress with the claimant's take-home pay of $75 per week, the distress comes to an average of $266.67 per week, or 3½ times the usual salary.

In presenting the variations of the formula, we have used the same figures. Where the case has been overtreated medically, or the medical bills are based on exorbitant rates per visit, and where more X rays and other diagnostic tests are used than is necessary, it is clear that higher valuations will be produced.

A further variation of the formula concerns a change in the multiplier from 3 to 4, 5, and even 10. This is usually justified on the theory that the multiplier of 3 refers to low-verdict areas, and also contemplates a case where there is a full recovery with no residual effects. Where the case is to be tried in a high-verdict area, or where there is some small permanent disability or facial scarring, a higher multiplier is used to cover either the verdict differential or the permanent condition.

1220 The Unit of Time Formula

This is an approach to the valuation of intangible items which is used exclusively by plaintiff's counsel. It begins with an arbitrary value being placed on the plaintiff's discomfort on a unit of time basis, so much per hour, day, week, or month. This unit value is multiplied by the number of hours, days, weeks, or months during which the discomfort continued. In cases where medical evidence indicated that the discomfort would continue beyond the date of evaluation or trial, projections are made to cover the future duration of the discomfort, and the same figures are applied to the anticipated discomfort to be suffered in the future, whether it be for a short period or for the remainder of the claimant's life.

As an illustration of the application of this formula, let us assume that we have a case in which the discomfort allegedly covered a period of 6 months and the arbitrary figure of 25¢ per hour is claimed as the reasonable value of the discomfort suffered. The plaintiff's attorney will concede that the claimant slept 8 hours a day and was therefore insensible to pain during that time. Therefore, the claim will be based only on the actual pain suffered, or 16 hours per day. The computation would be as follows:

16 hours @ 25¢	= $4.00 per day
6 months	= 180 days
Value of discomfort	= $720.00

The attorney will then argue that this figure only compensates the claimant for discomfort and does not take into consideration the value of the enjoyment of life of which the claimant has been deprived during the disability. The claimant likes to swim, bowl, fish, or engage in other sports but, because of the disability, was deprived of these pleasures. These items are arbitrarily valued at $3 per day, or $540 which, when added to the previous discomfort claim of $720, now makes the claim $1,260.

As a further item, the attorney could argue that the claimant was unable to perform his usual marital functions and that this loss of capacity during his disability, plus the humiliation and embarrassment, should have a value of at least another $2 per day, or $360, making the total $1,620. While other items could be and often are added to those already considered, the illustration will sufficiently set forth the form and substance of the procedure.

Plaintiffs' attorneys have also used this type of evaluation in statements to the jury in summation, implemented by the use of a blackboard on which the figures are placed. While some courts have permitted such arguments, there is a growing tendency on the part of the majority to whom the question has been presented to reject them.

The weakness of this formula approach is the same as we find in the others. There is no logical basis for the arbitrary assumptions of the values on which it is based. As one court analyzed it:

> The absurdity of a mathematical formula is demonstrated by applying it to its logical conclusion. If a day may be used as a unit-of-time in measuring pain and suffering, there is no logical reason why an hour or a minute or a second could not be used, or perhaps even a heart beat, since we live from heart beat to heart beat. If one cent were used for each second of pain, this would amount to $3.60 per hour, to $86.40 per twenty-four hour day, and to $31,536 per year. The absurdity of such a result must be apparent, yet a penny a second for pain and suffering might not sound unreasonable. The principle is the same, whether one uses a second, an hour or a day as the basic unit-of-time, because to the unit-of-time used one must assign some money value which has no foundation in the evidence. . . . [*Affett* v. *Milwaukee & Suburban Transit Corp.*, 106 N.W. 2d 274 (Wisconsin).]

1221 Factors Increasing Settlement Valuation

In some cases there are additional factors which increase the possibilities of a large verdict. These factors will increase the amount that the company would be well-advised to pay in settlement rather than to risk the trial of the case. Among the factors are:

1. Applicable law.
2. Nature of the offending instrumentality.
3. Locality of the accident.
4. Horror factor.
5. Personal and physical characteristics of the insured.
6. Character of defense witnesses.
7. Employment of an attorney.

1. Applicable Law. Where the facts give the claimant, for example, the advantage of the application of strict or absolute liability against the insured, or where the claimant has the benefit of a presumption of *res ipsa loquitur*, the applicable law favors the claimant, and the case will involve a jury question. In situations such as these—because the burden of proof which the claimant must sustain is light and the burden of explanation or defense is heavy—the claim poses a greater degree of danger to the company, and the claim representative will be persuaded to pay more in settlement than in the average case.

2. Nature of the Offending Instrumentality. Where the offending instrumentality is one which exposes the community or the claimant to an increased degree of peril because of its intrinsic nature, juries are apt to bring in larger verdicts. Such instrumentalities might consist of poisons, acids, explosives, and wild animals. Included in this area also would be instrumentalities which are not in themselves dangerous, but because of their poor maintenance expose people to greater danger. These might include poorly maintained premises in such dilapidated condition that they expose those entering them to additional risk of injury, or motor vehicles whose brakes, lights, and steering apparatus are not properly functional, and which are driven with the knowledge of the defective conditions.

Some jurors have a bias against such vehicles as taxicabs, motorcycles, and sports cars, and where any of these is involved, that factor may be persuasive of the necessity of a higher settlement valuation.

3. Locality of the Accident. This is a factor where the accident occurs at or near a nursing home, children's playground, school, hospital, or congested area. The negligent operation of the vehicle in those areas will have an influence on value.

4. Horror Factor. This is present when the act which caused the injury is reprehensible in nature or where the effects of the injury are such that the claimant presents a bizarre, grotesque, or gruesome appearance because of facial or head scarring, the enucleation of an eye, the amputation of a prominent member, such as a hand, foot, arm, or leg, or a severe mental or emotional disability. To illustrate the effect of this factor arising from the reprehensible nature of the act causing the injury, let us take two cases, both of which resulted in the death of a nine-month-old baby.

In the first case, the baby is held in its mother's lap while riding in an automobile. The defendant, a middle-aged schoolteacher, is driving her car in the opposite direction at a speed of approximately 25 m.p.h. The road is covered with snow and, in spite of her precautions, the schoolteacher loses control of the car and it sideswipes the vehicle in which the baby is riding. The baby falls from his mother's lap and sustains a fractured skull from which death ensues. The schoolteacher is technically chargeable with negligence in failing to keep her car under control, and, while the claim is actionable, there is no horror factor and no increased valuation is indicated.

In contrast to that case, let us assume that the nine-month-old baby is placed in a carriage and wheeled by his mother onto the front lawn. It is a beautiful summer day and the child is sleeping peacefully out in the sun. A truck comes down the street at a high rate of speed. The driver has a bottle of beer in one hand, and his other arm is around his girl friend who is riding with him. The truck goes out of control and runs onto the lawn and over the child, causing its death. The facts, as related by eyewitnesses, will indicate that the huge wheels passed completely over the baby's body, crushing it beyond recognition.

Both cases had the same result: the death of a nine-month-old baby. But the second case, which involved the horror factor because of the manner in which the accident was caused, will bring a much higher valuation at the hands of a jury than will the first. The second case also carries a major risk that a jury will impose punitive damages upon the truck driver and his employer. (See Section 1226 below.)

5. Personal and Physical Characteristics of the Insured. This factor is involved when the insured is likely to be a substandard witness because of age, appearance, language, or reputation. Jurors generally regard young drivers (especially teen-agers) as being irresponsible with respect to the operation of a motor vehicle. Older drivers may be viewed as having impairments of sight, reflexes, and response as to the apprehension and avoidance of the dangers of the highway. An insured whose appearance indicates a physical impairment, such as the absence of an arm or a leg, the wearing of extremely thick eyeglasses or the use of a hearing aid, may incline the jury to the belief that the physical impairment contributed to the causation of the accident. The insured's ability to use language to describe the event, his or her recall of the details of the event, as well as the appearance of sincerity, will all be taken into account. If any of these attributes are lacking—the language halting, rambling, and incoherent, or the recall of the past event hazy, or the appearance of sincerity questionable—the insured is a less-than-desirable witness. Similarly, a well-to-do personal appearance or reputation of wealth, where the claimant is a poor person, can count heavily against the insured.

6. Character of Defense Witnesses. Evaluation of the defense witnesses may disclose that they have an interest in the outcome of the lawsuit, are friends of the insured, have poor appearances, lack the ability to testify clearly, give the appearance of dishonesty, or have criminal records. If any of these conditions are present, the amount of reliance which can be placed upon them to establish the defense will be open to question.

7. Employment of an Attorney. Where some settlement negotiations have been conducted with the claimant, the appearance of an attorney in the case may influence the amount which will be required to settle the case. The attorney usually charges a contingent fee, based on one third to one half of the recovery. It stands to reason that, if the claimant's demand is $1,000, the case will have to bring $1,500 in settlement for him to net that amount after the attorney's fee is paid. Just how far the claim representative will be induced to go over the amount of the original settlement valuation will depend on the other factors of the case. These include the defenses available, the ability of the claimant's attorney and whether he or she is willing and able to try a case or is a "settler," and how near the trial date the settlement negotiations are held.

1222 Factors Decreasing Settlement Valuation

Among the factors which, if present, will decrease the amount that the company should be induced to pay in settlement are the:

1. Applicable law favoring the defendant.
2. Personal and physical characteristics of the claimant.
3. Credibility of the claimant's witnesses.
4. Responsibility of a codefendant.
5. Attorney's lack of control of the claimant.

1. Applicable Law Favoring the Defendant. This factor applies where the claimant is chargeable with contributory negligence or assumption of risk, or where, because of the facts of the event, the claimant will have difficulty in establishing the negligence of the defendant.

2. Personal and Physical Characteristics of the Claimant. As opposed to the appearance of the insured, the claimant's appearance may be such that he or she does not inspire credibility, has poor recall of the events, is hesitant in answering questions, or has some speech defect which makes the claimant difficult to understand. As in the case of the insured, the presence of a physical defect unrelated to the accident, such as the absence of an arm, leg, or eye, as well as a defect in sight or hearing (as evidenced by extreme magnification in eyeglass lenses or the wearing of a hearing aid), might induce the jury to believe that these defects had some part in the causation of the accident.

3. Credibility of Claimant's Witnesses. If the claim representative has reason to know that the claimant's witnesses will create a poor impression as to the believableness of their testimony because of their interest in the outcome, the value of these witnesses to the claimant may be discounted accordingly. This interest might be based upon bias, prejudice, or relationship to the claimant, or because of a record of convictions of crimes involving moral turpitude. Included among the claimant's witnesses would be the claimant himself, and the claimant's testimony and credibility should be subject to the same criteria.

4. Responsibility of a Codefendant. Where the insured is one of two or more joint tort-feasors, his or her liability is joint or individual. Where the other tort-feasor (or tort-feasors, as the case might be) are codefendants, or where they can be brought in by the insured as such, it is clear that the responsibility for the claimant's damage is divided among them. The claim representative will weigh the degree of danger posed by the case and will evaluate the probabilities of the insured being exonerated and the others held liable. If the chances of the insured are good, the claim representative may offer to make a small contribution to the settlement, if one is agreed upon, but ordinarily will not actively engage in settlement negotiations. If the probabilities of a successful defense for the insured are remote, the claim representative should engage in carrying on the negotiations, either alone or in concert with the representatives of the other defendants.

If the case is settled, it is reasonable for the claim representative to insist on some participation from the other defendants, or at least a contribution toward the amount paid. If participation or a contribution is refused, consideration will be given to disposition of the case by means of a covenant not to sue. In any case, the presence of one or more codefendants should reduce the amount that the company would be induced to pay in settlement.

5. Attorney's Lack of Control of the Claimant. This is an intangible element but can sometimes be an important factor in reducing the amount of settlement. The claim representative will usually know something about the claimant's background and occupation. Where the claimant is a migrant worker, a transient, or a person who does not stay in any one place for any appreciable period of time, the attorney may have some difficulty in having the claimant present in court at the time of trial. This is especially true where the attorney has made some financial advances to the claimant. Clearly, the attorney will not be able to establish a case without the client, and the attorney's anxiety to settle may be motivated by a desire to close the case before the client takes off for places unknown. Confronted with this problem, the attorney will usually settle for an amount less than the sum which would be required if this factor did not exist.

1223 Survival Claims

At common law the death of either plaintiff or defendant ended the litigation; to use legal terminology, the action "abated" with the death of either party. Legislation has changed the rule. At the present time, when either party to the litigation dies, the action may be brought or continued by or against the personal representative of the deceased. When the injured person dies, whether as a result of the accident or not, whatever cause of action that person had against a tort-feasor during his or her lifetime may be brought by the deceased's personal representative. For the cause of action to survive to the personal representative, it must have been such a cause of action as could have been asserted by the deceased had he or she lived. If the deceased settled the case while alive, or the statute of limitations had run against the claim, the deceased could not have asserted the claim had life continued. Therefore, in those two cases, there was no cause of action to survive, since the deceased did not have a cause of action which could be asserted at the time of death. The test is whether the deceased could have asserted the claim at the time of death. If so, then the action survives; otherwise it does not.

The survival statute merely allows the personal representative to take the place of the deceased and to perform whatever acts the deceased could have performed with relation to the case if death had not intervened. It does not give the personal representative any greater rights than those the deceased had; it does not alter the burden of proof nor does it in any way affect the running of the statute of limitations. The personal representative must sustain the burden of proof, producing evidence of liability, as well as evidence of damages, just as the deceased would have had to do if he or she personally brought the action. The statute of limitations generally will continue to run against the case just as if the deceased had lived. For example, let us assume that the deceased passed away one year, 11 months, and 29 days after the accident, and that the statute of limitations on personal injury cases is two years. The personal representative has exactly one day within which to bring the action. The statute generally will run two years after the accident, whether the injured person is alive or dead.

The measure of damages is exactly the same as in any other personal injury case, with the exception that the loss of earning capacity would be measured by the period from the date of the accident to the date of death, and the out-of-pocket expenses would be limited to those expenses incurred by the deceased during life. The obligation to pay for funeral expenses was not incurred during the deceased's lifetime, and therefore this is not an item of damages. It should be emphasized that the action brought by the personal representative is exactly the same action that the deceased could have brought had he or she lived. The personal representative is a substitute for the deceased, and whatever the deceased could have recovered while alive can be recovered by the personal representative—and nothing more. If the deceased was alive, he or she could not have recovered for funeral expense; neither can the personal representative in the absence of a statutory provision that permits this item to be included. The items of damage, then, are the out-of-pocket expenses, loss of earning capacity, and physical and mental distress incurred or suffered by the deceased during life.

Survival claims can be divided into three classes, according to the cause of death:

1. Death from causes other than the accident.
2. Instantaneous death caused by the accident.
3. Death due to the accident after a period of time.

1. Death from Causes Other than the Accident. Death may have occurred after the deceased had completely recovered from the effects of the accident, or may have occurred while the deceased was still under treatment, or still suffering disability as a result of the accident. In either case the measure of damages is the same, namely, the expenses incurred and the distress suffered up to the time of death. In the second case, where the deceased, had death not occurred, might have suffered for years from the effects of the injury, the result is exactly the same. The fact that the deceased might have so suffered is not an element of damage to be considered; the only measure is the suffering actually sustained.

2. Instantaneous Death. If death occurred instantly, or simultaneously with the happening of the accident, it is clear that the deceased has sustained no out-of-pocket expenses, no loss of earning capacity, and has suffered no distress; therefore the claim has no value. It must be emphasized that this conclusion relates to instantaneous death only, and if the deceased survived the accident, even for a matter of seconds, the case is not one of instantaneous death and must be considered under the third division.

3. Death Due to the Accident after a Period of Time. Death may occur seconds, minutes, weeks, or years after the happening of the accident. We use exactly the same measurement in all cases when it comes to damages. Let us assume that the claimant died 60 seconds after the happening of the accident, and that survival for that period of time can be established. Little or no out-of-pocket expenses were sustained, but the deceased may have been conscious during that minute and experienced severe physical distress. If he or she was unconscious during that minute, then no physical distress was suffered. The damages would be measured in such a case by the period of conscious pain and suffering, and if there was no conscious pain and suffering, the case has little or no value. The same criteria would be applied to all other cases in this class. If the deceased survived for a longer period of time but did not regain consciousness at any time after the accident and before death, there is no basis for a claim for conscious physical distress. But other items, such as out-of-pocket expenses and loss of earning capacity, must be taken into account.

Some states have combined the survival action with an action for wrongful death where there is a relationship between the two. The majority of the states, however, have statutes which completely disassociate the two causes of action. In any case, it is possible to have an action brought under the survival statute, and none under the wrongful death statute, for the reason that death was not the result of the accident. On the other hand, where the deceased survived for any period of time and then died as a result of the accident, there are two causes of action: one for the damages which the deceased sustained during his lifetime, and the other for damages for wrongful death.

1224 Wrongful Death

The cause of action for wrongful death did not exist at common law. It is a cause of action created by legislative enactment and, therefore, we must look to the statute itself to determine the measure of damages and the persons for whose benefit such damages may be sought. The first of these statutes was enacted in England in 1846 as the Fatal Accidents Act, more generally known as Lord Campbell's Act. The purpose of the act was to provide a means whereby the bereaved family of the accident victim could recover a sum of money which would be the equivalent of what they would have received from the victim had he lived. The family of the victim was frequently left destitute, and it was to relieve this situation that the act was passed.

No recovery was provided for the mental anguish and bereavement suffered by the members of the family. The measure of damages was based entirely upon the pecuniary loss suffered by each member of the family. This does not mean that damages are measured by the total future income that the deceased would have enjoyed had he lived, but by that portion of his income which could reasonably be expected to have been contributed to the family members. For example, a single man earning $100 per week regularly sent his mother $35 per week for her support. In the case of his death the mother's pecuniary loss would be $35 per week for the balance of *her* life. The obligation assumed by the son would continue only as long as his mother lived and would end with her death.

The loss of society, companionship, sexual relations (in the case of a surviving husband or wife), love, and affection does not represent a pecuniary loss, however great the loss might be. For that reason these items are not taken into account.

All of the American states have wrongful death statutes. Most of the states have enacted statutes similar to Lord Campbell's Act by providing for a recovery based upon the deceased's future contributions. Others have introduced variations of the original act, and still others provide for an entirely different measure of damages. Some states provide for a maximum limit of recovery, whereas others leave the amount of the award to the discretion of the jury with no limit whatsoever. The claim representative must be familiar with the wrongful death statute of the state and thoroughly understand the measure of damages. He or she also must keep abreast of legislative amendments to the statute.

While it is beyond the scope of this work to analyze the various statutes in detail, wrongful death statutes generally fall into one of four classifications: (1) punitive statutes, (2) statutes providing for damages based on loss to the estate, (3) statutes providing for damages based on contributions, and (4) combined death and survival statutes.

1. Punitive Statutes. Some of the earlier wrongful death statutes provided assessment of damages by way of punishment for causing the death of a human being, with no regard to the loss suffered by the survivors. The trend has been away from this notion, and today only two states award damages on this basis: Massachusetts (by statute) and Alabama (by judicial interpretation). The Massachusetts statute reads in part as follows:

> . . . For death of a person, exercising due care and not in one's employ, by negligence or wilful, wanton or reckless acts of one's self or servants, recovery may be had of not less than $5,000 or more than $50,000, according to the culpability of the defendants in the case.

This means that the amount of damages recoverable, subject to the monetary limitations set forth, is based upon the degree of negligence or "culpability" of the defendants. The greater the negligence, the greater the award; or the more wrongful the act, the greater the punishment to be inflicted.

The Alabama statute provides for the recovery of "such damages as the jury may assess" with no limitation as to the amount of recovery. The courts of that state have construed the statutory language to mean that damages should be proportioned to the degree of culpability.

2. Damages Based on Loss to the Estate. Among states that have this type of statute, there are three distinctly different approaches to the measurement of damages, each state using one of the three. These measurements are:

1. Net Loss to the Estate. The net earnings of the deceased, after subtracting the amount that would have been spent personally for food, clothing, shelter, and entertainment, are reduced to present value.

2. Gross Loss to the Estate. Damages are based on the earnings of the deceased over the work-life period, without any deduction for expenditures by the deceased. This would provide a greater recovery than if the actual loss sustained by the estate is reduced to present value.

3. Accumulation. Damages are based on what the deceased would have earned and saved during the work-life period (plus interest thereon), the damages being established by his past performance as to the percentage of earnings which were actually saved. This measurement offers the least recovery for the death of the breadwinner who expends most or all of the salary to sustain the family. The amount here is likewise reduced to present value.

Where there are survivors, and damages are based on the net loss to the estate, the result will be practically the same as would be the case where a Lord Campbell's Act type of statute was involved. In the two other situations, the amount of the recovery would differ considerably in that the second would provide for a greater recovery, and the third considerably less. In any case, where there are no survivors, this fact would not in any way alter the amount of the recovery under this type of statute whereas, under a Lord Campbell's Act type, there would be no pecuniary loss if there were no survivors, and there would be no recovery. Under this type of statute funeral expenses, since they represent a loss to the estate, are recoverable.

3. Damages Based on Contributions. The great majority of the states have enacted statutes of this type. They closely parallel Lord Campbell's Act, and provide for a recovery based on the probable future contributions to the beneficiaries by the deceased. Clearly, the length of the deceased's work-life, net income, and the life expectancy of each beneficiary will all have an influence on the value of the claim. For example, if a beneficiary should die prior to the trial, the period of the deceased's possible contributions to that beneficiary would be limited to the beneficiary's lifetime, or the period from the date of the deceased's death to the date of the beneficiary's death. Also, where the beneficiary is much younger than the deceased, it is clear that contributions by the deceased would continue only so long as he or she was able to earn. Therefore, the value of such a claim would be measured by the deceased's work-life. Where the beneficiary is older than the deceased, and the life expectancy of the beneficiary is less than the deceased's work-life, the recovery is measured by the life expectancy of the beneficiary rather than by the work-life of the deceased.

Since the recovery is measured solely by the pecuniary loss suffered by the beneficiaries, damages are limited to that measurement and no other. Funeral expenses ordinarily are not included (unless specifically provided for by the statute), nor is there any recovery for mental anguish or bereavement, or loss of society, companionship, love, and affection, since none of these represent a pecuniary loss. Some states regard the loss of the advice, help, instruction, and guidance which reasonably could have been expected to have been received by the beneficiaries from the deceased as a pecuniary loss and allow damages for such losses. The theory is that, if the beneficiaries sought such advice and guidance from other sources, it could be obtained by the payment of fees for such services.

Wrongful death claims based on the death of a child present a particularly troublesome problem. In the distant past, a child was an economic asset since the child could be set to work at a very early age, and, at common law, the wages of the child were the property of the father (the mother would have no common-law claim unless she was a widow, had been deserted by the father, or the child was illegitimate). The older cases refer to the wage-profit formula in evaluating claims for the death of a child, basing the recovery on the wages earned or expected to be earned by the child, less the anticipated costs of raising the child. The damages thus produced were limited to the period of the child's minority since the father had no right to the child's wages when the child came of age.

The situation is quite different at the present time. Children do not work at an early age. The costs of raising and educating a child usually far exceed any possible profit which a parent might receive from the child's work. As a matter of fact, in the majority of families—in the absence of special circumstances—the parents seldom receive any part of the child's earnings. In spite of these facts, evidence is offered of the child's possible earnings. Such evidence is highly speculative, but substantial awards have been made by juries who were undoubtedly swayed by the mental anguish and bereavement of the parents rather than the actual pecuniary loss.

Some states have approached the problem more honestly by providing a remedy in the wrongful death statute for mental anguish and bereavement of parents caused by the death of a minor child. The Florida Wrongful Death statute (Section 768.03) provides that the recovery in the case of the death of a minor child may be for the loss of the child's services and "such sum for the mental pain and suffering of the parents as the jury may assess."

4. Combined Death and Survival Statutes. Some statutes provide for one cause of action to recover for the damages sustained by the deceased before death and for the damage caused by the death itself. These statutes avoid some of the complications which arise where there are separate survival and wrongful death statutes, disposing of all claims arising out of the accident and death in the one action.

In all of these statutes the measure of damages is not affected by the fact that the survivors or the estate are the beneficiaries of life insurance policies carried by the deceased; the amounts so recovered are not allowed in mitigation of the damages. While the cases do not so state, it would seem that tacit recognition is being given to the collateral source rule in that recoveries from a collateral source do not diminish the tort-feasor's liability to respond in damages.

1225 Settlement Valuation of Wrongful Death

It is clear that, because of the variations between the wrongful death statutes, the method of establishing the settlement value will depend upon the provisions of the statute. Under statutes of the punitive type, it is practically impossible to anticipate, with any degree of accuracy, the amount of the jury verdict. Suffice it to say that consideration must be given to the facts of the accident, the tort-feasor's conduct, and the degree of fault charged against the tort-feasor. Clearly, the presence or absence of the horror factor will influence the verdict. As a guide, the claim representative can refer to verdicts in similar cases in the same area. While the outcome of other cases will not be conclusive—in the sense that juries cannot always be expected to follow the same verdict pattern—they will be persuasive of the jury thinking in the particular area in which the case is to be tried.

Where the measure of damages depends upon the income or contributions of the deceased, the value of these cases can be estimated by the use of the appropriate present value tables. To do this, however, the most important element to be established is the net income of the deceased, whether it will increase or decrease during the work-life period, and the portion of the income which would have been devoted to the deceased's subsistence. Again, it should be emphasized that the net income is the deceased's take-home pay and not his gross wages. In cases involving the net loss to the estate, or contributions, it becomes important to ascertain probable personal expenses; that is, the amount the deceased normally would expend for personal food, clothing, shelter, and entertainment. The net income, less this amount, will be the net loss to the estate, or the amount which is available for contributions.

We will consider a number of cases, with respect to the computation of estimated damages, where the recovery is based on the loss to the estate and where it is based on the deceased's contributions to the beneficiaries. The figures in all of the following examples do not contemplate any limitation as to the amount recoverable under the statute. If there is a maximum limit provided, and the computations exceed that amount, the limit of the statute will be controlling.

Damages Based on Loss to the Estate. Under this classification, there are the three approaches to the measurement of damages: net loss to the estate, gross loss to the estate, or accumulations. Let us assume that the deceased is 40 years of age at the time of his death. His take-home pay is $400 per month; his personal expenses are $250 per month, and he is able to save and accumulate $25 per month. Further assume that his wages will remain constant for the remainder of his work-life, and that there is no anticipated change in income, either increasing or decreasing it. According to Table 12–3, which shows monthly annuity for the duration of life at work (page 406), the present value of $1 per month, discounted at 5 percent, at age 40, is $152. And according to these figures, the computation of the value in each category is as follows.

Net Loss to the Estate	
Net income per month	$ 400.00
Personal expenses	250.00
Net loss	$ 150.00
Present value $1 per month	× 152.00
Present value	$22,800.00
Gross Loss to the Estate	
Net income per month	$ 400.00
Present value $1 per month	× 152.00
Present value	$60,800.00
Accumulations	
Savings per month	$ 25.00
Present value $1 per month	× 152.00
Present value	$ 3,800.00

In all of these cases, accuracy in the determination of the basic figures is essential. For example let us assume that, instead of a net income of $400 per month, investigation would have revealed that the deceased was employed on a time and overtime basis; that his income did not remain constant for the entire year and, over the period of one year (taking into consideration the slack season), his average income was $350—not $400. The difference would affect the present value figures in the first two categories considerably in that the net loss to the estate would be $15,200 as compared to $22,800, and the gross loss figure would be $53,200 as compared to $60,800. The difference in income would have no effect on the computation based on accumulations, unless the comparison between the deceased's personal expenses and his net income demonstrated the impossibility of any savings whatsoever, or indicated that the amount of saving must have been something less than claimed. In any event, it cannot be overemphasized that accuracy in the establishment of the basic figures is extremely important.

Damages Based on Contributions. In computing present value, which is based on contributions, we will have to consider the age of the beneficiary and his or her life expectancy, and the age and work-life expectancy of the deceased. If the beneficiary is older than the deceased, the obligation of contribution would continue only during the lifetime of the beneficiary, which in many cases is shorter than the work-life expectancy of the deceased. On the other hand, where the life expectancy of the beneficiary is greater than the deceased's work-life, the obligation to make contributions would continue only so long as the deceased was capable of producing an income. In addition, the health of the beneficiary might have an effect upon life expectancy, reducing it below the average expectancy. The same would be true of the health of the deceased. If, at the time of the accident, the deceased was suffering from some condition which would reduce work-life expectancy, this fact must be taken into consideration.

The amount of the contributions must be accurately verified. This can be done by examining canceled checks, past income tax returns, allocations of salary made to dependents, as well as books of account, paid bills, and other documents of similar nature. Also, the income of the deceased will sometimes furnish a clue as to whether the contributions were in fact made. If his income was such that all of it was needed to sustain himself, this would leave little room for contributions of anything but a very small payment. For example, if the deceased earned $100 per week, and his personal expenses were $90 per week, it is clear that the most that could be available for contributions to others would be $10 per week, or less. Any claim for contributions of more than $10 would be untenable and, undoubtedly, untrue. Examples 1, 2, 3, and 4, illustrate the use of the tables with reference to computing valuations in respect to damages based on contributions.

EXAMPLE 1

PROBLEM: Evaluation, one older beneficiary.
CLAIM: Wrongful death.
LAW: Compensatory damages to beneficiaries; no limit.
DECEASED: Age 38, unmarried, good health prior to accident.
CLAIMANT: Dependent mother, age 66.
HEALTH OF DEPENDENT: Excellent.
LIABILITY: Clear.
WAGES: Take-home pay $125 per week.
CONTRIBUTION: $35 per week to mother.

Valuation (commutation rate 5%)

With the mother as the sole dependent, her loss as a result of the accident is the loss of contributions from her son for the rest of her life. Therefore, since the son will outlive his mother, the measure of damages would be the present value of $35 per week ($1,820 annually) for the mother's life expectancy.

Present value of $1 per year (at age 66)*	$ 7.15921
Annual payment	× 1820
Present value	$13,029.76

*Table 12–2

EXAMPLE 2

Problem: Evaluation, two older beneficiaries.
Claim: (Same facts as No. 1.)
Claimants: Mother, age 66; father, age 69.
Health of Beneficiaries: Excellent.
Contributions: $35 weekly to both.
Assumption: Contribution equal to both parents.

Valuation (commutation rate 5%)

Loss is measured by the lives of both mother and father. Annual payment of $1,820 is divided equally, $910 to each.

Mother's Claim	
Present value $1 per year at age 66	$ 7.15921
Annual payment	×910
Present commuted value	$ 6,514.88
Father's Claim	
Present value $1 per year at age 69	$ 6.27048
Annual payment	×910
Present value	$ 5,706.13
Present value of both claims	$12,221.01

EXAMPLE 3

Problem: Evaluation, one younger beneficiary.
Claim: Wrongful death.
Law: Compensatory damages; no limit.
Deceased: Mechanic, regularly employed, age 38; married, no children, no previous health impairment.
Claimant:Wife, age 25.
Health of Beneficiary: Excellent.
Liability: Clear.
Wages: Take-home pay, $125 per week.
Contribution: Cost of maintenance of deceased (lunches, clothing, rent, transportation to and from work, and entertainment) computed at $75 per week; wife's portion of earnings, $50 per week.

Valuation (commutation rate 5%)

The wife's life expectancy at age 25 is 38.81 years. This is greater than the deceased's work-life expectancy of 22.99 years. Since the deceased's obligation is limited to the years during which he can produce income, the valuation will be based on the deceased's work-life expectancy.

Present value of $1 per year at age 38*	$ 158.62
Monthly contribution ($50 × 4)	×200
Present value	$31,724.00

*Table 12–3.

EXAMPLE 4

Problem: Evaluation, one younger and one older beneficiary.
Claim: Wrongful death.
Law: Compensatory damages; no limit.
Deceased: Mechanic, regularly employed, age 38; married, no children, no previous health impairment.
Claimant: Wife, age 25, and mother, age 70.
Health of Beneficiaries: Excellent.
Liability: Clear
Wages: Take-home pay, $125 per week.
Contributions: To mother, $15 per week; to wife, $45 per week; personal expenses of deceased, $65 per week.

Valuation (commutation rate 5%)

Mother's Claim	
Present value $1 per year at age 70*	$ 5.98022
Annual payment ($15 × 52)	×780
Present value	$ 4,664.57
Wife's Claim	
Present value $1 per month at age 38†	$ 158.62
Monthly payment ($45 × 4)	×180
Present value	$28,551.60

*Table 12–2. †Table 12–3.

The use of these particular present value tables is not mandatory as far as the jury is concerned. They are set forth as examples of a vast amount of data which will form, in part, the basis of expert testimony that the jury will be expected to weigh. Neither is the claim representative obligated to base his or her settlement values or estimated values on them. Their purpose is merely to serve as a guide to estimated values and for use in connection with reducing settlement demands. In any case, the claim representative will be guided by the specific facts of each case and by his or her experience and judgment in arriving at a settlement figure.

PUNITIVE DAMAGES

1226 Nature of Punitive Damages

Damages awarded by the courts in tort causes of action may be defined as pecuniary compensation or indemnity recoverable by any person who has suffered loss, detriment, or injury, whether to his or her person, property, or rights. The money damages so awarded may be *compensatory* or *punitive*.

Compensatory damages consist of an award of money which will reasonably compensate the injured person for the loss suffered up to the time of trial and, if the injury is a continuing one, the amount needed to indemnify the injured party against losses which will be incurred in the future. (See previous sections of this chapter—Sections 1201, 1210, 1211, and 1212, for example—for a discussion of these concepts.)

In addition to compensatory damages, most states permit the jury to award punitive damages—additional amounts by way of punishment where the defendant's conduct has been intentional, malicious, or outrageous. The award is made to the plaintiff over and above the amount of the compensatory damages to punish the defendant for his outrageous behavior and to prevent him from repeating the same offense.

Punitive damages may also be assessed against the employer or the principal for the acts of his or her servant or agent, even though the employer or principal did not participate in the occurrence and was unaware of it. Punitive damages may be assessed when any of the following situations are found to exist:

1. Where the principal authorized the act and the manner of its accomplishment, or ratified or approved the act after it was done.
2. Where the agent was not selected with due care and where the exercise of due care would have revealed the unfitness of the agent for the task.
3. Where the agent was employed in a supervisory or managerial capacity and performed the act within the scope of his authority.

Situation 1 merely states the fundamental rule of agency that, where a person performs an act through another under his control, he does the act himself. Therefore, having control of the method and means of doing the act, the principal is answerable for the entire act. The same thing is true where the principal ratifies or adopts the act as his own, after the offense has been committed.

Situation 2 refers to the duty of care in the selection of employees which the prinpcal must exercise in cases where others are exposed to a risk of injury. For example, *A* employs *B* as a janitor in his apartment house, giving him a master key. If *A* had checked *B*'s employment record, he would have ascertained that *B* had been discharged from his previous position because he viciously attacked a woman tenant. *B* then attacks a woman tenant in *A*'s apartment house, after gaining access to the apartment with the master key. *A* may be liable for punitive damages because his failure to exercise care in the selection of *B* exposed his tenants to an unreasonable risk of harm and, in employing *B* under those circumstances, *A* made *B*'s acts his own.

Situation 3 may seem to overlap Situation 2, but this is not entirely the case. Situation 3 refers to corporations or large firms where there has been no fault on the part of the employer, either in the selection or the retention of the employee. Punitive damages may be awarded against the employer because it employed the agent in a managerial capacity and his acts then became the acts of the employer.

1227 A Current Perspecitve on Punitive Damages

The doctrine of punitive damages has been a much-praised and much-criticized part of our civil justice system.

It has been praised because it allows juries to impose pecuniary punishment on defendants who are thought to be "guilty" of intentional wrongdoing, malice or conscious disregard for the safety of another. The doctrine has been criticized precisely because it permits the imposition of punishment, and punishment is the object of our *criminal* justice system. Compensation for loss is the object of our civil justice system. A civil jury that decides to punish a defendant is allowed to impose quasi-criminal penalties without the safeguards of due process and equal protection, and a higher burden of proof, that the criminal law affords to criminal defendants. Punitive damages also are criticized as a windfall to a plaintiff who has already received compensation.

Defense counsel and claim representatives frequently voice their concern that the pleading of punitive damages has become almost a routine strategy of plaintiffs' counsel. Concern about potential punitive damages verdicts skews the claim evaluation and settlement process. Cases that normally would be tried (or settled for a small amount) may be settled for a disproportionately large sum, because of the threat of a potentially ruinous punitive damages verdict. To an increasing extent, punitive damages verdicts in a jurisdiction represent the amount of maximum exposure of defendants, and are factors defendants must consider in formulating settlement positions and litigation strategies.

Defendants who have been on the receiving end of punitive damages verdicts have argued in numerous appellate cases in state and federal courts that punitive damages are unjustifiable and unfair. Several such cases have been heard by the U.S. Supreme Court. Appellants have offered various constitutional arguments, based on equal protection and/or due process, that juries should not be allowed unfettered freedom to impose punitive damages. A substantial number of the Justices have been sympathetic to such arguments. (See *TXO Production Corp.* v. *Alliance Resources Corp.*, 113 S.Ct. 2711 [1993].) A majority of the court may yet determine that punitive damages are unconstitutional because, under certain circumstances, they violate the Due Process Clause. At this writing, the Court has granted certiorari in at least one case in which such agruments will be presented again.

Many recent tort reform efforts also have focused on punitive damages. Several state legislatures in recent years have passed legislation placing caps (or maximum amounts) on punitive damages in certain cases, for example, or imposing a higher standing of proof as a prerequisite to an award of punitive damages.

Critics of punitive damages, since the 1994 elections, have had reason to be hopeful that Congress would enact significant federal tort reform legislation. In March 1995, the U.S. House of Representatives passed the Common Sense Legal Standards Reform Act, which would place a cap (or maximum) on punitive damages in all civil lawsuits at $250,000, or three times economic damages, whichever is greater. In May 1995, the Senate passed its own version of tort reform legislation—limited to products liability actions. The Senate bill limits punitive damages to two times compensatory damages or $250,000, whichever is greater; it also provides uniform standards for punitive awards. Passage of the two bills is a significant milestone in the history of punitive damages. However, differences in the House and Senate bills must be reconciled in conference committee before a bill can be sent to the president and, at this writing, a presidential signature is by no means certain.

Chapter 13

Settlement Negotiations and Termination

SETTLEMENT CONSIDERATIONS

1300 Nature and Purpose of Settlement

1301 Burden of Proof

1302 Qualifications for Settlement

1303 Nuisance Settlements

1304 Classification of Claims as to Liability

1305 Relationship of Injury to Settlement

1306 Liens

1307 Satisfaction of Liens

1308 Subrogation

1309 Subrogation by the United States

SETTLEMENT NEGOTIATIONS

1310 Order of Settlement

1311 Settlements by Joint Tort-Feasors

1312 The Settlement Interview

1313 First-Call Settlements

1314 Control of the Claimant

1315 Preparing for Settlement Negotiations

1316 The Offer

1317 When to Make an Offer

1318 When Not to Make an Offer

1319 Negotiations with Attorneys

1320 Increasing Offers

1321 Creating a Problem for the Claimant or Attorney

RELEASES

1322 What Is a Release?

1323 Effect of a Release

1324 Execution of the Release

1325 Releases by Individuals

1326 The Releasee

SETTLEMENT IN SPECIAL SITUATIONS

1327 Releases by or in Behalf of Minors

1328 Indemnifying Releases by the Parents

1329 Guardianship Proceedings and Friendly Suits

1330 Nominal or No Consideration Releases

1331 Releases by Partnerships or Corporations

1332 Settlements: Survival and Wrongful Death

1333 Covenants Not to Sue

1334 Mary Carter Agreements

1335 Loan Receipt Agreements

1336 Form of Guarantee or Loan Agreement

1337 Open-End Releases

1338 Advance Payments

1339 Settlement without Release

SETTLEMENT CONSIDERATIONS

1300 Nature and Purpose of Settlement

Settlement is the process by which parties having disputed matters between them reach an agreement as to what is due from one to the other. It contemplates a willingness on the part of each to forgo a legal remedy and to perform his or her part of the bargain if a satisfactory arrangement can be reached. In liability claims, a settlement usually involves the payment of money to the claimant as consideration for forebearance of the right to assert a cause of action against the insured. It is evidenced by the execution of a document, either a release or a covenant not to sue, plus an act by the opposing party, consisting of the transfer of the money to the claimant. To be an executed and binding settlement, both acts must be completed. While either act is yet to be done, the contract of settlement is executory and is subject to avoidance by the party who has performed.

For example, if the claimant signs a release and the money is not paid within a reasonable time, the claimant may consider the contract as breached. The claimant may seek to enforce the contract by suing the insurance carrier for damages for breach of contract, the damages being the amount which would have been received under the agreement. On the other hand, the claimant may consider that, since the contract has been breached, it is no longer binding, and assert the cause of action against the insured as if no contract of settlement had been made.

The claim representative will use the process of settlement as a means of terminating those cases which qualify for that type of treatment. He or she may be able to make the determination as to settlement immediately, or it may be necessary to conduct some investigation to reach such a conclusion. In any case, the claim representative must be persuaded that the claim involves a possible responsibility on the part of the insured and that the claimant has sustained provable damages. The claim representative will reject claims which do not involve any responsibility on the part of the insured, as well as claims in which there is responsibility, but in which the claimant has sustained no damages which are susceptible of proof.

1301 Burden of Proof

In determining the cases which qualify for settlement, consideration will be given to the facts and whether the claimant can meet the burden of proof which the law imposes. To recover, the claimant must cross the "bridge of proof" from accident to verdict. The claimant must be able to establish certain points, and to counter the defense of contributory negligence. This "bridge" may be illustrated as follows:

ACCIDENT { Negligence of the defendant } { Proximate cause } { Freedom from contributory negligence } { Damages } VERDICT

The claimant in a typical negligence case must prove that the defendant was negligent, that the defendant's negligence was the proximate cause of the accident, and that the damages were sustained as a result of the accident. In addition, he or she must be prepared to go forward with the evidence and to rebut any evidence that is offered that the claimant's own negligence contributed in some degree to the causation of the accident. The law requires that the claimant establish the case by a preponderance of evidence. This means that he or she must produce evidence which, when fairly considered, produces the stronger impression, has the greater weight, and is more convincing as to its truth than the evidence in opposition. It does not mean the greater number of witnesses, but it does mean that the testimony of witnesses will be weighted by the opportunity for knowledge, the information possessed, and the manner of testifying.

The claimant (or plaintiff) is not entitled to have the claim submitted to the jury until a prima facie, or basic, case has been made out. This means that the plaintiff must establish all the elements of the claim and offer proof of the existence of all the necessary parts of the cause of action. Should the plaintiff fail to establish one of the required items, the cause of action will fail, and there is nothing for the jury to consider. For example, if the claimant proves that the defendant was negligent but fails to prove that such negligence was the proximate cause of the accident, one of the necessary elements of the cause of action has not been established, and it must fail. If the claimant proves damages, and that they were proximately caused by the accident, but fails to prove the negligence of the defendant, the claim also will fail.

1302 Qualifications for Settlement

The settlement process is undertaken only where both parties to the controversy are willing to resolve their disputes by that means. In insurance claims the plaintiff is always willing to employ the settlement process. He or she has made a claim for a specific amount, and if the amount is paid, the demands have been met and there would be no reason to proceed to litigation. The claimant might be willing to forgo litigation and accept something less than the demand where payment will be made immediately. On the defense side, the insurance carrier is always interested in the disposition of its claims, but whether it is willing to make a payment or engage in settlement negotiation will depend upon the particular facts of each case.

It is the claim representative's duty, therefore, to determine at the earliest possible moment the cases which qualify for settlement discussion and those which do not. At the same time, he or she will make a determination in the qualified cases just how far the company will be willing to go in meeting the claimant's demands. The claim representative will consider the facts of the case and will apply rules regarding burden of proof to the situation. Cases thus subjected to examination will fall into one of three classifications: (1) clear liability, (2) doubtful liability, or (3) no liability.

Clear Liability. Where the responsibility of the insured defendant can be established and there is no defense available, the claim is regarded as one of clear liability. If a reasonable settlement can be agreed upon, these cases should be settled promptly. For example, if the insured hits a properly parked car and causes property damage to the parked vehicle, the insured's responsibility is clear and there is no defense available. The claimant is entitled to recover the reasonable value of the damage thus inflicted. The same thing would be true as to personal injuries if the car was occupied at the time of the accident and the occupants sustained injury.

Doubtful Liability. Cases occur in which the claimant can make out a prima facie case and, therefore, be entitled to submit the case to the jury, but where defenses also can be asserted, which, if believed by the jury, would require a defendant's verdict. These claims usually should be compromised, the extent of the compromise depending upon the strengths and weaknesses of the claimant's case as opposed to the strengths and weaknesses of the defense.

No Liability. In cases where the claim representative is convinced that the claimant cannot make out a prima facie case, or where the investigation reveals that the accident was caused solely by the negligence of a third party, there is no liability, and these claims should be rejected. For example, let us assume that the insured was properly and legally parked and the claimant's vehicle ran into it. Certainly there is no responsibility on the part of the insured, and the claimant would not be able to establish any negligence. Therefore, the claimant would not be able to establish the first element of the cause of action against the insured. If a claim is made by the claimant for damage to his vehicle, it should be resisted.

1303 Nuisance Settlements

When a claim is reported, the insurance company must create a file, establish a reserve for the claim, and enter the file and other information in its records. In the course of development the file is ultimately closed, either by payment or by the passage of time where no claim is asserted. Cases which qualify for settlement treatment are usually disposed of by that method, or are brought to trial by the claimant and disposed of by that means. In between these two classes of claims are those which have no merit, but which are being actively pressed by the claimant or the claimant's attorney, either by continuous demands for settlement or by the filing of a suit. The insurance company cannot close such a file while the claim is pending, and therefore it must expend clerical time, maintain its records, and include the claim in its open-file inventory for a variety of purposes.

Because the insurance industry is a business, it is cost-conscious and will, like any other business, attempt to reduce costs where possible. In the early days of the casualty industry, some companies felt that it was desirable to dispose of these nonmeritorious claims by a small payment in order to avoid the nuisance of keeping them open with its attendant burdens of record-keeping. For that reason nominal payments were made in order to close the files. Thus the terms "nuisance claims" and "nuisance value" were introduced into insurance terminology.

Insurance companies are divided in their approach to the handling of these claims. Some still follow the practice and feel they come out better in the final analysis by making the payment and buying a release for an amount which will be commensurate with what it would cost them to maintain the file and defend the lawsuit. The opponents of this view take the position that payment of these claims is a surrender to legal blackmail and, further, that payment of the claims will encourage the bringing of other and further claims of similar variety. They feel that claims should be disposed of strictly on merit and that no payment should be made unless the facts justify it. The handling of this type of claim will depend upon the company policy, as will the extent of the payment, if any, to be made.

Both sides, incidentally, agree that the terms "nuisance" and "nuisance value" have no place in insurance parlance and should not be used. Therefore they discourage the use of the terms.

1304 Classification of Claims as to Liability

Claims arising in areas of absolute liability, such as impurities in food, inherently dangerous operations, dangerous instrumentalities, and cases in which absolute liability is created by statute, come within the clear liability category. In addition, most companies regard the following situations, arising in automobile claims, as coming within the clear liability definition:

1. Pedestrian knockdown where the pedestrian is on the crosswalk, or, if a controlled intersection, crossing with the green light.
2. Defendant's car, out of control, mounts the sidewalk, knocking down one or more pedestrians, or causing property damage.
3. Rear-end hit, where defendant's car strikes the rear of the plaintiff's car, which is properly parked, or legally stopped on the highway, without any contributory negligence on the part of the plaintiff.
4. Wrong turns cases in which the defendant makes a right or a left turn from the wrong lane in front of following traffic.
5. Pull-out cases where the defendant's car pulls out from the curb and strikes the plaintiff's car, without any contributory negligence on the part of the plaintiff.

6. Unattended vehicle parked by the defendant on an incline rolls downhill without any interference by a third party.
7. Defendant driving from private driveway onto highway strikes pedestrian or cars on highway. This is regarded as clear liability whether the defendant is backing out or driving ahead.

These types of claims should be settled as promptly and as economically as possible.

Cases of doubtful liability usually qualify for a compromise settlement, but the amount the defendant should be willing to pay will vary with the facts of the particular case and the seriousness of the injury. If a compromise cannot be effected, most of these cases will have to be tried rather than settled for the full demand. Cases in this category are as follows:

1. Uncontrolled intersection cases where there is a question of fact as to which car entered the intersection first.
2. Controlled intersection cases where each driver claims the light was in his or her favor.
3. Where defendant made a left turn in the face of oncoming traffic and the plaintiff had an opportunity to stop and failed to do so.
4. Dart-out cases of a child crossing the street, not at the crosswalk but between two parked cars.
5. Passing on the right cases where plaintiff's vehicle, traveling in the same direction, passes on the right rather than the left, and where there are circumstances which may justify such action.

Examples of cases of no liability, which do not qualify for any settlement consideration whatsoever, irrespective of the seriousness of the injury, are as follows:

1. Injuries to trespassers, other than infants, caused by a defective condition of the premises, or by any cause other than the intentional act of the owner to injure them.
2. Injury to licensees occurring in a part of the premises outside the licensed area.
3. Rear-end hit where the defendant's car was properly parked or legally stopped on the highway and was hit in the rear.
4. Wrong turns where the plaintiff made a left turn in the face of oncoming traffic and the defendant had no opportunity to stop.
5. Stop sign cases where plaintiff's car went through a stop sign without regard to traffic moving in either direction.
6. Private driveway accidents where plaintiff's car came out of a private driveway or private road in the path of the defendant.
7. Dart-out cases involving an adult with no negligence on the part of the automobile operator.

1305 Relationship of Injury to Settlement

The nature and extent of the injury will have some influence upon the question of settlement. If the injuries are serious and of a permanent nature, or if there is a death claim involved where there are minor children, a sympathetic element may be introduced into the trial of the case. In those cases settlement consideration should also contemplate the possible jury reaction, and the amount estimated for settlement should be increased to cover these elements. Just how far the claim representative should be willing to go will be dictated by the eye appeal of the injury or the dependents involved. Experience gained from past cases, as well as current jury awards in similar cases, is the only guide that can be used. Since each case will have to stand on its own particular facts, the only possible guide that can be given in advance is a breakdown of the various types of cases and the general treatment which they should receive:

1. No Liability and Minor Injury. This claim clearly should not be settled, and if no claim is pressed, no action is required. If the claim is being pressed, on completion of the investigation there should be a prompt denial to the claimant with an explanation as to why the claim will not be paid.

2. No Liability and Serious Injury. The treatment of this case will depend upon the facts and the severity of the injury. In some cases, because of the facts of the accident, there may be a possibility of a loss of some vital evidence or the possibility of being unable to produce a disinterested witness upon whom the defendant's case depends. In others there may be extremely high costs of defense, together with a pathetic picture presented by the claimant. In such cases, a compromise settlement may be indicated. In cases where these elements are not present, even though the injury is severe, no settlement should be considered.

3. Doubtful Liability and Minor Injury. If the claimant is seriously pressing the claim, settlement should be consummated on the basis of the cost of trial and no more. Where the claimant is not seriously pressing the claim, no action is indicated, and it may be that the claim will be forgotten. In the latter case, if the claimant should later actively press the claim, then settlement treatment on the basis of the cost of trial may be considered.

4. Doubtful Liability and Serious Injury. Claims in this category normally require settlement on a compromise basis. The amount paid in settlement will depend upon the nature and the extent of the injury, and the figure should contemplate the impact of the sympathetic elements of the case on the jury.

5. Clear Liability Regardless of Injury. These cases should be investigated promptly, and, as soon as a definite determination is made as to liability and injury, efforts should be made to effect as economical a settlement as can be made commensurate with a fair and reasonable valuation.

1306 Liens

A lien is a charge, security, or encumbrance upon property. In liability insurance claims it is a charge that can be asserted against the property of the claimant (the settlement money) by another person because of some services rendered in connection with the claim. Liens either arise at common law or are created by statute. For example, at common law when an attorney is engaged, he or she has a lien on the client's cause of action for the payment of the fee. Therefore, if there is a settlement of the client's cause of action, the attorney may assert the right of lien against the settlement money. In all cases, the person paying the money must recognize the lien if on notice of its existence. Where the insurance carrier is on notice of the claimant's employment of an attorney, usually in the form of a letter from the attorney advising of such employment, the insurance carrier is bound to recognize that lien unless the attorney releases the lien or the lien is satisfied.

Should the insurance carrier pay over the money to the claimant, the attorney may sue the company for the fee. To avoid any problems, insurance carriers always add the name of the attorney as an additional payee on the settlement draft, so that the draft would be payable to "John Jones and Henry Brown, his attorney." Thus the draft, in order to be negotiated, would require the endorsements of both payees. The endorsement by the attorney is evidence that the lien has been satisfied. However, it sometimes happens that the claimant engages one attorney and, because of some dissatisfaction, discharges that attorney and engages another. In such a case, in the absence of a notice from the first attorney either that the lien has been satisfied or that the attorney is claiming no lien, the practice is to include the names of both attorneys as additional payees. In order to negotiate the draft, the claimant will need the endorsements of both attorneys, and the liens can be satisfied at that time. If the insurance carrier is not on notice of the employment of the attorney at the time the settlement is made and the money paid, it has no obligation to recognize the lien.

Some states have passed statutes which create a lien in favor of hospitals or doctors who have rendered treatment for an injury caused by the negligence of a third party. These laws usually provide for notice in the form of a direct notification to the tort-feasor. Or, where the name or address of the tort-feasor is unknown, the statute will usually provide for constructive notice in the form of a filing of the lien with some public official, such as the county clerk, county registrar, or similar officer. The statutes provide that where notification is given, either directly or constructively, the physician or hospital has a lien on the proceeds of the claimant's recovery which must be recognized by the insurance carrier paying the money. Failure to recognize the lien, where notice has been given, will subject the insurance carrier to liability to the physician or hospital for the amount of the bill.

Most workers' compensation laws provide that where the claimant was injured in the course of employment because of the negligence of a third party, the claimant has the right to claim compensation, proceed against the third party, or both. In case compensation is paid, the insurance carrier or the employer who made the payments is given a lien on the proceeds of the claimant's recovery from the third party to the extent of the compensation and medical expenses paid. Just as in any other lien, the third party is not bound to recognize the lien unless and until the third party has notice of its existence.

It should be emphasized that the liens of the hospital, physician, and compensation insurance carrier exist solely because they are granted by a statute. If there is no state statute creating the lien, then it has no existence in that state. On the other hand, the attorney's lien is a common-law lien and is in existence in all states. Therefore, the claim representative must be familiar with the laws respecting liens in all the states in which the insurer operates.

It may happen that there is more than one lien involved in a specific case, and a question may arise as to which lien has the priority. The rule is that the lien which is prior in time is prior in right. Since the attorney's lien attaches to the cause of action, it comes into existence prior to any other liens which attach to the proceeds of recovery. The cause of action existed before the recovery, and therefore the attorney's lien came into existence before any other. As to the liens which attach to the recovery, the lien filed first (by the giving of actual or constructive notice) is prior in right to liens filed subsequently.

1307 Satisfaction of Liens

Where a settlement is made or a verdict rendered for the plaintiff, a lien, properly asserted by notice to the defendant, can be extinguished only by payment or release by the lienholder. As to cases in which a verdict is rendered, there is no problem as far as the claim representative is concerned. He or she will issue the draft in payment of the judgment, with the claimant and all lienholders named as payees. Under those circumstances, it is no part of the claim representative's duty to either investigate or decide the merits of the lien, whether it is reasonable or not, or whether the claimant has any defenses which may be available against the lienholder. The claim representative has met his or her only duty when recognizing the lien by naming the lienholder as one of the payees. This is true even though the total amount of the liens exceeds the judgment.

The division of the draft is not a matter of any concern to the claim representative. It may happen that the claimant will request that the original draft be canceled and one issued to the claimant alone, or that separate drafts be issued to the claimant and each lienholder. The claim representative is under no duty to thus accommodate the claimant and should do so only when there is definite proof of the amount of each lien. In the event of an error, the company would be liable to the lienholder for the excess. Therefore, the better practice is to issue one draft and let the claimant work the problem out with the aid and assistance of an attorney.

Where a settlement is being made and where the amount of the settlement is adequate to meet the claims of the lienholders as well as the claimant, the same treatment should be given. Again, it is of no concern to the claim representative whether the amounts of the liens are reasonable. However, where a compromise settlement is being negotiated, the existence of liens may present obstacles, especially where the payments of the liens in full will leave little or nothing for the claimant. In such a case it might be to the advantage of the claim representative, in working out the settlement, to attempt to secure an agreement from the lienholders to release their respective liens for an amount less than the full lien. It should be emphasized again that the lienholder never has a cause of action directly against the tort-feasor arising from the accident. The lienholder's rights against the tort-feasor come into existence only when there is a settlement or verdict. In a compromise settlement case, especially where the liability is doubtful, the lienholder is interested in seeing a settlement made. If the case is tried and the verdict is in favor of the defendant, it is possible that the lienholder may never get any money. Therefore, in compromise cases, it is very often to the lienholder's advantage to reduce the amount of the claim so as to assure the settlement, rather than to insist on the full amount and to run the risk of getting nothing.

Clearly, the financial status of the claimant will have some influence on the lienholder's decision, as will the nature of the claim and the possibilities of a defendant's verdict. To illustrate, let us assume that the claimant is a laborer who is married and has four children. He has sustained a rather serious injury which necessitated hospitalization over an extended period of time. The hospital bill is $30,000, a lien has been properly filed, and the tort-feasor is on notice of its existence. The liability, however, is extremely doubtful, and it is only because of the seriousness of the claimant's injuries and the outside chance that the sympathy of the jury might persuade them to bring in a verdict for the plaintiff that the insurance carrier is induced to consider the matter of settlement at all.

The insurance carrier is willing to pay a top figure of $35,000 for a full release, including the hospital lien. The claimant will not settle for $5,000 which is all that would be left after the hospital lien is satisfied, but will settle if he can be guaranteed a payment of $20,000 net. In such a case, the claim representative will discuss the matter with the hospital and, if she can secure a commitment from them that they will release their lien for the payment of $15,000, the case can then be settled on the claimant's terms.

It should also be pointed out that the claimant is under no obligation to press the claim, in which case the hospital's lien is worthless. The hospital cannot compel him to press the claim and therefore, in the case illustrated, the hospital has much to gain by agreeing to the settlement of its lien and much to lose if it refuses. In a good many of these cases, the claim representative will have to work patiently with both parties, especially where the lienholder will release the claim for a certain amount and the claimant is unwilling to settle for the balance. In most instances the differences can be worked out and the settlement ultimately consummated.

1308 Subrogation

Subrogation technically means the substitution of one party for another with reference to a lawful claim, demand, or right. It arises by operation of either law or equity. Subrogation is a transfer which the law compels someone to make because of the circumstances. Under most compensation laws, for example, where the injury is caused by a third party and the employee claims compensation, the compensation insurance carrier is substituted for the claimant for the purpose of bringing suit against the third party after a specific period of time, if the claimant fails to do so. This is subrogation and comes about by operation of law when the period of time expressed in the statute has passed. No act, voluntary or otherwise, is required by the claimant. The cause of action passes to the compensation carrier in accordance with the provisions of the statute and the compensation carrier may assert the rights formerly held by the claimant.

In equity, subrogation is regarded as a legal fiction through which a person, not as a volunteer but because of some obligation (as in an insurance contract), pays the debt of another and is substituted to all the rights and remedies available to the creditor, who has been paid. The debt is treated, in equity, as still existing for the debt payer's benefit. Therefore, where a collision carrier has paid for damage to the insured's vehicle caused by the negligence of a third party, the collision carrier is the owner of the cause of action for damages to the vehicle as against the negligent third party.

1309 Subrogation by the United States

There are a number of situations where the U.S. government is required by law to render medical and hospital services to various classes of persons. These classes include members of the armed services, veterans who received treatment at Veterans Administration hospitals, seamen who are treated by the Public Health Service in marine hospitals, officers of the Public Health Service, officers and enlisted personnel of the Coast Guard, as well as military and naval cadets attending service academies. As to members of the Armed Forces, the obligation to furnish medical and hospital care extends not only to injuries or diseases occurring while in the course of duty, but also to injuries sustained while on authorized leave or furlough which are not sustained because of misconduct. Where any of these classes of persons is injured because of a tortious act of a third person, the question whether the United States could assert a claim against the third party for the value of the medical services rendered was an open one until legislation was finally enacted in 1962. The legislation (42 USCA 2651–2653) affects all classes of persons noted above, with certain exceptions.

This statute creates a cause of action on behalf of the United States to recover—for the reasonable value of the medical services rendered where the United States is required by law to render such service—as against a negligent third party. Under the statute, the right of the injured person is transferred or subrogated to the United States insofar as it relates to the medical treatment rendered. In addition, the United States may intervene in any legal proceeding as a party plaintiff and, if the injured person does not commence any legal proceeding within six months of the rendering of the first treatment, the United States may bring an action in its own name to recover for the reasonable value of the medical or hospital services rendered. This is not a lien statute. The United States owns a claim for medical services immediately upon the rendering of the first treatment. Therefore, if the claimant were to execute a release of his or her claim after treatment has been rendered, such release will not be binding on the United States; the claimant cannot release a claim which he or she does not own—a claim which is owned by the United States.

The right of the United States to recover is not, as would be the case in a lien statute, dependent upon the recovery by the claimant. Likewise, there is no provision requiring that the United States give notice to the responsible third party. It would seem that any settlement of cases in the category covered by the statute would be at the tort-feasor's peril and, if there was medical treatment rendered by the United States, that the release given by the claimant would not extinguish the right of the United States to recover, regardless of whether the tort-feasor was aware of the fact that treatment was rendered. Where the claim is released by the claimant prior to the rendition of treatment by the United States, it would seem that, under the statute, the United States would acquire no right against the tort-feasor. The statute provides for a transfer of the claimant's right against the third party insofar as it relates to the United States. If the claim has already been released, then the claimant has no right remaining and cannot transfer anything to the United States.

SETTLEMENT NEGOTIATIONS

1310 Order of Settlement

Where two or more claimants are injured, the order of contact, for the purposes of control, will be the most seriously injured first, the next most seriously injured second, and so on down to the claimant who is least seriously injured. The theory is that if it is impossible to control all the claimants, the next best thing is to control the serious cases, if possible. When it comes to settlement, the best method will consist of settling all the personal injury claims at one and the same time. If this cannot be done, the most seriously injured claimant should receive the first settlement consideration. The reason is that once one claim is settled, the other claimants may regard the settlement as an admission of liability even though, as a matter of law, it is not. Therefore, the remaining claimants may be more difficult to deal with and may make excessive demands. If there are to be excessive demands, it is better to receive them in the cases which are the less dangerous.

Obviously this cannot be a hard and fast rule, and circumstances will alter the procedure. Where there are three claimants, and two have completely recovered, and the seriously injured claimant is still under treatment with the outcome in doubt, settlement of the two claims that are ready for settlement should not be held up until the third claimant recovers sufficiently to discuss settlement. In such a situation, the claim representative should settle the less serious injury cases rather than run the risk of losing the claimants to an attorney because of the delay in settling. Group settlement discussions should be avoided and the claim representative should not discuss settlement with more than one claimant at one and the same time. The best climate for a settlement discussion is with each claimant alone.

In cases involving both property damage and personal injury claims, there once was a rule that no property damage claim would be settled until all the personal injury claims have been closed. These cases are generally automobile claims where two cars are involved.

Insurers today generally do not subscribe to this line of thinking. Most feel that where multiple claims are involved it is best to settle the claims as quickly as possible, whether small or large, or whether involving property damage or not. They feel that there is an advantage to be gained by settling as many claims as possible and that the severity factor should not determine the order of settlement. The advantages of this approach are: (1) The smaller cases are easy to settle and can be disposed of in a short period of time after the accident; (2) It minimizes the problem of keeping claimants under control in that the settlement of the smaller cases tends to keep the more serious cases under control; (3) It keeps the demands on the smaller cases within reasonable limits, which might not be the case if one of the more serious claims was settled for a large amount; and (4) It keeps the demands in the more serious claims at a lower figure because of the small amounts paid in the other cases. Where the injuries involved in some of the claims are of such severity that the demands will equal or exceed the policy limits, and the case is one for settlement, the second approach may afford a better chance of disposing of the cases within the policy limits than would the first.

Refusal to settle property damage claims where liability is clear would violate the Unfair Claims Practices Act in most states. Fair Claims Practices Acts, in effect in many states, are statutes that impose obligations on insurers in their dealings with claimants.

1311 Settlements by Joint Tort-Feasors

It frequently happens that the insured is one of two or more joint tort-feasors, all of whom are responsible for the accident. If the representatives of all the joint tort-feasors are in agreement that the case should be settled and the amount needed in settlement will be shared equally, then one claim representative can handle the settlement for the entire group and, if the case is settled, will obtain a copy of the release for all defendants. The releases will include the names of all joint tort-feasors. In such a situation it is better to have one claim representative speak for the group than to have all tort-feasors represented at the settlement conference. But if it cannot be avoided, there can be a conference at which all representatives are in attendance.

Unfortunately, where there are joint tort-feasors, they seldom agree as to the extent of their liability, and, as a consequence, one claim representative feels that the others should pay the major portion of the settlement with a small contribution from him. He may be motivated by the fact that he has low policy limits (which generally are not disclosed) or that his investigation indicates a possibility that his insured will not be involved. In any case, each claim must stand on its own facts, and the attitude taken by the claim representative will depend on the extent of his exposure, whether it be on the issue of liability or the matter of low-policy limits.

1312 The Settlement Interview

Settlements can be consummated by mail, telephone, or personal interview. Small cases usually qualify for disposition by one of the first two methods. A request can be made by mail or telephone for the bills incurred, either for medical treatment or property damage as the case may be; the case can be discussed by telephone, and a settlement agreed upon; or an offer of a settlement as a specific amount can be made by mail. A variation of the latter procedure could include sending the claimant a release form draft, endorsement of which will constitute a release. Small claims are those which involve a few hundred dollars. Company policy may dictate a larger or a smaller amount as the breaking point between which claims can be handled by mail or telephone and those which require a personal contact with the claimant.

Where a personal settlement interview is desirable, there are three elements which require consideration: (1) timing, (2) preparation, and (3) climate.

Timing. The settlement interview should take place as soon after the happening of the accident as possible, at a time when the claimant is willing and able to discuss settlement. The claim representative should not attempt to force the claimant into a settlement discussion when it is clear that the claimant wants to wait until some future date. The claim representative can endeavor to persuade the claimant that the time for settlement has arrived, but if the claimant is adamant in refusal to discuss the subject, arrangements should be made for it to take place at some future time.

For example, let us assume that the claimant says she is not ready to discuss settlement until she has had a final examination from her doctor, which is to take place within the next 10 days. The claim representative may attempt to persuade the claimant that the best judge of her physical condition is herself and, that if she feels well, there isn't much more the doctor can tell her. If the claimant is amenable to this argument, then the discussion can take place. Otherwise, if she insists that she will not settle the case until she sees her physician for a final examination, there is no point in even opening the discussion.

Should the claim representative insist on discussing settlement, and make an offer, it is obvious that, under the circumstances, the case will not be settled. However, one of two things may happen. The claimant will consult her physician as to the adequacy of the amount offered. The doctor might advise her that the amount is much too low and recommend a considerably higher figure or the employment of an attorney. The fact that the doctor doesn't know anything about settlement values will not prevent him or her from expressing an opinion. On the other hand, the physician may feel that the claimant's physical condition does not support the offer made and will counsel the claimant to see if she can get a little more, but in any case settle on the claim representative's terms. Then the doctor will give a report which will not justify the offer made by the claim representative. In either case, the claim representative has nothing to gain by insisting on making an offer. The practical effect will be to get the doctor into the discussion (if only indirectly), as the controlling influence as to whether the case will be settled.

The same principle would apply to fatal cases. After the accident, the claim representative should call and express sympathy to the dependents, but should not talk settlement until they are mentally ready to sit down and discuss financial matters. The worst thing that the claim representative could do would be to try to discuss settlement while the dependents are in the state of bereavement. Not only will the attempt be fruitless, but the claim representative will appear as a callous individual, devoid of human feelings, who is interested only in business and nothing else. This will be a tremendous obstacle to overcome when the time for actual settlement arrives. Occasionally, there will be a case where the dependents are interested and willing to talk settlement even before the funeral has taken place. If there is some indication of willingness to do so, there is no reason why the settlement discussion cannot take place immediately. But this is the exception rather than the rule.

Preparation. For the discussion to result in a settlement, both parties must be prepared to consummate the settlement. This means that the claimant should have all bills in itemized form, if necessary, and any other data needed, such as a certificate from the physician or an estimate of the damage to property. The claim representative should have completed a sufficient inquiry into the facts so as to know whether the insured was entirely responsible for the accident or partly chargeable with the injury. He or she should know just how far the company will want to go in meeting the claimant's demands and the limits of his or her authority to bind the company to a settlement.

Climate. This is an extremely important element. The settlement discussion should take place under the best possible circumstances with only the claim representative and the claimant present, or with the addition of the spouse or near relative. The more people present and participating, the more difficult the interview will be.

1313 First-Call Settlements

In some cases, it is possible to dispose of a claim by settlement when the initial contact is made. If the claim representative has sufficient information as to liability, such a settlement should be made on the first call. These settlements not only save considerable time for the claim representative but also save the company the expense of maintaining the file. Therefore, first-call settlements should be made wherever possible.

One word of caution should be added, however. If the claim representative has not completed enough of an inquiry to be reasonably certain of the responsibility of the insured, and if the claimant looks for a ''fast settlement'' for an amount which seems to be much less than the obvious value of the injuries as claimed, the claim representative should not be stampeded into making a settlement. Signs such as these point to a possible fraudulent claim, and further inquiry must be made before payment is made. Other danger signs are ridiculously low demands on a ''take it or leave it'' basis with the implication that, if the demand is not met at that moment, the claimant will engage counsel in the morning.

It is difficult to set a rule as to when the opportunity for a first-call settlement should not be grasped. Suffice it to say that if there is anything in the case—the claimant's anxiety to conclude the case or a lack of sufficient information as to liability—which raises a doubt in the claim representative's mind as to the good faith of the claim, further inquiry rather than quick settlement should be the rule. In other cases, first-call settlements should be encouraged.

1314 Control of the Claimant

Control of the claimant means that no attorney has been retained and that the claim representative is in control of the situation insofar as a settlement discussion with the claimant is concerned. When the claimant retains an attorney, the claim representative has lost control of the case. In most cases first-call settlements cannot be made, some because the claimant is still hospitalized or under treatment and others because the results of the injury as to permanency or temporary disability are unknown. If the claim representative is to maintain control of the case, he or she must make an immediate contact with the claimant, even though this first contact cannot possibly produce a settlement, and there must be frequent call-backs to check the claimant's progress. When the time for settlement arrives, the claim representative will be able to discuss settlement with the claimant and not with an attorney.

Generally, cases in the hands of attorneys cost more to settle than those in which the settlement is made with the claimant directly. For the most part, attorneys in personal injury cases work on a contingent fee basis, the fee being a percentage (usually at least one third) of the amount recovered.

The claim representative will not advise the claimant against the employment of an attorney. He or she will, however, point out that attorneys do not work for nothing and that it might be in the claimant's interest to wait and see whether the case can be settled satisfactorily without the employment of an attorney, in which case the claimant would have no attorney's fee to pay.

Another method of maintaining control of the case is through an immediate contact with the attending physician. A telephone call to the doctor—advising that the claim representative has seen the patient, and telling the doctor that in the event of a settlement, which appears favorable at this time, the claim representative will try to see that the doctor's bill is protected—will very often make the doctor a real participant in the case and all the more willing to cooperate with the claim representative. This is good psychology because no one wants to be ignored.

In many cases, the claim representative will merely ask the doctor for a report and say nothing about the case, nor show any interest in the doctor's bill. Under those circumstances nobody could blame the doctor for feeling left out and not caring to cooperate with the claim representative in settling the case, even when asked to do so in the later stages. Cooperation of the doctor can be a very valuable asset and should be cultivated. The doctor is much closer to the patent than a claim representative ever will be; the patient develops the habit of listening to the doctor in medical matters, and will continue that habit when the doctor talks about the settlement of the case. If the doctor's bill is to be protected, then the doctor's own interest is involved in the case.

1315 Preparing for Settlement Negotiations

In all cases involving the possible responsibility of the insured, there is a settlement value. This value is an amount that would be to the advantage of the claimant to accept and to the company's advantage to pay. Settlement negotiations are the means by which both parties seek to arrive at a figure agreeable to each. There is a certain amount of "horse trading" in this process, with the claimant seeking to get as much as possible for the injuries and the claim representative seeking to make a settlement at a reasonable figure, saving as much as possible for the company. There is no reason why this situation should be a secret, and if the claimant maintains that the claim representative is seeking a low-dollar settlement for the company, it should be freely admitted, while calling attention to the fact that the claim representative does not blame the claimant for trying to get as much as possible for the injury.

Before entering into settlement negotiations the claim representative will consider the relative bargaining positions of the parties, the advantages which the facts of the case give to the insurance company, and the disadvantages which will accrue if the case is not settled. He or she will consider the possibilities of the claimant's recovery, the possible amount of recovery, and the probability of a defense verdict. The claim representative will consider at least the one bargaining advantage which the insurance company has in all cases: that they can call the turn as to whether the case will be settled. They control the money, and if they decide not to go along with the claimant's settlement demand, no settlement can be made. There is nothing the claimant can do to force a payment at that moment. The claimant can force a payment only by bringing the case to trial and obtaining a verdict. Then there may be an appeal, if the facts so warrant. During the time from the demand to the verdict, there is no way that the claimant or the claimant's attorney can compel the company to disburse any funds. The company alone can decide whether it is to its advantage to pay some money in settlement before verdict or to make the claimant prove the case before any money is paid.

The objective of settlement negotiations is to make a contract. The contract will come into existence through the usual preliminary steps of an offer from one side and acceptance by the other. In these cases there will be consideration moving from each party to the other. The defendant will pay a certain sum of money to the claimant, in return for which the claimant will forgo the right to sue. As evidence of agreement to forgo legal rights, the claimant will execute a document, or contract, which we call a release.

In cases where there are other parties alleged to be jointly responsible, the claimant may wish to retain rights against such other joint tort-feasors and merely to release one defendant. In such a case, and in some states, the use of a covenant not to sue will accomplish this result. The claimant by means of that document does not relinquish the claim, but does promise not to sue the defendant in consideration of the payment of money.

1316 The Offer

The offer, as one of the elements in the formation of a contract, may be made by either party. It must be definite in its terms and is, in effect, a proposal to make a contract. The person to whom the offer is made may, by acceptance, create a binding contract. The offeror cannot make a binding contract, and there is nothing that the offeror can do after having made the offer to bring the contract into existence. A counteroffer is construed as a rejection of the original offer and terminates it. The counteroffer then becomes the only offer, and the person to whom it is made can create a contract by acceptance. There is no limit to the number of offers or demands that may be made, and each offer or demand will cancel the one previously made.

In insurance terminology we refer to "offer" and "demand" to distinguish between an offer made by the company and an offer made by the claimant or his attorney. They are both offers under contract law. Although we refer to the claimant's offer as a demand, the legal significance is the same. The insurance carrier's acceptance of the demand will create a contract.

Some attorneys like to proceed on the assumption that once an offer is made the company is bound by it, and that a counterproposal, in the form of a demand, does not release the company from its obligation to pay its original offer if it is accepted. This is not a true statement of the law. A counteroffer is a rejection and terminates the offer. If the attorney makes a counteroffer and it is not accepted by the company, then there is no offer open. Then the attorney will accept, or try to accept, the company's original offer. This so-called acceptance is, legally, another offer which the company can accept or reject as it sees fit.

1317 When to Make an Offer

There are two schools of thought as to whether the claim representative should make the initial offer. One school advocates the making of the first offer by the claim representative on the theory that, if the claimant has a much larger figure in mind, the offer of a much smaller amount will condition his or her thinking and lower the demands without subjecting the claimant to the necessity of exposing an opinion as to value. In a word, the claimant will not ask as much as was originally in mind if he or she hears an offer which is much lower. On the other hand, the fact that the offer is so disproportionate to the figure the claimant had in mind might drive the claimant to an attorney and terminate the possibility of a settlement directly with the claimant. It can be argued that in such a case the claim representative has lost nothing because, if the claimant's valuation was so high that it would be impossible to meet it, no settlement with the claimant could be consummated. In this way the problem of bringing the claimant into the area of a reasonable figure would be transferred to the attorney. The attorney would recognize the impossibility of the claimant's demand and would endeavor to bring the claimant's thinking as to value within reasonable and attainable limits.

The arguments against this course of dealing are impressive. When the claim representative makes the first offer he or she gives the claimant a bargaining advantage. The claimant will know exactly what the claim representative has in mind as to the amount the insurer is willing to pay. The claimant will have disclosed no information as to his position. The claim representative will not know whether the offered figure is too high or too low, from the claimant's standpoint. It is just as likely that the offer will be more than the claimant had in mind as it is that the offer will be considerably less. Therefore, the claim representative runs the risk either of overpaying the case or of losing the case to an attorney because the figure is regarded as too niggardly. He or she won't know in advance how the offer will be received. In making the first offer the claim representative is taking a calculated risk, one which, in the usual case, is unnecessary.

Most claim representatives subscribe to the second school. They feel the better procedure is to find out what the claimant's thinking is as to value. The claim representative can point out the out-of-pocket expenses and suggest that the claimant give some idea of what a reasonable settlement should be. If the claimant expresses a figure, then the claim representative can decide whether to make an offer or not, depending upon the amount of the claimant's demand and whether it is within reasonable limits.

Often the claimant will answer the question by asking another. He or she will inquire as to what the insurer usually pays in cases of this kind. The claim representative can then state that the insurer is willing to pay the out-of-pocket expenses and can then make a list of them. The claim representative can work this out on a piece of paper and ask the claimant's opinion of that figure. The claimant might accept the figures, or might request something more. The claimant will be asked to identify, in dollars, exactly what is meant by "something more."

Ultimately, the claim representative will wind up with a settlement demand. He or she can pay it or can endeavor to work it down to within what seems reasonable limits. This can be accomplished by means of a lower, or trading, offer, and as the claimant comes down in demand, the original offer can be raised.

1318 When Not to Make an Offer

The general rule is that an offer should not be made unless the amount of the offer is such that there is a possibility of the case being settled at or the near the amount offered. If the amount of the demand is so high that any offer the claim representative might be able to make will seem ridiculously small, no offer should be made. The task of the claim representative will be to reduce the demand before making any offer. If the demand cannot be reduced, there is no reason to make an offer which will not settle the case.

1319 Negotiations with Attorneys

The claim representative should bear in mind that in dealing with an attorney he or she is dealing with a limited agent, one who normally has no authority to settle the claim without specific authorization from the client. Therefore any negotiations are subject to the approval of the client, and no offer of settlement can be accepted without having been submitted to the client. Because the attorney is expected to have some knowledge of the value of the claim, there is no reason why the attorney should not be asked to make his or her demands known. The claim representative should not normally make the first or initial offer. Once the attorney has made a demand, usually considerably more than he or she expects to get, the claim representative may make a counteroffer. This offer can only be accepted by the client, and the attorney's agreement that the case is settled for that figure is still subject to the wishes of the client.

Some attorneys use this limited agent relationship as a vehicle for getting an increase in the offer. What sometimes happens is that the attorney agrees that the offer is fair and that he or she will submit it to the client. The attorney assures the claim representative that the client will accept it. However, the attorney later calls the claim representative and states that he or she could not get the client to accept the offer. The attorney may go to great lengths as to the arguments advanced to the client, that the client is a stubborn mule, but that he or she was finally able to get the client to agree upon another figure, larger than the offer but not too far above it. If the claim representative believes the story, the offer can be increased to meet the new demand, provided the facts in the file justify an increase. On the other hand, if the attorney's case is weak, the claim representative can stand on the original offer and refuse any increase.

In a variation of the same type of procedure, the attorney may make a demand, let us say, of $2,000. After some discussion the claim representative offers $500. The attorney will say that the offer must be submitted to the client but that the attorney is quite sure the client will not accept it. He or she will inquire of the claim representative as to whether the claim representative would be willing to pay $1,000, provided the attorney can get the client to accept it. If the claim representative answers this inquiry in the affirmative, he or she has increased the offer to $1,000, whether meaning to do so or not. If the case follows the usual course, the attorney will come back and say the client would not agree to $1,000, but the attorney was successful in securing the client's approval of a $1,500 figure. Since the difference between the offer and the demand is only $500, the claim representative should not let such a small difference stand in the way of a settlement.

By such a simple device, the attorney has obtained an increase in the offer to $1,000 and has placed the claim representative in a position where a demand of $1,500 does not seem too far out of line. The claim representative should meet the attorney's inquiry whether a payment of $1,000 would be made, if he or she can get the client to accept it, by stating that the offer is $500. It will remain open for a reasonable period of time. If it is not accepted, then the attorney has no offer. If the client wishes to make a demand of $1,000, the claim representative will consider it but cannot guarantee that the company will accept it. As far as the claim representative is concerned, the offer is $500 and no more.

In dealing with attorneys, the claim representative should consider the strengths and weaknesses not only of the insurer's case but also that of the attorney. There is no way the attorney can compel the company to settle the case. This can come only as the result of an agreement, and the claim representative is the one who can decide if the case will be settled or not. The claim representative should also recognize that most plaintiffs' attorneys handle these cases on a contingent fee basis, which means that the attorney will not receive a fee until some money is recovered by the client, by settlement or verdict. The attorney cannot spend money that is represented by open files in his office. Therefore the attorney has a pecuniary interest in the disposition of the claim, and cannot collect a fee until there is a recovery.

Some attorneys are settlers and rarely, if ever, try a case; if they have a case of sufficient severity, they will turn it over to trial counsel for trial. Where the case is forwarded to another attorney, the attorney of record loses part of the fee. Therefore, the claim representative should recognize those attorneys in the area who are of the settling type, and those who are able and willing to bring a case to trial. The settlers ultimately will abandon small cases in which no settlement can be made. They will forward the larger cases. A somewhat typical arrangement between counsel is that the trial counsel receives as his fee 25 percent of the recovery. If the original attorney has a contingent fee arrangement of 33⅓ percent it is clear, in a forwarded case, that his or her fee is reduced to 8⅓ percent. Figures of this sort should have some place in the claim representative's valuation of the case and should influence the case handling.

1320 Increasing Offers

The general rule is that an offer should not be increased unless there is a corresponding decrease in the demand. The reason is that an increase under those circumstances would serve no useful purpose and will impede the settlement negotiations rather than advance them. For example, if the demand is $1,000 and the claim representative offers $500, an increase in the offer to $600, without any action by the claimant, will immediately create the impression in the claimant's mind that the $500 was not a serious offer. The claimant will stand on the $1,000 demand until sure that the claim representative has reached a top figure. If the claim representative then raises the offer to $700, the claimant will feel sure the first offer of $500 was hardly serious, because there has been a $200 advance without any move being made on the part of the claimant. The increase in the offer only made the claimant suspicious of the claim representative's motives in offering that sum in the first place.

What should happen in such a case is that the claim representative should stand on the $500 offer until the claimant reduces his or her demand. When there is a reduction in the demand, then and only then should the claim representative even consider an increase in the offer. How much of an increase should be made will depend upon the circumstances—and the ultimate figure the claim representative has in mind as the top settlement value. If the claimant comes down $100, reducing the demand to $900, the claim representative does not have to increase the offer by the same amount. He or she can increase the offer to $550, or, if the circumstances dictate, increase the offer by the same amount.

The mere fact that there has been a decrease in the demand does not necessarily require that the claim representative increase the offer. He or she can stand on the original offer and attempt to force another and further decrease in the demand before making any move at all. Just what technique the claim representative uses depends on personal judgment and the circumstances of the case, in the sense of just how dangerous the claim representative thinks the case is. If it is a case of clear liability, the claim representative is justified in being more liberal in the increases; if it is a case of doubtful liability the claim representative may make small increases in the offer, or none at all.

1321 Creating a Problem for the Claimant or Attorney

Most claim representatives can recall at least one case involving serious injuries in which substantial offers of settlement were made and the offers were refused. The case went to trial and resulted in a verdict for the defendant. The result may have produced some amusement among the claim department personnel, but to the claimant it was a tragedy, and to the claimant's attorney an embarrassing nightmare. Not only has the attorney lost a fee, but he or she must explain to a seriously injured client why there was no recovery and, more important, why the attorney recommended the refusal of the offer (if he or she did) or why the attorney did not insist that the offer be accepted. No matter what the explanation is, the claimant will blame the attorney for the result and for the fact that no money was received for the injury.

An offer should be calculated to settle the case. It must be one which will merit consideration, and in serious cases (and in some not so serious), a realistic offer will create a problem for the claimant and the attorney who, in most cases, will accept the offer rather than risk the uncertainties of trial. The attorneys who represent plaintiffs are fully aware of these possibilities, which should also influence the claim representative in the handling of these matters.

RELEASES

1322 What Is a Release?

A release is a contract whereby the person executing the instrument (the releasor) gives up a right, claim, or privilege to the person against whom it might have been demanded or enforced (the releasee). To be a binding contract, it must be supported by a valuable consideration. The consideration passing from the releasee to the releasor in insurance claims is the payment of a sum of money, and the consideration passing from the releasor to the releasee is the extinguishment of the releasor's right to bring legal action to enforce the claim.

The contract of release is executed, or completed, when both parties have performed their respective obligations, namely, where the claimant has relinquished his or her right and as evidence thereof has signed the release, and the company has performed its obligation by making the payment of the money recited as the consideration. When both these things have happened, the release is a binding contract and may be interposed as a defense to any later action which the claimant might bring against the releasee. In the absence of fraud or other special circumstances, an executed release is a complete defense to any action which the claimant might seek to enforce against the releasee arising out of the same accident.

The contract of release is executory, or incomplete, when one party has performed his obligation and the other has not. Under such circumstances the nonperforming party usually has a reasonable time to perform. What would constitute a reasonable time will depend upon the circumstances. In liability insurance cases, where the claimant has signed the release, he or she is entitled to the money at once. The claimant may agree to some delay, perhaps a day or two; since he or she is entitled to the money at the time of signing the instrument, he or she may refuse the tender of the money if it is made at any other time. On the other hand, the claimant may accept it and, having accepted it, ratifies the contract and waives any breach which may have arisen because of the company's failure to pay the consideration at the time the release was signed.

Where one party has performed and the other has not, the performing party has an election of one of two remedies. The performing party may regard the contract as breached and sue the other party for damages for breach of contract. This is an action on the contract, and the measure of damages will be the amount which the person would have received if the contract had not been breached. In the other remedy, the performing party may also regard the contract as breached but consider that the breach by the opposite party has the effect of canceling the contract, thereby relieving the performing party from any obligations and permitting the pursuit of any other remedies which may be available.

For example, the claim representative agrees to settle a personal injury claim for $500 and the claimant signs a release for that amount. The claim representative promises to deliver the draft to the claimant within a few days but does not do so. The claimant can sue the releasee, on the contract, and the measure of damages will be the amount that would have been received had the contract been performed by the releasee, namely $500. Or the claimant may exercise his other option and regard the contract as a nullity because of the nonperformance by the releasee. The claimant may bring a tort action for personal injury as if no contract of release had ever been made. The executory contract of release, which was not performed by the releasee, will not be a defense to the cause of action for personal injuries. The measure of the claimant's damages in this case will be based on the usual special damages and general damages for discomfort and inconvenience. The release and the agreed consideration of $500 will not have any influence on the verdict, nor may evidence of the agreement be received by the court.

We may also consider a third situation. The claimant signs the release without receiving payment. One week later the claim representative tenders a draft to the claimant for the amount of the consideration. The claimant, within legal rights to do so, refuses the draft. The contract then remains an executory contract and the claimant may exercise either option as to the future course of action. It is clear, however, that the claimant would bring an action for personal injuries since he or she could have enforced the contract by merely accepting the draft. The claimant still has the option, if he or she chooses, to sue for breach of contract.

1323 Effect of a Release

Generally, an executed contract of release extinguishes any cause of action that the releasor may have against the releasee. It does not necessarily release any claim that the releasor may have against anyone other than the person named as the releasee. Therefore, the claim representative should be careful to include as releasees the names of all persons who qualify as insureds under the liability policy.

For example, let us assume that *A*, the named insured under an automobile policy, gives *B* permission to use the vehicle. *B* is involved in an accident while using the vehicle. When taking a release from the injured party, the adjuster should name as the releasees both *A* and *B*. *A* is the named insured and as such is entitled to the protection of the policy. *B* is likewise an insured under the policy and entitled to its protection. If *B* was acting as the agent of *A* at the time of the accident, *A* could be liable under the doctrine of *respondeat superior*. If *B* was not the agent of *A*, and this fact could be established, then *A* would have no liability. If it were alleged that *B* was acting as agent of *A*, the company might have a problem of proof. It certainly would be in a better position if it could interpose a release running to both *A* and *B* as a defense than to defend on the theory of no agency.

Also, state law generally makes the owner of the automobile liable where the vehicle is being used with the owner's permission, express or implied, irrespective of whether there is an agency relationship. It is for these and other reasons that the claim representative should include as releasees the names of all persons who could possibly qualify as insureds under the policy.

Where there are joint tort-feasors involved, the common-law rule was that the release of one of several joint tort-feasors releases all. For this rule to be applied, the person released had to occupy the position of a joint tort-feasor with relation to the other parties. If he or she did not, even though a release was given, the rule was not applicable. For example, in an automobile case, *A* is stopped for a traffic light. *B* stops behind her. *C* negligently strikes the stopped car of *B* and forces it into the stopped car of *A*, causing damage. The proximate cause of the accident clearly is the negligence of *C*. *B* was not guilty of any negligent act whatsoever. Because of his dislike of litigation, *B* settles with *A* for $100 and *A* executes a release to *B* for that amount. *A* later sues *C*. The release to *B* did not extinguish *C*'s liability. *B* was not a joint tort-feasor, and therefore the common-law rule has no application. The rule in most jurisdictions today is that a release of one joint tort-feasor is not intended to be a full satisfaction as against all, if it reserves rights against other tort-feasors.

The releasor can release only the claim which he or she has against the releasee. If the releasor has assigned the claim, in whole or in part, he or she can release only that part of the claim still owned. Personal injury claims may not be assigned, so we are concerned only with claims of property damage that can be assigned. If a property damage claim is assigned in whole or in part, and the tort-feasor has notice of the assignment, he or she must recognize the assignment, and a release from the original claimant or owner of the property damage cause of action will not protect the tort-feasor from the claim of the assignee. If there is no notice given of the assignment, the tort-feasor may deal with the claimant directly, and even though there has been an assignment of the cause of action, the failure of the assignee to give notice of the assignment (where knowledge of the assignment did not reach the tort-feasor from any other source) is fatal to the assignee's cause of action.

We will encounter this situation most frequently in connection with claims for property damage to automobiles which are covered by collision policies. If the collision carrier pays for its portion of the property damage loss, and the insurer of the tort-feasor has notice or knowledge of such payment, any settlement with the property damage claimant must be made in contemplation of the subrogation right of the collision carrier, and the release given by the property damage claimant will release only that portion of the claim which has not been assigned or subrogated to the collision carrier. On the other hand, if the insurer of the tort-feasor has no notice or knowledge of the payment by the collision carrier and the assignment to it, a release given by the property damage claimant will extinguish the entire claim.

Where the wrongdoer or insurance carrier has knowledge or notice of a subrogation right on the part of the collision carrier, they may still make a settlement with the property damage claimant to cover the deductible and also personal injuries, if any. Such a settlement would not extinguish the rights of the subrogee or assignee, but a release given by the claimant will effectively extinguish any rights or claims he or she might have against the wrongdoer. A release can be given by the claimant, which will not prejudice the rights of the collision carrier, by adding to the release: "It is understood and agreed that this release does not prejudice the subrogation claim of my collision insurance carrier above my $ _______ deductible." The inclusion of this paragraph, or one of similar wording, will enable the claimant to settle the claim without violating the insurance contract with the collision carrier.

1324 Execution of the Release

Printed release forms are used by all insurance carriers. All the claim representative has to do is to fill in the blank spaces properly and obtain the signature or signatures of the claimant or claimants. In accordance with an agreement between the insurance industry and the American Bar Association, filling in the blank spaces on a release prepared by the legal department of the insurance carrier does not constitute the practice of law. The printed general release forms are so worded that they can be used in either the singular or plural, depending upon whether the release is being executed by one person or more than one. In some cases, it may be desirable to take a special form of release because of special circumstances. These special release forms should be prepared by the company's legal department or an attorney.

The general release form has a blank space where the name or names of the persons released can be inserted. It is important that the claim representative include the names of every person (or firm, or corporation) entitled to the insurance protection of the policy so that the release will discharge and release any and all claims against them. It does not matter that the possibility of a claim against any of them is remote or unidentifiable. If they are entitled to the protection of the policy as additional insureds and they are concerned in the accident, however remotely, they should be named as releasees.

The release should be signed by the releasor, and the releasor's acknowledgment should be taken by a notary if possible. In small cases, the releasor's signature, witnessed by another person, will be acceptable. If no one else is present, the claim representative may sign as a witness. The reason for all this is that if it should become necessary at a later date to prove the release, one taken before a notary will be the easiest to prove—should the claimant deny executing the instrument. Where the signature has been witnessed by another person, it is best to obtain the address of such person so that, if it should become necessary to prove the release, the witness can be easily located. Where the claim representative signs the release, he or she can be used as a witness to the event. However, such testimony is not as effective as that of a notary or a disinterested witness.

The rule followed by most companies is that where the claim involves a substantial payment, or where the injuries are such that the results of the treatment are unknown, or where there is any possibility of future litigation because of a recurrence or aggravation of the condition, or for any other cause, the release should be notarized. In all other cases, witnesses who saw the release signed or the claim representative, are acceptable as witnesses to the document.

Since a release may have to be offered in evidence, the name of the insurance carrier should never appear as a releasee (except in Louisiana and Wisconsin where state statutes permit an action against the insurer), either alone or in connection with an action against the insured. Likewise there should be no notations made on the document, such as a company date stamp or comments of the supervisor, and there should be no alterations or erasures. If the claim representative has made a mistake in spelling, or any other error, it is better to use another form, rather than to correct the form by a strikeover or an erasure.

1325 Releases by Individuals

The release by an individual should be signed by the releasor signing his or her name in full (including first name, middle initial, and last name). If there is no middle initial or he or she normally signs by the use of initials only, then it is acceptable to have the releasor omit the middle initial (which he does not have) or to use initials only. The reason it is better to have the releasor sign his or her full name is that it makes identification easier to prove against a denial of the execution of the document. Married women must sign the releases with their given names, such as Mary Jones and not Mrs. John Jones. If for any reason it is necessary to identify her as a married person, and to have her release not only a claim which she has personally but also one which she owns as a result of her relationship to her husband, the release might show as the releasor, "Mary Jones, Individually, and as the wife of John Jones." This release should then be signed merely "Mary Jones."

The printed release forms recite that the releasor is over the age of 21 or of legal age. If there is any doubt in the claim representative's mind whether the releasor is of legal age, he should make inquiry and, if necessary, have the releasor present some proof of age. If the release is presented to the claim representative by the releasor's attorney, it is not necessary to make this inquiry. The claim representative can rely on the presenting of the release by the attorney as including a warranty that the release is legally executed.

Where the wife is injured, all states recognize the husband's cause of action for loss of consortium. Therefore, when a claim is settled with a married woman, it is necessary that both husband and wife join in the release so that both causes of action may be extinguished at one and the same time. The wife can release her claim for her injury but not her husband's claim for the loss of her services and for the medical expenses which she incurred and for which he is responsible. A release by the wife alone will then release only one part of the claim. A release from husband and wife might read "We, Mary Jones and John Jones, husband and wife," or "We, Mary Jones and John Jones, living together as husband and wife." The release should be signed by both.

Where the husband is injured, most states recognize a cause of action by the wife for loss of consortium, in accord with the Hitaffer rule [*Hitaffer* v. *Argonne Products,* 183 Fed. 2d 811]. Some states have considered the question and have rejected the rule, and still others have not considered the question at all. If there is any doubt in the claim representative's mind, or if the state in which the accident occurred has not passed on the question, it is recommended that a joint release be obtained. In such a case, the releasors should be described as "We, John Jones and Mary Jones, husband and wife," or "We, Mary Jones, as wife of John Jones, and John Jones, individually . . ." In either case, the intent is plain that the claim being released is that of John Jones and any claim that Mary Jones may have as the wife of John Jones.

It sometimes happens that both the husband and wife are injured in the same accident and it is necessary to settle the personal injury claims of both. A joint release should be taken because, in the case of the wife, in all states, the husband has a cause of action for the loss of consortium in addition to the wife's claim for personal injury. In the case of the husband's injury, in some states only he has a cause of action, and in others the wife has an additional claim for loss of consortium. The joint release should show the releasors to be, "We, Mary Jones, individually and as wife of John Jones, and John Jones, individually, and as husband of Mary Jones . . ." This wording would take care of a situation where there are claims for loss of consortium on the part of each for the injury to the other.

There are cases in which this is not possible because the injured person claims that one of the three following situations exist: (1) she is either divorced or separated from her husband; (2) her husband is serving in the Armed Forces; (3) her husband is absent from home on business but is expected to return.

An absolute divorce terminates the marriage and ends any marital rights either party may have. The divorced husband has no further right to his wife's services, nor is he responsible for her medical attention. He, therefore, has no cause of action for loss of consortium in the event of her injury. Where the claim representative is dealing with a divorced woman, he or she should note the fact of her divorce, and when and where it was obtained, in her statement. Then after settlement, if a claim is made by the former husband, the record of divorce can be readily located. These cases can be settled with the divorced woman as if she were single, which she legally is.

In the case of legal separation, called a limited divorce in some states, the same situation will prevail. Where the parties are separated, either by agreement or by a court decree, the husband has no further right to her services, nor is he responsible for her medical expenses. In such cases the woman usually has a copy of the separation agreement or the decree which can be examined, or she can tell the claim representative the name and address of her attorney who will have a copy of the papers. In any event, these cases can be settled with the claimant, and a release from her alone will extinguish the entire claim.

Where the husband enters the service he usually, on recommendation of his attorney or the armed force itself, provides his wife with a power of attorney, enabling her to transact the family business in his absence. Under this power of attorney she can release the husband's claim. It is best for the claim representative to make a copy of the power of attorney for the file. When this is done, the claim can be settled and the release signed by the wife alone. The releasor may be shown as "Mary Jones, for myself, and for and on behalf of my husband, John Jones, by virtue of the power invested in me by the power of attorney, dated ________ 19_____, executed by my husband, John Jones."

Handling the situation of the absent husband will require the exercise of judgment. The safest procedure would be to maintain control of the injured wife until the husband returns and the claim can be discharged by a settlement with both. If the claim representative is anxious to settle the case, and feels that it will be lost to an attorney if payment is not made, then the claim representative may take an individual release from the wife and leave a joint release with her to be executed by both her husband and her. It is clear that in following this method the claim representative is taking a calculated risk that the husband will refuse to sign the release, but in most cases he will do so. Upon the execution of the individual release by the wife, payment should be made. Most people will feel that, since the claim representative has shown good faith in making the payment, they are morally bound to execute the documents. In all cases where the individual or individuals sign the release in other than an individual capacity, the signature should be followed by the same description as appears in the release itself.

Some individuals operate their private businesses under a trade name, even though it is entirely owned by one person. Where it is advisable to settle a property damage or other claim involving the business, it is sometimes advisable to indicate on the release that the claim being discharged covers not only the claim by the individual but the claim of the business itself. Therefore, the releasor will be named as "Mary Jones, individually and as owner of the Colonial Cleaners," and the signature on the release will be followed by the same descriptive words. A variation of this could be used by having the releasor described as the Colonial Cleaners, and the release could be signed "Colonial Cleaners, by Mary Jones, sole owner." This type of handling refers only to businesses solely owned by one individual. It does not refer to partnerships or corporations, even though all of the stock of the corporation is owned by the individual and his or her family.

1326 The Releasee

Normally the release should run to the insured as the releasee. Since the insurance company is not a party to the accident or occurrence, the name of the company should not appear on the release. In states such as Louisiana and Wisconsin, the insurance carrier can be named as a defendant in cases in litigation. Prior to litigation, a release running to the insured will effectively protect the insurance company. If the company is a named defendant and the lawsuit is settled, then the company should be included as a releasee.

Where more than one of the insureds is involved in the accident, even remotely, it is best to add the names as releasees. For example, if *A* is driving *B*'s car (with *B*'s permission on *A*'s business) when the accident happened, it is best to have the release run to both *A* and *B*.

SETTLEMENT IN SPECIAL SITUATIONS

1327 Releases by or in Behalf of Minors

An infant or minor is a person who has not attained full legal age. In some states, this age is 18. The minor attains full legal age on the day before his or her 18th birthday and from that day forward can execute a complete and binding release even though the accident may have occurred during his or her minority. In some states, where the minor is legally married, both the husband and wife are considered capable of performing legal acts in their own behalf. With this exception, the infant during minority is under a legal disability and cannot give an effective legal release as far as claims for personal injury and property damage are concerned. In some states, a contract made by a minor, under these circumstances, is considered voidable at the option of the minor, while others regard the minor's contract as totally void. Therefore, in either case, a release given by the minor would afford the defendant little or no protection.

Where there has been an accident resulting in personal injuries to the minor child, the parents have lost the services of the child and, in addition, have had to assume the responsibility for medical expenses and other items needed for the care of the child's injury. At common law, and today, the parents have an independent cause of action for the loss of services of the infant. Therefore, when settling cases involving injuries to a minor, there are two causes of action which must be extinguished: first, the claim by the minor for the injuries, including pain and suffering and permanency, if any, and second, the claim for medical expense and loss of services by the parents.

Since the minor is under a legal disability and cannot act independently, someone of legal age must act for the minor. As to the parents' claim, the parents themselves can give a binding release. In cases involving small settlements a practice has grown whereby a release is taken from the parents to cover both claims. This will not effectively extinguish the claim of the minor for the injury. The procedure is used only on small cases where it is unlikely that any further claim will be made for or in behalf of the minor child. While it does not have any binding force legally, it is used nevertheless for psychological reasons, and in most cases, barring any unanticipated physical complication as far as the minor is concerned, no further claim will be made. It should not be used in major cases or those where there are possibilities of future permanency or recurrences of the injury. Such cases should be settled only by means of a court-approved settlement or a friendly suit, whichever the local practice dictates.

Since the release taken under these circumstances is not binding, it is customary to take a "no injury" statement from the parents in addition to the release. This statement will indicate that the infant has fully recovered from the effects of the injury, has returned to normal school activity or normal play activity, and has exhibited no evidence of the injury at the time the statement was taken. Also included should be the fact either that no medical treatment was required or that it consisted of several treatments and that the treatment has been concluded. A medical certificate or report from the attending physician might also be secured, indicating the trivial nature of the condition and that the patient was discharged as cured with no residual defects.

It is well to reemphasize that this procedure will not result in a binding release of the infant's claim, but will effectively extinguish the parents' cause of action for loss of services. Therefore most companies restrict the use of this procedure to cases involving small claims on the theory that cases of that size do not justify the expense of a court-approved settlement.

An emancipated child is one who has been freed from the power and authority of the family. This usually comes about by means of an agreement between the child and parents that the child, able to care for himself or herself, may leave home and make his or her own living, receive wages, and spend them as he or she pleases. The result is that the parent has made an entire surrender of the care, custody, and earnings of the child, as well as a complete renunciation of parental duties. In most states, the marriage of a child with the parent's consent, if the marriage is sanctioned by law, is construed to be a complete emancipation. Since the parent no longer has any obligation to care for the child and no right to the services and earnings of an emancipated child, in the case of injury to the child, the parent has no cause of action for either the medical expense or for the loss of the child's services.

While the emancipation of the child divests the parents of their interests, the fact of emancipation does not give the minor legal status to contract. His or her contracts are still subject to the disabilities of minority and may be avoided or disaffirmed by the infant. Therefore, the settlement of a personal injury claim with an emancipated child is subject to the same procedure which would be followed in connection with a settlement with any child.

1328 Indemnifying Releases by the Parents

Where a minor has sustained relatively trivial injuries, instead of following the procedure outlined in the preceding paragraph, some companies use a special form of release and indemnifying agreement. This agreement purports to release the claim of the parent for care and loss of services, and also the minor's claim for injuries. But, in addition, it contains an agreement by the parent that in the case of a claim by the minor, the parent will indemnify the releasor from any loss so sustained. This type of agreement is intended to be a general release of both the parents' and the infant's claims and, in addition, contains an affirmative agreement by the parent to indemnify and hold harmless the defendant against all loss occasioned by any action subsequently brought by or on behalf of the infant. It is generally agreed that, while the parent cannot effectively release the infant's claim by this means, the parent can release his or her own claim. The legal effect of the indemnity agreement may be open to question. It has not been considered in many cases.

Some courts have held the indemnity agreement to be contrary to public policy and void. Others consider the indemnity agreement valid, because it binds only the parent and does not affect the rights of the infant.

1329 Guardianship Proceedings and Friendly Suits

While the procedure used for settling infants' claims differs from state to state, the fundamental principle is the same. An infant's claim can be effectively released only by means of a court-approved settlement. The matter is submitted to the court in accordance with the rules of court of the state, and they might take the form of a guardianship proceeding or a friendly suit. In either case, both sides are usually represented by counsel. The court will be advised of the details of the settlement and will decide whether it is in the best interests of the infant that the settlement be made.

If the court decides against the acceptance of the settlement, the application will be denied, whereas if the court approves of the settlement, it will issue a judgment or order approving the settlement and the amount. Frequently, where large amounts are involved, the court will include in the order the person to whom the amount is to be paid and how the money is to be handled for the benefit of the infant. This sometimes takes the form of payment to a trustee who is ordered to invest the money for the infant and to disburse the funds only upon further order of the court. The defendant is bound to make the payment in accordance with the terms of the order to the person or persons designated.

1330 Nominal or No Consideration Releases

Where a person has been involved in an accident, he or she is a potential personal injury claimant even though denying having sustained any injury. In such cases, some companies follow the practice of taking a release from such a possible claimant, reciting as consideration a nominal amount, such as $1 or $5, or reciting that the release is being given for no consideration at all. Such releases have no legal effect whatsoever and are taken for psychological reasons. The theory is that such possible future claims are not likely to be pressed. There is, of course, the calculated risk that if anything of a serious nature develops, the claimant will seek legal advice and possibly make a claim. If that happens, the release will not afford the defendant very much protection, and in most cases the release will not be pleaded as a defense. Since this is a rare situation, it would seem that the nominal or no consideration release has a place in the handling of claims and, in an appropriate case, can be used.

1331 Releases by Partnerships or Corporations

A partnership is a joint business enterprise by two or more persons. It is created by a contract called a partnership agreement. Each partner, acting within the scope of the partnership business, is the agent of the other partners. Therefore, where a release is required of a partnership, the instrument may be signed by any one of the partners and is binding on the partnership as a whole and upon each other partner individually. As a general rule, no one other than a partner has the authority to execute a release, so that in these matters the claim representative must be certain that the release is from one of the partners. The claim representative should not be satisfied with a document signed by any other person, even if that person alleges that he or she is the manager of the partnership enterprise. The partner signing the release will sign his or her name under the firm name as a partner. The releasor in the instrument will be the name of the partnership, whether it consists of the names of the partners or is a fictitious name. For example, if the partnership name is *Jones & Smith,* the releasor's name will be given as "Jones & Smith, a partnership," and the release will be signed "Jones & Smith, by John Jones, partner." Where the partnership uses a fictitious name, the same form may be used, such as "J & S Auto Parts, a partnership," and the release signed "J & S Auto Parts, by John Jones, partner."

A corporation is an artificial person, created by law, which can function only through agents. It is created by compliance with the corporation law of the state in which it is located. This compliance usually consists of the filing of the articles of incorporation and the payment of a fee to the secretary of state. A corporation and only a corporation can use the designation "Inc." after the corporate name. The corporation is managed by a board of directors who may delegate certain duties of management to various officers and other officials.

Among the duties which can be delegated is the power to release claims which the corporation may have against others, and the power to execute the necessary documents as evidence thereof. When this power is delegated, there must be action by the board of directors, and the action must be entered on the minutes of the directors' meeting. Therefore, when the claim representative takes a release from a corporation, he or she must take it from the officer of the corporation who has the power to release claims and the power to execute the document. The releasor will be the corporation, and the document will be signed by the corporate name, plus the name of the officer executing the document.

For example, the releasor in the body of the release will be the *ABC Corporation,* and the document will be signed "ABC Corporation, by John Jones, Secretary." The officer then will affix the corporate seal. Since all releases by a corporation should be notarized, the notary's statement may read somewhat as follows:

> On the 15th day of November, 1990, before me came John Jones, to me known, who, being by me duly sworn, did depose and say that he resides at 124 Main Street, in the city of Anytown, County of Anycounty, State of Anystate, that he is the Secretary of the ABC Corporation, the corporation described in, and which executed, the foregoing instrument; that he knows the seal of the said corporation; that the seal affixed to said instrument is such corporate seal; that it was so affixed by order of the Board of Directors of said corporation and that he signed his name thereto by like order.

1332 Settlements: Survival and Wrongful Death

The survival statutes refer to the claim that the deceased had at the time of death. It consists of the special damages sustained, together with compensation for conscious pain and suffering. The action for these damages is maintainable by the personal representative of the deceased. The personal representative can be one who was appointed by the deceased during life, such as the executor under the deceased's last will and testament. If no such appointment has been made, the personal representative can be one who qualified as the administrator of the estate of the deceased and received such appointment from the probate court, which has jurisdiction over decedents' estates.

The personal representative is the person with whom the claim representative will settle, if settlement is indicated, and the settlement so made will be for the benefit of the heirs at law. Technically, the claim representative has only to deal with the personal representative and is not concerned with the manner in which the proceeds of the settlement are distributed to the heirs. As a practical matter, the claim representative may be dealing with the heirs at law, and the settlement agreed upon will be one that they approve, and the personal representative will merely go through the legal motions necessary to close out the case. In many cases, the claim representative will be confronted with a situation in which the victim died intestate (without a will) and will be dealing with the heirs directly. The settlement will be agreed upon, and then one of the heirs will qualify as the personal representative of the deceased, and the settlement will be concluded with that person. This requires a simple legal procedure in the probate court, but the proposed representative must be represented by counsel.

In some cases, the claim representative will agree that as part of the settlement the company will either provide counsel or pay for the reasonable counsel fees in connection with this proceeding. Where the heirs are represented by counsel, the claim representative should not make any agreement with respect to counsel fees unless it is to the company's advantage to do so. Where the heirs are represented by counsel, the claim representative will be dealing only with counsel, and the matter of attorney's fees is normally not a subject of settlement discussion. In an appropriate case, the claim representative could agree to add something to the settlement figure to take care of the attorney's fee, but in no case should the claim representative agree to pay the counsel fee to the attorney for the heirs directly. The reason behind this procedure is that the attorney cannot serve adverse interests. If he is representing one party, and is paid by the adverse party, there is a question of legal ethics involved; but more important, from the claim representative's perspective, the settlement may be opened to attack should the heirs ever seek to set it aside.

In a survival action, the measure of damages will be the amounts which the deceased could have recovered from the defendant had he or she lived. This would include any out-of-pocket expenses, such as medical, hospital, and surgical bills, property damage, loss of earning capacity, and, in addition, the value of conscious pain and suffering. These damages will be measured by the deceased's lifetime and will not include any expenses incurred after death, such as funeral expenses. To put it another way, the cause of action here is one which the deceased could have brought had he or she lived, and, therefore, the recovery is limited only to those items which the deceased could have claimed. The deceased never had a claim for funeral expenses during life since those expenses were not incurred. Therefore, as to the items which can be claimed in a survival action, if the deceased could have recovered for them had he or she lived, they are recoverable; otherwise they are not.

In a survival action it should be emphasized that the cause of the deceased's death has no bearing on the existence of the cause of action. The survival action may be maintained if the deceased had a cause of action at death. If death occurs from causes other than the injury, the action still may be maintained. However, if the deceased did not have a cause of action at death, then there is no action which can survive. This might come about where the deceased released the claim during life, or the case was tried and resulted in a verdict which was satisfied or a verdict for the defendant, or the claim was barred by the tolling of the statute of limitations. The survival action does not arise unless the deceased had a cause of action that could have been maintained at the time of death.

The same defenses which could have been interposed against the deceased can be interposed against the personal representative in the survival action. These include contributory negligence, assumption of risk, unavoidable accident, act of God, etc. Also, the personal representative is bound by the statute of limitations in exactly the same way as the deceased, so that the survival action must be brought within the period of limitation applicable to the original cause of action.

Where the claim representative is dealing with the heirs directly, there is no reason why a settlement cannot be made, even where the state law requires the appointment of an administrator of the estate. If the heirs can agree on the person (usually one of their number) who will qualify as administrator or (if so named in the deceased's will) as executor, the claim representative can settle the case. Then—taking from the proposed administrator a release, signed by her as administrator—to show good faith, the claim representative can turn over a draft to the administrator for the amount recited as the consideration in the release. The draft will be drawn to the order of the administrator and not to him or her personally.

For example, if the proposed administrator was Mary Jones, the draft would be drawn to the order of "Mary Jones, as Administrator of the Estate of Henry Jones, Deceased." This draft must be endorsed as drawn and Mary Jones cannot cash it until she can establish that she is the administrator. Therefore, all Mary Jones has to do to be able to secure the money is to qualify as the administrator and dispose of the money in accordance with the order of the court. The claim representative has no concern with respect to the distribution of the money, but is only concerned with obtaining a binding release. When the person qualifies as the administrator, the settlement is approved, and the draft properly cashed, the claim representative's task is at an end.

In some states, a settlement can be made with the heirs at law directly, without any reference to a personal representative. Where this procedure is permissible, it is suggested that the final papers be prepared by counsel.

Where the death of the deceased is caused by the wrongful act of the defendant, the deceased never owned a cause of action for his or her own wrongful death, and, both at common law and under our law today, since such a cause of action does not exist, it does not survive to the personal representative of the deceased. Therefore any action for wrongful death is separate and distinct from any claim that the deceased might have had during life, and the survival statutes have no relationship to that cause of action.

At common law, there was no recovery by the persons who sustained damages as a result of the wrongful death of another person upon whom they were dependent for support or from whom they could reasonably expect to receive some gifts during his or her lifetime and to receive a final gift in the form of a testamentary bequest at the time of death. The wrongful death cause of action was created solely by statute, solely for the benefit of the persons defined in the statute, and has no relationship to any other cause of action which the deceased may have had during life, which cause of action may have been asserted under the survival statutes by the deceased's representative.

The action for wrongful death is another and further action, owned by the persons for whose benefit the statute was passed, and the settlement of a cause of action which survived the deceased's death will have no influence one way or the other on the existence or the prosecution of the action for wrongful death. Nor is the existence of the wrongful death action dependent upon whether the survival action is brought. It could happen that the deceased had a cause of action at death, and the deceased's personal representative either never brought the action, or permitted the statute of limitations to run against it. In neither case would the cause of action for wrongful death be affected in any way.

For the cause of action to exist, it must meet the requirements of the statute. While state statutes vary as to the amount of damages recoverable and as to the basis of recovery, there is some agreement as to the basic criteria which must be met before the cause of action comes into existence. These qualifications usually are as follows:

> When the death of a person is caused by the wrongful act, neglect, or default, such as would, if death had not ensued, have entitled the person injured to maintain an action for damages resulting from the injury, the person who would have been liable in damages for the injury, if death had not ensued, shall be liable in an action for damages, notwithstanding the death of the person injured . . .

Before the wrongful death action can come into existence, two elements must be present: (1) liability, and (2) a maintainable cause of action for personal injury by the deceased at the time of death.

Liability. The accident and the death must have been caused by the "wrongful act, neglect or default" of the person sought to be charged, committed under circumstances which would have permitted the deceased to maintain an action for personal injuries had he or she lived. This means that the circumstances must create a responsibility on the part of the defendant, and that the same criteria for judging the deceased's personal injury action if he or she had lived would be applied to the wrongful death claim. If the deceased could not have recovered because of contributory negligence, assumption of risk, or because the accident was not due to the wrongful act, neglect, or default of the defendant, then the wrongful death action must fail.

A Maintainable Cause of Action. If for any reason, at the time of death, the deceased could not have maintained a cause of action for personal injury, then there is no wrongful death action maintainable. For example, if the deceased during her lifetime released the claim, then she did not have a cause of action at the time of death and would not have been entitled to maintain an action for personal injuries had she lived. In that case, the requirements of the statute could not be met. If the deceased had brought a cause of action against the defendant, and the case resulted in a judgment for the defendant, or a judgment for the plaintiff which had been satisfied, she would not have been entitled to maintain a cause of action for personal injuries at the time of death and the requirements of the statute could not be met. The same thing would be true if the statute of limitations had run against the claim before the deceased's death.

When the first two requirements are met, the action may be brought, but it may be brought only within the time limited in the statute and in the manner which the statute prescribes. The following is typical of one type of provision:

> Every action . . . shall be brought in the name of the administrator ad prosequendum of the decedent . . . except where the decedent dies testate and his will is probated, in which event the executor named in the will . . . shall bring the action. Every action . . . shall be commenced within two years after the death of the decedent and not thereafter.

This section of the statute provides for the method of bringing the action in the name of the administrator or the executor named in the will. While it is true that either of these persons is merely a nominal plaintiff, the fact remains that no other person may bring the action. In addition, the action is barred if the action is not begun within two years after the death of the decedent.

It should be noted that the statute has no reference whatsoever to the date of the accident. If the action is brought within two years of the date of the death of the decedent, it is timely. It should be emphasized, however, that the first two requirements must be met even before the action is maintainable. This means that there must have been a cause of action, based on the negligence of the defendant, which the deceased could have asserted if death had not ensued. If those two elements are present, the action may be brought by the administrator or the executor.

While the action is brought by a nominal plaintiff, namely the administrator or executor, it is brought for the benefit of certain persons. The statute may name the persons and their relationship to the deceased, or it may designate the beneficiaries of the action by reference to the state laws of descent and distribution. The following is the latter type: "The amount recovered in proceedings under this chapter shall be for the exclusive benefit of the persons entitled to take any intestate personal property of the decedent in the proportions in which they are entitled to take the same.'' This means that the beneficiaries of the action are the same persons who would be entitled to take the deceased's personal property if he or she had died without a will. Reference then would have to be had to the state statutes to determine who these people are, but it should be emphasized that the statute is a modification of the common law and is construed only by a strict interpretation of its language. The persons for whose benefit the action was created are those mentioned in the statute or those included by reference to other statutes.

Most of the statutes which are patterned after Lord Campbell's Act base the measure of damages on the pecuniary loss sustained by the persons for whose benefit the action may be brought. Therefore, the identity of such persons and the extent of their pecuniary loss will determine the settlement or verdict value. The claim representative will have to be familiar with the applicable wrongful death statute in all these cases, as well as the persons for whose benefit the action may be brought and the measure of their damages. Merely because a person has sustained a pecuniary loss through the death of the decedent is not enough to create a cause of action. That person must also be within the class of persons for whom the statute created the cause of action.

For example, the statute may identify the beneficiaries by reference to the laws of descent and distribution, as was the situation in the statute above quoted. In such laws the usual provision is that a surviving wife will take all of the deceased's personal property. If there is a surviving wife and child or children, the wife will be entitled to one third and the child or children two thirds of the personal property. Where either of these two situations obtain, the beneficiaries are limited to the wife, or the wife and child or children, to the exclusion of any other relatives, even though such relatives actually did sustain some pecuniary loss by reason of the death.

Another example: if a decedent left a surviving wife, she would be the only beneficiary, and even though he supported his parents or his brothers and sisters, none of them would have a cause of action, even though they had sustained a pecuniary loss.

When the claim representative has reached the point where settlement discussions are in order, he or she must be certain that the persons with whom he or she is dealing are those for whose benefit a recovery can be had. For example, if the beneficiaries are the wife and the child of the deceased, the claim representative must be certain that she is a legitimate wife. The same would be true as to the child. The claim representative must secure copies of the birth certificate and the marriage certificate.

The settlement can be made with the beneficiary and a draft may be made payable to the person who qualifies as the administrator in return for a release. The draft will be drawn to the order of the administrator, and the release will be signed by him (or her) as administrator. The draft cannot be cashed, if it is properly drawn to the administrator, until that person qualifies. When that happens, another release can be signed, if it is needed.

For example, if we assume that the claim representative is dealing with Mary Jones, the widow of John Jones, he or she can explain to Mary that she must qualify as administratrix of the estate. She will sign the release in such capacity, and the claim representative, in order to show good faith, will draw a draft to "Mary Jones, Administratrix of the Estate of John Jones, Deceased."

1333 Covenants Not to Sue

It sometimes happens in a case where there are joint tort-feasors that one will be willing to settle his or her share of the case and the other will not. If the claimant is willing to settle with the one, with the understanding that the settlement will not prejudice his or her rights against the other tort-feasor, this can be accomplished by the use of the covenant not to sue. Should the claimant give a release to one of several joint tort-feasors, the common-law rule is that the claimant has released the entire claim; at common law and in many states, the release of one releases all. Where a release cannot be used, the covenant not to sue can be utilized. It is an agreement that the claimant will not sue the tort-feasor with whom the agreement is made. The cause of action against all the joint tort-feasors remains unchanged. The claimant has merely agreed with one of them that he or she will not sue that tort-feasor. Such an agreement may read as follows:

> FOR AND IN CONSIDERATION of the payment of the sum of Fifty Thousand Dollars ($50,000), receipt of which is hereby acknowledged, the undersigned, his heirs, administrators, executors and assigns hereby expressly covenants and agrees forever to refrain from bringing suit or proceeding at law or in equity against JOHN JONES, his agents or assigns, either severally or jointly with any other person, on account of, or in any way growing out of, any and all known and unknown personal injuries and property damage resulting or to result from an accident that occurred on or about the 15th day of November, 1994, at or near First and Main Streets, Anytown, Anystate.
>
> It is understood and agreed that this payment is the compromise of a doubtful and disputed claim, and is not to be construed to be an admission of liability on the part of JOHN JONES, by whom liability is expressly denied.
>
> It is further understood that this is a covenant not to sue as to the above mentioned parties and not a release.

In legal effect this instrument does not release the claim, even against John Jones. It simply constitutes an agreement that the claimant will not sue John Jones on account of the accident. Should the claimant sue John Jones on the claim, John Jones could counterclaim for breach of contract. The amount recoverable on the counterclaim would be exactly the same amount that could be recovered on the claim.

1334 Mary Carter Agreements

In a lawsuit involving two or more codefendants, it sometimes happens that one of the codefendants executes an agreement with the plaintiff whereby the settling defendant guarantees that the plaintiff will receive a certain amount of money, regardless of the outcome of the lawsuit. If the verdict equals or exceeds the amount of money agreed upon, the plaintiff agrees to satisfy the judgment from the other defendants and the settling defendant will pay nothing. If the verdict is less than the amount agreed upon, the settling defendant will pay the difference between the agreed amount and the verdict. The agreement further provides that the existence of the agreement will not be revealed except by order of the court.

Some courts have characterized such an arrangement as a "collusive proceeding" with "immoral consideration."

In 1967, the Florida Appellate Court decided the case of *Booth* v. *Mary Carter Paint Co.* [202 So. 2d 8]. The heirs of the decedent Elsie Booth brought action against the Willoughby Trucking Company and the Mary Carter Paint Company as a result of a two-truck and one-auto accident which resulted in Mrs. Booth's death. Prior to trial, the defendant, Willoughby, and the plaintiffs entered into an agreement whereby Willoughby's exposure would be limited to $12,500. If the verdict exceeded $37,500, the plaintiff would satisfy the verdict against Mary Carter only. If the verdict was less than $37,500, the satisfaction of judgment would be against Mary Carter, but Willoughby agreed to pay up to $12,500 to make the recovery total $37,500. Finally, if there was a defense verdict, Willoughby agreed to pay the full $12,500. It was further agreed that the agreement would not be revealed to the other defendants, except by order of the court. Willoughby continued as a defendant and neither the court nor the jury was informed of the existence of the agreement. After a plaintiff's verdict of $15,000, Mary Carter sought a setoff on the theory that the agreement constituted a release by one of the tort-feasors. The court denied the motion and this was affirmed on appeal.

In a later Florida case, *Bill Currie Ford* v. *Cash* [252 So. 2d 407], the court upheld the validity of the Mary Carter agreement, and, in addition, held that the nonsettling defendant could not introduce the agreement on the theory that such an admission would prejudice the settling defendant. Other Florida cases have held that the Mary Carter agreement was not against public policy and upheld the lower court's refusal to void the agreement. [See *Ward* v. *Ochoa*, 284 So. 2d 385 and *Maule Indus. Inc.* v. *Rountree*, 284 So. 2d 389. In the latter case, the court did hold that the agreement was subject to discovery.]

1335 Loan Receipt Agreements

Another facet of the guarantee agreement is the loan receipt agreement, wherein the settling defendant provides the plaintiff with an interest-free loan with the understanding that, in the event of a verdict against one or both defendants, the plaintiff would execute against the nonsettling defendant and would reimburse the settling defendant out of the proceeds. The difference between this type of agreement and the guarantee agreements is that an actual payment of money is made, whereas in the guarantee there is only a promise to pay certain monies conditioned upon the outcome of the lawsuit. Some courts have held that the loan receipt agreement was in violation of the rule against contribution among joint tort-feasors and have construed it as a covenant not to sue, allowing a *pro tanto* reduction of the judgment against the nonsettling defendant. [See *Bolton* v. *Zeigler*, 111 Fed. Supp. 516 (Northern District of Iowa).]

There is a certain amount of confusion among the courts as to the validity of the loan agreements. If this device is contemplated, advice of counsel should be obtained by the claim representative before proceeding. In determining whether the loan agreement should be used, consideration should be given to the following: the present state of the law regarding loan agreements in the state in which the contract is to be executed; whether the courts of that state will uphold the validity of loan agreements; agreement as to the lender-defendant's maximum liability; the method of repayment; the possibilities of repayment; and last but not least the exposure of the lender and the codefendants. If it is determined that the possibilities of repayment are not very great, the possible settlement of the claim by means of a covenant not to sue should be considered, subject to advice of counsel.

1336 Form of Guarantee or Loan Agreement

The form of the loan agreement will vary according to the circumstances, the promise of repayment, and the maximum liability to which the lender will be exposed. As to the guarantee agreement (Mary Carter), there should be inserted in the agreement a paragraph setting forth the negligence of the other defendants and exonerating the settling defendant from liability. This paragraph is inserted to create some reluctance on the part of other defendants to offer the agreement in evidence, since in some cases the paragraph might be likely to influence the jury. The agreement usually contains a promise on the part of the plaintiff that the existenceof the agreement will not be disclosed except upon the order of the court. In some states the disclosure of the agreement is mandatory, so that the plaintiff cannot be held to the promise. Otherwise, the plaintiff is bound not to disclose the existence of the agreement except when ordered by the court to do so.

While the conditions of the guarantee agreement might vary with the circumstances, Figure 13–1 is a somewhat typical Mary Carter agreement.

1337 Open-End Releases

It sometimes happens that the claimant is reluctant to settle the claim for fear that some medical condition may develop and some further medical expense will be incurred; if the case is settled, obviously the claimant would have to absorb this expense. In order to terminate such a case, some companies use the open-end release. By means of this type of release, payment is made for the known items of damages, and, as an additional consideration for the release, the releasee agrees to pay for reasonable medical expenses incurred

FIGURE 13–1

JOHN DOE AND RACHEL ROE, CODEFENDANTS

WHEREAS, the undersigned counsel of record for the plaintiffs and the undersigned counsel of record for John Doe desire to resolve amicably between them the extent of the liability, exposure or possible contribution of the defendant, John Doe.

[Here a paragraph should be inserted setting forth the negligence of the other defendant (Rachel Roe) and exonerating John Doe, the settling defendant, from any responsibility for the causation of the accident.]

NOW, THEREFORE, the parties hereto agree as follows:

1. The maximum liability, exposure or financial contribution of John Doe shall be $10,000. [For the purposes of this form, we have chosen the sum of $10,000. The amount could be any agreed-upon amount.]
2. Such liability, exposure or financial contribution of the defendant John Doe shall abate to the extent that the plaintiffs are able to effect collection from the other defendant or his insurance carrier, as provided herein.
3. The purpose of this agreement is to guarantee the plaintiffs a recovery of at least $10,000 and to decrease the exposure of the defendant, John Doe. It is the intention of the parties hereto that this agreement shall be construed as a conditional agreement between them as to financial responsibility only, and it shall in no way constitute or be construed to constitute a release, settlement, admission of liability, or otherwise, and shall have no effect upon the trial of the case as to liability or the extent of damages, nor shall said agreement be revealed to the jury trying the said case.

The plaintiffs agree that, in the event of a verdict against Rachel Roe and her insurance carrier only or a joint verdict against defendants, Rachel Roe and John Doe, the plaintiffs will first collect said judgment against Rachel Roe and her insurance carrier. If the plaintiffs effect collection of $10,000 or more from Rachel Roe and her insurance carrier upon any such judgment, plaintiffs agree to execute a full and complete release of all liability to defendant, John Doe, without any payment by the latter.

Plaintiffs agree that, in the event of a verdict in favor of defendant, Rachel Roe, and her insurance carrier, and against defendant, John Doe, the latter will be furnished a full release and satisfaction upon payment of $10,000, regardless of said judgment amount.

within one year from the date of accident, provided that the treatment is rendered by a legally licensed physician or a legally constituted hospital. The form used for this purpose is designated as a ''Medical Expense Agreement;'' a typical one is shown in Figure 13–2.

Thus, by the use of this method of termination, not only does the company effectively close the case but, in the case of future complications, the intent of the agreement is to limit the recovery for future medical expense to the period of one year from the date of the accident or occurrence.

Figure 13–2

For and in consideration of the payment to me/us of the sum of ________________________________dollars ($____________) and in further consideration of the promise to pay the following additional reasonable and necessary medical expenses incurred by me/us within one year from an occurrence on _________________________ at or near _________________________ and directly resulting therefrom but only to the extent of my/our proportionate share of the statutory bodily injury financial/safety responsibility limits of $__________ per person and $__________ per occurrence, which amount shall be reduced by the payment received herewith.

Hospitals ____

Doctors ____

all of whom are expressly authorized to give to the bearer any information acquired by them while attending me/us in a professional capacity. I/we, being of lawful age, have released and discharged, and by these presents do for myself/ourselves, my/our heirs, executors, administrators and assigns, release, acquit and forever discharge the promisor(s) ____ and any and all other persons, firms, corporations of and from any and all actions, causes of actions, claims, demands, damages, costs, loss of service, expenses, compensation, and all consequential damage on account of, or in any way growing out of, any and all known and unknown personal injuries and death and property damage resulting or to result from the accident or occurrence above described.

1338 Advance Payments

For many years the insurance companies followed a system whereby no payment, partial or otherwise, would be made of any claim unless it was in full settlement of the claim. It was made only in return for a general release extinguishing the claim. Such a system may have had its merits, but it did create an adversary relationship between the injured person and the company, and, in addition, in serious injury cases it did have an adverse effect upon the injured person's rehabilitation. Therefore, in recent years many of the companies have adopted a system whereby in appropriate cases payments would be made to the injured person or to the doctor and hospital as the need accrued with the understanding that the payments thus advanced would be credited to the insured or the insurer in the event of a settlement or judgment.

Advance payments are usually made for one or more of the following items: (1) property damage sustained, (2) medical bills as incurred, (3) hospital bills as incurred, (4) usual take-home pay or an amount which will be needed for current living expense. Payments for these items as noted will be made periodically as required. When initiated, these payments will continue during the period of the injured person's disability and medical treatment and will continue even though the injured person subsequently retains an attorney.

Most companies require a receipt for each and every advance payment made. Figure 13–3 shows an example.

Some companies merely make an oral agreement with the injured person which is confirmed by letter with respect to the type of advance payments that will be made and when such payments will be made. This is usually confirmed by letter. When payments are made, the release form of endorsement common on most claim drafts is deleted and appropriate wording is inserted either on the face of the draft or on the reverse side explaining the payment, such as the following:

> Advance allowance for hospital expenses from November 1st to November 30th, 1990.
> Advance allowance for payment of Dr. Jones' bill for services rendered to date.
> Reimbursement for salary loss from November 1st to November 30th, 1990.
> Payment of repair costs to 1988 Chevrolet automobile.

If an attorney is employed by the injured person, and an advance payment agreement has been made, most companies will continue the advance payments through the attorney. Usually, a letter will be addressed to the attorney advising that advance payments have been made and that they will continue so long as the claimant is disabled. Of course, the company could take the position that the employment of an attorney ends the advance payment procedure, but the company has more to gain by continuing the process.

Where the advance payment procedure is continued, the attorney has the problem of determining what his or her fee is to be. Surely, the attorney cannot ex-

FIGURE 13–3

RECEIPT FOR ADVANCE PAYMENT
(This is not a release)

This is to acknowledge receipt of $____________ paid on behalf of ____________________ to be credited to the total amount of any final settlement or judgment in my/our favor for alleged damages resulting from an accident on ____________ 19___ at ____________.
I/We authorize the above sum to be distributed as follows: ____________
____

Date__________

____
Claimant

____
Spouse

____
Witness

____
Witness

pect the client to pay a percentage of the money which has already been paid voluntarily to the client. It would seem that the fee would be restricted to the amount that the attorney has been able to obtain through his or her efforts. However, this is a matter between the attorney and client in which the claim representative can have no interest.

Advance Payments as an Admission. Under the rules of evidence followed in most states, advance payments are not admissible in evidence on the question of liability nor is the fact that such payment has been made construed as an admission. Some states have adopted, in some form, the standard of the *Uniform Rules of Evidence* (Section 52) which provides as follows:

> (1) Evidence that a person has, in compromise or from humanitarian motives, furnished or promised to furnish money, or any other thing, act or service to another who has sustained or claimed to have sustained loss or damage, is inadmissible to prove his liability for the loss or damage or any part of it.

Even in states which have not as yet adopted this type of rule, it is extremely doubtful that evidence of advance payments would be admissible. Certainly a voluntary payment made by a third party (the insurance company) would not be binding on the insured defendant. In the absence of a special agreement, the insurance company is not the agent of the insured for the purpose of admitting liability. Therefore the action of the insurance company could not be admitted in evidence to establish the liability of the insured.

Selection of Advance Payment Cases. All cases do not qualify for advance payment treatment. The use of this technique is usually restricted to cases involving clear liability and moderate to severe injuries. In doubtful liability cases, each case will have to be judged on its own merits and a decision made as to the prospects of successfully defending the claim.

Each company using the advance payment system has devised its own program for its utilization and the cases to which it will be applied. Some apply it to cases of minimum severity, and others limit its use to severe injuries only, and then only in clear liability cases.

Advance Payments and the Policy Limits. In considering the use of advance payments, the company must at all times be aware of the possible consequences to the insured. In a case where the policy limits are high and the prospects of any verdict approaching that figure are slight, there is normally no problem. It is where the policy limits are low and the injuries severe that a question arises. The company has undertaken to indemnify and defend the insured up to the limits of the policy. If the company has undertaken advance payments and the amount paid reaches the policy limits, a problem may arise as to the responsibility of the company to defend a subsequent lawsuit. In ordinary cases, when the policy limits have been exhausted, there may be no further obligation on the part of the company to defend or to assume the costs of defense. Therefore, if the advance payment technique is to be used in such cases, it can be adopted only where the insured is in agreement with the procedure. If the insured will not agree, the system cannot be used. The insured has every right to expect that the insurance company will meet all the terms of the insurance contract. There is nothing in the insurance contract that would permit advance payments to be made at the expense of the insured. Therefore, if the policy limits have been exhausted by means of advance payments, the insured may institute an action on the policy with a possible successful result. The company's rights and obligations under its duty to defend are complex and vary from state to state. Advice of counsel should be sought before the company takes steps to limit or curtail this duty owed to the insured.

Advance Payment Credit. The understanding between the injured person and the company is that the company will be entitled to credit for all payments made in advance against any future settlement or judgment with respect to the claim. Where there is a settlement, no particular problem is encountered, since no final settlement will be made unless credit is given for the advance payments made. When the case proceeds to judgment, and credit for the payments made is thereafter sought, the question arises as to whether the fact of the advance payments should be offered in evidence by the defendant so that it might have some influence on the amount which the jury will award. In *Edwards* v. *Passarelli Bros.* [221 N.E. 2d 708 (Ohio)], the insurance carrier advanced $1,574.25 prior to the trial. The jury award was $10,000. The defendant paid the amount of the judgment and costs in full less the advance payments of $1,574.25. The defendant then sought a satisfaction of judgment on motion, basing its contention on the receipt for advance payments which the claimant had signed. On appeal, the court said:

> . . . In essence, plaintiff is attempting to recover $11,574.25 from a $10,000.00 judgment.
>
> Here plaintiff has received $1,574.25 from defendant's insurer and has signed a receipt therefor. The receipt is clear and unambiguous. It states that a certain sum has been paid on behalf of a named person for alleged damages resulting from a certain accident and that such sum is to be credited to any final settlement or judgment won by the receiver of such certain sum. These terms are self-explanatory. Should there be no final settlement or judgment, nothing remains to be done, and the receiver of such sum has benefitted by that amount. However, should a final settlement occur between the parties, or should the issue proceed through the courts to final judgment, then a sum equal to the advance payment is to be credited to such final settlement or judgment.

The court further recognized that it would be a distinct advantage to the plaintiff if the defendant were required to introduce evidence of the advance payment agreement, whether it be in writing or the result of letters sent to the claimant. The jury no doubt would be influenced by the fact that an insurance company had voluntarily made the payments which would be taken into account in determining the issue of liability. In addition, the fact of insurance would be in evidence. Having in mind that the claimant had already received a certain amount of money, the jury might be persuaded to award a larger amount which would be over and above that which the plaintiff had already received. Generally, if the jury is not aware of the fact that the claimant had already received the advance payments, it would seem that the jurors are more likely to determine the issue of damages on the merits.

Advance Payments and the Statute of Limitations. In some cases the running of the statute of limitations may complicate the system of advance payments. This is especially true in states which have a one-year statute applicable to bodily injury claims. Clearly, if advance payments are continued up to and perhaps beyond the date the statute ran, the insurance company could be accused of misleading the claimant and creating a false sense of security. This would in some cases enable the claimant to allege that the insurance company has waived the running of the statute, especially in cases where some payments were made after the statute ran against the case. Thus, the insurer has the option of either (1) waiving the running of the statute or (2) putting the claimant on notice that the statute is about to run.

1. Waive the Statute. Payments can be continued until the claimant has recovered, and then if needed a final settlement can be made. The continuation of the payments would seem to waive the running of the statute. The danger here is that if a final settlement is not made to the satisfaction of the claimant, there is always the possibility of litigation, and this after the statute of limitation has tolled.

2. Put the Claimant on Notice. Even though advance payments are being made and the date of the tolling of the statute is approaching, the insurer can put the claimant on notice by letter advising that within a certain period of time (usually 30–60 days) a final settlement must be made and, if this is not done, the insurer will no longer be responsible for further payments of any kind. In some cases this notice will result in immediate litigation and in others a final settlement might be consummated.

As to the approach to be taken, the decision will have to be made on the merits of the case, the possibility of litigation and the prospects for a final settlement on an equitable basis. A few states require that, where advance payments are being made, the insurer notify the claimant in writing of the date on which the statute of limitations will run. In the absence of such notice, the statute will not be tolled.

Payments to Others. It sometimes happens that it will be to the company's advantage to pay the medical and hospital bills directly to the doctor or hospital. This is especially necessary in states where there are lien laws favoring either the hospital or doctor or both. Agreement can be made with the claimant that such a payment be made after he or she has submitted an unpaid bill. In transmitting the payment, it is suggested that a letter be addressed to the payee with a copy to the claimant which would read as follows:

We are pleased to enclose our draft/check in the sum of $____________ in payment of your bill covering services rendered from ____________ to ____________ and consisting of the following:

Hospitalization, operating room, X rays, etc.

This payment is being made direct to you at the request of ____*(Claimant's name)*____.

When payment is made in this fashion, the claim representative will find that the payee generally will be cooperative in furnishing authorized medical information and hospital records.

1339 Settlement without Release

In an effort to increase the number of first-call settlements, some companies follow the technique of a settlement without release in small cases (usually under $1,000) where the amount of the claimant's damage is low and has already been ascertained. No release or receipt is required, and the case is paid with the understanding that, if the claimant should incur any further expense in connection with the accident, the company will be glad to consider it. This is sometimes referred to as a "walk-away" settlement. The claimant has received full compensation for damages and there would be no reason to make any further claim unless other injuries or other expenses are discovered. Generally, if the entire amount of the claim is ascertainable, the entire procedure can be concluded with one call, either in person or even by telephone. Such cases will eliminate the necessity for call-backs and ultimately will save the company a certain amount of claim expense.

If the entire amount is not ascertainable on the first call, the advance payment technique can be used with respect to the known damage and an agreement reached that the company will pay the reasonable amount of the outstanding items.

Chapter 14

A Note on Bibliography and Miscellaneous Areas of the Law

1400 Bibliographical Note: Legal Reading and Research

1401 Researching Various Areas of the Law

1402 Computer-Assisted Legal Research

1400 Bibliographical Note: Legal Reading and Research

The preceding sections offer the reader an overview of certain areas of the law. The purpose is to provide a basic, working knowledge of those aspects of the law (and their practical applications) that appear to be of greatest professional concern to the claim representative. This type of overview—within a volume of manageable, readable size and scope—requires a process of selection. It has been necessary to omit certain topics that would be of interest to some individual readers.

This section is offered for the assistance of the reader who may want to learn more about a subject treated in these pages, or may find it necessary to do research on new and different topics. These suggestions and references may prove helpful to the claim representative who finds himself or herself in the position of wanting more information.

There are many useful single volume and multivolume treatises available, which may be of benefit to the reader seeking further details on specific subjects. Many of these should be available at most county law libraries, generally located in the county courthouse and open to the public. The library at any local law school should have virtually all of these references among its holdings.

A law library can be a forbidding environment. Much of the natural apprehension that a claim representative may feel can be dispelled by asking the librarian for help. The assistance of a capable law librarian can put vast resources at your disposal.

1401 Researching Various Areas of the Law

General References. Comprehensive treatments of the law can be found in such multivolume "legal encyclopedias" as *American Jurisprudence* and *Corpus Juris Secundum* (which may be translated as "the body of law, second series"). The titles of these works suggest the breadth of their approach. The titles are often abbreviated as *Am.Jur.* and *C.J.S.*. The claim representative looking for a general discussion of a topic, or a starting point for in-depth research, might begin by looking into one of these encyclopedic sets of books.

Another multivolume set of books, *American Law Reports* (generally abbreviated as A.L.R.) offers detailed summaries of the case law on particular subjects. For example, a claim representative doing research on products liability might run across a reference such as: "Annot., *Products Liability: Modern status of rule that there is no liability for patent or obvious dangers*, 35 A.L.R.4TH 861 (1985)." This means that the pertinent case law on that issue is summarized and discussed at page 861 of volume 35 of the fourth series of A.L.R., issued in 1985. The same citation can guide the reader to even more recent court decisions, listed in the "Later Case Service" volumes of A.L.R.

The claim representative occasionally may be confused by legal phrases couched in Latin or French or by terminology which (although expressed in the English language) seems to fall short of being "plain English." There are several useful legal dictionaries; the best-known of these is *Black's Law Dictionary*, available at virtually any law library.

The "general references" discussed above in this section should form part of the "core" holdings of just about any law library at just about any law school or county courthouse. The claim representative who spends a few hours looking into these volumes and learning how to use them (as well as learning how to use the other resources of his or her local law library) will have a useful foundation for future legal reading and research.

Tort Law. *Prosser on Torts* is one of the most famous and widely used treatises (or hornbooks) in the legal universe. It has been through a number of editions and, most currently, is available as Prosser and Keeton, *Law of Torts* (5th edition 1984).

Two useful softbound volumes are *Kionka's Torts in a Nutshell: Injuries to Persons and Property* and *Malone's Torts in a Nutshell: Injuries to Family, Social and Trade Relations*. Each is a volume in the "Nutshell" series published by a major law book publisher. Many of the books in this series (on such topics as admiralty, contracts, conflict of laws, legal research, to name only a few) are available in law libraries, or at the college and university bookstores that sell textbooks for courses at your local law school. While designed for law students, one or more of these concise volumes could be considered useful additions to the claim representative's library. *Legal Research in a Nutshell* is an instructive guide for the claim representative or student looking for additional guidance in the intricacies of legal research.

Insurance. Among the comprehensive and authoritative multivolume treatises on the law of insurance are *Couch on Insurance*, *Appleman on Insurance*, and *Long on Liability Insurance*. Less exhaustive (but quite accessible and useful) is a one volume treatise by Keeton and Widiss on *Insurance Law*. An examination of the index of one of these detailed, scholarly treatises can lead the claim representative to the appropriate sections that discuss virtually any insurance law topic that is likely to be of interest. Two other books, devoted more to practical, litigation-oriented problems and their solutions, are: Windt, *Insurance Claims and Disputes*; and Ostrager and Newman, *Handbook on Insurance Coverage Disputes*.

Such treatises are supplemented or published in revised editions from time to time, in order to keep them reasonably current as new cases are decided and new statutes enacted.

Other Areas of the Law. The burgeoning law of products liability has given rise to several specialized multivolume treatises, such as Frumer and Friedman, *Products Liability*, and Hursh and Bailey, *American Law of Products Liability*.

For that matter, just about every area of the law has its authoritative, multivolume standard reference, from *Benedict on Admiralty* to *Larsen on Workmen's Compensation*. While valuable for anyone doing in-depth research, the usual needs of most claim representatives can probably be met by dipping into one of the less specialized references cited above. For example, *Prosser on Torts* not only covers the law of torts in detail, but provides substantial information on such areas of the law as workers' compensation, products liability, professional liability, and damages. As another example, unless a claim representative is a specialist in a narrow field, it is likely that seeking out the appropriate entry in *C.J.S.* or *Am.Jur.* will provide all that he or she needs to know about admiralty, aviation, workers' compensation, and a host of other specialized subjects.

Periodicals. All law libraries contain enormous numbers of volumes of "law reviews." Every major law school publishes its law review several times a year. Each issue typically contains scholarly articles on legal topics, and notes and comments on recent decisions of note. A lawyer who practices in a particular state will need to be familiar with the law review published by each law school in his or her state. The claim representative should also know about these "local" law reviews. In addition, most state bar associations publish a periodical magazine or journal, as do many city or county bar associations. These law reviews and law journals are excellent sources of information on recent cases and other developments in the law in your jurisdiction, and the claim representative would be well-advised to have some acquaintance with them.

"Loose-Leaf Services." The generic title of "services" is often used to refer to weekly or biweekly or monthly periodicals, usually consisting of reports of recent judicial decisions or legislative developments or regulatory agency actions in a particular area of the law. Such services are available in many specialized areas. They have the advantage of being comprehensive and timely. The lawyer who specializes in, say, products liability, environmental law, taxation, employment law, or life and health insurance will certainly subscribe to some of them.

Many such loose-leaf periodical services can be found in any law library and can be a good source of current, if specialized, information for the claim representative.

As mentioned above, a capable law librarian can be an excellent guide to the vast resources available in a modern law library. A reasonable command of those resources can be of invaluable assistance to the claim representative.

No amount of library expertise, however, can be a substitute for advice of local counsel, whether in-house or outside counsel. The law is not a set of books filled with immutable, "black letter" rules. Library reading and research can provide you with valuable information and a grounding in important rules. But a lawyer who practices in the state and federal courts in your jurisdiction will be in the best position to understand and interpret the distinctive body of common law and statutory law that has developed in your state, as well as the procedures and court rules that govern local practice.

1402 Computer-Assisted Legal Research

The claim representative should be aware of the enormous resources available through computer-assisted legal research. Extensive legal research data bases (such as LEXIS or WESTLAW), enable a person to do accurate and comprehensive legal research in a far shorter time than is possible through traditional forms of law library research.

The researcher typically taps into these data bases through a telephone connection, using a personal computer. A wide variety of searches can be done by computer, using selected words and/or phrases to instruct the data base. It can be commanded, for example, to retrieve pertinent cases on a particular issue decided by the appellate courts in a particular jurisdiction—or in a broad range of jurisdictions. The computer data base can also help greatly in "shepardizing," that is, finding citations in other cases to an earlier decision that is of particular interest to the researcher. Many other references (such as law- and business-related newspaper and magazine articles) are available through on-line computer services.

Access to WESTLAW or LEXIS (as well as basic instruction in their use and information about the costs involved) often can be obtained through a local law school library or county law library.

Appendix

Glossary of Legal and Insurance Terms

These materials are provided simply for quick reference to a few of the legal and insurance terms a claim representative may encounter. The glossary should not be considered a substitute for detailed legal references, such as an authoritative and comprehensive law dictionary.

ab initio From the beginning.

accident An unexpected or sudden event. Some insurance policies define accident, or *accidental means*, in the contract itself. In this situation, the wording of the contract will govern the meaning contemplated by the parties, and not the dictionary definition.

accountable Responsible, liable.

acknowledgment Formal declaration before an authorized official by one who has executed an instrument, that it was done voluntarily.

act of God An act occasioned exclusively by the violence of nature apart from any human agency.

action The legal demand made before a court by which one seeks to enforce one's right to recover from another party; a lawsuit.

action ex contractu Action for breach of a contract.

action ex delicto A legal action arising out of a breach of duty; action in tort.

actual authority In the law of agency, the authority a principal confers on the agent, or allows the agent (either expressly or implied by) to believe himself or herself to possess.

actual cash value The fair or reasonable cash price for which property could be sold in the market. It is the greatest amount the insured can recover in most policies indemnifying for damage to property, except in states where valued policy laws are in effect.

additur The power of a trial court to increase the amount of an inadequate award made by a jury.

administrator A person to whom letters of administration (authority to administer the estate of a deceased person) given by the court to collect assets of the estate, pay its debts, and distribute the assets, similar to an executor, who is a representative appointed by the will of the deceased.

admissions Voluntary statements as to the existence of certain facts.

affiant One who makes a written, sworn statement of fact (or affidavit).

affidavit A written statement of fact sworn to by the party making it before an officer authorized to administer an oath.

affirmative warranty An affirmation of existence of a fact at the time an insurance policy is entered into. A *promissory warranty* requires that something be done or not done after the policy has taken effect.

agency A relationship in which one person is authorized to act for or represent another. For discussion of various types of agency, see Sections 632 to 649 of this book.

ambiguity Doubt or uncertainty about the meaning of a term or expression used in a written instrument.

answer Initial pleading by the defendant in a lawsuit responding to the plaintiff's complaint, e.g., denying the plaintiff's allegations or alleging other facts to defeat them.

appeal The process by which a party asks a higher court to review an adverse decision by a lower court.

application The preliminary request, declaration, statement, or petition in writing made by a party seeking an insurance policy.

arbitration The submission for determination of a disputed matter to private unofficial persons selected by the parties or appointed in a manner provided by law or by agreement of the parties.

arising out of and in the course of employment Workers' compensation acts provide for compensating an employee whose injury arises out of and in the course of employment, i.e., an injury resulting from a risk reasonably incident to the employment.

assault An intentional, unlawful, apparently violent show of force toward another. **Battery** consists of the actual execution of the act offered in an assault.

assign To make over or transfer to another.

assured A person who has been insured against losses or perils covered by the insurance policy.

attachment A remedy by which the plaintiff acquires a lien upon the property or effects of the defendant for satisfaction of a judgment. The purpose is to take the defendant's property into legal custody.

attest To bear witness to; to swear to; to certify.

attorney In the most general sense, one who acts for another.

attorney-at-law A lawyer or advocate.

attorney-in-fact A person authorized by another to act in his or her behalf. This authority is conferred by a written instrument called a *power of attorney*.

attorney's lien The right of an attorney-at-law to hold or retain in his or her possession the money or property of a client to assure payment of attorneys' fees.

audit In insurance, an examination of the insured's books and payroll records to determine the premium due.

award The decision or determination rendered by an arbitrator.

bad faith Dishonesty; activity implying or involving actual or constructive fraud, or a design to mislead or deceive another, or to avoid fulfilling some duty or some contractual obligation. See *good faith*.

bailee A person who is entrusted with or who has possession of property belonging to another.

bailment A delivery of goods or personal property by one person to another on a temporary basis.

battery Wrongful physical contact with another without his or her consent.

beneficiary A person for whose benefit a contract or trust is made; the person to whom the proceeds of an insurance policy are payable.

binder A temporary memorandum of agreement to enter into an insurance contract.

breach of contract Failure to perform a promise or to comply with a term of a contract.

broker An agent employed to enter into contracts. In insurance, an individual or organization which acts as the representative of the insured in writing insurance contracts.

burden of proof The necessity of affirmatively proving facts in dispute between the parties in a lawsuit.

cancellation Termination of a contract. In insurance, termination of a contract (before its expiration) by either the insured or the company.

Carlisle tables Life annuity tables, compiled at Carlisle, England, about 1780 and sometimes used by actuaries as one of the bases for estimating life expectancy.

carrier One who transports persons or property. Common carriers are those who undertake to carry members of the general public.

casualty Accident; event resulting from sudden, unexpected or unforeseen cause.

caveat emptor *Let the buyer beware*. The rule that a purchaser must examine, judge, and test for himself or herself.

certiorari A writ or demand from a higher court to a lower court requesting the record of a case for purposes of review.

chattel An item of personal property.

claim The allegation of a right to recover for a loss, e.g., one which may be covered by an insured's policy contract.

claimant One who claims or asserts a right or claim.

classification of risks A term used in insurance with reference to the nature of articles insured and to the occupation and business of the applicant.

client A person who employs or retains an attorney to advise and act for him or her.

code A systematic body of law; a collection or revision of laws.

coinsurance A relative division of risk between insurer and insured, taking effect only when the actual loss is partial and less than the amount of the policy.

collusion An agreement between two or more persons to commit fraud.

common law The body of law derived from the judgments of courts, distinguished from laws made by legislatures.

comparative negligence The doctrine by which the negligence of the parties is compared in terms of percentages of fault; recovery is barred or damages reduced in proportion to the amount of the plaintiff's fault.

complaint The initial document filed in a civil lawsuit, including a statement of the harm suffered by the plaintiff and a specific request for relief by the court.

compulsory insurance Any form of insurance that is required by the state. For example, in some states, automobile liability insurance is compulsory for all owners of automobiles; workers' compensation insurance is compulsory for employers in most states.

concurrent insurance Where two or more insurance policies cover the same interest, or identical property; overlapping insurance.

condition A clause in a contract or agreement which may suspend, rescind, or modify the principal obligation; conditions may be *positive* (requiring that a specified event shall happen or an act be done), *restrictive*, or *negative* (the latter imposing an obligation not to do a particular thing).

conservator A guardian or preserver appointed by the court to manage the person and/or the estate of an incompetent person.

consideration Something of value promised to induce a contracting party to enter into a contract.

constructive loss Sometimes referred to as *constructive total loss*. Loss resulting from extensive damage to property that renders it valueless to the insured or prevents its restoration or repair except at a prohibitive cost.

contempt An act in willful disregard or disobedience of a public authority, especially a judge.

contempt of court Any act calculated to embarrass, hinder, or obstruct the court in the administration of justice, or lessen its authority or dignity.

contractual liability Liability assumed under any contract or agreement, express or implied.

contributory negligence A plaintiff's failure to exercise due care, which contributes to his or her injury.

conversion An act that deprives an owner of his or her property without the owner's permission for an indefinite time.

corporation An artificial person or legal entity created by the authority of state law, consisting of an association of numerous individuals; regarded in law as having a personality and existence distinct from that of its members, as well as the capacity of continuous succession.

costs Expenses of a lawsuit awarded to the successful party (and recoverable from the losing party) for costs incurred in prosecuting or defending the suit.

covenant not to sue An agreement by one who undertakes not to sue to enforce a right of action against another.

damages A pecuniary compensation or indemnity which may be recovered in the courts by any person who has suffered loss or injury through the wrongful act of another.

declaration A statement by the applicant or the insured with regard to the circumstances of the risk; statements made by the insured as to the existence of certain facts on which the insurance company relies in entering into the contract.

defendant The person against whom relief or recovery is sought in a lawsuit.

delictum A tort, wrong, injury, or offense.

disclaimer The refusal or denial of a claim. In insurance law, a denial by the insurance carrier that the policy of insurance covers the circumstances claimed by the insured.

discovery Disclosure and exchange of information between parties to a lawsuit.

earned premium The amount at any time during the life of the policy which would compensate the company for the protection furnished for the expired portion of the policy term. Since insurance premiums are paid in advance, the premium is not earned until the protection required by the policy has actually been afforded to the insured.

endorsement A supplementary agreement attached to an insurance policy that changes its conditions or coverage.

excess insurance The amount of insurance which is available only when losses exceed those covered by a primary policy or retained by the insured.

experience The loss record of an insured, or a class of insurance coverage over a period of years.

experience rate A special rate for casualty insurance available to an insured because of satisfactory experience; this rate is a deviation from the manual rate.

extraterritoriality Operation of laws beyond the physical limits of a state enacting those laws.

falsus in uno, falsus in omnibus *False in one thing, false in everything*. If testimony of a witness on a material issue is willfully false and given with intent to deceive, the jury may disregard all of the witness's testimony.

family automobile doctrine Also referred to as the family car or the family purpose doctrine: that any household member using the automobile, with the owner's permission, becomes the owner's representative, for whose negligence the owner is responsible. It is a form of vicarious liability.

fellow servant rule Rule that an employer is not liable for injuries to an employee caused by the negligence of a fellow employee engaged in the same general business, if employer has exercised due care.

fidelity bond A contract of fidelity insurance; a guarantee of personal honesty of an officer or employee, indemnifying against that person's wrongful acts.

fiduciary A person or corporation having the duty created by his or her undertaking to act primarily for another's benefit, creating a relationship implying and necessitating great confidence and trust on the one part and a high degree of good faith on the other.

financial responsibility law A statute requiring motorists to furnish evidence of ability to pay damages either before or after an accident has occurred.

fleet policy An insurance contract covering a number of automobiles specifically designated, or providing automatic coverage of all automobiles owned by the insured.

good faith Honesty of intention and unwillingness to take any conscious advantage of another.

goods Every species of personal property.

guardian A person lawfully invested with the legal right and duty of caring for the person or property of another person, who is considered incapable of administering his own affairs.

hazard In insurance law, the risk or probability that the insured event may occur.

hearsay Evidence proceeding solely from repetition of what one has heard others say, not from the witness's personal knowledge.

imputed negligence Negligence that is not directly attributable to a person, but that of someone in privity with that person.

increase in hazard In insurance, a change in the circumstances of a risk, making a loss more probable.

independent contractor One who contracts to do a piece of work according to his or her own methods and without being subject to the control of the employer, except as to the result of the work.

inherently dangerous Danger inhering in an instrumentality or condition, requiring special precautions to prevent injury.

injunction A judicial order requiring the person to whom it is directed to do, or refrain from doing, something.

insurable interest An interest in property that would make the loss of the property a pecuniary loss to the insured. Every interest in property, or any relation thereto or liability in respect thereof, of such nature that a contemplated peril might directly damage the insured, is an insurable interest.

insurance A contract whereby, for a consideration (premium), one party agrees to compensate the other for specified losses caused by certain perils.

interstate commerce Transportation of persons or property between the states.

ipso facto *By the fact itself.*

joint and several A liability is said to be joint and several where the plaintiff may sue one, some, or all of the tort-feasors, at his or her option.

judgment The official decision of a court regarding the rights of the parties to a lawsuit.

judgment creditor One who has obtained an enforceable judgment of a court.

judgment debtor A person against whom judgment has been entered.

judicial notice The act by which a court will, of its own motion and without the production of evidence, recognize the existence and truth of certain facts.

latent defect A hidden defect; a defect in an article known to the seller but not to the purchaser, and not discoverable by ordinary observation.

lease Any contract that creates the relationship of landlord and tenant; contract for use of lands or buildings.

legal representative One who stands in place of and represents the legal interests of another; often refers to *executors* or *administrators.*

legally liable Responsibility under the law; liability imposed by law or by contract.

liability A legally enforceable obligation. In insurance terminology an important distinction is made between *liability imposed by law*, which means an obligation forced upon a person because of his or her acts or omissions, and the broader term *legal liability* which embraces all pecuniary obligations, including liability assumed by contract. With certain exceptions, most liability insurance policies protect merely against liability imposed by law and exclude any liability assumed by contract.

malice The intentional doing of a wrongful act with an intent to inflict an injury; ill will or evil.

malpractice Professional misconduct or unreasonable lack of skill.

manual rates Insurance costs for a particular area of business, as published in the pertinent manual. These rates are usually fixed by a rating bureau. Discounts from manual rates are sometimes allowed because of favorable loss experience.

merchantability Reasonable fitness of an article for the general purpose for which it shall have been sold. Where the article sold is ordinarily used in only one way, its fitness for that particular use is impliedly warranted.

misrepresentation A false statement of fact or false representation, a statement calculated to deceive or mislead.

nuisance That which annoys and disturbs one in possession of his or her property, unreasonably interfering with its ordinary use or occupation; everything that endangers life or health, gives offense to senses, violates the laws of decency, or obstructs reasonable use of property.

oath An affirmation of the truth of a statement.

obligation Any enforceable duty assumed by or imposed by law upon a person.

obligee The person in whose favor an obligation is contracted.

obligor The person who has engaged to perform some obligation.

occupancy In insurance contracts, refers to the type and character of the use of property; in a homeowners' policy implies actual use of the house as a dwelling place, not absolutely continuous but as a place of usual return.

occupational disease Disease gradually contracted in usual and ordinary course of employment, and caused by the employment.

ocean marine insurance Any form of marine coverage while the subject of the insurance is on water: "wet marine." Insurance on ships and cargo on inland lakes and rivers also comes under the general classification of ocean marine insurance. *Inland marine insurance* properly refers to any risk *not* on water assumed by a marine insurance company, such as personal property floaters and the like.

omnibus clause A provision in the automobile liability policy which extends coverage to any person legally responsible for the operation of the insured automobile, and to any person operating the car with the permission of the named insured.

opinion evidence Evidence of what a witness thinks or infers; distinguished from personal knowledge of the facts in dispute.

order In legal practice, every direction of a court or judge made or entered in writing and not included in a judgment; an application for an order is a *motion*.

ordinary care That degree of caution which the ordinary person of reasonable prudence would use under any given set of circumstances.

ostensible agency An implied or apparent agency that exists where one person allows another to believe that a third person is his or her agent.

ostensible authority The apparent authority that a principal allows a third person to believe the agent possesses.

parol evidence Oral or verbal evidence, as opposed to evidence in writing; evidence that is given by witnesses in court.

parol evidence rule When parties put their agreement in writing, this rule provides that all previous oral agreements merge in the writing and a contract, as then written, cannot be modified or changed by parol evidence in the absence of mistake or fraud in the preparation of the writing.

parties The persons who take part in any act or contract, or who are either plaintiffs or defendants in a lawsuit.

partnership A contract between two or more persons to conduct a business involving a proportional sharing of the profits and losses.

perjury The act of lying under oath by a witness in a judicial proceeding.

plaintiff The person who initiates a lawsuit.

possession Ownership or control of property.

power of attorney An instrument authorizing another to act as one's agent or attorney.

precedent A court that provides an example of authority for a later, similar case on a similar question of law.

premium The consideration paid by an insured to an insurance underwriter.

preponderance of evidence Greater weight of evidence, or evidence which is more credible and convincing than the evidence offered by the opponent.

prima facie *At first sight*. On the face of it.

prima facie case A case that will support a favorable finding, unless contradicted and overcome by other evidence.

principal The employer of an agent who gives authority to an agent or attorney to act for him or her.

privity of contract The relationship that exists between contracting parties.

probate The process of proving a will and distributing property.

probative facts. Evidentiary facts; facts that prove other facts.

proximate cause The real cause of something; the cause that produces the injury, and without which it would not have occurred.

rate In insurance, the agreed factor in determining an insurance premium.

reasonable care That degree of care a person of ordinary prudence would exercise in similar circumstances.

reckless Indifferent to consequences of an act, or willfully disregarding danger to others.

reinsurance A contract by which an insurer agrees that a third party will insure it against loss or liability by reason of the original risk insured against.

release Relinquishment of a right by one person to the person against whom the right might have been enforced.

relevancy Applicability to a disputed issue in a lawsuit.

remittitur The power of a trial court to decrease the amount of an award made by a jury.

remote cause In the law of negligence, a cause that would not ordinarily lead to the event that took place.

representation A statement, express or implied, made by one contracting party to the other that persuades the other party to enter into the agreement.

res gestae *Things done*. Everything said and done as part of a transaction.

Res gestae is an exception to the hearsay rule; it renders acts and declarations, which constitute a part of the things done and said, admissible in evidence even though they would otherwise be excluded as hearsay evidence or self-serving declarations.

res ipsa loquitur *The thing speaks for itself*. Rebuttable presumption that the defendant was negligent, based upon proof that the thing causing an accident was in the defendant's exclusive control, and that the accident ordinarily would not happen without negligence.

res judicata *A thing decided*. An issue which was in controversy and has been decided by a court; that decision is conclusive between the parties in the same action or subsequent proceeding.

rescind To annul a contract; to abrogate it from the beginning and restore the parties to the positions they would have occupied had no contract been made.

respondeat superior *Let the master answer*. An employer is liable in certain circumstances for the wrongful acts of an employee. It is a type of vicarious liability.

slander The speaking of false words that cause injury to another.

subpoena A court order to a witness to appear and give testimony.

subpoena duces tecum A subpeona ordering a witness to appear and produce documents.

subrogation The substitution of one person (such as an insurance company that has paid a claim) in the place of another with reference to the claim, so that the one who is substituted succeeds to the rights of the other in pursuing a legal remedy.

surety One who insures or guarantees payment or performance, if the principal fails.

tort A wrongful act which may form the basis for a civil action.

trespasser One who wrongfully enters upon another's premises.

unilateral mistake Mistake or misunderstanding about the terms of a contract.

verdict The formal decision by a jury in a trial.

vicarious liability Legal liability for the acts of another, e.g., one's agent or employee.

waiver The voluntary relinquishment of a known right.

willful Intentional; reckless.

Index

A

Absolute liability. See Strict or absolute liability
Acceptance by conduct, 138
Acceptance of claim, 6
Acceptance of offer, 138
Accident description
  automobile case, 319–320
  general liability claim, 322–323
  workers' compensation claims, 325–328
Accords, 157–158
Act of God, 44, 100–101
  carrier liability, 185–186
  innkeeper liability, 184–185
Administrators, 169–170
ADR. See Alternative dispute resolution
Advance payments, 481–486
  as evidence, 483
  on settlements, 485
Affett v. *Milwaukee & Suburban Transit Corp.*, 420
Agency, 18. See also Law of Agency
  parent-child relationship, 115
Agent
  attorneys, 168
  authority to act, 161
  control by principal, 161
  by emergency, 166–167
  employee as, 164
  family purpose doctrine, 242–243
  fiduciary, 168–169
  independent contractors issue, 170–172
  liability to principal, 175
  liability to third persons, 175
  and subagent, 166
  trustees, 169–170
  types of, 162–163
  unauthorized acts, 176
Allen v. *Wm. P. McDonald Corporation*, 70
Allergy defense, 210–211
Allergy test. See Patch test
Alsteen v. *Gehl*, 84
Alternative dispute resolution, 38–39
  providers, 39
Ambiguities, in contracts, 148
Ambulances, 235–236
American Insurance Association, 252
American Law Institute, 18, 204, 207, 391
American Law of Products Liability (Hursh and Bailey), 486
American Law Reports, 488
American Motorists Insurance Co. v. *E. R. Squibb & Sons, Inc.*, 222
American National Standards Association, 219
Anatomy. See also Diseases
  blood, 370–373
  circulatory system, 357–358
  clavicle and scapula, 355–356
  cranium and face, 354–355
  eye function, 367–368
  head, 360–362
  the heart, 368–370
  joints, 356
  lower extremities, 356
  muscular system, 356–357
  nervous system, 357
  skeleton, 354
  spinal column, 355
  thoracic cage, 355
  upper extremities, 356
Anthracosis, 374
Apparent agent. See Implied agent
Appleman on Insurance, 489
Applicable law factor, 420
Arbitration agreements, 155
Archibald v. *Braverman*, 73
Arthritis, 364–365
Asbestosis, 375
Assault, 74–75
Assignment of contract, 148
Assisted negotiation, 39
Association-reaction test, 284
Assumption of risk, 98–99, 209, 210, 244
Attorney
  contingent fees, 150–151
  control of claimant, 451–451
  limited agents, 168
  loss of settlement, 460
  negotiation on settlement, 454–455, 457–459
  offer to, 455–457
Attorney-client privilege, 287
Attractive nuisance doctrine, 68–71. See also Nuisance
  creation of the dangerous condition, 71
  dangerous condition, 69–71
  nature of children, 71
Automobile insurance
  compulsory, 250–251
  no fault, 253–254
  personal injury plan benefits, 253–255
  state laws, 251
  tort exemption, 255–256
Automobiles
  Consumer Product Safety Act, 199
  enhanced injury, 198
  family purpose doctrine, 242–243
  guest defined, 246
  guest statutes, 245–246
  law of torts, 240–261
  National Traffic and Motor Vehicle Safety Act, 199
  road worthiness, 198
  safe design, 197–198
  seat belt defense, 239–240
  statutory liability of the owner, 243

traveling in same direction, 230
unregistered, 250
Autopsy reports, 293

B

Babinski sign, 354
Bailee
conversion of property, 183
liability to third persons, 180–181
sole benefit of, 180
Bailment
contrasted with sale or exchange, 177
definition of, 176–177
degrees of care required, 179–180
distinguished from custody, 177–178
distinguished from rental, 178
and theft or conversion, 178–179
types of, 179
types of liability, 179–186
Bailor
liability, 180
sole benefit of, 179–180
Battery, 42, 74–75
Benedict on Admiralty, 489
Beneficiary contracts, 155–156
Bennet Drug Stores, Inc. case, 193
Bill Currie Ford v. *Cash*, 478
Binding arbitration, 39
Black's Law Dictionary, 488
Blood
grouping and transfusion, 373–374
hematoma, 375
Hr factors, 373–374
red cells, 371
Rh factor, 373
thrombosis and embolism, 372–373
white cells, 371
Blood grouping and transfusions, 373–374
Blood test for intoxication, 376–377
Blunk v. *Allis-Chalmers Manufacturing Company*, 209
Bogen v. *Bogen*, 119
Bolten v. *Zeigler*, 479
Bone conduction, 353
Booth, Elsie, 478
Booth v. *Mary Carter Paint Co.*, 478
Borrowed servant rule, 167
Both ways rule, 241
Breach of condition, use of waiver and estoppel, 146–147
Breach of warranty, 191
manufacturers, 215
retailers, 215–216
Breathalyzer, 377
Bridge of proof, 439
Bristol-Myers Co. v. *Gonzales*, 201
Broderson v. *Rainier National Park Co.*, 152
Brown v. *Parker*, 120
Bruises. See Contusions
Burden of proof, 265, 270
Bursitis, 365

C

California Court of Appeals, 73
California Supreme Court, 64, 73
Clark v. *Rental Equipment Co.*, 267
Carpini v. *Pittsburgh and Weirton Bus Company*, 197
Casualty claim. See Claim
Causation, personal injury claims, 351–352
Caveat emptor rule, 187–188, 194
Cellulitis, 366
CFR. See Code of Federal Regulations
Challenges to jurors, 35
Chancery courts
and appellate courts, 20
injunction remedy, 19
origin, 19
reformation remedy, 20
rescission remedy, 20
Charitable immunity doctrine, 130
Charitable institutions, 129–130
Cherokee Laboratories v. *Rogers*, 16
Choroid, 367
Ciafalo v. *Vic Tanny Gyms, Inc.*, 152
Cippollone v. *Liggett Groups Inc.*, 213
Circuit Court of Appeals for the District of Columbia, 105
City of Austin v. *Daniels*, 125
Civil Aeronautics Board, 293, 294
Civil Aeronautics Reports, 293–294
Civil damage laws. See Dram shop acts
Civil suit procedure, 24–39
alternative dispute resolution, 38–39
the answer, 29–30
claim representatives duty in litigation, 37
claim representatives duty in trial preparation, 37–38
the complaint, 25–27
court charge, 36
discovery proceedings, 30–32
duties of claim representative, 28
investigation, 24
judge and jury functions, 33–34
jury selection, 34–35
motions, 32–33
motions after verdict, 37
opening statements, 35
overdue process problem, 29
receipt of process by insured, 27–28
subpoenas, 33
summons, 24–25
time extensions, 28–29
the trial, 35–36
verdict, 36
waiver of a jury, 34
Claim
definition of, 1
first-party, 1
third-party, 2
Claimant, 32, 217. See also Defendant; Plaintiff
attorney's lack of control, 424
credibility of witnesses, 423
personal and physical characteristics of, 422
responsibility of a codefendant, 423–424
termination, 6–7
Claim representative
duties, 5–7
employment, 2
and evidence, 263
as fiduciary agent, 169
functions, 4
investigation of product liability, 217–219
negotiations with attorneys, 457–459
required knowledge, 7
responsibilities, 3–4
Claims evaluation. See also Damages; Offer; Settlement
formula methods, 415–419
personal injury, 414–415
purpose and scope, 379–381
three-times-the-medical formula, 416–418
time of, 425–426
unit of time formula, 418–419
Clark v. *Ruidoso-Honda Valley Hospital*, 122
Clark v. *Ticehurst*, 193
Clear liability, 441
Coagulation of blood, 371–372
Code of Federal Regulations, 22–24
Collateral source rule, 387
Colles fracture, 359
Commercial General Liability (CGL) policy, 221
Commission, 46
Common carriers
and exculpatory contracts, 186
liability, 185–186
private, 186
Common law
and arbitration, 155

duties recognized by, 45
judicial authority, 13
jurisdiction, venue, and forum shopping, 17–18
law of place, 13–14
origin, 9
origin of equity, 18–19
reasonably prudent person standard, 46–47
Restatement of the Law, 18
rights and duties under, 10
separation of crimes and torts, 9
significant contracts rule, 14–17
stare decisis doctrine, 11
statute law modifications, 11–12
in the United States, 12–13
Common Sense Legal Standards Reform Act, 436–437
Comparative negligence, 97–98, 210
modified form, 97–98
pure form, 97
slight versus gross negligence, 98
Comparison, 300–301
Compensatory damages, 381, 434–435. See also Punitive damages
Competent evidence, 264
Component suppliers, 205
Comprehensive General Liability policy. See Commercial General Liability (CGL) policy
Compression fracture, 359
Compromise negotiation, 6–7
Compulsory automobile insurance, 243, 250–251
Congress
creation of regulatory agencies, 22–24
preemptive statutes, 22
Consideration
accord and satisfaction, 157–158
in contracts, 132, 138–139
Consortium, 104–106
damages for loss, 389–391
Hitaffer rule, 105–106
loss of, 94
Constitution of the United States, 15, 20, 77, 245
creation of the court system, 21–22
Consumer Product Safety Commission, 199
Contra-coup fracture, 359
Contract law, 18
Contracts
accord and satisfaction, 157–158
ambiguities, 148
assignments, 148
attorney contingent fees, 150–151
beneficiary, 155–156
to compound a crime, 149–150
conditions, 145
covenant not to sue, 160
duration of, 133–134
elements of, 132
exculpatory, 151–153
fraud, 142–143
hold harmless agreements, 153–155
laws governing, 148–149
leases, 156–157
mistake of fact, 141–142
nonwaiver and reservation of rights, 147–148
offer, 133–141
parol evidence rule, 143
to procure evidence, 150
releases, 158–160
representations, 143–144
void and voidable, 141
waiver and estoppel, 146–147
warranties, 144
Contribution, 111–112
Contributory negligence, 94–96, 244
assumption of risk, 209
both ways rule, 241
and highway use, 248
imputed, 95–96, 241–242
at intersections, 247–248
last clear chance, 96
product liability defense, 187–188, 208–210
seat belt defense, 239–240
Contributory negligence defense, 210
Contusions, in head injuries, 361
Conversion, 43
of property, 78
Couch on Insurance, 489
Court Based Dispute Resolution Programs, 38
Court records, 296–297
Covenant not to sue, 111, 160
Coverage. See also Insurance; Liability insurance
investigation of, 301–302
Crisci v. *Security Insurance Company of New Haven*, 85
Critical evidence, 219–221, 224, 305–306
Cunningham v. *State*, 153
Currie v. *Fitting*, 94

D

Damages, 81. See also Claims evaluation; Offer; Settlement
claimant duty to establish, 383–384
claimant duty to mitigate, 384–386
collateral source rule, 387–388
effect of religious belief, 386–387
factors decreasing settlement, 422–424
factors increasing settlement, 420–422
and investigation, 302
and life expectancy, 401–402
loss of consortium, 389–391
loss of earning capacity, 396–399
nature of, 380–382
out-of-pocket expenses, 396
permanent disability, 399–401
personal injury, 395–399
for physical injury, 75
and a preexisting physical disability, 388–389
present value of future, 404–408
proof in slander and libel, 76
property, 391–395
purpose of claims evaluation, 379–380
single recovery rule, 382
survival claims, 424–426
time of valuation rule, 382–383
work-life expectancy, 402–404
wrongful death claim, 426–429
wrongful death statutes, 93–94
Day v. *Barber-Colman Co.*, 213
Death, of a minor child, 94
Death on the High Seas by Wrongful Act, 97
Defamation, 43
libel and slander, 75–76
Defective condition, rule, 206
Defendant, 32, 33. See also Claimant; Plaintiff
answer to plaintiff, 29–30
receipt of process, 27–28
trial evidence, 36
Defense. See Tort defenses; Tort immunities
Defense Research Institute, 402
Degrees of care, 48
Delaware Supreme Court, 245
Demonstrative evidence, 263
Department of Health and Human Services, 23
Depressed fracture, 359
Deutsch v. *Connecticut Co., 383*
Diagnostic signs, 354
Diagnostic tests, 353–354
Diagrams, as evidence, 335–339
Diglio v. Jersey Central Power and Light Company, 70
Dillon v. *Legg*, 73
Dippel v. *Sciano*, 210
Discovery proceedings, 30–32
Diseases. See also Anatomy
bacterial infections, 375–376

compressed-air, 374
epilepsy, 362
etiology, 352 lung, 374–375
Dislocation, classifications, 360
Distributors, as sellers, 205
Diversity jurisdiction, 18
Diversity of citizenship, 18
Documentary evidence, 263
Document Collection, Review and Production, 37 For the Defense 9 (Schoemaker), 32
Dogs, injuries caused by, 89
Doubtful liability, 441
claims, 443
extent of injury, 444
Dram shop acts, 83–84
Duckworth v. *Ford Motor Company*, 212
Due care, 237–238
Due Process Clause, 436

E

Eagle-Pitcher Industries, Inc. v. *Liberty Mutual Insurance Company*, 222
Early neutral evaluation, 38
Earning capacity, loss of, 416
Edwards v. *Passarelli Bros.*, 484
Electrocardiogram, 353–354
Elmore v. *American Motors*, 207
Embolism, 372–373
Emergency, disabled vehicles, 237–238
Emergency rules of the road, 235–236
Emotional distress. See Mental distress
negligent infliction of, 71–73
English Sale of Goods Act, 195
Epilepsy, 362
Equitable Society for the Assurance of Life and Survivorship, 401
Equity
origin in common law, 19
remedies under, 19–20
Essential services benefits, 254, 260
no-fault insurance, 254
Estoppel, in contract law, 146–147
Etiology, of disease, 352
Evaluation function, 6
Evans v. *General Motors Corporation*, 197, 198
Evidence. See also Investigation
admissibility, 263–264
admissibility of public records, 291–297
admissions against interest, 278–279
admissions by agent, 284
admissions by conduct, 283
attorney-client privilege, 287
bookkeeping entries, 280
contracts to procure, 150
conviction in traffic court, 281
conviction of prior crimes, 281–283
court records, 296–297
deception tests, 284
diagrams, 335–339
expert testimony, 266–270
hearsay rule, 276–277
husband-wife relationship, 286–287
interstate commerce commission records, 297
intoxication, 378
irrebuttable presumptions, 271–272
judicial notice, 274–275
liability insurance, 285–286
nature of, 263
and offers to compromise, 285
pain and suffering declarations, 278
photographs, 289
physical facts, 333–334
physician-patient privilege, 287–288
plea of guilty to traffic charge, 280–281
precautions to prevent harm, 284–285
presumptions and inferences, 270–271
priest-penitent privilege, 288–289
prior contradictory statements, 279–280
privileged communications, 286
qualifications of witnesses, 265–266
res gestae statements, 276, 277, 278, 320, 323 *res ipsa loquitur* rule, 272–274
testimony in prior proceedings, 279
verification process, 340–348
videos, 289–290
vital statistics records, 296
weight of, 264–265
X rays, 290
Examination
of an object, 341
medical, 342–347
of scene, 341–342
Exculpatory contracts
applied to bailments, 183–184
and common carriers, 186
compared to hold harmless agreements, 154–155
effects of infancy, 153
signed agreements, 152
unsigned agreements, 153
Executors, 169–170
Expert testimony, 266–270
basis for, 268
need for, 266–268
Eye, 367–368

F

Fair Claims Practices Act, 450
False imprisonment, 43, 80
False statement, 75
Family immunity doctrine
and death of a spouse, 118–119
effect of divorce or separation, 118
effect of insurance, 121–122
and emancipated children, 121
parent and child, 120–121
rejection of interspousal doctrine, 119–120
Family purpose doctrine, 242–243
Fatal Accidents Act of 1846. See Lord Campbell s Act
Federal Aviation Act, 23, 293, 294
Federal Aviation Administration, 23
Federal Cigarette Labeling and Advertising Act, 213
Federal District Court for the Southern District of New York, 16
Federal Employers Liability Act, 22, 97
Federal Food, Drug, and Cosmetic Act, 23
Federal Food Additives Act, 23
Federal Hazardous Substances Labeling Act, 23–24
Federal income tax returns, 294
Federal Insecticide, Fungicide and Rodenticide Act (FIFRA), 213
Federal Judicial Center, 38
Federal Jury Instruction Guide, 270
Federal Rules of Civil Procedure, 24
Federal Rules of Evidence, 266, 269
Federal Tort Claims Act, 122, 123
Fedor v. *Mauwehu Council, Boy Scouts of America, Inc.*, 153
Fire apparatus, 236
Fitzgerald v. *Valdez*, 121
Food and Drug Administration, 23
Formula methods of claims evaluation, 416–420
Foreseeability
doctrine, 54–55
motor vehicle operation, 55–56
ownership of public premises, 56–57
product liability, 57
rescue doctrine, 57–58
Forster v. *Manchester*, 78
For The Defense (Jones), 402
Forum non conveniens, 17
Fractures
classification, 358–360
treatment of, 360
Fraud, in contracts, 142–143
Freehe v. *Freehe*, 119
FTCA. See Federal Tort Claims Act

Funeral expenses, 254, 260
  no-fault insurance, 255
Fussner v. *Andert*, 94

G

Garst v. *General Motors Corporation*, 268
Gelbman v. *Gelbman*, 121, 122
General agent, 162–163
General contractor, 171–172
General damages, 381
General liability cases, witness statements, 322–324
General Obligations Law, 111
Gray v. *American Radiator and Standard Sanitary Corporation*, 216
Greenman v. *Yuba Power Products Company*, 197, 212
Greenstick fracture, 359
Gross negligence, 49
Guardians, 170
Guest statutes, automobiles, 245–246

H

Hagans v. *Oliver Mach. Company*, 268
Handbook on Insurance Coverage Disputes (Ostranger and Newman), 489
Harvey v. *Fridley Medical Center*, 267
Hazardous product cases
  additional defendants, 222–223
  exposure theory, 222
  investigation, 223–225
  manifestation theory, 222
Hearsay rule, 276–277
Heart, 368–370
Hernia, 364
Hertzog v. *Harrison Island Shores, Inc.*, 152
Hitaffer rule, 105, 465
Hitaffer v. *Argonne Products*, 105, 465
Hold harmless agreement, 90
  in contract law, 153–154
  types, 154–155
Hooker Chemical and Plastics Co., 223
Horror factor, 421
Hostile witness, 308
Hr factors, 373–374
Hunt v.*Firestone Tire and Rubber Company*, 209
Hypothetical question, 341

I

Illinois Supreme Court, 205
Impacted fracture, 359
Implied agent, 163
Implied warranties, 194
Imprisonment, 80
Imputed negligence, 113
Income continuation benefits, 254
  no-fault insurance, 254
Income contribution benefits, 259–260
Incomplete fracture, 359
Incontrovertible physical facts doctrine. See Judicial notice
Incubation period, 376
Indemnity, 112
Independent contractors
  and agency, 170–172
  joint tort-feasors, 114
Index Bureau, 348
Individual rights, court protection of, 10
Inducement, in fraud, 20
Inducement in fraud, 142, 143
Infants, voidable contracts, 153
Inflammatory diseases, 365–366
Injunction, 19
Injuries. See also Personal injury claims
  descriptions, 321
In loco parentis, 115
Innkeeper liability, 184–185
Inquiry, 299
Insurance. See also Coverage; Liability insurance
  effect on family immunity doctrine, 121–122
  first-party coverage, 1
  third-party coverage, 2
Insurance broker, 163
Insurance Claims and Disputes (Windt), 489
Insurance Company of North America v. *Forty-Eight Insulations, Inc.*, 222
Insurance industry
  offer and demand, 133
  representations, 143–144
Insurance Law (Keeton and Widiss), 489
Intention, to harm, 74
Intentional tort, 42–43
Internal Revenue Code, 398
Interrogatories, 30–32
Intersections, 247–248
Interspousal immunity doctrine. See Family immunity doctrine
Interstate Commerce Commission, 23, 251, 297
Interstate Commerce Commission Act, 23
Intervening cause, 52–54
Intoxication
  as evidence, 377–378
  tests, 377
Intoxication tests, 291–292, 377–378
Investigation. See also Evidence
  of claim, 5–6
  critical evidence, 305–306
  nature of, 298–301
  outline of, 303–306
  purpose of, 301
  scope of, 301–302
  witnesses, 306–312
Investigation plan, 219–225
Invitation, revocation, 63
Invitee, 61–62
Iris of eye, 367–368

J

Joint and several liability
  combination of both, 109–110
  concurrent, 108–109
  contribution and indemnity, 111–112
  successive, 109
Joint enterprise
  and agency, 165–166
  negligence, 114
Joint tort-feasors, 108–113, 241. See also Tort-feasors
  contribution law, 112–113
  covenant not to sue, 160
  General Obligations Law, 111
  indemnity and contribution, 215–216
  release of one rule, 110–111
  restrictive release, 160
  and third-party conduct defense, 211–212
Joint Tortfeasors Contribution Laws, 215–216
Jones, Professor David D., 402
Jones Act, 97
Judge, trial role, 33–34
Judge Hosted Settlement Conferences, 38
Judicial notice, 274–275
Jury
  reasonably prudent person standard, 34
  selection, 34–35
  trial role, 33–34
  waiver of, 34
Justice v. *Gatchell*, 245

K

Kansas Supreme Court, 16
Keeton, Professor, 252
Kilberg v. *Northeast Airlines, Inc.*, 15, 16
Kionka's Torts in a Nutshell, 488

L

Lack of privity rule, 188
Landlord-tenant relationship, 66–68
Lange v. *Holt*, 386
Larsen on Workmen's Compensation, 489
Larsen v. *General Motors Corporation*, 198
Lasegue sign, 354
Last clear chance rule, 96–97
Law of agency, 18. See also Agency
  direct liability of principal, 174
  and joint enterprise, 165–166
  and partnership, 165
  relationships, 164–166
  respondeat superior doctrine, 164, 172, 243
  scope of agency, 172–174
  special and general employers, 167–168
Law of place
  and contracts, 148–149
  significant contracts rule, 14–17
Law of the forum, 14–17
Law of torts. See also Torts
  compared to law of contract, 42
  definition of tort, 40–42
  intentional tort, 42–43
  liability without fault, 43–44
  negligence, 43, 44–45
Law of Torts (Prosser and Keeton), 488
Legal Research in a Nutshell, 488
Legal standards of intoxication, 377
Lex fori. See Law of the forum
LEXIS, 490
Lex loci delicti. See Law of place
Liability. See also Products liability; Strict liability
  for acts of indemnitor, 154–155
  bailee to third person, 180
  bailor to bailee, 180
  bailor to third person, 181
  common carrier, 185–186
  hazardous products cases, 222
  innkeepers, 184–185
  investigation of, 302
  limitation in bailment, 182–183
  market share theory, 203
  and private carriers, 186
  third person to bailee, 181–182
  third person to bailor, 182
  without fault, 43–44
  wrongful death, 474–475
Liability, vicarious,, 113–117
Liability insurance. See also Coverage; Insurance
  automobile, 251
  family immunity doctrine, 117–122
  waiver and estoppel, 146–147
Libel, 43, 75–76
License
  area of premise, 62
  revocation, 63
  and social guests, 60–62
Licensees, 60
Lie-detector tests, 284
Life expectancy
  tables, 403–408
  work, 403
Life Expectancy Discount table, 408
Limited agent, 163
Lockett v. *General Electric Company*, 202
Long on Liability Insurance, 489
Lord Campbell's Act, 92, 426, 427, 428, 476
Loss of use, 392–394
Love, William T., 222
Love Canal case, 222
Lymphadenitis, 366
Lymphangitis, 366

M

MacNeal Memorial Hospital v. *Cunningham*, 205
MacPherson v. *Buick Motor Company*, 190
Magee v. *Wyeth Laboratories,Inc.*, 211
Magistrate Hosted Settlement Conferences, 38
Maintainable cause of action, 475–477
Malice, 81
Malicious abuse of legal process, 43
Malicious prosecution, 43, 80–81
  damages, 81
Malicious use of process. See Wrongful civil proceedings
Malone's Torts in a Nutshell, 488
Malpractice, statute of limitations, 103
Manufacturers
  breach of warranty, 195–196
  duty to warn, 199–202
  product liability, 189–190
  safe design and production, 196–199
  as sellers, 205
  strict liability, 211
Manufacturers identification, 202–203
Mariorenzi v. *Joseph DiPonte, Inc.*, 65
Market share theory, 203
Market value, 392
  items devoid of, 392
Married Women's Acts, 118
Mary Carter Paint Company, 478
Material evidence, 264
Maule Indus. Inc. v. *Rountree*, 478
McBurney's sign, 354
McDaniel v. *Atlanta Coca-Cola Bottling Company*, 78
McDaniel v. *Sinn*, 16
Mediation, 38
Medical examiner, 345
Medical expense benefits, 254, 258
  no-fault insurance, 254
Medical knowledge, 349–351
Medical malpractice. See Malpractice
Medical report, 346–347
Medical standards of intoxication, 376–377
Mental distress, 415–416
Metal-Matic, Inc. v. *The Eighth Judicial District*, 216
Michael v. *Warner-Chilcott*, 201
Minitrial, 39
Mistake of fact, in contracts, 141–142, 143
Model Code of Evidence, 278
Morton v. *Bengay*, 57
Moschkau v. *Sears, Roebuck and Company*, 193
Mosier v. Carney, 119
Moss v. Fortune, 152
Motorists
  assured clear distance rule, 228
  compliance with traffic signs, 222–230
  compulsory automobile insurance, 250–251
  driver negligence, 242, 246–247
  failure to see traffic warning signs, 230
  financial responsibility law, 250
  and pedestrians, 247
  rights and duties, 227–228
  and roadway workers, 248–249
  rules of the road, 228
  seat belt defense, 239–240
  service process on nonresidents, 251
  state licensing regulations, 249
  statutory liability of owner, 243, 251
  unregistered vehicles, 225
  vehicles traveling at right angles, 233
  vehicles traveling in opposite directions, 232

vehicles traveling in the same direction, 230–232
vicarious liability, 240–242
vicarious liability of nonowner, 243
violating rules in an emergency, 233
Motor vehicle accident reports, 291
Multiple fracture, 359
Myotitis, 365

N

National Conference of Commissioners on Uniform State Laws, 195
National Safety Council, 219
National Traffic and Motor Vehicle Safety Act, 199
National Traffic Safety Agency, 199
Negligence, 43, 191
causal relationship, 47
damages, 47
establishing, 35
failure to comply with standards, 46–47
foreseeability rule, 54–58
gross, 48–49
intervening cause, 52–54
legal duty owed, 44–46
ordinary, 48
parent-child relationship, 115–116
proximate cause, 238–239
slight, 48
state of the art defense, 213
Negligence per se, 47–48
failure to use seat belts, 240
lack of driver's license, 249
sales in violation of a statute, 193–194
Negligent entrustment, 242
Negligent sales, 193
Neighborhood canvas, 309
Neighborhood check, 347
Neuritis, 365–366
New York Court of Appeals, 15, 190, 239–240
Niagara County v. *Utica Mutual Insurance Company*, 223
Niagara Falls Board of Education, 223
No-fault auto insurance, 252–255
arbitration under no-fault statutes, 256–257
claims administration under, 257–261
settlement of claims and disputes, 261
subrogation under, 256
third-party claims, 256
No liability claims, 441, 443
Nonbinding arbitration, 38–39
Nonbinding summary jury trials, 39
Nuisance. See also Attractive nuisance doctrine
basis of liability, 82–83
claims, 442

O

O'Connell, Professor, 252
Offer, 133–137. See also Claims evaluation; Damages; Settlement
acceptance of, 138
to attorney or agent, 133–136
capacity to make, 139–141
consideration of, 138–139
duration of, 133–134
termination of, 137
through authorized agent, 136–137
Oklahoma Supreme Court, 16
Oliveria v. Oliveria, 120
Omission, 47
Opportunity, in driving, 239
Oral depositions, 30–32
Oral evidence, 263
Osteomyelitis, 365–366
Ownership, duties of, 58–71

P

Palsgraf v. *Long Island Railroad*, 54, 55
Papas v. *Upjohn Co.*, 213
Pardue v. *City of Sweetwater*, 70
Parent-child relationship, 115–117
agency exception, 115
negligent parent, 115–116
parent participation in tort, 116–117
statute modification of imputed negligence, 116–117
Partnership, agent and, 165
Passengers, rights and duties, 244
Patch test, 354
Pathologic fracture, 359
Pearson v. *Northeast Airlines, Inc.*, 15, 16
Pecuniary punishment, 436
Periostitis, 366
Personal injury claims, 366. See also Injuries
arthritis, 364–365
calculating damages, 408–434
causation, 351–352
common injuries, 366
compressed-air disease, 374
diagnostic signs, 354
diagnostic tests, 353–354
disc injuries, 363
and disclaimers defense, 214
disease etiology, 352
epilepsy, 362
fractures, 358–360
head injuries, 360–362
hematoma, 375
hernia, 364
indemnity and contribution, 215–216
infection, 375–376
inflammatory diseases, 365–366
intoxication tests, 376–377
lengths of disability, 366–367
lung diseases, 374–375
medical knowledge, 349–351
spinal or back injuries, 362–363
trauma, 352
traumatic neurosis, 363
whiplash, 364
x rays, 352–353
Personal injury protection programs
benefits, 254–255
no fault, 251–261
payments and penalties, 261
tort exemption, 255–256
Personal jurisdiction, 17
Personal property, loss of use, 392–393
Phlebitis, 366
Photographs, as evidence, 334–335
Physical distress, 415–416
Physical facts, 333–334
Pinkerton National Detective Agency, Inc. v. *Stevens*, 78
Plaintiff, 32. See also Claimant; Defendant
burden of proof, 35–36, 219
choice of place, 14–17
complaint, 25–27
defendant's answer to, 29–30
Plasma, 371
Poepping v. *Linderman*, 119
Police cars, 236
Police records, 292
Presumptions
civil cases, 271–272
irrebuttable, 271–272
Prima facie case, 36, 83, 191, 257
Prime contractor. See General contractor
Principal
control of agent, 161–162
direct liability, 174
liability to agent, 176
Privacy rights, 76–78
Privilege, defense of defamation, 76
Probable cause, 81
Products
anticipated uses, 199–202

assembly, 193
dangers, 192–193
negligent sales, 193
patch test, 208
safe design, 197–199
safe manufacture, 196–197
sales in violation of statute, 193–194
testing and inspection, 192
used for unintended purposes, 208–209

Products liability. See also Liability; Strict liability
allergy and susceptibility, 210–211
breach of warranty, 194
caveat emptor rule, 187–188
contributory negligence defense, 210
defective condition, 206
disclaimers defense, 214
duty to warn, 199–202
early concepts, 190–191
elimination of privity requirement, 191
general characteristics, 187–190
government specifications defense, 213
investigation process, 217–225
long-arm statutes, 216–217
manufacturer and distributor, 195–196
manufacturer duties, 196–202
manufacturer identification, 202–203
physical harm rule, 208
retailer negligence, 191–194
seller engaged in business, 204–206
state of the art defense, 213
statute of limitations, 214–215
strict liability tort, 203–204
third-party conduct defense, 211–212
unintended use rule, 208–209
unreasonable danger, 207
user or consumer, 207

Products Liability (Frumer and Friedman), 489

Property ownership, 58–71
area of invitation or license, 62
attractive nuisance doctrine, 68–71
duties of, 58–59
invitee, 61–62
landlord and tenant, 66–68
licensees, 60
modifications of occupiers liability, 64–65
police officers and fire fighters in the line of duty, 63–64
revocation of invitation or license, 63
social guests, 60–61
trespassers, 59–60

Prosser on Torts, 488

Pro tanto reduction, 479

Proximate cause rule, 49–51, 238–239
bodily injuries, 51
consequential injuries, 52
medical treatment complications, 51–52
sine qua non test, 49
substantial factor rule, 51

Public Health Service, 445

Public Service Commission Accident Reports, 293

Punitive damages, 434–437. See also Compensatory damages
current perspective on, 436–437
nature of, 434–435

Q

Quasi-governmental theory, 129–130

Quid pro quo. See Consideration

R

Rappaport v. *Nichols*, 84

Real property, loss of use, 393–394

Reasonable care, 227

Reasonable doubt, 265

Reasonable man standard. See Reasonably prudent person standard

Reasonably prudent person standard, 46–47, 95
and motorists, 227

Receivers, 169–170

Red blood cells, 371

Reformation, 19

Rejection of claim, 6

Releases, 158–160, 460–467
by or in behalf of children, 467–469
effect of, 462–463
execution of, 462–463
by individuals, 464–467
nominal or no consideration, 470
open-end, 479–481
by parents, 469
by partnership or corporation, 470–471
the releasee, 467

Relevant evidence, 264

Representations, prior to contract, 143

Rescission, 19

Res gestae statements, 276, 277, 278, 320, 323

Res ipsa loquitur rule, 206
in evidence, 272–274

Respiratory test, 284

Respondeat superior doctrine, 112, 240, 243, 462

Restatement of the Law of Torts, 18, 391

Restatement (Second) of the Law of Torts, 69, 77, 85, 196, 204, 205, 210, 241

Restatement (Second) on Conflict of Laws, 15

Restrictive release, 111

Retailers
breach of warranty, 194
as sellers, 205–206

Retina, 367

Reynard v. *Bradshaw*, 158

Rh factor, 373

Richards v. *United States*, 16

Romberg sign, 354

Rowland v. *Christian*, 64, 65

Rule of certainty, 383

Rules of the road
commercial vehicles, 238
disabled vehicles, 237–238
emergencies, 233
emergency vehicles, 235–236
entering highway, 234
highway regulations, 227
intersections, 233
motorcycles and bicycles, 236
no contact cases, 238–239
parked vehicles, 236–237
passing, 230–231, 232
and pedestrians, 227
railroad crossings, 234–235
reduction of speed or stopping, 231
school buses, 235
stop signs, 234
traffic signs, 229–230
turns, 231–232

S

Saeter v. *Harley Davidson Motor Company*, 210

Santiago v. *Package Machinery Company*, 211

Satisfaction of accord, 157–158

Sclera, 367

Scope of agency, 172–174
deviation from, 173–174

Seat belt defense, 239–240

Selective service records, 295

Senders v. *Baird*, 69

Services, in consortium, 390

Settlement. See also Claims evaluation; Damages; Offer
advance payments, 481–486

burden of proof, 439–440
claimant control, 453–454
clear liability, 442–443
covenant not to sue, 477
doubtful liability, 441
first-call, 453
guarantee or loan agreement, 479
increasing an offer, 459–460
interview, 451–453
by joint tort feasors, 450–451
and liens, 445–447
loan receipt agreements, 478–479
Mary Carter agreements, 478
nature and purpose, 439
negotiations, 454–455
negotiations with attorneys, 457–459
no liability, 441
nuisance claims, 441–442
offer, 455–457
order of, 449–450
qualifications for, 440–441
relation to injury, 444
and subrogation, 448–449
survival and wrongful death, 471–477
value, 394–395
without release, 486
Sex, in consortium, 389
Sidewalks, 247
Signed agreements, 152
Silicosis, 374
Sills v. *Massey-Ferguson*, 207
Silver v. *Silver*, 245
Sindell v. *Abbott Laboratories*, 203
Sine qua non test, 49
Sioux City R. R. v. *Stout*, 68
Skahill v. *Capital Airlines*, 16
Slander, 43, 75–76
Snellen test, 354
Social guests, 60–61
Social Security, 295
Society, in consortium, 389–390
Special damages, 381, 399
Special employer, 167
Spier v. *Barker*, 239
Spinal injuries, 362–363
disc injuries, 363
whiplash, 364
Sprain fracture, 359
Spruill v. *Boyle-Midway, Inc*, 209
Stare decisis doctrine, 11
Statements
automobile claims, 318–322
by children, 332
by disabled persons, 331–332
form and substance, 318
general liability claims, 322–324
by illiterates, 331
negative, 332–333
recorded, 317–318
serious injury and death claims, 329–331
signed, 314–316
structure of 312–314
taken in hospitals, 328–329
through interpreters, 331
workers compensation claims, 324–328
Statute, duties arising from, 45–46
Statute of limitations, 101–103
Stellate fracture, 359
Sterling Drug Inc. v. *Cornish*, 211
Stevens v. *Allis-Chambers Manufacturing Company*, 210
Stress fracture, 359
Strict liability, 191. See also Liability; Products liability
dangerous instrumentality doctrine, 190–191
manufacturers, 190–191
product liability, 189–190
retailers, 205–206
retailers and manufacturers, 203–204
state of the art defense, 213
unintended product use, 208–209
Strict or absolute liability
animals as dangerous instrumentalities, 87–89
dangerous instrumentality doctrine, 86–87
unhazardous operations doctrine, 89–90
Subcontractor, 170–171
Subject-matter jurisdiction, 17
Subpoena, 33
for public records, 292
Subpoena duces tecum, 33
for public records, 296
Substantial factor rule, 50, 55
foreseeability, 54
Sun Shipbuilding and Dry Dock Company, 202
Superintendent of Documents, 292
Supreme Court of Idaho, 245
Supreme Court of Illinois, 216
Supreme Court of North Carolina, 119
Supreme Court of Rhode Island, 65
Supreme Court of the United States, 245
Surveillance, 347–348
Survival claims
death by a wrongful act, 91–94
wrongful death, 426–434
Survivor benefits, 254, 260
no-fault insurance, 255
Systolic blood pressure test, 284

T

Tampa Drug Company v. *Wait*, 193
Tart v. *Register*, 387
Tendinitis, 365
Tenosynovitis, 365
Termination function, 6–7
Theory of defense, 302–303
Thibault v. *Sears, Roebuck and Company*, 201
Third-party conduct liability defense, 211–212
Third party neutral, 39
Thompson v. *Hagan*, 245
Three-times-the-medical evaluation formula, 416–418
Thrombosis, 372–373
Tort defenses. See also Tort immunities
product liability, 208–215
Tort-feasors, 41, 53, 91, 121. See also Joint tort-feasors
responsibility for acts, 175
Tort immunities, 117–130. See also Tort defenses
Federal Tort Claims Act, 122–123
governmental immunity, 123–129
institutions, 129–130
intra family, 117–122
quasi-governmental theory, 129–130
trust fund theory, 129–130
Tort liability, nuisance as a basis of, 82–83
Tort parties, 104–107
consortium, 104–106
minors and insane persons, 107–108
prenatal injuries, 106–107
Torts. See also Law of torts
classification of, 42–44
in common law, 10
created by common law, 43–44
created by statute, 44
crime distinguished from, 9
damages sustained, 41
intentional, 74–86
legally protected rights, 41
parent-child, 114–117
wrongful invasion of rights, 41
wrongful legal proceedings, 85
Torts (Prosser and Keeton), 65, 99, 130
Tort theory, 204
Traffic court hearings, 292
Transferred intent, 43
Trauma, 352
Trespass, 79–80
Trespasser, 59–60
ab initio, 63
Trustees, 169–170
Trust fund theory, 129

Truth, defense of defamation, 76
Turntable case, 68
TXO Production Corp. v. *Alliance Resources Corp.*, 436

U

UCC. See Uniform Commercial Code
Ultrahazardous operations doctrine, hold harmless agreement, 154
Unavoidable accident, 99–100
Underwriters Laboratories, 219
Unemployment compensation records, 295–296
Unfair Claims Practices Act, 450
Uniform Act, 291
Uniform Arbitration Act, 39
Uniform Commercial Code, 195–196, 214, 215
Uniform Contribution Act, 111
Uniform Rules of Evidence, 483
Uniform Sales Act, 195
United States Coast Guard, 448
United States Code, 22
United States Code Annotated, 22
United States Court of Appeals, 20
United States Department of Labor, 402
United States House of Representatives, 436
United States Life Tables, 402
United States Supreme Court, 16, 20, 213, 436
Unit of time evaluation formula, 419–420
Universal agent, 162
Unsigned agreements, 153
USC. See United States Code
USCA. See United States Code Annotated

V

Vandermark v. *Ford Motor Company*, 212
Verification, 299–300, 340–348
  disability claims, 347–348
  by experts, 340–342
  through index bureau, 348
  medical examination, 342–347
  by neighborhood check, 347
  by surveillance, 347–348
  by videotape, 348
Veterans Administration, 448
  records, 294–295
Vicarious liability, 113–117
  auto owners, 240–242
  employer-employee, 114
  husband-wife, 117
  or imputed negligence, 113
  owner and independent contractor, 114
  parent-child, 114–117
Videotape, verification by, 348
Visibility, in driving, 239
Vital statistics records, 296
Vital Statistics of the United States, 402
Void, *ab initio*, 141
Voir dire examinations, 34
Voluntary acts, 46

W

Wage-profit formula, 94
Waiver, in contract law, 146–147
Ward v. *Ochoa*, 478
Warranty
  of fitness, 194
  of merchantability, 194
  prior to contract, 143, 144–145
  strict liability, 189
  of title, 194
Warranty theory, 203–204
Watchdogs, 89
Waube v. *Warrington*, 72
Weather reports, 292
Weber test, 354
WESTLAW, 490
White blood cells, 371
Williams v. *Klemesrud*, 84
Willoughby Trucking Company, 478
Winterbottom v. *Wright*, 190
Witnesses
  appearance of, 311
  children, 332
  classification of, 307–308
  definition of, 306–307
  disabled, 331–332
  education of, 311–312
  expert, 307
  expert testimony, 266–270
  friendly or unfriendly, 307–308
  hearsay rule, 276–277
  illiterate, 331
  interested in outcome, 308
  interviewing, 309–311, 312–314
  locating, 308–309
  multiple statements, 333
  negative, 332–333
  non-English speaking, 331
  prior contradictory statements, 279–280
  qualifications of, 265–266
  recorded statements, 317–318
  signed statements, 314–316
  statements in automobile claims, 318–322
  statements in general liability claims, 322–323
  statements in workers' compensation claims, 324–328
  statements taken in hospitals, 328–329
  testimony in prior proceedings, 279
Workers' compensation cases, deduction under no-fault insurance, 260–261
Work-life expectancy, future damages, 404–408
Writ of certiorari, 20
Wrong-doer. See Tort-feasors
Wrongful civil proceedings, 82
Wrongful death, 90–94
  beneficiaries, 92–93
  settlement valuation, 430–434
  survival actions, 90–91
Wrongful death statutes
  based on contributions, 428–429
  based on loss to the estate, 428
  beneficiary rights, 92–93
  combined with survival, 429–430
  damage, 93–94
  death of a minor child, 94
  defenses, 94
  English law, 92–94
  punitive, 427
Wrongful invasion of rights, 41
Wycko v. *Gnodtke*, 94

X

X rays
  as evidence, 290, 344–345
  in injury claims, 353

Y

Yarrow v. *Sterling Drug Company*, 201

Z

Zayre of Atlanta, Inc. v. *Sharpton*, 85
Zone of danger theory, 72